FEDERAL REPORTS ON POLICE KILLINGS

Ferguson, Cleveland, Baltimore, and Chicago

United States Department of Justice

MELVILLE HOUSE
BROOKLYN · LONDON

**FEDERAL
REPORTS
ON POLICE
KILLINGS**

First Melville House Printing: June 2017

Melville House Publishing   8 Blackstock Mews
            46 John Street   and   Islington
      Brooklyn, NY 11201   London N4 2BT

mhpbooks.com
facebook.com/mhpbooks
@melvillehouse

ISBN: 978-1-61219-654-1

Designed by Fritz Metsch

Printed in the United States of America
10 9 8 7 6 5 4 3 2 1

Contents

Federal Report on Police Killings

Federal Officials Close Investigation into Death of Trayvon Martin

Department of Justice
Office of Public Affairs

FOR IMMEDIATE RELEASE
Tuesday, February 24, 2015

The Justice Department announced today that the independent federal investigation found insufficient evidence to pursue federal criminal civil rights charges against George Zimmerman for the fatal shooting of Trayvon Martin on Feb. 26, 2012, in Sanford, Florida. Prosecutors from the Justice Department's Civil Rights Division, officials from the FBI, and the Justice Department's Community Relations Service met today with Martin's family and their representatives to inform them of the findings of the investigation and the decision.

"The death of Trayvon Martin was a devastating tragedy. It shook an entire community, drew the attention of millions across the nation, and sparked a painful but necessary dialogue throughout the country," said Attorney General Eric Holder. "Though a comprehensive investigation found that the high standard for a federal hate crime prosecution cannot be met under the circumstances here, this young man's premature death necessitates that we continue the dialogue and be unafraid of confronting the issues and tensions his passing brought to the surface. We, as a nation, must take concrete steps to ensure that such incidents do not occur in the future."

Following the shooting, a team of some of the department's most experienced civil rights prosecutors and FBI agents conducted a comprehensive, independent investigation of the events of Feb. 26, 2012. The federal investigation was opened and conducted separately from the state of Florida's investigation of the shooting under local laws. Once the state initiated the second-degree murder prosecution, federal investigators began monitoring the state's case and halted active investigation in order not to interfere with the state's trial. Federal investigators provided reports of interviews and other evidence they obtained to the state's prosecution team.

Shortly after Zimmerman's acquittal in state court on July 13, 2013, federal investigators resumed active investigation. Federal investigators reviewed all of the material and evidence generated by the state of Florida in connection with its investigation and prosecution of Zimmerman, including witness statements, crime scene evidence, cell phone data, ballistics reports, reconstruction analysis, medical and autopsy reports, depositions, and the trial record. Federal investigators also independently conducted 75 witness interviews and obtained and reviewed the contents of relevant electronic devices. The investigation included an examination of police reports and additional evidence that was generated related to encounters Zimmerman has had with law enforcement in Florida since the state trial acquittal. In addition, federal authorities retained an independent biomechanical expert who assessed Zimmerman's descriptions of the struggle and the shooting.

The federal investigation sought to determine whether the evidence of the events that led to Martin's death were sufficient to prove beyond a reasonable doubt that Zimmerman's actions violated the federal criminal civil rights statutes, specifically Section 3631 of Title 42 of the U.S. Code or Section 249 of Title 18 of the U.S. Code, as well as other relevant federal criminal statutes. Section 3631 criminalizes willfully using force or threat of force to interfere with a person's federally protected housing rights on account of that person's race or color. Section 249 criminalizes willfully causing bodily injury to a person because of that person's actual or perceived race. Courts define "willfully" to require proof that a defendant knew his acts were unlawful, and committed those acts in open defiance of the law. It is one of the highest standards of intent imposed by law.

The federal investigation examined whether Zimmerman violated civil rights statutes at any point during his interaction with Martin, from their initial encounter through the fatal shooting. This included investigating whether there is evidence beyond a reasonable doubt that Zimmerman violated Section 3631 by approaching Martin in a threatening manner before the fatal shooting because of Martin's race and because he was using the residential neighborhood. Investigators also looked at whether there is evidence beyond a reasonable doubt that Zimmerman violated Section 3631 or Section 249, by using force against Martin either during their struggle or when shooting Martin, because of Martin's race.

"Although the department has determined that this matter cannot be prosecuted federally, it is important to remember that this incident resulted in the tragic loss of a teenager's life," said Acting Assistant Attorney General Vanita Gupta of the Civil Rights Division. "Our decision not to pursue federal charges does not condone the shooting that resulted in the death of Trayvon Martin and is based solely on the high legal standard applicable to these cases."

After a thorough and independent investigation into the facts surrounding the shooting, federal investigators determined that there is insufficient evidence to prove beyond a reasonable doubt a violation of these statutes. Accordingly, the investigation into this incident has been closed. This decision is limited strictly to the department's inability to meet the high legal standard required to prosecute the case under the federal civil rights statutes; it does not reflect an assessment of any other aspect of the shooting.

The Justice Department is committed to investigations of allegations of bias-motivated violence and will continue to devote the resources required to ensure that allegations of civil rights violations are fully and completely investigated. The department aggressively prosecutes criminal civil rights violations whenever there is sufficient evidence to do so.

Department of Justice Report Regarding the Criminal Investigation into the Shooting Death of Michael Brown by Ferguson, Missouri Police Officer Darren Wilson

MARCH 4, 2015

I. INTRODUCTION

At approximately noon on Saturday, August 9, 2014, Officer Darren Wilson of the Ferguson Police Department ("FPD") shot and killed Michael Brown, an unarmed 18-year-old. The Criminal Section of the Department of Justice Civil Rights Division, the United States Attorney's Office for the Eastern District of Missouri, and the Federal Bureau of Investigation ("FBI") (collectively, "The Department") subsequently opened a criminal investigation into whether the shooting violated federal law. The Department has determined that the evidence does not support charging a violation of federal law. This memorandum details the Department's investigation, findings, and conclusions. Part I provides an introduction and overview. Part II summarizes the federal investigation and the evidence uncovered during the course of the investigation, and discusses the applicable federal criminal civil rights law and standards of federal prosecution. Part III provides a more in-depth summary of the evidence. Finally, Part IV provides a detailed legal analysis of the evidence and explains why the evidence does not support an indictment of Darren Wilson.

The Department conducted an extensive investigation into the shooting of Michael Brown. Federal authorities reviewed physical, ballistic, forensic, and crime scene evidence; medical reports and autopsy reports, including an independent autopsy performed by the United States Department of Defense Armed Forces Medical Examiner Service ("AFMES"); Wilson's personnel records; audio and video recordings; and internet postings. FBI agents, St. Louis County Police Department ("SLCPD") detectives, and federal prosecutors and prosecutors from the St. Louis County Prosecutor's Office ("county prosecutors") worked cooperatively to both independently and jointly interview more than 100 purported eyewitnesses and other individuals claiming to have relevant information. SLCPD detectives conducted an initial canvass of the area on the day of the shooting. FBI agents then independently canvassed more than 300 residences to locate and interview additional witnesses. Federal and local authorities collected cellular phone data, searched social media sites, and tracked down dozens of leads from community members and dedicated law enforcement email addresses and tip lines in an effort to investigate every possible source of information.

The principles of federal prosecution, set forth in the United States Attorneys' Manual ("USAM"), require federal prosecutors to meet two standards in order to seek an indictment. First, we must be convinced that the potential defendant committed a federal crime. See USAM § 9-27.220 (a federal prosecution should be commenced only when an attorney for the government "believes that the person's conduct constitutes a federal offense"). Second, we must also conclude that we would be likely to prevail at trial, where we must prove the charges beyond a reasonable doubt. See USAM § 9-27.220 (a federal prosecution should be commenced only when "the admissible evidence will probably be sufficient to sustain a conviction"); Fed R. Crim P. 29(a)(prosecution must present evidence sufficient to sustain a conviction). Taken together, these standards require the Department to be convinced both that a federal crime occurred and that it can be proven beyond a reasonable doubt at trial.In order to make the proper assessment under these standards, federal prosecutors evaluated physical, forensic, and potential testimonial evidence in the form of witness accounts. As detailed below, the physical and forensic evidence provided federal prosecutors with a benchmark against which to measure the credibility of each witness account, including that of Darren Wilson. We compared individual witness accounts to the physical and forensic evidence, to other credible witness accounts, and to each witness's own prior statements made throughout the investigations, including the proceedings before the St. Louis County grand jury ("county grand jury"). We worked with federal and local law enforcement officers to interview witnesses, to include re-interviewing certain witnesses in an effort to evaluate inconsistencies in their accounts and to obtain more detailed information. In so doing, we assessed the witnesses' demeanor, tone, bias, and ability to accurately perceive or recall the events of August 9, 2014. We credited and determined that a jury would appropriately credit those witnesses whose accounts were consistent with the physical evidence and consistent with other credible witness accounts. In the case of witnesses who made multiple statements, we compared those statements to determine whether they were materially consistent with each other and considered the timing and circumstances under which the witnesses gave the statements. We did not credit and determined that a jury appropriately would not credit those witness accounts that were contrary to the physical and forensic evidence, significantly inconsistent with other credible witness accounts, or significantly inconsistent with that witness's own prior statements.

Based on this investigation, the Department has concluded that Darren Wilson's actions do not constitute prosecutable violations under the applicable federal criminal civil rights statute, 18 U.S.C. § 242, which prohibits uses of deadly force that are "objectively unreasonable," as defined by the United States Supreme Court. The evidence, when viewed as a whole, does not support the conclusion that Wilson's uses of deadly force were "objectively unreasonable" under the Supreme Court's definition. Accordingly, under the governing federal law and relevant standards set forth in the USAM, it is not appropriate to present this matter to a federal grand jury for indictment, and it should therefore be closed without prosecution.

II. SUMMARY OF THE EVIDENCE, INVESTIGATION, AND APPLICABLE LAW

A. Summary of the Evidence

Within two minutes of Wilson's initial encounter with Brown on August 9, 2014, FPD officers responded to the scene of the shooting, and subsequently turned the matter over to the SLCPD for investigation. SLCPD detectives immediately began securing and processing the scene and conducting initial witness interviews. The FBI opened a federal criminal civil rights investigation on August 11, 2014. Thereafter, federal and county authorities conducted cooperative, yet independent investigations into the shooting of Michael Brown.

The encounter between Wilson and Brown took place over an approximately two-minute period of time at about noon on August 9, 2014. Wilson was on duty and driving his department-issued Chevy Tahoe SUV westbound on Canfield Drive in Ferguson, Missouri when he saw Brown and his friend, Witness 101, walking eastbound in the middle of the street. Brown and Witness 101 had just come from Ferguson Market and Liquor ("Ferguson Market"), a nearby convenience store, where, at approximately 11:53 a.m., Brown stole several packages of cigarillos. As captured on the store's surveillance video, when the store clerk tried to stop Brown, Brown used his physical size to stand over him and forcefully shove him away. As a result, an FPD dispatch call went out over the police radio for a "stealing in progress." The dispatch recordings and Wilson's radio transmissions establish that Wilson was aware of the theft and had a description of the suspects as he encountered Brown and Witness 101.

As Wilson drove toward Brown and Witness 101, he told the two men to walk on the sidewalk. According to Wilson's statement to prosecutors and investigators, he suspected that Brown and Witness 101 were involved in the incident at Ferguson Market based on the descriptions he heard on the radio and the cigarillos in Brown's hands. Wilson then called for backup, stating, "Put me on Canfield with two and send me another car." Wilson backed up his SUV and parked at an angle, blocking most of both lanes of traffic, and stopping Brown and Witness 101 from walking any further. Wilson attempted to open the driver's door of the SUV to exit his vehicle, but as he swung it open, the door came into contact with Brown's body and either rebounded closed or Brown pushed it closed.

Wilson and other witnesses stated that Brown then reached into the SUV through the open driver's window and punched and grabbed Wilson. This is corroborated by bruising on Wilson's jaw and scratches on his neck, the presence of Brown's DNA on Wilson's collar, shirt, and pants, and Wilson's DNA on Brown's palm. While there are other individuals who stated that Wilson reached out of the SUV and grabbed Brown by the neck, prosecutors could not credit their accounts because they were inconsistent with physical and forensic evidence, as detailed throughout this report.

Wilson told prosecutors and investigators that he responded to Brown reaching into the SUV and punching him by withdrawing his gun because he could not access less lethal weapons while seated inside the SUV. Brown then grabbed the weapon and struggled with Wilson to gain control of it. Wilson fired, striking Brown in the hand. Autopsy results and bullet trajectory, skin from Brown's palm on the outside of the SUV door as well as Brown's DNA on the inside of the driver's door corroborate Wilson's account that during the struggle, Brown used his right hand to grab and attempt to control Wilson's gun. According to three autopsies, Brown sustained a close range gunshot wound to the fleshy portion of his right hand at the base of his right thumb. Soot from the muzzle of the gun found embedded in the tissue of this wound coupled with indicia of thermal change from the heat of the muzzle indicate that Brown's hand was within inches of the muzzle of Wilson's gun when it was fired. The location of the recovered bullet in the side panel of the driver's door, just above Wilson's lap, also corroborates Wilson's account of the struggle over the gun and when the gun was fired, as do witness accounts that Wilson fired at least one shot from inside the SUV.

Although no eyewitnesses directly corroborate Wilson's account of Brown's attempt to gain control of the gun, there is no credible evidence to disprove Wilson's account of what occurred inside the SUV. Some witnesses claim that Brown's arms were never inside the SUV. However, as discussed later in this report, those witness accounts could not be relied upon in a prosecution because credible witness accounts and physical and forensic evidence, *i.e.* Brown's DNA inside the SUV and on Wilson's shirt collar and the bullet trajectory and close-range gunshot wound to Brown's hand, establish that Brown's arms and/or torso were inside the SUV.

After the initial shooting inside the SUV, the evidence establishes that Brown ran eastbound on Canfield Drive and Wilson chased after him. The autopsy results confirm that Wilson did not shoot Brown in the back as he was running away because there were no entrance wounds to Brown's back. The autopsy results alone do not indicate the direction Brown was facing when he received two wounds to his right arm, given the mobility of the arm. However, as detailed later in this report, there are no witness accounts that could be relied upon in a prosecution to prove that Wilson shot at Brown as he was running away. Witnesses who say so cannot be relied upon in a prosecution because they have given accounts that are inconsistent with the physical and forensic evidence or are significantly inconsistent with their own prior statements made throughout the investigation.

Brown ran at least 180 feet away from the SUV, as verified by the location of bloodstains on the roadway, which DNA analysis confirms was Brown's blood.

Brown then turned around and came back toward Wilson, falling to his death approximately 21.6 feet west of the blood in the roadway. Those witness accounts stating that Brown never moved back toward Wilson could not be relied upon in a prosecution because their accounts cannot be reconciled with the DNA bloodstain evidence and other credible witness accounts.

As detailed throughout this report, several witnesses stated that Brown appeared to pose a physical threat to Wilson as he moved toward Wilson. According to these witnesses, who are corroborated by blood evidence in the roadway, as Brown continued to move toward Wilson, Wilson fired at Brown in what appeared to be self-defense and stopped firing once Brown fell to the ground. Wilson stated that he feared Brown would again assault him because of Brown's conduct at the SUV and because as Brown moved toward him, Wilson saw Brown reach his right hand under his t-shirt into what appeared to be his waistband. There is no evidence upon which prosecutors can rely to disprove Wilson's stated subjective belief that he feared for his safety.

Ballistics analysis indicates that Wilson fired a total of 12 shots, two from the SUV and ten on the roadway. Witness accounts and an audio recording indicate that when Wilson and Brown were on the roadway, Wilson fired three gunshot volleys, pausing in between each one. According to the autopsy results, Wilson shot and hit Brown as few as six or as many as eight times, including the gunshot to Brown's hand. Brown fell to the ground dead as a result of a gunshot to the apex of his head. With the exception of the first shot to Brown's hand, all of the shots that struck Brown were fired from a distance of more than two feet. As documented by crime scene photographs, Brown fell to the ground with his left, uninjured hand balled up by his waistband, and his right, injured hand palm up by his side. Witness accounts and cellular phone video prove that Wilson did not touch Brown's body after he fired the final shot and Brown fell to the ground.

Although there are several individuals who have stated that Brown held his hands up in an unambiguous sign of surrender prior to Wilson shooting him dead, their accounts do not support a prosecution of Wilson. As detailed throughout this report, some of those accounts are inaccurate because they are inconsistent with the physical and forensic evidence; some of those accounts are materially inconsistent with that witness's own prior statements with no explanation, credible for otherwise, as to why those accounts changed over time. Certain other witnesses who originally stated Brown had his hands up in surrender recanted their original accounts, admitting that they did not witness the shooting or parts of it, despite what they initially reported either to federal or local law enforcement or to the media. Prosecutors did not rely on those accounts when making a prosecutive decision.

While credible witnesses gave varying accounts of exactly what Brown was doing with his hands as he moved toward Wilson—i.e., balling them, holding them out, or pulling up his pants up—and varying accounts of how he was moving—*i.e.,* "charging," moving in "slow motion," or "running"—they all establish that Brown was moving toward Wilson when Wilson shot him. Although some witnesses state that Brown held his hands up at shoulder level with his palms facing outward for a brief moment, these same witnesses describe Brown then dropping his hands and "charging" at Wilson.

B. Initial Law Enforcement Investigation

Wilson shot Brown at about 12:02 p.m. on August 9, 2014. Within minutes, FPD officers responded to the scene, as they were already en route from Wilson's initial radio call for assistance. Also within minutes, residents began pouring onto the street. At 12:08 p.m., FPD officers requested assistance from nearby SLCPD precincts. By 12:14 p.m., some members of the growing crowd became increasingly hostile in response to chants of "[We] need to kill these motherfuckers," referring to the police officers on scene. At around the same time, about 12:15 p.m., Witness 147, an FPD sergeant, informed the FPD Chief that there had been a fatal officer-involved shooting. At about 12:23 p.m., after speaking with one of his captains, the FPD Chief contacted the SLCPD Chief and turned over the homicide investigation to the SLCPD. Within twenty minutes of Brown's death, paramedics covered Brown's body with several white sheets.

The SLCPD Division of Criminal Investigation, Bureau of Crimes Against Persons ("CAP") was notified at 12:43 p.m. to report to the crime scene to begin a homicide investigation. When they received notification, SLCPD CAP detectives were investigating an armed, masked hostage situation in the hospice wing at St. Anthony's Medical Center in the south part of St. Louis County, nearly 37 minutes from Canfield Drive. They arrived at Canfield Drive at approximately 1:30 p.m. During that time frame, between about 12:45 p.m. and 1:17 p.m., SLCPD reported gunfire in the area, putting both civilians and officers in danger. As a result, canine officers and additional patrol officers responded to assist with crowd control. SLCPD expanded the perimeter of the crime scene to move the crowd away from Brown's body in an effort to preserve the crime scene for processing.

Upon their arrival, SLCPD detectives from the Bureau of Criminal Identification Crime Scene Unit erected orange privacy screens around Brown's body, and CAP detectives alerted the St. Louis County Medical Examiner ("SCLME") to respond to the scene. To further protect the integrity of the crime scene, and in accordance with common police practice, SLCPD personnel did not permit family members and concerned neighbors into the crime scene (with one brief exception). Also in accordance with common police practice, crime scene detectives processed the crime scene with Brown's body present. According to SLCPD CAP detectives, they have one opportunity to thoroughly investigate a crime scene before it is forever changed upon the removal of the decedent's body. Processing a homicide scene with the decedent's body present allows detectives, for example, to accurately measure distances, precisely document body position, and note injury and other markings relative to other aspects of the crime scene that photographs may not capture.

In this case, crime scene detectives had to stop processing the scene as a result of two more reports of what sounded like automatic weapons gunfire in the area at 1:55 p.m. and 2:11 p.m., as well as some individuals in the crowd encroaching on the crime scene and chanting, "Kill the Police," as documented by cell phone video. At each of those times, having exhausted their existing resources, SLCPD personnel called emergency codes for additional patrol officers from throughout St. Louis County in increments of twenty-five. Livery drivers sent to transport Brown's body upon completion of processing arrived at 2:20 p.m. Their customary practice is to wait on scene until the body is ready for transport. However, an SLCPD sergeant briefly stopped them from getting out of their vehicle until the gunfire abated and it was safe for them to do so. The SLCME medicolegal investigator arrived at 2:30 p.m. and began conducting his investigation when it was reasonably safe to do so. Detectives were at the crime scene for approximately five and a half hours, and throughout that time, SLCPD personnel continued to seek additional assistance, calling in the Highway Safety Unit at 2:38 p.m. and the Tactical Operations Unit at 2:44 p.m. Witnesses and detectives described the scene as volatile, causing concern for both their personal safety and the integrity of the crime scene. Crime scene detectives and the SLCME medicolegal investigator completed the processing of Brown's body at approximately 4:00 p.m, at which time Brown's body was transported to the Office of the SLCME.

C. Legal Summary

1. The Law Governing Uses of Deadly Force by a Law Enforcement Officer

The federal criminal statute that enforces Constitutional limits on uses of force by law enforcement officers is 18 U.S.C. § 242, which provides in relevant part, as follows:

> Whoever, under color of any law, . . . willfully subjects any person . . . to the deprivation of any rights, privileges, or immunities secured or protected by the Constitution or laws of the United States [shall be guilty of a crime].

To prove a violation of Section 242, the government must prove the following elements beyond a reasonable doubt: (1) that the defendant was acting under color of law, (2) that he deprived a victim of a right protected by the Constitution or laws of the United States, (3) that he acted willfully, and (4) that the deprivation resulted in bodily injury and/or death. There is no dispute that Wilson, who was on duty and working as a patrol officer for the FPD, acted under color of law when he shot Brown, or that the shots resulted in Brown's death. The determination of whether criminal prosecution is appropriate rests on whether there is sufficient evidence to establish that any of the shots fired by Wilson were unreasonable, as defined under federal law, given the facts known to Wilson at the time, and if so, whether Wilson fired the shots with the requisite "willful" criminal intent.

i. The Shootings Were Not Objectively Unreasonable Uses of Force Under 18 U.S.C. § 242

In this case, the Constitutional right at issue is the Fourth Amendment's prohibition against unreasonable seizures, which encompasses the right of an arrestee to be free from "objectively unreasonable" force. *Graham v. Connor*, 490 U.S. 386, 396-97 (1989). "The 'reasonableness' of a particular use of force must be judged from the perspective of a reasonable officer on the scene, rather than with the 20/20 vision of hindsight." *Id.* at 396. "Careful attention" must be paid "to the facts and circumstances of each particular case, including the severity of the crime at issue, whether the suspect poses an immediate threat to the safety of the officers or others, and whether he is actively resisting arrest or attempting to evade arrest by flight." *Id.* Allowance must be made for the fact that law enforcement officials are often forced to make split-second judgments in circumstances that are tense, uncertain, and rapidly evolving. *Id.* at 396-97.

The use of deadly force is justified when the officer has "probable cause to believe that the suspect pose[s] a threat of serious physical harm, either to the officer or to others." *Tennessee v. Garner*, 471 U.S. 1, 11 (1985); *see Nelson v. County of Wright*, 162 F.3d 986, 990 (8th Cir. 1998); *O'Bert v. Vargo*, 331 F.3d 29, 36 (2d Cir. 2003) (same as *Garner*); *Deluna v. City of Rockford*, 447 F.3d 1008, 1010 (7th Cir. 2006), *citing Scott v. Edinburg*, 346 F.3d 752, 756 (7th Cir. 2003) (deadly force can be reasonably employed where an officer believes that the suspect's actions place him, or others in the immediate vicinity, in imminent danger of death or serious bodily injury).

As detailed throughout this report, the evidence does not establish that the shots fired by Wilson were objectively unreasonable under federal law. The physical evidence establishes that Wilson shot Brown once in the hand, at close range, while Wilson sat in his police SUV, struggling with Brown for control of Wilson's gun. Wilson then shot Brown several more times from a distance of at least two feet after Brown ran away from Wilson and then turned and faced him. There are no witness accounts that federal prosecutors, and likewise a jury, would credit to support the conclusion that Wilson fired at Brown from behind. With the exception of the two wounds to Brown's right arm, which indicate neither bullet trajectory nor the direction in which Brown was moving when he was struck, the medical examiners' reports are in agreement that the entry wounds from the latter gunshots were to the front of Brown's body, establishing that Brown was facing Wilson when these shots were fired. This includes the fatal shot to the top of Brown's head. The physical evidence also establishes that Brown moved forward toward Wilson after he turned around to face him. The physical evidence is corroborated by multiple eyewitnesses.

Applying the well-established controlling legal authority, including binding precedent from the United States Supreme Court and Eighth Circuit Court of Appeals, the evidence does not establish that it was unreasonable for Wilson to perceive Brown as a threat while Brown was punching and grabbing him in the SUV and attempting to take his gun. Thereafter, when Brown started to flee, Wilson was aware that Brown had attempted to take his gun and suspected that Brown might have been part of a theft a few minutes before. Under the law, it was not unreasonable for Wilson to perceive that Brown posed a threat of serious physical harm, either to him or to others. When Brown turned around and moved toward Wilson, the applicable law and evidence do not support finding that Wilson was unreasonable in his fear that Brown would once again attempt to harm him and gain control of his gun. There are no credible witness accounts that state that Brown was clearly attempting to surrender when Wilson shot him. As detailed throughout this report, those witnesses who say so have given accounts that could not be relied upon in a prosecution because they are irreconcilable with the physical evidence, inconsistent with the credible accounts of other eyewitnesses, inconsistent with the witness's own prior statements, or in some instances, because the witnesses have acknowledged that their initial accounts were untrue.

ii. Wilson Did Not Willfully Violate Brown's Constitutional Right to Be Free from Unreasonable Force

Federal law requires that the government must also prove that the officer acted willfully, that is, "for the specific purpose of violating the law." *Screws v. United States*, 325 U.S. 91, 101-107 (1945) (discussing willfulness element of 18 U.S.C. § 242). The Supreme Court has held that an act is done willfully if it was "committed" either "in open defiance or in reckless disregard of a constitutional requirement which has been made specific or definite." *Screws*, 325 U.S. at 105. The government need not show that the defendant knew a federal statute or law protected the right with which he intended to interfere. *Id.* at 106-07 ("[t] he fact that the defendants may not have been thinking in constitutional terms is not material where their aim was not to enforce local law but to deprive a citizen of a right and that right was protected"); *United States v. Walsh*, 194 F.3d 37, 52-53 (2d Cir. 1999) (holding that jury did not have to find defendant knew of the particular Constitutional provision at issue but that it had to find intent to invade interest protected by Constitution). However, we must prove that the defendant intended to engage in the conduct that violated the Constitution and that he did so knowing that it was a wrongful act. *Id.*

"[A]ll the attendant circumstances" should be considered in determining whether an act was done willfully. *Screws*, 325 U.S. at 107. Evidence regarding the egregiousness of the conduct, its character and duration, the weapons employed and the provocation, if any, is therefore relevant to this inquiry. *Id.* Willfulness may be inferred from blatantly wrongful conduct. *See id.* at 106; *see also United States v. Reese*, 2 F.3d 870, 881 (9th Cir. 1993) ("Intentionally wrongful conduct, because it contravenes a right definitely established in law, evidences a reckless disregard for that right; such reckless disregard, in turn, is the legal equivalent of willfulness."); *United States v. Dise*, 763 F.2d 586, 592 (3d Cir. 1985) (holding that when defendant "invades personal liberty of another, knowing that invasion is violation of state law, [defendant] has demonstrated bad faith and reckless disregard for [federal] constitutional rights"). Mistake, fear, misperception, or even poor judgment does not constitute willful conduct prosecutable under the statute. *See United States v. McClean*, 528 F.2d 1250, 1255 (2d Cir. 1976) (inadvertence or mistake negates willfulness for purposes of 18 U.S.C. § 242).

As detailed below, Wilson has stated his intent in shooting Brown was in response to a perceived deadly threat. The only possible basis for prosecuting Wilson under 18 U.S.C. § 242 would therefore be if the government could prove that his account is not true—*i.e.*, that Brown never punched and grabbed Wilson at the SUV, never attempted to gain control of Wilson's gun, and thereafter clearly surrendered in a way that no reasonable officer could have failed to perceive. There is no credible evidence to refute Wilson's stated subjective belief that he was acting in self-defense. As discussed throughout this report, Wilson's account is corroborated by physical evidence and his perception of a threat posed by Brown is corroborated by other credible eyewitness accounts. Even if Wilson was mistaken in his interpretation of Brown's conduct, the fact that others interpreted that conduct the same way as Wilson precludes a determination that he acted for the purpose of violating the law.

III. SUMMARY OF THE EVIDENCE

As detailed below, Darren Wilson has stated that he shot Michael Brown in response to a perceived deadly threat. This section begins with Wilson's account because the evidence that follows, in the form of forensic and physical evidence and witness accounts, must disprove his account beyond a reasonable doubt in order for the government to prosecute Wilson.

A. Darren Wilson's Account

Darren Wilson made five voluntary statements following the shooting. Wilson's first statement was to Witness 147, his supervising sergeant at the FPD, who responded to Canfield Drive within minutes and immediately spoke to Wilson. Wilson's second statement was made to an SLCPD detective about 90 minutes later, after Wilson returned to the FPD. This interview continued at a local hospital while Wilson was receiving medical treatment. Third, SLCPD detectives conducted a more thorough interview the following morning, on August 10, 2014. Fourth, federal prosecutors and FBI agents interviewed Wilson on August 22, 2014. Wilson's attorney was present for both interviews with the SLCPD detectives. Two attorneys were present for his interview with federal agents and prosecutors. Wilson's fifth statement occurred when he appeared before the county grand jury for approximately 90 minutes on September 16, 2014.

According to Wilson, he was traveling westbound on Canfield Drive, having just finished another call, when he saw Brown and Witness 101 walking single file in the middle of the street on the yellow line. Wilson had never before met either Brown or Witness 101. Wilson approached Witness 101 first and told him to use the sidewalk because there had been cars trying to pass them. When pressed by federal prosecutors, Wilson denied using profane language, explaining that he was on his way to meet his fiancée for lunch, and did not want to antagonize the two subjects. Witness 101 responded to Wilson that he was almost to his destination, and Wilson replied, "What's wrong with the sidewalk?" Wilson stated that Brown unexpectedly responded, "Fuck what you have to say." As Wilson drove past Brown, he saw cigarillos in Brown's hand, which alerted him to a radio dispatch of a "stealing in progress" that he heard a few minutes prior while finishing his last call. Wilson then checked his rearview mirror, and realized that Witness 101 matched the description of the other subject on the radio dispatch.

Wilson requested assistance over the radio, stating that he had two subjects on Canfield Drive. Wilson explained that he intended to stop Brown and Witness 101 and wait for backup before he did any further investigation into the theft. Wilson reversed his vehicle and parked in a manner to block Brown and Witness 101 from walking any further. Upon doing so, he attempted to open his driver's door, and said, "Hey, come here." Before Wilson got his leg out, Brown responded, "What the fuck are you gonna do?" Brown then slammed the door shut and Wilson told him to "get back." Wilson attempted to open the door again. Wilson told the county grand jury that he then told Brown, "Get the fuck back," but Brown did not comply and, using his body, pushed the door closed on Wilson.

Brown placed his hands on the window frame of the driver's door, and again Wilson told Brown to "get back." To Wilson's surprise, Brown then leaned into the driver's window, so that his arms and upper torso were inside the SUV. Brown started assaulting Wilson, "swinging wildly." Brown, still with cigarillos in his hand, turned around and handed the items to Witness 101 using his left hand, telling Witness 101 "take these." Wilson used the opportunity to grab Brown's right arm, but Brown used his left hand to twice punch Wilson's jaw. As Brown assaulted Wilson, Wilson leaned back, blocking the blows with his forearms. Brown hit Wilson on the side of his face and grabbed his shirt, hands, and arms. Wilson feared that Brown's blows could potentially render him unconscious, leaving him vulnerable to additional harm.

Wilson explained that he resorted to his training and the "use of force triangle" to determine how to properly defend himself. Wilson explained that he did not carry a taser, and therefore, his options were mace, his flashlight, his retractable asp baton, and his firearm. Wilson's mace was on his left hip and Wilson explained that he knew that the space within the SUV was too small to use it without incapacitating himself in the process. Wilson's asp baton was located on the back of his duty belt. Wilson determined that not only would he have to lean forward to reach it, giving more of an advantage to Brown, but there was not enough space in the SUV to expand the baton. Wilson's flashlight was in his duty bag on the passenger seat, out of his reach. Wilson explained that his gun, located on his right hip, was his only readily accessible option.

Consequently, while the assault was in progress and Brown was leaning in through the window with his arms, torso, and head inside the SUV, Wilson withdrew his gun and pointed it at Brown. Wilson warned Brown to stop or he was going to shoot him. Brown stated, "You are too much of a pussy to shoot," and put his right hand over Wilson's right hand, gaining control of the gun. Brown then maneuvered the gun so that it was pointed down at Wilson's left hip. Wilson explained that Brown's size and strength, coupled with his standing position outside the SUV relative to Wilson's seated position inside the SUV, rendered Wilson completely vulnerable. Wilson stated that he feared Brown was going to shoot him because Brown had control of the gun. Wilson managed to use his left elbow to brace against the seat, gaining enough leverage to push the gun forward until it lined up with the driver's door, just under the handle. Wilson explained that he twice pulled the trigger but the gun did not fire, most likely because Brown's hand was preventing the gun from functioning properly. Wilson pulled the trigger a third time and the gun fired into the door. Immediately, glass shattered because the window had been down, and Wilson noticed blood on his own hand. Wilson initially thought he had been cut by the glass.

Brown appeared to be momentarily startled because he briefly backed up. Wilson saw Brown put his hand down to his right hip, and initially assumed the bullet went through the door and struck Brown there. Wilson then described Brown becoming enraged, and that Brown "looked like a demon." Brown then leaned into the driver's window so that his head and arms were inside the SUV and he assaulted Wilson again. Wilson explained that while blocking his face with his left hand, he tried to fire his gun with his right hand, but the gun jammed. Wilson lifted the gun, without looking, and used both hands to manually clear the gun while also trying to shield himself. He then successfully fired another shot, holding the gun in his right hand. According to Wilson, he could not see where he shot, but did not think that he struck Brown because he saw "smoke" outside the window, seemingly from the ground, indicating to him a point of impact that was farther away.

Brown then took off running. Wilson radioed for additional assistance, calling out that shots were fired. Wilson then chased after Brown on foot. Federal prosecutors questioned Wilson as to why he did not drive away or wait for backup, but instead chose to pursue Brown despite the attack he just described. Wilson explained that he ran after Brown because Brown posed a danger to others, having just assaulted a police officer and likely stolen from Ferguson Market. Given Brown's violent and otherwise erratic behavior, Wilson was concerned that Brown was a danger to anyone who crossed his path as he ran.

Wilson denied firing any shots while Brown was running from him. Rather he kept his gun out, but down in a "low ready" position. Wilson explained that he chased after Brown, repeatedly yelling at him to stop and get on the ground. Brown kept running, but when he was about 20 to 30 feet from Wilson, abruptly stopped, and turned around toward Wilson, appearing "psychotic," "hostile," and "crazy," as though he was "looking through" Wilson. While making a "grunting noise" and with what Wilson described as the "most intense aggressive face" that he had ever seen on a person, Brown then made a hop-like movement, similar to what a person does when he starts running. Brown then started running at Wilson, closing the distance between them to about 15 feet. Wilson explained that he again feared for his life, and backed up as Brown came toward him, repeatedly ordering Brown to stop and get on the ground. Brown failed to comply and kept coming at Wilson. Wilson explained that he knew if Brown reached him, he "would be done." During Brown's initial strides, Brown put his right hand in what appeared to be his waistband, albeit covered by his shirt. Wilson thought Brown might be reaching for a weapon. Wilson fired multiple shots. Brown paused. Wilson explained that he then paused, again yelled for Brown to get on the ground, and again Brown charged at him, hand in waistband. Wilson backed up and fired again.

The same thing happened a third time where Brown very briefly paused, and Wilson paused and yelled for Brown to get on the ground. Brown continued to "charge." Wilson described having tunnel vision on Brown's right arm, all the while backing up as Brown approached, not understanding why Brown had yet to stop. Wilson fired the last volley of shots when Brown was about eight to ten feet from him. When Wilson fired the last shot, he saw the bullet go into Brown's head, and Brown "went down right there." Wilson initially estimated that on the roadway, he fired five shots and then two shots, none of which had any effect on Brown. Then Brown leaned forward as though he was getting ready to "tackle" Wilson, and Wilson fired the last shot.

Federal prosecutors questioned Wilson about his actions after the shooting. Wilson explained that he never touched Brown's body. Using the microphone on his shoulder, Wilson radioed, "Send me every car we got and a supervisor." Within seconds, additional officers and his sergeant arrived on scene. In response to specific questions by federal prosecutors, Wilson explained that he had left his keys in the ignition of his vehicle and the engine running during the pursuit, so he went back to his SUV to secure it. In so doing, he was careful only to touch the door and the keys. Wilson then walked over to his sergeant, Witness 147, and told him what happened. Both Wilson and Witness 147 explained that Witness 147 told Wilson to wait in his SUV, but Wilson refused, explaining that if he waited there, it would be known to the neighborhood that he was the shooter. Wilson explained that the atmosphere was quickly becoming hostile, and he either needed to be put to work with his fellow officers or he needed to leave. Per Witness 147's orders, Wilson drove Witness 147's vehicle to the FPD. It was during the drive that Wilson realized he was not bleeding, but had what he thought was Brown's blood on both hands.

As soon as Wilson got to the police department, he scrubbed both hands. When federal prosecutors challenged why he did so in light of the potential evidentiary value, Wilson explained that he realized after the fact that he should not have done so, but at the time he was reacting to a potential biohazard while still under the stress of the moment. Wilson then rendered his gun safe and packaged it with the one remaining round in an evidence envelope. When federal prosecutors further questioned why he packaged his own gun, Wilson explained that he wanted to ensure its preservation for analysis because it would prove what happened. At first, he hoped Brown's fingerprints or epithelial DNA from sweat on his hand might be present from when Brown grabbed the gun. But then Wilson actually saw blood on the gun, and assumed that since he was not bleeding, the blood likely belonged to Brown, and therefore, Brown's DNA would be present.

During Wilson's interview with federal authorities, prosecutors and agents focused on whether he was consistent with his previous statements, the motivation for his actions, and his training and experience relative to when the use of deadly force is appropriate. Federal prosecutors challenged Wilson with specificity about why he stopped Brown and whether he was aware that Brown and Witness 101 were suspects in the Ferguson Market robbery. Similarly, prosecutors challenged Wilson about his decision to use deadly force inside the SUV, to chase after Brown, and to again use deadly force on Brown in the roadway. Wilson responded to those challenges in a credible manner, offering reasonable explanations to the questions posed.

At the time of his interview, federal prosecutors and agents were aware of the autopsy, DNA, and ballistics results, as detailed below. Wilson's account was consistent with those results, and consistent with the accounts of other independent eyewitnesses, whose accounts were also consistent with the physical evidence. Wilson's statements were consistent with each other in all material ways, and would not be subject to effective impeachment for inconsistencies or deviation from the physical evidence. Therefore, in analyzing all of the evidence, federal prosecutors found Wilson's account to be credible.

B. Physical and Forensic Evidence

1. Crime Scene

As noted above, SLCPD detectives from the Bureau of Criminal Identification, Crime Scene Unit processed the scene of the shootings. During processing, they photographed and took video of the crime scene, including Brown's body and Wilson's SUV. They measured distances from Brown's body, Wilson's SUV, and various pieces of evidence. As described in detail below, they recovered twelve spent shell casings. One was located on the ground between the driver's door and back passenger door of the SUV and another was located near the sidewalk, diagonally across from the driver's door. Seven casings and one spent projectile were located in the general vicinity of Brown's body. Those casings were located on the ground next to the left side of his body (on the south side of Canfield Drive), with four closer to his body, and three in the grassy area of the sidewalk. The projectile was located on the right side of Brown's body (on the north side of Canfield Drive). Three additional casings were further east, or further away from where Brown came to rest. Crime scene detectives also recovered a spent projectile fragment from the wall of an apartment building located east of Brown's body, in the direction toward which Wilson had been shooting. As described below, crime scene detectives noted apparent blood in the roadway approximately 17 feet and 22 feet east of where Brown's body was found and east of the casings that were recovered, consistent with Brown moving toward Wilson before his death. There was no other blood found in the roadway, other than the pool of blood surrounding Brown's body.

Crime scene detectives recovered Brown's St. Louis Cardinals baseball cap by the driver's door of the SUV. Two bracelets, one black and yellow, and the other beaded, were found on either side of the SUV. Brown's Nike flip flops were located in the roadway, the left one near the front of the driver's side of the vehicle, approximately 126 feet west of where Brown's head came to rest, and the right one in the center of the roadway, 82.5 feet west of where Brown's head came to rest and just south of the center line. This is consistent with witness descriptions that Brown, wearing his socks, described as bright yellow with a marijuana leaf pattern, ran diagonally away from the SUV, crossing over the center line.

Prior to transport of Brown's body, the SLCME medicolegal investigator documented the position of Brown's body on the ground. Brown was on his stomach with his right cheek on the ground, his buttocks partially in the air. His uninjured left arm was back and partially bent under his body with his left hand at his waistband, balled up in a fist. His injured right arm was back behind him, almost at his right side, with his injured right hand at hip level, palm up. Brown's shorts were midway down his buttocks, as though they had partially fallen down.

The forensic analysis of the seized evidence is detailed below:

2. Autopsy Findings

There were three autopsies conducted on Michael Brown's body. SLCME conducted the first autopsy. A private forensic pathologist conducted the second autopsy at the request of Brown's family. AFMES conducted the third autopsy at the Department's request.

The SLCME, AFMES, and the private forensic pathologist were consistent in their findings unless otherwise noted. Brown was shot at least six and at most eight times. As described below, two entrance wounds may have been re-entry wounds, accounting for why the number of shots that struck Brown is not definite.

Of the eight gunshot wounds, two wounds, a penetrating gunshot wound to the apex of Brown's head, and a graze or tangential wound to the base of Brown's right thumb, have the most significant evidentiary value when determining the prosecutive merit of this matter. The former is significant because the gunshot to the head would have almost immediately incapacitated and immobilized Brown; the latter is significant because it is consistent with Brown's hand being in close range or having near-contact with the muzzle of Wilson's gun and corroborates Wilson's account that Brown struggled with him to gain control of the gun in the SUV.

The skin tags, or flaps of skin created by the graze of the bullet associated with the right thumb wound, indicate bullet trajectory. They were oriented toward the tip of the right thumb, indicating the path of the bullet went from the tip of the thumb toward the base. Microscopic analysis of the wound indicates that Brown's hand was near the muzzle of the gun when Wilson pulled the trigger. Both AFMES and SLCME pathologists observed numerous deposits of dark particulate foreign debris, consistent with gunpowder soot from the muzzle of the gun embedded in and around the wound. The private forensic pathologist called it gunshot residue, opining that Brown's right hand was less than a foot from the gun. The SLCME pathologist opined that the muzzle of the gun was likely six to nine inches from Brown's hand when it fired. AFMES pathologists opined that the particulate matter was, in fact, soot and was found at the exact point of entry of the wound. The soot, along with the thermal change in the skin resulting from heat discharge of the firearm, indicates that the base of Brown's right hand was within inches of the muzzle of Wilson's gun when it fired. AFMES pathologists further opined that, given the tangential nature of the wound, the fact that the soot was concentrated on one side of the wound, and the bullet trajectory as detailed below, the wound to the thumb is consistent with Brown's hand being on the barrel of the gun itself, though not the muzzle, at the time the shot was fired.

The presence of soot also proves that the wound to the thumb was the result of the gunshot at the SUV. As detailed below, several witnesses described Brown at or in Wilson's SUV when the first shot was fired, and a bullet was recovered from within the driver's door of the SUV. There is no evidence that Wilson was within inches of Brown's thumb other than in the SUV at the outset of the incident. Additionally, according to the SLCME pathologist and the private forensic pathologist, a piece of Brown's skin recovered from the exterior of the driver's door of the SUV is consistent with skin from the part of Brown's thumb that was wounded. It is therefore a virtual certainty that the first shot fired was the one that caused the tangential thumb wound.

The order of the remaining shots cannot be determined, though the shot to Brown's head would have killed him where he stood, preventing him from making any additional purposeful movement toward Wilson after the final shots were fired. The fatal bullet entered the skull, the brain, and the base of the skull, and came to rest in the soft tissues of the right face. The trajectory of the bullet was downward, forward, and to the right. Brown could not have been standing straight when Wilson fired this bullet because Wilson is slightly shorter than Brown. Brown was likely bent at the waist or falling forward when he received this wound. It is also possible, although not consistent with credible eyewitness accounts, that Brown had fallen to his knees with his head forward when Wilson fired this shot. However, the lack of stippling and soot indicates that Wilson was at least two to three feet from Brown when he fired.

The remaining gunshots, like the thumb wound, were all on Brown's right side and none of them would have necessarily immediately immobilized Brown. The lack of soot and stippling indicates that the shots were fired from a distance of at least two to three feet. However, as described below, because of environmental conditions and because Brown's shirt was blood soaked, it was not suitable for gunshot residue analysis to determine muzzle-to-target distance. Therefore, we cannot reliably say whether gunshot residue on Brown's shirt might have provided evidence of muzzle-to-target distance. Regardless, gunshot residue is inherently delicate and easily transferrable.

In addition to the thumb wound and the fatal shot to the head, Brown sustained a gunshot wound to his central forehead, with a corresponding exit wound of the right jaw. The bullet tracked through the right eye and right orbital bone, causing fractures of the facial bones. Brown sustained another gunshot wound to the upper right chest, near the neck. The bullet tracked though the right clavicle and upper lobe of the right lung, and came to rest in the right chest. Brown sustained another entrance wound to his lateral right chest. The bullet tracked through and fractured the eighth right rib, puncturing the lower lobe of the right lung. The bullet was recovered from the soft tissue of the right back. The AFMES pathologists and the private forensic pathologist opined that the right chest wound could have been a re-entry wound from an arm wound as described below, and the clavicle wound could have been a re-entry wound from the bullet that entered Brown's forehead and exited his jaw. The SLCME pathologist also allowed for the possibility of re-entry wounds, but did not opine with specificity due to the variability of such wounds.

Brown also sustained a gunshot wound to the front of the upper right arm, near the armpit, with a corresponding gunshot exit wound of the back of the upper right arm. The remaining gunshot wounds were also to the right arm. These bullet trajectories are described according to the standard anatomic diagram, that is, standing, arms at sides, palms facing forward. That said, Brown sustained a gunshot wound to the dorsal (back) right forearm, below the elbow. The bullet tracked through the bone in the forearm, fracturing it, and exiting through the ventral (front) right forearm. Finally, Brown sustained a tangential or graze gunshot wound to the right bicep, above the elbow.

Given the mobility of the arm, it is impossible to determine the position of the body relative to the shooter at the time the arm wounds were inflicted. Therefore, the autopsy results do not indicate whether Brown was facing Wilson or had his back to him. They do not indicate whether Brown sustained those two arm wounds while his hands were up, down, or by his waistband. The private forensic pathologist opined that he would expect a re-entry wound across Brown's stomach if Brown's hand was at his waistband at the time Wilson fired. However, as mentioned, there is no way to know the exact position of Brown's arm relative to his waistband at the time the bullets struck. Therefore, these gunshot wounds neither corroborate nor discredit Wilson's account or the account of any other witness. However, the concentration of bullet wounds on Brown's right side is consistent with Wilson's description that he focused on Brown's right arm while shooting.

The autopsy established that Brown did not sustain gunshot wounds to his back. There was no evidence to corroborate that Wilson choked, strangled, or tightly grasped Brown on or around his neck, as described by Witness 101 in the summary of his account below. There were no bruises, abrasions, hemorrhaging of soft tissues, or any other injuries to the neck, nor was there evidence of petechial hemorrhaging of Brown's remaining left eye. The private forensic pathologist opined that although the lack of injury does not signify the absence of strangulation, it would be "surprising," given Brown's size, if Wilson attempted to strangle Brown. The private forensic pathologist explained that the act of strangling is often committed by the stronger person, as it is rarely effective if attempted by the person of smaller size or weaker strength.

Brown sustained a one inch superficial incised wound to the right middle of the front of his left arm. SCLME differed with AFMES, characterizing this wound as an abrasion, but AFMES opined that this was more like a cut, consistent with being caused by broken window glass. Brown also sustained abrasions to the right side of the head and face, including abrasions near the right forehead, the lateral right face, and the upper right cheek, consistent with Brown falling and impacting the ground with his face. The private forensic pathologist opined that the severity of these abrasions could have been caused by involuntary seizures as Brown died. He also opined, as did the SLCME pathologist, that these abrasions were consistent with Brown impacting the ground upon death and sliding on the roadway due to the momentum from quickly moving forward.

According to the AFMES and SCLME pathologists, Brown also had small knuckle abrasions, but the pathologists could not link them to any specific source. The SLCME pathologist opined they may have been inflicted post mortem, while the AFMES pathologist opined that they were too small to determine whether they were caused pre or post-mortem. The private forensic pathologist did not note any knuckle abrasions or injury to Brown's hands, explaining that he would expect Brown to have knuckle injury if Wilson sustained broken bones, but not necessarily bruising. AFMES pathologists likewise concurred that lack of injury to Brown's hands is not inconsistent with bruising to Wilson's face.

3. DNA Analysis

The SLCPD Crime Laboratory conducted DNA analysis on swabs taken from Wilson, Brown, Wilson's gun, and the crime scene. Brown's DNA was found at four significant locations: on Wilson's gun; on the roadway further away from where he died; on the SUV driver's door and inside the driver's cabin area of the SUV; and on Wilson's clothes. A DNA mixture from which Wilson's DNA could not be excluded was found on Brown's left palm.

Analysis of DNA on Wilson's gun revealed a major mixture profile that is 2.1 octillion times more likely a mixture of DNA from Wilson and DNA from Brown than from Wilson and anyone else. This is conclusive evidence that Brown's DNA was on Wilson's gun.

Brown is the source of the DNA found in two bloodstains on Canfield Drive, approximately 17 and 22 feet east of where Brown fell to his death, proving that Brown moved forward toward Wilson prior to the fatal shot to his head.

Brown's DNA was found both on the inside and outside of the driver's side of the SUV. Brown is the source of DNA in blood found on the exterior of the passenger door of the driver's side of the SUV. Likewise, a piece of Brown's skin was recovered from the exterior of the driver's door of the SUV, consistent with Brown sustaining injury while at that door. Brown is also the source of the major contributor of a DNA mixture found on the interior driver's door handle of the SUV. A DNA mixture obtained from the top of the exterior of the driver's door revealed a major mixture profile that is 6.9 million times more likely a mixture of DNA from Wilson and DNA from Brown than from Wilson and anyone else.

Brown's DNA was found on Wilson's uniform shirt collar and pants. With respect to the left side of Wilson's shirt and collar, it is 2.1 trillion times more likely that the recovered DNA mixture is DNA from Wilson and DNA from Brown than from Wilson and anyone else. Similarly, with respect to a DNA mixture obtained from the left side of Wilson's pants, it is 34 sextillion times more likely that the mixture is DNA from Wilson and DNA from Brown than from Wilson and anyone else. Brown is also the source of the major male profile found in a DNA mixture found in a bloodstain on the upper left thigh of Wilson's pants.

DNA analysis of Brown's left palm revealed a DNA mixture with Brown as the major contributor, and Wilson being 98 times more likely the minor contributor than anyone else.

DNA analysis of Brown's clothes, right hand, fingernails, and clothes excluded Wilson as a possible contributor.

4. Dispatch Recordings

According to FPD records, at about 11:53 a.m., a dispatcher called out a "stealing in progress" at the address of Ferguson Market while Wilson was in the midst of a sick infant call. During his interview with federal officials, Wilson told prosecutors and agents that he heard the call on his portable radio, but did not hear the specifics about the location of the "stealing in progress." He also stated that he heard that one of the suspects was wearing a "black shirt," that they had stolen cigarillos, and were going toward the Quick-Trip. The actual description given was that of a "black male in a white t-shirt," "running toward the Quick-Trip," and that "he took a whole box of Swisher cigars." Two officers, Witness 145 and Witness 146, the same two FPD officers who first responded to Canfield Drive after the shooting, responded to the Ferguson Market. At approximately 11:56 a.m., Witness 145, via radio, added, "He's with another male. He's got a red Cardinals hat, white t-shirt, yellow socks, and khaki shorts."

Wilson left the sick call at approximately 11:58 a.m., after EMS arrived to transport the mother and sick child to the hospital. Twenty-seven seconds later, Wilson radioed to Witness 145 and Witness 146, "Do you guys need me?," corroborating that Wilson was aware of the theft at Ferguson Market prior to his encounter with Brown. Witness 145 responded that the suspect "disappeared into the woodwork." Wilson, having not heard him, asked the dispatcher to "relay." The dispatcher then clarified, "He thinks that they . . . disappeared." Wilson then said "clear," indicating that he understood.

Wilson drove his police SUV west on Canfield Drive, where he encountered Brown and Witness 101 walking east in the middle of the street. Wilson's last recorded radio transmission occurred at approximately noon when he called out, "Put me on Canfield with two and send me another car," consistent with Wilson's account that he radioed for backup once he interacted with Brown and Witness 101.

Several radio transmissions followed from dispatch and from Officer 145 seeking a response from Wilson to no avail. About one minute and forty seconds following Wilson's last transmission, Witness 145 called out to send the supervising sergeant to Canfield Drive and Copper Creek Court, the location of the shooting incident. There were no recorded radio transmissions from Wilson from the time Wilson called for assistance to the time that Witness 145 called for a supervisor.

As noted above, Wilson stated that he also radioed for backup after the initial shots when Brown ran from the SUV, and then again after he shot Brown to death. According to Wilson, as he left the shooting scene, he realized that his radio must have switched from channel 1, which he had been using, to channel 3 during the initial struggle. Channel 3 is a dedicated channel for the North County Fire Department. It only receives transmissions, and therefore, officers cannot use that channel to transmit messages to dispatch. While this is not definitive evidence that Wilson attempted to call for assistance both after the initial shots in the SUV and after he killed Brown, it offers a plausible explanation for the lack of radio transmissions. Moreover, as detailed below, there are several witnesses who state that Wilson paused in the SUV after

Brown took off running, arguably giving him enough time to attempt to radio dispatch. Likewise, several witnesses saw Wilson appear to use his shoulder microphone after Brown fell to the ground, presumably to radio dispatch.

5. Ballistics

Witness 143, a firearms and toolmarks examiner with the SLCPD, conducted the ballistics analysis for the St. Louis County Police Laboratory. Witness 144, an FBI firearms and toolmarks examiner, conducted gunshot residue analysis and reconstructed the shooting incident.

i. Wilson's Firearm and Projectiles Fired

There were a total of five projectiles, and a fragment from another projectile, recovered from the crime scene and Brown's autopsy. There were a total of 12 shell casings recovered from the crime scene. Wilson's gun can hold up to 13 rounds, 12 in the magazine and one in the chamber. Witness 143 test-fired Wilson's Sig Sauer S&W .40 caliber semi-automatic pistol, noting apparent blood on the gun. He compared the test bullets and casings to those seized as evidence from Brown's body and the crime scene. Witness 143 confirmed that all 12 shell casings were fired from Wilson's gun, consistent with the one round remaining in the gun after the shooting. Witness 143 also confirmed that four of the recovered projectiles, as well as the recovered fragment, were fired from Wilson's gun. The remaining projectile, recovered from the inside of the driver's door of Wilson's SUV, was too damaged to conclusively find that it came from Wilson's gun.

ii. Projectile Recovered from SUV

Witness 144 conducted a shooting incident reconstruction of the interior driver's door panel of Wilson's SUV to determine the trajectory of the bullet that was recovered there. The trajectory of the bullet was at a downward angle from left to right, striking the armrest near the interior door handle, entering the door from inside the SUV, and coming to rest inside the door. This is consistent with Wilson's description of the initial gunshot.

Witness 144 conducted gunshot residue analysis on the inside of the driver's door. Particulate and vaporous lead residues found on the interior driver's door panel near the interior window weather stripping and on the interior side frame of the driver's door were, like the recovery of the bullet itself, consistent with the discharge of a firearm. These residues were unsuitable for muzzle-to-target distance determinations. However, vaporous lead residues rarely are deposited at a distance greater than 24 inches, consistent with Wilson discharging his firearm while seated in the driver's seat, less than two feet from the driver's door.

iii. Gunshot Residue on Brown's Shirt

Witness 144 conducted gunshot residue analysis on Brown's shirt. For the most part, gunshot residue analysis can only determine whether defects in an item, i.e., the holes in his shirt, are the result of gunshots. Analysis cannot determine the directional travel of bullets.

Witness 144 examined seven holes in the shirt. Gunshot residues in the form of nitrite and bullet wipe lead residues were found near some of the holes. This does not necessarily suggest that the remaining holes were not created by bullets. According to Witness 144, lack of gunshot residue could be due to the possibility of intervening conditions, like large amounts of blood, environmental conditions, or the way the shirt was folded and packaged.

Likewise, the presence of nitrite residues tells very little. Nitrite residues were found near three holes in Brown's right sleeve, and one hole in the right chest of this shirt. Test-firing of the gun showed that nitrite residues appear at a muzzle-to-target distance of eight feet or less, consistent with Wilson's description and several other witness descriptions that Wilson and Brown were about eight feet apart during the final shots. However, the residues were not in a measurable pattern. This means that they may not even be associated with the specific holes in the shirt that they are near, but rather may be just indiscriminate residue from any of the shots, including the close range shots at the SUV, or transferred from one shot to another during the handling and packaging of the clothes.

6. Fingerprints

Wilson's gun was not tested for the presence of Brown's fingerprints. After SLCPD crime scene detectives recovered Wilson's gun, they submitted the gun for DNA analysis rather than for fingerprints analysis. The detectives told federal prosecutors that they knew that typically testing for one would preclude testing for the other, and there was a high likelihood of DNA given the presence of apparent blood on the gun. They also knew that even according to Wilson, Brown never had sole possession of the gun, and if Brown ever had control of the gun at all, it was only when Brown's hand was over Wilson's hand during a struggle for the gun, lessening the likelihood of fingerprints. Furthermore, based on their training and experience, there was a greater likelihood of finding a DNA profile on the gun than lifting fingerprints with enough fine ridge detail to make it suitable for comparison. Because the gun was swabbed in its entirety, it could not later undergo latent fingerprint analysis.

SLCPD crime scene detectives lifted five latent fingerprints from the outside of the driver's door of the SUV. Two were unsuitable for comparison; one was determined to be Wilson's fingerprint; and the remaining two prints, although suitable for comparison, belonged to neither Brown nor Wilson. The leather interior of the SUV was unsuitable for recovering latent prints. Fingerprint examiners also tested Wilson's duty belt for fingerprints, but none recovered was suitable for comparison.

7. Audio Recording of Shots Fired

Witness 136 was in his apartment using a video chat application on his mobile phone when the shooting occurred. According to Witness 136, he heard "maybe three" gunshots followed by a five to six second pause. After those first gunshots, Witness 136 recorded the remainder of his chat and turned it over to the FBI. The recording is about 12 seconds long and captured a total of 10 gunshots. The gunshots begin after the first four seconds. The recording then captured six gunshots in two seconds. There was a three second pause, followed by a seventh gunshot. There was a quick pause of less than one second before the final three-shot volley within two seconds. The recording was not time-stamped. As detailed below, this recording is consistent with several credible witness accounts as well as Wilson's account, that he fired several volleys of shots, briefly pausing between each one.

8. Wilson's Medical Records

Paramedics examined Wilson when he returned to the FPD after the shooting, and recommended that he go to the hospital for follow-up treatment. Wilson sought medical treatment at Christian Northwest Hospital within two hours of the shooting. Witness 117, a nurse practitioner, examined Wilson. For the purpose of making a medical diagnosis, Witness 117 questioned Wilson about what happened. Wilson stated that he was twice punched in the jaw. Witness 117 noted acute or fresh pink scratch marks on the back of Wilson's neck as well as swelling to his jaw. Wilson sustained a contusion of the mandibular joint or jaw area, but did not break his jaw or any other bones. According to Witness 117, Wilson's injuries were consistent with his description of what transpired.

Wilson submitted to a drug and alcohol screen. His blood alcohol content was 0.00% and he tested negative for cocaine, marijuana metabolites, amphetamines, opiates, and phencyclidine, the chemical commonly known as PCP.

9. Brown's Toxicology

A toxicologist with the St. Louis University (SLU) Toxicology Laboratory and the Chief of the Division of Forensic Toxicology at AFMES each conducted blood and urine screens on samples collected from Brown's body. Brown tested positive for the presence of cannabinoids, the hallucinogenic substances associated with marijuana use. The SLU Toxicology Laboratory found 12 nanograms per milliliter of Delta-9-THC, the active ingredient in marijuana, where AFMES found 11 nanograms per milliliter of Delta-9-THC in Brown's blood.

According to both laboratories, these levels of Delta-9-THC are consistent with Brown having ingested THC within a few hours before his death. This concentration of THC would have rendered Brown impaired at the time of his death. As a general matter, this level of impairment can alter one's perception of time and space, but the extent to which this was true in Brown's case cannot be determined. THC affects individuals differently depending on unknown variables such as whether Brown was a chronic user and the concentration of the THC ingested.

10. Ferguson Market Surveillance Video

At approximately 11:53 a.m. on August 9, 2014, about ten minutes prior to the shooting, Brown and Witness 101 went to Ferguson Market, a nearby convenience store. Surveillance video shows Brown stealing several packages of cigarillos and then forcefully shoving the store clerk who tried to stop him from leaving the store without paying. Evidence of this theft and assault likely would be admissible by the defense in a prosecution of Wilson because it is relevant to show Brown's state of mind at or near the time of the shooting, and arguably corroborates Wilson's self-defense claim.

Surveillance cameras captured the incident without audio. SLCPD detectives, FBI agents, and federal prosecutors jointly interviewed the store employees who were present at the time. The employees, a father (the clerk who was assaulted) and his adult daughter, are of Indian origin. The father does not speak English well, and therefore, was not as able as his daughter to recount with specificity what Brown said during the incident.

The video depicts Brown and Witness 101 entering the store and proceeding to the front counter. Brown stood at the register, as Witness 101 waited behind him. Brown asked the clerk behind the counter for cigarillos. The clerk put a package of cigarillos on the counter. Brown then "snatched" the package of cigarillos from the counter. Using his left hand, Brown reached behind him and gave them to Witness 101. Brown then reached over the counter, as Witness 101 described and the video shows, and took additional packages of cigarillos. In so doing, Brown dropped some of the cigarillos and had an exchange with the clerk during which he refused to pay. Witness 101 then placed the cigarillos that Brown had given him back on the register counter, as Brown picked up his stolen goods from the floor.

Brown and Witness 101 proceeded to the exit and the clerk, who is about 5'6" and 150 lbs, attempted to stop them. The clerk first tried to hold the store door closed to prevent Brown's exit. However, Brown shoved the clerk aside, and as Witness 101 walked out the door, Brown menacingly re-approached the clerk. According to the store employees, Brown, looking "crazy" and using profane language, said something like, "What are you gonna do about it?" Brown then exited the store and the clerk's daughter called 911.

C. Witness Accounts

As the first responding investigators, SLCPD detectives interviewed witnesses on Canfield Drive within the first few hours of the shooting. One week later, on August 16, 2014, in an effort to identify additional witnesses who may have been reluctant to speak with local law enforcement, the FBI conducted a neighborhood canvass of more than 300 residences. Federal and county authorities largely conducted additional interviews jointly, unless a witness expressed discomfort with the presence of either federal agents or SLCPD detectives. To evaluate the merits of a potential federal prosecution, federal prosecutors and FBI agents conducted follow-up interviews. Many witnesses also testified before the county grand jury. Unless otherwise noted, witnesses did not know, or know of, Brown or Wilson prior to the shooting.

For ease of review, this report divides the summaries of witness accounts into three sections based on the nature and credibility of their accounts to a jury. First, the report summarizes the accounts of those witnesses whose statements have been materially consistent, are consistent with the physical evidence, and that are mutually corroborative. For these reasons, prosecutors determined these witness accounts were reliable and would be credible to jurors. This section is further broken down into subsections for those witness accounts that support Wilson's claim of self-defense and those that support a criminal prosecution of Wilson. Of course, to support a prosecution of Wilson under 18 U.S.C. § 242, the weight of the evidence from those witness accounts that support a prosecution must be prove the violation beyond a reasonable doubt to twelve reasonable jurors. A prosecution will fail if the credible evidence creates "reasonable doubt" of Wilson's guilt by supporting Wilson's statements that he acted reasonably and in self-defense. The second section of summaries contains those accounts that neither inculpate

Wilson nor fully corroborate Wilson's account. These witnesses, regardless of whether prosecutors determined their accounts to be credible, would not strengthen the government's case in a prosecution of Wilson. The third section of summaries contains those witness accounts that are inconsistent with the physical and forensic evidence, materially inconsistent with that witness's own prior statements, or those witnesses who have recanted large portions of their accounts, admitting that they did not in fact witness the shooting as they initially claimed. Therefore, for this last category of witnesses, federal prosecutors either could not rely on their accounts to support a prosecution of Darren Wilson or did not consider their accounts in making a prosecutive decision.

1. Witnesses Materially Consistent with Prior Statements, Physical Evidence, and Other Witnesses and Therefore, Give Credible Accounts

i. Witnesses Materially Consistent with Prior Statements, Physical Evidence, and Other Witnesses Who Corroborate That Wilson Acted in Self-Defense

a. Witness 102

Witness 102 is a 27-year-old bi-racial male. Witness 102 gave three statements. First, SLCPD detectives interviewed him; second, FBI agents interviewed him; third, Witness 102 testified before the county grand jury.

Witness 102 was doing house repairs on a residence on Canfield Drive when the shooting occurred. Witness 102 first noticed Brown and Witness 101 walking down Canfield Drive about 20 minutes prior to the shooting when he went to his truck to retrieve a broom. Brown's size initially drew Witness 102's attention. When Witness 102 later came back outside to get another tool, he noticed Wilson's SUV parked in the middle of the street at an angle, with the driver's side closer to the center of the street. Witness 102's vantage point was street level, about 450 feet from the SUV with a view of the driver's side of the SUV.

According to Witness 102, he saw Brown standing on the driver's side of the SUV, bent over with his body through the driver's window from the waist up. Witness 102 explained that Brown was "wrestling" through the window, but he was unable to see what Wilson was doing. After a few seconds, Witness 102 heard a gunshot. Immediately, Brown took off running in the opposite direction from where Witness 102 was standing. Witness 102 heard something metallic hit the ground. Witness 102 thought that he had just witnessed the murder of a police officer because a few seconds passed before Wilson emerged from the SUV. Wilson then chased Brown with his gun drawn, but not pointed at Brown, until Brown abruptly turned around at a nearby driveway. Witness 102 explained that it made no sense to him why Brown turned around. Brown did not get on the ground or put his hands up in surrender. In fact, Witness 102 told investigators that he knew "for sure that [Brown's] hands were not above his head." Rather, Brown made some type of movement similar to pulling his pants up or a shoulder shrug, and then "charged" at Wilson. It was only then that Wilson fired five or six shots at Brown. Brown paused and appeared to flinch, and Wilson stopped firing. However, Brown charged at Wilson again, and again Wilson fired about three or four rounds until Brown finally collapsed on the ground. Witness 102 was in disbelief that Wilson seemingly kept missing because Brown kept advancing forward. Witness 102 described Brown as a "threat," moving at a "full charge." Witness 102 stated that Wilson only fired shots when Brown was coming toward Wilson. It appeared to Witness 102 that Wilson's life was in jeopardy. Witness 102 was unable to hear whether Brown or Wilson said anything.

Witness 102 did not see Brown's friend, Witness 101, at any time during the incident until Witness 101 "came out of nowhere," shouting, "'They just killed him!'" Witness 101 seemed to be shouting toward a blue Monte Carlo that had stopped behind Wilson's SUV. Witness 101 then ran off. Witness 102 explained that once he saw officers putting up police tape, he went down to the scene and began telling another onlooker what he had witnessed. Witness 102 later learned via a "friend" on Facebook that his voice was inadvertently captured on another bystander's cell phone recording. Federal prosecutors reviewed this recording and Witness 102 identified his voice on the recording when he testified before the county grand jury. In it, Witness 102 can be heard correcting someone else who was recounting what he heard from others, that Wilson "stood over [Brown] and shot while on the ground." In response, Witness 102 stated that Wilson shot Brown because Brown came back toward Wilson. Witness 102 "kept thinking" that Wilson's shots were "missing" Brown because Brown kept moving.

Witness 102 did not stay on Canfield Drive long after the shooting, but rather started to leave the area after about five minutes because he felt uncomfortable. According to Witness 102, crowds of people had begun to gather, wrongly claiming the police shot Brown for no reason and that he had his hands up in surrender. Two black women approached Witness 102, mobile phones set to record, asking him to recount what he had witnessed. Witness 102 responded that they would not like what he had to say. The women responded with racial slurs, calling him names like "white motherfucker."

Witness 102 called 911 the following day to report what he saw. He then went to the FPD on Monday, August 11, 2014, where he was referred to the SLCPD. Witness 102 explained that he came forward because he "felt bad about the situation," and he wanted to "bring closure to [Brown's] family," so they would not think that the officer "got away with murdering their son." He further explained that "most people think that police are bad for 'em up until the time they're in need of the police," and he felt that witnesses would not come forward to tell the truth in this case because of community pressure.

As described above, all of Witness 102's statements were materially consistent with each other, with physical and forensic evidence, and with other credible witness accounts. Witness 102 does not have a criminal history. Therefore, if called as a defense witness in a prosecution of Darren Wilson, this witness's account would not be vulnerable to meaningful cross-examination and would not be subject to impeachment due to bias or inconsistencies in his prior statements. Accordingly, after a thorough review of all the evidence, federal prosecutors determined his account to be credible and likewise determined that a jury appropriately would credit his potential testimony.

b. Witness 103

Witness 103 is a 58-year-old black male who gave two statements. First, Witness 103 was reluctant to meet with SLCPD detectives, FBI agents, and federal prosecutors because he has no particular allegiance to law enforcement. Witness 103 is a convicted felon who served time in federal prison, and has a son who was shot and injured by law enforcement during the commission of a robbery. Witness 103 expressed concerns because there were signs in the neighborhood of Canfield Drive stating, "snitches get stitches." Therefore, he agreed to be interviewed only on the condition of confidentiality. Witness 103 later testified before the county grand jury.

According to Witness 103, he was driving his blue pickup truck in the opposite direction of Wilson's SUV, and ended up virtually next to the driver's side of the SUV when it stopped. Relative to Witness 102, Witness 103 had a similar, but much closer view of the driver's side of the SUV. If the parked SUV is viewed as dividing Canfield Drive in half, both Witness 102 and Witness 103 were on the same side, with a view of Brown's back as he ran from Wilson, and a view of Brown's front as he ran toward Wilson.

When Witness 103 stopped his truck on Canfield Drive, although he did not see what led up to it, he saw Brown punching Wilson at least three times in the facial area, through the open driver's window of the SUV. Witness 103 described Wilson and Brown as having hold of each other's shirts, but Brown was "getting in a couple of blows." Wilson was leaning back toward the passenger seat with his forearm up, in an effort to block the blows. Then Witness 103 heard a gunshot and Brown took off running. Wilson exited the SUV, appeared to be using his shoulder microphone to call into his radio, and chased Brown with his gun held low.

Witness 103 explained that Brown came to a stop near a car, put his hand down on the car, and turned around to face Wilson. Brown's hands were then down at his sides. Witness 103 did not see Brown's hands up. Wanting to leave, Witness 103 began to turn his car around in the opposite direction that Brown had been running when he heard additional shots. Witness 103 turned to his right, and saw Brown "moving fast" toward Wilson. Witness 103 then drove away.

Witness 103 had a passenger in his truck. Although Witness 103 tried to facilitate contact between federal and state authorities and the passenger, the passenger refused to identify himself or provide any information.

When Witness 103 was initially subpoenaed to testify before the county grand jury, he expressed even more reluctance than he did during his investigative interview, this time alleging memory loss. However, he ultimately testified consistently with his original account, with the physical and forensic evidence, and with other credible witness accounts. Therefore, if called as a defense witness in a federal prosecution of Darren Wilson, Witness 103 would be subject to limited impeachment for his two felony convictions, including a theft conviction, but his apparent antipathy toward law enforcement would bolster testimony that corroborates Wilson. Accordingly, after a thorough review of all the evidence, federal prosecutors determined his account to be credible, and likewise determined that a jury appropriately would credit his potential testimony.

c. Witness 104

Witness 104 is a 26-year-old bi-racial female. Witness 104 gave three statements. SLCPD detectives interviewed her, federal prosecutors and agents interviewed her, and she testified before the county grand jury.

Witness 104 was in a minivan that had been traveling in the opposite direction of Wilson, and came to a halt in front of Wilson's SUV, and somewhat behind, yet adjacent to Witness 103's blue pickup truck. Witness 104 was on the same side of the SUV as Witness 102 and Witness 103. She was seated in the middle row behind the driver's seat of the minivan, leaning over toward the center, with a direct view of Brown running away from Wilson, a frontal view of Brown coming back toward Wilson, and the shooting thereafter. Witness 104 is the adult daughter of the two witnesses in the driver and passenger front seats, Witness 105 and Witness 106, respectively. She is the sister of Witness 107, who was seated in the middle row passenger seat to her right.

According to Witness 104, she was leaning over, talking to her sister, Witness 107, when she heard two gunshots. She looked out the front window and saw Brown at the driver's window of Wilson's SUV. Witness 104 knew that Brown's arms were inside the SUV, but she could not see what Brown and Wilson were doing because Brown's body was blocking her view. Witness 104 saw Brown run from the SUV, followed by Wilson, who "hopped" out of the SUV and ran after him while yelling "stop, stop, stop." Wilson did not fire his gun as Brown ran from him. Brown then turned around and "for a second" began to raise his hands as though he may have considered surrendering, but then quickly "balled up in fists" in a running position and "charged" at Wilson. Witness 104 described it as a "tackle run," explaining that Brown "wasn't going to stop." Wilson fired his gun only as Brown charged at him, backing up as Brown came toward him. Witness 104 explained that there were three separate volleys of shots. Each time, Brown ran toward Wilson, Wilson fired, Brown paused, Wilson stopped firing, and then Brown charged again. The pattern continued until Brown fell to the ground, "smashing" his face upon impact. Wilson did not fire while Brown momentarily had his hands up. Witness 104 explained that it took some time for Wilson to fire, adding that she "would have fired sooner." Wilson did not go near Brown's body after Brown fell to his death.

Witness 104 explained that she first saw Brown's friend, Witness 101, when he took off running as soon as the first two shots were fired. She never saw him again.

All three of Witness 104's statements were consistent with each other, consistent with the physical and forensic evidence, and consistent with other credible witness accounts. Witness 104 does not have a criminal history. Therefore, if called as a defense witness in a prosecution of Darren Wilson, this witness's account would not be vulnerable to meaningful cross-examination and would not be subject to impeachment due to bias or inconsistencies in prior statements. Accordingly, after a thorough review of all the evidence, federal prosecutors determined her account to be credible, and likewise determined that a jury appropriately would credit her potential testimony.

d. Witness 105

Witness 105 is a 50-year-old black female. She gave two statements. SLCPD detectives interviewed her, and federal prosecutors explained the nature of the two parallel criminal investigations to Witness 105 prior to her testimony before the county grand jury. Witness 105 was driving a minivan in which Witness 104, her daughter, was seated behind the driver's seat in the middle row. Her husband, Witness 106, was next to her in the front passenger seat, and her other daughter, Witness 107, was seated behind her husband and next to Witness 104. Witness 105 had been traveling east on Canfield Drive, when she stopped in front of Wilson's vehicle with a view of the driver's side of his vehicle. Her view was also of the back of Brown as he first ran away, and then the front of Brown as he turned around and came back toward Wilson.

According to Witness 105, Wilson was driving a car, not an SUV, and a gunshot drew her attention to the vehicle. She noticed Brown's hands on Wilson's "car." Brown then ran eastbound and Wilson chased after him, gun in hand but held low. Witness 105 explained that Brown put his hands up "for a brief moment," and then turned around and made a shuffling movement. Wilson told Brown to "get down," but Brown did not comply. Instead, Brown put his hands down "in a running position." Witness 105 could not tell whether Brown was "charging" at Wilson or whether his plan was to run past Wilson, but either way, Brown was running toward Wilson. According to Witness 105, Wilson only shot at Brown when Brown was moving toward him. She could not see Brown's hands as he was running, but saw him reaching down as he began to fall to the ground. Witness 105 saw Wilson shoot Brown in the face before he began to stumble. Once Brown was on the ground, it appeared to Witness 105 that Wilson was calling out on the radio using his shoulder microphone.

When Witness 105 contacted SLCPD detectives, she was reluctant to identify herself and ultimately met with them in a library parking lot. She explained that she was coming forward because in speaking with her neighbors, she realized that what they believed had happened was inconsistent with what actually happened. She further explained that that she had not been paying attention to media accounts, and had been unaware of the inaccuracies being reported.

Both of Witness 105's statements were consistent with each other, materially consistent with the physical and forensic evidence, and consistent with other credible witness accounts in all material ways. Witness 105 has no criminal history. If called as a defense witness in a prosecution of Darren Wilson, this witness's account would be subject to limited impeachment on her ability to accurately perceive what occurred, *e.g.*, that she perceived Wilson driving a car, rather than an SUV. However, that line of cross-examination does not undermine the overall consistency of her account with other credible witness accounts and with the physical evidence. Accordingly, after a thorough review of all the evidence, federal prosecutors determined her account to be largely credible and likewise determined that a jury appropriately would credit her potential testimony.

e. Witness 108

Witness 108 is a 74-year-old black male who claimed to have witnessed the shooting, stated that it was justified, but repeatedly refused to give formal statements to law enforcement for fear of reprisal should the Canfield Drive neighborhood find out that his account corroborated Wilson. He was served with a county grand jury subpoena and refused to appear.

During the initial canvass of the crime scene on August 9, 2014, in the hours after the shooting, SLCPD detectives approached Witness 108, who was sitting in his car on Canfield Drive. They asked if he witnessed what happened. Witness 108 refused to identify himself or give details, but told detectives that the police officer was "in the right" and "did what he had to do," and the statements made by people in the apartment complex were inaccurate. Both state and federal investigators later attempted to locate and interview Witness 108, who repeatedly expressed fear in coming forward. During the investigators' attempts to find Witness 108, another individual reported that two days after the shooting, Witness 108 confided in her that he "would have fucking shot that boy, too." In saying so, Witness 108 mimicked an aggressive stance with his hands out in front of him, as though he was about to charge. SLCPD detectives finally tracked down Witness 108 at a local repair shop, where he reluctantly explained that Wilson told Brown to "stop" or "get down" at least ten times, but instead Brown "charged" at Wilson. Witness 108 told detectives that there were other witnesses on Canfield Drive who witnessed the same thing. An SLCPD detective and federal prosecutor again tracked down Witness 108 in hopes of obtaining a more formal statement. However, Witness 108 refused to provide additional details to either county or federal authorities, citing community sentiment to support a "hands up" surrender narrative as his reason to remain silent. He explained that he would rather go to jail than testify before the county grand jury.

Witness 108 has no criminal history. Witness 108's accounts, although quite general, are clearly exculpatory as to Wilson and consistent with other credible evidence. His reluctance to testify in opposition to community sentiment lends further credence to his account.

f. Witness 109

Witness 109 is a 53 year-old black male. Like Witness 108, Witness 109 claimed to have witnessed the shooting, stated that it was justified, and repeatedly refused to give formal statements to law enforcement for fear of reprisal should the Canfield Drive neighborhood find out that his account corroborated Wilson. He was served with a county grand jury subpoena and refused to appear. Likewise, Witness 109 repeatedly refused to formally meet with SLCPD detectives, FBI agents, or federal and county prosecutors.

Law enforcement identified Witness 109 through a phone call that he made to the SLCPD information line at 5:19 p.m. on the day of the shooting. During that six-minute recorded call, the operator transferred Witness 109 to an SLCPD detective, and Witness 109 provided the following information, repeatedly refusing to meet with detectives in person. Witness 109 stated that he did not want his phone number traced, and would deny everything if it was traced. Witness 109 stated that he did not know Brown or his friend, Witness 101. However, he was calling because Witness 101, whom he described as the "guy with the dreads," lied on national television. Witness 109 described Brown and Witness 101 walking on the center line of the street when the officer asked them to get out of street. Brown responded something to the effect of, "Fuck the police." According to Witness 109, Wilson got out of his vehicle and Brown, the "young guy that died," hit him in the face. Witness 109 explained that Wilson reached for what appeared to be a taser but dropped it, and then grabbed a gun. Witness 109 explained that Brown reached for Wilson's gun. Although Witness 109's description was somewhat disjointed, he also stated that at first Brown ran away from Wilson, but then kept coming toward Wilson. Wilson told Brown to stop and lie down, but Brown failed to comply. Witness 109 said that Wilson fired in self-defense, explaining that Wilson did not shoot to kill at first, but "he unloaded on him when [Brown] wouldn't stop." Witness 109 said that "a lot of people saw that it was justified," ending the call by stating, "I know police get a bad rap, but they're here to protect us."

Federal and county prosecutors and investigators tried to no avail to interview Witness 109. True to his word on that initial phone call, he would not discuss what he saw. He did, however, acknowledge that he placed a call to the SLCPD information line.

Witness 109 does have a criminal history that would be admissible in federal court. Witness 109 has a misdemeanor theft conviction from 1985 and a felony arrest, both of which likely would be inadmissible in federal court for impeachment purposes. Witness 109's account is exculpatory as to Wilson and although Witness 109 may be subject to limited impeachment, the majority of his description is consistent with the physical and forensic evidence, and consistent with other credible witness accounts. Community sentiment and therefore his reluctance to testify on behalf of Wilson would likely bolster his account.

g. Witness 113

Witness 113 is a 31-year-old black female. She was interviewed one time by FBI agents during their canvass on August 16, 2014, and gave an account that generally corroborated Wilson, but only after she was confronted with untruthful statements she initially made in an effort to avoid neighborhood backlash. When local authorities tried to serve Witness 113 with a subpoena to testify before the county grand jury, she blockaded her door with a couch to avoid service.

Witness 113 was on her brother's balcony, located opposite and to the left of the aforementioned minivan, when she first saw Brown walking in the street. Contrary to other witness accounts, Witness 113 saw what she believed to be three black males walking in the street, and two police vehicles present, calling into question whether she actually witnessed the beginning of the incident. She explained that one of the police officers told Brown and his friends to go on the sidewalk, and then subsequently called Brown over to his vehicle, where a struggle occurred.

Witness 113 then gave an account that was contrary to physical evidence, internally inconsistent, and admittedly untrue. She first explained that Brown ran east, away from Wilson, as Wilson shot at him. However, she then explained that she watched as Brown ran west past Wilson, who shot Brown right next to the SUV. Witness 113 stated that Wilson fired shots into Brown's back as he lay flat on his stomach on the ground. When the FBI told Witness 113 that the autopsy results and other evidence were inconsistent with her account, she admitted that she lied. She explained to the FBI that, "You've gotta live the life to know it," and stated that she feared offering an account contrary to the narrative reported by the media that Brown held his hands up in surrender.

Witness 113 then admitted that she saw Brown running toward Wilson, prompting Wilson to yell, "Freeze." Brown failed to stop and Wilson began shooting Brown. Witness 113 told the FBI that it appeared to her that Wilson's life was in danger. She explained there was a pause in the shots before the firing resumed, but Witness 113 had ducked down for cover and did not see anything after the first volley of shots.

Witness 113 was with her brother and boyfriend when the shooting occurred. Witness 113 refused to provide their contact information, and they both repeatedly evaded law enforcement's attempts to meet with them.

Witness 113 has no criminal history that would be admissible in federal court. Witness 113 has past arrests but no convictions, which likely would be inadmissible in federal court. In a federal prosecution, if served and called to testify on behalf of Wilson, federal prosecutors could subject Witness 113 to cross-examination due to her admittedly untruthful statements during the first part of her interview with the FBI. However, her reasons for being untruthful, coupled with the fact that she immediately changed course when her statements were challenged, give her account reliability. Accordingly, prosecutors did not discount her narrative in its entirety, but rather in examining all of the evidence, considered this witness's account in making a prosecutive decision.

h. Witness 134

Witness 134 is a 36-year-old white female. She was interviewed one time by federal authorities. At the time of her interview with federal agents and prosecutors, she was Wilson's fiancée and was Wilson's field training officer in 2011. Prosecutors considered her potential bias when interviewing Witness 134, but sought out and evaluated her account for several reasons. First, as noted below in the legal analysis, to make a determination as to whether a potential civil rights defendant has the requisite criminal intent, prosecutors must consider a subject officer's training as part of an evaluation of his overall understanding of when the use of deadly force is permissible. Second, Witness 134 spoke to Wilson minutes after the shooting, while he was arguably still under the stress of the situation and immediately after he perceived it. It is possible that in a prosecution of Wilson, defense counsel would be permitted to introduce Wilson's initial statements to Witness 134 through the "present sense impression" or "excited utterance" hearsay exceptions. Fed. R. Evid. 803(1); 803(2).

Witness 134 explained that when she was Wilson's field training officer for the FPD, he did not require a lot of training because he had prior experience as a law enforcement officer. Wilson knew and understood that he was permitted to use physical force when he or someone else was met with a physical threat. As Wilson's training officer, she never had concerns as to whether he understood when he was permitted to use force.

Witness 134 was on light duty on August 9, 2014, working at the police department building because she was pregnant. She was working the same shift as Wilson and was waiting to join him for lunch. Witness 134 stated that when Wilson arrived at the FPD at about 12:15 p.m., he did not seem like himself. His face was red and puffy, consistent with injury. Knowing something was wrong, she asked Wilson what happened. Wilson responded, "I just killed someone." Wilson also told her that he had washed blood from his hands.

Witness 134 also explained that other than facial injuries, she did not notice additional injuries or blood on Wilson, but she did notice blood on the hammer of his gun, still holstered in his belt. Wilson asked her to retrieve latex gloves for him, which Wilson then used to clear and package his gun. Witness 134 did not actually see Wilson do this because her back was to him, although she could hear what he was doing. She also saw the envelope, presumably containing the gun, sealed with evidence tape, but did not know who eventually took it to an evidence locker.

Prior to packaging his gun, Wilson gave Witness 134 a narrative consistent with the accounts he later gave throughout the course of the investigation. Federal agents and prosecutors asked Witness 134 to be specific about what Wilson told her at the police department in the immediate aftermath as opposed to subsequent conversations that they have had since the shooting. Witness 134 was certain that Wilson told her the following: He told Brown and his friend to get out of the street, but did not say anything "ignorant" that would anger them. As Wilson was passing Brown and his friend, he saw cigarillos in Brown's hand and noticed Witness 101's black shirt and realized that they matched the description of the suspects involved in the "stealing in progress." As Brown was attacking Wilson, Wilson explained that in his mind, he went through the weapons available to him on his gun belt. He knew that he had no choice but to use his gun.

Wilson explained to Witness 134 that he was able to shoot inside the SUV, but did not know where the bullet went and whether it hit Brown. Brown ran off and Wilson chased him, explaining to Witness 134 that "all of a sudden," Brown stopped, turned around, and started "charging" him. Witness 134 explained that although she could not remember the exact words Wilson said he used, he said something like, "Get on the ground," trying to get Brown to stop. However, Wilson told her that Brown did not stop and continued to charge at Wilson. Wilson fired at Brown and continued to do so until Brown was on the ground because Brown "just wouldn't stop."

Witness 134 explained that Wilson was shaken, but confident that he did the right thing in the moment, although he became worried in the few minutes that followed the shooting because the neighborhood was quickly becoming hostile.

Witness 134 explained that in all of their conversations, Wilson had been adamant that Brown's hands were not up, but rather, Brown's right hand was in his waistband with his left hand in a fist, as though he was running. Witness 134 said that she was relieved to see the results of the private autopsy in the media because it showed a series of shots in Brown's right arm, consistent with Wilson's explanation that he had tunnel vision during the shooting.

After learning of Witness 101's account alleging that Wilson grabbed Brown's throat by reaching out the driver's window and then subsequently shooting him while he was surrendering, Wilson told Witness 134 that Witness 101 was not present for the shooting because he saw Witness 101 run off as soon as Brown handed him the cigarillos during the assault at the SUV window. Wilson and Witness 134 agreed that the notion that a police officer would attempt to pull an individual into his vehicle, especially someone as big as Brown, is contrary to training. Wilson described Brown as Hulk Hogan–like, such that he could have easily overpowered Wilson.

Witness 134 has no criminal history. If called as a defense witness in a prosecution of Darren Wilson, Witness 134 would be subject to cross-examination due to obvious bias. However, her account of what Wilson told her is consistent with Wilson's previous statements, with other credible witness accounts, and with the forensic and physical evidence. Accordingly, having met Witness 134 and considered her manner and demeanor, federal prosecutors found her account credible. Nonetheless, because of Witness 134's relationship with Wilson and because most of her information came directly from Wilson, prosecutors did not heavily rely on her account when making a prosecutive decision.

ii. Witnesses Consistent with Prior Statements, Physical Evidence, and Other Witnesses Who Inculpate Wilson

There are no witnesses who fall under this category.

2. Witnesses Who Neither Inculpate Nor Fully Corroborate Wilson

i. Witness 107

Witness 107 is a 30-year-old black female. Witness 107 was seated in the passenger seat in the middle row of a minivan that was stopped opposite Wilson's SUV at the time of the shooting. Witness 107 was seated next to her sister Witness 104 and behind her father, Witness 106. Witness 105, her mother, was seated in the driver's seat. However, when Witness 107 initially described what happened, she mistakenly thought she was in the front passenger seat and forgot that her father was present. She also mistakenly thought that they had been driving in the same direction as Wilson.

Witness 107 gave three statements. First, an SLCPD detective and an FBI agent jointly interviewed her. Federal prosecutors and agents conducted a follow-up interview to address inconsistencies with the physical evidence in her original account. Witness 107 also testified before the county grand jury.

According to Witness 107, she was looking at her mobile phone when she heard two gunshots. She looked up and out the front windshield, and saw Brown run away from Wilson. Witness 107 mistakenly thought that Wilson was standing toward the front of the passenger side of the police vehicle, and could not remember whether the vehicle was an SUV or a car. Wilson then chased after Brown and drew his gun, shooting three times. Contrary to the autopsy results, Witness 107 stated that Wilson shot Brown in the leg and hip as Brown was running away. Brown then turned around and briefly put his hands with up, palms forward, near his shoulders, as though he was "giving up." But then Brown put his hands down, one of them holding his chest, as he came back toward Wilson, though Witness 107 was unsure whether Brown was stumbling or running. Wilson fired the last shots from 10 to 15 feet away from Brown, and kept shooting as Brown was falling to the ground.

Witness 107 explained that immediately following the shooting, her mother drove to a nearby parking lot. She and her family members discussed what they witnessed, and they all seemed to have witnessed different things. Her sister, Witness 104, for example, was adamant that Brown "charged" at Wilson, whereas Witness 107 expressed uncertainty. The family also could not reach a consensus as to the number of shots fired.

When Witness 107 met with federal prosecutors and agents, she was visibly shaken by what she witnessed, articulating the difficulty of watching someone die. However, given the differences among what she and her family saw, and realizing that she was factually incorrect about the direction of the police vehicle, the location where Wilson stood, and where the bullets struck Brown, she was not certain about what she believed she witnessed.

Witness 107 has one prior misdemeanor arrest that likely would not be admissible in federal court. As detailed above, Witness 107 was admittedly mistaken or unsure about some of what she perceived, rendering her account vulnerable to effective cross-examination. Regardless of credibility, her account does not inculpate Darren Wilson and does not support a federal prosecution.

ii. Witness 106

Witness 106 is a 45-year-old white male. As mentioned, he was seated in the front passenger seat of a minivan, driven by his wife, Witness 105. Witness 106's daughters, Witness 104 and Witness 107, were seated in the middle row of the minivan, behind the driver and front seat passenger, respectively. According to Witness 106, although his wife saw Wilson emerge from what she remembered was a police car, he first saw Wilson and Brown when they were in the street. It initially looked to Witness 106 like Brown had a gun and there was a firefight happening, although he has since realized that not to be the case. Regardless, Witness 106's overall impression was that he witnessed a police officer "taking down a gunman in a residential neighborhood before anyone else got hurt." It was for that reason that Witness 106 agreed to speak with SLCPD detectives. He otherwise does not "have any love" for law enforcement, having served 18 years in prison. Witness 106 also testified before the county grand jury.

Witness 106 explained that he first saw Brown as he ran from Wilson. Wilson fired one shot which seemed to hit Brown in the leg because Brown appeared to stagger. Brown's arms then "briefly flung" out and he turned around to face Wilson. Witness 106 then explained that even though the neighborhood had been talking about Brown having his "hands up," Brown "did not have his hands up." Brown's arms were down at his sides, such that Witness 106 could not even see Brown's hands. Witness 106's vantage point was over Wilson's shoulder. Witness 106 saw Brown walk toward Wilson and thought that Brown was about to shoot Wilson, as Wilson shot Brown until he fell to his death. Wilson was about six to 10 feet from Brown when he fired the final shots at Brown.

Witness 106's account is inconsistent with the physical and forensic evidence and other credible witness accounts. He has a conviction for sexual abuse that would likely be admissible in federal court as impeachment evidence, although his bias tends to bolster his account. Regardless of its credibility, Witness 106's account does not inculpate Darren Wilson and therefore does not support a federal prosecution.

iii. Witness 110

Witness 110 is a 51-year-old black male who is married to Witness 111. Witness 110 spoke to SLCPD detectives on two occasions. As noted below, the second interview occurred because Witness 111 was too upset to complete the first interview. Witness 110 also testified before the county grand jury.

Witness 110 and Witness 111 first came into contact with SLCPD detectives because they were attending a social function the evening of August 9, 2014. The couple told a friend, an attorney, what they had witnessed, and the friend called the SLCPD on their behalf. SLCPD detectives responded to the venue of the social function to interview Witness 110 and Witness 111, but they were reluctant to speak to law enforcement, fearing retaliation from people in the community. They agreed to speak only on the condition of confidentiality. However, during that initial contact with SLCPD detectives, Witness 111 began crying and could not talk about what she witnessed. Witness 110 was too shaken to give a full account, but he did explain that earlier that day, he and his wife were at the Canfield Green Apartments complex visiting Witness 110's elderly mother and brother, Witness 112. He then gave a brief account which he detailed a few days later when he met again with SLCPD detectives.

According to Witness 110, he and Witness 111 were driving on Canfield Drive when they noticed Brown and his friend, Witness 101, walking in the center of the street and had to veer around them to avoid hitting them. Witness 111 commented to Witness 110, "Why don't they just get on the sidewalk?" As they were pulling into the driveway of the building they were visiting, they noticed Wilson driving in the opposite direction. During his initial interview with SLCPD detectives, Witness 110 explained that while in the driveway, he noticed Brown standing beside the driver's door of the SUV, with the upper portion of his body inside the driver's area of the SUV. Witness 110 did not mention this during his second interview with SLCPD detectives or when he testified in front of the county grand jury.

Witness 110 then explained that he and Witness 111 went up to the second floor apartment balcony, located opposite and off to the right of the minivan with Witness 104, Witness 105, Witness 106, and Witness 107. Their vantage point was of the passenger side of the SUV, followed by the right profile of Brown as he ran away from Wilson, and then the left profile of Brown as he turned around and moved toward Wilson.

Witness 110 stated that he witnessed an exchange between Wilson, Brown, and Witness 101, but did not hear what was said. Wilson reversed his vehicle, using it to block Brown and Witness 101. Brown and Wilson engaged in a back and forth "scuffle," although Witness 110 could not see exactly what happened because the SUV blocked his view of Brown. They then heard a shot and Witness 101 "disappeared." Brown remained at the SUV and the scuffle continued until there was a second gunshot and Brown took off running. When Brown reached a nearby driveway, he stopped and looked down at his hand, which Witness 111 noted had blood on it. Witness 110 believed that Brown looked at his left hand. Brown put his hands out at his sides, palms up, as though asking,

"What the heck?" Brown then moved toward Wilson with his hands in that same position, and Wilson shot Brown. Brown then paused, the shooting stopped, and then Brown advanced again. Witness 110 stated that Wilson shot Brown only when Brown was moving toward him, and did not shoot at Brown as he ran away. Witness 110 initially told SLCPD detectives that Brown moved "quickly," although he testified in the county grand jury that he could not describe how Brown was moving toward Wilson, though he was not "charging" or "running." At no time were Brown's hands up in surrender or otherwise.

Witness 110 has no criminal history. As noted, Witness 110's second interview was consistent with his grand jury testimony, though partially inconsistent with what he initially told SLCPD detectives. Nonetheless, Witness 110's account was consistent with the physical and forensic evidence. Regardless of the credibility of his account, it does not inculpate Wilson, and therefore does not support a federal prosecution.

iv. Witness 111

Witness 111 is a 48-year-old black female who is married to Witness 110. As mentioned, she was too upset to speak with SLCPD detectives on the evening of August 9, 2014, but did speak to law enforcement on August 18, 2014, when she was jointly interviewed by SLCPD detectives, FBI agents, and federal prosecutors. Federal authorities also met with Witness 110 at that time. Witness 111 subsequently testified before the county grand jury.

Witness 111's account is consistent with the account of Witness 110, with two exceptions. First, when she witnessed Brown turn around after fleeing from Wilson, Witness 111 explained that Brown looked down at his right hand, which was bleeding. This is contrary to Witness 110, who said that Brown looked down at his left hand and did not mention seeing blood. Second, Witness 111 described Brown as moving back toward Wilson in "slow motion," where Witness 110 at one time described Brown walking "quickly," but later could not characterize his pace. According to Witness 111, at no time were Brown's hands up in surrender or otherwise.

Witness 111 has no criminal history. Witness 111's statements were consistent with each other, and with the physical and forensic evidence, and therefore, Witness 111 would not be vulnerable to cross-examination on those grounds. However, Witness 111 was especially distraught during her investigatory interview, stating that she, too, has a teenage son and commenting that she wished Wilson had used a form of less lethal force. Her bias could subject her to effective cross-examination, and led federal prosecutors to question whether her bias was affecting her ability to accurately recall events. Regardless, Witness 111's account does not inculpate Wilson, and therefore does not support a federal prosecution.

v. Witness 115

Witness 115 is a 32-year-old black male. Witness 115 gave three investigatory statements and was interviewed by the media on several occasions. First, SLCPD detectives interviewed Witness 115 within hours of Brown's death. Second, federal agents and prosecutors conducted a follow-up interview, during which they challenged Witness 115 on what he actually witnessed as opposed to what he assumed had taken place. Witness 115 also testified before the county grand jury.

According to Witness 115, he was in his second floor apartment at the time of the shooting, on the same side of the SUV as the minivan occupied by Witness 104, Witness 105, Witness 106, and Witness 107, but with a view of Brown's right profile as he was coming back toward Wilson. Just before noon, Witness 115 was in his bedroom when he heard what he thought was an altercation. He described hearing "strong voices" or loud grunts, but could not make out specific words or sounds. Witness 115 went to his window and looked through horizontal blinds by pushing them apart. He saw Brown at the driver's door of the SUV and "arms were being exchanged." Federal prosecutors and agents asked Witness 115 to demonstrate Brown's actions, and he did so by making a fist and a punching motion. Witness 115 demonstrated that Wilson had his arm bent across his chest in a defensive position, but he was reluctant to state that Brown "punched" Wilson. However, after federal prosecutors played Witness 115's own cell phone video back to him, he acknowledged that on the video, recorded right after Brown died, he narrated, "Dude was all up in his car; dude was punching on him," and that "dude" was Brown. Witness 115 explained that his initial impression was that Brown was punching Wilson because Brown was on the outside, standing on the street, and appeared to have the upper hand.

Witness 115 explained that he suddenly saw both Brown and his friend, Witness 101, who had been standing toward the front part of the SUV, start running. Witness 115 did not know why they started to run and he did not hear a gunshot, though he acknowledged that the suddenness with which they ran was consistent with a shot being fired. Brown ran down the middle of the street and Witness 101 started to crouch down by a white Monte Carlo. According to Witness 115, Wilson then got out of his SUV, gun drawn, and immediately fired shots as he began to quickly walk in Brown's direction. With each shot, Witness 101 ducked down a little more, creeping around the Monte Carlo until he went from the driver's side to the passenger side, and out of Witness 115's view. Witness 115 explained that while he was watching Witness 101, he was not watching Brown, who had disappeared from his range of view once he ran from Wilson.

Witness 115 stated that there was a pause in the shooting and he used this opportunity to go out on his balcony to get a better look. As he did, he realized that he left his mobile phone on his dresser. He went back to his bedroom, re-trieved his phone, and returned to his balcony. At the same time, he called to his wife, Witness 124, who joined him with their three children. By the time Witness 115 saw Brown again, Brown was walking back toward Wilson with his arms folded across his stomach. Witness 115 said he "assumed" that Wilson had shot Brown in the stomach, although he did not see this happen. This as-sumption is inconsistent with the autopsy findings.

Witness 115 stated that he did not see Brown with his hands up and Brown did not appear to be surrendering. Rather, Brown looked as though he was slowly going down to the ground as he walked toward Wilson. Wilson then fired another volley of shots and Brown fell to the ground with one arm under him and the other at his side. Consistent with Wilson's account, Witness 115 explained that once Brown was on the ground, Wilson kept his gun drawn and appeared to be talking in his radio on his shoulder. According to Witness 115, at no time did Wilson touch Brown's body.

Witness 115 described the crowds that began to form immediately after the shooting, as people began to gather and talk about what happened. Witness 115 explained that although he initially spoke to SLCPD detectives only four hours after the incident, by then, he had already discussed the incident with Witness 124 and with a passerby on the street. He explained that this passerby can be heard on Witness 115's cell phone video, attempting to correct Witness 115, as Witness 115 narrated that Brown had been punching Wilson.

Witness 115 expressed that he felt comfortable with federal prosecutors and agents who were questioning him about assumptions and inconsistencies. However, Witness 115 was concerned that because of the constant talk in the neighborhood and his multiple media appearances without the presence of a lawyer, he may have unwittingly made inconsistent statements in the past.

Witness 115 has one prior misdemeanor conviction, which likely would be inadmissible in federal court as impeachment evidence. Witness 115 is vulner-able to effective cross-examination because he did not witness significant parts of the shooting and based parts of his account on assumption. Regardless of credibility, Witness 115's account does not inculpate Darren Wilson and there-fore does not support a federal prosecution.

vi. Witness 141

Witness 141 is a 19-year-old black male who moved out of Missouri after the shooting. Witness 141 gave three statements. First, FBI agents based in Texas interviewed him. Federal prosecutors and agents conducted a follow-up inter-view. Finally, Witness 141 testified before the county grand jury.

According to Witness 141, he was sitting on his balcony when he saw Brown and Witness 101 walking down the middle of Canfield Drive. Witness 141 knew

Brown through a friend, but did not have regular interaction with him. Unrelated to the shooting incident, Witness 141 went into his apartment to retrieve his mobile phone. While inside, he heard gunshots, prompting him to go back out to the balcony. Witness 141 saw Wilson pointing his gun at Brown, who had his hand across his front torso or waist. Brown never had his hands up in surrender or otherwise. Brown appeared to be stumbling or walking toward Wilson, who fired about five to seven shots at Brown from a distance of about eight feet. Brown collapsed to the ground. Witness 141 did not see Witness 101 anywhere. Witness 141 used his mobile phone to record a video in the aftermath of Brown's death.

Witness 141 testified before the county grand jury that he thought that after Wilson fired the first shot, the additional shots were "excessive," an opinion that would be inadmissible in federal court, and a misstatement of the applicable federal law. Witness 141 based that opinion on the fact that he did not perceive Brown to be a physical threat. However, he acknowledged that he did not see what led up to the initial shots, and did not see Brown run from Wilson, turn around to face Wilson, or any of Brown's actions during that time. Rather, he only saw Wilson shoot Brown as Brown moved toward him.

Witness 141 has no criminal history. Witness 141's statements were consistent with each other, but he did not witness large parts of the incident. Regardless of whether his account is credible, it does not inculpate Darren Wilson and therefore does not support a federal prosecution.

vii. Witness 114

Witness 114 is a 75-year-old black female. She gave two statements. First, she was interviewed by the FBI, and she later testified before the county grand jury.

Witness 114 saw the initial interaction between Brown and Wilson from her second floor window. Witness 114's view was of the passenger side of Wilson's SUV. Witness 114 saw Brown and Witness 101 walking in the middle of Canfield Drive, when Wilson stopped his SUV and leaned his head out of the driver's window as though saying something to Brown. Brown then made some sort of hand gesture, indicating to Witness 114 that he was responding to Wilson. Wilson continued driving, but then jerked back his SUV and parked it at an angle, with the back of the SUV closer to the center of the street. According to Witness 114, Brown remained there, while Witness 101 kept walking. She did not see Witness 101 again.

Next, Witness 114 saw Wilson hold onto Brown, though she was unsure how the physical contact began. Witness 114 stated that Wilson and Brown were "tussling," explaining that she could see Brown's hands inside the SUV by looking through the passenger side window. However, she did not see any other part of his body go into the SUV because Brown was standing straight up. From her perspective, it looked like Brown was trying to pull away. Yet Witness 114 acknowledged that had Wilson un-holstered his gun in the manner he described, it was also possible, given Brown's position, that Brown reached for Wilson's gun.

Witness 114 watched Brown run from the SUV, followed by Wilson with his gun drawn, until they both disappeared from her line of sight. She heard two gunshots followed by six more gunshots, but did not see Wilson fire any shots. Witness 114 changed her clothes and went down to street level to see Brown's body in the street.

Witness 114 has no criminal history. Witness 114's statements were consistent with each other, however, she did not see the majority of the shooting. Accordingly, her account does not inculpate Wilson and therefore does not support a federal prosecution.

viii. Witness 129

Witness 129 is a 22-year-old black male. He gave two statements. First, FBI agents interviewed him as part of their canvass on August 16, 2014. Second, Witness 129 testified before the county grand jury.

Witness 129 was outside his apartment when he saw Brown and his friend, Witness 101, walking in the middle of Canfield Drive. Wilson pulled up next to them in his SUV. Brown and Witness 101 kept walking and Wilson backed up to cut them off. Brown and Wilson then engaged in a "scuffle." Witness 129's view was of the passenger side of the SUV. Therefore, although he could tell that Wilson remained in the driver's seat of the SUV while Brown was standing outside of the SUV, Witness 129 could not describe exactly what Brown and Wilson were doing or how the upper half of Brown's body was positioned relative to the SUV. Witness 129 then heard a gunshot, but Brown remained at the SUV and the scuffle continued for another 20 to 30 seconds. A second shot then went off and Brown ran eastbound down Canfield Drive. Witness 129 explained that Witness 101 ducked behind a white car, ran around it, and went in the other direction. Wilson got out of the SUV and fired one or two shots, though Witness 129 did not see whether the shots struck Brown, nor did he see what Brown was doing, because a nearby building blocked his view.

Witness 129 has no criminal history. Witness 129's statements were materially consistent with each other and consistent with other credible evidence. However, Witness 129's account does not inculpate Wilson, and therefore does not support a federal prosecution.

ix. Witness 116

Witness 116 is a 16-year-old black male. He gave three statements. First, he met with SLCPD detectives within hours of the shooting in the presence of his father and father's girlfriend. He subsequently met with federal agents and prosecutors. Finally, he testified before the county grand jury.

Witness 116 explained that he was in his apartment watching television when he heard screams, prompting him to go to the window and look out of the vertical blinds. Witness 116 saw Brown with his hands inside the driver's side of the SUV. He then saw Wilson take out what appeared to be a taser. Wilson shot the taser one time, but missed, which is why Witness 116 surmised that Wilson took out his gun. Brown's friend, Witness 101, took off running somewhere into the apartment complexes.

Wilson shot once or twice, and Brown, with arms at his sides, ran out of view. Witness 116 looked away because he assumed that Brown had been apprehended. He then heard five or six more shots and looked back out the window to see Brown dead on the ground. Witness 116 did not see what happened leading up to Brown standing by the SUV.

Witness 116's statements were consistent, but he also mistakenly believed that Wilson used a taser. Regardless of the reliability of his account, Witness 116 did not witness significant parts of the shooting. Like several of the witnesses in this section of the report, that which he did see does not inculpate Darren Wilson and therefore does not support a federal prosecution.

3. Witnesses Whose Accounts Do Not Support a Prosecution Due to Materially Inconsistent Prior Statements or Inconsistencies With the Physical and Forensic Evidence

i. Witness 101

Witness 101 is a 22-year-old black male who was walking in the middle of Canfield Drive with Brown when they encountered Wilson. Witness 101 made multiple statements to the media immediately following the incident that spawned the popular narrative that Wilson shot Brown execution-style as he held up his hands in surrender. These media interviews occurred prior to Witness 101 giving his two statements. First, FBI and SLCPD jointly interviewed Witness 101 on August 13, 2014, in the presence of Witness 101's mother, Witness 101's two attorneys, and an individual who explained that he was in charge of Witness 101's personal security. Witness 101 subsequently testified before the county grand jury.

According to Witness 101, he and Brown had been friends for about two to three months as of the day of the shooting. Witness 101 viewed himself as a role model or mentor to Brown. Witness 101 came into contact with Brown on August 9, 2014, at about 7:00 a.m. At some point between then and just prior to noon, he and Brown decided to go to Ferguson Market to get cigarillos. Witness 101 could not recall in detail what the pair was doing in those five intervening hours, other than to explain that they were playing video games and talking. However, Witness 101 explained that just prior to going to Ferguson Market, Brown engaged in a 25-minute conversation about marijuana with one of two contractors who were working in the apartment complex.

Witness 101 explained that when they went to Ferguson Market, Brown stole cigarillos from behind the counter as though he was entitled to them, and then subsequently shoved the store clerk, who was substantially smaller in stature than Brown, who was 6'5" and 289 lbs. Witness 101 initially minimized these events when speaking with law enforcement, but then acknowledged to the county grand jury that Brown was surprisingly aggressive. Brown's behavior caught Witness 101 off guard because it was uncharacteristic of Brown and contrary to Brown's usual behavior. Witness 101 expected to encounter the police when they left Ferguson Market because he heard the clerk say he was going to call the police. Witness 101 described Brown's behavior as "bold" when Brown openly carried the stolen cigarillos as they walked down Canfield Drive.

Witness 101 and Brown were walking eastbound, single-file, on Canfield Drive in the center of the street on the yellow line when they encountered Wilson driving in the opposite direction in his marked FPD SUV. Witness 101 explained that they had not been obstructing traffic, although several cars had to avoid Brown and Witness 101 as they drove by. Wilson told them to "get the fuck on the sidewalk," and Witness 101 responded that they were "not but one minute from their destination." Brown and Witness 101 did not move onto the sidewalk, but continued to walk in the middle of the street. As Wilson drove past them, he reversed his SUV and parked it at an angle, blocking both lanes in the road and almost hitting them, asking, "What did you just say?" According to Witness 101, Wilson attempted to open the driver's side in an "aggressive" and "forceful" manner. The door opened less than an inch because of Brown and Witness 101's proximity to the door. The door quickly bounced off of Brown and Witness 101 and shut on Wilson. According to Witness 101, this angered Brown. Witness 101 also stated that he understood how Wilson could have perceived that Brown shut the door on him.

According to Witness 101, Wilson then reached out the window and up with his left hand, grabbing Brown by the throat. The private forensic pathologist termed such an action "surprising," based on the autopsy results and his experience as a forensic pathologist. Wilson and Brown engaged in a "tug of war," during which Wilson unsuccessfully tried to pull Brown toward the SUV as Brown attempted to pull away, while still holding the cigarillos. Witness 101 told county and federal investigators that Brown told Wilson, "Get the fuck off me. We're not doin' anything wrong. Leave us the fuck alone." However, Witness 101 explained that even though Wilson had his grip on Brown, Brown had the upper hand both because of his stature and his physical position relative to the car. As Witness 101 told investigators, Wilson would have to be "super-human" to "overpower" Brown. Witness 101 told the county grand jury that Brown was getting "the best of the officer" because Wilson was only using his left hand. During this tug of war, Wilson's grip gradually slipped from Brown's throat to his shirt, down to his shoulder and arm. Although Witness 101 told the county grand jury that Wilson gripped Brown's right arm, Witness 101 told investigators that Wilson mostly was gripping Brown's shirt by pulling it down over Brown's forearm. According to Witness 101, at no point did Brown ever strike, punch, or grab any part of Wilson. He could offer no explanation as to how Wilson sustained injury, other than to speculate that it was the result of their "tug of war."

As the "tug of war" continued, Brown was then able to turn to his right toward Witness 101 and hand off the cigarillos with both hands. Brown then put his left hand on the door frame under the rearview mirror, while Wilson, using his left hand, maintained hold of Brown's right arm or sleeve. According to Witness 101, Wilson used his right hand to grab hold of Brown's left arm, although it is unclear from Witness 101's accounts whether he actually saw that happen or assumed it happened. Wilson, also using his right hand, then took out his gun and said, "I'm going to shoot." Witness 101 saw Wilson holding the gun and aiming it out the window when Wilson again started to say, "I'm going to shoot."

Witness 101 explained that Wilson fired, hitting Brown in the torso. Witness 101 described blood on the right side of Brown's torso. At the time of the shot, Brown was standing straight, his midsection up against the door, with his left hand down at his side and Wilson gripping Brown's right arm. Contrary to the autopsy results, particularly with regard to the thumb wound and the round recovered from the inside of the driver's door, Witness 101 was adamant that Wilson neither fired a shot within the SUV, nor did Brown have his hand(s) near the gun when the first shot was fired. Witness 101 explained that Wilson fired the shot and "the bullet traveled outside the car and struck [Brown] in the chest." Witness 101 was equally adamant that Brown's hands and arms never entered the SUV, telling investigators that the only hand that would have been "free" would have been Brown's left hand, and that hand neither entered the vehicle nor "reached for" Wilson's gun. However, when he testified before the county grand jury, Witness 101 made room for the possibility that Brown's arm entered the SUV when he was not looking.

According to Witness 101, after the first shot, Brown and Witness 101 simultaneously ran eastbound, away from the SUV. Witness 101 explained that he got ahead of Brown, such that his back was to both Brown and Wilson. Fearing for his life, Witness 101 crouched down among the cars that had now stopped in the middle of the street because of the parked SUV. Witness 101 attempted to get into a nearby car, a gray Sunfire, but the occupants would not allow him inside. Brown ran past Witness 101, telling him, "Keep running, bro." After a pause, Witness 101 explained that he heard Wilson emerge from the SUV. Witness 101 stood up and watched "in plain sight" as Wilson passed him and chased after Brown.

According to Witness 101, Wilson then fired a second shot which appeared to strike Brown in the back. Brown's arms were not raised at that time. During his investigative interview, Witness 101 stated that the bullet "definitely struck [Brown] in the back." During his county grand jury testimony, Witness 101 stated that the bullet likely "grazed" Brown's arm, acknowledging that since he had made his original statements, he had watched media reports of the privately-commissioned autopsy of Brown. Witness 101 said that he assumed that had Brown not been struck, he would have kept on running. Instead, Brown stopped. Brown put his hands up above his head, in the air, and turned around to face Wilson. In so doing, one arm was lower than the other, though Witness 101 could not say whether it was the left or right arm. According to Witness 101, Brown then stated, "I don't have a gun" or "I'm unarmed." Brown started to say it again, but Wilson, while walking toward Brown, fired one volley of at least four shots and Brown fell to his death. Wilson never said a word; he never commanded Brown to stop or freeze. Witness 101 was steadfast that Brown fell to the ground right where he initially stopped and turned around. At most, Brown took a half-step forward, but he did not move toward Wilson. Witness 101 was also steadfast that Brown never put his hand(s) near his waist. As described earlier, the physical evidence establishes that Brown moved forward about 20 feet toward Wilson, and the SLCME medicolegal investigator found Brown with his left hand at his waistband.

Witness 101 also told the county grand jury that he "stood and watched face-to-face as every shot was fired as [Brown]'s body [fell] to the ground," but was unaware that Wilson shot Brown in the face and head until he saw media reports of the privately-commissioned autopsy. Until then, he thought the only shots were to Brown's "upper region" and chest.

Witness 101 ran from the scene, saying, "He just killed my friend." Witness 101 went home and changed his shirt, so he later would not be recognized by the police. By the time he went back to the scene of the shooting, the streets were crowded with people, but, contrary to the dispatch recordings and cellular phone video, there were no police officers on scene. When police officers did arrive, he did not want to speak with them. Instead, Witness 101 went to Brown's grandmother's home and told her and other family members what happened. With the encouragement of Brown's family, Witness 101 went back out onto the street and gave an interview to the media.

During his testimony before the county grand jury, Witness 101 acknowledged that he had discussed the incident with another witness, Witness 118. Witness 101 explained that he was friendly with Witness 118, and noticed her standing on her balcony when he and Brown first encountered Wilson on Canfield Drive. He explained that he was surprised that so many other witnesses came forward because Witness 118 was the only person he saw outside, and she was the only person who saw the incident from the "first shot to the last shot." However, as detailed below, Witness 118 was not out on her balcony for the majority of the incident, and it is unknown at what point she actually witnessed the shootings, if at all.

Witness 101 has a misdemeanor conviction for a crime of dishonesty likely admissible in federal court as impeachment evidence. As described above, material parts of Witness 101's account are inconsistent with the physical and forensic evidence, internally inconsistent from one part of his account to the next, and inconsistent with other credible witness accounts that are corroborated by physical evidence. It is also unclear whether Witness 101 had the ability to accurately perceive the shootings. Witness 101 likely crouched down next to a white Monte Carlo as Wilson chased Brown. The Monte Carlo was facing west with a view of the passenger side of the SUV. Brown ran in the opposite direction that the Monte Carlo was facing. Witness accounts vary as to whether Witness 101 was ducking for cover on the passenger side of the Monte Carlo with his back to the shooting, or whether he fled the scene prior to the final shots being fired. Both Witness 101's inconsistencies and his ability to perceive what happened, or lack thereof, make his account vulnerable to effective cross-examination and extensive impeachment. Accordingly, after a thorough review of all of the evidence, federal prosecutors determined material portions of Witness 101's account lack credibility and therefore determined that his account does not support a prosecution of Darren Wilson.

ii. Witness 123

Witness 123 is a 29-year-old black male who gave two statements. First, he was jointly interviewed by FBI agents and SLCPD detectives. Second, he testified before the county grand jury.

Witness 123 was in the front passenger seat of a white Monte Carlo that was traveling west on Canfield Drive behind Wilson before Wilson stopped his SUV. Witness 133, a black female, was driving the Monte Carlo. Witness 123 first observed Brown and his friend, Witness 101, walking in the street in the opposite direction of the SUV. It seemed to Witness 123 that Brown and Witness 101 failed to comply with a directive from Wilson because the SUV quickly swerved back, and stopped while Brown and Witness 101 were still standing on the yellow line in the middle of the street.

The SUV was then positioned such that Witness 123 and Witness 133 had a view of its passenger side. Therefore, although Witness 123 described a tussle involving Brown at the driver's window, he could not be more specific. During the tussle, Witness 101 looked startled and ran off. Witness 123 then heard a gunshot and told Witness 133 to back up. He heard a second gunshot just as Brown was running past the driver's window of the Monte Carlo. Witness 123 ducked after the second shot and, therefore, could not see if Brown was injured. Between four and six seconds later, he looked out the front windshield to see Wilson emerge from the SUV with his gun held low. At about the same time, Witness 101 approached the Monte Carlo's passenger side door, which Witness 123 had already opened to allow him more room to duck. Witness 101 asked if he could get into their car, but Witness 123 would not permit him to do so, instead instructing him to duck down. Witness 123 then turned his attention to Witness 133, who was shaking. While Witness 123 attempted to calm Witness 133, Witness 101 disappeared and they never saw him again.

Witness 123 explained to the FBI and the SLCPD that he turned around and watched through the back window as Brown turned around with hands halfway up, shoulder height, and crunched up as though he was about to go to the ground. Witness 123 did not know what prompted Brown to turn around. He then heard a volley of about five shots in addition to the two initial shots, and Brown fell forward to his death, palms face forward and arms tucked under him. Witness 123 told the county grand jury that he saw Brown turn around and hold his hands up. Wilson shot Brown three times and Brown fell to the ground dead. Contrary to the physical evidence, Witness 123 explained that Brown died where he turned around and did not move toward Wilson. After the final shots, Wilson appeared to be looking at his (Wilson's) arms.

Witness 133 quickly drove around the SUV and away from the scene after the shooting. Witness 123 and Witness 133 subsequently discussed what they had seen with each other while watching media reports.

Witness 123 has no criminal history. Witness 123's accounts to investigators and to the county grand jury were inconsistent with the physical and forensic evidence, making him vulnerable to effective cross-examination. His focus was split among the driver of the vehicle, Witness 101, and the shooting itself. For those reasons, prosecutors questioned his ability to accurately perceive the incident and could not rely upon his account to support prosecution of Darren Wilson.

iii. Witness 133

Witness 133 is a 33-year-old black female who gave three statements. SLCPD detectives first interviewed Witness 133 within hours of the shooting. She subsequently met with federal agents and prosecutors who questioned her more in-depth. She then testified before the county grand jury.

As previously noted, Witness 133 was driving a white Monte Carlo west on Canfield Drive when she was forced to stop behind Wilson's SUV. Witness 123 was seated in Witness 133's front passenger seat. Witness 133 initially saw Brown and Witness 101 walking down the center line of the street in the opposite direction in which she was traveling. Wilson stopped his SUV alongside Brown and Witness 101, and it appeared to Witness 133 that "something had to have been said between the two parties." However, Witness 133 could not hear anything. Once the SUV stopped, her vantage point was of its passenger side. She was able to see that there was some sort of "tussle" on the driver's side of the SUV between Wilson, who was seated in the SUV, and Brown, whose feet she could see moving underneath the SUV. The SUV was shaking. Witness 101, who was standing closer to the front of the SUV, was trying to see what was happening.

Witness 133 then heard a gunshot from within the SUV. Witness 133 stated that the "suspect who got shot, backed up, and seemed amazed." Both Brown and Witness 101 then ran eastbound past her vehicle down Canfield Drive. The gunshot "terrified" Witness 133, and when she saw Wilson get out of the SUV, she immediately ducked down for cover. It was then that Witness 101 appeared at her passenger side door, asking if he could get in the car, saying "Can you get me away from here? It's crazy." Witness 133 refused to allow Witness 101 into her car, instead telling him to duck. Witness 123, Witness 133, and Witness 101 all ducked for cover together. During her interview with federal authorities, Witness 133 added that she likely "blacked out" while all of this was happening.

Shortly thereafter, Witness 133 looked in her rearview mirror, and saw Brown's face, indicating to her that Brown had turned to face Wilson. She described hearing two or three shots and then Brown fell to the ground. At some point, Witness 101 disappeared, but having been focused on Brown, she did not know where he went or when he left. Wanting to leave quickly, Witness 133 drove on the grass and around the SUV to get out of the area.

During both her interview with SLCPD and her follow-up interview with federal agents and prosecutors, Witness 133 was repeatedly asked if there was anything else that she saw or anything she thought investigators would need to know. In both instances, Witness 133 denied knowing any more information, telling federal authorities that she had given "everything [she's] got." However, she expressed sorrow as the mother of a teenaged son.

Despite her repeated assurances that she saw nothing else, Witness 133 testified before the county grand jury that when she looked in the rearview mirror, Brown had his hands up before he fell to his death. When questioned by the county prosecutor about providing this new information, Witness 133 acknowledged that the transcripts from her prior statements were correct, and that she told SLCPD detectives, FBI agents and federal prosecutors everything she could think of that was important. Witness 133 never offered an explanation as to why she did not previously disclose that Brown's hands were up. Witness 133 also acknowledged that she has been watching the news and "hands up" had become the "mantra" of the protesters.

Witness 133 has no criminal history. Witness 133's repeated omission of a material detail that goes directly to whether Wilson used unreasonable force, coupled with the fact that she told federal authorities that she "blacked out" before later testifying that she saw Brown's hands up, would subject her to effective cross-examination if called as a prosecution witness. It calls into question whether she actually saw Brown's hands at all, had "blacked out," or had been distracted by Witness 101. Accordingly, federal prosecutors determined material portions of her account to be unreliable, and therefore it does not support a prosecution of Darren Wilson.

iv. Witness 119

Witness 119 is a 15-year-old black male. He initially told SLCPD detectives that he witnessed the shooting. However, he later recanted, telling federal agents and prosecutors that he lied to SLCPD detectives because he just wanted to be involved in the investigation. Witness 119 reiterated the same thing to county prosecutors and did not testify before the county grand jury.

Witness 119 initially spoke to SLCPD detectives within hours of the shooting, while standing on Canfield Drive. In part because of the chaos around him during the interview, and in larger part because he was lying, much of Witness 119's initial account did not make sense. Witness 119 seemed to claim that Wilson shot Brown in the side from out of the window of the SUV, possibly while he was still driving. Wilson then chased after Brown, and ultimately shot him to death in the head while Brown had his hands in the air.

Federal agents and prosecutors sought to follow up with Witness 119 to clarify his account. Witness 119 readily admitted that he never saw the shooting, but was sitting near a flowerbed playing video games on his phone when he heard gunshots. Witness 119 could not see the SUV from his vantage point. He and his brother waited until the gunshots stopped before going to the scene because they did not want to get hit by a stray bullet. By the time they arrived on scene, Brown was dead. Witness 119 claimed that he told the police that he was a witness because he was traumatized and because he "wanted to be a part of it."

Because Witness 119 admitted that he gave a false account, federal prosecutors did not consider his account in the prosecutive decision.

v. Witness 125

Witness 125 is a 23-year-old black female. She initially told law enforcement that she witnessed the shooting, but later recanted, claiming that she wanted to be involved from the outset and therefore lied to investigators.

SLCPD detectives briefly interviewed Witness 125 during their initial canvass after the shooting. Witness 125 claimed that she was asleep for the first two gunshots. Her boyfriend, Witness 131, told her to get up and go to the window. Witness 125 then gave an internally inconsistent account, first saying that Brown's arms were by his waist, followed by his hands going up. When asked for clarification, she said the same thing in reverse, explaining that it all occurred while Brown was kneeling.

In an effort to reconcile this inconsistency and help inform the prosecutive decision, federal prosecutors sought to meet with Witness 125. Witness 125 refused to meet with federal prosecutors but did meet with FBI agents. She reiterated that she was asleep during the first few shots, but then went to her window where she witnessed Brown standing with his hands up in surrender. Although she could not see who was shooting Brown due to a tree blocking her line of sight, Witness 125 explained that she witnessed two volleys of shots, one which caused Brown to grab his torso with his left hand and a second volley causing his head to snap back before he fell to the ground. Witness 125 did not see Brown move from his position. Despite saying otherwise in her recorded statement to the SLCPD, she denied telling FBI agents that she originally told SLCPD detectives that Brown was kneeling prior to his death.

When Witness 125 appeared at the St. Louis County Prosecutor's Office to testify before the county grand jury, she was accompanied by an attorney. Prior to her testimony, Witness 125 told the county prosecutors that she lied to the FBI and to SLCPD detectives. Witness 125 was then given immunity from federal prosecution for making material false statements to federal agents so long as she testified truthfully in the grand jury. She testified that she did not, in fact, witness any part of the incident, but claimed she did so because she wanted to be "part of something." She claimed that a friend in the community told her to tell the SLCPD and the FBI what her boyfriend saw, but to claim it as her own.

Witness 125 has no criminal history. Because Witness 125 admitted that she gave false accounts, federal prosecutors did not consider her accounts in the prosecutive decision.

vi. Witness 131

Witness 131 is a 22-year-old black male. As previously mentioned, Witness 131 is the fiancé of Witness 125, who first told SLCPD detectives and then FBI agents that she saw Wilson shoot Brown while he had his hands in the air, and then admitted to county prosecutors that she lied to law enforcement and did not, in fact, see anything. Witness 131 gave two statements, first to FBI agents and then he testified before the county grand jury.

Witness 131 told the FBI that he was in his apartment when he heard three gunshots, prompting him to call Witness 125 to come look out their living room window. However, he changed his account when he testified before the county grand jury, claiming that he only called to his fiancée once the shooting had stopped.

Witness 131 stated that he initially did not see Wilson, but saw only Brown, who was taking a few steps forward. Witness 131 testified before the county grand jury that his view was somewhat obstructed, but he also saw Witness 101 run across the yard. Witness 131 then heard about five more shots, and watched as Brown grabbed his torso with his left hand, while holding his right hand in the air, in front him at a 45 degree angle. Witness 131 then heard another volley of shots and Brown's arms dropped. Brown fell to his knees and collapsed face down in the street. Witness 131 explained to the FBI that once Brown stopped moving forward, the shooting stopped. It was then that Witness 131 noticed a police officer approach Brown just as other officers arrived on scene.

Despite Witness 131 telling the FBI that Brown was shot only when he moved forward, he testified to the contrary in front of the county grand jury. There, he testified that Brown stood still as he was shot to death and denied that Brown moved forward at all. When county prosecutors confronted Witness 131 with his inconsistency, he denied that he said anything different to the FBI.

Witness 131 has no criminal history. Witness 131's accounts are inconsistent with each other, and his most recent version is inconsistent with the physical and forensic evidence. He also claimed that his fiancée was present for something she admitted she did not witness. Accordingly, based on a thorough review of all of the evidence, federal prosecutors determined his account not to be credible, and it therefore does not support a prosecution of Darren Wilson.

vii. Witness 112

Witness 112 is a 62-year-old black male who was with his brother, Witness 110, and sister-in-law, Witness 111, when he witnessed the shooting. As described above, they witnessed the shooting from the second floor balcony located opposite and off to the right of the minivan occupied by Witness 104, Witness 105, Witness 106, and Witness 107. Their view was of the passenger side of the SUV, followed by the right profile of Brown as he ran away from Wilson, and then the left profile of Brown as he turned around and moved toward Wilson.

Witness 112 gave three investigative statements, and he also spoke to the print media. He spoke first with SLCPD detectives. He then met with federal prosecutors and agents, and subsequently testified before the county grand jury.

Witness 112 agreed to meet with SLCPD detectives only because he spoke to his pastor, and realized that what he witnessed was "weighing on [him]." Witness 112 explained that Witness 101 could not have seen what he is claiming to have seen in his media interviews. According to Witness 112, he was sitting by his bedroom window when he saw Brown and Witness 101 walking in the center of the street. Witness 112 knew Brown from the neighborhood and always found him to be respectful.

Witness 112 saw Wilson's SUV pass Brown and Witness 101, and then back up. Witness 112 then went out to his balcony to get a better view. Once there, he saw a "tussling" at the SUV, and acknowledged that he did not know whether Wilson grabbed Brown or vice versa. However, Witness 112 was adamant that, contrary to what he kept hearing from people in his neighborhood, at least one of Brown's arms was inside the SUV. Wilson fired a shot from within the SUV, likely in an effort to get Brown off of him because Brown was so big. After that initial shot, Brown looked startled and took off running. Witness 101 took off running as well, and did not reappear until much later, once Brown's body was covered.

Witness 112 explained that it appeared that Brown stopped running because either the pain or shock hit him. Brown turned around, and looked down, as though checking himself for injury. In so doing, Witness 112 explained that Brown raised his arms partly, palms up, clarifying that he "didn't have his hands all the way up." Brown then moved his arms out at a 35 to 45 degree angle, as if to say, "What?" It was then that Wilson trained his gun on Brown, and as Brown moved forward, Wilson repeatedly yelled, "Stop!" When Brown failed to stop, Wilson fired shots. Brown's arms went limp at his sides, but he kept moving toward Wilson, though Witness 112 characterized it as "not in a menacing way." Witness 112 explained that at no time did Brown say a word. Instead, Witness 112 yelled out from his balcony for Brown to stop, but Brown kept slowly advancing, bent forward, and Wilson kept shooting.

When Witness 112 subsequently met with federal agents and prosecutors, he gave a similar account, except that he steadfastly claimed that when Brown turned around in the roadway, he held his arms up in surrender, at ninety degree angles with his palms facing out. When asked about his previous description, Witness 112 became agitated and angry, and refused to listen to a recording of his previous statement. He was unable to explain the difference in his accounts, and why his statement had changed. Witness 112 similarly described that Brown held his hands up in surrender when he testified before the county grand jury.

Subsequent to his meeting with federal authorities and his appearance before the county grand jury, Witness 112 gave an "anonymous" interview to the local print media. Although Witness 112 never identified himself, based on the account given that was almost verbatim to his initial SLCPD interview and the proximity in time to his county grand jury testimony, federal and county prosecutors and investigators recognized that it was Witness 112. In that media interview, Witness 112 reverted to his initial version that he told

SLCPD detectives, explaining that Brown did not have his hands up in surrender, but rather partly raised his arms, palms up, checking for injury. This stood in stark contrast to what he told the FBI and federal prosecutors, and to his testimony in the county grand jury.

Witness 112 has a felony conviction for stealing from 18 years ago that likely would be inadmissible in federal court as impeachment evidence. Witness 112 made it clear in all of his statements that he believes that Wilson should not have shot and killed Brown, stating that it was "overkill," without offering more of an explanation. Witness 112's accounts are inconsistent as to whether Brown held his hands up in surrender, and his most recent account is that Brown's hands were not up in surrender. Because federal prosecutors cannot discern the truth among Witness 112's versions, and his most recent account does not inculpate Wilson, federal prosecutors cannot rely upon it to support a prosecution of Darren Wilson.

viii. Witness 135

Witness 135 is a 20-year-old black female. She was walking on Canfield Drive at the time of the initial interaction between Brown and Wilson. She gave three statements. The FBI first interviewed Witness 135 during their canvass on August 16, 2014, and she subsequently met with federal prosecutors. She then testified before the county grand jury.

According to Witness 135, as she was standing on the south side of the street, she saw Wilson's SUV back up and bump up against Brown and his friend. Brown then "charged over" to the driver's side of the SUV and put his arms inside the driver's window. She was unable to see what transpired inside the vehicle because the width of Brown's back obstructed her view. She did, however, explain that Brown's arms were moving aggressively and his head, shoulders, and top half of his body were in the window.

Witness 135 stated that this interaction lasted about 15 seconds during which time she saw a gun fall to the ground and then heard a gunshot. She moved to a nearby tree where she initially waited, and then continued her walk home. Brown ran anywhere from five to 10 steps, and then turned around to face Wilson who had emerged from the SUV seconds after Brown took off running. Witness 135 explained that she was both walking away and scanning the street as this was happening, so she did not see the entire incident. She recalled that as Brown turned around, he put his hands up with his arms, "scrunched up," pulled tight against his body, palms out at about shoulder height. According to Witness 135, Brown was hunched forward, though he took a few steps backward, and was shot about five times before he fell to his death. According to Witness 135, there was only this one additional volley of shots after the initial shot, Brown never moved forward, and Wilson never shot Brown as he was running away.

Witness 135 readily acknowledged to federal prosecutors that she has poor vision, and was not wearing her contact lenses on the date of the shooting. She was able to see shapes and figures, but could not see details or facial expressions from where she stood once Brown ran from the SUV. Because the physical evidence proves that Brown moved forward before he fell to his death, federal prosecutors and agents asked Witness 135 if it was possible that Brown moved forward, but she did not see it. Witness 135 responded that it was possible, not only because of her vision problems but because she was not watching Brown the entire time. Instead, she was scanning the block, and was worried for her own safety due to the ringing of gunshots.

Witness 135 explained to federal prosecutors that Brown's friend ran off as soon as the first shot was fired and she never saw him again. However, she described a similarly built black male with dreadlocks who was later running around the Canfield apartments, saying something to the effect of, "The police shot my friend and his hands were up." Witness 135 explained that quickly became the narrative on the street, and to her frustration, people used it both as an excuse to riot and to create a "block party" atmosphere.

During her county grand jury testimony, Witness 135 characterized Wilson's actions as "murder," an opinion that would be inadmissible in federal court. When county prosecutors pressed her for an explanation, she stated that she sees it that way because Wilson should have used a taser, night stick, or similar weapon. Witness 135 also stated that when she saw the gun drop by the SUV, she assumed it belonged to Brown, acknowledging that it was not unreasonable for Wilson to think that Brown had a weapon. Witness 135 also testified about her own negative experience with the FPD, when an officer arrested her and "basically beat [her] up." That officer was not Darren Wilson, nor did she ever have prior interactions with Wilson.

Witness 135 has no criminal history. As detailed above, Witness 135's initial account was inconsistent with the forensic and physical evidence and inconsistent with other credible witness accounts. She admittedly was unsure of what she saw, both because she was distracted and because she has poor vision. Because of her admitted inconsistencies along with her questionable ability to have accurately perceived what happened, federal prosecutors determined material parts of this witness's account to lack reliability and therefore, her account does not support a prosecution of Darren Wilson

ix. Witness 124

Witness 124 is a 31-year-old black female. As previously noted, Witness 124 is the wife of Witness 115. In addition to testifying before the county grand jury, Witness 124 gave two interviews to law enforcement, first to SLCPD detectives and then to FBI agents during their canvass one week after the shooting.

In her initial interview to SLCPD detectives, Witness 124 explained that she was on the phone and eating when her husband, Witness 115, called to her, "Baby, Look out the window. They're shooting." She went to the window and saw Brown running from Wilson, who was walking and steadily shooting at Brown from behind. Brown then disappeared from her sight, making her think that Brown got away. However, Brown then reappeared and came back toward Wilson. Witness 124 then joined Witness 115 on the balcony with their three children. Once on the balcony, Witness 124 saw Wilson shoot Brown in the chest area, firing two shots, followed by three shots until Brown tipped over and fell to the pavement. She further told the SLCPD detective that Brown had nothing in his hands, and Wilson did not go near Brown's body. At no point did Witness 124 describe Brown's arm across his torso as her husband described. At no point did she describe Brown's hands up in surrender.

However, during her interview with the FBI, Witness 124 described that she first saw Wilson's SUV when Wilson tried to run over Brown and Witness 101. This directly contradicts her prior statement that Witness 115 called to her to look out the window after the first shots were fired. During her FBI interview, Witness 124 also added that she saw Brown turn around and put his hands up. This also directly contradicts her initial statement in which she claimed that Brown disappeared from sight and that she did not see him until he reappeared in her line of sight. Witness 124 also added that, contrary to virtually every other witness account, Wilson walked toward Brown and shot him to death.

Witness 124 has no criminal history. In an effort to reconcile the apparent inconsistencies in Witness 124's accounts and determine what she actually witnessed as opposed to what she may have heard from others, federal prosecutors sought to meet with her. However, Witness 124 failed to appear for a scheduled meeting and refused to reschedule at any time or place of her convenience. Therefore, federal prosecutors did not have the opportunity to assess her credibility and determine which parts of her account, if any, were accurate. Because the substance of her two investigative accounts stood in stark contrast to each other, without further explanation, federal prosecutors determined her accounts not to be credible and therefore did not consider them in its prosecutive decision.

x. Witness 127

Witness 127 is a 27-year-old black female who gave three investigative statements, including testifying before the county grand jury. SLCPD detectives initially interviewed Witness 127 within two hours of the shooting. She subsequently appeared in the media several times. Federal agents and prosecutors interviewed Witness 127, in the presence of her lawyer, because parts of her account were inconsistent with the physical evidence.

According to Witness 127, she was driving east on Canfield Drive, traveling in the opposite direction of Wilson's SUV. and heard tires screeching as she rounded a curve. When she pulled up to where the SUV was stopped, Witness 127 saw Brown "rassling" at the driver's window. Brown's head was bent at the window, with his palms on the outside of the door. Witness 127 said that it looked like Brown was either pushing off of the door or pulling away and that someone was pulling him into the car, in a "tug of war" manner. However, she did not see anyone or anything pulling Brown. At the same time this was happening, Witness 127 was looking at her mobile phone, trying to no avail to record what was transpiring "because it didn't look right." Witness 127 then heard a gunshot, but did not see blood or injury. She said that Brown broke free, indicating that it looked like Brown's right shirtsleeve was being pulled, though she could not see anything pulling it.

Upon hearing that gunshot, Witness 127 drove around the SUV and turned left into a nearby parking lot. She parked her car and got out. By that time, she saw Brown running and heard shots being fired. Witness 127 did not actually see Wilson exit the SUV, but she saw him chase after Brown. Witness 127 described volleys of gunshots without specificity. She explained that once she was out of her car, she began walking on the sidewalk as the shooting continued. She saw Brown's body make a jerking movement such that his hands started going up involuntarily. In one quick motion, Brown turned around with his hands up at right angles at his shoulders. Wilson then shot him, and Brown fell to his death where he stood. Witness 127 did not see injury to either of Brown's hands when his hands were up. Witness 127 was adamant that, contrary to DNA evidence with regard to the blood east of Brown's body, Brown never moved toward Wilson. She insisted that he fell to his death right where he turned around. She was equally adamant that Brown's hands remained outside the SUV during the initial interaction between Wilson and Brown, despite forensic and physical evidence to the contrary. When questioned by federal prosecutors and then by county prosecutors during her county grand jury testimony, she disallowed any possibility that perhaps her perception was compromised because she was using her phone, driving, and parking, among other reasons. Additionally, Witness 127 appeared in the media with her friend, Witness 118, allowing for the possibility that their accounts became conflated .

Witness 127 has no criminal history. Although Witness 127's statements are materially consistent with each other, significant portions are contrary to the forensic and physical evidence and inconsistent with credible witness accounts. Witness 127 was unable to give reasonable explanations as to why the physical evidence might be inconsistent with what she remembers, and therefore prosecutors were left to conclude that she inaccurately perceived material portions of the shootings either because of the stress of incidents or because she was distracted. Accordingly, after a thorough review of the evidence, fed-

eral prosecutors determined material portions of this witness's account not reliable and therefore cannot be used to support prosecution of Darren Wilson.

xi. Witness 118

Witness 118 is a 19-year-old black female who lives in the Canfield Green neighborhood and knew Brown through a mutual friend, Witness 120. Witness 118
also knew Witness 101, with whom she became friendly when she moved into
the neighborhood. Prior to the shootings, Witness 118 and Witness 101 social-
ized almost weekly. Witness 118 denied speaking with Witness 101 since the
shootings, contrary to what Witness 101 said during his testimony before the
county grand jury. However, Witness 118 acknowledged speaking to Witness
120 about the shooting. As detailed later in this memorandum, Witness 120
was admittedly untruthful about what he claimed to have witnessed.

Witness 118 gave three investigative statements, and testified before the
county grand jury. A SLCPD detective initially interviewed Witness 118 approximately two hours after the shooting. She subsequently appeared in the
media several times. During those media interviews, Witness 118 added details that she did not report to local law enforcement, claiming in the news
that she saw the "whole scenario play out." In an effort to evaluate the inconsistencies between her statements to law enforcement and her statements to
the media as well as inconsistencies with physical evidence, federal agents and
prosecutors interviewed Witness 118 in the presence of her lawyer.

During her initial SLCPD interview, Witness 118 stated that just before the
shooting, she was in her apartment when she heard the screech of tires and
thought someone might be hurt. She then heard three gunshots and went to
look out her bedroom window. Witness 118 denied to the SLCPD detective
that she witnessed any "tussle" at the side of the SUV. In fact, her view was
of the passenger side of the SUV, which would have limited her ability to see
a struggle at the driver's side even if she had looked out the window in time.

Witness 118 told the SLCPD detective that she then saw Wilson get out
of the SUV and run in a hurry. She did not see anyone else at that time. She
left her bedroom window to go to her patio door when she heard no less than
four more shots. Those shots occurred about 30 seconds after the first three
shots. Witness 118 thought someone was trying to shoot Wilson. She did not
see Brown until she got to her patio door, when she peeked through the blinds
to see him running. While looking through her glass door, she was distracted
for about 10 to 30 seconds by Witness 101 ducking behind a black Monte Carlo
and trying to hide. Witness 101 was creeping westward, toward the front of the
Monte Carlo, with his back to Wilson and Brown as they ran east on Canfield
Drive.

Witness 118 told the SLCPD detective that she then looked back toward Brown as he turned around, put his hands in the air, and got shot two times. Brown fell to the ground face down, with his arms at 90 degree angles on either side of his head, contrary to what the crime scene photos depict and the SLCME medicolegal investigator noted, *i.e.,* Brown's left hand was at his waistband and his right hand was down at his side.

At the conclusion of the interview with the SLCPD, Witness 118 assured the detective that what she reported was her best recollection of the incident and that she was not leaving anything out. Nonetheless, Witness 118's accounts to the media and to federal prosecutors and agents were different from her initial statement to the SLCPD, even though her grand jury testimony was ultimately more consistent with her initial SLCPD account.

Witness 118 claimed to the media that she "saw" screeching tires as the SUV swerved at Brown and Witness 101. She further claimed that she watched Brown as he was reaching, pulling, and "hassling" through the window of the SUV, in what appeared to be "arm wrestling." Witness 118 told the media that Wilson was pulling Brown into the SUV while Brown was trying to flee. She claimed to have seen the first gunshots hit Brown as he pulled away and fled. She also claimed that she saw a bullet strike a nearby building, but acknowledged that she inferred this because she saw SLCPD detectives attempting to remove one from a building wall.

Witness 118 added to her media narrative that Wilson shot Brown in the back from three feet away and that Brown never moved back towards Wilson. Physical evidence is inconsistent with both of those added details. Also, contrary to her initial account, Witness 118 told federal agents and prosecutors that Brown's arms were at his sides and his hands were around his hips when he came to rest on the ground.

When federal prosecutors and agents challenged the inconsistencies in her accounts, Witness 118 conceded that she likely assumed facts that she did not witness herself based on talking with other residents in the Canfield Green complex and watching the news, but was not specific about which facts. Witness 118 also added that she did not have a lawyer when she was first interviewed by the SLCPD, though there was nothing to indicate that interview was custodial or coercive and Witness 118 expressed no apprehension or hesitation when speaking with the SLCPD.

Witness 118 has no criminal history. Witness 118's accounts are riddled with internal inconsistencies, inconsistencies with the physical and forensic evidence, and inconsistencies with credible witness accounts. Her attention was admittedly diverted away from the shooting when she watched Witness 101 ducking for cover and she acknowledged that her account was also based on assumption and media coverage. Accordingly, after a thorough review of the evidence, federal prosecutors determined the various versions of this witness's account to lack credibility and therefore it does not support a prosecution of Darren Wilson.

xii. Witness 122

Witness 122 is a 46-year-old white male. He was laying drain pipe on Canfield Drive with Witness 130 on the morning of the shooting. Witness 122 gave six statements, including testimony before the county grand jury. SLCPD detectives and an FBI agent twice jointly interviewed him, and SLCPD detectives once independently interviewed him. Witness 122 and Witness 130 authored one-page written statements on advice of a former boss. Witness 122 and Witness 130 claimed that they did not discuss what they witnessed, though Witness 130 admitted that they read each other's statements after they were written. Witness 122 gave a media interview on the condition of anonymity. As noted throughout this memorandum, federal prosecutors interviewed many potential witnesses in an effort to assess credibility and reconcile internal inconsistencies and inconsistencies with physical evidence, as is necessary to make a fair prosecutive decision. Witness 122 agreed to meet with federal prosecutors only after assurances that he would not be held against his will at the FBI office, claiming that he had heard of instances where individuals go to the FBI office and do not emerge for days.

According to Witness 122, Witness 122 and Witness 130 (collectively, "the contractors") twice encountered Brown during the morning of the shootings, first when Brown was alone and then when Brown was with Witness 101. Witness 122 and Brown did most of the talking, and the topics included God and smoking marijuana. About 20 minutes after their last conversation with Brown, the contractors heard a loud bang. Witness 122 saw Brown running, staggering, or falling forward. Contrary to the autopsy results, Witness 122 described Brown being shot in the back and "knew he had gotten hit." In fact, both contractors claimed to have witnessed bullets go through Brown and exit his back, as evidenced by his shirt "popping back" and "stuff coming through." However, in his interview with federal prosecutors, Witness 122 explained that he thought that Brown was shot in the back and stumbled until he saw media reports about the autopsy commissioned by Brown's family. After learning about that autopsy, he realized that Brown was not shot in the back and admittedly changed his account.

Witness 122 also claimed that Brown put his right hand to the ground to regain his balance when he was hit and as he turned around. According to both contractors, Brown then turned around with his hands up and repeatedly screamed "Okay!" as many as eight times, an exclamation heard by no other witness. When Witness 122 demonstrated the position of Brown's hands for federal prosecutors and agents, he wavered from a position of surrender to one indicative of a person trying to maintain balance.

Contrary to the autopsy results establishing that the shot to the top of Brown's head would have incapacitated Brown almost immediately, both contractors insisted that Brown continued to move toward Wilson as far as 20, 25, or even 30 feet after the final shots. Witness 122 described Brown as walking "dead on his feet, and then he just fell forward." Later, both contractors admitted that they did not actually see Brown fall to the ground, because their view was obstructed by the corner of a building.

Witness 122 insisted that there were three officers present during the shootings, demonstrating the inaccuracy of his perception. Witness 122 described three uniformed police officers engaged with Brown in a "triangle formation" at the time of the shootings. Witness 122 described a heavyset, older officer, and two "skinny, little people," one of whom was possibly a female and the other with dark hair and a moustache, who was a head shorter than the heavyset officer. Witness 122 described the shooter as the heavyset officer. Witness 122 explained that the heavset officer shot until he ran out of bullets, and then the shorter officer with the moustache trained his gun on Brown, but did not shoot. These statements cannot be reconciled with the fact that Wilson was the only officer present when Brown was shot and that Wilson has a slim build.

Witness 122 also explained that he did not see Witness 101 at all during the shooting itself, and did not understand how Witness 101 could claim to see everything if he was hiding behind a car. Witness 122 also said that contrary to what was reported in the media, Brown did not say, "Don't shoot."

The contractors, apparently unwittingly, were captured on a widely circulated video taken several minutes after the shooting while responding officers were securing the scene with crime scene tape. That video depicts another individual yelling, "He wasn't no threat at all," as Witness 122 put his hands up and stated, "He had his fucking hands in the air." As detailed below, two other witnesses, Witness 128 and Witness 137, each took credit for making the statement, "He wasn't no threat at all." Both of those witnesses have since acknowledged to federal agents and prosecutors that they did not, in fact, know whether Brown was a threat.

According to the Brown family, Witness 122 called them after the shooting and told them that he had seen Wilson shoot Brown execution-style as Brown was on his knees holding his hands in the air. However, Witness 122 denied making any statements about the nature of the shooting to the Brown family. As mentioned, despite his earlier statements, Witness 122 recanted the claim that he actually saw Brown fall dead to the ground.

Witness 122 has no criminal history. As detailed above, material portions of Witness 122's accounts are irreconcilable with the physical and forensic evidence. These accounts are also inconsistent with each other and inconsistent with credible witness accounts. Accordingly, after a thorough review of all of the evidence, federal prosecutors determined this witness's accounts not to be credible and therefore do not support a prosecution of Darren Wilson.

xiii. Witness 130

Witness 130 is a 26-year-old white male. As previously noted, he was laying drain pipe on Canfield Drive with Witness 122, on the morning of the shooting. Witness 130 gave five statements, including testimony before the county grand jury. SLCPD detectives and an FBI agent twice jointly interviewed him, and SLCPD detectives once independently interviewed him. Like Witness 122, Witness 130 authored a one-page written statement on advice of a former boss. Witness 122 and Witness 130 claimed that they did not discuss what they witnessed, though Witness 130 admitted that they read each other's statements after they were written. Like Witness 122, Witness 130 gave a media interview on the condition of anonymity.

As noted, Witness 122 and Witness 130 twice encountered Brown during the morning of the shootings, first when Brown was alone and then when Brown was with Witness 101. Witness 122 and Brown did most of the talking, and Witness 130 admitted that at times, Brown seemed paranoid and aggressive, clenching his fists and causing Witness 130 some concern. Witness 130 thought Brown "was not in his right mind," based upon how paranoid he seemed.

About 20 minutes after their last conversation with Brown, Witness 130 heard a loud bang. Witness 130 stepped around the corner of an apartment building that was obstructing his view, and saw Brown "fast walk[ing]" east on Canfield Drive. According to both contractors, Brown then turned around with his hands up and repeatedly screamed "Okay!" as many as eight times, an exclamation heard by no other witness According to Witness 130, after Brown turned around, he continued to stumble or otherwise approach Wilson, although he did not know whether Brown was speeding up to come after Wilson, or whether his momentum was carrying him forward. Wilson then fired at least seven shots, but as Witness 130 told the grand jury, Wilson only fired when Brown moved forward. Witness 130 described Wilson "unloading his clip" into Brown, although Witness 130 acknowledged that Brown put his arms down after the third shot.

Witness 130 explained that Wilson backed up as Brown approached him. Contrary to the autopsy results establishing that the shot to the top of Brown's head would have incapacitated Brown almost immediately, like Witness 122, Witness 130 insisted that Brown continued to move toward Wilson as far as 20, 25, or even 30 feet after the final shots. Contrary to his initial account, Witness 130 admitted that he did not actually see Brown fall to the ground because his view was obstructed by the corner of a building.

Witness 130 has no criminal history. Federal prosecutors attempted to meet with Witness 130 to evaluate inconsistencies in his various statements. Witness 130 refused to meet with federal prosecutors, making reliance on his account problematic because his statements are inconsistent with each other, inconsistent with the physical and forensic evidence, and inconsistent with credible witness accounts. Therefore, federal prosecutors could not rely on Witness 130's account to support a prosecution of Darren Wilson.

xiv. Witness 142

Witness 142 is a 48-year-old black male. Witness 142 briefly spoke to SLCPD detectives within hours of the shooting incident and denied that he witnessed the shooting. However, the SLCPD and the FBI then followed up with Witness 142 after SLCPD detectives learned that Witness 142 called in to an Atlanta-based podcast on August 11, 2014, where he described the shootings. Witness 142 then testified before the county grand jury.

During the podcast, Witness 142 explained that he was sitting on his front patio when he heard the first gunshot. He then moved closer to get a better look at what he termed a "scuffle," and saw "the brother (referring to Brown) leaning over into the window." Witness 142 further described Brown's "upper body in the windshield." The podcast announcer then asked if what "the officer is saying is true," relative to what happened at the SUV. Witness 142 responded, "yes." Witness 142 explained that Brown then took off running and Wilson chased after him. Witness 142 thought that Wilson shot at Brown while Brown was running away. Brown then turned around and came back toward Wilson. Wilson "unloaded on him" and Brown fell to the ground.

The podcast announcer then asked if Brown's hands were up. Witness 142 responded, "Well, I don't know. I didn't see that." He went on to explain that "the crowd" was saying that Brown's hands were up, and that he was ducking to avoid getting hit by gunfire. The announcer later asked, "If you had to say from your opinion, was it justified?" Witness 142 paused and then said, "yes," referencing the scuffle in the SUV. However, he then stated that Wilson should not have shot at Brown while Brown was "fleeing the scene," an opinion that would be inadmissible in federal court and a misstatement of applicable federal law.

SLCPD detectives recognized Witness 142's voice on the podcast from their initial canvass of Canfield Drive, when Witness 142 denied seeing anything. Therefore, an SLCPD detective and an FBI agent interviewed Witness 142 again in an effort to determine what he actually saw. However, during that interview, Witness 142 again changed his account from what he stated on the podcast. Witness 142 told the SLCPD detective and the FBI agent that he was inside his apartment and heard one gunshot. He looked out his patio sliding glass door and saw the driver's side of a police SUV, where Brown was "tussling" with

Wilson, who was inside the SUV. Witness 142 stated that Wilson was tugging on Brown's shirt collar. Even though Brown's back was to him, Witness 142 saw Brown's hands against the SUV and Wilson's hands grabbing Brown's shirt. He denied seeing any part of Brown's body inside the SUV. Brown then pushed away from the SUV and "sprinted" east on Canfield Drive. Wilson, with his gun on his hip, immediately got out of the SUV and chased Brown. After that, Witness 142 does not know what happened, claiming that a concrete barrier obstructed his view.

Witness 142 admitted that on the podcast, he stated that Brown's head was inside the SUV, but claimed that he lied, though he could offer no explanation for doing so. He recalled saying that Wilson shot Brown as Brown was running away, though he admitted to law enforcement that he did not see that happen. Witness 142 clarified that he thought Wilson was shooting at Brown because everything happened in a matter of seconds. He also acknowledged that he told the podcast announcer that he saw Brown stop, turn around, and come back at Wilson. However, he told the SLCPD detective and the FBI agent that he only assumed that Brown did those things, based on Brown's body facing west in the street. Witness 142 told law enforcement that he stayed outside in the street for hours after the shooting, hearing people say that Brown had his hands up. However, he did not see Brown with his hands up. Witness 142 stood by his initial statement that the shooting was justified, though he stated that he did not actually see what happened. He further told law enforcement that he originally lied to SLCPD detectives on the day of the shooting, when he claimed to not have seen anything. Witness 142 explained that he was afraid and did not want to get involved.

Witness 142 has no criminal history. Witness 142 changed his account and could offer no explanation as to why he did so, and his most recent account is inconsistent with credible witness accounts and inconsistent with forensic and physical evidence. Accordingly, federal prosecutors determined that they could not credit either one of his accounts. Regardless, his accounts do not inculpate Darren Wilson and therefore do not support a prosecution.

xv. Witness 138

Witness 138 is a 22-year-old black male. The SLCPD first interviewed Witness 138 about five hours after the shooting. The interview was very brief and federal prosecutors and agents sought to interview him to obtain more detailed information. Witness 138 repeatedly ignored attempts by federal authorities to meet with him when he lived in St. Louis. He then moved out of state. Again, Witness 138 failed to respond to messages left by county and federal authorities, and refused to appear before the county grand jury. Finally, an FBI agent and federal prosecutor tracked down Witness 138 outside of his mother's house in Kentucky. Witness 138's account to federal authorites stood in stark contrast to what he initially told the SLCPD.

Witness 138 told SLCPD that on the day of the shooting, he was watching television in his apartment when he heard one gunshot, causing him to run outside. Brown had kicked off his flip flops and started running away from Wilson, who had emerged from his SUV with his gun drawn. Wilson ran east after Brown, past Witness 101 who was by a white Monte Carlo. Wilson shot Brown as he was running away. Brown then turned around, "threw his hands up," and said something. Initially, Witness 138 stated that he could not hear what Brown said. Then he explained that Brown said something with the word "shoot" in it. By the end of the interview, Witness 138 stated that Brown said, "Please don't shoot." Brown then fell to his knees, and Wilson shot him again. Other police officers arrived on the scene, and Wilson got into a different police vehicle than the one in which he arrived, and left the scene.

Witness 138 told federal authorities that Brown and Witness 101 came to his house the morning of the shooting, prior to their walk to Ferguson Market. They made plans to smoke marijuana later in the day and Brown and Witness 101 told Witness 138 that they were going to get cigarillos and would return. Thereafter, Witness 120 arrived at Witness 138's house. While Witness 138 and Witness 120 were talking in the doorway, Witness 138 heard two gunshots. He ran toward the gunshots, while Witness 120 ran in a different direction. Witness 138 saw Wilson "walk quickly" toward Brown. Unlike what he told the SLCPD detective, Witness 138 said that while going after Brown, Wilson was yelling "stop" or "freeze." Also contrary to his initial account, Witness 138 said that he did not hear Brown say anything. He saw Brown stop and put his hands up, shoulder height at 90 degree angles. Because he heard gunfire, Witness 138 ducked for cover, face-first in the dirt where two white contractors were working. Witness 138 remained in that position until the incident was over, and he looked up and saw Brown dead on the ground.

Witness 138 told federal authorities that Brown fell to the ground in the exact place where he first turned around and did not move forward toward Wilson. Because this is inconsistent with the physical evidence and other credible accounts, federal authorities asked Witness 138 if it was possible that Brown moved toward Wilson. Witness 138 explained that Brown could have moved forward, could have put his arms down, and in fact, he did not know what Brown did for the majority of the shooting because he was face-first in the dirt. He did not look up until Brown was already dead. Witness 138 described the position of Brown's body as having his hands at right angles next to his head, contrary to photographic evidence and the observations of the SLCME medicolegal investigator.

After Brown was killed, Witness 101 ran over to Witness 138 in shock. Witness 101 left the scene to change his clothes, and then returned. According to Witness 138, at the insistence of Witness 101's uncle and pastor, Witness 101 gave an interview to the media. Witness 138 explained that he was "stupid" to stand next to Witness 101 as he appeared on camera.

In response to federal authorities questioning about Wilson's description of Brown as "Hulk Hogan," Witness 138 said that Brown was more like the World Wrestling Federation wrestler "Big Show" in stature, but not in personality. Brown was intimidating because of his size, and Witness 138 understood how Wilson could generally perceive him as a threat. Witness 138 explained that he was friendly with Brown, and although it would surprise him if Brown attacked a police officer, it also surprised him to see the surveillance video of Brown shoving a store clerk, as it was uncharacteristic of him. In the days leading up to his death, Brown was acting out of character, speaking about his desire to get away from the struggles of life.

Witness 138 has no criminal history. There are significant inconsistencies between his two accounts, with the physical and forensic evidence, and with credible witness accounts. Accordingly, after a thorough review of the evidence, federal prosecutors determined this witness's first account to lack credibility. His second account, regardless of credibility, does not inculpate Wilson. Therefore, these accounts do not support a prosecution of Darren Wilson.

xvi. Witness 132

Witness 132 is a 25-year-old black male. He spoke with FBI agents on three occasions. First, Witness 132 met with FBI agents during their canvass on August 16, 2014. At that time, Witness 132 stated that he did not see the shooting or hear the gunshots. However, he stated that his wife may have seen some of the incident. Ten days later, two other FBI agents followed up with his wife. She indicated that she did not see anything, but Witness 132, contrary to what he stated before, claimed to have witnessed the shooting of Brown. Finally, Witness 132 spoke again to the FBI, claiming her memory of the shooting was "blurry."

During her second encounter with the FBI, contrary to all accounts that Wilson was driving westbound, Witness 132 said that he, Witness 132, was driving eastbound behind two FPD marked SUVs. Each SUV had two police officers, all of whom were white. According to Witness 132, the first SUV stopped in the middle of the street, cutting off Brown and running over his feet. Brown then "punched into the police car" because he was angry. In return, the police officer, to whom Witness 132 referred as "Ears," reached down and shot Brown. Witness 132 explained that Brown tried to run, but again, the officer shot Brown right where he stood, about five feet from the SUV. Brown half-turned, fell to his knees, and put his hands up. The officer shot Brown eight or nine more times. This all occurred on the passenger side of the vehicle.

After that interview with the FBI, Witness 132 actively and successfully evaded service of a county grand jury subpoena. Federal and county prosecutors independently and repeatedly tried to contact Witness 132 to no avail in an effort to reconcile the inconsistencies in his statements. However, Witness 132 ignored phone calls, hung up on the prosecutors, and pretended he was not at home. Witness 132 moved out of state and the FBI tracked him down in Georgia. Witness 132 refused to meet with federal prosecutors and told the FBI that the events of August 9, 2014 were "blurry," he could not remember what happened, and he was starting a new chapter in his life.

Witness 132 has no criminal history. Witness 132's second statement is starkly inconsistent with what he initially told law enforcement, is inconsistent with forensic and physical evidence, and is inconsistent with credible witness accounts. Federal prosecutors determined his account to inherently lack credibility, and did not consider it when making a prosecutive decision.

xvii. Witness 121

Witness 121 is a 36-year-old black female who twice spoke to federal authorities, and then testified before the county grand jury.

FBI agents initially interviewed Witness 121 in the presence of three other people during the FBI canvass on August 16, 2014. Her account was confusing and hard to follow, made more confusing by the three other individuals who interjected their thoughts into her account. Nonetheless, Witness 121 initially told the FBI that she saw Brown and Witness 101 walking in the street and she also saw an SUV with two police officers. The police officer on the driver's side of the SUV reached out from within the vehicle and grabbed Brown by the collar. She assumed that the officer had his hand on his gun when he grabbed Brown. She heard a gunshot which struck Brown in the upper chest, leaving a red spot on Brown's shirt. Witness 121 explained that the officer then immediately fired a second shot. Witness 121 seemed to suggest that the second shot happened while Brown was still by the SUV, prompting him to run; at another point during the same interview, Witness 121 suggested that the second shot occurred as Brown was running. She did not know whether that second shot struck Brown. She also explained that the second police officer emerged from the vehicle, though Witness 121 could not provide a description of him, nor be specific about when he emerged. Witness 121 explained that after Brown took off running, Brown put his hands up, walked toward Wilson, and then Wilson shot him. She further stated that Wilson walked over to Brown and "emptied" his gun into Brown, and that Brown "finally fell" after the last shot.

In contrast, however, during her follow up interview with federal prosecutors, Witness 121 explained that based on her vantage point, she did not see the initial interaction between Wilson and Brown. She explained that she had been standing by a dumpster, smoking a cigarette and talking on her phone when a gunshot drew her attention to the SUV. Once she heard the first shot, she became terrified and got ready to run, but instead watched Brown run from the SUV. Witness 121 made no mention of the second shot during her second interview. Likewise, Witness 121 denied that the second officer got out of the vehicle.

As before, Witness 121 explained that after Brown took off running, he put his hands up, walked toward Wilson, and then Wilson shot Brown. However, unlike in her first interview, Witness 121 denied that Wilson walked over to Brown and "emptied his gun" into him. Although she admitted making that prior statement, Witness 121 could offer no explanation for saying something that was inconsistent with the physical evidence and the accounts of almost all other witnesses. Instead, she described a chaotic scene and broke down in tears, acknowledging that she did not know what led up to the shooting. Witness 121 tearfully stated that she "didn't see that young man do anything wrong," empathizing with Brown's mother because her own mother lost a child.

Witness 121 confirmed during her interview with federal authorities that Wilson did not fire any shots while Brown was running way. According to Witness 121, the only shots fired were the first one and the volley of shots as Brown was walking toward the officer with his hands up in surrender. Contrary to how Brown's body was found and photographed when he fell to his death, Witness 121 was certain that Brown's body landed in the same position that his hands were in when he was standing, at right angles adjacent to his head.

Contrary to every other witness account and mobile phone video taken in the immediate aftermath of the shooting, Witness 121 explained that Wilson then checked Brown's pulse while his body lay on the ground. When federal prosecutors pressed her on this, Witness 121 acknowledged that perhaps she was mistaken. She stated that she was unsure which police officer checked his pulse and it likely happened after the police tape went up.

When asked about Witness 101's presence, Witness 121 explained that she had been looking back and forth between Brown and Witness 101 during the shooting. However, Witness 101's whereabouts were unclear throughout both of her accounts. During her first interview, Witness 121 stated that Witness 101 took off running when the initial shots were fired. During the second interview, she first stated that Witness 101 stood by the SUV and vomited on the street. When federal prosecutors asked if crime scene investigators would find vomit on the street to corroborate her claim, Witness 121 admitted that she did not see, but rather heard from others, that Witness 101 vomited on the street. Federal prosecutors and agents repeatedly urged Witness 121 to describe what she herself witnessed. It was then that she stated that Witness 101 had been crouched down, below car level, before he ran from the scene.

When Witness 121 appeared before the county grand jury, she again testified inconsistently. She testified that while she witnessed the shooting, she was standing next to Witness 126. As detailed below, Witness 126's account was internally inconsistent and inconsistent with physical evidence. She also claimed that Witness 137 tossed a cigarette down to her from a balcony above. Witness 137, as detailed below, admitted to being untruthful when he was first interviewed by the FBI, giving an account inconsistent with the physical evidence.

Reverting back to her initial account, Witness 121 testified before the county grand jury that even though her view was of the passenger side of the SUV, contrary to the physical evidence and other credible witnesses, Brown's hands were never inside the SUV. She also added that she heard Witness 101 tell Wilson that he and Brown "weren't that far" from where they were going.

Further, even though she admitted to federal prosecutors that she never heard Brown say anything, Witness 121 told the county grand jury that Brown screamed, "I give up!" as Wilson faced him in the roadway, gun drawn. However, she claimed that she was too far away to hear Wilson say anything.

Witness 121 has no criminal history. Witness 121 admittedly made false statements during her initial interview, her accounts are inconsistent with each other, inconsistent with the physical and forensic evidence, inconsistent with credible accounts, and she demonstrated bias in favor of Brown's family. Accordingly, after a thorough review of all of the evidence, federal prosecutors determined this witness's accounts to lack credibility and therefore do not support a prosecution of Darren Wilson.

xviii. Witness 126

Witness 126 is a 53-year-old black female. She is the godmother of Witness 137. Witness 126 gave two statements, first to the FBI and then to the county grand jury. During the course of her interview with the FBI, Witness 126 stated that her godson had been shot by police.

According to Witness 126, she suffers from memory loss and is under psychiatric care. Her account to the FBI was brief and is inconsistent with the autopsy results. She claimed that she was outside of her apartment during the shooting, never mentioning Witness 121 who claimed to be with Witness 126 at the time. Witness 126 saw Brown on his knees with his hands up, as Wilson was coming toward him and shooting at him. Brown then fell face down to the ground. Wilson went over to him, and similar to what her godson, Witness 137, said, "finished him off." When the FBI told Witness 126 that her account was contrary to the evidence, she became belligerent, grabbed the recording device, shut it off, and would not return it to the agents.

When the agents retrieved it, and turned the recording device back on, Witness 126 admitted that she initially lied. She stated that she never saw Wilson inflict gunshot wounds on Brown. Rather, she saw him running from behind, and then fall to his knees with his hands in the air. She then saw Wilson walking toward Brown, followed by a "click click" sound. Wilson had bruising and redness on the right side of his face. Someone then tapped her on the shoulder and she turned away. She heard nine gunshots in total, and by the time she turned back around, Brown was dead on the ground.

Witness 126 stated that she had spoken with Brown before. They discussed college and helping senior citizens. Brown told her that "everything he used to do, he wouldn't do it anymore."

Witness 126 telephoned the FBI the day after her interview to schedule an interview because she did not remember meeting with the agents and giving her account.

When Witness 126 testified before the county grand jury, she claimed to suffer from memory loss, but then recounted everything she had eaten for breakfast and every pill she had taken on the morning of August 9, 2014. Then she testified that she heard several shots, came out onto the parking lot, and saw Brown on his knees as Wilson fired shots into his head. She denied being untruthful to the FBI, and denied that she admitted to being untruthful to the FBI.

After Witness 126 testified before the county grand jury, she told the state prosecutor that she recorded the shooting on her mobile phone. However, she had since dropped the phone in the toilet. When the state prosecutor told her that forensic experts may still be able to recover the data, Witness 126 stated that she got mad and threw the phone in the junk yard.

Witness 126 has several felony arrests and a misdemeanor conviction that likely would be inadmissible in federal court as impeachment evidence. However, Witness 126 was admittedly untruthful to the FBI, suffers from memory loss, and provided internally inconsistent accounts that are also inconsistent with the physical and forensic evidence and credible witness accounts. Her account would be subject to extensive cross examination. Accordingly, federal prosecutors determined this witness's account to lack credibility and therefore it does not support a prosecution of Darren Wilson.

xix. Witness 137

Witness 137 is 40-year-old black male. After the shooting, Witness 137 had learned that Brown was his nephew's friend. He is the godson of Witness 126. He gave two law enforcement statements and testified before the county grand jury. Witness 137 first met with FBI agents on August 16, 2014, during their neighborhood canvass. Witness 137 also gave an interview to the media which was widely circulated throughout various media outlets. The account to the media and to the FBI was both internally inconsistent and inconsistent with the physical evidence. Therefore, federal agents and prosecutors subsequently met with Witness 137 in an attempt to assess inconsistencies and clarify his statement.

In his initial account during the neighborhood canvass, Witness 137 stated that he was on his porch using his mobile phone when he heard a gunshot. He looked out from his porch and saw Brown running away from a police officer who was chasing him. The police officer shot Brown in the back. "Realiz[ing] he was shot," Brown turned around with his hands up in surrender. Brown walked toward the officer and as he did so, the officer "closed in on him" until they were less than an arm's length apart. The officer fired "every round" into Brown, killing him "execution" style. Witness 137 explained that the officer shot Brown in the lower abdomen, chest, and then the "head shot." Witness 137 stated that after Brown fell forward, "the officer stood over him and finished him off." Witness 137 stated that the officer shot Brown in the head both when he was still standing and then when he was on the ground. Although Witness 137 stated that Brown fell to his knees for the final shots, and the last words Brown said were "Don't shoot," he also stated that Brown was lying on the ground when the final bullets were fired. Witness 137 referred to how clear the "visual" of events was to him.

Throughout the interview, Witness 137 also referred to events that preceded the initial gunshots even though he admitted that he did not see those events. He also discussed the interaction at the SUV, the location of recovered bullets, and the type of clip in the officer's gun.

During their follow-up interview with Witness 137, federal prosecutors and agents asked Witness 137 to describe only what he saw. Witness 137 once again stated that the sound of a gunshot drew his attention. When he moved further onto his porch, he said that he heard another shot, and saw Brown turn around with his hands up. Referencing the arm graze wound that was widely reported in the news after the privately-commissioned autopsy, Witness 137 stated that he believed that wound caused Brown to turn around. He then saw the officer backing up while firing shots as Brown walked at a "steady pace" of about ten steps in total toward him. According to Witness 137, there was no pause in the succession of shots, and Brown kept walking, even after he was shot in the torso. Witness 137 stated, "that's all I seen," explaining that he did not see Brown fall to the ground because that occurred in a blind spot. However, he was able to see the officer walk away, call for back up, and appear to be discombobulated. It was then that Witness 137 walked over to the scene where Brown's body lay in the street.

Contrary to his previous statement, Witness 137 denied that the officer shot Brown from less than an arm's length away, denied that he saw the officer shoot Brown execution-style; denied that the officer shot Brown when he was on the ground; denied that the officer "finished him off;" and denied that Brown's last words while on his knees were "Don't shoot." Witness 137 explained that he initially told the FBI that the officer stood over Brown and shot him execution-style while on his knees because he "assumed" that to be true. Witness 137 based his assumptions on the sound of the bullets and "common sense" from living in the community, despite claiming to have a "clear visual" of events.

Witness 137 also identified his voice on the aforementioned video taken in the aftermath of the shooting depicting the two contractors. As mentioned, Witness 137 was one of two people who claimed to be off camera shouting, "He wasn't no threat at all," because he did not perceive Brown to be a threat. However, Witness 137 acknowledged that contrary to what he originally told the FBI, the only part he saw was Brown moving back toward the officer. He did not witness what transpired at the SUV, did not witness Brown run from the SUV, and he did not witness Brown fall to his death. Therefore, Witness 137 agreed that he did not know whether Brown was a physical threat before or after the portion that Witness 137 claimed to see.

Witness 137 has previously been convicted of second-degree murder and armed criminal action which likely would be admissible in federal court as impeachment evidence. Additionally, Witness 137 was untruthful to the FBI during his initial interview, and untruthful in his media accounts. Although he later recanted most of what he claimed to have seen, he was unable to offer a credible explanation as to why he was not truthful at the outset, leaving federal prosecutors to question what, if anything, he actually did witness. His accounts are inconsistent with each other, inconsistent with the physical and forensic evidence, and inconsistent withcredible witness accounts. Accordingly, after a thorough review of the evidence, federal prosecutors determined this witness's accounts not to be credible and therefore do not support a prosecution of Darren Wilson.

xx. Witness 128

Witness 128 is a 23-year-old black male who has made three different statements to law enforcement and testified before the county grand jury. He initially had a telephone interview with an investigator from the St. Louis County Prosecutor's Office and then an additional interview with that same investigator and the FBI. Both interviews were materially inconsistent with the physical evidence. Federal agents and prosecutors interviewed Witness 128 again in an effort to evaluate some of the inconsistencies.

According to Witness 128's initial accounts, he was driving east on Canfield Drive when he witnessed the shooting. It is unclear what Witness 128 initially saw because in one interview, he stated that he saw the police vehicle quickly back up. In another interview, he stated that by the time he pulled up, Wilson had already stopped his vehicle. Witness 128 stated that he then saw Brown struggling to get away from Wilson, who was choking Brown with both hands, while Witness 101 stood behind Brown. Witness 128 then heard a gunshot and saw the impact of the bullet, initially giving little detail but subsequently adding that Wilson held the gun out the window with his right hand while holding Brown with his left hand, and firing the gun into Brown's left chest.

Brown broke free and ran about 15 feet while Witness 101 ducked down between the police vehicle and the car right behind it. Witness 128 explained that while Wilson was still seated in the vehicle with the door closed, Wilson "let more shots go." Brown appeared to get hit by four rounds in the middle of his back. Brown "slowed up" and turned around, although Witness 128 later stated that Brown continued running another 20 or 25 feet before he turned around.

Wilson then emerged from the SUV about five seconds after he fired four or five rounds, and "patiently" walked toward Brown in "lazy pursuit." Brown "threw his hands up, clean in the air." Initially, Witness 128 stated that Brown said, "Don't kill me," but later admitted that he did not actually hear Brown or Wilson say anything. Wilson then fired two shots at "point blank range" from within two feet. The shots hit Brown in the face and Brown fell to the ground. Wilson then fired four or five shots into Brown's back after Brown was already dead, face first on the ground. Witness 128 then drove by Wilson and asked him why he shot Brown. Wilson told Witness 128 to "shut the fuck up," "mind [his] own business," and "keep going." Witness 128 then pulled into his complex and parked, staying away because he did not want to get shot himself. According to Witness 128, there were no other people or cars on the street, except for a white pick-up truck behind him.

Federal prosecutors and agents met with Witness 128 and challenged him on internal inconsistencies and statements he made that were inconsistent with physical evidence. Contrary to his previous account, he stated that when he pulled up on Canfield Drive, he saw Brown in the driver's side window of the SUV from his mid-chest up. He stated that Brown and Wilson were pulling on each other's shirts until Brown backed up. Wilson then held his gun out the window and fired a shot. As a result, Brown ran from the vehicle. Contrary to his previous statement to the FBI, Witness 128 told federal prosecutors that although he heard additional shots, he did not see them because he ducked down in his vehicle. For the first time, Witness 128 mentioned the presence of a female passenger in his vehicle. He could not identify the passenger, but explained that during the shooting, his attention was diverted to her because he was trying to keep her calm, as she had become hysterical.

Witness 128 explained that when he stopped ducking for cover, he saw Brown coming back toward Wilson with his hands up. Witness 128 stated that Wilson shot Brown, causing him to fall face down to the ground. He maintained that Wilson then stood over Brown and shot into his back. When federal prosecutors asked him to reconcile those final shots with the autopsy report that shows that Brown was not shot in the back, Witness 128 said he may have hallucinated but could not offer more of an explanation. He also admitted that much of what he initially said was assumption.

As mentioned, Witness 128 was one of two witnesses who identified his voice on the aforementioned video taken in the aftermath of the shooting depicting the two contractors. Witness 128 claimed to be the person off camera shouting, "He wasn't no threat at all," because he did not perceive Brown to be a threat. However, Witness 128 acknowledged that he did not know what happened at the SUV. Contrary to what he originally told the FBI, he did not see Brown run from the SUV, was mistaken about the final shots fired, and therefore did not know whether Brown was a threat to Wilson.

Witness 128 also admitted that he spoke to Brown's mother on the day of the shooting and shared details of the shooting. Witness 128 told Brown's mother that Wilson shot Brown at point blank range while his hands were up, and that even after Brown fell to his death, Wilson stood over Brown and fired several more times. Witness 128 also told several neighbors his inaccurate version of what happened, as they were gathering in the minutes and hours after the shooting. Several individuals identified Witness 128 through description as someone who was going around spreading a narrative that Brown was shot with his hands up in surrender.

Witness 128 has been convicted of multiple felonies including crimes of dishonesty, all of which would be admissible in federal court as impeachment evidence. Witness 128's accounts are inconsistent with each other, inconsistent with the forensic and physical evidence, and inconsistent with credible witness accounts. Accordingly, after a thorough review of the evidence, federal prosecutors determined this witness's accounts to lack credibility and therefore do not support a prosecution of Darren Wilson.

xxi. Witness 140

Witness 140 is a 45-year-old white female who gave two statements to law enforcement and testified before the county grand jury. Witness 140 contacted SLCPD detectives in September 2014, claiming to have been a witness to the shooting of Brown, but too fearful to come forward when it happened. She explained that she decided it was time to come forward because she knew the case was being presented to the county grand jury and she was "tired of hearing that the officer is guilty." SLCPD and the FBI jointly interviewed Witness 140, who completely corroborated Wilson's account. Although the physical and forensic evidence was consistent with her account, the timing of her disclosure and the details of her narrative caused investigators to question her veracity. Therefore, federal prosecutors and agents conducted a follow-up interview.

During her follow-up interview, as in her initial account, Witness 140 claimed that she inadvertently ended up on Canfield Drive because she got lost on her way to visit a friend in Florissant, whom she had not seen in about 25 years. Witness 140 explained that she did not have a cell phone or a GPS, and was prone to getting lost. She pulled into the Canfield Green apartment complex to ask for directions, getting out of her car to do so. When federal prosecutors asked her why, as a woman, she would get out of her car in an unfamiliar neighborhood, she explained that she wanted to smoke a cigarette. Thereafter, while standing on the sidewalk, smoking a cigarette with a man from whom she was getting directions, she saw Wilson's SUV drive in the opposite direction of Brown and Witness 101, who were walking in the middle of the street. Witness 140 explained that she saw Wilson stop, speak to Brown and Witness 101, pull forward, and then back up. Wilson then tried to open the door of the SUV, but Brown punched it shut. Witness 101 grabbed the rearview mirror, bending it inward and catching his bracelet which broke and fell to the ground.

The specificity of this description initially caused SLCPD detectives concern because it mimicked an obscure media article which offered theories about how the SUV rearview mirror came to be folded inward and how beaded bracelets, found at the scene, landed on the ground. During Witness 140's follow-up interview, federal prosecutors asked her about this online article and Witness 140 acknowledged reading it prior to meeting with SLCPD detectives, possibly using it to fill in gaps in her memory.

According to Witness 140, she saw a struggle by the SUV, explaining that Brown was bent forward such that the top portion of his body, starting at the navel, was in the SUV. She described "childish wrestling" or "fist fighting" that ensued. She heard one gunshot from within the SUV, and then saw Brown run away, as Wilson shouted, "Stop. Freeze. I'm gonna shoot." Wilson fired a second gunshot as he got out of the SUV. Witness 140 described it as a possible "warning shot" because Brown did not "even flinch," indicating to her that he was not hit. Wilson then pursued Brown, who "made it further than where he got shot." Brown then turned around as Brown's arms flew upward, and Wilson stopped pursuing him. Brown bent forward in a "football-type" mode, hands balled up in fists, and "started charging." Witness 140 explained that Brown looked like "he was on something." Wilson looked panicked as he repeatedly shot Brown in the arm. Brown, however, kept coming at Wilson, who backed up as Brown closed the distance. Witness 140 heard a volley of four shots, a pause, and then two more shots before Brown fell to his death and "it got gross."

Witness 140 explained that she did not see Witness 101 after the initial interaction at the SUV until he reappeared five to 10 minutes after the shooting with his black t-shirt draped over his "wife-beater" tank top. This description matched how Witness 101 appeared in media interviews in the aftermath of the shooting. Also, seeing Witness 101 reappear conflicted with Witness 140's explanation that she immediately left Canfield Drive after the last shots because she was the only white woman in a neighborhood that was quickly growing hostile.

Investigators also questioned Witness 140 about the route she took out of the complex, which looks navigable on a map, but in reality is blocked by a concrete street barrier. Witness 140 responded that she is not good with directions, and was unsure the route she took. Since the shooting incident, she has acquired both a GPS and a mobile phone.

Witness 140 stated that she went immediately home and told no one about what she witnessed except her ex-husband. However, when SLCPD detectives attempted to verify this, Witness 140's ex-husband reported that Witness 140 has a tendency to lie. Witness 140's response was that her ex-husband was distrustful that the detectives were who they claimed to be. Nonetheless, Witness 140 acknowledged that she suffers from bouts of mania because she does not take her medicine for bipolar disorder and she suffered traumatic brain injury from a car crash several years ago.

Witness 140 also admitted to federal prosecutors that although she told no one about what she had witnessed, she posted comments on websites and Facebook about the shooting. Her comments were blatantly profane and racist. Furthermore, she was involved in developing a fundraising organization for first responders, and had a picture of a "thin blue line" as her Facebook profile picture.

During her testimony before the county grand jury, Witness 140 admitted that she did not get lost on Canfield Drive while en route to visit a high school friend, but rather she purposely went to Canfield Drive that day because she fears black people and was attempting to conquer her fears. However, in an effort to bolster he testimony, Witness 140 provided county prosecutors with a daily journal she claimed to keep, with one entry that documented the events of August 9. While that entry was detailed, all of the other entries were generic and sporadic.

Witness 140 was twice convicted of passing bad checks, felonies that are crimes of dishonesty and likely admissible in federal court as impeachment evidence. Although Witness 140's account of this incident is consistent with physical and forensic evidence and with credible witness accounts, large parts of her narrative have been admittedly fabricated from media accounts, and her bias in favor of Wilson is readily apparent. Accordingly, while her account likely is largely accurate, federal prosecutors determined that the account as a whole was not reliable and therefore did not consider it when making a prosecutive decision.

xxii. Witness 139

Witness 139 is 50-year-old black female. She made two statements, including her county grand jury testimony. As detailed below, Witness 139's initial account was riddled with inconsistencies from one sentence to the next. She was unable to provide a coherent narrative, and when she was asked to clarify, Witness 139 would respond with "you know what I mean," answer with a non sequitur, or break down in sobs. The details that she did provide were largely inconsistent with the physical evidence. Witness 139 was similarly incoherent and inconsistent when she testified before the county grand jury, unable to provide any sort of linear narrative.

Witness 139 reluctantly came to the NAACP office in St. Louis to meet with SLCPD detectives, FBI agents, and federal prosecutors. Through hysterical tears, she expressed fear in speaking with law enforcement because she felt pressured by the community to make a statement about what she had purportedly witnessed. She explained that ever since she gave a media interview, people have been anonymously calling her. Witness 139 explained that these calls made her feel threatened, though she could not articulate how or why she felt threatened.

According to Witness 139, at about 2:30 to 3:00 p.m., she was driving eastbound on Canfield Drive, in the same direction she claimed Wilson's "four door car" was traveling, and the same direction in which Brown and Witness 101 were walking. She had difficulty distinguishing between Brown and Witness 101. Witness 139 stated that she was behind the police car, but pulled over to let him pass. Wilson then stopped his car to speak with Brown and Witness 101, though Witness 139 was inconsistent about whether two or three cars pulled past her and drove off or whether there were two or three cars in front of her when Wilson stopped. Witness 139 stated that Wilson told Brown and Witness 101 to use the sidewalk, but then said that she could not actually hear words. Rather, she just heard a deep voice. Either Brown or Witness 101 then walked toward the front of the police car and Wilson grabbed that person. Witness 139 could not be more descriptive, explaining that she had answered her mobile phone while this was happening.

Witness 139 explained that Wilson reached for his gun and held it straight out of the driver's side window, firing one or two shots. Later in her interview, she described Wilson holding the gun on the window frame when firing. Either way, Witness 139 explained that while this was happening, Witness 101 ran behind the police car. Brown was standing by the driver's side window, close enough to touch the car. However, she later described Brown being closer to the headlights of the car. When she saw those first gunshots, Witness 139 put her head down on the steering wheel, covering her eyes. Wilson then got out of his car, stood over Brown, and kept shooting. If Witness 139 was initially driving behind Wilson, she would have had the same vantage point as Witness 123 and Witness 133 in the white Monte Carlo, and therefore, would have been unable to see the driver's side of Wilson's vehicle and much of what she described.

Also inconsistent with what she initially described, Witness 139 said that

Brown ran from the police car after the first two shots. She first claimed that Wilson shot Brown in the back as Brown was running, which caused Brown to turn around. Witness 139 also stated that Wilson was still getting out of his car when Brown turned around, making it unclear if Wilson shot at Brown as he was running away. To that end, Witness 139 also stated that she was not sure if the bullet struck him in the back. Regardless, Brown turned around, never moving forward from where he stood. According to Witness 139, Brown fell to the ground dead with his hands next to his head at right angles because his hands had been up. Wilson then fired at least three shots as Brown was lying face down on the ground. Witness 139 saw that Brown was bleeding from his back. When asked how she was able to witness the final shots if she had her head down in her arms, Witness 139 explained that she put her head down in her arms after the first two shots, but she could still see because she was peeking. Witness 139 claimed that when she asked Wilson if she could check on Brown because she is a nurse, he told her to "get the fuck on."

Witness 139 has no criminal history. Witness 139's account was incoherent and inconsistent throughout, markedly inconsistent with the physical and forensic evidence, and inconsistent with credible witness accounts. Wilson was driving an SUV westbound at noon, not a car eastbound at 2:30 p.m.; Wilson fired the first shot inside the SUV, not straight out the window; Brown moved toward Wilson and did not fall to his death where he turned around, nor did he die within an arm's length of the police vehicle; and Wilson did not stand over Brown and shoot him causing him to bleed from the back. Accordingly, federal prosecutors determined this witness's account not to be credible and therefore it does not support a prosecution of Darren Wilson.

xxiii. Witness 120

Witness 120 is a 19-year-old black male who said he was Brown's best friend and Witness 101's "cousin." Brown was staying with Witness 120 the night before the shooting occurred, during which time they did "a whole lot of talking about God" and "about the problems that [they have] been going through." Witness 120 explained that it seemed like Brown was "going through a phase."

Witness 120 gave three statements, including his testimony before the county grand jury. FBI agents and SCLPD detectives initially interviewed Witness 120 in the presence of his lawyer and his uncle. Witness 120 gave an internally inconsistent account that was also inconsistent with physical evidence. Federal prosecutors and agents interviewed Witness 120, with his lawyer present, in an attempt to determine what he actually witnessed.

According to Witness 120's initial account, he was on the phone on the third floor of his sister's apartment when he heard a gunshot. He instantly hopped up to look out the window because he knew that Brown and Witness 101 were walking to the store to get cigarillos to smoke marijuana later that day. When he looked out the window, Witness 120 saw Brown, who was facing the window, drop to his knees with his hands in the air, blood coming from his left shoulder and ribcage. Brown's back was to the police vehicle. Witness 101 was next to Brown. Brown told Witness 101 to "run for your life." However, later in the same interview, Witness 120 stated that Witness 101 told him (Witness 120) that he, Witness 101, ran away after that first shot. When Witness 120 testified before the county grand jury, he said that he did not see Witness 101 until after the shooting was over.

According to Witness 120, Wilson then got out of the police cruiser, and positioned himself "a step away" from Brown, who stated, "Please don't shoot me." Wilson then shot Brown "point blank" in the head and Brown fell on his side. Wilson then fired eight more shots while Brown was on the ground, one of which grazed his arm.

During his follow-up interview with federal prosecutors and federal agents, Witness 120 stated that he was asleep when Brown and Witness 101 left to go to the store. He woke to the sound of a gunshot. Witness 120 then repeated the same account as before: He went to the window and saw Brown on his knees with his hands up, situated about five feet from the police vehicle. Brown said, "Please don't shoot me," and Wilson fired a shot into Brown's head at "point blank" range. However, during the second interview, Witness 120 acknowledged that he never saw Wilson emerge from his vehicle and never saw any injury on Brown. Instead, he claimed that after that second shot, he ran downstairs and heard two volleys of four shots each with a pause in between. By the time he got downstairs, the gunfire had ended. Witness 120 explained that although he did not see the shots, common sense dictates that those eight shots struck Brown. He also explained that he based most of his recanted account on what people "in the community told [him]."

Although Witness 120 recanted most of his original statement, his version to federal prosecutors was still inconsistent with the autopsy results. Likewise, Witness 120 gave an inconsistent account to the county grand jury, admittedly based on rumor and hearsay, and motivated by his allegiance to his friend. When grand jurors questioned Witness 120 about inconsistencies with physical evidence, he dismissed the question, stating that Brown "was assassinated for what reason."

Witness 120's claim that Brown's body was found five feet from the police vehicle is inconsistent with the crime scene; Witness 120's description that Wilson shot Brown at point blank range is inconsistent with the autopsy results; Witness 120's description that he was at home at the time the first shots were fired is inconsistent with Witness 138's description that Witness 120 was at Witness 138's house when the shots were fired.

Witness 120 has a felony arrest that likely would be inadmissible in federal court as impeachment evidence. In addition to his accounts being riddled with inconsistencies with each other, the physical and forensic evidence, and credible witness accounts, Witness 120's account is driven by apparent bias for his friend. Accordingly, federal prosecutors determined his account to lack credibility and it does not therefore support a prosecution of Darren Wilson.

xxiv. Witness 148

Witness 148 is a 26-year-old black female who did not report to federal authorities that she witnessed the shooting until late February, 2015. Witness 148 briefly spoke to federal prosecutors via telephone to provide a summary of what she witnessed on August 9, 2014. Based on that description, federal prosecutors and agents subsequently met with Witness 148 in person.

According to Witness 148, she was driving eastbound on Canfield Drive, traveling in the same direction as Brown and Witness 101. She drove past Wilson, who was driving his SUV, and Brown and Witness 101 who were walking in the street, but right next to the curb of the sidewalk. Contrary to all other evidence, they were not in the middle of the street. She heard Wilson say, "Get the fuck on the sidewalk," and she heard either Brown or Witness 101 respond that they were near their "destination." Suspecting something was going to happen between Wilson and Brown and Witness 101 because she is from Chicago and is used to bad interactions with police, she slowed down and watched over her right shoulder, out her back window. She heard tires "screech" and saw the SUV reverse back.

Witness 148 pulled her vehicle into a nearby parking lot and parked because she wanted to see what would happen next. She told her four-year-old son to wait in her car while she got out of her vehicle and watched as Brown and Wilson engaged in a struggle on the driver side of the SUV. Witness 148 stated her that her vantage point was of the passenger side of the SUV, but she could nonetheless see Brown using his hands to push off the driver's door as Wilson pulled Brown toward the SUV. She heard Brown repeatedly state, "I didn't do anything," as Wilson stated, "Stop resisting." Despite being in a parking lot and on the opposite side of the SUV as Brown, Witness 148 stated that Brown "looked scared and it's not like he's a giant or anything." Witness 148 also stated that Brown never put his hands inside the SUV window, despite forensic and physical evidence to the contrary. However, she ultimately acknowledged to prosecutors that because she could not see the driver's side of the SUV, she did not know whether Brown put his hands inside the SUV window.

According to Witness 148, her son then got out of her vehicle because he wanted to watch what was happening. Witness 148 heard a gunshot. Witness 148 got down on the grass and covered her child's body with her own to protect him. While doing so, she watched Witness 101 and then Brown run from the SUV. After that, Witness 101 disappeared and she never saw him again. Wilson then emerged from the SUV and fired at least two shots. Brown flinched, arch-ing his body back as though the bullet had "grazed" him. Brown then turned around and put his hands up in right angles at shoulder-height in a sign of sur-render. He then dropped to his knees, and started to say something like, "I don't have a -," but was cut off as Wilson walked toward Brown firing at least six shots, killing Brown. Witness 148 described Wilson as "possessed" based on the "look in his eyes," as though "he wasn't human." It is unclear based on Witness 148's description how she was able to see both the look in Wilson's eyes and Brown trying to speak as he was surrendering, all at the same time.

Witness 148 was initially adamant that, contrary to DNA evidence in the roadway and credible witness accounts that establish otherwise, Brown never moved forward from the spot where he turned around to face Wilson. When prosecutors specifically asked her about this, Witness 148 acknowledged that because he son was squirming on the ground and she feared for his safety, her attention may have been diverted during the shooting, and therefore she may have missed parts of it. Nonetheless, she repeated that Wilson shot Brown as he was "surrendering."

When prosecutors and agents pressed Witness 148 as to why it took her nearly seven months to come forward and report what she witnessed, she explained that she feared the FPD. She maintained that she did not tell anyone—"not one living soul"—about what she witnessed on August 9, 2014. Witness 148 stated however, that she was she was not going to live in fear and therefore went to Ferguson every day since the shooting until the day of the county grand jury's decision on November 24, 2014. She protested and marched, but never shared with anyone what she witnessed, including her god-daughter who started a "Michael Brown movement." However, Witness 148 met a close friend of the Brown family after a Martin Luther King Day protest. Several weeks after that, she told the friend what she had witnessed and ultimately met with Brown's mother. Witness 148 explained that as a mother herself, she wanted to share with Brown's mother what happened to Brown.

Federal prosecutors asked Witness 148 why she chose not report to the FBI or the SLCPD, since her distrust was specific to the FPD. Witness 148 explained that she did not know that either of those agencies was investigating, despite the fact that she went to Ferguson everyday for three months and admittedly, read media reports about the shooting in the hours, days, and weeks after it occurred.

Witness 148 has felony convictions including conviction for a crime of dis-honesty that would be admissible in federal court as impeachment evidence. Her account is inconsistent with the physical and forensic evidence, inconsis-tent with undisputed facts, *i.e.* Brown and Witness 101 were in fact walking in the middle of the street, and she admittedly did not see portions of the inci-dent based on her vantage point and because she was protecting her child from gunfire. Similar to Witness 140, even if Witness 148 was present on Canfield Drive on August 14, 2014, and saw parts of the incident, Witness 148's account is inherently unreliable and subject to extensive cross-examination based on how she obtained her information and what motivated her to come forward. She did not report what she witnessed for nearly seven months without any reasonable explanation for the delay, giving her ample opportunity to research the facts in the form of media stories and county grand jury transcripts; she has an apparent distrust of the police (she told federal prosecutors at the outset of her interview that she "didn't trust police at all"); she is upset that "Darren Wilson got away" with what she believes to be a crime and then subsequently engaged in months of protests, but yet she failed to report it to the FBI, not because of distrust, but because she was unaware of the federal investigation. This is difficult to reconcile in light of both her daily visits to Ferguson while the FBI was canvassing the area and her regular internet searches about the shooting. For these reasons, federal prosecutors did not credit her account and could not rely upon it to support a prosecution of Darren Wilson.

xxv. Other Individuals Who Did Not Witness the Shootings

Throughout the course of the two investigations, FBI agents and SLCPD detectives both jointly and independently monitored social media, print media, and local and national television broadcasts and news reports in an effort to locate potential witnesses and sources of information. Investigators tracked down several individuals who, via the aforementioned media, claimed to have witnessed Wilson shooting Brown as Brown held his hands up in clear surrender. All of these purported witnesses, upon being interviewed by law enforcement, acknowledged that they did not actually witness the shooting, but rather repeated what others told them in the immediate aftermath of the shooting.

For example, one individual publicly posted a description of the shooting during a Facebook chat, explaining that Brown "threw his hands up in the air" as Wilson shot him dead. A Twitter user took a screenshot of the description and "tweeted" it throughout the social media site. When the SLCPD and the FBI interviewed the individual who made the initial post, he explained that he "gave a brief description of what [he] was hearing from the people that were outside" on Canfield Drive, but he did not witness the incident itself. Similarly, another individual publicly "tweeted" about the shooting as though he had just witnessed it, even though he had not.

Likewise, another individual appeared on a television program and discussed the shooting as if he had seen it firsthand. When law enforcement interviewed him, he explained that it was a "misconception" that he witnessed the shooting. He spoke to the host of the show because he was asked if he wanted to talk about the shooting. In so doing, he was inaccurately portrayed as a witness.

Another individual recorded the aforementioned video of the contractors taken in the aftermath of the shootings. When an FBI agent and federal prosecutor met with that individual, he explained that because the video had been widely circulated in the media, many people incorrectly believed that he had witnessed the shooting. He did not witness the shootings, and was initially unsurprised to hear gunshots because it was not uncommon to hear gunfire in the neighborhood. He started recording after the gunshots abated by placing his iPad in the ground-level window of his basement apartment. He provided federal authorities with that video and other videos taken minutes after the shooting. Several videos captured conversations of bystanders on Canfield Drive, standing by police tape as paramedics covered Brown's body with two more sheets in addition to the one that was already covering him. During those conversations, bystanders discussed what transpired, although none of what was recorded was consistent with the physical evidence or credible accounts from other witnesses. For example, one woman stated that the officer shot at Brown from inside his vehicle while the SUV was still moving and then the "officer stood over [Brown] and pow-pow-pow."

Because none of these individuals actually witnessed the shooting incident and admitted so to law enforcement, federal prosecutors did not consider their inaccurate postings, tweets, media interviews, and the like when making a prosecutive decision.

IV. LEGAL ANALYSIS

The evidence discussed above does not meet the standards for presentation of an indictment set forth in the USAM and in the governing federal law. The evidence is insufficient to establish probable cause or to prove beyond a reasonable doubt a violation of 18 U.S.C. § 242 and would not be likely to survive a defense motion for acquittal at trial pursuant to Federal Rule of Criminal Procedure 29(a). This is true for all six to eight shots that struck Brown. Witness accounts suggesting that Brown was standing still with his hands raised in an unambiguous signal of surrender when Wilson shot Brown are inconsistent with the physical evidence, are otherwise not credible because of internal inconsistencies, or are not credible because of inconsistencies with other credible evidence. In contrast, Wilson's account of Brown's actions, if true, would establish that the shootings were not objectively unreasonable under the relevant Constitutional standards governing an officer's use of deadly force. Multiple credible witnesses corroborate virtually every material aspect of Wilson's account and are consistent with the physical evidence. Even if the evidence established that Wilson's actions were unreasonable, the government would also have to prove that Wilson acted willfully, *i.e.* that he acted with a specific intent to violate the law.

As discussed above, Wilson's stated intent for shooting Brown was in response to a perceived deadly threat. The only possible basis for prosecuting Wilson under Section 242 would therefore be if the government could prove that his account is not true—i.e., that Brown never punched and grabbed Wilson at the SUV, never struggled with Wilson over the gun, and thereafter clearly surrendered in a way that no reasonable officer could have failed to perceive. Not only do eyewitnesses and physical evidence corroborate Wilson's account, but there is no credible evidence to disprove Wilson's perception that Brown posed a threat to Wilson as Brown advanced toward him. Accordingly, seeking his indictment is not permitted by Department of Justice policy or the governing law.

A. Legal Standard

To obtain a conviction of Darren Wilson at trial for his actions in shooting Michael Brown, the government must prove the following elements beyond a reasonable doubt: (1) that Wilson was acting under color of law; (2) that he acted willfully; (3) that he deprived Brown of a right protected by the Constitution or laws of the United States; and (4) that the deprivation resulted in bodily injury or death. The Constitutional right at stake depends on Brown's custodial status at the time Wilson shot him. *See Graham*, 490 U.S. at 395; *Loch v. City of Litchfield*, 689 F.3d 961, 965 (8th Cir. 2012). In this case, Wilson had attempted to stop and possibly arrest Brown. The rights of an arrestee are governed by the Fourth Amendment's prohibition against unreasonable searches and seizures, which includes the right to be free from excessive force during the course of an arrest. *See Nelson v. County of Wright*, 162 F.3d 986, 990 (8th Cir. 1998). Under the Fourth Amendment, an officer's use of force must be "objectively reasonable" under the facts and circumstances known to the officer at the time he made the decision to use physical force. *Id*. Establishing that the intent behind a Constitutional violation is "willful" requires proof that the officer acted with the purpose "to deprive a person of a right which has been made specific either by the express terms of the Constitution or laws of the United States or by decisions interpreting them." *See United States v. Lanier*, 520 U.S. 259, 267 (1997), *citing Screws v. United States*, 325 U.S. 91 (1945). While the officer need not be "thinking in Constitutional terms" when deciding to use force, he must know what he is doing is wrong and decide to do it anyway. *Screws* at 106-07. Mistake, panic, misperception, or even poor judgment by a police officer does not provide a basis for prosecution under Section 242. *See United States v. McClean*, 528 F.2d 1250, 1255 (2d Cir. 1976) (inadvertence or mistake negates willfulness for purposes of 18 U.S.C. § 242).

There is no dispute that Wilson, who was on duty and working as a patrol officer for the FPD, acted under color of law when he shot Brown, or that the shots resulted in Brown's death. The determination of whether criminal prosecution is appropriate rests on whether there is sufficient evidence to establish that any of the shots fired by Wilson were unreasonable given the facts known to Wilson at the time, and if so, whether Wilson fired the shots with the requisite "willful" criminal intent, which, in this case, would require proof that Wilson shot Brown under conditions that no reasonable officer could have perceived as a threat.

B. Uses of Force

Under the Fourth Amendment, a police officer's use of physical force against an arrestee must be objectively reasonable under the circumstances. *Graham*, 490 U.S. at 396-97 (1989). "The 'reasonableness' of a particular use of force must be judged from the perspective of a reasonable officer on the scene, rather than with the 20/20 vision of hindsight." *Id.* at 396. "Careful attention" must be paid "to the facts and circumstances of each particular case, including the severity of the crime at issue, whether the suspect poses an immediate threat to the safety of the officers or others, and whether he is actively resisting arrest or attempting to evade arrest by flight." *Id.* Allowance must be made for the fact that law enforcement officials are often forced to make split-second judgments in circumstances that are tense, uncertain, and rapidly evolving. *Id.* at 396–97.

The use of deadly force is justified when the officer has "probable cause to believe that the suspect pose[s] a threat of serious physical harm, either to the officer or to others." *Tennessee v. Garner*, 471 U.S. 1, 11 (1985); *see Nelson*, 162 F.3d at 990; *O'Bert ex. rel. Estate of O'Bert v. Vargo*, 331 F.3d 29, 36 (2d Cir. 2003) (same as *Garner*); *Deluna v. City of Rockford*, 447 F.3d 1008, 1010 (7th Cir. 2006), *citing Scott v. Edinburg*, 346 F.3d 752, 756 (7th Cir. 2003) (deadly force can be reasonably employed where an officer believes that the suspect's actions place him, or others in the immediate vicinity, in imminent danger of death or serious bodily injury). An officer may use deadly force under certain circumstances even if the suspect is fleeing. "Where the officer has probable cause to believe that the suspect poses a threat of serious physical harm, either to the officer or to others, it is not constitutionally unreasonable to prevent escape by using deadly force. Thus, if the suspect threatens the officer with a weapon or there is probable cause to believe that he has committed a crime involving the infliction or threatened infliction of serious physical harm, deadly force may be used if necessary to prevent escape, and if, where feasible, some warning has been given." *See Garner*, 471 U.S. at 11-12.

An officer may not, on the other hand, use physical force, deadly or otherwise, once a threat has been neutralized. This is true even if the suspect threatened an officer's life—or that of another—prior to being brought under control. *See Moore v. Indehar*, 514 F.3d 756, 762 (8th Cir. 2008); *Nelson*, 162 F.3d at 990. For that reason, every instance in which Wilson shot Brown could potentially be prosecuted if the deployment of deadly force was objectively unreasonable in the particular circumstance. We must therefore determine whether, each time he fired his weapon, the available evidence could prove that Wilson acted reasonably or unreasonably in light of the facts available to him at the time. In particular, we must examine whether the available evidence shows that Wilson reasonably believed that Brown posed a threat of serious bodily harm to Wilson himself or others in the community, or whether Brown clearly attempted to surrender, prior to any of the shots fired by Wilson.

1. Shooting at the SUV

The evidence establishes that the shots fired by Wilson while he was seated in his SUV were in self-defense and thus were not objectively unreasonable under the Fourth Amendment. According to Wilson, when he backed up his SUV and attempted to get out to speak with Brown, Brown blocked him from opening the door. Brown then reached through the window and began to punch Wilson in the face, after which he reached for and gained control of Wilson's firearm by putting his hand over Wilson's hand. As Brown was struggling for the gun and pointing it into Wilson's hip, Wilson gained control of the firearm and fired it just over his lap at Brown's hand. The physical evidence corroborates Wilson's account in that the bullet was recovered from the door panel just over Wilson's lap, the base of Brown's hand displayed injuries consistent with it being within inches of the muzzle of the gun, and Wilson had injuries to his jaw consistent with being struck. Witnesses 102, 103, and 104 all state that they saw Brown with the upper portion of his body and/or arms inside the SUV as he struggled with Wilson. These witnesses have given consistent statements, and their statements are also consistent with the physical evidence.

In contrast, the two primary witnesses who state that Wilson instigated the encounter by grabbing Brown and pulling him toward the SUV and that Brown's hands were never inside the vehicle are Witnesses 101 and 127. Both of those witnesses have given accounts that are inconsistent with the forensic and physical evidence. For example, both witnesses insisted that Wilson shot Brown in the back as he fled and that they saw shots hit Brown in the back. These statements are contradicted by all three autopsies, which concluded that Brown had no entry wounds to his back. Both witnesses also insist that, after he turned to face Wilson, Brown raised his hands, never moved forward, and never reached for his waistband. While Brown might well have briefly raised his hands in some fashion (see below), the physical evidence in the form of the blood on the ground establishes that he did move forward and that he fell to the ground with his left hand near his waistband. Both of these accounts are further undermined by the witnesses' physical inability to perceive what they claim to have seen. Witness 101 was hiding behind a vehicle for significant portions of the incident and Witness 127 was looking at her cell phone, attempting to make a video recording of the encounter, and driving her car. Given the deficiencies in the accounts of these two witnesses, federal prosecutors credited the accounts of Witnesses 102, 103, 104, and Wilson and concluded that Brown did in fact reach for and attempt to grab Wilson's gun, that Brown could have overpowered Wilson, which was acknowledged even by Witness 101, and that Wilson fired his weapon just over his own lap in an attempt to regain control of a dangerous situation.

Under well-established Fourth Amendment precedent, it is not objectively unreasonable for a law enforcement officer to use deadly force in response to being physically assaulted by a subject who attempts to take his firearm. *See, e.g., Nelson,* 162 F.3d at 990-91 (holding that it was not objectively unreasonable for officer to shoot at a suspect through a closet door after suspect attempted to grab his gun, hit him in the head with an asp, and pushed him into closet). The government therefore cannot meet its burden of establishing probable cause to a grand jury or proving beyond a reasonable doubt to twelve trial jurors that the shots fired by Wilson at the SUV were unreasonable. These shots are thus not prosecutable violations of 18 U.S.C. § 242.

2. Wilson's Subsequent Pursuit of Brown and Shots Allegedly Fired as Brown Was Running Away

The evidence does not support concluding that Wilson shot Brown while Brown's back was toward Wilson. Witnesses, such as Witness 118, Witness 128, Witness 139 and others, who claim to have seen Wilson fire directly into Brown's back, gave accounts that lack credibility because the physical evidence establishes that there were no entry wounds to Brown's back, although there was a wound to the anatomical back of Brown's right arm, and a graze wound to Brown's right arm. Also, other witnesses who say that Wilson fired at Brown as he ran have given accounts that are not credible because significant aspects of their statements are irreconcilable with the physical evidence, such as Witness 101 and 127, whose statements are suspect for the reasons noted above. Similarly, Witness 124 claims to have seen Wilson following behind Brown while steadily firing at him. However, Witness 124 dramatically changed her accounts of what she saw between the time of her first statement to the SLCPD and second statement to the FBI. She refused to meet with the federal prosecutors to clarify her varying accounts. Also, her account was dramatically different from that of her husband, Witness 115, who was standing next to her during the incident. Witness 115 stated that he thought he saw Wilson fire once at Brown as he was running away, but other aspects of his account lack credibility for the reasons set forth above, *i.e.* he did not witness significant parts of the shooting and based parts of his account on assumption. Witnesses 128 and 137 initially claimed that Wilson fired at Brown while he was running away, but then acknowledged that they did not see what Wilson and Brown were doing at this point and thus do not know whether Wilson fired at Brown as he was running away. Witnesses 105 and 106 thought they saw Wilson fire at Brown as he was running, but describe seeing Brown hit in the leg and back in a manner that does not match the autopsy findings. Accordingly, there is no credible evidence that establishes that Wilson fired at or struck Brown's back as Brown fled.

3. Shots Fired After Brown Turned to Face Wilson

The evidence establishes that the shots fired by Wilson after Brown turned around were in self-defense and thus were not objectively unreasonable under the Fourth Amendment. The physical evidence establishes that after he ran about 180 feet away from the SUV, Brown turned and faced Wilson, then moved toward Wilson until Wilson finally shot him in the head and killed him. According to Wilson, Brown balled or clenched his fists and "charged" forward, ignoring commands to stop. Knowing that Brown was much larger than him and that he had previously attempted to overpower him and take his gun, Wilson stated that he feared for his safety and fired at Brown. Again, even Witness 101's account supports this perception. Brown then reached toward his waistband, causing Wilson to fear that Brown was reaching for a weapon. Wilson stated that he continued to fear for his safety at this point and fired at Brown again. Wilson finally shot Brown in the head as he was falling or lunging forward, after which Brown immediately fell to the ground. Wilson did not fire any additional shots. Wilson's version of events is corroborated by the physical evidence that indicates that Brown moved forward toward Wilson after he ran from the SUV, by the fact that Brown went to the ground with his left hand at (although not inside) his waistband, and by credible eyewitness accounts.

Wilson's version is further supported by disinterested eyewitnesses Witness 102, Witness 104, Witness 105, Witness 108, and Witness 109, among others. These witnesses all agree that Brown ran or charged toward Wilson and that Wilson shot at Brown only as Brown moved toward him. Although some of the witnesses stated that Brown briefly had his hands up or out at about waist-level, none of these witnesses perceived Brown to be attempting to surrender at any point when Wilson fired upon him. To the contrary, several of these witnesses stated that they would have felt threatened by Brown and would have responded in the same way Wilson did. For example, Witness 104 stated that as Wilson ran after Brown yelling "stop, stop, stop," Brown finally turned around and raised his hands "for a second." However, Brown then immediately balled his hands into fists and "charged" at Wilson in a "tackle run." Witness 104 stated that Wilson fired only when Brown moved toward him and that she "would have fired sooner." Likewise, Witness 105 stated that Brown turned around and put his hands up "for a brief moment," then refused a command from Wilson to "get down" and instead put his hands "in running position" and started running toward Wilson. Witness 105 stated that Wilson shot at Brown only when Brown was moving toward him. These witnesses' accounts are consistent with prior statements they have given, consistent with the forensic and physical evidence, and consistent with each other's accounts. Accordingly, we conclude that these accounts are credible.

Furthermore, there are no witnesses who could testify credibly that Wilson shot Brown while Brown was clearly attempting to surrender. The accounts of the witnesses who have claimed that Brown raised his hands above his head to surrender and said "I don't have a gun," or "okay, okay, okay" are inconsistent with the physical evidence or can be challenged in other material ways, and thus cannot be relied upon to form the foundation of a federal prosecution. The two most prominent witnesses who have stated that Brown was shot with his hands up in surrender are Witness 101 and Witness 127, both of whom claim that Brown turned around with his hands raised in surrender, that he never reached for his waistband, that he never moved forward toward Wilson after turning to face him with his hands up, and that he fell to the ground with his hands raised. These and other aspects of their statements are contradicted by the physical evidence. Crime scene photographs establish that Brown fell to the ground with his left hand at his waistband and his right hand at his side. Brown's blood in the roadway demonstrates that Brown came forward at least 21.6 feet from the time he turned around toward Wilson. Other aspects of the accounts of Witness 101 and Witness 127 would render them not credible in a prosecution of Wilson, namely their accounts of what happened at the SUV. Both claim that Wilson fired the first shot out the SUV window, Witness 101 claims that the shot hit Brown at close range in the torso, and both claim that Brown did not reach inside the vehicle. These claims are irreconcilable with the bullet in the SUV door, the close-range wound to Brown's hand, Brown's DNA inside Wilson's car and on his gun, and the injuries to Wilson's face.

Other witnesses who have suggested that Brown was shot with his hands up in surrender have either recanted their statements, such as Witnesses 119 and 125, provided inconsistent statements, such as Witness 124, or have provided accounts that are verifiably untrue, such as Witnesses 121, 139, and 132. Witness 122 recanted significant portions of his statement by acknowledging that he was not in a position to see what either Brown or Wilson were doing, and who falsely insisted that three police officers pursued Brown and that the shooter was heavy set (in contrast to the slimly-built Wilson). Similar to Witness 128, Witness 122 told Brown's family that Brown had been shot execution-style. Witness 120 initially told law enforcement that he saw Brown shot at point-blank range as he was on his knees with his hands up. Similar to Witness 138, Witness 120 subsequently acknowledged that he did not see Brown get shot but "assumed" he had been executed while on his knees with his hands up based on "common sense" and what others "in the community told [him.]" There is no

witness who has stated that Brown had his hands up in surrender whose statement is otherwise consistent with the physical evidence. For example, some witnesses say that Wilson only fired his weapon out of the SUV, (*e.g.* Witnesses 128,
101, and 127) or that Wilson stood next to the SUV and killed Brown right there
(*e.g.* Witnesses 139, 132, 120). Some witnesses insist that Wilson shot Brown in
the back as he lay on the ground. (*e.g.* Witnesses 128 and 139). Some witnesses
say that Wilson shot Brown and he went to the ground immediately upon turning to face Wilson. (*e.g.* Witnesses 138, 101, 118, and 127). Some say Wilson went
to the ground with his hands raised at right angles. (*e.g.* Witnesses 138, 118, and
121). Again, all of these statements are contradicted by the physical and forensic
evidence, which also undermines the credibility of their accounts of other aspects of the incident, including their assertion that Brown had his hands up in a
surrender position when Wilson shot him.

When the shootings are viewed, as they must be, in light of all the surrounding circumstances and what Wilson knew at the time, as established by the
credible physical evidence and eyewitness testimony, it was not unreasonable
for Wilson to fire on Brown until he stopped moving forward and was clearly
subdued. Although, with hindsight, we know that Brown was not armed with
a gun or other weapon, this fact does not render Wilson's use of deadly force
objectively unreasonable. Again, the key question is whether Brown could reasonably have been perceived to pose a deadly threat to Wilson at the time he
shot him regardless of whether Brown was armed. Sufficient credible evidence
supports Wilson's claim that he reasonably perceived Brown to be posing a
deadly threat. First, Wilson did not know that Brown was not armed at the time
he shot him, and had reason to suspect that he might be when Brown reached
into the waistband of his pants as he advanced toward Wilson. *See Loch v. City
of Litchfield*, 689 F.3d 961, 966 (8th Cir. 2012) (holding that "[e]ven if a suspect is
ultimately 'found to be unarmed, a police officer can still employ deadly force if
objectively reasonable.'") (quoting *Billingsley v. City of Omaha*, 277 F.3d 990, 995
(8th Cir. 2002)); *Reese v. Anderson*, 926 F.2d 494, 501 (5th Cir. 1991) ("Also irrelevant is the fact that [the suspect] was actually unarmed. [The officer] did not
and could not have known this."); *Smith v. Freland*, 954 F.2d 343, 347 (noting that
"unarmed" does not mean "harmless) (6th Cir. 1992). While Brown did not use
a gun on Wilson at the SUV, his aggressive actions would have given Wilson
reason to at least question whether he might be armed, as would his subsequent
forward advance and reach toward his waistband. This is especially so in light
of the rapidly-evolving nature of the incident. Wilson did not have time to determine whether Brown had a gun and was not required to risk being shot himself
in order to make a more definitive assessment.

Moreover, Wilson could present evidence that a jury likely would credit that
he reasonably perceived a deadly threat from Brown even if Brown's hands were
empty and he had never reached into his waistband because of Brown's actions

in refusing to halt his forward movement toward Wilson. The Eighth Circuit Court of Appeals' decision in *Loch v. City of Litchfield* is dispositive on this point. There, an officer shot a suspect eight times as he advanced toward the officer. Although the suspect's "arms were raised above his head or extended at his sides," the Court of Appeals held that a reasonable officer could have perceived the suspect's forward advance in the face of the officer's commands to stop as resistance and a threat. As the Court of Appeals explained:

> Although [the suspect] had by this time thrown his firearm in the snow, . . . [the officer] did not observe that action. Instead of complying with [the officer's] command to get on the ground, [the suspect] turned and moved toward the officer. [Plaintiffs], noting that [the suspect's] arms were raised above his head or extended at his sides, suggest that [the suspect] was simply trying to find a suitable place to get on the ground, because his truck sat near a tree and snowbank. But even if [the suspect's] motives were innocent, a reasonable officer on the scene could have interpreted [the suspect's] actions as resistance. *It is undisputed that [the suspect] continued toward [the officer] despite the officer's repeated orders to get on the ground . . . Thus, a reasonable officer could believe that [the suspect's] failure to comply was a matter of choice rather than necessity.*

> *Loch*, 689 F.3d 961, 966 (8th Cir. 2012) (emphasis added).

Were the government to prosecute Wilson, the court would instruct the jury using *Loch* as a foundation. Given the evidence in this matter, jurors would likely conclude that Wilson had reason to be concerned that Brown was a threat to him as he continued to advance, just as did the officer in *Loch*.

In addition, even assuming that Wilson definitively knew that Brown was not armed, Wilson was aware that Brown had already assaulted him once and attempted to gain control of his gun. Wilson could thus present evidence that he reasonably feared that, if left unimpeded, Brown would again assault Wilson, again attempt to overpower him, and again attempt to take his gun. Under the law, Wilson has a strong argument that he was justified in firing his weapon at Brown as he continued to advance toward him and refuse commands to stop, and the law does not require Wilson to wait until Brown was close enough to physically assault Wilson. Even if, with hindsight, Wilson could have done something other than shoot Brown, the Fourth Amendment does not second-guess a law enforcement officer's decision on how to respond to an advancing threat. The law gives great deference to officers for their necessarily split-second judgments, especially in incidents such as this one that unfold over a span of less than two minutes. "Thus, under *Graham*, we must avoid substituting our personal notions of proper police procedure for the instantaneous decision of the officer at the scene. We must never allow the theoretical, sanitized world of our imagination to replace the dangerous and complex world that policemen face every day." *Smith*, 954 F.2d at 347 (6th Cir. 1992). *See also Ryburn v. Huff*, 132 S. Ct. 987, 991-92 (2012) (courts "should be cautious about second-guessing a police officer's assessment, made on the scene, of the danger presented by a particular situation"); *Estate of Morgan v. Cook*, 686 F.3d 494, 497 (8th Cir. 2012) ("The Constitution ... requires only that the seizure be objectively reasonable, not that the officer pursue the most prudent course of conduct as judged by 20/20 hindsight vision." (citing *Cole v. Bone*, 993 F.2d 1328, 1334 (8th Cir. 1993)) "It may appear, in the calm aftermath, that an officer could have taken a different course, but we do not hold the police to such a demanding standard." (citing *Gardner v. Buerger*, 82 F.3d 248, 251 (8th Cir. 1996) (same))). Rather, where, as here, an officer points his gun at a suspect to halt his advance, that suspect should be on notice that "escalation of the situation would result in the use of the firearm." *Estate of Morgan* at 498. An officer is permitted to continue firing until the threat is neutralized. *See Plumhoff v. Rickard*, 134 S.Ct. 2012, 2022 (2014) ("Officers need not stop shooting until the threat has ended").

For all of the reasons stated, Wilson's conduct in shooting Brown as he advanced on Wilson, and until he fell to the ground, was not objectively unreasonable and thus not a violation of 18 U.S.C. § 242.

C. Willfulness

Even if federal prosecutors determined there were sufficient evidence to convince twelve jurors beyond a reasonable doubt that Wilson used unreasonable force, federal law requires that the government must also prove that the officer acted willfully, that is, with the purpose to violate the law. *Screws v. United States*, 325 U.S. 91, 101-107 (1945) (discussing willfulness element of 18 U.S.C. § 242). The Supreme Court has held that an act is done willfully if it was "committed" either "in open defiance or in reckless disregard of a constitutional requirement which has been made specific and definite." *Screws*, 325 U.S. at 105. The government need not show that the defendant knew a federal statute or law protected the right with which he intended to interfere. *Id*. at 106–107 ("[t]he fact that the defendants may not have been thinking in constitutional terms is not material where their aim was not to enforce local law but to deprive a citizen of a right and that right was protected"); *United States v. Walsh*, 194 F.3d 37, 52-53 (2d Cir. 1999) (holding that jury did not have to find defendant knew of the particular Constitutional provision at issue but that it had to find intent to invade interest protected by Constitution). However, we must prove that the defendant intended to engage in the conduct that violated the Constitution and that he did so knowing that it was a wrongful act. *Id*.

"[A]ll the attendant circumstance[s]" should be considered in determining whether an act was done willfully. *Screws*, 325 U.S. at 107. Evidence regarding the egregiousness of the conduct, its character and duration, the weapons employed and the provocation, if any, is therefore relevant to this inquiry. *Id.* Willfulness may be inferred from blatantly wrongful conduct. *See id.* at 106; *see also United States v. Reese*, 2 F.3d 870, 881 (9th Cir. 1993) ("Intentionally wrongful conduct, because it contravenes a right definitely established in law, evidences a reckless disregard for that right; such reckless disregard, in turn, is the legal equivalent of willfulness."); *United States v. Dise*, 763 F.2d 586, 592 (3d Cir. 1985) (holding that when defendant invades personal liberty of another, knowing that invasion is violation of state law, defendant has demonstrated bad faith and reckless disregard for federal constitutional rights). Mistake, fear, misperception, or even poor judgment do not constitute willful conduct prosecutable under the statute. *See United States v. McClean*, 528 F.2d 1250, 1255 (2d Cir. 1976) (inadvertence or mistake negates willfulness for purposes of 18 U.S.C. § 242).

As discussed above, Darren Wilson has stated his intent in shooting Michael Brown was in response to a perceived deadly threat. The only possible basis for prosecuting Wilson under section 242 would therefore be if the government could prove that his account is not true—*i.e.*, that Brown never assaulted Wilson at the SUV, never attempted to gain control of Wilson's gun, and thereafter clearly surrendered in a way that no reasonable officer could have failed to perceive. Given that Wilson's account is corroborated by physical evidence and that his perception of a threat posed by Brown is corroborated by other eyewitnesses, to include aspects of the testimony of Witness 101, there is no credible evidence that Wilson willfully shot Brown as he was attempting to surrender or was otherwise not posing a threat. Even if Wilson was mistaken in his interpretation of Brown's conduct, the fact that others interpreted that conduct the same way as Wilson precludes a determination that he acted with a bad purpose to disobey the law. The same is true even if Wilson could be said to have acted with poor judgment in the manner in which he first interacted with Brown, or in pursuing Brown after the incident at the SUV. These are matters of policy and procedure that do not rise to the level of a Constitutional violation and thus cannot support a criminal prosecution. *Cf. Gardner v. Howard*, 109 F.3d 427, 430–31 (8th Cir. 1997) (violation of internal policies and procedures does not in and of itself rise to violation of Constitution).

Because Wilson did not act with the requisite criminal intent, it cannot be proven beyond reasonable doubt to a jury that he violated 18 U.S.C.§ 242 when he fired his weapon at Brown.

VI. CONCLUSION

For the reasons set forth above, this matter lacks prosecutive merit and should be closed.

Investigation of the Cleveland Division of Police

United States Department of Justice
Civil Rights Division

United States Attorney's Office
Northern District of Ohio

DECEMBER 4, 2014

U.S. DEPARTMENT OF JUSTICE

The Honorable Frank G. Jackson Mayor
City of Cleveland Cleveland City Hall 601 Lakeside Avenue
Cleveland, Ohio 44114

Dear Mayor Jackson:

The Department of Justice has completed its civil pattern or practice investigation of the Cleveland Division of Police ("CDP" or "the Division"). We have concluded that we have reasonable cause to believe that CDP engages in a pattern or practice of the use of excessive force in violation of the Fourth Amendment of the United States Constitution. We have determined that structural and systemic deficiencies and practices—including insufficient accountability, inadequate training, ineffective policies, and inadequate engagement with the community—contribute to the use of unreasonable force.

Our investigation under the Violent Crime and Law Enforcement Act of 1994, 42 U.S.C. § 14141 ("Section 14141") focused on allegations of excessive force by CDP officers. Section 14141 makes it unlawful for government entities, such as the City of Cleveland and CDP, to engage in a pattern or practice of conduct by law enforcement officers that deprives individuals of rights, privileges, or immunities secured by the Constitution or laws of the United States. The investigation was conducted jointly by the Civil Rights Division and the United States Attorney's Office for the Northern District of Ohio. This letter is separate from, and does not address, any criminal investigation that may be conducted by the Department of Justice.

We opened our investigation after a series of incidents of potential excessive force revealed a rift between CDP and certain segments of the communities it serves. An investigation into one of those incidents by the Ohio Attorney General concluded that the incident was the result of a "systemic failure" by CDP. Numerous leaders and organizations in Cleveland called on us to open an investigation into CDP, including a member of the U.S. Congress, leaders of several different religious communities, civil rights and community groups, and ultimately you, Mayor Jackson. Our investigation found that the concerns raised by community members, civic leaders, and other law enforcement agencies are well-founded.

We recognize the challenges faced by officers in Cleveland and in communities across the nation every day. Policing can be dangerous. At times, officers must use force, including deadly force, to protect lives, including their own.

The use of force by police should be guided by a respect for human life and human dignity, the need to protect public safety, and the duty to protect individuals from unreasonable seizures under the Fourth Amendment. A significant amount of the force used by CDP officers falls short of these standards. Although CDP has taken some steps to improve the Division's use of force policies and procedures, these initiatives, by themselves, have been insufficient. The need for sustainable reform is highlighted by the fact that just over a decade ago the Department of Justice completed its first investigation of the Cleveland Division of Police. That investigation raised concerns and resulted in recommendations that are starkly similar to the findings in this letter. The voluntary reforms undertaken at that time did not create the systems of accountability necessary to ensure a long-term remedy to these issues.

Throughout our investigation, CDP's leadership has been receptive to our preliminary feedback and technical assistance. We also received cooperation from the patrol officers and supervisors we met, which we value greatly. We recognize that the men and women of CDP want to do their jobs effectively and appropriately. They are trying to do a tough job as best they can. CDP's officers serve the public at great risk. They are working under quite difficult circumstances and we appreciate their willingness to serve. However, as outlined in this letter, more work is necessary to ensure that officers have the proper guidance, training, support, supervision, and oversight to carry out their law enforcement responsibilities safely and in accordance with individuals' constitutional rights. We appreciate your expressed willingness to embrace many of the changes we have highlighted in our conversations with CDP during this investigation. We will continue to work collaboratively with you, the Division's leadership, and other stakeholders to develop sustainable reforms that will resolve our findings. The Statement of Principles that we agreed to on December 2, 2014, is a critical first step in moving toward reform, and we applaud the City's willingness to make its intent to collaborate with us explicit. However, if we cannot reach an appropriate resolution, Section 14141 authorizes the Department of Justice to file a civil lawsuit to "eliminate the pattern or practice" of police misconduct. 42 U.S.C. § 14141.

We thank the members of Cleveland's diverse communities for bringing relevant information to our attention and for sharing their experiences with us. We are encouraged by the many individuals who took an active interest in our investigation and who offered thoughtful recommendations, including community advocates, religious leaders, and members of CDP's patrol officer and management unions. We appreciate those individuals who came forward to provide information about specific encounters with CDP, even when recounting those events was difficult. We also thank the officers who shared information about the many challenges they face. We know that many residents care deeply about preventing the types of incidents described in this letter even as they have a genuine interest in supporting the men and women of CDP who uphold their oaths and work to protect the people of Cleveland.

We appreciate the cooperation and professionalism that you, CDP, and other city officials have displayed during our investigation. We received invaluable assistance from the Division's leadership, and officers. Based on this cooperation, we are optimistic that we will be able to work with the City and CDP to address our findings. We are encouraged that, just two days ago, we agreed to a Joint Statement of Principles to guide our negotiations to remedy the constitutional violations we found. Together, by promoting constitutional policing, we will make CDP more effective and will help build the community's trust in the Division.

I. SUMMARY OF FINDINGS

Our investigation concluded that there is reasonable cause to believe that CDP engages in a pattern or practice of using unreasonable force in violation of the Fourth Amendment. That pattern manifested in a range of ways, including:

- The unnecessary and excessive use of deadly force, including shootings and head strikes with impact weapons;
- The unnecessary, excessive or retaliatory use of less lethal force including tasers, chemical spray and fists;
- Excessive force against persons who are mentally ill or in crisis, including in cases where the officers were called exclusively for a welfare check; and
- The employment of poor and dangerous tactics that place officers in situations where avoidable force becomes inevitable and places officers and civilians at unnecessary risk.

Officers may be required to use force during the course of their duties. However, the Constitution requires that officers use only that amount of force that is reasonable under the circumstances. We found that CDP officers too often use unnecessary and unreasonable force in violation of the Constitution. Supervisors tolerate this behavior and, in some cases, endorse it. Officers report that they receive little supervision, guidance, and support from the Division, essentially leaving them to determine for themselves how to perform their difficult and dangerous jobs. The result is policing that is sometimes chaotic and dangerous; interferes with CDP's ability to effectively fight crime; compromises officer safety; and frequently deprives individuals of their constitutional rights. Based on our investigation, we find that the Division engages in a pattern or practice of using excessive force in violation of the Fourth Amendment.

Like most police departments the Department of Justice has investigated, the majority of the force used by CDP officers is reasonable and not in violation of the Constitution. Nonetheless, we found that CDP officers engage in excessive force far too often, and that the use of excessive force by CDP officers is neither isolated, nor sporadic. In fact, as we indicated when we met with the City in October 2014, determining whether a pattern or practice of the unreasonable use of force exists was not a close case. Thus, even if people have differing views regarding the propriety of any single incident, it would not change the ultimate conclusion that there is a broader pattern or practice of unreasonable force. Our findings, however, do not mean that any individual officers have acted with criminal intent, a wholly different and higher legal standard that is beyond the scope of this letter and this investigation.

We have concluded that these incidents of excessive force are rooted in common structural deficiencies. CDP's pattern or practice of excessive force is both reflected by and stems from its failure to adequately review and investigate officers' uses of force; fully and objectively investigate all allegations of misconduct; identify and respond to patterns of at-risk behavior; provide its officers with the support, training, supervision, and equipment needed to allow them to do their jobs safely and effectively; adopt and enforce appropriate policies; and implement effective community policing strategies at all levels of CDP.

The pattern or practice of unreasonable force we identified is reflected in CDP's use of both deadly and less lethal force. For example, we found incidents of CDP officers firing their guns at people who do not pose an immediate threat of death or serious bodily injury to officers or others and using guns in a careless and dangerous manner, including hitting people on the head with their guns, in circumstances where deadly force is not justified. Officers also use less lethal force that is significantly out of proportion to the resistance encountered and officers too often escalate incidents with citizens instead of using effective and accepted tactics to de-escalate tension. We reviewed incidents where officers used Tasers, oleoresin capsicum spray ("OC Spray"), or punched people who were already subdued, including people in handcuffs. Many of these people could have been controlled with a lesser application of force. At times, this force appears to have been applied as punishment for the person's earlier verbal or physical resistance to an officer's command, and is not based on a current threat posed by the person. This retaliatory use of force is not legally justified. Our review also revealed that officers use excessive force against individuals who are in mental health crisis or who may be unable to understand or comply with officers' commands, including when the individual is not suspected of having committed any crime at all.

In addition to the pattern or practice of excessive force, we found that CDP officers commit tactical errors that endanger both themselves and others in the Cleveland community and, in some instances, may result in constitutional violations. They too often fire their weapons in a manner and in circumstances that place innocent bystanders in danger; and accidentally fire them, sometimes fortuitously hitting nothing and other times shooting people and seriously injuring them. CDP officers too often use dangerous and poor tactics to try to gain control of suspects, which results in the application of additional force or places others in danger. Critically, officers do not make effective use of de-escalation techniques, too often instead escalating encounters and employing force when it may not be needed and could be avoided. While these tactical errors may not always result in constitutional violations, they place officers, suspects, and other members of the Cleveland community at risk.

Principal among the systemic deficiencies that have resulted in the pattern or practice we found is the Division's failure to implement effective and rigorous accountability systems. The fact that we find that there are systemic failures in CDP, however, should not be interpreted as inconsistent with holding officers accountable in any particular incident. Individual CDP officers also bear responsibility for their own actions once afforded due process of law. Any effort to force a decision between systemic problems and individual accountability is nothing more than an effort to set up a false choice between two important aspects of the same broader issues that exist at CDP. Force incidents often are not properly reported, documented, investigated, or addressed with corrective measures. Supervisors throughout the chain of command endorse questionable and sometimes unlawful conduct by officers. We reviewed supervisory investigations of officers' use of force that appear to be designed from the outset to justify the officers' actions. Deeply troubling to us was that some of the specially-trained investigators who are charged with conducting unbiased reviews of officers' use of deadly force admitted to us that they conduct their investigations with the goal of casting the accused officer in the most positive light possible. This admitted bias appears deeply rooted, cuts at the heart of the accountability system at CDP, and is emblematic of the type of practice that justifies a finding under Section 14141.

Another critical flaw we discovered is that many of the investigators in CDP's Internal Affairs Unit advised us that they will only find that an officer violated Division policy if the evidence against the officer proves, beyond a reasonable doubt, that an officer engaged in misconduct—an unreasonably high standard reserved for criminal prosecutions and inappropriate in this context. This standard apparently has been applied, formally or informally, for years to these investigations and further supports the finding that the accountability systems regarding use of force at CDP are structurally flawed. In actuality, we found that during the time period we reviewed that officers were only suspended for any period of time on approximately six occasions for using improper force. Discipline is so rare that no more than 51 officers out of a sworn force of 1,500 were disciplined in any fashion in connection with a use of force incident over a three-and-a half-year period. However, when we examined CDP's discipline numbers further, it was apparent that in most of those 51 cases the actual discipline imposed was for procedural violations such as failing to file a report, charges were dismissed or deemed unfounded, or the disciplinary process was suspended due to pending civil claims. A finding of excessive force by CDP's internal disciplinary system is exceedingly rare. A member of the Office of Professional Standards (or "OPS"), which, among other duties, has been charged with investigating use of deadly force incidents, stated that the office has not reviewed a deadly force incident since 2012. CDP's systemic failures are such that the Division is not able to timely, properly, and effectively determine how much force its officers are using, and under what circumstances, whether the force was reasonable and if not, what discipline, change in policy or training or other action is appropriate.

The current pattern or practice of constitutional violations is even more troubling because we identified many of these structural deficiencies more than ten years ago during our previous investigation of CDP's use of force. In 2002, we provided initial observations regarding CDP's use of force and accountability systems and, in 2004, we recommended that the Division make changes to address some of the deficiencies we identified. CDP entered into an agreement with us, but that agreement was not enforced by a court and did not involve an independent monitor to assess its implementation. The agreement did require CDP to make a variety of changes, including revising its use of force policy and establishing new procedures for reviewing officer-involved shootings. In 2005, we found that Cleveland had abided by that agreement and it was terminated. It is clear, however, that despite these measures, many of the policy and practice reforms that were initiated in response to our 2004 memorandum agreement were either not fully implemented or, if implemented, were not maintained over time. It is critical that the City and the Division now take more rigorous measures to identify, address, and prevent excessive force to protect the public and to build the community's trust. We believe that a consent decree and an independent monitor are necessary to ensure that reforms are successfully implemented and sustainable. We are encouraged that the City also recognizes that these measures are essential to sustainable reform in the Joint Statement of Principles.

Finally, CDP's failure to ensure that its officers do not use excessive force and are held accountable if they do, interferes with its ability to work with the communities whose cooperation the Division most needs to enforce the law, ensure officer safety, and prevent crime. Instead of working with Cleveland's communities to understand their needs and concerns and to set crime-fighting priorities and strategies consistent with those needs, CDP too often polices in a way that contributes to community distrust and a lack of respect for officers— even the many officers who are doing their jobs effectively. For example, we observed a large sign hanging in the vehicle bay of a district station identifying it as a "forward operating base," a military term for a small, secured outpost used to support tactical operations in a war zone. This characterization reinforces the view held by some—both inside and outside the Division—that CDP is an occupying force instead of a true partner and resource in the community it serves. While CDP's leadership recently adopted a new community policing initiative, the Division must undergo a cultural shift at all levels to change an "us-against-them" mentality we too often observed and to truly integrate and inculcate community oriented policing principles into the daily work and management of the Division.

Although we did not investigate CDP's search, seizure, and arrest practices, our force review revealed concerns we would be remiss not to address. The documents we reviewed to determine the lawfulness of CDP's force practices often described stops, searches, and arrests by officers that appear to have been unsupported. Notwithstanding the limited nature of this review, what we saw suggests that some CDP officers violate individuals' Fourth Amendment rights by subjecting them to stops, frisks, and full searches without the requisite level of suspicion. Individuals were detained on suspicion of having committed a crime, with no articulation or an inadequate articulation in CDP's own records of the basis for the officer's suspicion. Individuals were searched "for officer safety" without any articulation of a reason to fear for officer safety. Where bases for detentions and searches were articulated, officers used canned or boilerplate language. Supervisors routinely approved these inadequate reports without seeking additional information from the officers about the circumstances that justified the encounter that ultimately concluded with a use of force. Given the possibility that CDP's practices in this regard violate the Constitution and the near certainty that they breed more distrust in the community, we have asked that the Division work with us to address these concerns as well, and we appreciate your commitment in the Joint Statement of Principles to address these issues.

We recognize that the Division has started to implement some reforms to address concerns raised by the Department of Justice, the community and others, but much more is needed. As the City recognized in entering into the Joint Statement of Principles, the failure to take even more remedial action places residents at risk of excessive force and further alienates the Division from the communities it serves. We believe the City's commitment to an Agreement with us that will be entered as a consent order in federal court is crucial to making these remedies effective. Making constitutional policing a core Division value, and building systems of real accountability that carry out that value, will support the vast majority of CDP officers who strive to and do uphold their oaths to protect and serve the City of Cleveland. This will foster trust with the community, allowing all CDP officers to perform their jobs more safely and effectively.

II. BACKGROUND

The Department began this investigation in March 2013 in the wake of serious allegations that CDP officers use excessive force, and that the Division fails to identify, correct, and hold officers accountable for using force in violation of the

Constitution. Several incidents eroded community confidence and suggested there were serious flaws in CDP's use of force practices, including the Division's ability and willingness to hold officers accountable for unlawful, improper, or unsafe conduct. In January 2011, a police helicopter video emerged showing that, earlier that month, officers used excessive force against an unarmed man who had led police on a chase. The force—which included kicks to his head— was used after the man had surrendered to officers and was handcuffed and prone on the ground. None of the officers involved had written a report as to either using or witnessing any force at all, and no officers were appropriately disciplined for failing to report the use of force. In addition, even after the incident received significant attention and the man was prosecuted for his flight, none of the many police officers on the scene identified the officers who had used force that night. As a result, the officers who improperly used force could not be held accountable for their conduct.

In March 2011, the Cleveland Plain Dealer began an analysis of CDP's use of force and, over the next several months, ran a series of articles that described significant problems with CDP's force practices, based on a review of publicly available data. The Plain Dealer reported that CDP officers often engaged in force that appeared to be excessive and in violation of policy; that CDP failed to identify excessive force incidents; failed to conduct adequate supervisory reviews of force incidents; and failed to adequately discipline a small group of officers who were involved in a disproportionate number of use of force incidents, many of which appear to have been unreasonable. The Plain Dealer also reported that, between October 2005 and March 2011, CDP officers used Tasers 969 times, all but five of which the Division deemed justified and appropriate (a 99.5% clearance rate which one police expert said "strains credibility"). *The Plain Dealer* analyzed similar CDP force data in 2007 and found that supervisors reviewed 4,427 uses of force over four years and justified the force in every single case.

On November 29, 2012, over 100 Cleveland police officers engaged in a high speed chase, in violation of CDP policies, and fatally shot two unarmed civilians. The incident inflamed community perceptions, particularly in the African-American community, that CDP is a department out of control and that its officers routinely engage in brutality. The incident began when Timothy Russell and his passenger Malissa Williams drove past the Justice Center in downtown Cleveland, at which point officers and witnesses outside the Justice Center heard what they believed to be a shot fired from the car. It now appears that what they actually heard was the car backfiring. A massive chase ensued, involving at least 62 police vehicles, some of which were unmarked, and more than 100 patrol officers, supervisors, and dispatchers—about 37 percent of the CDP personnel on duty in the City. The pursuit lasted about 25 minutes, at times reaching speeds of more than 100 miles per hour. During the chase, some of the confusing and contradictory radio traffic incorrectly indicated that the occupants of the car may be armed and may be firing from the car. Other radio traffic did not support that conclusion. No supervisor asserted control over the chase, and some even participated. CDP now admits that the manner in which the chase occurred was not in accordance with established CDP policies. The chase finally ended outside the City's borders, in an East Cleveland school parking lot, with CDP vehicles located in front of and behind Mr. Russell's car. In circumstances that are still being disputed in court, thirteen CDP officers ultimately fired 137 shots at the car, killing both its occupants. Mr. Russell and Ms. Williams each suffered more than 20 gunshot wounds. The officers, who were firing on the car from all sides, reported believing that they were being fired at by the suspects. It now appears that those shots were being fired by fellow officers.

The Office of the Ohio Attorney General and its Ohio Bureau of Criminal Investigation and Identification ("BCI") conducted an investigation of the incident, at the conclusion of which BCI issued a report that raised serious questions about CDP's policies, training, supervision, communication, and technology. In an accompanying statement, the Ohio Attorney General, Mike DeWine, said it was a "miracle" that no law enforcement officer was killed during the incident and added, "Our two month investigation reveals that we are dealing with a systemic failure in the Cleveland Police Department. Command failed. Communications failed. The System failed." On December 27, 2012, Cleveland's mayor publicly requested that the Civil Rights Division of the Department of Justice review CDP's use of force policies. Subsequently, six CDP officers were indicted for their actions on November 29, 2012. The City recently agreed to pay $3 million to settle a civil lawsuit filed by the families of Mr. Russell and Ms. Williams. In conducting our investigation, we did not assess whether the officers involved in this incident violated the law. This matter is subject to an ongoing criminal prosecution and this findings letter is not intended to interfere with that process in any manner. Nor did we find predication to investigate whether CDP's practices discriminate against minority groups or otherwise deprive individuals of the protections provided by the Equal Protection Clause of the Fourteenth Amendment. We include the November 29, 2012, incident here to describe the serious allegations facing the Division when we began our investigation and the community distrust that CDP must grapple with in ensuring it provides effective and constitutional policing services to all segments of the Cleveland community. We also note that many of the concerns regarding policies, training, supervision, accountability, and equipment that were implicated by that incident were confirmed during our investigation, as set out below. Thus, our investigation revealed a clear pattern or practice of use of excessive force by officers without specific consideration of the November 29, 2012 incident.

III. METHODOLOGY

Our evaluation of CDP's use of force was informed by many sources, including: (1) witness interviews and hundreds of individuals participating in community town hall meetings; (2) the Division's officers, supervisors, and command staff; (3) other stakeholders in the City, including elected representatives of the patrol officer and management unions, the Office of Professional Standards and the Civilian Police Review Board, members of religious communities, and other community leaders; (4) Division documents, including reports documenting officers' use of deadly and less lethal force and materials associated with those reports; (5) Division policies, procedures and training materials, and (6) analysis provided by our expert police consultants.

Throughout our investigation, we sought information relevant to the Division's use of force and worked to gain a comprehensive understanding of the Division, including its leadership, systems of accountability, operations, and community engagement. We conducted multi-day onsite tours in Cleveland in March 2013, April 2013, June 2013, December 2013, February 2014, and July 2014. Collectively during these investigative tours, we met with command staff, most of the district commanders, officers of various ranks and leadership, and officers within the Internal Affairs Unit, among others. We accompanied officers and supervisors in their zone cars during various shifts and in every district. The Division briefed us on changes to its policies and practices. We met with representatives from the officers' and supervisors' unions. In addition to these onsite tours, which involved representatives from both the United States Attorney's Office and the Civil Rights Division, the United States Attorney's Office maintained a steady presence in Cleveland, attending community group meetings and visiting the districts to speak with officers and supervisors.

We also sought to learn more from individuals and groups who had direct interactions with the Division, and whom CDP is sworn to protect. We held multiple community town hall meetings in different regions of the City. During each of our onsite tours in Cleveland, we met with individuals who were willing to talk to us about their experiences with the police. In addition, we conducted three visits to Cleveland, in September 2013, May 2014, and October 2014 focused solely on talking to members of the community. We heard community members' concerns through outreach at community events, recreation centers, local businesses, and public housing units. We met with religious leaders, community activists, and representatives from several organizations that provide services to Clevelanders who are homeless or have a mental illness. We interviewed individuals who had either witnessed or been subjected to force by CDP officers. We verified these accounts where possible by reviewing available documentary, photographic, and video support, as well as Division records.

We were aided in our review by several expert police consultants who have significant experience in constitutional and best-practices policing, including reducing improper uses of force, ensuring officer safety and accountability, and promoting respectful police interactions with the community. Some of these consultants, who have worked for decades in police positions ranging from patrol officer to Chief, joined us during our onsite tours of the Division, participated in one or more of our town hall meetings, conducted interviews with civilians and officers, and accompanied officers and supervisors in their zone cars. The experience and knowledge of these nationally-recognized law enforcement experts has helped to inform our findings.

We reviewed an extensive volume of documents provided to us by the Division, including nearly 600 reports and investigations of officers' uses of force covering a three-year period. We reviewed more than 500 Use of Less Lethal Force Reports for uses of force that occurred between January 2012 and July 2013 and approximately 60 reports produced by the Division's Use of Deadly Force Investigation Team ("UDFIT") between 2010 and 2013, including every deadly force incident that occurred between January 2012 and April 2013. We closely analyzed these documents and applied the relevant legal standards to determine whether the Division's use of force was legally justified. Our review of individual use of force reports and investigations, along with our consultants' opinions on these documents, informed our investigation into whether a pattern or practice of excessive force exists.

To evaluate the causes of, and the factors contributing to, the use of unreasonable force, we reviewed internal and external CDP documents addressing a variety of operational issues, including policies and procedures, training, and investigations. For example, our conclusions about CDP's supervision and accountability systems are based on interviews of relevant staff, a review of policies and procedures, approximately 50 Internal Affairs investigations, more than 100 civilian complaint investigations, spreadsheets tracking outcomes of civilian complaints, and spreadsheets tracking disciplinary actions. This represented all of the 2012 and 2013 Internal Affairs investigations provided by CDP and a sample of the civilian complaints filed in 2012 and 2013.

We note that CDP's inability to produce key documents raises serious concerns regarding deficiencies in the Division's systems for tracking and reviewing use of force and accountability-related documents. These documents are necessary to assess whether officers are using force appropriately, to hold officers accountable for unreasonable uses of force, and to gauge the need for additional training, tactical reviews, or policy changes. CDP did not, for example, produce deadly force investigations that occurred after April of 2013 despite multiple requests. CDP was not able to produce some 2012 use of less lethal force reports until more than a year after our initial request for documents and failed to provide a justification for this delay. CDP reported that there were dozens of additional Internal Affairs investigations conducted during the time period we reviewed, but failed to provide these documents despite multiple requests. CDP was also unable to provide final dispositions for every civilian complaint, including complaints filed two years ago. Similarly, to date CDP has not been able to provide Taser firing histories which we requested over five months ago.

These are fundamental documents and pieces of information that should be readily accessible to CDP's leadership to inform decision-making. Instead, it appears that, at best, CDP is too often operating with incomplete or inaccurate information about its force practices. While we understand that CDP leadership may have informal ways to gather more information, a modern police force of CDP's size must have more formalized and structured mechanisms in place. CDP's inability to track the location of critical force-related documents is itself evidence of fundamental breakdowns in its systems and suggests that any internal analysis or calculation of CDP's use of force is likely incomplete and inaccurate. It also suggests that CDP does not accept that they are accountable for documenting and explaining their decisions in such matters to civilian leadership, the City, and the community as a whole.

Not only is CDP unable to track important force-related information, but it also appears that CDP's information is incomplete because some uses of force may not have been reported. CDP recently asserted in our meetings with them that total arrests involving a use of force have declined over the past eight years, as have the percentage of arrests which involve a use of force. CDP also asserted that Taser use declined significantly from 2009 to 2013. However, our review of a sample of 2012 arrest records for persons charged with resisting arrest suggests that some uses of force are not being reported. For the months of February, June and August 2012, there were 111 resisting arrest incidents, and for seven of these—over six percent—CDP acknowledges that no use of force report can be located. Furthermore, in all but one of these seven incidents, the arrest reports describe police action that constitutes force as defined by CDP policy, and the remaining one strongly suggests that reportable force was used. In the face of such underreporting, CDP's determination that uses of force have declined is not wholly reliable. The inability to produce Taser firing histories compounds our concerns about the reliability of the data and undermines the assertion that Taser uses have declined.

IV. FINDINGS

We have reasonable cause to believe that CDP engages in a pattern or practice of using unconstitutional force in violation of the Fourth Amendment. Our review revealed that Cleveland police officers use unnecessary and unreasonable force in violation of the Constitution at a significant rate, and in a manner that is extremely dangerous to officers, victims of crimes, and innocent by-standers. This pattern of unreasonable force manifests itself in CDP's use of deadly force, use of less lethal force, including Tasers, and use of force against restrained people and people in crisis.

A pattern or practice may be found where incidents of violations are re-peated and not isolated instances. *Int'l Bd. of Teamsters v. United States*, 431 U.S. 324, 336 n.16 (1977) (noting that the phrase "pattern or practice" "was not in-tended as a term of art," but should be interpreted according to its usual mean-ing "consistent with the understanding of the identical words" used in other federal civil rights statutes). Courts interpreting the terms in similar statutes have established that statistical evidence is not required. *Catlett v. Mo. Highway & Transp. Comm'n*, 828 F.2d 1260, 1265 (8th Cir. 1987) (interpreting "pattern or practice" in the Title VII context). A court does not need a specific number of incidents to find a pattern or practice, and it does not need to find a set number of incidents or acts. *See United States v. W. Peachtree Tenth Corp.*, 437 F.2d 221, 227 (5th Cir. 1971) ("The number of [violations] . . . is not determinative. . . . In any event, no mathematical formula is workable, nor was any intended. Each case must turn on its own facts."). Although a specific number of incidents and statistical evidence is not required, our review found that CDP officers use un-necessary and unreasonable force in violation of the Constitution a significant percentage of the time that they use force.

A. CDP officers engage in a pattern or practice of unconstitutional force.

Our review revealed that Cleveland police officers violate basic constitutional precepts in their use of deadly and less lethal force at a rate that is highly sig-nificant. Claims that officers have used excessive force during an arrest or de-tention are governed by the Fourth Amendment's reasonableness standard. *Graham v. Connor*, 490 U.S. 386, 394 (1989). "Determining whether the force used to effect a particular seizure is 'reasonable' under the Fourth Amendment requires a careful balancing of the nature and quality of the intrusion on the individual's Fourth Amendment interests against the countervailing govern-mental interests at stake." *Id.* at 396 (internal quotations and citations omitted). The reasonableness of a particular use of force is based on the totality of the circumstances and "must be judged from the perspective of a reasonable officer on the scene, rather than with the 20/20 vision of hindsight." *Id.* As the Sixth Circuit has stated:

> The Court has identified three factors that lower courts should consider
> in determining the reasonableness of force used: (1) the severity of the

crime at issue; (2) whether the suspect posed an immediate threat to the safety of the police officers or others; and (3) whether the suspect actively resisted arrest or attempted to evade arrest by flight. These factors are not an exhaustive list, as the ultimate inquiry is "whether the totality of the circumstances justifies a particular sort of seizure."

Baker v. City of Hamilton, Ohio, 471 F.3d 601, 606-07 (6th Cir. 2006) (citations omitted).

The most significant and "intrusive" use of force is the use of deadly force, which can result in the taking of human life, "frustrat[ing] the interest of . . . society . . . in judicial determination of guilt and punishment." *Tennessee v. Garner*, 471 U.S. 1, 9 (1985). Use of deadly force (whether or not it actually causes a death) is permissible only when an officer has probable cause to believe that a suspect poses an immediate threat of serious physical harm to the officer or another person. *Id.* at 11. A police officer may not use deadly force against an unarmed and otherwise non-dangerous subject, *see Garner*, 471 U.S. at 11, and the use of deadly force is not justified in every situation involving an armed subject. *Graham*, 490 U.S. at 386. The Sixth Circuit has recognized that "even when a suspect has a weapon, but the officer has no reasonable belief that the suspect poses a danger of serious physical harm to him or others, deadly force is *not* justified." *Bouggess v. Mattingly*, 482 F.3d 886, 896 (6th Cir. 2007) (emphasis in original). In order to justify the use of deadly force, an officer's "sense of serious danger about a particular confrontation" must be both "particularized and supported." *Id.* at 891. In making our determination under Section 14141 it is not necessary to show that there is a pattern or practice of intentional or criminal misconduct by individual officers in their unreasonable use of force, and we make no such finding in this letter.

We determined that, as part of the pattern or practice of excessive force, officers fire their guns in circumstances where the use of deadly force is not justified, including against unarmed or fleeing suspects who do not pose a threat of serious harm to officers or others. We also discovered incidents in which CDP officers draw their firearms and even point them at suspects too readily and in circumstances in which it is inappropriate. In part as a result of this dangerous practice, which is both inappropriate and tactically unsound, officers strike people on the head with their guns in circumstances that do not justify deadly force. CDP officers use less lethal force—including Tasers, OC Spray, and strikes to a suspect's body—against individuals who pose little, if any, threat, or who offer minimal resistance, including those who are handcuffed, already on the ground, or otherwise subdued. CDP officers too hastily resort to using Tasers, often in a manner that results in excessive force and demonstrates a pervasive use of poor and dangerous tactics. CDP officers also use Tasers and other forms of less lethal force against individuals with mental illness or under the influence of drugs or alcohol or who have a medical condition affection their cognitive abilities, or who may be unable to comply with officers' demands. Collectively, these practices make up a pattern or practice of constitutional violations.

1. CDP officers shoot at people who do not pose an imminent threat of serious bodily harm or death to the officers or others.

In reaching our conclusion that CDP engages in a pattern or practice of excessive force, we identified several cases in which officers shot or shot at people who did not pose an immediate threat of death or serious bodily injury to officers or others. An incident from 2013 in which a sergeant shot at a victim as he ran from a house where he was being held against his will is just one illustration of this problem. "Anthony" was being held against his will inside a house by armed assailants. When officers arrived on scene, they had information that two armed assailants were holding several people inside the home. After officers surrounded the house, Anthony escaped from his captors and ran from the house, wearing only boxer shorts. An officer ordered Anthony to stop, but Anthony continued to run toward the officers. One sergeant fired two shots at him, missing. According to the sergeant, when Anthony escaped from the house, the sergeant believed Anthony had a weapon because he elevated his arm and pointed his hand toward the sergeant. No other officers at the scene reported seeing Anthony point anything at the sergeant.

The sergeant's use of deadly force was unreasonable. It is only by fortune that he did not kill the crime victim in this incident. The sergeant had no reasonable belief that Anthony posed an immediate danger. The man fleeing the home was wearing only boxer shorts, making it extremely unlikely that he was one of the hostage takers. In a situation where people are being held against their will in a home, a reasonable police officer ought to expect that someone fleeing the home may be a victim. Police also ought to expect that a scared, fleeing victim may run towards the police and, in his confusion and fear, not immediately respond to officer commands. A reasonable officer in these circumstances should not have shot at Anthony.

Another incident from 2012 in which an officer shot a man who was lawfully armed and appeared to be cooperating with the officers' orders further illustrates this problem. Two officers observed "Brian" walking with an open container of beer. When officers asked Brian to stop, he initially refused and walked to a nearby porch, set down his beer and then, according to the resulting report, turned towards the officers' zone car in a manner that indicated he was going to speak with them. The first officer reportedly saw a gun in Brian's waistband, yelled "gun," and pointed his service weapon at Brian. The second officer reported that, in response, Brian raised his hands above his head and informed the officers that he had a concealed handgun license. The second officer moved behind Brian to begin to handcuff him. According to this officer's report, Brian then lowered his hands "a bit" below ear level. Then, the first officer fired a shot that struck Brian in the abdomen. According to reports, Brian's injuries were significant enough that he required immediate lifesaving measures. While the officer who fired the shot alleged that Brian had reached for his weapon, that account conflicts with the statement provided by the officer's partner and the eight civilian witnesses who were on or near the porch at the time Brian was shot, none of whom reported seeing Brian reach for his gun. Numerous witnesses reported that Brian was attempting to cooperate with officers and began lowering his hands in response to an officer's order that he place his hands behind his back.

The officer's use of deadly force in these circumstances was unreasonable. The Sixth Circuit has recognized that a suspect's "mere possession of a weapon is not enough to satisfy [an officer's] burden" of establishing that the use of deadly force was reasonable. *See Bouggess*, 482 F.3d at 896. The shooting officer's partner and all of the civilian witnesses confirmed that Brian informed the officers that he had a handgun license. Brian took the precise steps advised by the Ohio Attorney General's Office when a person carrying a concealed handgun is stopped for law enforcement purposes. The weight of the evidence suggests that Brian was attempting to comply with officers' orders and did not pose an imminent threat of serious bodily harm to the officers or others, and the officer should not have fired his weapon.

We also reviewed incidents where CDP officers shot at people who were fleeing in vehicles as the vehicle was moving away from the officer and the suspects' flights did not pose a threat of serious bodily harm to anyone, rendering the use of deadly force at that point unreasonable. Shooting at a fleeing suspect violates the Constitution when the fleeing suspect does not pose a threat of serious bodily harm to the officer or others. In the Sixth Circuit, "it has been clearly established . . . for the last twenty years that a criminal suspect 'ha[s] a right not to be shot unless he [is] perceived to pose a threat to the pursuing officers or to others during flight.'" *Sample v. Bailey*, 409 F.3d 689, 699 (6th Cir. 2005) (citing *Robinson v. Bibb*, 840 F.2d 349, 351 (6th Cir. 1988)); *cf. Plumhoff v. Rickard*, 527 U.S. ___ , 134 S. Ct. 2012, 2021 (2014) (finding officers' use of deadly force against fleeing suspect reasonable where suspect engaged in "outrageously reckless driving," leading officers on a chase that exceeded 100 miles per hour and passing more than two dozen vehicles, several of which were forced to alter course); *Hocker v. Pikeville City Police Dep't*, 738 F.3d 150, 152, 158 (6th Cir. 2013) (finding police officers' use of deadly force reasonable where officers shot an intoxicated suspect, whom the court found to be a continuing threat, after he led the officers on a seven-mile, high-speed chase at night, then reversed his vehicle, slamming into an officer's patrol car and moving it thirty feet while an officer was temporarily trapped inside). In the words of the Supreme Court, "[i]t is not better that all felony suspects die than that they escape." *Garner* at 11.

Shooting at vehicles creates an unreasonable risk unless such a real and articulable threat exists. First, it is difficult to shoot at a moving car with accuracy. Missed shots can hit bystanders or others in the vehicle. Second, if the driver is disabled by the shot, the vehicle may become unguided, making it potentially more dangerous. The dangers of this practice are recognized in Division policy, in fact. The problem is, however, that the restrictions created by this policy are not consistently enforced. Both the May 2007 and the March 2013 CDP Use of Force policies state, "Firing at or from a moving vehicle is rarely effective and presents extreme danger to innocent persons . . ." In its 2013 review of CDP's use of force policies and practices, the Police Executive Research Forum ("PERF") recommended that CDP policy be changed to prohibit the discharge of firearms at or from a moving vehicle unless deadly physical force is being used against the police officer or another person present, by means other than the moving vehicle. In making this recommendation, PERF noted that shooting at a moving vehicle is dangerous because "it does not result in a stopped vehicle—it simply raises the chances of danger from an uncontrolled vehicle." We commend CDP for adopting PERF's recommendation regarding shooting at moving vehicles in its most recent Use of Force policy, which was revised in August 2014. However, it is too soon to determine whether CDP's actual practices will also change in light of the new policy. CDP's Use of Force policies revised in May 2007 and March 2013 both prohibited officers from shooting at vehicles that were no longer a threat, yet we found that officers nonetheless have done so.

In an incident from 2010, an officer shot a fleeing individual. There, officers had responded to a home because a woman reported that her ex-boyfriend was outside calling her and making threats. As officers were arresting the suspect ("Charles"), "David," who had been sitting in the passenger seat of the car in which he had arrived with Charles, started the car as if to leave. An officer approached the car, pointed his gun at David, and ordered him to turn the car off. According to the officer, David then cut the wheels to the left and sped off so that the vehicle brushed against the officer, pushing him backwards. In response, the officer reported, he fired one round at the driver as he drove off, striking him in the back of the shoulder. Again, while the officer might well have been in danger when the car was next to him, the initial threat posed by David to the officer had ended by the time the officer shot at David, and the officer did not articulate any basis for believing that David was a threat to anyone else. Under these circumstances, the officer's use of deadly force was unreasonable.

These incidents are examples of precisely the type of deadly force prohibited by the Fourth Amendment. *See Smith v. Cupp*, 430 F.3d 766, 773-74 (6th Cir. 2005) (officer violated the Fourth Amendment when he shot at a suspect fleeing in a stolen police cruiser because the officer fired his weapon "after the police cruiser was past" and the potential danger to the public from the suspect's driving off "was not so grave as to justify the use of deadly force"); *Sigley v. City of Parma Heights*, 437 F.3d 527, 537 (6th Cir. 2006) (officer was not entitled to qualified immunity for shooting a suspect fleeing in a vehicle where he "sh[ot] [the suspect] in the back when he did not pose an immediate threat to other officers"). We found many additional deadly force incidents that violated the Fourth Amendment in our review. These shootings also violated the CDP policy in place at the time, which prohibited shooting at vehicles that no longer pose an imminent threat.

2. CDP officers hit people in the head with their guns in situations where the use of deadly force is not justified.

In our review of CDP's use of force, we also found that CDP officers use their guns to strike people in the head in circumstances where the use of deadly force is not justified. Striking someone in the head with an impact weapon is deadly force, as CDP's own policies recognize. Our review of deadly force investigations revealed that CDP officers have hit suspects in the head with their pistols in circumstances that do not warrant deadly force. This practice is partially a result of tactical errors where officers drawn their firearms at inappropriate times. In these circumstances, when officers ultimately engage physically with suspects, they do so while holding a firearm. This is an extremely dangerous practice, increasing the risk of an accidental discharge—which has happened on more than one occasion involving CDP officers—and the risk that a suspect will gain control of the weapon. It also limits the less-lethal options an officer has available to bring an actively resisting subject under control because one of his hands is occupied holding the firearm.

In an incident from 2012 that illustrates this problem, an officer's gun discharged when he struck a suspect in the head with it. The officer, who was off-duty and dressed in civilian clothes, observed what he believed to be a drug transaction take place involving two vehicles and about six suspects. The officer approached them without calling for backup and told them to leave. When "Eric" got out of one of the cars, the officer drew his handgun, pointed it at Eric, and ordered Eric to the ground, identifying himself as a CDP officer but not showing a badge. A witness reported that she saw a man, later identified as the officer, holding a gun to Eric's face while Eric asked repeatedly for the officer to show his badge and expressed disbelief that he was an officer. One of the occupants of the car later told police that he thought they were being robbed.

The officer then began wrestling with Eric with his gun still drawn. During the struggle, the officer struck Eric in the head with the weapon, at which time the weapon discharged. Eric then broke free from the officer and ran away. The officer reported that he did not know whether the bullet struck Eric, but that Eric was bleeding from the face as he ran away. The extent of Eric's injuries is unclear based on the documents CDP provided.

This use of deadly force was not reasonable and was quite dangerous for the arrestee, the officer, and the public. An officer's use of deadly force is not justified where a suspect physically resists arrest but poses no imminent danger of serious physical harm to the officer or another. *See Bouggess*, 482 F.3d at 891 ("It cannot reasonably be contended that physically resisting arrest, without evidence of the employment or drawing of a deadly weapon, and without evidence of any intention on the suspect's part to seriously harm the officer, could constitute probable cause that the suspect poses an imminent danger of *serious* physical harm to the officer or to others."). Additionally, the officer's actions could reasonably be predicted to escalate the situation because he engaged with Eric while off-duty without any means to identify himself as a police officer and without communicating with 911 or dispatch for back up. Moreover, the officer's decision to physically engage with the suspect while holding his gun was dangerous. Barring extremely rare circumstances, an officer should never do this. This officer could have killed this suspect with his blow, and he also risked shooting the suspect, himself, or innocent bystanders.

Another example of this dangerous and unlawful practice is an incident from 2011 in which an officer struck an unarmed man in the head with his gun after the man had committed a minor, nonviolent offense. "Fred" had tried to shoplift a bottle of wine and a can of beer from a supermarket. The officer, who was working secondary employment at the supermarket, ordered Fred to stop as he was exiting the store. Instead of stopping, Fred ran. The officer followed him and, even though he did not claim to have seen a weapon, approached Fred with his gun drawn and ordered him to the ground. Fred said, "Shoot me." The officer again ordered Fred to the ground, and Fred again said, "Shoot me." As the officer stepped toward Fred, Fred moved toward the officer. The officer then hit Fred on the left side of his head with his gun, forced him to the ground, and handcuffed him. The strike to Fred's head resulted in a laceration that required four staples to close. Again, this use of deadly force against a man who was not armed, had committed a minor offense, and who presented only a minimal threat to the officer was unreasonable and dangerous.

While officers are sometimes required to use force during the course of their duties, they are always required to do so within the constitutional parameters of the Fourth Amendment. Far too often, however, Cleveland police officers use deadly force where they do not have probable cause to believe anyone is in immediate, serious danger. In some instances, their use of deadly force places themselves and others in serious danger. This unjustified use of deadly force violates the Constitution and poses unacceptable risks to the Cleveland community.

3. CDP officers use less lethal force that is disproportionate to the resistance or threat encountered.

Our review of CDP's use of force also found that, in instances in which it is reasonable for officers to resort to some level of force in response to an individual's actions, CDP officers too frequently resort to a type of force that is unreasonable in light of the resistance or threat encountered. Force, including less lethal force, is excessive if the level of force used is disproportionate to the resistance or threat encountered. *Ciminillo v. Streicher*, 434 F.3d 461, 469 (6th Cir. 2006) ("[I]n this Circuit, it was clearly established that individuals had a general right to be free from unreasonable use of non-lethal force."). CDP officers use less lethal force—including Tasers, OC Spray, and strikes to a suspect's body—against individuals who pose little, if any, threat, or who offer minimal resistance, including those who are handcuffed, already on the ground, or otherwise subdued. CDP officers too hastily resort to using Tasers, and they do so in a manner that results in excessive force a significant percentage of the time and demonstrates a pervasive use of poor and dangerous tactics. CDP officers also use Tasers and other forms of less lethal force against individuals with mental illness or impaired faculties, or who may be unable to comply with officers' demands.

a. Head and body strikes.

CDP officers also use less lethal force on people who are handcuffed or otherwise subdued and pose little or no threat to officers. This practice contravenes well-settled law. *See Champion v. Outlook Nashville, Inc.*, 380 F.3d 893, 902 (6th Cir. 2004) (The Sixth Circuit has "consistently held that various types of force applied after the subduing of a suspect are unreasonable and a violation of a clearly established right."). One egregious incident in which officers resorted to an excessive amount of force, mentioned briefly in the Background section of this letter, occurred in January 2011. On the day in question, officers apprehended Edward Henderson after he fled from the police in a vehicle, leading officers on a chase that lasted about six minutes. Mr. Henderson then pulled over, exited his van, and sat on a highway guardrail. When CDP officers approached, Mr. Henderson walked into a group of trees. As one officer approached with his service weapon drawn, Mr. Henderson responded to commands to lay prone on the ground and spread his arms and legs. Infrared video from a CDP helicopter involved in the pursuit shows numerous officers approaching Mr. Henderson, including one with a gun drawn. The helicopter officer comments, "Looks like they got the male in custody." After Mr. Henderson was restrained, prone on his stomach, officers began kicking Mr. Henderson, and other officers appear to be striking him as well. Mr. Henderson was subsequently brought to the hospital with a broken orbital bone. The force officers used in this incident against an unarmed man, prone on the ground and surrounded by CDP officers, was unnecessary and excessive.

In another incident, an officer punched a handcuffed 13 year-old boy in the face several times. Officers had arrested the juvenile for shoplifting. While "Harold" was handcuffed in the zone car, he began to kick the door and kicked an officer in the leg. In response, the 300 pound, 6'4" tall officer entered the car and sat on the legs of the 150 pound, 5'8" tall handcuffed boy. Harold was pushing against the officer with his legs, but was handcuffed and posed no threat to the officer. Nevertheless, the officer continued to sit on Harold and punched him in the face three to four times until he was "stunned/dazed" and had a bloody nose. In considering the reasonableness of an officer's use of force, courts "must . . . consider the size and stature of the parties involved." *Solomon v. Auburn Hills Police Dep't*, 389 F.3d 167, 174 (6th Cir. 2004) (finding that a 120 pound, 5'5" tall woman posed "no immediate threat" to the safety of officers who weighed between 230 and 250 pounds and stood at least 5'8" tall). Moreover, this unreasonable use of force appears to have been designed to punish the boy rather than to control him. The Fourth Amendment does not permit force to be used for punishment. *See, e.g., Baker v. City of Hamilton*, 471 F.3d 601, 607 (6th Cir. 2006) (finding that officer used "unjustified and gratuitous" force when he struck a suspect in the knee because "the purpose of this hit was not to subdue . . . but rather to punish him"); *Bultema v. Benzie County*, 146 F. App'x 28, 37-38 (6th Cir. 2005) (unpublished) ("[R]egardless of what the suspect may have done to the police officer prior to the arrest, the police officer is constitutionally prohibited from exacting retribution once the suspect has been subdued.").

b. Tasers and OC Spray.

Our review also found that CDP officers use their Tasers and OC Spray inappropriately. Tasers are a valuable tool for law enforcement, but they are also a weapon that exerts a significant amount of force on the person and cannot be used without adequate justification for such a high level of force. One court described the effect of a Taser on a person this way: "The impact is as powerful as it is swift. The electrical impulse instantly overrides the victim's central nervous system, paralyzing the muscles throughout the body, rendering the target limp and helpless. . . . The tasered person also experiences an excruciating pain that radiates throughout the body." *Bryan v. McPherson*, 590 F.3d 767, 773 (9th

Cir. 2009). CDP officers, however, do not treat their Tasers as weapons which deliver such a high level of force. We found, for example, that officers use Tasers as a weapon of first resort instead of employing lower level force options. We reviewed incidents where officers immediately resorted to the Taser despite the presence of other officers who could help contain the individual using lower levels of force, or where de-escalation techniques might have proved more effective than using force. We also found that officers tase people who are handcuffed and that, in some cases, multiple officers deployed Tasers simultaneously or a single officer deployed a Taser multiple times when only a single use was justified.

Additionally, CDP officers misuse the so-called "drive stun mode" of their Tasers. A Taser may be used in two different ways—either by discharging the pair of darts, which remain connected to the main unit by a conductive wire, or by applying the Taser directly to a person's body while pulling the trigger. In the first method, an electrical circuit is complete that temporarily incapacitates a subject. The second method, called drive stun mode, inflicts pain as a compliance measure without incapacitating the subject. The practice of using Tasers in drive stun mode as a pain compliance tactic should be reserved for situations where other less painful tactics cannot be used and, in fact, may have limited effectiveness because, when used repeatedly, it may even exacerbate the situation by inducing anger in the subject. In its August 2013 report to CDP, PERF recommended that CDP discourage the use of drive stun as a pain compliance tactic, and CDP agreed to do so. PERF also recommended that CDP permit officers to use drive stun only to supplement the probe mode to complete the circuit or as a countermeasure to gain a safe distance between an officer and a subject, but CDP declined to do so, without explanation. In practice, we found that CDP officers frequently use the Taser in drive stun mode.

In one incident that illustrates CDP's inappropriate use of Tasers, an officer used his Taser to drive stun a 127-pound juvenile twice as two officers held him on the ground. Officers believed that "Ivan" matched the description of a possible fleeing suspect wanted for harassing store customers and stealing. Officers chased Ivan on foot, caught up to him, and tackled him. The officers alleged that the 127-pound juvenile "continued to resist" as they both held him on ground, prompting one of the officers to deploy his Taser twice in the juvenile's back in drive stun mode, even though both officers were holding him down. In this incident, the use of the Taser in any mode was unreasonable. There were two officers present and the juvenile was already on the ground and could have been controlled using lesser force.

In another instance from 2013, officers tased a handcuffed, fleeing prisoner, and then drive stunned him twice after having lost control of him while placing him in the back of a zone car. When officers initially confronted the individual, "Jason," he falsely identified himself, so they decided to arrest him for "falsification." They placed him in handcuffs and patted him down for weapons. Finding none, they attempted to place him in the back of the zone car. While they were doing so, the handcuffed Jason somehow managed to escape from the two officers and began running in the middle of the street. The officers gave chase and, when Jason did not comply with commands to stop, one officer attempted to tase him "to stop the male from causing himself severe injuries from falling or being struck." This rationale offered by the officer should have been sufficient on its own for CDP to find this use of force unjustified, as suspects normally fall after being tased. Justifying the use of a Taser to stop a feeling, handcuffed person from falling is simply not credible. *See, e.g., Bryan*, 590 F.3d at 773 (officer's use of Taser caused the subject to fall face-first onto asphalt, shattering four front teeth and causing facial contusions). Jason continued running, but according to the officers, he eventually tripped and fell to the ground. When the officers caught up to him, they attempted to hold Jason down, but the handcuffed Jason "continued to resist and not comply" with orders. Despite the fact that there were two officers present, the officers drive-stunned Jason twice while he was handcuffed and on the ground. This use of force was unreasonable. The suspect was already on the ground and was in handcuffs. The decision to drive stun him twice appears to have been made more to punish Jason for running rather than to gain control of him, which could have been accomplished with less force, if any. *See Baker*, 471 F.3d at 607; *Bultema*, 146 F. App'x at 37-38. In addition to problems with the tasings, the fact that two officers completely lost control of a handcuffed suspect is concerning. This incident of tasing a person who was already handcuffed, a practice that on its face is quite hard to justify, was not the only time we saw it occur. And each and every time we saw officers write that they had tased a handcuffed suspect, the use of force was approved up the chain of command.

Officers also have unnecessarily and unreasonably used OC spray against handcuffed people. A particularly troubling incident occurred in February 2013, when CDP officers placed a so-called "spit sock" on a mentally ill suspect, "Kent," then sprayed OC spray over the spit sock while Kent was handcuffed and in the back of a zone car. Officers apparently then forced him to continue wearing the spit sock. The incident began when officers responded to a male who called 911 and threatened to "blow up the government," among other threats. Numerous zone cars responded to Kent's home. Officers placed Kent in handcuffs and, because he was spitting on them, they placed a spit sock, a hood which helps prevent the transfer of diseases from spitting, over his head. They then placed him in a zone car. Kent began to kick at the rear windows of the zone car, and a sergeant opened the door and ordered Kent to stop. Kent tried to spit on the sergeant and began kicking the window again. The sergeant then sprayed OC spray in the man's face, over the spit sock. CDP records reflect that Kent was not immediately decontaminated, but rather was transported and not decontaminated until he arrived at the hospital. The use of OC spray was unnecessary. Moreover, spraying Kent through a spit sock, then requiring him to wear it, is cruel and amounts to unnecessary punishment. Yet, this tactic was not even questioned by the chain of command.

4. CDP officers use unreasonable force, including Tasers, against individuals with mental illness, individuals in medical crisis, and individuals with impaired faculties.

Another aspect of the pattern we found is that CDP officers too often use unreasonable force against individuals with mental illness, individuals in medical crisis, and individuals with impaired faculties who may be unable to comply with officers' demands or who may respond to officers erratically for reasons beyond their control. We recognize the challenges that people with mental illness, especially people in mental health crisis, pose to the delivery of police services. It is critical that CDP practices, particularly use of force practices, adequately take into account the population of people with mental illnesses CDP officers encounter and serve. The law requires officers to consider suspects' diminished capacity in assessing the appropriate level of force to use. *See Champion v. Outlook Nashville, Inc.*, 380 F.3d 893, 904 (6th Cir. 2004) (assessing reasonableness of force used on autistic detainee, finding, "[t]he diminished capacity of an unarmed detainee must be taken into account when assessing the amount of force exerted."); *see also Sheehan v. City of San Francisco*, 743 F.3d 1211, 1231-33 (9th Cir. 2014) (holding that Title II of the Americans with Disabilities Act applies to arrests). In *Martin v. City of Broadview Heights*, 712 F.3d 951, 954-55 (6th Cir. 2013), a mentally unstable 19-year-old, who was naked and "speaking quickly and nonsensically" died after officers repeatedly struck him in his face, back, and ribs; handcuffed him; and continued to restrain him face-down against the ground. The Sixth Circuit held that officers violated clearly established law when they failed to take into account that the arrestee was unarmed and "exhibited conspicuous signs that he was mentally unstable." *Id.* at 962. The Court found that the Fourth Amendment required the officers "to de-escalate the situation and adjust the application of force downward," and that "the officers ignored Martin's diminished mental state and used excessive force to control him." *Id.*

CDP officers, especially the majority who are not specially trained on this issue, do not use appropriate techniques or de-escalate encounters with individuals with mental illness or impaired faculties to prevent the use of force and, when force is used, officers do not adjust the application of force to account for the person's mental illness. In many of the incidents we reviewed, officers' interactions with individuals with mental illness were precipitated by calls for assistance from concerned family members or civilians, and did not involve any allegations that a crime had been committed. The Sixth Circuit has recognized that "the fact that a plaintiff [alleging excessive force] . . . ha[s] committed no crime clearly weigh[s] against a finding of reasonableness." *Ciminillo*, 434 F.3d at 467.

We reviewed one incident where—in response to a request for assistance—a CDP officer tased a suicidal, deaf man who committed no crime, posed minimal risk to officers and may not have understood officers' commands. "Larry's" mother had requested CDP's assistance because her son, who has bipolar disorder and communicates through sign language, was holding broken glass against his neck and threatening suicide. When officers arrived, Larry went into the bathroom and sat on the edge of a half-filled tub. The officers followed and, without confirming that Larry could communicate through notes, wrote him a note saying that he needed to go to the hospital. Larry waved his hands "aggressively," which the officers interpreted as refusal. One of the officers then grabbed Larry's arm. Larry pulled back, "struggling" with the officer. The other officer then yelled "Taser" and pointed his finger at his Taser. Larry continued to struggle, so the officer tased Larry in his chest. This use of force was unreasonable. As an initial matter, Larry may not have understood officers' commands. But even more importantly, Larry was not a threat to officers—he simply was pulling away from an officer, refusing to leave the bathroom, and he was not suspected of any crime. Officers should have attempted additional crisis intervention techniques instead of resorting to force against this suicidal male.

In another incident involving the use of a Taser against a person in crisis, a CDP officer tased a man, despite the fact that he was suffering a medical emergency and was strapped onto a gurney in the back of an ambulance, because he was verbally threatening officers. Two officers had been flagged down because the man was having seizures and, at the time, was lying on the sidewalk. When the officers spoke with "Mark," he told them that he suffers from grand mal seizures and that he had been drinking. Officers called EMS and, while waiting for EMS to arrive, observed Mark have at least four more seizures. When EMS arrived, officers assisted him into the ambulance, where he was strapped onto a gurney. Once strapped down, Mark became angry and threatened to punch one of the officers and one of the medics. He then tried to unstrap himself from the gurney and balled his fist, stating that he would prefer to walk home. One of the officers then unholstered his Taser, told Mark to calm down, and threatened three times to tase him. Mark continued to try to stand up while threatening to beat the officer. The officer then drive stunned Mark on his top left shoulder. Mark had committed no crime, was strapped down and was in the midst of a medical crisis. His repeated seizures may also have left him confused and disoriented. Indeed, there is no indication that Mark could carry out his threat against the officers, particularly when he was strapped to the gurney. The officers' decision to tase him under these circumstances was unreasonable and may have been counterproductive. *See* 2011 ECW Guidelines, at 14 (Using a Taser "to achieve pain compliance may have limited effectiveness and, when used repeatedly, may even exacerbate the situation by inducing rage in the subject").

We found several problems with officers' use of force on people who show obvious signs that they are under the influence of phencyclidine ("PCP") that resulted in constitutional violations, including many instances in which CDP officers unreasonably deployed their Tasers multiple times. These are highly volatile and dangerous situations. Based on our review of force reports, these encounters appear to be very common in Cleveland. Despite their prevalence, CDP fails to adequately address and train its officers to effectively respond to these volatile situations. We have seen these ill-prepared officers respond by using excessive force against these individuals, placing themselves and others in danger. In one such instance, officers deployed their Tasers 12 times against a man who was in the street, naked, and high on PCP, including eight times in drive stun mode. In another incident, officers repeatedly tased a handcuffed man who was high on PCP, again using the drive stun mode. The goal in addressing a dangerous situation should be to use the amount of force needed to protect the officer and the public, not to continually inflict pain on a suspect who is unable to rationally comply with police commands.

B. CDP officers commit tactical errors that endanger the Cleveland Community and reduce officer safety as well.

We found that CDP officers commit tactical errors that endanger themselves and other members of the community and may result in the use of excessive force. They too often carelessly and accidentally fire their weapons, at times seriously injuring people who were not a serious threat to officers and placing bystanders at unwarranted risk of serious injury and death. We also found that CDP officers too often fail to de-escalate confrontations and instead engage in questionable and dangerous tactics which place them in danger or result in their use of force that may not have been necessary. While these tactical errors may not always result in constitutional violations, they do at times, and moreover they place officers, suspects, and other members of the Cleveland community at risk. Especially in light of the broader pattern and practice we have observed, these incidents are legally significant.

1. CDP officers carelessly fire their weapons, placing themselves, subjects, and bystanders at unwarranted risk of serious injury or death.

We reviewed incidents in which officers carelessly or accidentally fired their weapons, at times critically injuring people, in instances where it may not have been appropriate to have drawn their firearms at all. An officer's decision to reach into a man's vehicle while the officer had his gun drawn and in his hand resulted in the officer shooting the man in the chest. "Nathan" had tried to make a right turn from the center lane, cutting off and almost colliding with a car that was proceeding straight through the intersection. It was 2:30 in the morning, and the area was crowded with pedestrians who had emptied out of the local bars and restaurants. Nathan was unable to complete the right turn because the street was blocked off, but by this time there were pedestrians crossing behind his vehicle, such that he could not back up into his lane. Consequently, he was stuck in the middle of the intersection, blocking traffic. At this point, an officer approached Nathan's vehicle with his gun drawn. The records of the incident provide no written basis to explain why he drew his gun, which is in itself a troubling fact. In his videotaped statement, the officer merely said he felt "uneasy" because he could not see Nathan's hands. With his gun pointed at Nathan, the officer ordered Nathan to turn off his ignition and to show the officer his hands. The officer claims Nathan did not obey these commands and that he had his right hand down where the officer could not see it. Nathan claims that he had his hands up and was afraid to move them because the officer was pointing his gun at him. When Nathan did not comply, the officer himself attempted to turn off the vehicle. To do so, he leaned his entire upper body into the car and, with his right hand, attempted to turn off the car. Meanwhile, his gun was in his left hand, pointed at Nathan, and his finger was on the trigger. He claims that he then felt force on his hand "like [Nathan] was trying to grab my weapon." The gun discharged, striking Nathan, who had been stopped originally for a potentially unlawful left turn, once in the chest.

This shooting resulted from poor tactics by the officer—both in pulling and pointing his gun and reaching into the car. These tactics resulted in an unnecessary and unreasonable use of force which, at the very least, resulted from the officer having made the dangerous choice to reach into a vehicle while holding his weapon. CDP's current use of force policy, which was in place at the time of this incident, prohibits officers from reaching into vehicles at all, let alone with their gun in their hands, because it is "extremely dangerous and can result in the officer being dragged by the vehicle." It is hard to believe that the officer would have made the decision to lean into the car to try to turn off the ignition if he really thought Nathan might be armed or reaching for a weapon. His decision to reach in with his gun in his hand, with his finger on the trigger, is even more difficult to explain and, in this instance, resulted in the shooting of an unarmed man who had been involved only in a minor traffic incident.

We reviewed incidents where officers accidentally shot their guns while pursuing suspects. In one instance, an officer's decision to draw his gun while trying to apprehend an unarmed hit-and-run suspect resulted in him accidentally shooting the man in the neck. The man was critically injured. One pattern we have observed is that CDP officers do not consider carefully enough their actions in drawing their weapons and pointing them at suspects, actions which may be necessary in some circumstances but which should be far from routine and fundamentally change the tenor of a police-civilian encounter.

We found that officers sometimes draw, point and/or fire their weapons without considering their environment, or the potential harm to bystanders or nearby residents. Officers do not adequately consider the potential destination of rounds fired especially if, as often happens, they miss their intended targets. In an incident from 2011 officers fired 24 rounds in a residential neighborhood, striking nearby houses and vehicles. Officers had responded to a scene where "Oscar" had allegedly shot his girlfriend and threatened to shoot officers, a very serious and dangerous situation. Nine officers arrived to find Oscar on the porch, waving a gun, and at times putting it to his head. Apparently suicidal, Oscar repeatedly told officers to shoot him. Officers approached with weapons drawn, telling Oscar to drop the gun. Oscar refused and began walking down the street, telling officers they would have to kill him. Officers followed. Oscar again put the gun to his head and then pointed it at officers. In response, five officers fired a total of 24 rounds. Three of the five officers fired more than six rounds each. By the time CDP officers stopped firing, six rounds had struck nearby residences; eleven rounds struck a pickup truck parked along a curb; two other rounds struck a second nearby parked pickup; and one round struck the passenger side pillar of an automobile parked along the curb. Oscar ended up in critical condition with gunshot wounds to his right buttocks, right calf, right foot, and left hip.

While we are not concluding that this response represents an application of unreasonable force, this incident illustrates several tactical errors that resulted in too many officers firing too many shots, placing residents of a neighborhood at risk of serious injury. CDP officers failed to follow basic, generally accepted techniques for responding to an armed suspect threatening suicide. For example, although there were nine officers on the scene, it appears that no one person was commanding or controlling the scene. A supervisor or the first-responding officer should have designated various locations from which the officers could seek cover and contain the movement of the suspect. No negotiator was called to the scene. Instead, the officers responding to the scene were unsupervised and grouped together with little or no cover. As a result of these poor tactics, officers placed themselves in harm's way and increased the likelihood that multiple officers would fire their weapons in response to a threat by the suspect. In this instance, the first CDP officer who opened fire appeared justified in doing so because the suspect pointed his weapon at officers. Other officers reported they fired their weapons because they thought the suspect was firing at them. He was not—the suspect's gun was later determined to be inoperable. A police force must be trained to deal with situations in which officers are firing their weapons and take efforts to ensure that officers are firing in response to suspect fire and not in response to fire from other officers. While no residents were inadvertently struck by the errant rounds, the actions CDP officers took in response to Oscars' actions created a scenario in which they unnecessarily subjected neighborhood inhabitants and one another to a heightened risk of death or serious injury.

2. CDP officers use other dangerous and poor tactics, placing members of the Cleveland community at risk.

We also found additional instances in which CDP officers used inappropriate and dangerous tactics that resulted in uses of force that may have been avoidable. We reviewed instances in which officers used force when they should have de-escalated the situation and used a lower level of force, or perhaps avoided the need to use force at all. This is especially true, and troublesome, in the instances described above in which officers used force against people who were in a mental health crisis. But we observed this troubling pattern in other contexts as well, especially where police officers essentially lost their patience with people who were not cooperating or who were verbally abusive to officers.

We also found other instances of poor and dangerous tactics that may have resulted in constitutional violations or other dangerous situations. When handcuffing or searching a suspect, for example, we found incidents in which Cleveland police officers lost control of the suspect, requiring the officers to use force that would not have been necessary had they used sound tactics in the first place that would have enabled them to maintain control. In one incident that illustrates this problem, officers lost control of a suspect during a pat down, used force to gain control of him, and then failed to locate a loaded gun on the suspect before placing him in the zone car and transporting him to jail. In May 2013, two officers approached "Paul" because he looked "suspicious" and might have been urinating in front of a store. After approaching Paul, an officer patted him down "for officer's safety." During the pat down, an officer located a kitchen knife. The officer then informed Paul that he was under arrest. Paul tried to pull away, but the officer's finger got caught in Paul's clothing, breaking the officer's finger. The other officer on scene then stepped in and "tackled" Paul, who was "actively resisting." Once Paul and the officer were on the ground, the officer punched Paul several times, including in his forehead, in the back of his head, and in the middle of his back. The officer who punched Paul did not write a report, and so it is impossible to tell how many times he punched Paul in the head, or the level of resistance he was encountering that he felt necessitated this use of force. The officers reported to the supervisor the conclusory, boilerplate statement that Paul was "actively resisting." The first officer then assisted in the struggle and the two were able to get Paul handcuffed. After transporting Paul to the Central Prison Unit for booking, the officers found a loaded gun in Paul's coat pocket.

Aside from the fact that the officer only used the boilerplate "actively resisting" language in the CDP report, it is troubling that officers lost control of a suspect while they were patting him down. This incident is not discussed because we are making a finding that the officer used too much force, but rather because it is impossible to tell from the record whether the amount of force used was appropriate or not and because the written record demonstrates that the officers' tactical errors exacerbated a very dangerous situation. Similarly, in the incident discussed above, involving "Jason," a handcuffed suspect escaped while officers were placing him in the zone car. To protect the community, officers must be able consistently to conduct basic police functions without losing control of suspects. Moreover, their loss of control of Paul and Jason required them to use greater force against these suspects, which otherwise may not have been necessary. Last, in Paul's case it obviously is extremely troubling that officers placed an armed man in the back of their zone car because they failed to find the loaded gun when they finally were able to complete the pat down.

Police officers are charged with the ultimate responsibility of protecting the public and keeping the peace—and they may employ the use of force, including deadly force, to do so. However, any use of force must be within the confines of the Fourth Amendment, and we have reasonable cause to believe that CDP officers engage in a pattern or practice of resorting to unreasonable amounts of force when encountering subjects. As discussed further below, the reasons underlying CDP's pattern of unreasonable force vary from its inadequate accountability systems to its failure to embrace and incorporate the concepts of community policing at all levels of CDP.

C. Systemic Deficiencies Cause or Contribute to the Excessive Use of Force.

Police departments have the ability and responsibility to detect and take steps to prevent the use of unreasonable force by their officers. The components of an effective use of force accountability system are well known. Police departments must ensure appropriate training in how and when to use force, and provide the supervision necessary for sufficient oversight of officers' use of force. Departments must also provide their officers clear, consistent policies on when and how to use and report force. Departments must implement systems to ensure that force is consistently reported and investigated thoroughly and fairly, using consistent standards and without regard to improper external factors or biases. The force investigation serves as the basis for reviewing the force incident to determine whether the officer acted both lawfully and consistently with departmental policy, as well as to determine whether the incident raises policy, training, tactical, or equipment concerns that need to be addressed for officer and civilian safety. Use of force aggregate data and trends should be monitored to enable the Division to identify and address emerging problems before they result in significant or widespread harm. CDP fails in all of these areas, and this has created an environment that permits constitutional violations. It has also created an atmosphere within CDP in which there is little confidence in the fairness of the disciplinary process—a lack of confidence which extends from the rank and file all the way to the highest levels of the Division and City leadership. Along with police practitioners, courts have long acknowledged that deficiencies in systems and operations can unequivocally lead or contribute to constitutional violations.

1. CDP Does Not Ensure that Officers Adequately Report the Force they Use.

A good accountability system begins with an appropriate record of the facts of an incident. That record is far too often lacking at CDP. To help ensure that misconduct and unsafe tactics are identified and can be prevented in the future, the facts of every use of force beyond unresisted handcuffing must be documented accurately and then reviewed fairly and thoroughly. Proper use of force reporting and review are essential parts of any police department's efforts to ensure that its officers are using force in a manner that complies with the Constitution and case law. Cleveland police officers do not adequately document force incidents, rendering it quite often impossible to tell how much force they have used and why.

Until recently, when a use of force incident occurred, each officer at the scene was not required to write a report documenting the incident. Instead, in the case of less lethal force, one officer (not even necessarily the one who applied the force) would typically write a report intended to summarize the actions and observations of every officer on scene. These summary reports made it impossible to discern whose account of events was being reported, making it difficult to hold any one officer accountable for his or her actions. Because only one officer was required to sign the report, there was no indication that the other named officers agreed with or even saw the description of events set forth in the report. Moreover, the officer writing the less lethal force report frequently was not the officer who used the force. At the time of our investigation, this practice was consistent with CDP policy.

CDP's use of force reports also suffer from additional deficiencies. Officers' reports repeatedly do not adequately convey the force they have used or why, and CDP therefore has no way of evaluating whether its officers are using force that is excessive, against policy, or that implicates tactical, training, or equipment concerns. Officers use canned or boilerplate language that does not describe with sufficient particularity the type of force they used. They say, for example, that they "employed a takedown maneuver" or that they "took [the subject] to the ground" or even "escorted [the subject] to the ground." This language does not adequately describe the level and type of force used for a supervisor to review and ensure that the force was within constitutional limits. Officers also commonly are unclear regarding exactly how they used a Taser—i.e., whether darts were deployed or whether drive stun was used. In some instances, when officers employ a Taser, they will use it multiple times without justifying each successive use. Officers also fail to adequately describe the level of the threat, if any, posed by those against whom force was used. They justify their use of force with non-specific language about subjects' actions such as "continued to resist" or "took an aggressive stance." And they frequently justify force by expressing a fear that a subject had a weapon without articulating any basis for that fear.

These deficiencies in officers' report writing and other shortcomings regarding use of force reporting are due, at least in part, to inadequacies in CDP's policies. Officers are giving to their supervisors precisely what is required of them, and supervisors are not requiring enough. In short, there is a boilerplate culture when it comes to use of force reporting. Though CDP has revised and improved its force and related policies, the current policies still provide insufficient guidance to officers on how to report force and what information the reports must contain. There is no requirement, for example, that officers describe with specificity the force they used, or the resistance they encountered. Instead, officers are directed to fill out the "action response continuum" section of the Division's "Use of Less Lethal Force Report." This section of the form contains a series of check boxes, with descriptions such as "other deadly force," "wrestling/pushing member," "striking," and "punching." The policies also contain no prohibition on using conclusory or boilerplate language to describe an officer's or suspect's actions. Additionally, CDP policy does not consider pointing a firearm at someone to be a use of force, and therefore officers are not required to report when they have done so. These shortcomings in CDP's policies inhibit supervisors' ability to review force and ensure that it is within constitutional limits.

In addition to inadequate policy guidance, we are also concerned that policies, as they exist, are not being followed a significant amount of the time. For example, it appears that force sometimes is not being reported at all, despite CDP policy that requires officers to report any force beyond unresisted handcuffing. During our interviews, officers and command staff alike evinced a poor understanding of when force must be reported. One commander stated that he does not believe a shove to be a use of force. Officers also told us that far from punishing an officer who failed to report a use of force, some supervisors discourage officers from reporting force. The policy requires that, when officers use force, they are to notify a supervisor, who is to come to the scene and, in the case of less lethal force, conduct a full investigation. Officers told us that some supervisors express annoyance that they have been called to the scene and have to perform the work necessary to conduct a use of force investigation. Officers reported to us that they sometimes do not call supervisors to the scene of a use of force (and do not otherwise report it) for fear of getting on the wrong side of their supervisor. Officers also told us that some supervisors, upon arriving on scene and assessing the force, instruct officers not to report it, especially where the person upon whom force was used did not receive any injuries.

Finally, none of the approximately 10 officers who participated in or witnessed the use of force against Edward Henderson, described above, filed the required written use of force report or otherwise documented that they had used or witnessed any force against Mr. Henderson. This is despite the fact that Henderson was taken to the hospital with a broken orbital bone and that numerous other officers were on the scene. In other words, officers did not report the force knowing that anyone who conducted an even cursory review of the situation would be able to determine that some force was used. Of course, documenting the incident would likely have required an officer to state the identity of those officers who applied the force in writing, something that has not occurred to this day. This example of an excessive use of force only came to light when the video of the incident surfaced. To date, no officers have identified any of the officers who used force in this incident, and no officers have been disciplined for failing to report this incident.

2. Supervisory Investigations of Force are Inadequate.

Compounding the problem of inadequate reporting, supervisors conduct insufficient reviews of officers' uses of less lethal force. They make little effort to determine the level of force that was used and whether it was justified. In some cases, supervisors take steps to justify a use of force that, on its face, was unreasonable. Of the hundreds of force incidents we reviewed, supervisors almost never found the force to be unreasonable. That is a record that is simply not credible even in the very best police department. Supervisors also fail to identify and rectify tactical deficiencies that place officers, suspects, and the community at serious risk of harm. In short, the Division is not identifying and preventing unlawful force committed by its officers.

Pursuant to CDP policy, whenever an officer uses force, the officer is to immediately notify a supervisor—typically a sergeant—who is to respond to the scene. In the case of less lethal force, the supervisor is to conduct an "objective, impartial, and complete investigation" of the use of force, by taking action that

includes interviewing all witnesses, reviewing all known videos and audio evidence, and checking the officers' reports for accuracy and completeness. GPO
2.1.01, Use of Force, §V.E (rev. Aug. 8, 2014). After completing the investigation,
the supervisor is required to write a synopsis of the event, including an evaluation of whether the force used was appropriate and in compliance with CDP
policy. The complete investigation packet is then to be sent up the chain of
command to a deputy chief, with approvals and appropriate recommendations
required at each level.

In practice, these supervisory investigations are cursory and too often
appear to be designed from the outset to justify officers' actions. The supervisory synopses often fail to identify necessary information that is missing in
the initial officers' reports, and not only do these inadequate reports not result
in discipline, but supervisors all the way up the chain of command sign off on
these deficient reports. Often, the language included in the supervisor's synopsis is simply a repetition of the language included in the officer's report that
itself is facially insufficient. The hundreds of less lethal force reports we reviewed were almost entirely devoid of any analysis by anyone in the chain of
command regarding whether the force was reasonable. Instead, they simply
state that use of force was within Division guidelines. It is almost as if the goal
of the chain of command in many incidents is *not* to create a complete record
of the incident that can be subjected to internal and external review, instead of
the opposite.

More specifically, supervisors fail to reconcile or to follow up on key facts or
discrepancies between officers', witnesses', and suspects' accounts, or discrepancies between the force described and injuries sustained by subjects, or any
other available evidence. Supervisors have even failed to hold officers accountable after discovering that officers misreported the force they used. In one incident, in which an officer apparently choked "Gwendolyn," a woman who was
handcuffed to a chair, the officer had written in his report that a fellow officer
had "attempted to grab the offender in the chest area." After reviewing security camera footage of the incident, however, the supervisor wrote that the
officer had grabbed the subject "by the front of the neck." The supervisor did
not take any action or follow up in any way on the fact that the officers had
mischaracterized the force they used. Instead, the supervisor approved this use
of force and did not feel the need to express any opinion regarding the fact
that the officer was minimizing the extent of the incident. The captain who
reviewed the investigative packet took no issue with the force used, the different characterizations of the force, or the numerous other deficiencies in the
investigation. Instead, he approved the use of force, noting that "although [he]
would not normally condone grabbing a handcuffed prisoner by the neck," the
limited space in the room and Gwendolyn's attempt to kick the officer justified
the officer's use of force. Supervisors' failure to follow up on discrepancies in

force reporting undermines CDP's accountability systems and allows unreasonable force to continue.

Indeed, supervisors' analyses of use of force incidents is superficial at best and, at its worst, appears to be designed to justify their subordinates' unreasonable use of force. The incident in which the officer punched the handcuffed 13-year-old in the face three to four times illustrates this problem. There, the officer weighed twice what the handcuffed boy weighed, and there was at least one other officer present who could have helped control him. The supervisor who reviewed the incident noted the size difference, the presence of other officers, and the fact that the boy was handcuffed, yet nevertheless found that this clearly excessive and punitive use of force was "arguably the best response." He justified the face punches because the boy had kicked the officer and attempted to escape the zone car. The supervisor failed to even consider that the punches might have been retaliatory (perhaps because the officer was angry) and unnecessary to secure the boy. He said that, while "at first review" other tactics such as joint manipulation, assistance from other officers, pressure point control, and other tactics might have been considered, to do so would be to view the incident with the benefit of hindsight and therefore inappropriate. This abdication of supervisory responsibility allows unreasonable uses of force to continue unchecked.

In addition to failing to identify and address excessive uses of force, supervisors fail to identify officers who have used poor or dangerous tactics, or who have broken Division rules relating to use of force, and may be in need of additional training or other corrective action. For example, we saw instances in which officers enlisted the assistance of passersby or bystanders to help gain control of and handcuff a suspect. While it is laudable for the public to seek to help the police, this practice of actively seeking public intervention is extremely dangerous and unprofessional—the person could easily be injured, or could interfere with or undermine the officer's efforts or, worse, attempt to hurt the officer or reach for the officer's weapon. Or, the person might use excessive force or tactics that violate the law or CDP policy. In none of these instances did a supervisor note that this practice was inappropriate or recommend training or counseling to discourage it. Moreover, some CDP officers justify the use of unreasonable force against handcuffed or restrained people by asserting that they have lost control of suspects. The use of force against handcuffed suspects should always be subjected to great scrutiny because it generally is unnecessary. Instead, we found instead that this practice is tolerated—that it is effectively presumed that each time an officer applies force to a handcuffed person that it is one of the rare cases when it was necessary —and, as a result, the practice is tacitly authorized by the Division.

In our review of these investigations, we saw no accountability for supervisors who conducted inadequate less lethal force investigations. In almost all instances, these inadequate reports and investigations were approved all the way up the chain of command with no comment. We saw very few instances in which supervisors up the chain of command conducted any analysis to determine if the use of force was Constitutional and within the established guidelines of CDP. By tolerating supervisors' failures to investigate uses of force, CDP misses the opportunity to correct dangerous behavior, and instead sends the message that there is little institutional oversight or concern about officers' use of force.

On a systemic, Division-wide level, our review of CDP policies and practices revealed that CDP does not examine and analyze force reports to detect common patterns and trends regarding officers' uses of force. Such analyses would help CDP identify disproportionate types of force, which can implicate a need for policy revisions as well as an adjustment to the supervisory review process. As discussed more thoroughly in this letter's section on Training, these analyses can also help pinpoint important topics for training or re-training.

As discussed in more detail later, one root cause of these deficiencies in supervisor review of use of force is a lack of experienced, well-supported, well-trained supervisors. Supervisors also reported that their workloads are simply unmanageable. Sergeants told us that "it's the worst job in the department" and "the work never stops," noting that they might be responsible for five less lethal force investigations during one shift in addition to various other duties. Sergeants also reported that they are isolated from others who have similar positions in different parts of the City, which could be an important source of training and support, and there are too few lieutenants to provide needed guidance and support. For instance, some sergeants reported that they may only see the Lieutenant assigned to their platoon once each week. More broadly, supervisors appeared to have difficulty balancing their responsibility to effectively lead, manage, and hold officers accountable. The level of discomfort with these responsibilities is an indication that CDP is not providing supervisors with the training, guidance, resources, or support required to perform their jobs effectively. Many of these individuals enter the force wanting to excel at their work and serve the public, but they report that their enthusiasm and morale is quickly sapped by a structure that does not provide them with the tools they need to succeed in their jobs.

3. CDP's Internal Review Mechanisms are Inadequate.

Inadequacies in CDP's internal investigation and review mechanisms also contribute to the pattern or practice of unreasonable force that we identified. CDP has several components that share responsibility for investigating officers' alleged violations of criminal law or Division policy and holding officers accountable if violations are found: the Use of Deadly Force Investigation team, the Office of Professional Standards, the Internal Affairs Unit, and the Inspection Unit. CDP has several policies and manuals that attempt to define the varying responsibilities of these components, but we found that the division of labor was unclear, allowing violations of Division policies to slip between the cracks. Moreover, some responsibilities conferred to particular components by policy are not fulfilled in practice. For example, CDP policy dictates that the Office of Professional Standards, which is primarily responsible for investigating civilian complaints, and the Internal Affairs Unit both investigate an officer's use of deadly force to determine if the officer violated Division policy. In practice, the Office of Professional Standards apparently has not conducted a proper investigation of an officer's use of deadly force since 2012.

During interviews, some members of CDP's staff expressed confusion about which component is responsible for carrying out which particular duties and why. Even with full access to CDP's staff, policies, and procedures, we found the Division's accountability systems to be difficult to navigate; it is unlikely that civilians seeking information on how a particular complaint or investigation will be handled will find a clear answer. Moreover, the lack of clarity regarding who is responsible for what interferes with competent investigations and consistent and fair adjudication of discipline.

a. CDP Fails to Adequately Investigate and Hold Officers Accountable for Misconduct.

Our review found that several of CDP's systems for investigating and holding officers accountable for the use of excessive force are flawed, including Internal Affairs, the Use of Deadly Force Investigation Team, and the Tactical Review Committee. In some cases, these flaws prevented the Division from holding officers accountable for serious misconduct. The deficiencies were apparent in both the quality of the investigations and the outcome of those investigations. The quality of the investigations is compromised by investigators' apparent bias in favor of clearing the officer instead of objectively pursuing all of the available facts—a bias that more than one investigator actually admitted to our team. Many investigations also lacked key documents and appeared incomplete, further undermining their quality. And CDP's improper use of *Garrity* warnings may severely interfere with investigations and prosecutions of criminal misconduct by officers.

i. The Internal Affairs Unit and the Use of Deadly Force Investigation Team do not conduct thorough and objective investigations of alleged officer misconduct.

CDP's Internal Affairs Unit is responsible for providing guidance to supervisors regarding officers' alleged involvement in criminal activity and "investigat[ing] all incidents as directed by the Chief of Police." Internal Affairs also investigates any allegation that a CDP officer violated Division policy, unless the allegation arose out of the use of deadly force. Deadly force investigations are conducted by the Division's Use of Deadly Force Investigation Team ("UDFIT"). The UDFIT team does not determine whether the use of deadly force violated criminal law or Division policy, however. It only investigates the incident. Internal Affairs then reviews the UDFIT file and conducts any additional investigation necessary to determine if the officer violated Division policies. CDP's chain of command also reviews the UDFIT file, and it is forwarded to the Prosecutor's Office for review.

While the investigations conducted by the UDFIT team are more thorough than less lethal force investigations, we observed deficiencies in how detectives approached uses of deadly force that were not clearly justified. The reviews appeared to be biased in favor of clearing the officer as opposed to gaining a full and objective understanding of the incident. During officer interviews, for example, detectives asked leading questions, failed to ask important follow-up questions, and failed to resolve inconsistencies. In some instances, investigators failed to take basic investigatory steps. These failures resulted in determinations in favor of the officer that may not have been justified had an adequate investigation been conducted. Indeed, during our interviews with UDFIT investigators, one UDFIT investigator told us that he assumed the officer's use of force was reasonable in 98 percent of the cases. Other UDFIT investigators told us that they intentionally cast an officer in the best light possible when investigating the officer's use of deadly force.

Similarly, our review of Internal Affairs (or "IA") investigations found they frequently lacked key documents, such as transcripts or comprehensive summaries of officer interviews. The quality of investigations, including deadly force investigations, is further compromised by the investigators' failure to ask key questions and take important investigatory steps. Even more troubling, however, is that multiple IA investigators are applying an inappropriate standard of proof when conducting administrative investigations. When we specifically asked several IA investigators what standard they applied, they struggled to find an answer before deciding on "beyond a reasonable doubt." Only one IA investigator responded with the less stringent—and appropriate—"preponderance of the evidence" standard. That raises the probability that for years the great majority of IA investigations have been using a "beyond a reasonable doubt" criminal law standard. These failures fundamentally undermine CDP's ability to hold officers accountable. Indeed, we reviewed investigations where it was clear that CDP should have taken swift action to address an officer's conduct but failed to do so. For example, Internal Affairs reviewed the 2013 incident in which an officer shot at a victim as he ran from the house where he was being held against his will. Internal Affairs determined that there were no violations of Division policy and recommended that the investigation be closed without further action. This is an unacceptable outcome. This case almost resulted in tragedy, and it arose from circumstances that are likely to repeat themselves. At a minimum, Internal Affairs should have recognized the need for remedial training.

In another incident discussed earlier, an off-duty officer without any means of identifying himself as an officer inappropriately approached a group of suspects without backup and struck a civilian in the head with his service weapon during a struggle. The officer's use of force in this incident was excessive and he demonstrated poor tactical decisions that placed him and others in danger. Internal Affairs determined that the officer's actions were justified and that no further action should be taken. In addition to failing to recommend further action, in both of the above examples, the officers were referred to in the files by investigators as the "victim," despite the fact that the officers had used excessive force, in one instance against a crime victim the officer had come to rescue.

ii. CDP applies *Garrity* protections too broadly.

CDP applies *Garrity* protections too broadly, potentially compromising criminal prosecutions of officers who have committed acts of criminal misconduct. *Garrity v. New Jersey*, 385 U.S. 493 (1967) prohibits a police department from compelling an employee, through the threat of termination, to provide self-incriminating statements and then subsequently using those statements in a criminal prosecution. However, departments can and should give officers the opportunity to provide voluntary statements. Officers may be willing to give statements without being compelled to do so. Indeed, in many instances, an officer's willingness to provide a statement at the outset of the investigation allows the investigation to proceed more quickly, expeditiously resolves questions of officer misconduct, and identify opportunities to improve tactical and scenario-based training.

CDP has not developed an appropriately nuanced approach when providing *Garrity* warnings and protections to officers' statements regarding their uses of force. It is our understanding that the county prosecutor determines whether officers will receive *Garrity* protections regarding the use of deadly force. Although the prosecutor should be consulted and precautions should be taken to make sure the criminal investigation is not tainted, in all use of force incidents CDP should make an independent determination of when and whether to issue *Garrity* warnings in order to ensure that it meets its obligation to administratively investigate potential violations of CDP's policies in a timely manner. Even more importantly, however, CDP's current practice, as mandated by its Internal Affairs manual, is to provide *Garrity* warnings and protections for all statements made in administrative investigations. In at least some of these instances, however, officers may not be entitled to *Garrity* protections. For *Garrity* to apply, the officer must have wanted to invoke his or her Fifth Amendment rights, but was prevented from doing so by the threat of termination. These circumstances will not be present in all administrative investigations. As a result of CDP's current practices, officers' statements cannot be used in a criminal case even though officers may have been willing to provide statements without being compelled to do so, or may not have been entitled to *Garrity* protections at all. This overly-broad invocation of *Garrity* may result in the exclusion of important evidence from an investigation, including exculpatory evidence that would clear the officer. Moreover, while CDP's procedures note that "[e]very measure shall be taken to ensure that a one-way fire wall will exist between concurrent criminal and administrative investigations" to prevent the compelled statement or any information derived from that statement from being used in the criminal investigation, CDP's policies do not outline how this should occur. This failure may result in tainted criminal prosecutions.

Internal Affairs also fails to adequately investigate civilian complaints that officers used excessive force. Per policy, when the Office of Professional Standards receives a civilian complaint that it determines includes allegations of criminal misconduct, including excessive force, it is to refer the case to Internal Affairs for investigation. As discussed in the following section, investigations of misconduct referred to Internal Affairs through the civilian complaint process were routinely substandard—they are often limited to an interview of the complainant and the collection of basic documents. Internal Affairs failed to take additional necessary steps to investigate these allegations.

iii. CDP does not implement appropriate corrective measures.

Finally, our review of CDP's practices for implementing corrective measures, including discipline against individual officers and changes in tactics or training, revealed several troubling practices. For example, we found instances where an investigation was complete and administrative charges were brought, but the case remained "pending" for an unreasonably lengthy period. In some cases, the reason for the delay was unclear and in other cases the reason for the delay was clear, but not legitimate. We reviewed one instance, for example, where CDP delayed its disciplinary process because of a pending civil case. According to OPS records, the Police Review Board sustained the complaint but, nearly four years later, the case continues to be listed as "pending" in documents tracking CDP's disciplinary decisions. A pending civil case is not a valid reason for delaying CDP's internal disciplinary processes. It can be many years before a civil lawsuit is fully resolved. This practice prevents the Division from swiftly holding officers accountable and sends a message to other officers that they need not fear discipline for their actions.

Also of concern is CDP's threshold for determining that officers have been held accountable for serious misconduct. For example, CDP reported to us that from 2010 through early May 2014, 51 officers had been disciplined related to uses of force. Our review of the particular incidents to which CDP referred showed that discipline for the majority of cases involved either procedural infractions such as failure to submit a timely report, or instances where officers actually suffered no consequences because hearings were not held in time or charges were dismissed for other unexplained reasons. CDP's portrayal of these cases as officers being disciplined in connection with use of force indicates a problematic view of what constitutes holding officers accountable.

Similarly, as part of its deadly force review process, CDP has established a Tactical Review Committee that is responsible for "review[ing] relevant documents, confer[ring] with appropriate technical experts, and decid[ing] recommendations on training, tactics, and equipment issues," but this committee is not being appropriately utilized. CDP policy states that the Tactical Review Committee is to review all deadly force incidents once any criminal, UDFIT, and administrative reviews are complete, yet it appears that, in practice, tactical reviews do not always occur. Though we requested all documents regarding all reviews completed by the Tactical Review Committee between January 1, 2010 and June 28, 2013, we received only 15 reviews from that time period. CDP provided none from 2010 and 2013, and only seven from 2011 and eight from 2012. For context, CDP officers were involved in 23 use of deadly force incidents in 2011 and 22 use of deadly force incidents in 2012. We understand the Tactical Review Committee does not necessarily review a use of deadly force incident during the same calendar year in which the use of force took place, particularly if the incident took place late in the year. Nevertheless, these delays in the review process are unacceptable and allow failures in policy, training, and tactics to continue, potentially resulting in the further use of excessive force due to the same deficiency. We found that eight of the 15 deadly force incidents reviewed were not reviewed until at least a year had passed; four additional incidents were not reviewed until three or four years had passed. Two of the incidents reviewed in 2012 occurred in 2008, and two other incidents reviewed in 2012 occurred in 2009. The utility of these reviews, three to four years after the incident occurred, is greatly diminished.

Even when these reviews are completed, however, many of them are inadequate. Reviewers devoted no more than a single page to many incidents and failed to identify basic failures in training and tactics. Tactical reviews should examine every aspect of a call from dispatch to disposition, and reviewing officers should offer substantive commentary and analysis. Yet many reviewing officers do no more than write "Reviewed" on the form. In three of the tactical reviews, training was recommended, but we did not see any evidence that the recommendations were adopted. We also note that CDP has no equivalent process to review less lethal force incidents, even if the less lethal force resulted in serious injuries. Because of these failures, the Tactical Review Committee does not perform its intended function and undermines CDP's ability to identify and address deficiencies that are resulting in the use of excessive force.

b. CDP Fails to Adequately Investigate Civilian Complaints of Officer Misconduct.

An effective and transparent system for investigating civilian complaints of misconduct is a critical element of a police department's accountability system to prevent the use of excessive force. The Charter of the City of Cleveland requires OPS to conduct "a full and complete investigation" of each complaint of police misconduct filed by a civilian. CDP's policies recognize that, in order to ensure that officers "serve the community in a[n] . . . accountable manner," there should be "a readily accessible process" to submit complaints of misconduct. CDP's investigations of these complaints should be "timely and thorough" to both "protect citizens from police misconduct and members from complaints that are retaliatory, manipulative or simply misunderstanding of police protocol." *Id.* But is apparent that the reality falls far short of the written policies on these matters. Our review revealed that CDP's investigations are neither timely nor thorough, that civilians face a variety of barriers to completing the complaint process, and that the system as a whole lacks transparency. As a result, CDP falls woefully short of meeting its obligation to ensure officer accountability and promote community trust.

During our previous investigation of CDP, completed in 2004, we noted significant concerns regarding the civilian complaint process. We concluded that OPS was understaffed; investigators were not provided with the guidance and resources necessary to do their jobs effectively; investigations were untimely; civilians' access to the complaint process was limited; and some complaints that should have been investigated were not. More than ten years later, these problems remain and, in some cases, have worsened. Current deficiencies in the complaint process include impossibly high caseloads for investigators, the inappropriate and premature rejection of civilians' complaints, substandard investigations, significant delays in completing investigations, and the failure to document and track outcomes.

We discovered a troubling pattern of OPS inappropriately rejecting complaints that may have warranted an investigation. Specifically, CDP policy permits complaints to be "administratively withdrawn" in limited circumstances.

For example, the OPS administrator has the authority to administratively withdraw "[c]omplaints regarding citizens receiving Uniformed Traffic Tickets (UTT)," but only "if the complaint is based entirely on the belief that the citizen did not deserve the UTT . . . because they did not violate the law." Despite this strict limitation, we reviewed examples of OPS withdrawing complaints that alleged that an officer engaged in misconduct. The alleged misconduct occurred during the issuance of a ticket, but the complaint was not "based entirely on the belief that the citizen did not deserve the UTT." Instead, it alleged that the officer violated the law or Division policy. These complaints should have been investigated.

In other instances, OPS inappropriately closed or administratively withdrew civilians' complaints solely for "lack of response" or "lack of cooperation." OPS's manual only permits administrative withdrawal on this basis where there is no other information on which to base an investigation. In addition, investigators must first have made diligent efforts to reach the complainant. In practice, however, OPS routinely closes cases after little effort to reach the complainant and despite other information upon which to base an investigation. When complainants "fail to cooperate" with an investigation, CDP should continue the investigation when it has enough information to do so, because CDP has an independent interest in ferreting out misconduct by its officers. Indeed, it has an obligation to do so. Complainants may seek to withdraw complaints or fail to continue to cooperate for reasons wholly unrelated to the merits of their complaints. Moreover, a policy of discontinuing investigations where complainants fail to cooperate may result in subtle or overt efforts by investigators or officers to discourage complainants from proceeding.

When a civilian's complaint is accepted for investigation, investigations are frequently delayed and substandard. OPS does not have sufficient investigative staff to investigate complaints in a timely and thorough manner. Some investigators reported that, while they would prefer to conduct more comprehensive investigations, their staggering caseloads make it impossible to take even some basic investigative steps such as seeking out witnesses or visiting the scene of the alleged misconduct. Underscoring the dire need for additional OPS investigators, our recent review revealed that, on average, complaints take six months to complete, which is far longer than is appropriate. We saw many complaints that took more than a year to resolve—a delay that is unreasonable both to the civilian looking for resolution and the officers who bear the burden of recalling the details of the incident. OPS staff reported that, due to the sheer volume, "We just can't touch some complaints." For dozens of complaints, we saw no record they were ever resolved, indicating that the complaints simply fell through the cracks—an unacceptable outcome in a functioning civilian complaint process.

OPS investigations are also frequently substandard. The OPS Manual provides little guidance on the steps that should be taken in order to conduct a thorough investigation, leaving officers to their own devices and resulting in investigations that are inconsistent in content and quality. The investigations we reviewed consistently lacked basic follow up, such as going to the scene and seeking out witnesses. Even when a complaint alleges that an officer engaged in serious misconduct, the entire investigative file may consist only of officer statements, the complainant's signed form and recorded interview, and little, if any, additional documentation. Pursuant to policy, OPS investigators do not interview the involved officer unless the officer requests an oral interview in lieu of a written response. As a result, OPS investigators must rely on written questions and answers to probe the validity of a civilian's complaint, to assess inconsistencies in police reports, or to evaluate the officer's credibility in re-counting his or her version of events. Therefore, an effective investigative in-terview of an officer is impossible. This undermines the investigative process. Additionally, in many of the OPS files we reviewed, it was not clear whether an investigation ever took place or whether the complaint was ever resolved.

CDP's complaint intake process makes it difficult for complainants to suc-cessfully make complaints in the first instance. In 2002, we asked that CDP "work with the appropriate union officials to permit the CDP to investigate all citizen complaints, whether signed and written in the complainant's hand-writing or not." However, pursuant to CDP policy, the Division still does not investigate all of the complaints it receives—only those that are signed by the complainant. Thus, CDP will not accept anonymous or third-party complaints. This process, which appears to be a result of the Collective Bargaining Agree-ment between the City and the officer's union, appears to be designed to make it difficult for victims of police misconduct to successfully make complaints. The City must work with the unions to ensure that it is able to investigate all complaints, including from anonymous and third party complainants, whether signed or unsigned.

Once OPS completes its investigation of a complaint, the civilian Police Review Board reviews it and reaches a disposition. The Board's review of these investigations is likewise inadequate. First, the Board's review is based on in-adequate information. Investigators are not invited to attend meetings and, as a result, Board members have no opportunity to discuss cases with the inves-tigators who are the most familiar with them. Additionally, the Board has in-explicably instructed investigators not to include an officer's prior complaint and disciplinary history in the investigative file. The Board's failure to assess an officer's prior conduct interferes with its evaluation of the credibility of the current complaint and impedes its ability to discern potential patterns of mis-conduct.

Second, the Board's decisions lack transparency, which, in turn, undermines accountability. The Board's case files frequently lack final dispositions and, when dispositions are included, there is no evidence of the Board's rationale supporting its decisions. The problems inherent in this practice are demonstrated when the Board sustains a complaint and recommends discipline. The Board members play no role in any disciplinary conference. Rather, OPS investigators, who were excluded from the Board's decision-making process, are required to defend the Board's disposition and disciplinary recommendations at the Chief's conferences. Neither the Chief nor the investigators have the benefit of knowing the Board's rationale. The Board's failure to justify its decisions in writing makes the civilian review process less transparent, places an unnecessary burden on investigators, and increases the likelihood that the Board's decisions will be overturned. Moreover, when the Board's recommendations are overturned, complainants are not informed of this fact, further reducing the transparency of the process. This system is likely to produce ill-informed decisions and unfounded results.

Finally, the Police Review Board and OPS are not fulfilling their obligation to review deadly force incidents. Under the City Charter, the Police Review Board has immense power to review deadly force incidents. The Board may issue subpoenas, compel witnesses, and order that relevant documents be produced. Moreover, the OPS Manual requires OPS and the Board to review deadly force investigations and requires that the OPS Administrator be called to the scene following a use of deadly force. After reviewing a use of deadly force investigation, the Board has the authority to hold a public hearing on the incident or recommend a change in police procedure. The Use of Deadly Force Investigation Team's manual further permits OPS to decide that an officer should be charged with violating Division policy or receive reinstruction or training.

In practice, Board members and OPS staff reported that they have little involvement in the review of deadly force incidents. The Board has not reviewed an UDFIT investigation since early 2012. This failure undermines community confidence. If the Board and OPS were to appropriately utilize their authority, they could serve as the community's eyes and ears during deadly force investigations, increasing the transparency of the process, and giving voice to the community's concerns by shaping CDP policy and ensuring that any officer who uses deadly force without justification is held accountable and that those who are justified benefit from the community's confidence that the review process was fair and effective.

CDP's civilian complaint system, as a whole, is disorganized and ineffective. CDP was only able to produce a fraction of the case files we requested, and the files produced were often incomplete and lacked basic information about dispositions and outcomes. CDP does not have systems in place to track its performance or decision-making regarding civilian complaints. CDP should have such tracking ability, including the types of complaints it receives, against which officers, and whether those complaints were sustained, unfounded, administratively withdrawn, or closed for other reasons, and what, if any, discipline resulted. CDP should also have mechanisms in place to accurately collect, analyze, and report the critical information that can be derived from civilian complaints, such as areas where additional officer training may be necessary. In addition, CDP has no systems in place to track the performance of OPS and the Police Review Board. While the OPS Manual requires that OPS issue periodic reports and statistical analyses, we found no evidence that this occurs. OPS has not produced an Annual Report that we were shown in three years. Given these deficiencies, and others detailed above, CDP's complaint process has little legitimacy in a City that would benefit greatly from an effective system for addressing the community's concerns regarding its police force.

4. CDP Officers are Inadequately Supported and Trained.

Our review of reports and investigations of officers' use of force, both deadly and less lethal, revealed that CDP officers lack some of the basic support, skills, and knowledge required to safely and effectively respond to situations that commonly arise in law enforcement encounters. We saw evidence that officers do not know how to safely and effectively control subjects. In some cases, officers reported that they lost control of handcuffed subjects and in many instances officers were unable to handcuff a subject, at times resulting in the application of significant force, or in the enlisting of a passerby to help gain control of the subject. We also saw officers' over-reliance on Tasers, and a propensity to too readily draw and even point their firearms, which may be a result of officers' lack of confidence that they will be able to control a situation. Officers also sometimes do not appear to know how to safely handle firearms. We saw too many incidents in which officers accidentally shot someone, either because they fired their guns accidentally, or because they shot the wrong person. In additional incidents, it was pure luck that officers did not accidentally shoot a suspect, a bystander, or another officer. CDP needs to ensure that its officers are properly trained; that the training is reinforced through ongoing training and instruction; and that officers are consistently held accountable for failing to abide by their training. Its failure to do so has contributed to the pattern or practice of excessive force that we identified and has placed officers and the community in danger.

CDP does not have effective mechanisms in place to ensure that its officers have received training that is adequate in its content, quality, and quantity. It is critical for a major city police department the size of Cleveland's to have in place ways to evaluate and analyze its training, and to build and revise training programs based on an objective review of trends identified in force reports, civilian complaints, and disciplinary proceedings, as well as changes in the law and emerging issues in the field. CDP lacks many of these mechanisms.

CDP provides its recruit classes with more than the minimum number of hours required by the state, and the number of hours it provides is similar to other departments of its size. However, CDP has not engaged in enough analysis to determine whether the number of hours overall and the content of the training it provides are sufficient for its recruits, or whether the content of the training has been absorbed by the recruits by examining their behavior once they leave the academy. CDP does not devote enough time to some important use of force topics. For example, CDP does not devote enough time to teaching its recruits about its use of force policies. Many officers told us that they do not understand the use of force policies. In its August 2013 report, PERF noted that CDP was only providing four hours of classroom instruction to recruits regarding the basis and legal background of its use of force policies, and that civil liability was also included in this single four-hour block. As stated above, civil liability is a wholly different concept than following CDP policies, and it too often seems to drive the basic review of a use of force incident at CDP. It appears that, since the report was issued, CDP has added an additional four-hour class regarding constitutional issues and CDP use of force policies. If true, one day may still be insufficient for a topic as important as use of force policies.

CDP also has not conducted sufficient analysis to determine whether its in-service training is sufficient or appropriate. Based on our review, not enough in-service training hours are devoted to use of force topics. CDP does have an in-service Training Review Committee that reviews the curriculum and lesson plans for in-service training programs. The committee also develops training topics and is tasked with ensuring that training complies with relevant laws and policies. However, there appears to be little hard analysis behind the committee's methods—members have no data analysis or any other tool with which to analyze training needs. The committee does review use of force investigations and determines whether training topics can be gleaned from those incidents. However, as described below, these measures are insufficient.

CDP should regularly be examining and analyzing force reports to identify deficiencies in training. Currently, the Division does not engage in any analysis of force reports to discover trends, including whether the reports indicate there may be a department-wide issue in a particular area. Indeed, when we asked CDP to provide us with all less lethal force reports for a given time period, it was not able to produce them in a coherent or organized fashion. It is clear that CDP itself has not attempted to analyze these reports to discover on its own the trends we identified during our review. For example, during our review of deadly force investigations, we discovered that many officers do not safely handle their firearms, and they make poor decisions as to whether it is appropriate or safe to fire them. In more than one incident we reviewed, including the November 29, 2012, shooting deaths of Ms. Williams and Mr. Russell, officers justified having fired their guns on the stated belief that the suspect was firing at them when in fact the gunfire was coming from other officers. We also saw instances in which officers shot someone and claimed that the shooting was accidental. Alarming trends such as these should be identified by the Division and then training should be evaluated to ensure that, in the future, officers have received training sufficient in content and quality to correct these obvious deficiencies.

We also discovered that officers do not effectively de-escalate situations, either because they do not know how, or because they do not have an adequate understanding of the importance of de-escalating encounters before resorting to force whenever possible. They also are sometimes unable to safely and effectively control subjects, resulting in dangerous situations and situations in which officers resort to more force than would have been required had the officer been well-trained. Many officers told us they believe they do not receive enough training, especially scenario-based training and training on appropriate techniques to control subjects. That should change.

CDP also does not provide sufficient and current training on new and revised policies. When a policy is revised, even significantly so, officers are advised of that change in roll-call. Officers informed us that no training accompanies that advisement—the new or revised policy simply is distributed to officers and read aloud. The officer in charge of the training division informed us that no training on that revised policy will occur until the next in-service training, which may be many months away. During our investigation, we observed the inadequacies of this practice with regard to two policies that recently had been revised. CDP recently changed its vehicle pursuit policy to, among other things, limit the crimes for which officers may pursue suspects. This change is important, and in line with national best practices. Officers, however, expressed that they did not understand why the change was made or how it should be implemented. They also expressed their feelings that it was simply an inappropriate overreaction to the November 29, 2012, pursuit and would interfere with their ability to do their jobs effectively. We observed a similar reaction to the Division's decision in response to our recommendation, and consistent with national best practices, to require all officers who observe or use force to write their own report documenting what they saw and did. Again, officers did not understand why the change was made, how it should be implemented, or how it would benefit them. If officers had received formal, coherent training on these policy revisions, including how they will benefit officers and increase safety, their reactions may have been more positive. Moreover, this training would have allowed CDP to ensure that all officers understand the policies and could be held accountable for abiding by them.

CDP also fails to ensure that officers abide by their training and that the practices taught in the academy reflect the actual practices of the Division. For example, we reviewed CDP's curriculum for its training regarding report writing and found that it appropriately instructs officers to avoid police jargon and canned, inexact phrases such as "furtive movement," "suspicious activity," and "suspect resisted." However, we consistently found these phrases and similar ones throughout officers' reports, and these reports were accepted and even endorsed by supervisors. We also saw frequent instances in which officers clearly violated CDP policy, and these violations were neither identified nor corrected by supervisors. And, in most of the instances of excessive force we identified, supervisors all the way up the chain of command approved the use of force as appropriate. Regardless of what officers learn in the academy or in-service training, in the field officers learn that policy violations, unsafe practices, and—ultimately—excessive force are all acceptable to CDP when supervisors fail to hold officers accountable to the policies and training that are in place.

5. CDP's Use of Force Policy is Still Deficient.

Deficiencies in CDP's use of force policy also contribute to the pattern or practice of excessive force that we found. The use of force policy has changed, but the policy in place at the time of our investigation was confusing, at times conflicted with the law, and did not provide sufficient guidance to officers. Indeed, many officers reported to us that they did not understand the policy and, more generally, did not understand what level of force they were permitted to use under what circumstances. In August 2014, the Division revised its use of force policy to provide additional guidance to officers as to when and how officers may use force. We are encouraged by the Division's efforts to revise the policy and its stated commitment to reform. We still have some concerns about the revised policy, however, as well as the Division's implementation of this and other significant policy changes.

The revised policy remains confusing about when officers may use various levels of force and appears to authorize some of the excessive force we found in our review. For example, the "action response" continuum, which officers are to fill out as part of their less lethal force report, includes an actual check box for hitting someone on the head with a firearm. As an initial matter, it is unclear why a less lethal force report includes a section for deadly force options. It is also unclear why CDP appears to be categorizing hitting someone with a gun as a conventional response when force is needed. This is uniformly understood to be a dangerous practice that should never be permitted except in very unusual and exigent circumstances in which the use of deadly force is authorized; yet, it was a practice we saw CDP officers engaging in too frequently. Additionally, the policy's definition of "Actively Resistant/Self-

Destructive Behavior" includes a warning that officers are to be "particularly vigilant of persons presenting cues of an imminent attack" and, as an example of such a cue, lists "yawning with outstretched arms" and "glancing around, assessing the environment." Officers cannot meaningfully apply this definition, given that the policy appears to authorize significant force, including the use of Tasers, against people because they are yawning with outstretched arms or are glancing around, but do not pose an immediate threat. The policy's definition of "Actively Resistant/Self-Destructive Behavior" also includes the action of ingesting narcotics, and thus indicates that an appropriate response may include the use of the Taser. Tasing someone who is trying to destroy evidence by swallowing it can cause the person to choke and die.

The revised force policy also lacks sufficient guidance as to how force should be reported. It does not require specificity in officers' descriptions of the force used and resistance encountered. Instead, it directs officers to describe the force and resistance by checking boxes in the "Action Response section" on the related form. There is no requirement in the policy that an additional explanation of each of these actions be included in a narrative. The revised force policy still does not include the pointing of a firearm at a person in the definition of force, and does not require officers to report having pointed a firearm at a person. The dangers inherent in such a policy choice have played themselves out in Cleveland—officers draw and/or point their firearms too quickly, perhaps because they do not think of it as something that must be justified by the circumstances they are facing. As we have seen, officers' decisions to draw their firearms have resulted in unnecessary escalations of force, accidental discharges, and dangerous hands-on encounters with suspects while officers are holding their guns. Another consequence of failing to include this action as a reportable use of force is that supervisors do not even know that it has occurred unless it resulted in the use of force or occurred in conjunction with other types of force. Even in these instances, investigators do not investigate the propriety of the officer's decision to have drawn the gun in the first place and instead make conclusory statements about it being done "for officer safety." As a result, no one in CDP knows how often officers are pointing their firearms or under what circumstances, and the Division is unable to identify and rectify training and tactical concerns that this behavior may raise.

This is an example of how a policy decision has enormous ramifications for CDP's ability to engage in effective community policing. When officers point their guns at people without proper justification, even if the encounter does not progress any further, it can be a traumatic event for the citizen. Done enough, communities can come to feel as if they are under siege. Then, instead of seeing the police as an agency that is there to protect them and their communities, they come to see officers as a force that is there to control them through fear. This mentality fosters distrust of the police, reduces cooperation, and interferes with CDP's ability to fight crime while ensuring officer safety.

Officers also reported that official policy does not reflect the practices of the Division, in part because they do not have the technology or equipment to follow policy. A near-universal refrain from officers was that the policies are used to discipline officers when a significant event comes to light, even where the officer's actions reflected the practice of the entire Division and instructions from supervisors. In other words, officers believe that high publicity events are treated differently in terms of discipline by CDP than uses of force that no one is watching. If true, that would also tend to erode community confidence in the police. Although officers do not want to be disciplined, of course, they are more willing to accept consequences when they believe that the result, whether they agree with it or not, is not influenced by external factors but is driven wholly by the facts, the law, and policies that govern their actions.

CDP has expressed a willingness to revise its policies, and has proactively sought input from the Department of Justice and others as to how its policies should be revised. The Division also has quickly responded to suggestions regarding deficiencies in its policies. That is laudable, however, its response has not always been effective. For example, we raised with CDP our concern that not all officers who use or witness force are required to report it. CDP agreed to begin requiring officers to write these reports. While we are encouraged by the Division's response to that feedback, the implementation of this change was carried out haphazardly. Though CDP has now changed its policy to require all officers at the scene of a use of force to write a narrative describing the incident, initially, a deputy chief simply sent an email to the command staff informing them that, effective immediately, all officers on the scene of a less lethal force incident are each to complete a memorandum, to be included in the investigative file, detailing their actions. Officers informed us that they were told of the change in roll-call, but received no explanation of the reasoning behind the change, nor did they receive any training on what it meant or how to implement it. They expressed confusion over what it meant and why it was being required.

Officers told us that they view that process as typical of the way policy changes are implemented at CDP, and they expressed frustration over not knowing exactly what policies and procedures are currently in effect. According to officers, policy changes are usually communicated to officers through "Divisional Notices," with no explanation or training. Moreover, the changes are not reflected in the official policy manual and there is no indication, even in the electronic version of the manual, that a Divisional Notice was issued that changed the requirements of a particular policy. Consequently, officers are confused as to which policies are in effect and have no way of knowing if they are referencing current CDP policy when looking to the manual for guidance as to their actions. Additionally, CDP has no way of holding officers accountable for failing to adhere to policy changes that have been implemented where it is unclear which policy currently is in effect.

6. CDP's Early Intervention System is Inadequate.

CDP does not use an adequate early intervention system to help identify risky and problematic trends in officer behavior before a pattern or practice of misconduct arises, such as the pattern or practice of excessive force that we found here. An early intervention system is a tool used by police departments to provide individualized supervision and support to officers and to manage risk. Specifically, an early intervention system is one or more databases that track various officer activities, including uses of force, civilian complaints, stops, and arrests. An effective early intervention system both tracks this activity and allows the department to analyze patterns of behavior by individual officers or groups of officers to identify those who might be in need of support or intervention from the department. An early intervention system is not a mechanism for imposing discipline. Instead, the goal of an early intervention system is to manage the potential risk to officers, the department, and the community by taking corrective action and providing officers with resources—such as counseling, training, additional supervision, or monitoring, and action plans for modifying future behavior—before serious problems occur.

CDP's early intervention system is ineffective and poorly utilized. Until very recently, it was voluntary and officers identified for inclusion in the program could choose whether or not to participate. This is contrary to national standards and our 2002 recommendation that CDP make participation mandatory. In January of 2014, CDP drafted a revised policy and reported that it is transitioning to a mandatory early intervention program. This is an important and necessary improvement. CDP also reported that it is in the process of securing software that will allow the Division to electronically link data from various components that provide information about officers' activities, including the Internal Affairs Unit and the Office of Professional Standards. It is too early to assess whether CDP will be able to effectively integrate their data analysis through this new software.

However, the system CDP intends to implement still has significant failings. It will not be effective in disrupting problematic patterns of behavior before they occur because the indicators CDP tracks are too limited and those that are tracked may not provide timely information. CDP's draft policy regarding its revised early intervention program appropriately states that the intent of the program is to "intervene before discipline is required. It is designed to prevent inappropriate conduct which may, without intervention, rise to a level where discipline becomes necessary." We found, however, that the substantive provisions of the policy and CDP's practices fall short of this goal. Some of the indicators tracked in the current system only provide information that is untimely and based on past events. Moreover, there are additional factors that CDP's early intervention system should be tracking, including criminal allegations and civil claims against officers, in order to provide a more complete picture of officers' activities and potential need for intervention.

Finally, although CDP is tracking some relevant performance indicators, it is not clear when those indicators trigger an assessment of whether intervention is required. Although the revised policy refers to "pre-determined thresholds," such thresholds have not been determined. A precise threshold should be standardized for all officers and incorporated into CDP's policy.

7. CDP Is Not Engaging in Community Policing Effectively at All Levels of the Division.

We began our investigation in the aftermath of a series of high profile incidents that contributed to and highlighted an enormous amount of distrust between CDP and certain communities it serves. Members of racial, ethnic, and language minorities, expressed public outrage at the way they perceive that their communities are treated by CDP. Reports of the enormous amount of force that culminated in the fatal shooting of two unarmed African-Americans in East Cleveland on November 29, 2012; the revelation that officers were caught on tape kicking an African-American man in the head, who was handcuffed, prone on the ground, and appeared to have surrendered, and then did not report having used any force; and claims by a Latino family that officers chased and forcibly handcuffed their teenage son who has Down syndrome while looking for robbery suspects who did not resemble the boy, all had brought to the fore the distrust that had been percolating between the police and the community for years. This level of distrust between the police and the community interferes with CDP's ability to work with the various communities it serves to effectively fight crime and ensure the safety of the people of Cleveland.

A police department dedicated to community policing not only reactively responds to calls for service but also proactively works with the community to create safer, more secure neighborhoods by identifying and addressing the root causes of crime. In so doing, the community and the police department together promote greater public safety. This type of police-community partnership is desperately needed in Cleveland. Recently, CDP put into place a new community policing philosophy, including a mission statement and an emphasis on community engagement, professionalism, and respect; has created new community policing goals that include initiating neighborhood improvement plans and working with community groups to create a safer city; and has launched new community policing training. While these initiatives are encouraging, it is far too early to determine their thoroughness, effectiveness, or success. At this point, we can only assess CDP's community policing efforts based on those policies, training, and tactics in place throughout the course of our investigation.

During our investigation, we found that CDP's method of policing contributes to the community's distrust of and lack of respect for officers—officers escalate situations instead of diffusing them and using them as an opportunity to build trust and rapport; officers draw their service weapons on people who are suspected of minor crimes or who do not otherwise pose a threat; and officers use force against people in mental health crisis after family members have called the police in a desperate plea for assistance. Any attempt CDP makes to establish and maintain a positive and beneficial relationship with the community is potentially also undermined by the frequency with which officers appear to stop and search people without meeting the requisite threshold of reasonable suspicion or probable cause. As noted previously in the Summary section of this letter, it appears preliminarily that officers often subject people to stops and searches without the requisite level of suspicion. In addition, despite the fact that we are making no finding regarding racial profiling, we must report that when we interviewed members of the community about their experiences with the police, many African-Americans reported that they believe CDP officers are verbally and physically aggressive toward them because of their race. We also found that, when community members attempt to file complaints about mistreatment at the hands of CDP officers, they are met with barriers and resistance.

Given this backdrop, a comprehensive community policing strategy must be a central component of any police reform in Cleveland. An effective community policing strategy enables law enforcement agencies and the individuals and organizations they serve to develop solutions to problems and increase trust in the police. Community policing involves building partnerships between law enforcement and the people and organizations within its jurisdiction; engaging in problem-solving through proactive measures; and managing the police agency to support community partnerships and community problem-solving. And it translates to all ranks, sectors and units of a police department.

In recent years, and throughout the course of our investigation, CDP's concept of community policing has been implemented only superficially. CDP does participate in many programs that are aimed at building relationships with the community to enhance the services it provides. It has a community policing unit. It participates in multidisciplinary efforts, like STANCE and through the Cleveland Rape Crisis Center, to reach out to community members and groups. Its commanders host and attend community meetings to hear citizen complaints. It participates in federal/state/local task forces that encourage data driven policing and cooperative law enforcement. These efforts are to be praised and recognized. They should, we believe, be continued and enhanced. But these programmatic efforts are not enough. True community policing, discussed herein, must encompass a philosophy of how individual officers interact with and view the communities that they police each and every day. It is about more than attending meetings; it is about how officers talk to and act towards the people they encounter every day. That ethos needs significant improvement throughout CDP.

During our tours, we additionally observed that neither command staff nor line officers were able to accurately or uniformly describe what community policing is or how CDP implements a community policing model. Our review revealed in addition to the programmatic aspects of community policing, that CDP's community policing strategy, at least until recently, has consisted of three elements: a Bureau of Community Policing and district Community Service Units that perform limited community policing functions; supervisors instructing patrol officers to get out of their zone cars and walk around the community while providing little additional guidance or training; and monthly CDP-sponsored community meetings that do not appear to attract the members of the community who have the most strained relationships with the police. This model is insufficient to address the disconnect that currently exists between CDP and some members of the community. CDP's failure to implement a proactive, positive relationship with all of the communities it serves in order to address community concerns and issues has created an environment in which CDP officers will likely have to resort to force more often than they would otherwise.

In a well-run community policing program, the concepts that underpin community policing would permeate all aspects and functions of the police department. CDP lacks many comprehensive strategies that make a community policing program effective. The Bureau of Community Policing consists of one section to which 18 individuals, 16 of whom are officers, are assigned. According to documents provided by CDP, their duties include assisting patrol officers with traffic control; running crime prevention programs in schools and elsewhere; acting as crossing guards at schools; teaching students about substance abuse and gang violence; and recruiting new officers to the force. Yet, we also learned that in recent years CDP has greatly reduced its involvement in key programs in the Cleveland Municipal School System. CDP should ensure that its community policing efforts are comprehensive, and focus on schools and children in addition to neighborhoods in order to build trust. According to an assignment posting provided by CDP, the officers assigned to the Community Services Units within the districts are charged with focusing on quality of life issues by attending community meetings, addressing drug activity, responding to the District Commander's crime initiatives, and performing riot and crowd control functions. While some of these functions assigned to the Bureau of Community Policing and the Community Service Units are part of community policing, they are only a small part of an effective community policing model. Indeed, several Community Services Unit officers we spoke with told us that they did not consider the functions they performed to be community policing. Those officers said they spend much of their time addressing burglaries, traffic, and drug problems.

Many district commanders, as well as former Chief McGrath, told us that supervisors tell patrol officers to get out of their zone cars, walk around, and get to know residents and store owners. Although we observed that some officers were engaged in thoughtful and effective community policing strategies, we found that there is no organizational support for community policing activities. Instead, they are ad hoc and officer specific. One officer with whom we spent time during a ride-along greeted many residents by name and stopped to speak with some of them. Children in the neighborhood called out to him and waved as he drove by. The officer told us, however, that he got to know members of the community due to his own interest in doing so and that such actions were not mandated by command staff. He does it because like many officers in CDP he cares, but not because it is required as part of his job. A sergeant we spoke with in the same district confirmed that the officer was acting entirely on his own initiative with no encouragement from command staff. But personal dedication and commitment, even if present in a large number of good and honest CDP officers, is not a modern strategy for an organization of the size and importance of CDP. For instance, one district commander we spoke with affirmatively stated that his patrol officers are not held accountable for community policing and are trained solely to answer radio calls in order to "put out fires and move the problem" because, he said, "that is what police do." Several officers we rode with stated that they got out of their zone cars or initiated contact with civilians only when responding to calls. Officers also indicated that they were too busy responding to calls to take time to do anything else, such as walking through neighborhoods or business districts.

Deficiencies in CDP's community policing efforts are, to a certain extent, not surprising. Even with the advent of CDP's new community policing philosophy, we are aware of no CDP policies regarding community policing. We have seen no formal, systemic community policing plan to ensure officers are interacting with civilians; and we have seen no efforts to analyze those interactions and to use the information gained to improve CDP's ability to fight crime. In addition, performance evaluations of officers do not include a community policing component.

We also saw evidence that some officers hold views that are incompatible with community policing principles, and that this attitude is tolerated and encouraged by at least some members of command staff. A former actual Commander of community policing for CDP told us that he believes the culture within CDP is antithetical to a community policing mentality and that officer training instills in officers an "us-against-them" mentality. During an interview with one district commander, he referred to his district as a "forward operating base," and we later observed a large sign hanging in the vehicle bay of that district station identifying it as such. Such metaphors have no place in a community-oriented police department. While a stray comment here or there would not itself be worthy of report, leadership and messaging do matter, especially in light of the other findings and observations set forth in this letter.

CDP policy places responsibility for establishing community policing strategies for the Division with the Deputy Chief of Field Operations. Nonetheless, Chief Williams, who at the time was Deputy Chief of Field Operations, told us that CDP has no Division-wide community policing strategy and instead relies on district commanders to establish community policing plans. Many district commanders told us that they have an excellent relationship with those they police, citing, for example, their monthly meetings with community members. We attended several of these meetings, and indeed, those in attendance evinced respect and appreciation for CDP. However, as set forth above, these meetings are not a strategy for every day community policing and they attract a small number of people who reflect only a fraction of the communities CDP serves. Citizens need to know not only the "brass," but they need a trusting relationship with the patrol officers who are in their communities every single day. Many Cleveland residents fear and mistrust CDP and feel that they are in an adversarial relationship with the Division. Although it is harder to accomplish, more needs to be done to try to involve the members of the community who have a less favorable view of CDP.

On another occasion, a commander noted that he had tried to address crime outside of the usual responses to calls for service by contacting the law department and a City councilperson about ways to address the theft of scrap metal, which is a primary problem in his district. Such actions can be an important part of community policing, as a successful community policing strategy depends on cooperation between the police department and other government entities within the city. However, this commander's personal efforts again appear to be an exception to CDP's overall policing strategy, which relies very little on communication and proactive daily partnerships with those they police.

CDP has taken some initial steps to establish an effective community policing approach to interacting with the people of Cleveland and proactively addressing crime. Holding community meetings, encouraging officers to get to know residents, working with the city council and other government entities, and other strategies are all basic building blocks of an effective community policing framework. But much more must be done. CDP must target the communities where distrust of the police is most pervasive. Community meetings must entail a broader representation of community members and must dig deeper into how those members can work with officers to prevent crime. In addition, community policing principles must be formalized and inculcated into the culture of the Division. Underpinning all of CDP's efforts must be a community-oriented philosophy that positions community members and groups as partners in an effort to proactively problem-solve together.

8. CDP's Approach to Individuals in Crisis Is Underdeveloped.

CDP's crisis intervention policies and practices are underdeveloped, and CDP has not yet fully integrated these practices into its response to individuals in crisis, resulting in the use of unreasonable force against these individuals. When individuals experience a mental health crisis, law enforcement officers often are the first responders. In many of these situations, officers have been called to the scene by concerned family members who are only seeking help for their loved ones. Frequently, these individuals in crisis have not committed any crime. Too often in Cleveland, however, officers handle these difficult situations poorly and end up resorting to unconstitutional force against people in crisis. Although CDP has invested in improving its response to people in crisis over the last few years, critical work still remains to ensure that officers' interactions with people in crisis are appropriate.

CDP contracts with Cuyahoga County's Alcohol, Drug Addiction, and Mental Health Services ("ADAMHS") to provide some of its officers with crisis intervention training. Once officers have completed this 40-hour block of training, CDP designates them as crisis intervention team ("CIT") officers. Many officers describe this training as the best and most effective training they have ever received while at CDP. The problem, however, is that frequently these trained officers are not the people responding to calls of people in crisis in real time. That needs to change. Currently, at the beginning of each shift, supervisors are to inform dispatchers which zone cars have CIT officers so that dispatchers may assign CIT officers to assist with calls involving individuals experiencing a mental health crisis. However, CDP policy only requires dispatchers to "attempt" to dispatch a CIT officer to a call involving a person in mental health crisis. If CIT officers are already on other assignments, dispatchers are allowed to send only non-CIT officers. Partly as a result of this practice, officers who have not received CIT training are dispatched to handle calls involving individuals in crisis. We saw no evidence that CDP's staffing plan or car plan attempts to ensure that there is adequate CIT coverage or that CIT officers are assigned to shifts with a greater need for their skills.

As discussed above, we reviewed force reports in which officers responded to a call, often from a family member, to assist with an individual in mental health crisis, and the officers used excessive force to control the situation. Had officers used proper de-escalation techniques, it is possible these situations could have been resolved without resorting to force. In many of the problematic incidents we reviewed in which officers used excessive force against a person in crisis, no CIT officer was on scene. The presence of a properly trained CIT officer might have improved the safety of the person in crisis, the person's family, and the officers present.

CDP must change its policies and procedures to require CIT officers to respond to every incident involving an individual in known mental health crisis, even if a non-CIT officer who is first on scene must immediately begin addressing the situation. CDP must also ensure that enough officers respond to these calls. CDP's policy currently requires two officers to respond to calls involving individuals with mental illness. According to the documentation provided by CDP, however, it is common for only one CDP officer to respond to such a call. To ensure that CIT officers are always available in all parts of the city to respond whenever an encounter with someone in mental health crisis occurs, CDP needs to conduct an analysis to determine whether it currently has enough CIT officers and whether it is deploying those officers effectively, and then correct any discovered deficiencies.

In addition to ensuring that it has a sufficient number of CIT officers, CDP must also ensure that its personnel, including its officers and dispatchers, are adequately trained. When choosing which officers will attend CIT training, CDP should select only those officers who have volunteered for the training. All other patrol officers must be given basic training to ensure that they have a general working knowledge of how to respond to and assist individuals who are mentally ill. This will allow patrol officers both to recognize when someone might be experiencing a mental health crisis so that the officer may request the assistance of a CIT officer, and to safely and effectively handle the situation until that CIT officer arrives. Currently, CDP recruits are not receiving sufficient basic mental health training, and it does not appear that CDP has offered any in-service mental health training since at least 2010. CDP's training also must emphasize to all officers that they are to employ verbal de-escalation techniques whenever practicable as a first resort when encountering individuals experiencing a mental health crisis, regardless of whether the individual is violating or has violated the law. CDP policy currently limits the definition of "crisis" in the mental health context to situations when there is no law violation. CDP must expand this definition.

Finally, CDP should establish at least one CDP officer to act as a mental health liaison to facilitate communication between CDP and members of the mental health community. A police department can best serve and respond to individuals with mental illness when it has strong partnerships with mental health professionals, advocacy organizations, and others in the mental health community. CDP needs to involve these partners when creating and revising CDP policies, procedures, and training regimens related to crisis intervention. CDP should also solicit feedback from the mental health community on a regular basis regarding the efficacy of its CIT program. The CIT coordinator can establish and facilitate these relationships and should be available at all times as a resource for families, advocates, caregivers, and others in the mental health community.

One cannot overstate the importance of a robust CIT program. A well-trained cadre of CIT officers, together with patrol officers armed with a basic understanding of mental illness and how it can affect individuals, would provide the proper foundation CDP needs to effectively assist individuals with mental illness. A fully implemented CIT program also would improve the safety of officers as well as individuals with mental illness and their family members. A comprehensive crisis intervention program requires CDP to partner effectively with advocates, service providers, and families in the mental health community to ensure officers are appropriately assisting individuals experiencing mental health crises. While we recognize that CDP has taken significant steps to interact more appropriately with individuals with mental illness, it is imperative that CDP take additional measures to ensure that officers encountering people with mental illness consistently do so in a manner that respects their constitutional rights and provides them with the assistance they need.

9. CDP Equipment, Technology, and Staff Planning are Inadequate.

CDP's failure to appropriately allocate resources—including staffing and equipment— contributes to the pattern or practice of unconstitutional force. In addition, Cleveland police officers are not given the basic equipment, the physical structures, and the technology required to perform their jobs safely and effectively. We found that patrol officers are sent out to perform dangerous jobs without the ability to effectively communicate with the Division or with each other. Consequently, all too often they are placed in a position where they do not have the ability to learn basic information about the civilians with whom they interact. Asking officers to perform their duties without adequate technology, an appropriate staffing plan, a sufficiently professional workspace, or routine and functioning equipment is dangerous to the officer, undermines public safety and is unfair. It also cannot help but drain officer morale and diminish their patience in dealing with the members of the public they encounter.

We recognize that City budgets are severely constrained and that police departments around the country must make difficult decisions about where they will allocate resources at the expense of other needs of the department. We realize that these financial realities have become worse in recent years and that Cleveland has been particularly hard hit. We do not underestimate the difficulty the City and the Division finds itself in, and we recognize that Division leadership struggles with these decisions and their potential ramifications for the hard working men and women of the Cleveland Division of Police. However, the City must provide adequate resources to allow for constitutional and effective policing. As much as any building, stadium, or other public works project, a well-run, professional and constitutional police presence is the foundation of a healthy city in our democracy. Moreover, the City and the Division must work together to ensure that limited resources are allocated thoughtfully and effectively.

An effective police force needs a staffing plan that distributes personnel based on the expected workload at various times during the day. The plan must be systematically designed to use resources effectively, balancing personnel between specialized units, taking advantage of officers with particular skills, and conserving resources by civilianizing certain positions. An effective staffing plan could also help alleviate some of the Division's budget problems. For example, many jobs that could be performed by civilians are currently occupied by sworn officers. These include administrative desk jobs and crime scene technicians.

As described above, we found that field supervisors are failing in some of the most fundamental aspects of their responsibilities—reviewing and investigating the uses of force of the officers under their command, and correcting dangerous tactical choices that place the officer and others at risk. The number of officers a sergeant supervises—the sergeant's "span of control"—is a critical factor affecting the adequacy of supervision. Any span of control should take into account the level of activity and type of units being supervised. Additionally, law enforcement agencies such as CDP should deploy its staff to ensure "unity of command," a system in which officers report consistently to one sergeant, and, in most cases, officers and their supervisors have the same days off and the same schedules. That system is meant to ensure that supervisors know their subordinates' strengths and weaknesses, allowing them to better direct their work. CDP does not employ a unity of command structure and, because it has not conducted an adequate staffing study, it does not know whether its span of control is appropriate. An appropriate staffing analysis would allow the Division to know whether it needs more sergeants, or whether to deploy staff differently in order to allow for unity of command and a thoughtful span of control.

While CDP has taken some steps to improve the equipment it provides to officers—for example, it has provided officers with new portable radios relatively recently—other basic equipment is either outdated or nonexistent. For instance, officers lack effective zone car computers, called Mobile Data Computers ("MDCs"), which allow them to effectively access the computer-aided dispatch ("CAD") system. MDCs are essential tools for effective policing and for officer safety. When officers conduct a vehicle stop, officer safety requires that they run the license plate through the computer prior to approaching the vehicle to determine information about the vehicle and its likely driver—for example, whether the vehicle was stolen or involved in a crime, or whether its registered owner is wanted for a crime or has outstanding warrants. Not all of CDP's zone cars have computers and, of those that do, the computers do not all reliably work. Even the MDCs that do work properly do not give officers access to CAD or CDP's Records Management System. CAD includes vital information such as the nature of the call, whether anyone involved is armed, whether shots were fired, how many officers currently are on scene, a description of any suspects, direction of flight, and more. As a consequence, when officers make stops, they often cannot use their computers to obtain this critical information. Leadership reported that officers can request this information through dispatch. In reality, however, this solution is impractical. Officers reported that it takes far too long for officers to receive this type of information through dispatch. Moreover, the radio channel frequently is being used for more pressing and emergent situations, and officers are reluctant to intrude with these types of requests for basic information. One officer who does not have an MDC told us that she will not make traffic stops after dark because, without easily being able to run the license plate, she considers such situations to be too dangerous.

In part because they do not have functioning computers and access to the information in the CAD system, officers use their personal cell phones to communicate when in the field, to talk with their supervisors, to run checks on license places and suspects, to find locations, and to take photographs. The pervasive use of personal cell phones is problematic, particularly because CDP lacks any policy covering this subject. For example, when officers send text messages and take photographs, they potentially are creating evidence, and CDP has no protocol in place for how such evidence will be handled, preserved, or disclosed to prosecutors and defense attorneys. Nor is there any protocol for how this potentially important information will be transmitted to CDP's databases. It also interferes with CDP's ability to hold officers accountable for their actions, because it is impossible to discern what information officers had and when they had it.

The condition of officers' equipment and facilities also makes it difficult for them to comply with some policies and contributes to low officer morale. There are not enough computers at the district stations for officers to be able to easily write their reports, including use of force reports, in a timely manner. At the Fourth District, for example, there was until recently only one computer for all patrol officers. A second computer was added just before our April 2014 visit. Another serious equipment problem facing CDP officers is the condition of the force's vehicle fleet. Officers in all Districts stated that most of the cars are old and in poor repair. Many are out of service, or "bad ordered," at any given time, meaning that there are insufficient cars available to fully staff shifts. Because of the poor condition of CDP's vehicles, officers told us that some of them carry auto repair equipment and other maintenance materials which they have purchased at their own expense. These problems undermine CDP's ability to have sufficient supervisory review and places officers at risk.

Again, we acknowledge and understand the difficult financial strain on the City and the Division. However, the City must allocate its resources in a way that allows for constitutional policing. The City recently has chosen to spend a significant amount of money on body-worn cameras for some CDP officers. Body-worn cameras are an emerging technology that will likely be a very effective law enforcement tool and we applaud that decision. However, many officers do not even have working computers in their cars. There are many pressing concerns facing the Division, and a failure to thoughtfully assess the Division's needs and prioritize effectively affects officers' and supervisors' ability to do their jobs and erodes morale.

V. CONCLUSION

We recognize that many Cleveland officers have pursued their profession in order to effect positive change within the City and they make great sacrifices to do dangerous work. All of the residents of the City of Cleveland should recognize that as well. Respect and trust must go both ways. As the Sixth Circuit has noted, police officers are charged with the ultimate responsibility of protecting the public and keeping the peace—and they may employ the use of force, including deadly force, to do so. *See Hayes v. Memphis Police Dep't*, 634 F.2d 350, 352 (6th Cir. 1980). However, any use of force must be within the confines of the Fourth Amendment, and we have found that CPD engages in a pattern or practice of using unreasonable amounts of force in violation of the Constitution. While CDP has taken initial steps to implement new policies and procedures designed to remedy some of the deficiencies described in this letter, it is imperative that the City and the Division now take more rigorous measures to identify, address, and prevent excessive force to protect the public and to rebuild the community's trust. To that end, we believe the only effective mechanism to address these significant problems is to reach a consent decree that provides for a monitor to oversee the implementation of systemic reform in the CDP. The City's agreement, as reflected in the Join Statement of Principles, is a critical step on the path to reform.

We share your desire to ensure that the City of Cleveland has an effective, accountable police department that controls crime, ensures respect for the Constitution, and earns the trust of the public it is charged with protecting. Recent events have galvanized many in the community to join the public discourse over the future of the Cleveland Division of Police and its relationship with the community. We look forward to working with you, the Division, and the community to address our findings and to restore public trust and promote constitutional policing in Cleveland.

Sincerely,

VANITA GUPTA
Acting Assistant Attorney General
Civil Rights Division
Department of Justice

STEVEN M. DETTELBACH
United States Attorney
Northern District of Ohio

INVESTIGATION OF THE
BALTIMORE CITY POLICE DEPARTMENT

U.S. DEPARTMENT OF JUSTICE
CIVIL RIGHTS DIVISION

AUGUST 10, 2016

EXECUTIVE SUMMARY

Today, we announce the outcome of the Department of Justice's investigation of the Baltimore City Police Department (BPD).[1] After engaging in a thorough investigation, initiated at the request of the City of Baltimore and BPD, the Department of Justice concludes that there is reasonable cause to believe that BPD engages in a pattern or practice of conduct that violates the Constitution or federal law. BPD engages in a pattern or practice of:

1. making unconstitutional stops, searches, and arrests;
2. using enforcement strategies that produce severe and unjustified dispari- ties in the rates of stops, searches and arrests of African Americans;
3. using excessive force; and
4. retaliating against people engaging in constitutionally protected expression.

This pattern or practice is driven by systemic deficiencies in BPD's policies, train- ing, supervision, and accountability structures that fail to equip officers with the tools they need to police effectively and within the bounds of the federal law.

We recognize the challenges faced by police officers in Baltimore and other communities around the country. Every day, police officers risk their lives to uphold the law and keep our communities safe. Investigatory stops, arrests, and force—including, at times, deadly force—are all necessary tools used by BPD officers to do their jobs and protect the safety of themselves and others. Providing policing services in many parts of Baltimore is particularly chal- lenging, where officers regularly confront complex social problems rooted in poverty, racial segregation and deficient educational, employment and housing opportunities. Still, most BPD officers work hard to provide vital services to the community.

The pattern or practice occurs as a result of systemic deficiencies at BPD.

---

[1] The Special Litigation Section of the Civil Rights Division conducted the investigation pursuant to the Violent Crime Control and Law Enforcement Act of 1994, 42 U.S.C. § 14141 ("Section 14141"), Title VI of the Civil Rights Act of 1964, 42 U.S.C. § 2000d, the Omnibus Crime Control and Safe Streets Act of 1968, 42 U.S.C. § 3789d ("Safe Streets Act"); and the Americans with Disabilities Act of 1990, 42 U.S.C. §§ 12131–12134. The investigation did not examine the actions of officers involved in Freddie Gray's arrest on April 12, 2015, or the merits of any criminal or civil proceedings connected to that incident.

The agency fails to provide officers with sufficient policy guidance and training; fails to collect and analyze data regarding officers' activities; and fails to hold officers accountable for misconduct. BPD also fails to equip officers with the necessary equipment and resources they need to police safely, constitutionally, and effectively. Each of these systemic deficiencies contributes to the constitutional and statutory violations we observed.

Throughout our investigation, we received the full cooperation and assistance of BPD and the City of Baltimore. We interviewed current and former City leaders, including current BPD Commissioner Kevin Davis and former commissioners. We also interviewed current and former officers throughout the BPD command structure. We participated in ride-alongs in each district, interviewed numerous current and former officers individually, and met with the leadership of the Baltimore City Lodge No. 3 of the Fraternal Order of Police, which represents all sworn BPD officers. We are also heard from hundreds of people in the broader Baltimore community who shared information with our investigation. We met with religious organizations, advocacy groups, community support organizations, neighborhood associations, and countless individuals who provided valuable information about their experiences with BPD. We thank everyone for sharing their experiences and insights with us.

In addition to these interviews, we reviewed hundreds of thousands of pages of documents, including all relevant policies and training materials used by the Department since 2010; BPD's database of internal affairs files from January 2010 through March 2016; BPD's data on pedestrian stops, vehicle stops, and arrests from January 2010 to May 2015; incident reports describing stops, searches, arrests, and officers' use of non-deadly force from 2010 to 2015; all files on deadly force incidents since 2010 that BPD was able to produce to us through May 1, 2016; and investigative files on sexual assault cases from 2013 to 2015. We were assisted by a dozen current and former law enforcement leaders and experts with experience on the issues we investigated, and we retained statistical experts to analyze BPD's data on its enforcement activities.[2]

In the course of our investigation, we learned there is widespread agreement that BPD needs reform. Almost everyone who spoke to us—from current and former City leaders, BPD officers and command staff during ride-alongs and interviews, community members throughout the many neighborhoods of Baltimore, union representatives of all levels of officers in BPD, advocacy groups, and civic and religious leaders—agrees that BPD has significant problems that have undermined its efforts to police constitutionally and effectively.

---

2 In addition, the Department of Justice's Office of Community Oriented Policing Services (COPS) has been engaged in a collaborative reform process with the City and BPD. The COPS office has continued to provide technical assistance to BPD during our investigation, along with other components of the Department of Justice.

As we note in this report, many of these people and groups have documented those problems in the past, and although they may disagree about the nature, scope, and solutions to the challenges, many have also made efforts to address them. Nevertheless, work remains, in part because of the profound lack of trust among these groups, and in particular, between BPD and certain communities in Baltimore. The road to meaningful and lasting reform is a long one, but it can be taken. This investigation is intended to help Baltimore take a large step down this path.

Recent events highlight the critical importance of mutual trust and cooperation between law enforcement officers and the people they serve. A commitment to constitutional policing builds trust that enhances crime fighting efforts and officer safety. Conversely, frayed community relationships inhibit effective policing by denying officers important sources of information and placing them more frequently in dangerous, adversarial encounters. We found these principles in stark relief in Baltimore, where law enforcement officers confront a long history of social and economic challenges that impact much of the City, including the perception that there are "two Baltimores:" one wealthy and largely white, the second impoverished and predominantly black. Community members living in the City's wealthier and largely white neighborhoods told us that officers tend to be respectful and responsive to their needs, while many individuals living in the City's largely African-American communities informed us that officers tend to be disrespectful and do not respond promptly to their calls for service. Members of these largely African-American communities often felt they were subjected to unjustified stops, searches, and arrests, as well as excessive force. These challenges amplify the importance of using policing methods that build community partnerships and ensure fair and effective enforcement without regard for affluence or race through robust training, close supervision, data collection and analysis, and accountability for misconduct.

Starting in at least the late 1990s, however, City and BPD leadership responded to the City's challenges by encouraging "zero tolerance" street enforcement that prioritized officers making large numbers of stops, searches, and arrests—and often resorting to force—with minimal training and insufficient oversight from supervisors or through other accountability structures. These practices led to repeated violations of the constitutional and statutory rights, further eroding the community's trust in the police.

Proactive policing does not have to lead to these consequences. On the contrary, constitutional, community-oriented policing is proactive policing, but it is fundamentally different from the tactics employed in Baltimore for many years. Community policing depends on building relationships with all of the communities that a police department serves, and then jointly solving problems to ensure public safety. We encourage BPD to be proactive, to get to know Baltimore's communities more deeply, build trust, and reduce crime together with the communities it serves.

Fortunately, the current leadership of the City and the BPD already have taken laudable steps to reverse this course, including by revising BPD's use of force policies, taking steps toward enhancing accountability and transparency throughout the Department by, for example, beginning to equip officers with body worn cameras, and taking steps toward improving and expanding its community outreach to better engage its officers with the community they serve. Still, significant challenges remain.

Unconstitutional Stops, Searches, and Arrests

BPD's legacy of zero tolerance enforcement continues to drive its policing in certain Baltimore neighborhoods and leads to unconstitutional stops, searches, and arrests. Many BPD supervisors instruct officers to make frequent stops and arrests—even for minor offenses and with minimal or no suspicion—without sufficient consideration of whether this enforcement strategy promotes public safety and community trust or conforms to constitutional standards. These instructions, coupled with minimal supervision and accountability for misconduct, lead to constitutional violations.

- Stops. BPD officers recorded over 300,000 pedestrian stops from January 2010–May 2015, and the true number of BPD's stops during this period is likely far higher due to under-reporting. These stops are concentrated in predominantly African-American neighborhoods and often lack reasonable suspicion.
- BPD's pedestrian stops are concentrated on a small portion of Baltimore residents. BPD made roughly 44 percent of its stops in two small, predominantly African-American districts that contain only 11 percent of the City's population. Consequently, hundreds of individuals—nearly all of them African American—were stopped on at least 10 separate occasions from 2010–2015. Indeed, seven African-American men were stopped more than 30 times during this period.
- BPD's stops often lack reasonable suspicion. Our review of incident reports and interviews with officers and community members found that officers regularly approach individuals standing or walking on City sidewalks to detain and question them and check for outstanding warrants, despite lacking reasonable suspicion to do so. Only 3.7 percent of pedestrian stops resulted in officers issuing a citation or making an arrest. And, as noted below, many of those arrested based upon pedestrian stops had their charges dismissed upon initial review by either supervisors at BPD's Central Booking or local prosecutors.

- Searches. During stops, BPD officers frequently pat-down or frisk individuals as a matter of course, without identifying necessary grounds to believe that the person is armed and dangerous. And even where an initial frisk is justified, we found that officers often violate the Constitution by exceeding the frisk's permissible scope. We likewise found many instances in which officers strip search individuals without legal justification. In some cases, officers performed degrading strip searches in public, prior to making an arrest, and without grounds to believe that the searched individuals were concealing contraband on their bodies.

- Arrests. We identified two categories of common unconstitutional arrests by BPD officers: (1) officers make warrantless arrests without probable cause; and (2) officers make arrests for misdemeanor offenses, such as loitering and trespassing, without providing the constitutionally-required notice that the arrested person was engaged in unlawful activity.

- Arrests without probable cause: from 2010–2015, supervisors at Baltimore's Central Booking and local prosecutors rejected over 11,000 charges made by BPD officers because they lacked probable cause or otherwise did not merit prosecution. Our review of incident reports describing warrantless arrests likewise found many examples of officers making unjustified arrests. In addition, officers extend stops without justification to search for evidence that would justify an arrest. These detentions—many of which last more than an hour—constitute unconstitutional arrests.

- Misdemeanor arrests without notice: BPD officers arrest individuals standing lawfully on public sidewalks for "loitering," "trespassing," or other misdemeanor offenses without providing adequate notice that the individuals were engaged in unlawful activity. Indeed, officers frequently invert the constitutional notice requirement. While the Constitution requires individuals to receive pre-arrest notice of the specific conduct prohibited as loitering or trespassing, BPD officers approach individuals standing lawfully on sidewalks in front of public housing complexes or private businesses and arrest them unless the individuals are able to "justify" their presence to the officers' satisfaction.

Discrimination against African Americans

BPD's targeted policing of certain Baltimore neighborhoods with minimal oversight or accountability disproportionately harms African-American residents. Racially disparate impact is present at every stage of BPD's enforcement actions, from the initial decision to stop individuals on Baltimore streets to searches, arrests, and uses of force. These racial disparities, along with evidence suggesting intentional discrimination, erode the community trust that is critical to effective policing.

- BPD disproportionately stops African-American pedestrians. Citywide, BPD stopped African-American residents three times as often as white residents after controlling for the population of the area in which the stops occurred. In each of BPD's nine police districts, African Americans accounted for a greater share of BPD's stops than the population living in the district. And BPD is far more likely to subject individual African Americans to multiple stops in short periods of time. In the five and a half years of data we examined, African Americans accounted for 95 percent of the 410 individuals BPD stopped at least 10 times. One African American man in his mid-fifties was stopped 30 times in less than 4 years. Despite these repeated intrusions, none of the 30 stops resulted in a citation or criminal charge.
- BPD also stops African American drivers at disproportionate rates. African Americans accounted for 82 percent of all BPD vehicle stops, compared to only 60 percent of the driving age population in the City and 27 percent of the driving age population in the greater metropolitan area.
- BPD disproportionately searches African Americans during stops. BPD searched African Americans more frequently during pedestrian and vehicle stops, even though searches of African Americans were less likely to discover contraband. Indeed, BPD officers found contraband twice as often when searching white individuals compared to African Americans during vehicle stops and 50 percent more often during pedestrian stops.
- African Americans similarly accounted for 86 percent of all criminal offenses charged by BPD officers despite making up only 63 percent of Baltimore residents.
- Racial disparities in BPD's arrests are most pronounced for highly discretionary offenses: African Americans accounted for 91 percent of the 1,800 people charged solely with "failure to obey" or "trespassing"; 89 percent of the 1,350 charges for making a false statement to an officer; and 84 percent of the 6,500 people arrested for "disorderly conduct." Moreover, booking officials and prosecutors decline charges brought against African Americans at significantly higher rates than charges against people of other races, indicating that officers' standards for making arrests differ by the race of the person arrested.
- We also found large racial disparities in BPD's arrests for drug possession. While survey data shows that African Americans use drugs at rates similar to or slightly exceeding other population groups, BPD arrested African Americans for drug possession at five times the rate of others.

BPD deployed a policing strategy that, by its design, led to differential enforcement in African-American communities. But BPD failed to use adequate policy, training and accountability mechanisms to prevent discrimination, despite longstanding notice of concerns about how it polices African-American communities in the City. BPD has conducted virtually no analysis of its own data to ensure that its enforcement activities are non-discriminatory, and the Department misclassifies or otherwise fails to investigate specific complaints of racial bias. Nor has the Department held officers accountable for using racial slurs or making other statements exhibiting racial bias. In some cases, BPD supervisors have ordered officers to specifically target African Americans for stops and arrests. These failures contribute to the large racial disparities in BPD's enforcement that undermine the community's trust in the fairness of the police. BPD leadership has acknowledged that this lack of trust inhibits their ability to forge important community partnerships.

Use of Constitutionally Excessive Force

Our review of investigative files for all deadly force cases from 2010 until May 1, 2016, and a random sample of over eight hundred non-deadly force cases reveals that BPD engages in a pattern or practice of excessive force. Deficiencies in BPD's policies, training, and oversight of officers' force incidents have led to the pattern or practice of excessive force that we observed. We identified several recurring issues with BPD's use of force:

- First, BPD uses overly aggressive tactics that unnecessarily escalate encounters, increase tensions, and lead to unnecessary force, and fails to de-escalate encounters when it would be reasonable to do so. Officers frequently resort to physical force when a subject does not immediately respond to verbal commands, even where the subject poses no imminent threat to the officer or others. These tactics result from BPD's training and guidance.
- Second, BPD uses excessive force against individuals with mental health disabilities or in crisis. Due to a lack of training and improper tactics, BPD officers end up in unnecessarily violent confrontations with these vulnerable individuals. BPD provides less effective services to people with mental illness and intellectual disabilities by failing to account for these disabilities in officers' law enforcement actions, leading to unnecessary and excessive force being used against them. BPD has failed to make reasonable modifications in its policies, practices, and procedures to avoid discriminating against people with mental illness and intellectual disabilities.
- Third, BPD uses unreasonable force against juveniles. These incidents arise from BPD's failure to use widely-accepted tactics for communicating and interacting with youth. Instead, officers interacting with youth rely on the same aggressive tactics they use with adults, leading to unnecessary conflict.

- Fourth, BPD uses unreasonable force against people who present little or no threat to officers or others. Specifically, BPD uses excessive force against (1) individuals who are already restrained and under officers' control and (2) individuals who are fleeing from officers and are not suspected of serious criminal offenses.
- Force used on restrained individuals: we found many examples of BPD officers using unreasonable force on individuals who were restrained and no longer posed a threat to officers or the public.
- Force used on fleeing suspects: BPD officers frequently engage in foot pursuits of individuals, even where the fleeing individuals are not suspected of violent crimes. BPD's foot pursuit tactics endanger officers and the community, and frequently lead to officers using excessive force on fleeing suspects who pose minimal threat. BPD's aggressive approach to foot pursuits extends to flight in vehicles.
- We also examined BPD's transportation of detainees, but were unable to make a finding due to a lack of available data. We were unable to secure reliable records from either BPD or the jail regarding injuries sustained during transport or any recordings. Nonetheless, we found evidence that BPD: (1) routinely fails to properly secure arrestees in transport vehicles; (2) needs to continue to update its transport equipment to protect arrestees during transport; (3) fails to keep necessary records; and (4) must implement more robust auditing and monitoring systems to ensure that its transport policies and training are followed.
- Our concerns about BPD's use of excessive force are compounded by BPD's ineffective oversight of its use of force. Of the 2,818 force incidents that BPD recorded in the nearly six-year period we reviewed, BPD investigated only ten incidents based on concerns identified through its internal review. Of these ten cases, BPD found only one use of force to be excessive.

Retaliation for Activities Protected by the First Amendment

BPD violates the First Amendment by retaliating against individuals engaged in constitutionally protected activities. Officers frequently detain and arrest members of the public for engaging in speech the officers perceive to be critical or disrespectful. And BPD officers use force against members of the public who are engaging in protected speech. BPD has failed to provide officers with sufficient guidance and oversight regarding their interactions with individuals that implicate First Amendment protections, leading to the violations we observed.

Indications of Gender Bias in Sexual Assault Investigations

Although we do not, at this time, find reasonable cause to believe that BPD engages in gender-biased policing in violation of federal law, the allegations we received during the investigation, along with our review of BPD files, suggests that gender bias may be affecting BPD's handling of sexual assault cases. We found indications that officers fail to meaningfully investigate reports of sexual assault, particularly for assaults involving women with additional vulnerabilities, such as those who are involved in the sex trade. Detectives fail to develop and resolve preliminary investigations; fail to identify and collect evidence to corroborate victims' accounts; inadequately document their investigative steps; fail to collect and assess data, and report and classify reports of sexual assault; and lack supervisory review. We also have concerns that officers' interactions with women victims of sexual assault and with transgender individuals display unlawful gender bias.

Deficient Policies, Training, Supervision, and Accountability

BPD's systemic constitutional and statutory violations are rooted in structural failures. BPD fails to use adequate policies, training, supervision, data collection, analysis, and accountability systems, has not engaged adequately with the community it polices, and does not provide its officers with the tools needed to police effectively.

- BPD lacks meaningful accountability systems to deter misconduct. The Department does not consistently classify, investigate, adjudicate, and document complaints of misconduct according to its own policies and accepted law enforcement standards. Instead, we found that BPD personnel discourage complaints from being filed, misclassify complaints to minimize their apparent severity, and conduct little or no investigation. As a result, a resistance to accountability persists throughout much of BPD, and many officers are reluctant to report misconduct for fear that doing so is fruitless and may provoke retaliation. The Department also lacks adequate civilian oversight—its Civilian Review Board is hampered by inadequate resources, and the agency's internal affairs and disciplinary process lacks transparency.
- Nor does BPD employ effective community policing strategies. The Department's current relationship with certain Baltimore communities is broken. As noted above, some community members believe that the Department operates as if there are "two Baltimores" in which the affluent sections of the City receive better services than its impoverished and minority neighborhoods. This fractured relationship exists in part because

of the Department's legacy of zero tolerance enforcement, the failure of many BPD officers to implement community policing principles, and the Department's lack of vision for engaging with the community.

- BPD fails to adequately supervise officers through policy guidance and training. Until recently, BPD lacked sufficient policy guidance in critical areas, such as bias-free policing and officers' use of batons and tasers. In other areas, such as its policy governing "stop and frisk," BPD policy conflicts with constitutional requirements. The Department likewise lacks effective training on important areas, such as scenario-based training for use of force, an adequate Field Training program; and supervisory or leadership training.

- BPD also fails to collect data on a range of law enforcement actions, and even when it collects data, fails to store it in systems that are capable of effective tracking and analysis.

- Partly as a result, the BPD does not use an effective early intervention system to detect officers who may benefit from additional training or guidance to ensure that they do not commit constitutional and statutory violations.

- In addition, BPD fails to adequately support its officers with adequate staffing and material resources. The Department lacks effective strategies for staffing, recruitment and retention, forcing officers to work overtime after long shifts, lowering morale, and leading to officers working with deteriorated decision-making skills. Moreover, BPD lacks adequate technology infrastructure and tools that are common in many similar-sized law enforcement agencies, such as in-car computers. These technology deficits create inefficiencies for officers and inhibit effective data collection and supervision. The City must invest in its police department to ensure that officers have the tools they need to properly serve the people of Baltimore.

Notwithstanding our findings, we are heartened by the support for police reform throughout BPD the City, and the broader Baltimore community. Based on the cooperation and spirit of engagement we witnessed throughout our investigation, we are optimistic that we will be able to work with the City, BPD, and the diverse communities of Baltimore to address the issues described in our findings and forge a court-enforceable agreement to develop enduring remedies to the constitutional and statutory violations we found. Indeed, although much work remains, BPD has already begun laying the foundation for reform by self-initiating changes to its policies, training, data management, and accountability systems.

To that end, the Department of Justice and the City have entered into an

Agreement in Principle that identifies categories of reforms the parties agree must be taken to remedy the violations of the Constitution and federal law described in this report. Both the Justice Department and the City seek input from all communities in Baltimore on the reforms that should be included in a comprehensive, court-enforceable consent decree to be negotiated by the Justice Department and the City in the coming months, and then entered as a federal court order.

As we have seen in jurisdictions across America, it is possible for law enforcement agencies to enhance their effectiveness by promoting constitutional policing and restoring community partnerships. Strengthening community trust in BPD will not only increase the effectiveness of BPD's law enforcement efforts, it will advance officer and public safety in a manner that serves the entire Baltimore community. Together with City officials and the people of Baltimore, we will work to make this a reality.

I. BACKGROUND

A. Baltimore, Maryland

Baltimore is the largest city in the state of Maryland with a population of approximately 621,000. The Baltimore metropolitan area's 2.7 million residents make it the nation's 21st largest urban center. The City's population is approximately 63 percent African American, 30 percent white, and 4 percent Hispanic or Latino.[3] While the City hosts a number of successful institutions and businesses,[4] most economic measures show that large portions of Baltimore's population struggle economically. Compared to national averages, Baltimore exhibits: lower incomes, with a median household income nearly 20 percent lower than the national average; higher poverty rates, with 24.2 percent of individuals living below the federal poverty level[5]; elevated unemployment, with a rate hovering around 7 percent, and average unemployment rates per month that were 50 percent higher than the national average from 2014 to 2015.[6] Baltimore also scores below national averages in education: 80.9 percent of the population has graduated from high school, while 27 percent has a bachelor's degree or higher.[7] In most grades and subjects, the percentage of students below basic proficiency in Baltimore was twice the rate seen in Maryland as a whole.[8]

These socioeconomic challenges are pronounced among Baltimore's African-American population, owing in part to the City's history of government-sponsored discrimination. Schools and many other public institutions in the

---

3 U.S. Census Bureau, "American FactFinder-Results," accessed April 11, 2016, http://factfinder.census.gov/faces/tableservices/jsf/pages/productview.xhtml?src=CF.

4 For example, Baltimore is the headquarters for Johns Hopkins University Hospital, Under Armour, Inc., and Legg Mason, Inc., among many others.

5 U.S. Census Bureau, "American FactFinder-Results," accessed April 11, 2016, http://factfinder.census.gov/faces/tableservices/jsf/pages/productview.xhtml?src=CF.

6 Department of Labor, Local Area Unemployment Statistics (LAUS) - Workforce Information & Performance, https://www.dllr.state.md.us/lmi/laus/.

7 Bureau, "American FactFinder - Results." Nationally, over 88 percent of adult Americans have high school diplomas and 32 percent hold a bachelor's degree or higher.

8 National Center for Education Statistics Institute of Education Sciences, 2009 National Assessment of Educational Proficiency data explorer, http://nces.ed.gov/nationsreportcard/naepdata/dataset.aspx.

City remained formally segregated until the 1950s, and stark residential segregation has marked the City's history. In 1910, Baltimore became the first city in America to pass an ordinance establishing block-by-block segregation, a policy that was followed by other discriminatory practices, including restrictive covenants, aggressive redlining, a contract system for housing loans, and racially targeted subprime loans.[9] This legacy continues to impact current home ownership patterns, as Baltimore remains among the most segregated cities in the country.[10] In 2008, the City of Baltimore sued Wells Fargo under the Fair Housing Act, alleging that the company steered minority homebuyers into subprime loans. To settle this litigation, Wells Fargo agreed to provide $4.5 million in lending assistance to Baltimore residents and $3 million to address issues connected to foreclosures.[11] Certain neighborhoods, such as all of the census tracts in South Baltimore, have been at least 90 percent white since the 1970s. Other areas, including all of the tracts in Cherry Hill, Sandtown-Winchester, and Upton/Druid Hill, have been at least 90 percent black for the past five census periods and are currently more than 95 percent black.[12]

This history of racial discrimination has created persistent racial disparities in economic opportunity and education. Roughly 100,000 African American Baltimore residents live in poverty, accounting for more than three-fourths of Baltimoreans who do so. Many communities, particularly low-income communities, confront grave challenges with respect to upward mobility. Indeed, a recent Harvard University study found that Baltimore has the least upward mobility in America. In the nation's 100 largest jurisdictions, Baltimore's children face the worst odds of escaping poverty.[13] Consequently, the unemployment rate among African Americans is roughly double that of white individuals. In addition, white adults are 3.5 times more likely than black adults to have earned a bachelor's degree. African Americans are also significantly less likely

---

9 See generally Antero Pietila, NOT IN MY NEIGHBORHOOD (2010).

10 Frey W.H., New Racial Segregation Measures for States and Large Metropolitan Areas: Analysis of the 2005–2009 American Community Survey, http://censusscope.org/ACS/Segregation.html.

11 Similarly, Wells Fargo paid $234 million to settle a Fair Housing Act and Equal Credit Opportunity Act suit brought by the U.S. Department of Justice that alleged discriminatory lending practices against minorities, including payments to the City of Baltimore and many Baltimore residents that were alleged victims of the discriminatory practices. Wells Fargo agreed to provide $5.7 million in down payment assistance and pay an additional $1.6 million directly to victims with homes in the City.

12 Place Matters for Health in Baltimore: Ensuring Opportunities for Good Health for all, Joint Center for Political and Economic Studies, November 2012, 19-20; 9. http://jointcenter.org/docs/40925_JCBaltimoreReport.pdf

13 Raj Chetty and Nathaniel Hendren, The Impacts of Neighborhoods on Intergenerational Mobility, Harvard University, April 2015. http://www.equality-of-opportunity.org/images/nbhds_exec_summary.pdf.

to hold a high school diploma.[14] Moreover, white children make up one percent or less of the student body in numerous schools that serve disproportionately low-income children, perpetuating segregation by race and class.[15]

The impacts of segregation and economic inequality are further evident in lead poisoning patterns across Baltimore. The City has nearly three times the national rate of lead poisoning among children. This burden weighs heaviest on poor, African-American communities. The areas with the highest percentage of children with elevated blood lead levels are the heavily African-American neighborhoods of Sandtown-Winchester/Harlem Park (7.4 percent), Midway/Coldstream (6.1 percent), and Edmondson Village (5.3 percent).[16] According to the Center for Disease Control, even low levels of lead are associated with learning and behavioral problems, including decreased cognitive performance.[17]

While crime rate in urban America has declined significantly since the 1990s, Baltimore has experienced violent crime rates relatively higher than many other large cities. According to data from the Federal Bureau of Investigation, in 2014 Baltimore had the sixth highest rate of violent crimes out of the country's 76 cities with at least 250,000 residents. Baltimore's violent crime rate is roughly equal to that of Cleveland, albeit lower than the rate of violent crime in Detroit, Memphis, and Milwaukee.18 This past year reflected a notable surge in violence. On a per-capita basis, 2015 was the deadliest year in Baltimore's history with 344 homicides. The City's overall gun violence increased more than 75 percent compared to the previous year, with more than 900 people shot. As in other major cities, gang activity and a drug economy are also prominent fea-

---

14 Place Matters for Health in Baltimore: Ensuring Opportunities for Good Health for all, Joint Center for Political and Economic Studies, November 2012, 11. http://jointcenter.org /docs/40925_JCBaltimoreReport.pdf

15 Ayscue, J. B., & Orfield, G. (2015). School district lines stratify educational opportunity by race and poverty. Race and Social Problems, 7(1), 5–20. doi:http://dx.doi.org.ezproxy .princeton.edu/10.1007/s12552-014-9135-0

16 Vital Signs, Baltimore Neighborhoods Indicator Alliances, http://bniajfi.org/wp-content /uploads/2014/04/VS12_Children_and_Health.pdf.

17 Center for Disease Control, "Childhood Lead Poisoning Data, Statistics, and Surveillance," accessed June 14, 2016, http://www.cdc.gov/nceh/lead/data/index.htm.; U.S. Department of Health and Human Services, National Toxicology Program Monograph: Health Effects of Low-Level Lead, June 2012, http://ntp.niehs.nih.gov/ntp/ohat/lead/final /monographhealtheffectslowlevellead_newissn_508.pdf; Aimin Chen et al., "Lead Exposure, IQ, and Behavior in Urban 5- to 7-Year-Olds: Does Lead Affect Behavior Only by Lowering IQ?," Pediatrics 119, No. 3 (March 1, 2007): e650–58, doi:10.1542/peds.2006-1973.

18 In Section II.B, infra, we compare law enforcement activity in these cities with enforcement actions taken by BPD.

tures of Baltimore's crime landscape, although Baltimore residents use drugs at similar rates to the national average.[19]

Despite such challenges, Baltimore remains a vibrant cultural center in the region. It has a significant concentration of educational, medical, cultural, and sports institutions, and a rich collection of neighborhoods. As we heard throughout our investigation, residents take great pride in their neighborhoods and their City as a whole, and have invested deeply in them. These residents are supported by a vast array of community leaders, grassroots organizations, and service providers, and together they comprise a resilient and diverse collection of communities.

B. The Baltimore Police Department

The Baltimore Police Department, or BPD, is the eighth largest municipal police department in the nation. BPD employs nearly 3,000 personnel, including approximately 2,600 sworn officers, although this number has declined over the last year. The Department is led by a police commissioner appointed by the mayor of Baltimore and approved by the Baltimore City Council. The current commissioner is Kevin Davis, who was appointed interim commissioner by Mayor Stephanie Rawlings-Blake on July 8, 2015, and sworn into the position permanently on October 19, 2015.

Most BPD officers work in either the Patrol Division or the Criminal Investigations Division, each of which is overseen by a chief.[20] Patrol officers are divided geographically among nine police districts that include local police stationhouses, referred to as district headquarters. Each district has a captain and is led by a major whose primary responsibility is directing enforcement activities and supervising officers. BPD currently employs approximately 1,300 patrol officers who have primary responsibility for responding to calls for service and patrolling Baltimore streets.

The Criminal Investigation Division and Operational Investigation Division house BPD's specialized units, such as the Homicide Section, and the Special Investigation Section, which focus on investigating violent offenders, gangs, and gun crimes across Baltimore. The Division includes units that per-

---

19 According to data collected by the Substance Abuse and Mental Health Services Administration, 42.9 percent of Baltimore residents over age 12 have used marijuana, compared to 40.7 percent nationally. For drugs other than marijuana, SAMHSA reports that 3.28 percent of Baltimore adults have used these drugs within the past 30 days, compared to 3.35 percent nationally.

20 BPD also has an Administrative Bureau that consists of booking, human resources, information services, inspections, and other management functions.

form tactical operations, use special weapons, and serve warrants. The names of these specialized enforcement units have changed several times over the past decade. Special enforcement units have previously been called the Violent Crime Impact Division (VCID), Violent Crime Impact Section (VCIS), and the Violent Repeat Offender Unit (VRO). BPD also assigns a small number of officers to its Community Collaboration Division, which focuses on building police-community relations throughout the City.

The Department has a complex process for accountability that is detailed in Section III(C), *infra*. BPD allows district supervisors to resolve complaints of officer misconduct that are deemed less serious offenses, carrying punishment of no more than a three-day suspension. Complaints deemed to allege more serious misconduct are assigned to the Internal Investigation Division. In addition, Baltimore established a Civilian Review Board to provide a public voice in BPD's accountability process. Members of the public can lodge complaints with the Board directly, and BPD is required by statute to share with the Board all complaints it receives that fit within certain categories, including excessive force and discourtesy. The Board is authorized to conduct parallel investigations and make disciplinary recommendations. In practice, however, the Board's role has been diminished by severely limited investigative resources, inconsistent complaint referrals from BPD, and the City's failure to fill the Board's seats.

BPD officers are represented by the Fraternal Order of the Police Lodge No. 3 (FOP), which has a collective-bargaining contract with the City and serves as the sole collective-bargaining agent for officers below the rank of lieutenant, making membership inclusive of both line officers and their direct supervisors. In addition to the FOP, the Vanguard Justice Society, Inc., is a membership organization that advocates on behalf of minority officers. BPD did not hire its first African-American officer until 1937 and did not allow minority officers to drive patrol cars until 1966. Prior to 1966, the Department's small number of African-American officers were required to work foot patrol and were not permitted to work in predominantly white neighborhoods. In recent years, the Department has made efforts to attract and promote minority candidates. As of 2015, African Americans accounted for approximately 42 percent of BPD officers. About one-fifth of BPD officers are women. Most BPD officers are neither originally from Baltimore nor live in the City, and many commute long distances to work at the Department. Indeed, BPD leadership informed us that roughly three-fourths of BPD officers live outside the Baltimore City limits.

BPD coordinates with several auxiliary law enforcement agencies, and has done so increasingly in recent years to compensate when districts do not have sufficient officers to staff shifts. These agencies include the Baltimore School Police, the police force of the Baltimore City Public School System. Baltimore School Police officers have all the powers of law enforcement officers in the state, including arrest powers.[21] A memorandum of understanding between the Public School System and BPD authorizes the school police to "exercise full police power anywhere within the jurisdiction of the City of Baltimore," and to assist in investigations and follow-up in criminal cases.[22] The deployment plan for the school police indicates that these officers are assigned to foot patrol, bike units, and mobile response units outside of schools.[23] These officers also respond to calls for service in the City when BPD patrol shifts are understaffed.

C. BPD's Enforcement Priorities and Relationship with the Baltimore Community

Baltimore's legacy of government-sanctioned discrimination, serious health hazards, and high rates of violent crime have persisted and compounded for years—making Baltimore a challenging city to police fairly and effectively. Indeed, officers convey that working in Baltimore affords a uniquely intense and demanding experience. One member of BPD recently asserted, "a five-year cop in the city has the equivalent experience of a ten-year cop anywhere else."[24] These challenges are amplified by long-simmering distrust of law enforcement from segments of the Baltimore community. Indeed, when asked when community distrust of Baltimore law enforcement began, a former top city official deadpanned to Justice Department officials, "1729"—the year of the City's founding. These tensions hardened during the 1990s and 2000s as the City responded to increasing violent crime rates by emphasizing an aggressive, "zero tolerance" policing strategy that prioritized making large numbers of stops, searches, and arrests—often for misdemeanor street offenses like loitering and disorderly conduct. Throughout the 1990s and 2000s, arresting large numbers of people for minor offenses was central to BPD's enforcement paradigm; in 2005, BPD made more than 108,000 arrests, most for nonviolent offenses.

Arrest numbers declined starting in the late 2000s in response to falling crime rates and efforts to move towards a more holistic policing model focused on building community partnerships. Indeed, current BPD Commissioner Davis and his predecessor, Anthony W. Batts, have both acknowledged publicly that the zero tolerance approach to policing eroded community trust

---

21 Md. Code Ann., Educ. §§4–318 (c) and (d)(1) (2015).

22 Memorandum of Understanding between the Baltimore City Public School System and Baltimore Police Department at 1–2 (June 27, 2007).

23 Marshall T. Goddwin, Chief, Baltimore School Police Force, *Deployment For SY 2015/2016*, July 2, 2015.

24 Fraternal Order of Police Lodge 3, Blueprint for Improved Policing, 5, http://www.fop3.org /wp-content/uploads/2015/05/blueprint.pdf.

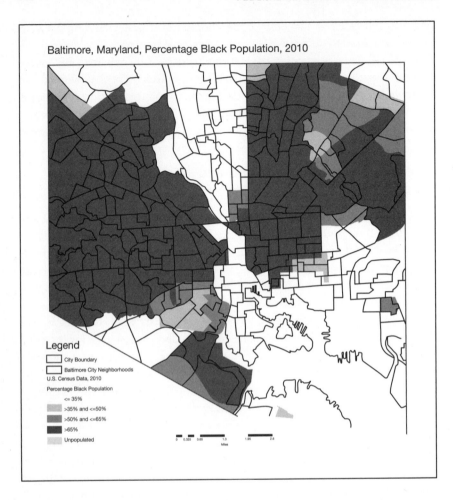

Baltimore, Maryland, Percentage Black Population, 2010

Legend

City Boundary

Baltimore City Neighborhoods

U.S. Census Data, 2010

Percentage Black Population

<= 35%

>35% and <=50%

>50% and <=65%

>65%

Unpopulated

and impeded efforts to build partnerships that are central to effective policing. Despite these efforts, however, the legacy of zero tolerance persists in
many aspects of the Department's enforcement. Many supervisors who were
inculcated in the era of zero tolerance continue to focus on the raw number
of officers' stops and arrests, rather than more nuanced measures of performance. As one example of this approach, supervisors frequently encourage
officers to "clear corners"—an instruction many officers understand to stop,
disperse, or arrest groups of individuals standing on public sidewalks. The
continued emphasis on these types of "stats" drives BPD's tendency to stop,
search, and arrest significant numbers of individuals on Baltimore streets—
often without requisite legal justification and in situations that put officers in
adversarial encounters that have little connection to public safety. Although
arrest numbers have declined from their peak in the mid-2000s, BPD officers

made over 200,000 arrests and 300,000 pedestrian stops in the five years of data we examined.[25]

A diverse array of stakeholders has highlighted problems with BPD's policing strategy. For example, the Fraternal Order of Police's 2012 Blueprint for Improved Policing in Baltimore advocates discontinuing the practice of rewarding statistically driven arrests, noting:

> [N]umbers drive everything in the BPD, which has led to misplaced priorities. As a result, officers in the BPD feel pressure to achieve numbers for perception's sake . . . The focus on assigning blame for less-than-satisfactory numbers . . . rather than problem-solving, is completely unproductive and weakens the collective morale of the BPD.[26]

City officials also admit that the Department's approach has been problematic. Mayor Rawlings-Blake has long recognized the need for reform and repeatedly criticized the aggressive policing strategies championed in the years before her term. In September 2013, she told residents, "As this conversation is going on, there is an anxiety that is building in some of our communities that we're going back to a time when communities felt like their kids were under siege . . . I want to allay any concerns out there that that is the tactic we're going to return to. That's not going to happen."[27] And in the fall of 2014, her administration noted that the zero tolerance strategy "ignited a rift between the citizens and the police, which still exists today" and that there is a "broken relationship" between law enforcement officials and community members.[28]

The larger Baltimore community has voiced similar concerns. News outlets, community advocates, and grassroots organizations have frequently criticized Baltimore's approach to policing. In 2006, the ACLU of Maryland sued BPD over its alleged pattern of making high numbers of unlawful stops and arrests. In addition, the police department has long faced allegations of unreasonable force. In some of these allegations, the police interactions were fatal. In

---

25 As explained further in Section II.A, the true number of pedestrian stops is likely several times higher than the recorded figure due to BPD's under-reporting.

26 Fraternal Order of Police Lodge 3, Blueprint for Improved Policing, 8–9, http://www.fop3 .org/wp-content/uploads/2015/05/blueprint.pdf

27 Luke Broadwater and Eric Cox, "Governor's Push for More Arrests Causing 'Anxiety' in Baltimore, Mayor Says," Baltimore Sun, September 25, 2013, http://www.baltimoresun.com /news/maryland/politics/blog/bs-md-ci-srb-arrests-20130925-story.html.

28 John Fritze, "Rawlings-Blake Criticism Highlights Debate over Police Strategy under O'Malley," Baltimore Sun, October 13, 2014, http://www.baltimoresun.com/news/maryland /politics/bs-md-police-omalley-politics-20141007-story.html.

others, Baltimore residents were left severely and permanently injured. In September 2014, the Baltimore Sun published "Undue Force," an article documenting cases of alleged police brutality and the millions of dollars the city has paid to settle lawsuits alleging that officers used excessive force. The article notes that more than 100 people have won court judgments or settlements related to allegations of brutality and civil rights violations since 2010.[29] More recently, No Boundaries Coalition, a resident-led advocacy organization operating in West Baltimore, released a report in March 2016 detailing stories of police misconduct told by witnesses and victims in the Sandtown-Winchester neighborhood. The community recollections reveal a belief that there is racism in law enforcement, unnecessary force and verbal abuse, an "us-versus-them" attitude among police officers, a lack of positive interactions with the police, and strong feelings of recrimination, resentment, fear, and mistrust among residents.[30]

In 2012, Mayor Rawlings-Blake hired Commissioner Batts to initiate reforms throughout the police department. The following year, Commissioner Batts issued *Public Safety in the City of Baltimore*, a five-year plan intended to "reduce crime, improve service, increase efficiency, redouble community engagement, and provide for the highest standards of accountability and ethical integrity."[31] The report discussed numerous challenges facing BPD, including: equipment, accountability, training, and communication failures; strained police-community relations, and low community engagement; and decreased morale and motivation among officers.[32] The report included an internal survey that revealed that only 14 percent of BPD employees believed the Baltimore community supports the police department. The report also laid out a plan for improving BPD's work in these areas. During a similar time period, the City substantially increased the resources of the police department. While the city faces serious budget constraints, the fiscal year 2016 police budget was approved at $476 million, representing a dramatic increase from the 2010 police budget of $340 million.

As the reform plans Commissioner Batts initiated were in their early stages, the unrest following the death of Freddie Gray in police custody in April 2015 demonstrated the deep and enduring divide between police officers and parts of the Baltimore community. Commissioner Davis acknowledged that BPD's legacy of zero tolerance enforcement contributed to these tensions: "Some of

---

29 Mark Puente, "Undue Force," Baltimore Sun, September 28, 2014, http://data.baltimoresun .com/news/police-settlements/.

30 No Boundaries Coalition, Over-Policed, Yet Underserved, March 2016, http://www.no-boundariescoalition.com/wp-content/uploads/2016/03/No-Boundaries-Layout-Web-1.pdf.

31 Anthony Batts, Public Safety in the City of Baltimore: A Strategic Plan for Improvement, 2013, 5.

32 Id. at 45–48.

things that we did in the past, like zero tolerance policing, didn't work and arguably led in part to the unrest that we experienced in 2015."[33] He has also acknowledged that improved relations with City residents require BPD to change its culture.[34] The desire for such reform is apparent. Commissioner Davis began a "History of Baltimore" speakers-series in early 2016 to provide officers with an understanding of the City's historical background. The topics, which range from housing and segregation to the development of Baltimore's port, were selected to provide a deeper appreciation of the diverse communities that the police serve. The release of a new Core Operating Procedures Manual during the summer of 2016 also represents an attempt to improve standards and guidelines with respect to officers' use of force.

We commend these efforts, but find that significant obstacles remain to achieving the change necessary to ensure that BPD's policing is both effective and constitutional. As described below, we find that BPD has engaged in a pattern or practice of conduct that violates the constitutional and federal statutory rights of City residents, and that the Department lacks sufficient systems to minimize these violations.

D. Federal Involvement

Numerous federal components have assisted BPD's reform efforts in recent years. In October 2014, Mayor Rawlings-Blake and Commissioner Batts requested to enter a collaborative reform process with the Department of Justice's Office of Community Oriented Policing Services (COPS). This federal review involved an assessment of BPD's policies, training, and operations as they related to the use of force and interactions with the members of the community. Through this process, subject matter experts identified by the COPS office began to examine BPD's community policing and engagement efforts and provided additional resources and trainings, such as peer-to-peer exchanges to facilitate sharing best practices from other police departments. Over the past several years, the Office of Justice Programs also awarded Byrne Justice Assistance grants to BPD, to support certain initiatives, including: a comprehensive review of BPD's technology systems and capabilities; an analysis of BPD's grant development efforts and strategy; and a customized workshop for BPD

---

33 Mary Rose Madden, "Baltimore Police Chief Wants To Reform Department," *NPR: All Things Considered*, April 24, 2016, http://www.npr.org/2016/04/24/475511963/baltimore-police-chief-wants-to-reform-department.

34 Kevin Rector, Justin George, and Mark Puente, "Baltimore's New Police Commissioner Has a Full Plate — and an Opportunity," *Baltimore Sun*, July 12, 2015, http://www.baltimoresun.com/news/maryland/bs-md-davis-challenges-20150711-story.html.

command staff to effectively develop and manage crime analysis capabilities. In response to another request from City leadership, the Justice Department provided federal law enforcement resources to help the City combat its crime and public safety challenges in August 2015. Following this initial assistance, the Bureau of Alcohol, Tobacco, Firearms and Explosives, the Federal Bureau of Investigation, the Drug Enforcement Administration, and the U.S. Marshals Service all agreed to make a longer term commitment of resources to law enforcement efforts in Baltimore.[35]

The death of Freddie Gray and ensuing unrest occurred during the early stages of the collaborative reform efforts between BPD and COPS. These events underscored the critical lack of trust between BPD and a significant portion of the City's residents, especially African Americans. After reviewing information it had received about BPD's police practices and receiving requests from Mayor Rawlings-Blake, members of Congress, and numerous other members of the Baltimore community, the Justice Department determined BPD warranted a comprehensive civil rights investigation to determine whether the Department engaged in a pattern or practice of constitutional and statutory violations. The Civil Rights Division thus opened a formal investigation into BPD on May 8, 2015. Since the civil rights investigation opened, the COPS office has continued to provide technical assistance to BPD.

Our investigation recognizes that, as Commissioner Davis aptly noted, Baltimore officers "have the burden to address racism and poverty and education and homelessness." These problems, which confront officers every day on the street and are not their responsibility alone to fix, are nevertheless intertwined with crime conditions across the City. But this burden on officers does not excuse BPD's violations of the constitutional and statutory rights of the people living in these challenging conditions. We find that BPD's practices perpetuate and fuel a multitude of issues rooted in poverty and race, focusing law enforcement actions on low-income, minority communities in a manner that is often unnecessary and unproductive. In other words, BPD's law enforcement practices at times exacerbate the longstanding structural inequalities in the City by encouraging officers to have unnecessary, adversarial interactions with community members that increase exposure to the criminal justice system and fail to improve public safety.

---

35 During this same time period, the Office of Justice Programs Office for Civil Rights initiated a language access compliance review of BPD, and that review is still ongoing.

II. BPD ENGAGES IN A PATTERN OR PRACTICE OF CONDUCT THAT VIOLATES THE UNITED STATES CONSTITUTION AND LAWS, AND CONDUCT THAT RAISES SERIOUS CONCERNS

The Civil Rights Division of the United States Department of Justice opened this investigation pursuant to the Violent Crime Control and Law Enforcement Act of 1994, 42 U.S.C. § 14141 ("Section 14141"), Title VI of the Civil Rights Act of 1964, 42 U.S.C. § 2000d ("Title VI"), and the Omnibus Crime Control and Safe Streets Act of 1968, 42 U.S.C. § 3789d ("Safe Streets Act" or "SSA"), and Title II of the Americans with Disabilities Act of 1990 (ADA), 42 U.S.C. §§ 12131–12134. Section 14141 prohibits law enforcement agencies from engaging in a pattern or practice of conduct that violates the Constitution or laws of the United States. Where such a pattern or practice exists, Section 14141 grants the Attorney General authority to bring suit for equitable and declaratory relief to remedy it. A pattern or practice exists where violations are repeated rather than isolated. *Int'l Bd. of Teamsters v. United States*, 431 U.S. 324, 336 n.16 (1977) (noting that the phrase "pattern or practice" "was not intended as a term of art," but should be interpreted according to its usual meaning "consistent with the understanding of the identical words" used in other federal civil rights statutes). An unlawful pattern or practice does not require any specific number of incidents. *United States v. W. Peachtree Tenth Corp.*, 437 F.2d 221, 227 (5th Cir. 1971) ("The number of [violations] . . . is not determinative. . . . In any event, no mathematical formula is workable, nor was any intended. Each case must turn on its own facts."); *see also Stastny v. S. Bell Tel. & Tel. Co.*, 628 F.2d 267, 278 (4th Cir. 1980) (holding in the context of employment discrimination that a plaintiff may show a pattern or practice through statistical evidence or a "sufficient number of instances of similar discriminatory treatment"). Title VI and its implementing regulations prohibit recipients of federal financial assistance, such as BPD, from discriminating on the basis of race, color, or national origin. Title VI provides that no person shall "be excluded from participating in, be denied the benefits of, or be subjected to discrimination under any program or activity receiving [f]ederal financial assistance" based on race. 42 U.S.C. § 2000d. The Title VI implementing regulations ban recipients of federal funds from using "criteria or methods of administration" that have an unnecessary disparate impact based on race. 28 C.F.R. § 42.104(b)(2). The Safe Streets Act likewise prohibits law enforcement practices that cause disparate impact based on race except where such impact is necessary to achieve nondiscriminatory objectives. *See* 28 C.F.R. § 42.203. The ADA, which applies to BPD's services, programs, and activities, including on-the-street encounters, arrests, and transportation to a hospital for mental health evaluation, *See* 42 U.S.C. § 12132; 28 C.F.R. § 35.130(a); requires BPD to "make reasonable modifications in policies, practices, or procedures when the modifications are necessary to avoid discrimination on the basis of disability." 28 C.F.R. § 35.130(b)(7); *Title II Technical Assistance Manual* § II-3.6100, at 14.

Our investigation finds that BPD engages in a pattern or practice of conduct that implicates our statutory authority. This pattern or practice is rooted in BPD's deficient supervision and oversight of officer activity, leading directly to a broad spectrum of constitutional and statutory violations. This lack of supervision and oversight includes BPD's failure to use effective and widely-accepted methods to supervise officers, collect and analyze data on officer activity, and classify, investigate, and resolve complaints of misconduct. This pattern or practice is also manifested in several ways that violate specific constitutional and statutory provisions: (1) BPD stops, searches, and arrests individuals on Baltimore streets without the reasonable suspicion or probable cause required by the Fourth Amendment; (2) BPD disproportionately stops, searches, and arrests African Americans in violation of Title VI and the Safe Streets Act, and this disparate impact, along with evidence suggesting intentional discrimination against African Americans, exacerbates community distrust of the police; (3) BPD uses unreasonable force in violation of the Fourth Amendment; (4) BPD violates the First Amendment rights of Baltimore residents by using force or otherwise retaliating against individuals exercising constitutionally protected activity, such as public speech and filming police activity; and (5) BPD's use of force against individuals with mental health disabilities or experiencing crisis violates the Americans with Disabilities Act. To illustrate these violations, throughout this letter we provide several examples of each type of violation that we found during our investigation. In some sections we provide more examples to illustrate the variety of circumstances in which the violation occurs, while in others we focus on one or two examples that demonstrate the nature of the violations we found. The number of examples included in a particular section is not indicative of the number of violations we found. These examples comprise a small subset of the total number of incidents upon which we base our conclusions.

We make these findings after a comprehensive 14-month investigation into BPD's practices. To gain the broadest possible perspective on the challenges facing BPD, our investigation involved reviewing an exhaustive set of documents and meeting with hundreds of officers, community members, city leaders, and other stakeholders. In total, we reviewed hundreds of thousands of pages of documents, including all relevant policies and training materials used by the Department since 2010; BPD's database of internal affairs files; a random sample of about 800 case files on non-deadly force incidents; files on all deadly force incidents since 2010 that BPD was able to produce to us through May 1, 2016; a sample of several hundred incident reports describing stops, searches, and arrests; investigative files on sexual assault cases; databases maintained by BPD and the State of Maryland containing information on hundreds of thousands of pedestrian stops, vehicle stops, and arrests; and many others. Throughout our review, we were assisted by a dozen law enforcement experts from across the country with expertise on the issues we investigated.

Our investigation also relied on numerous interviews with current and former BPD officers and city officials. At all times, BPD leadership took a cooperative and professional approach to our investigation and provided important insights into the challenges facing the Department. We met at length with current Commissioner Kevin Davis, former Commissioner Anthony Batts, and leaders throughout the BPD command structure. We visited each of BPD's nine police districts, where we met district leadership and spoke with line officers. We also accompanied line officers on dozens of ride-alongs that took place in every district. Line officers shared many key insights during these ride-alongs and other interviews. We are grateful for their candor in discussing the serious challenges they face and their genuine interest in preventing the types of issues discussed in our findings. We are likewise grateful to the leadership of the Baltimore Fraternal Order of Police, which met with us on multiple occasions and invited us to speak to union members at a lodge dinner. The Vanguard Justice Society similarly invited us to speak with their members and provided highly relevant information. To gain the broadest possible perspective on the challenges facing BPD, we also met with current and former officials in City government, including current and former elected officials and prosecutors from the State's Attorney's Office.

As in all of our investigations, we also met with large numbers of people in the broader Baltimore community. Our community outreach included meetings at churches and with religious leaders; meeting with advocacy and community support organizations; attending a variety of neighborhood gatherings, from formal meetings of neighborhood associations to summer barbecues; and canvassing neighborhoods on foot to collect stories about interactions with the police. We also met individually with numerous individuals who contacted us to share information. In sum, we met with more than 500 individuals during our investigation. We are extremely thankful for the many members of the Baltimore community who came forward to share information with us, even when doing so involved reliving difficult personal experiences. We are left with the firm impression that, despite the significant obstacles to restoring community trust in BPD, there is a deep desire across diverse elements of the City for a police force that is responsive, effective, and fair.

A. BPD MAKES UNCONSTITUTIONAL STOPS, SEARCHES, AND ARRESTS

We find that BPD engages in a pattern or practice of making stops, searches, and arrests in violation of the Fourth and Fourteenth Amendments and Section 14141. BPD frequently makes investigative stops without reasonable suspicion of people who are lawfully present on Baltimore streets. During stops, officers commonly conduct weapons frisks—or more invasive searches—despite lacking reasonable suspicion that the subject of the search is armed. These practices escalate street encounters and contribute to officers making arrests without probable cause,[36] often for discretionary misdemeanor offenses like disorderly conduct, resisting arrest, loitering, trespassing, and failure to obey. Indeed, BPD's own supervisors at Central Booking and prosecutors in the State's Attorney's Office declined to charge more than 11,000 arrests made by BPD officers since 2010.

1. BPD's Unconstitutional Stops, Searches, and Arrests Result in Part from Its "Zero Tolerance" Enforcement Strategy

The pattern of constitutional violations described below result in part from BPD's "zero tolerance" enforcement strategy, dating to the early 2000s. That strategy prioritized attempts to suppress crime by regularly stopping and searching pedestrians and arresting them on any available charges, including discretionary misdemeanor offenses. Recent BPD leadership, including the two most recent police commissioners, has acknowledged some of the problems created by this zero tolerance approach to enforcement and has attempted to shift BPD's focus to a more holistic policing model with greater emphasis on building community partnerships. For example, in April 2015 BPD enacted a new policy on misdemeanor "quality of life" offenses that instructed officers that "a verbal warning and counseling is preferable to a criminal/civil citation, and a criminal/civil citation is preferable to an arrest." Despite these laudable efforts, however, the legacy of the zero tolerance era continues to influence officer activity and contribute to constitutional violations.

---

36 As detailed in Section II(C) below, these street encounters also contribute to officers' pattern or practice of using excessive force.

Indeed, many BPD supervisors who were trained under the prior enforcement paradigm continue to encourage officers to prioritize short-term suppression, including aggressive use of stops, frisks, and misdemeanor arrests. A current BPD sergeant recently endorsed this approach to policing, posting on Facebook that the "solution to the murder rate is easy. Flex cuffs and a line at [Central Booking]. CJIS code 2-0055." CJIS 2-0055 is the offense code entered for loitering arrests. Similarly, a flyer celebrating loitering arrests was posted in several BPD districts. The flyer depicted three officers from one of BPD's specialized units known as Violent Crime Impact Division, or VCID, leading a handcuffed man wearing a hoodie along a city sidewalk towards a police transport van, with the text "VCID: Striking fear into loiters [sic] City-wide." And a deployment memo posted in one of BPD's districts in the summer of 2015 likewise encouraged officers to suppress crime through "proactive enforcement," including "stop and frisk," "street level drug enforcement," "warrant checks," "foot patrol," "car stops," and "quality of life" arrests.

These influences have contributed to BPD officers making large numbers of stops, searches, and arrests, often with dubious justification. From January 2010–May 2014, BPD officers recorded over 301,000 pedestrian stops. And the true number of stops is likely far higher because BPD officers do not document stops consistently. BPD's data suggests that stops are significantly underreported. In 2014 alone, BPD officers recorded approximately 124,000 stops, but an internal audit found that officers completed reports for only 37 out of a sample of 123 investigative stops captured on the computer-aided dispatch (CAD) system. If this audit accurately captures BPD's overall rate of reporting stops in 2014, it indicates that officers made roughly 412,000 stops *that year*

alone, which is more than seven times the average number of stops that BPD reported per year from 2010 to 2015. Other measures suggest that even this estimate may be conservative. BPD's 2014 audit of handgun charges that arose from stops found that officers did not complete a stop form in a single one of the 335 cases. These data are consistent with interviews and observations during the Justice Department's investigation, which revealed that many officers fill out stop reports rarely, if at all. In short, our investigation suggests that BPD officers likely make several hundred thousand pedestrian stops per year[37] in a city with only 620,000 residents.

Moreover, BPD's data show that these stops are concentrated on a small segment of the City's population. From 2010–2014, BPD officers in the Western and Central Districts recorded more than 111,500 stops—roughly 44 percent of the total stops for which officers recorded a district location.[38] Yet these are the two least populated police districts in Baltimore, with a combined population of only 75,000, or 12 percent of City residents.[39] These districts include the City's central business district and several poor, urban neighborhoods with mostly African-American residents.[40] In these districts, police recorded nearly 1.5 stops per resident over a four-year period. This data reveals that certain Baltimore residents have repeated encounters with the police on public streets and sidewalks. Indeed, the data show that one African-American man was stopped 34 times during this period in the Central and Western Districts alone, and several hundred residents were stopped at least 10 times. Countless individuals—including Freddie Gray—

---

37 During this period, BPD policy required officers to record all stops on a form titled "Stop and Frisk." Some of the activity recorded by officers on this form may reflect encounters that do not require reasonable suspicion, such as voluntary social contacts and witness interviews. The large majority of stops recorded, however, appear to reflect situations in which the subject is not free to leave and reasonable suspicion is required. This conclusion stems from interviews with officers who explained that they completed a "Stop and Frisk" form only when making an investigative stop, and analysis of a sample of over 7,000 stops examined by Justice Department investigators, which revealed that 73 percent of stops involved officers detaining subjects at least long enough to complete a warrant check. The stop data discussed here thus overwhelmingly reflect stops that require reasonable suspicion. In 2015, BPD addressed this issue by changing its documentation protocols so that officers complete "citizen/police contact" forms for voluntary field interviews and a "Form 309" for investigative detentions, weapons frisks, and searches.

38 Officers recorded district information in approximately 254,000 out of 301,000 total recorded stops.

39 Population data on BPD's police districts was provided by the Department and was compiled from the U.S. Census Bureau's 2014 American Community Survey 5-year data.

40 According to 2014 estimates from the U.S. Census Bureau, African Americans account for 83 percent of the population in the Central District and 96 percent in the Western District.

were stopped multiple times in the same week without being charged with a crime.[41]

The data likewise indicate that these encounters produce large numbers of arrests. While a significant portion of these arrests reflect BPD's efforts to combat violent crime in Baltimore City, more than 25,000 arrests were for non-violent misdemeanor offenses for which officers have significant discretion about whether to make an arrest. BPD arrested approximately 6,500 people for disorderly conduct, 4,000 for failing to obey a police officer, 6,500 for trespassing, 1,000 for "hindering" or impeding, 3,200 for "interference," 760 for being "rogue and vagabond," and 650 for playing cards or dice. These highly discretionary offenses often are not an effective way to promote public safety and are subject to abuse. Indeed, supervisors at Central Booking and local prosecutors dismissed a significant percentage of these charges upon their initial review of arrest documents. This initial review resulted in dismissal of 1 in 6 of these highly discretionary charges. Over 20 percent of all disorderly conduct charges and 25 percent of failure to obey charges were dismissed.

Careful oversight is necessary to ensure that these frequent street encounters and arrests do not result in constitutional violations. Our investigation finds, however, that BPD has amplified the risk of constitutional violations in its street enforcement efforts by relying on inadequate policies, training, supervision, and accountability mechanisms. The Department does not collect reliable data on stops and searches, has no mechanism for identifying patterns or trends in its officers' stops, searches, and arrests, and conducts little substantive review of officers' reasons for taking particular enforcement actions. Indeed, BPD has failed to take corrective action even where third parties—including local prosecutors—have identified officers who may be making stops, searches, or arrests in violation of the Constitution. As a result, the pattern or practice of constitutional violations described below has persisted for many years, undermining trust in law enforcement and impeding BPD's ability to form community partnerships that are essential to effective policing.

2. BPD Unconstitutionally Stops and Searches Pedestrians

The Fourth Amendment protects individuals from unreasonable seizures "when they step from their homes onto the public sidewalks." *Delaware v. Prouse*, 440 U.S. 648, 663 (1979). Contrary to this principle, we find reasonable

---

41 The data show that BPD recorded stops of Freddie Gray on February 16th and 20th, 2014. The data nonetheless record only three total stops of Freddie Gray between 2010 and 2015. These records further indicate that BPD officers under-report pedestrian stops. Although BPD arrested Mr. Gray at least four times from 2010–2014 on charges stemming from street encounters, none of these arrests have a corresponding stop report in BPD's data.

cause to believe that BPD officers regularly stop and search individuals who are lawfully present on Baltimore's streets, despite lacking the constitutionally required indicia that criminal activity is afoot.

Our findings are based on statistical analysis of stop outcomes, interviews with officers and community members, complaints filed against BPD, and our review of a random sample of several hundred incident reports that officers completed for arrests that stemmed from pedestrian stops. Officers' descriptions of the underlying stops in these incident reports revealed frequent constitutional deficiencies. We were unable to systematically analyze the sufficiency of reasonable suspicion in *all* stops made by BPD officers—as opposed to the subset of stops leading to arrest—because most BPD stop reports do not describe the facts establishing reasonable suspicion for a stop.[42] By limiting our review to stops that resulted in arrest, we focused on cases where officers presumably had stronger indicia of criminality to justify a stop compared to stops in which the investigation proved fruitless. It is troubling that this review nonetheless found repeated constitutional violations during stops and searches by BPD officers.

a. BPD Stops Pedestrians Without Reasonable Suspicion

Our investigation reveals a widespread pattern of BPD officers stopping and detaining people on Baltimore streets without reasonable suspicion that they are involved in criminal activity. This conduct violates the Fourth Amendment, which allows police officers to briefly detain an individual for investigation where the officers possess reasonable suspicion that the person is involved in criminal activity, *Terry v. Ohio*, 392 U.S. 1, 21 (1968). To satisfy this standard, officers "must be able to point to specific and articulable facts" supporting an inference of criminal activity; an "inchoate and unparticularized suspicion or hunch" is insufficient. *Id.* at 27.

Terry's particularity requirement is not satisfied where an officer deems a person to be acting suspiciously but fails to explain the specific basis of that suspicion. The police "must do more than simply label a behavior as suspicious to make it so"; rather, the police must also be able to . . . articulate why a particular behavior is suspicious" *United States v. Massenburg*, 654 F.3d 480, 491 (4th Cir. 2011) (citations and internal quotation marks omitted). Standing alone, an individual's unexplained presence in a high crime area is not sufficient to establish reasonable suspicion. *Illinois v. Wardlow*, 528 U.S. 119, 124 (2000) (citation omitted); *United States v. Slocumb*, 804 F.3d 677, 682–83 (4th Cir.

---

42 As explained further below, the failure to capture the facts supporting reasonable suspicion on stop forms also precludes BPD supervisors from substantively reviewing the basis for stops and correcting officer behavior, where necessary.

2015) (finding that officers lacked reasonable suspicion to stop a man who was present in a high crime area late at night, acting nervously, and conducting himself in a way that seemed "inconsistent" with his stated reasons for being at the location). Nor is an individual's decision to move away from police "in a normal, unhurried manner." *United States v. Sprinkle*, 106 F.3d 613, 617–18 (4th Cir. 1997) (officers lacked reasonable suspicion to stop individual who covered his face with his hand to conceal his identity and drove away from police at normal speed); *cf. United States v. Bumpers*, 705 F.3d 168, 175–76 (4th Cir. 2013) (finding reasonable suspicion where an apparent trespasser in high crime area "dodge[d] the police" by "walking away 'at a fast pace'"). Notwithstanding these requirements, officers may always approach individuals to make social contact and ask them to answer questions voluntarily. The cases discussed in this section involve situations in which BPD officers' descriptions of an encounter indicate that the person stopped was not free to leave and reasonable suspicion was therefore required.

BPD officers routinely violate these standards by detaining and questioning individuals who are sitting, standing, or walking in public areas, even where officers have no basis to suspect them of wrongdoing. The lack of sufficient justification for many of BPD's pedestrian stops is underscored by the extremely low rate at which stops uncover evidence of criminal activity. In a sample of over 7,200 pedestrian stops reviewed by the Justice Department, only 271—or 3.7 percent—resulted in officers issuing a criminal citation or arrest. Expressed a different way, BPD officers did not find and charge criminal activity in 26 out of every 27 pedestrian stops. Such low "hit rates" are a strong indication that officers make stops based on a threshold of suspicion that falls below constitutional requirements. *See Floyd v. City of New York*, 959 F. Supp. 2d 540, 575 (S.D.N.Y. 2013) (finding that a hit rate of 12 percent in pedestrian stops indicated that the stops were not supported by reasonable suspicion).

Despite the low rate of stops uncovering evidence of crimes, BPD supervisors often direct officers to make frequent stops as a crime suppression technique. Many of the unlawful stops we identified appear motivated at least in part by officers' desire to check whether the stopped individuals have outstanding warrants that would allow officers to make an arrest or search individuals in hopes of finding illegal firearms or narcotics. *Cf. Utah v. Strieff*, 579 U.S. __, slip op. at 8 (June 20, 2016) (holding that search incident to arrest was valid based on the discovery of an arrest warrant, even when the initial stop was unconstitutional, because "the stop was an isolated instance of negligence" and there was "no indication that this unlawful stop was part of any systemic or recurrent police misconduct"); *see also* 579 U.S. __, slip op. at 10–11 (Sotomayor, J., dissenting) (warning that police may make unlawful stops in hopes of uncovering outstanding warrants, subjecting individuals to "humiliations" and "indignity").[43] Indeed, where individuals lack identification allowing officers to check for warrants, officers sometimes detain and transport them to booking facilities to check their identification via fingerprinting—an unconstitutional detention even where officers have reasonable suspicion to make the initial investigative stop. *See, e.g., United States v. Zavala*, 541 F.3d 562, 579–80 (5th Cir. 2008) (90-minute detention in which subject was handcuffed, placed in a police car, and transported to different location "morphed from a *Terry* detention into a de facto arrest").

Officers' own reports describe this facially unconstitutional conduct. For example, an officer in the Northeast District noted in an incident report that he observed a 22-year-old African American male walking through an area "known to have a high rate of crime and [drug] activity." After watching the subject turn into an alley, the officer—despite possessing no specific information indicating that the man was involved in criminal activity—stopped and questioned him. The officer's report does not identify any evidence of wrongdoing uncovered during the *Terry* stop. Nonetheless, the report explains that the officer transported the man to BPD's Northeast District headquarters to "properly identif[y]" him because the subject "was reluctant to give any information about himself or his actions." After this custodial detention likewise uncovered no evidence of wrongdoing, the subject was finally released. This stop lacked reasonable suspicion at the outset, far exceeded the temporal limits even for valid *Terry* stops, *see infra* at 39, and violates BPD's policy requiring officers to contact supervisors when a *Terry* stop lasts for more than 20 minutes. But a BPD supervisor nonetheless signed off on the incident report describing this unlawful stop and detention.

In some cases, unconstitutional stops result from supervisory officers' explicit instructions. During a ride-along with Justice Department officials, a BPD sergeant instructed a patrol officer to stop a group of young African-American males on a street corner, question them, and order them to disperse. When the patrol officer protested that he had no valid reason to stop the group, the sergeant replied "Then make something up." This incident is far from anomalous. A different BPD sergeant posted on Facebook that when he supervises officers in the Northeast District, he encourages them to "clear corners," a term many officers understand to mean stopping pedestrians who are standing on city sidewalks to question and then disperse them by threatening arrest for minor offenses like loitering and trespassing. The sergeant wrote, "I used to say at roll call in NE when I ran the shift: Do not treat criminals like citizens. Citizens want that corner cleared." Indeed, countless

---

43 Consistent with this concern, BPD officers indicated that they conducted a warrant check in 73 percent of all pedestrian stops the Justice Department analyzed—including many stops that lacked reasonable suspicion.

interviews with community members and officers describe "corner clearing" scenarios, in which BPD officers stop, question, disperse, or arrest individuals in public areas based on minimal or no suspicion of highly discretionary offenses.

Such unlawful stops erode public confidence in law enforcement and escalate street encounters, sometimes resulting in officers deploying unnecessary force or committing additional constitutional violations. For example, on a cold January evening in 2013, an officer approached and questioned an African-American man crossing the street in a "high crime area" while wearing a hooded sweatshirt. The officer lacked any specific reason to believe the man was engaged in criminal activity, but, according to the incident report prepared by the supervisory officer on the scene, the officer "thought it could be possible that the individual could be out seeking a victim of opportunity."[44] This unsupported speculation furnishes no basis to conduct a stop. Nonetheless, multiple officers questioned the man and seized a kitchen knife that the man acknowledged carrying. When the man asked the officers to return his knife, the officers ordered the man to sit down and then forced him to the ground when the man "persisted to ask for his knife." The man yelled "you can't arrest me" and resisted his detention. Although there was no basis to detain the man, two officers attempted to handcuff and shackle him, while one officer struck him "in the face, ribs, and back" with fists. The man continued to resist being shackled as additional officers arrived, one of whom tased the man twice to prevent him from "escap[ing] the scene." After officers handcuffed the man, they transported him to Union Memorial Hospital for medical care. The man was not charged with any offense. The sergeant who responded to the scene confirmed that the involved officers tased the man twice and hit him in the face with their fists, yet the sergeant's report of the incident concluded that the "officers showed great restraint and professionalism."

In sum, we find that BPD officers frequently stop pedestrians on Baltimore streets without reasonable suspicion that they are engaged in criminal activity. This pattern is evidenced by the extremely low rate at which BPD's inves-

---

44 To justify the stop, officers also noted that the man put his hands in the pockets of his sweatshirt as they approached. However, given that the encounter occurred on a cold January evening and officers observed the man "shivering," placing hands inside a sweatshirt adds minimally, if at all, to any objective suspicion the officers possessed. *See United States v. Burton*, 228 F.3d 524, 529 (4th Cir. 2000) (holding that where suspect refused to speak with police or remove his hand from his pocket, "something more is required to establish reasonable suspicion that criminal activity is afoot"); *United States v. Patterson*, 340 F.3d 368, 370–72 (6th Cir. 2003) (holding that officers lacked reasonable suspicion where suspect placed hands in his pockets and walked away from police); *United States v. Davis*, 94 F.3d 1465, 1468–649 (10th Cir. 1996) (holding that officers lacked reasonable suspicion to stop a known gang member who ignored officers' orders to take his hands out of his pockets).

tigative stops yield evidence of criminality and officers' own descriptions of their conduct. The frequency of these unlawful stops subjects certain Baltimore communities to repeated constitutional harms.

b. BPD Searches Individuals During Stops Without Legal Justification

During pedestrian and vehicle stops, BPD officers regularly escalate encounters by conducting unlawful searches. This practice includes two types of conduct: (1) officers conducting weapons pat downs or "frisks" where they lack reasonable suspicion that a subject is armed and dangerous; and (2) pre-arrest strip searches in public areas. Both types of conduct result from systemic deficiencies in policy, training, and oversight.

i. Unconstitutional Frisks

BPD officers commonly frisk people during stops without reasonable suspicion that the subject of the frisk is armed and dangerous. This practice contravenes the principle that "before an officer places a hand on the person of a citizen in search of anything, he must have constitutionally adequate, reasonable grounds for doing so." *United States v. Powell*, 666 F.3d 180, 185 (4th Cir. 2011) (citation and internal quotation marks omitted). Before frisking a person stopped on the street or in a vehicle, officers must have reasonable suspicion—based on specific, particularized information—that a person is armed and dangerous. *See, e.g., Arizona v. Johnson*, 555 U.S. 323, 326–27 (2009). This requirement is distinct from the justification needed to make the underlying stop. *See Powell*, 666 F.3d at 186 n.5 (noting that the justification for making a stop "differs from . . . whether a lawfully detained person may be armed and dangerous and thus subject to a *Terry* frisk"). The assessment of reasonable suspicion to frisk is based on the totality of the circumstances; it is insufficient, standing alone, that a subject has a prior record of arrests for violent charges, *id. at* 184–86, was stopped in a high crime area, *Maryland v. Buie*, 494 U.S. 325, 335 (1990), or was stopped late at night, *Papachristou v. City of Jacksonville*, 405 U.S. 156, 163 (1972). Where reasonable suspicion to conduct a frisk exists, officers must limit the scope of the search to a pat down of "the outer layers of the suspect's clothing." *United States v. Holmes*, 376 F.3d 270, 275 (4th Cir. 2004). Once an officer establishes that a person is not armed, "that officer exceeds the permissible scope of a *Terry* frisk if he continues to search the suspect." *United States v. Swann*, 149 F.3d 271, 274–75 (4th Cir. 1998); *Minnesota v. Dickerson*, 508 U.S. 366, 378 (1993) (an officer exceeds the scope of a permissible frisk by "squeezing, sliding and otherwise manipulating the contents of defendant's pocket" after determining that the pocket did not contain a weapon) (citation and internal quotation marks omitted).

Yet for many years, suspicionless frisks have been a common feature of BPD's street enforcement efforts. Officers and community members told Justice Department investigators that frisks—often made under the guise of "officer safety" but without identifying any specific basis for believing that a person is armed—are a common feature of BPD's stops. Officers' own descriptions of frisks in their incident reports support this conclusion. For example, on a spring evening in 2010 officers responded to a call complaining that drug sales were occurring at a particular location. Officers arrived at the scene and observed several African-American individuals "standing and sitting at the location." Absent information that these individuals were armed or otherwise dangerous, the officers nonetheless approached and immediately frisked them. Officers disclosed the frisk in an incident report, explaining that they performed the frisk "for officer safety." Although the officers provided no information that suggested the individuals were armed or dangerous, BPD supervisors signed off on the report. Our review of incident reports and interviews with several hundred community members indicate that the unconstitutional frisk practice is widespread. We were unable to precisely quantify the scope of these unconstitutional frisks, however, because BPD does not reliably record when officers conduct a frisk.

BPD's misapplication of the *Terry* frisk standard subjects Baltimore residents to embarrassing invasions of privacy and needlessly escalates encounters with law enforcement. In one typical case, a BPD officer unlawfully frisked an African-American man after a traffic stop for driving with headlights off. Because the driver "looked nervous" as the officer approached, the officer ordered the driver and his passenger to exit the vehicle and stand on the side of the road. The officer then frisked the passenger, which included a public pat down of the passenger's groin. The officer identified no basis for frisking the passenger other than the *driver's* "nervous" appearance—far short of the required showing of particularized facts pointing to the presence of a weapon. *See Powell*, 666 F.3d at 183, 185, 187 (no reasonable suspicion to frisk man during a vehicle stop for a burned out light even where officers had information that the man had prior arrests for armed robbery). In another incident, an officer approached an African-American man walking on a sidewalk in November 2010 in an area the officer stated was "known for violent crime and narcotics distribution." When the officer "attempted to interview him about his activities," the man fled. According to the report the officer filed the day of the incident, he chased the man and deployed his taser because the man "refused to comply with my orders to stop." The taser prongs hit the man on the back but failed to stop him. As the chase continued, the officer reloaded his taser cartridge and again fired probes into the fleeing man's back. After catching up with the man, the officer used his taser yet again—this time in drive stun mode—detained the man for investigation, and conducted a weapons frisk. The report provides no reason to believe the man was armed.[45] The frisk and investigation found no weapon or other evidence of wrongdoing. The man—after being tased multiple times, taken to the ground, and frisked—was released without charges.

Even where BPD officers properly initiate a frisk based on reasonable suspicion that a person is armed or dangerous, we found instances in which the scope of those frisks exceeded the brief pat down of the "outer layers of the suspect's clothing" that *Terry* prescribes. *See, e.g., Holmes*, 376 F.3d at 275. While "[a] n officer is not justified in conducting a general exploratory search for evidence under the guise of a stop-and-frisk," *United States v. Brown*, 188 F.3d 860, 866 (7th Cir. 1999) (citing *Dickerson*, 508 U.S. at 378), BPD officers commonly frisk individuals in a way that seems intended to find small packages of narcotics rather than weapons. In cases reviewed by the Justice Department, officers reached inside of subjects' clothing, asked subjects to remove articles of clothing, and squeezed pockets to detect small bags that may contain illegal drugs.

ii. BPD Conducts Unconstitutional Strip Searches

In addition to impermissible *Terry* frisks, our investigation found many instances in which BPD officers strip-searched individuals without justification—often in public areas— subjecting them to humiliation and violating the Constitution. Strip searches are "fairly understood" as "degrading" and, under the Fourth Amendment, are reasonable only in narrow circumstances. *Safford Unified Sch. Dist. #1 v. Redding*, 557 U.S. 364, 375 (2009). Strip searches are never permissible as part of a pre-arrest weapons frisk. *See Holmes*, 376 F.3d at 275 (weapons frisks must be limited to the outer layers of a suspect's clothing). Following a lawful arrest, the reasonableness of a strip search turns on "the scope of the particular intrusion, the manner in which it is conducted, the justification for initiating it, and the place in which it is conducted." *Bell v. Wolfish*, 441 U.S. 520, 559 (1979). Absent specific facts indicating that an arrestee is concealing a weapon or contraband, officers may not strip search a person incident to arrest for an offense that is not "commonly associated by its very nature with the possession of weapons or contraband." *Logan v. Shealy*, 660 F.2d 1007, 1013 (4th Cir. 1981). Moreover, courts have "repeatedly emphasized the necessity of conducting a strip search in private." *Amaechi v. West*, 237 F.3d 356, 364 (4th Cir. 2001) (finding strip search unreasonable where it was conducted in public view). BPD policy likewise recognizes that strip searches should be conducted

---

45 More than a month later, the officer filed a supplemental report claiming that he "decided to frisk [the man] based on my suspicion that he was armed," citing the man's presence in a high crime area, his loose clothing, the fact that he "looked back over his shoulder," and that the man ran past a dumpster where he could have theoretically discarded a weapon or narcotics.

only "under very limited and controlled circumstances" and that "strip search-ing . . . [] suspects in public view or on a public thoroughfare is forbidden."

Nevertheless, our investigation found that BPD officers frequently ignore these requirements and strip-search individuals prior to arrest, in public view, or both. Numerous Baltimore residents interviewed by the Justice Depart-ment recounted stories of BPD officers "jumping out" of police vehicles and strip-searching individuals on public streets. BPD has long been on notice of such allegations: in the last five years BPD has faced multiple lawsuits and more than 60 complaints alleging unlawful strip searches. In one of these incidents—memorialized in a complaint that the Department sustained—officers in BPD's Eastern District publicly strip-searched a woman following a routine traffic stop for a missing headlight. Officers ordered the woman to exit her vehicle, remove her clothes, and stand on the sidewalk to be searched. The woman asked the male officer in charge "I really gotta take all my clothes off?" The male officer replied "yeah" and ordered a female officer to strip search the woman. The female officer then put on purple latex gloves, pulled up the woman's shirt and searched around her bra. Finding no weapons or contraband around the wom-an's chest, the officer then pulled down the woman's underwear and searched her anal cavity. This search again found no evidence of wrongdoing and the officers released the woman without charges. Indeed, the woman received only a repair order for her headlight. The search occurred in full view of the street, although the supervising male officer claimed he "turned away" and did not watch the woman disrobe. After the woman filed a complaint, BPD investiga-tors corroborated the woman's story with testimony from several witnesses and by recovering the female officer's latex gloves from the search location. Officers conducted this highly invasive search despite lacking any indication that the woman had committed a criminal offense or possessed concealed con-traband. The male officer who ordered the search received only a "simple rep-rimand" and an instruction that he could not serve as an officer in charge until he was "properly trained."

An African-American teenager recounted a similar story to Justice Depart-ment investigators that involved two public strip searches in the winter of 2016 by the same officer. According to the teenager, he was stopped in January 2016 while walking on a street near his home by two officers who were looking for the teenager's older brother, whom the officers suspected of dealing narcotics. One of the officers pushed the teenager up against a wall and frisked him. This search did not yield contraband. The officer then stripped off the teenager's jacket and sweatshirt and frisked him again in front of his teenage girlfriend. When this search likewise found no contraband, the officer ordered the teen-ager to "give your girl your phone, I'm checking you right now." The officer then pulled down the teenager's pants and boxer shorts and strip-searched him in full view of the street and his girlfriend. The officers' report of the incident disputes this account, claiming that they did not conduct a strip search and instead recovered narcotics from the teenager during a consensual pat down. No narcotics were ever produced to the teenager's public defender, however, and the State's Attorney's Office dismissed the drug charges for lack of evidence. The teenager filed a lengthy complaint with BPD describing the incident and identifying multiple witnesses. The teenager recounted to us that, shortly after filing the complaint, the same officer approached him near a McDonald's restaurant in his neighborhood, pushed the teenager against a wall, pulled down his pants, and grabbed his genitals. The officer filed no charges against the teenager in the second incident, which the teenager believes was done in retaliation for filing a complaint about the first strip search.

Other complaints describe similar incidents in which BPD officers conduct public strip searches of individuals who have not been arrested. For example, in September 2014, a man filed a complaint stating that an officer in the Central District searched him several days in a row, including "undoing his pants" and searching his "hindquarters" on a public street. When the strip search did not find contraband, the officer told the man to leave the area and warned that the officer would search him again every time he returned. The man then filed a complaint with Internal Affairs and identified the officer who conducted the strip search by name. When Internal Affairs investigators pressed the man to provide a detailed description of the officer, the man recalled that the officer "had red patches with sergeant stripes" on his uniform. The investigator recognized this description as patches worn by the officer in charge of a shift and confirmed that the officer named by the man was working as an officer in charge in the Central District on the dates the man alleged he was strip-searched. Internal Affairs nonetheless deemed the complaint "not sustained" without further explanation.

Deficient oversight and accountability has helped perpetuate BPD's use of unlawful strip searches. Although the Department's policy limits strip searches to specific, narrow circumstances following an arrest, BPD supervisors have failed to ensure that officers comply with this policy and internal affairs officials have not adequately investigated frequent complaints that officers violate it. BPD does not separately categorize or track complaints alleging unlawful strip searches. But our manual review of BPD's Internal Affairs database revealed more than 60 such complaints in the last six years—only one of which was sustained. In response to dozens of other strip search complaints, IA has deemed them "administratively closed," classified them solely for "administrative tracking," or found them not sustained—after minimal, if any, investigation. For example, in 2015 an African American man filed a complaint stating that he was strip-searched by an officer whom BPD eventually fired in 2016 after numerous allegations of misconduct. The man stated that the officer ordered him out of his vehicle during a traffic stop and searched the vehicle without the man's consent. When the stop of the vehicle did not uncover contraband, the officer pulled down the man's pants and underwear, exposing his genitals on the side of a public street, and then strip-searched him. The officer seized marijuana and cash during the strip search and allegedly told the man that the officer would return his money and drugs if the man provided information about more serious crimes. The complaint stated that when the man did not provide this information, the officer arrested him and turned over only part of the confiscated money, keeping more than $500. Despite the serious charges in this complaint and the officer's lengthy record of alleged misconduct, IA deemed it "administratively closed" without interviewing the complainant. This type of inadequate oversight has allowed BPD's unlawful strip search practice to continue.

3. BPD Makes Unconstitutional Arrests

Our investigation likewise found reasonable cause to believe that BPD's approach to street-level crime suppression has contributed to officers making thousands of unlawful arrests over the past five years. This pattern has three main components: (1) warrantless arrests made without probable cause in violation of the Fourth Amendment; (2) arrests for minor offenses, such as failure to obey and trespassing, in circumstances that violate the Due Process Clause's requirement to provide fair notice of prohibited conduct; and (3) investigative detentions that exceed the limits of *Terry* and constitute arrests.

a. BPD Arrests Individuals Without Probable Cause

The Fourth Amendment requires that arrests be supported by probable cause. *See, e.g, Dunaway v. New York*, 442 U.S. 200, 207–13 (1979); U.S. CONST. AM. IV. Probable cause requires "a probability or substantial chance of criminal activity" and is evaluated by examining "the totality of the circumstances." *Illinois v. Gates*, 462 U.S. 213, 243 n.13 (1983). It "require[s] . . . the kind of fair probability on which reasonable and prudent people, not legal technicians, act." *Florida v. Harris*, 133 S. Ct. 1050, 1055 (2013) (internal quotations omitted). Police may satisfy the probable cause requirement by obtaining a warrant prior to arrest or determining that probable cause exists in the field. *Gerstein v. Pugh*, 420 U.S. 103, 113–14 (1975). Our investigation determined that, when BPD officers make arrests in the field without a warrant, they often do so without probable cause.

Data maintained by the State of Maryland shows that, from November 2010–July 2015, BPD made thousands of arrests that reviewing officials declined to charge. The State's data records information about each person arrested, the arresting agency, all charges levied, and whether reviewing officials found that the charges were adequately supported. This data captures several stages of review of officers' justification for each arrest. When a BPD officer makes a warrantless arrest and brings the arrestee to Central Booking, a supervisor at booking determines whether to commit the arrestee into jail; release the arrestee on bond, on their own recognizance, or with a citation; or to nullify the arrest and release the arrestee without charge. For all cases except where an arrestee is released without charge, a representative from the State's Attorney's Office then conducts an initial review of the charging documents to ensure that they recite probable cause. This review usually occurs the same day as the arrest and looks only at the officer's stated justification for the arrest, not evidence from any other source. In some cases, the State's Attorney's review finds that an arrest lacks probable cause or otherwise should not result in filed charges.

Analysis of this data reveals that, from November 2010–July 2015, supervisors at Central Booking released 6,736 arrestees without charge. Prosecutors from the State's Attorney's Office declined to charge an additional 3,427 cases, explicitly finding that 1,983 of the underlying arrests lacked probable cause. In sum, BPD officers made 10,163 arrests that authorities immediately determined did not merit prosecution—an average of roughly 200 arrests per month.

BPD's pattern of making arrests without probable cause is most pronounced with non-felony offenses that stem from street encounters between officers and residents. For example, during the last five years prosecutors and booking supervisors rejected 1,350 disorderly conduct charges—20 percent of the total. Arrests for other highly discretionary, non-violent offenses were nullified at even higher rates. Officials rejected 24 percent of disturbing the peace charges, 23 percent of failure to obey charges, and 24 percent of hindering charges. Officials likewise rejected 156 trespassing charges, comprising roughly 5 percent of the total. And these numbers almost certainly understate the extent of BPD's problematic arrests, as they reflect only cases dismissed during preliminary review based on facial deficiencies in officers' reports, not arrests later shown to be invalid during pretrial hearings or at trial.

Indeed, our review of a random sample of 150 incident reports describing the probable cause for these discretionary arrests found that officers frequently recite facially inadequate justifications. In particular, these reports reveal that officers often arrest individuals for "trespassing" where the person arrested was standing on a public street that bordered property owned by the City or a private party. Such conduct is not criminal. "[I]ndividuals in this country have significant liberty interests in standing on sidewalks and in other public places." *City of Chicago v. Morales*, 527 U.S. 41, 54 n.19 (1999) (quoting Brief for the United States as Amicus Curiae 23).

Several examples highlight this pattern. In June 2011, an officer dispatched in response to suspected drug sales observed an African-American male fitting the basic description of one of the suspects. The officer wrote in his report that the suspect was standing on a public street "in front of" property owned by "the mayor and city council of Baltimore City." When the officer approached, the man "became nervous and could not provide a valid explanation for being at this location." Lacking any further evidence suggesting that the man was involved in narcotics sales or other criminal activity, the officer nonetheless transported the man to the Western District headquarters for "debriefing" and then to Central Booking, where the man was charged with trespassing. The man was not charged with any other offense, and the officer's account of the encounter furnishes no basis for the trespassing arrest. Rather, it shows that the man was merely standing lawfully on a public street. In January 2010, officers similarly approached a man who was "standing in front of 1524 Mount Mor Ct looking around" and who walked away when he saw officers. Officers stopped the man and arrested him when he "could not provide a valid explanation for *being in front of* 1524 Mount Mor Ct," a part of the Gilmore Homes public housing complex. In another case, an officer arrested an African-American man observed "standing in front of 578 Orchard St." The officer's report explained that when he approached, the man "began to walk east bound on Orchard St attempting to elude the officer." The officer stopped the man and asked him "why was he *standing in front of* 578 Orchard St and if he knew the resident" who resided there. When the man replied that he did not know the resident, the officer arrested him for trespassing. The officers' accounts of these and many similar incidents describe facially unlawful arrests for conduct that is not criminal.

b. BPD Arrests People Lawfully Present on Baltimore Streets in Violation of Due Process

BPD's application of city ordinances banning loitering, trespassing, and failing to obey an officer's order violates the Fourteenth Amendment. Citing these provisions, BPD frequently arrests people who are lawfully present on public sidewalks without providing the constitutionally required notice that they are engaging in prohibited conduct. These arrests are unconstitutional under the void-for-vagueness doctrine where they are made in circumstances that "fail to provide the kind of notice that will enable ordinary people to understand what conduct it prohibits." *Morales*, 527 U.S. at 56 (invalidating city ordinance that defined loitering as "to remain in one place with no apparent purpose."). Where conduct—like loitering—is generally lawful, police may make arrests only where the arrestees violated the ordinance knowingly. *See id.* at 57–58.[46]

Moreover, absent clear standards and an intent element, a "dispersal order itself is an unjustified impairment of liberty" and cannot form the basis of an

---

46 We do not address whether Baltimore City ordinances criminalizing loitering, failing to obey, and trespassing are facially unconstitutional.

arrest for failure to obey. *Id.* at 58. The Court of Special Appeals of Maryland has criticized BPD's application of the Baltimore's anti-loitering ordinance for precisely these reasons. *See Williams v. Maryland*, 780 A.2d 1210 (Md. Ct. App. 2001). The *Williams* court reversed a defendant's narcotics conviction after finding that the defendant's underlying arrest for loitering violated due process. The court noted that, although BPD officers claimed the man was part of a group that was impeding pedestrian traffic on a sidewalk, there was no "evidence even remotely supporting an inference of scienter" or that the defendant had notice that such conduct was illegal. *Id.* at 1217. Moreover, the court held that such notice must include a specific description of the prohibited conduct; officers could not provide sufficient notice by "[t]elling someone merely that he is 'loitering' and that if he does not move on he will be arrested." *Id.* at 1218.

The same vagueness problem exists in BPD's enforcement of trespassing statutes against individuals who are standing on sidewalks adjacent to public housing or private establishments. Indeed, a federal district court in Maryland has expressed concern about the type of highly discretionary trespassing arrests that BPD utilizes. *See Diggs v. Housing Authority*, 67 F. Supp. 2d 522, 532–35 (D. Md. 1999). There, the court enjoined enforcement of the City of Frederick's trespassing ordinance and noted that a "policy of issuing citations to persons with 'no apparent legitimate reason' for being on Housing Authority property may raise serious due process concerns in light of the Supreme Court's recent decision in *Chicago v. Morales*." *Diggs*, 67 F. Supp. at 534 n.19.

BPD's arrests of "loiterers" for trespassing and failing to obey orders to disperse frequently fall short of these due process standards. BPD often arrests people standing on streets or sidewalks for "trespassing" when they cannot provide a reason for their presence that officers deem acceptable. Our review found numerous cases in which BPD officers arrested individuals on sidewalks near public housing complexes or private businesses simply because officers determined that the arrestees had "no legitimate purpose" or "no business" in the area—precisely the type of vague, subjective trespassing standard invalidated in *Morales*. *See* 527 U.S. at 56 (finding unconstitutionally vague a statute that permitted arrest of "loiterers" who lack an "apparent purpose"); *see also Diggs*, 67 F. Supp. 2d at 534 n.19 (questioning arrests premised on having 'no apparent legitimate reason' for being on Housing Authority property").

For example, in April 2010, BPD officers approached five African Americans sitting on a brick wall in front of a private business. Officers wrote in their report that they "approached the group to ascertain their purpose for sitting on the wall in front of this location." When the individuals responded that they "were 'just chillin,'" officers arrested them for trespassing because the men "could not give a valid purpose for being on [the property]." Officers provided no warning before arresting the men and did not charge them with any other offense. Later the same month, a different BPD officer approached "two males sitting on the steps of 110 North Fremont Ave," a street that borders a public housing complex. When the men "attempted to get up and walk away," the officer stopped them and "asked what they were doing on the property."[47] The men responded that they were "just talking." The officer then—without any warning—arrested the men for trespassing because "neither was able to provide any legitimate explanation for being on the Housing Authority property." In September 2011, a BPD officer similarly arrested a man "loitering directly beside the 2501 E. Preston Street Greater Missionary Baptist Church." The officer made the arrest after asking the man "why he was in the area" and learning that the man "had no business near the area of the [church's] steps." Each of these arrests violates constitutional due process requirements because the arrested individuals lacked notice that their apparently innocent behavior was unlawful.

We found evidence that BPD supervisors have explicitly condoned trespassing arrests that do not meet constitutional standards, and evidence suggesting that trespassing enforcement is focused on public housing developments. A shift commander for one of BPD's districts emailed a template for describing trespassing arrests to a sergeant and a patrol officer. The template provides a blueprint for arresting an individual standing on or near a public housing development who cannot give a "valid reason" for being there—a facially unconstitutional detention. Equally troubling is the fact that the template contains blanks to be filled in for details of the arrest, including the arrest data and location and the suspect's name and address, but does not include a prompt to fill in the race or gender of the arrestee. Rather, the words "black male" are automatically included in the description of the arrest. The supervisor's template thus presumes that individuals arrested for trespassing will be African American.

BPD likewise makes constitutionally deficient arrests of people who fail to obey officers' unlawful orders to disperse. BPD policy requires that, prior to making such an arrest, officers warn people allegedly loitering that their specific conduct is illegal. Yet our review found that officers frequently do not provide this warning or indicate only that a person must disperse because he or she is "loitering"—an instruction that is unconstitutionally vague. See Williams, 780 A.2d at 1218 (due process requires more than "telling someone merely that he is 'loitering' and that if he does not move on he will be arrested."). Instead, we found numerous "failure to obey" arrests made without the required warning and premised on an officer's subjective dissatisfaction with a person's stated reason for standing or sitting on a public sidewalk.

---

47 Officers lacked reasonable suspicion to make the initial stop, as the men were observed only sitting on steps and then walking down a public sidewalk.

Trespassing Wording

ON **(Date)** AT APPROXIMATELY **(Time)** OFFICER JOHN DOE WAS WORKING IN A UNIFORM CAPACITY IN THE **(Address in Housing Location)** WHICH IS A HIGH DRUG TRAFFICKING AREA AND AN AREA KNOWN FOR VIOLENT CRIMES. OFFICER DOE OBSERVED A BLACK MALE LATER IDENTIFIED AS **(Name of Suspect)** (LOITERING, INVOLVED IN NARCOTIC ACTIVITY, ETC) IN THE **(Address)**. OFFICER DOE THEN APPROACHED **(Suspect)** AND ASKED HIM WAS HE A RESIDENT OF THE **(Name of Development)** PUBLIC HOUSING DEVELOPMENT, WHICH HAS SIGNS POSTED "NO TRESPASSING" PLACED IN A CONSPICUOUS MANNER THROUGHOUT THE DEVELOPMENT. **(Suspect)** ADVISED OFFICER DOE THAT HE WAS NOT A RESIDENT OF **(Development)** OFFICER DOE THEN ASKED **(Suspect)** WHAT WAS HIS REASON FOR BEING ON HOUSING PROPERTY, AT THIS POINT **(Suspect)** COULDN'T GIVE A VALID REASON FOR BEING ON HOUSING PROPERTY. **(Suspect)** WAS THEN PLACED UNDER ARREST AND TRANSPORTED TO CBIF FOR PROCESSING.

In October 2011, for example, an officer approached a group of African-American men standing on a sidewalk "within 100 feet of Amko liquor store." All but two of the men left when the officer approached. The officer stopped the two remaining men and warned them that they were "loitering" by blocking pedestrian traffic and that they were "trespassing near a liquor store." The officer then told the men "to leave the area, to stop loitering . . . and to stop trespassing near the liquor store." When one of the men replied, "I'm not leaving, I'm going to stay and finish talking to my brother," the officer arrested him for failing to obey. The order the man failed to obey—a general instruction not to "loiter" or trespass "near a liquor store"—falls far short of the notice required to support an arrest. Similarly, in July 2011 officers approached three males standing on the sidewalk in front of Crazy John's restaurant on East Baltimore Street because they were purportedly "obstructing pedestrian traffic in a public walkway." After several warnings, the officer ordered the men to leave the area and informed them that they would be arrested if they "returned." The three men then walked away and crossed the street, where they resumed "hang[ing] out." When the officer followed the men to their new location, the men walked farther down Baltimore Street, "taunted" the officer, and then ran away. Forty minutes later, the officer saw the men walking down an adjacent street while "attempting to come back on the 400 block of Baltimore Street" and arrested them for failure to obey the order not to "return." This arrest is premised on an unconstitutionally vague order not to return to a public street for an indeterminate time period.

These and similar arrests identified by our investigation reflect BPD officers exercising nearly unfettered discretion to criminalize the act of standing on public sidewalks. Absent clear warning about the specific types of conduct that will result in such arrests, this practice fails to provide notice required by the Due Process Clause and risks arbitrary and discriminatory enforcement. *See Kolender v. Lawson*, 461 U.S. 352, 357 (1983).[48] Accordingly, these arrests are unconstitutional.

c. BPD Unlawfully Detains Individuals for Investigation, Effectively Arresting Them Without Probable Cause

Our investigation further revealed that BPD officers unlawfully detain persons for extended periods of time—sometimes for at least several hours—without probable cause. These detentions constitute arrests and violate the Fourth Amendment. BPD does not process these detentions as arrests; instead officers use them to: (1) detain and question people suspected of crimes in hopes of uncovering evidence supporting an arrest; and (2) facilitate custodial interrogations of witnesses or other people with knowledge of suspected crimes. Neither purpose vitiates the requirement that officers must have probable cause to exceed the constitutional limits on investigative detentions.

"[D]etention for custodial interrogation—regardless of its label—intrudes so severely on interests protected by the Fourth Amendment as necessarily to trigger the traditional safeguards against illegal arrest." *Dunaway*, 442 U.S. at 216; *see also Brown v. Illinois*, 422 U.S. 590, 605 (1975) (detention in a police station without probable cause "for investigation or for questioning" violates the Fourth Amendment). The Fourth Amendment likewise prohibits officers extending detentions "for the purpose of gathering additional evidence to justify the arrest." *County of Riverside v. McLaughlin*, 500 U.S. 44, 56 (1991); *see also Brown*, 422 U.S. at 605 (station house detention and questioning "in the hope that something might turn up" requires probable cause). While *Terry* allows officers to detain individuals for brief investigation where officers have reasonable suspicion that criminal activity is afoot, *Terry* stops may not "resemble a traditional arrest." *Hiibel v. Sixth Judicial District Court*, 542 U.S. 177, 186 (2004). Courts have resisted putting precise limits on the permissible duration of *Terry* stops, but have found 90-minute detentions unconstitutional. *See United States v. Place*, 462 U.S. 696, 709–10 (1983); *accord United States v. Watson*, 703 F.3d 684 (4th Cir. 2012) (investigative detention for three hours without probable cause constituted an unlawful custodial arrest under the Fourth Amendment); *Zavala*, 541 F.3d at 579–80 (90-minute detention in which subject was transported to different location constituted "a de facto arrest"); *United States v. Chamberlin*, 644 F.2d 1262, 1266–67 (9th Cir. 1980) (placing a suspect in the back of a police car for twenty minutes while the officer pursued another suspect exceeded the limits of a *Terry* stop).

---

48 Indeed, as set forth in Section II(B), *infra*, these practices have resulted in highly discriminatory outcomes.

While BPD does not formally document investigative detentions, we found troubling indications that BPD officers use such detentions as a regular part of investigating people suspected of criminal activity. Local prosecutors described this practice to Justice Department officials as BPD officers making arrests without probable cause on the street, then hours later deciding to "un-arrest" when detention and questioning failed to uncover additional evidence. Our review of BPD documents confirmed that BPD uses these unlawful detentions.

For example, in October 2010, an officer responded to a call for suspected burglary that indicated several African-American men were using a green truck to carry away a furnace. The officer arrived on the scene and approached three African-American men who were standing around a green truck with a furnace in the back. In response to the officer's questions, one of the men stated that he was helping the other men move the furnace, which had been found in a nearby alley. The officer detained the men while he conducted a canvass of the area, which did not find any property from which the furnace could have been removed. Despite failing to identify evidence suggesting the men were involved in a burglary, the officer nonetheless placed all three men in custody and transported them to the Western District headquarters "for further investigation." While the men were held at the station, the officer reviewed a CitiWatch camera that confirmed their explanation that they moved the furnace from an alley. After detaining the men for 1 hour and 40 minutes, the officer released them. BPD records contain no indication that the men consented to their detention, much less to being detained for nearly two hours. In other cases, BPD officers have likewise stopped individuals based on reasonable suspicion, transported them to precincts for fingerprinting and further investigation, then ultimately released them more than an hour later when the investigation failed to uncover probable cause to make an arrest. *See supra*, at 29. These custodial detentions violate the Fourth Amendment, which forbids extending *Terry* stops "for the purpose of gathering additional evidence to justify [an] arrest." *Riverside*, 500 U.S. at 56; *see also Brown*, 422 U.S. at 6025 (station house detention and questioning "in the hope that something might turn up" requires probable cause).

4. BPD's Unconstitutional Stops, Searches, and Arrests Result from a Longstanding Practice of Overly Aggressive Street Enforcement with Deficient Oversight and Policy Guidance

BPD's pattern of making unconstitutional stops, searches, and arrests arises from its longstanding reliance on "zero tolerance" street enforcement, which encourages officers to make large numbers of stops, searches, and arrests for minor, highly discretionary offenses. This approach to street-level enforcement magnifies the importance of providing officers with robust policies and training and overseeing officer activity with comprehensive accountability systems. Yet BPD failed to collect reliable data, conducted minimal oversight of enforcement activities, and forced officers to rely on policies that provide insufficient guidance or, in several important areas, facially misstate constitutional requirements. Taken together, these deficiencies contribute to widespread constitutional violations.

a. Baltimore Leadership Prioritized "Zero Tolerance" Crime Suppression Tactics for Many Years

Starting in the late 1990s, Baltimore City and BPD leadership expressly adopted a policing model that embraced the principles of "zero tolerance" street enforcement. According to City and BPD leaders past and present, as well as media reports, Baltimore City based its approach in part on tactics developed by the New York Police Department and brought in consultants from NYPD's program to oversee its implementation in Baltimore.[49] As we heard from BPD officers and leaders, as well as numerous community members, the strategy involved BPD officers making widespread use of pedestrian stops and searches in a purported effort to seize guns and narcotics and deter crime. BPD supervisors encouraged officers to issue citations and make arrests for low-level "quality of life" offenses, including loitering, trespassing, disorderly conduct, failure to obey, and disturbing the peace. As part of this strategy, BPD leadership pressured officers to increase the number of arrests and to "clear corners," whether or not the officers observed criminal activity. The result was a massive increase in the quantity of arrests—but a corresponding decline in quality. Of the 100,000 arrestees that BPD processed through Central Booking in 2004,[50] more than one in five were released without charge.[51] Although our investigation did not analyze data on the number of stops and searches that took place during the same time period, it is doubtless that they far exceeded the number of arrests.

From the beginning, some community members and policymakers questioned the value of the policy, arguing that it could lead to harassment of residents without an appreciable reduction in crime. Zero tolerance enforcement made police interaction a daily fact of life for some Baltimore residents and provoked widespread community disillusionment with BPD, as well as calls from activists, former police officers, and state officials to adopt new practices. The strategy also created disillusion within the Department. According to the

---

49 *See, e.g.*, Gerard Shields, *O'Malley is wooing zero-tolerance gurus*, BALTIMORE SUN, Oct. 2, 1999, http://articles.baltimoresun.com/1999-10-02/news/9910020227_1_jack-maple-violent-crime-police-commissioner (last accessed Aug. 5, 2016).

50 At the time, Baltimore City had a population of approximately 650,000 residents.

51 JUSTICE POLICY INSTITUTE, BALTIMORE BEHIND BARS 10 (2010).

police union president at the time, some officers referred to the stop-and-frisk program as a "VCR detail," standing for "violation of civil rights."[52]

In June 2006, the ACLU of Maryland and the NAACP filed a lawsuit alleging that BPD was illegally arresting thousands of residents every year. The complaint asserted that BPD had not properly trained officers on the legal standard necessary to make an arrest, and had placed pressure on supervisors to bolster numbers, leading to citizens being improperly detained without probable cause. Shortly after the suit was filed, BPD began to take steps to decrease its reliance on zero tolerance policing. In the late 2000s, under Baltimore Police Commissioner Frederick H. Bealefeld III, the number of arrests, and arrestees released without charge, began to decrease.[53] In 2010, BPD and the City entered into a settlement to resolve the ACLU lawsuit, with BPD agreeing to adopt policies rejecting its former zero tolerance strategy and make changes to existing policies and procedures. The settlement established an Independent Auditor to evaluate BPD's progress toward adopting stop and arrest practices consistent with the Constitution. In 2015, BPD published a number of amended policies, including one addressing the core legal elements of quality of life offenses, in which it cautioned that verbal warnings, counseling, and citations are preferable to arrest. The policy states that arrest should only take place where the quality of life violation was committed in the officer's presence, and the officer has an objectively reasonable belief that arrest is necessary under the facts and circumstances or to otherwise protect the officer and citizens of Baltimore.

Current Baltimore Police Commissioner Kevin Davis and former Commissioner Anthony Batts have acknowledged that BPD's zero tolerance strategy damaged community relationships and created obstacles to effective policing. Both commissioners have publicly supported a more holistic policing model focused on rebuilding and leveraging community trust. Nevertheless, the practices of officers on the street have continued to reflect many of the problematic aspects of the previous strategy, resulting in a pattern of unconstitutional conduct. These problematic practices are reflected in our findings. BPD's failure to engage in meaningful change was also noted in the reports of the Independent Auditor established by the ACLU lawsuit settlement agreement. At the end of the four-year monitoring period, the Auditor determined that BPD had not reached full compliance on more than half of the conditions of the agreement. Failure to consistently and adequately report arrests and engage in meaningful oversight of street-level enforcement was, and remains, a recurring problem.

---

52 Gus G. Sentementes, *Police step up frisking tactic*, BALTIMORE SUN, Nov. 13, 2005, http: //articles.baltimoresun.com/2005-11-13/news/0511130098_1_frisking-deter-crime-police-officers (last accessed Aug. 5, 2016).

53 JUSTICE POLICY INSTITUTE, BALTIMORE BEHIND BARS 10 (2010).

All of the Auditor's reporting indicated that arrest reports for quality of life offenses did not meet the requirements of BPD departmental policies. The final report from 2014 noted that there was no systematic improvement in reporting for these offenses during the monitoring period.

One of the reasons that the intended move away from zero tolerance policing has not sufficiently curbed BPD's practice of unconstitutional street-level enforcement is a persistent perception among officers that their performance continues to be measured by the raw numbers of stops and arrests they make, particularly for gun and drug offenses. Many officers believe that the path to promotions and favorable treatment, as well as the best way to avoid discipline, is to increase their number of stops and make arrests for these offenses. By frequently stopping and searching people they believe might possess contraband, with or without requisite reasonable suspicion, officers aim to improve their statistical output, which will in turn reflect favorably in their performance reviews. During shifts observed by Justice Department investigators, patrol officers actively sought out corners to clear and indicated that they believed they were obligated to move groups of people standing on sidewalks, whether or not the individuals in the groups appeared to be engaged in criminal conduct. Several officers demonstrated a mistaken understanding of the law, expressing that a group standing in front of a business or a vacant lot was necessarily loitering or trespassing on the property.

These views are reinforced by BPD's mid-level supervisors, many of whom served in the Department during the height of the zero tolerance strategy and continue to embrace its principles. Some officers we interviewed expressed frustration with supervisory pressure to prioritize drug and gun arrests over community policing and longer, more intensive investigations. One officer acknowledged the futility of breaking up a crowd of "loiterers" because the crowd would simply relocate to a different store or corner. Yet supervisors still encourage officers to "clear corners" and engage in blanket enforcement of low-level offenses, as demonstrated by the incident discussed in Section II.A., *supra*, in which the officer's supervisor encouraged him to "make something up" in order to disperse residents who were gathered peaceably on a street corner. Other officers told us that they were denied the opportunity to work overtime because supervisors believed they did not make enough stops and arrests.

This pressure from supervisors not only contributes to constitutional violations, but can also result in poor tactical decision-making that imperils the lives of officers and innocent civilians. In one incident we reviewed, an officer observed a gathering of people talking, eating, and waiting for food outside a late-night restaurant after bars had closed. None of the people appeared to be committing any crimes. But rather than monitoring the group or calling for backup in case of trouble, the officer decided to attempt to disperse the gathering alone. The officer reported that he decided to do this because he believed his supervisor would not be happy if he saw the area had not been cleared. As a result of his decision to clear the corner, the officer ended up in a physical altercation with a man who refused to leave. Alone and surrounded by an unfriendly crowd, the officer fired his service weapon at a man he feared was about to kick him. The bullet struck two people, at least one of whom was not involved in the incident. Despite the officer's serious tactical mistakes, reviewing supervisors did not report any errors and concluded that the officer had acted appropriately.

b. Deficient Policies, Training, and Oversight

BPD exacerbates the risk that its aggressive street enforcement tactics will lead to constitutional violations by failing to use effective policies, training, oversight, and accountability systems. While these deficiencies are discussed in greater depth in Section III, *infra* at 128-54, several failings are particularly relevant to BPD's pattern or practice of making unlawful stops, searches, and arrests.

i. BPD Policies and Training Materials Do Not Equip Officers to Police Effectively and Constitutionally

Important BPD policies and training materials either misstate the law or are too vague to provide meaningful guidance to officers about operative constitutional standards. As a result, officers committed to constitutional policing are often not equipped to provide it.

For example, BPD's newly adopted order titled "Quality of Life Offenses— Core Legal Elements" from April 2015 does not accurately explain the legal requirements for making loitering arrests. The order includes a section discussing special considerations for a violation of the Baltimore City Code prohibiting loitering, but fails to mention the requirement that officers may not arrest individuals for loitering until they have been told what specific conduct is prohibited, warned that a violation of law is occurring, and still refuse to desist. As discussed above, BPD's stops policy likewise misstated the applicable legal standard until 2015 by not requiring officers to have suspicion that a person is armed and dangerous prior to conducting a weapons frisk. Other policies are insufficiently specific to provide effective guidance to officers. For example, General Order 4-94, "Strip Searches and Body Cavity Searches," requires officers to obtain a warrant in order to conduct a body cavity search "unless exigent circumstances exist to justify a warrantless search." However, the policy provides officers with no guidance about what would constitute sufficient exigent circumstances to justify an immediate, warrantless body cavity search.[54]

Several key training materials likewise fail to provide officers with an understanding of relevant constitutional requirements. For example, a lesson plan from a 2009 stop and frisk training indicates that "Investigative contacts of citizens by members of this agency will be conducted with articulable reason." The confusing reference to "articulable reason" misstates the *Terry* standard requiring reasonable suspicion based on specific and articulable facts. The lesson plan later instructs that the member "must be able to articulate reasonable suspicion or belief a crime has been or will be committed to perform a stop & frisk." This similarly misstates the relevant law, as it indicates that the same standard of suspicion is required for both an investigatory stop and a subsequent frisk—contrary to the requirement that an officer possess separate reasonable suspicion that an individual is armed and dangerous prior to initiating a frisk. Throughout the training, and on the reporting form, stop and frisk are consistently mentioned together, suggesting to officers that frisks are a matter of course during any stop. The training likewise does not mention that weapons frisks must be limited to a pat down of a person's outer clothing.

BPD leadership recognized the deficiencies in its stop and frisk guidance and updated the Department's policy on field interviews, investigative stops,

---

54 Other policies related to searches and seizures, though not directly related to our findings, are similarly troubling. For example, BPD General Order J-7 (January 5, 2004), "Search and Seizure Warrants" states that "Immediate entry may be initiated if sounds, conversations or other activity coming from within the premises leads you to believe that activity is occurring which may indicate a potential threat of physical harm to police officers/occupants, evidence is being destroyed, or a suspect is escaping." However, this does not accord with constitutional requirements. Prior to "forcibly entering a residence, police officers 'must knock on the door and announce their identity and purpose.'" *Bellotte v. Edwards*, 629 F.3d 415, 419 (4th Cir. 2011) (quoting *Richards v. Wisconsin*, 520 U.S. 385, 387 (1997)). While it is true that exigent circumstances may sometimes justify a "no-knock" entry, "police must have a reasonable suspicion that knocking and announcing their presence, under the particular circumstances, would be dangerous or futile, or that it would inhibit the effective investigation of the crime by, for example, allowing the destruction of evidence." *Bellotte*, 629 F.3d at 420 (citation omitted). "Generic" threats and dangers "raised at the most general level" are not particularized enough to establish exigent circumstances. *Id.* at 424 n.2. Entry without knocking based on mere speculation is likewise not reasonable under the Fourth Amendment. *Id.* at 423. The BPD policy also permits immediate entry, even in the absence of exigent circumstances, where there has been no response within 20 seconds of knocking on the door. This is not in accord with applicable law. Although 15–20 seconds may be a sufficient amount of time to wait if officers have reason to believe the delay gives rise to exigent circumstances, "in a case with no reason to suspect an immediate risk of frustration or futility in waiting at all, the reasonable wait time may well be longer when police make a forced entry, since they ought to be more certain the occupant has had time to answer the door." *United States v. Banks*, 540 U.S. 31, 41 (2003); *see also Hudson v. Michigan*, 547 U.S. 586, 590 (2006) ("Our reasonable wait time standard is necessarily vague.") (internal quotation marks and citations omitted).

weapons pat-downs and searches in 2015 to reflect a more accurate statement of the law. The new policy also requires that commanding officers provide trainings and conduct audits to ensure members engage appropriately and within policy, and fulfill reporting requirements. However, trainings have yet to be administered to the majority of field officers, and supervisors have not consistently audited reports or held officers accountable for failing to comply with the updated policy.

ii. BPD Lacks Effective Oversight and Accountability of Stops, Searches, and Arrests

BPD fails to use effective measures to review stops, searches, and arrests to identify and correct constitutional violations or provide counseling and support to its officers. BPD conducts minimal substantive review of the justification for particular stops, searches, and arrests, and does not sufficiently collect and analyze data to identify problematic patterns in these activities. Consequently, BPD relies almost exclusively on its complaint system to identify constitutional violations. These practices are not sufficient to ensure constitutional policing.

Substantive review of stops, searches, and arrests: BPD supervisors conduct minimal substantive review of officers' justifications for stops, searches, and arrests. Although BPD policy instructs officers to document all stops, frisks, and searches on a stop form, it lacks an effective means to identify and address unconstitutional behavior. For most of the period covered by our review, BPD officers recorded stops on a "Stop and Frisk" form that typically did not record an officer's reasons for making a stop or initiating a frisk. As a result, BPD officers did not document the facts justifying a stop or search except in cases that resulted in an arrest or use of force, for which officers were required to complete an incident report or use of force report. This information deficit precluded supervisory review for the large majority of stops that do not lead to arrests or citations—stops for which such review is imperative. BPD attempted to address this data collection issue through a policy change in 2015, when it began requiring officers to document the basis for *Terry* stops and frisks on a "Form 309" and instructing supervisors to review these justifications. But this process has not generated robust review. While supervisors usually review stop reports, they almost universally sign off on the bases for stops and searches—even where officers describe facially unlawful activity. Indeed, BPD supervisors told us they view their role as merely "documenting" officer activity, not reviewing it for compliance with policy and law. Moreover, our ride-alongs and officer interviews revealed that many officers who make *Terry* stops that do not lead to arrest report that they conducted only a voluntary "field interview"—or no stop at all—to avoid the new documentation requirements. And BPD has not audited its field reports or CAD data to root out this practice.

We found similar deficiencies throughout BPD's review of officers' justifications for arrests. As with stops and frisks, BPD front line supervisors consistently sign off on incident reports describing the basis for warrantless arrests,
even where the reports describe egregious constitutional violations. Indeed,
our review did not identify a single arrest questioned by a front line supervisor.
And as with stops, BPD supervisors told us that they see their role as documenting officer activity, not reviewing to ensure it conforms to constitutional
standards.

Data collection and pattern analysis: BPD likewise fails to collect and
analyze data to identify patterns in officers' stops, searches, and arrests. Despite a long record of public outcry and numerous complaints regarding illegal
stops, searches, and arrests for low level offenses, BPD has never consistently
collected and analyzed data regarding the number, type, and nature of its investigatory stops. BPD enters certain information from stop forms into an
electronic database, but the limited types of data and inconsistent data entry
practices preclude analysis. Indeed, BPD does not conduct any statistical analysis of its stops or searches using these data, nor are the data entered into BPD's
early intervention system to help identify officers whose activities may warrant
further scrutiny. This lack of meaningful data analysis hinders BPD's ability to
manage its officers effectively.

The inability to analyze data keeps BPD from identifying important trends,
curbing unlawful practices, and assisting officers or units that may benefit from
additional training or support. For example, BPD's data systems cannot identify whether specific officers or units bear a disproportionate share of responsibility for illegal stops and searches. During the course of our investigation,
we received a large number of anecdotes specifically identifying plainclothes
officers enforcing violent crime and vice offenses (the names and organization
of the units have changed multiple times over the years covered by the investigation) as particularly aggressive and unrestrained in their practice of stopping individuals without cause and performing public, humiliating searches.
A disproportionate share of complaints likewise accuse plainclothes officers of
misconduct. Yet much of BPD's stop data does not even identify the unit of
the officers involved in the stop, making unit-level analysis impossible. Indeed,
BPD's data on roughly half of the 300,000 stops recorded from 2010–2014 contain no information about the units of the officers who made the stop.

BPD similarly fails to track data on arrests made by officers. Although BPD
enters information on arrests in a basic database, the Department conducts no
analysis to identify trends in the type, frequency, or quality of arrests made by
particular officers or units. For example, one measure that could be used to
assess whether individual officers or units are engaged in a pattern of illegal
arrests would be to monitor arrest outcomes to determine if prosecutors filed
or dismissed charges in cases stemming from arrests by certain officers, units,

or supervisors. Doing so would identify officers who make arrests that cannot be prosecuted due to lack of probable cause, failure to collect evidence in a constitutional manner, or other improprieties. Tracking arrest outcomes is an important tool for imposing accountability as well as identifying officers who would benefit from additional training, guidance, or other early intervention. Yet BPD does not take any steps to track or identify officers or units who make arrests that cannot be prosecuted, or to identify supervisors who sign off on such arrests.

Even where prosecutors have provided BPD with specific information on problematic officers who routinely make improper arrests, searches, or seizures, the Department has failed to meaningfully investigate the information or take appropriate action. For several years, the State's Attorney's Office maintained a "Do Not Call" list of officers that prosecutors should not subpoena to testify because prosecutors determined that the officers did not testify credibly about their enforcement actions. Although the State's Attorney's Office regularly shared this list with BPD, the Department rarely used the information to identify officers who may need support or discipline. As a result, problematic officers remain on the street, detaining, searching, and arresting people even though the State's Attorney's Office has determined that it cannot prosecute a crime based on the officers' testimony. The State's Attorney's Office no longer maintains a written "Do Not Call" list, but prosecutors informally maintain a registry of problematic BPD officers who cannot be used to support criminal prosecutions. In recent years, the State's Attorney's Office has contacted BPD leadership on several occasions to identify officers that prosecutors determined can no longer testify credibly due to misconduct. In most of these cases, BPD leadership took no action against the identified problem officers.

B. BPD DISCRIMINATES AGAINST AFRICAN AMERICANS IN ITS ENFORCEMENT ACTIVITIES

We find reasonable cause to believe that BPD engages in a pattern or practice of discriminatory policing against African Americans. Statistical evidence shows that the Department intrudes disproportionately upon the lives of African Americans at every stage of its enforcement activities. BPD officers disproportionately stop African Americans; search them more frequently during these stops; and arrest them at rates that significantly exceed relevant benchmarks for criminal activity. African Americans are likewise subjected more often to false arrests. Indeed, for each misdemeanor street offense that we examined, local prosecutors and booking officials dismissed a higher proportion of African-American arrests upon initial review compared to arrests of people from other racial backgrounds. BPD officers also disproportionately use force—including constitutionally excessive force—against African-American subjects. Nearly 90 percent of the excessive force incidents identified by the Justice Department review involve force used against African Americans.

In the early 2000s, BPD began a "zero tolerance" enforcement strategy that encouraged officers to make frequent stops, searches, and arrests for misdemeanor offenses. This strategy overwhelmingly impacted the City's African-American residents and predominantly African-American neighborhoods. BPD has had notice of concerns about its policing of African-American communities for many years, yet it has failed to take adequate steps to ensure that its enforcement activities are non-discriminatory. The Department did not implement a "Fair and Impartial Policing" policy until 2015 and conducted virtually no analysis of its own data to assess the impact of its enforcement activities on African-American communities. BPD likewise has failed to effectively investigate complaints alleging racial bias—often misclassifying complaints to preclude any meaningful investigation. In some cases, BPD supervisors have ordered their subordinates to target African Americans specifically for heightened enforcement. We also found numerous examples of BPD officers using racial slurs or making other statements that exhibit bias against African Americans without being held accountable by the Department. These racial disparities and indications of intentional discrimination erode community trust that is a critical component of effective law enforcement. We heard repeatedly from community members who believed they were treated disrespectfully or singled out for enforcement because of their race. BPD leadership acknowledges that its legacy of zero tolerance enforcement in certain neighborhoods has damaged community partnerships and has taken steps to begin improving the Department's relationship with African-American communities. While we applaud these steps, significant work remains.

In addition to harming its relationship with the broader community, BPD's racially disparate enforcement violates the Safe Streets Act and Title VI of the Civil Rights Act of 1964. These statutes prohibit law enforcement practices that disparately impact African Americans unless the practices are necessary to achieve non-discriminatory objectives. *Cf. Gallagher v. Magner*, 619 F.3d 823, 837 (8th Cir. 2010) (in the related context of Fair Housing Act litigation, an official action that causes racially disparate impact may be justified only by showing that the action "has a manifest relationship to legitimate, non-discriminatory objectives"); *Albemarle Paper Co. v. Moody*, 422 U.S. 405, 425 (1975) (finding in the Title VII employment discrimination context that an employer may rebut prima facie showing of disproportionate impact by proving that the requirement causing disparate impact has a "manifest relationship to the employment in question"). Title VI provides that no person shall "be excluded from participating in, be denied the benefits of, or be subjected to discrimination under any program or activity receiving [f]ederal financial assistance" based on race. 42 U.S.C. § 2000d. The Title VI implementing regulations ban recipients of federal funds from using "criteria or methods of administration" that have an unnecessary disparate impact based on race. 28 C.F.R. § 42.104(b)(2). The Safe Streets Act likewise proscribes law enforcement practices that cause disparate impact based on race except where such impact is necessary to achieve nondiscriminatory objectives. *See* 28 C.F.R. § 42.203.

1. BPD's Enforcement Activities Disproportionately Impact African Americans

There is overwhelming statistical evidence of racial disparities in BPD's stops, searches, and arrests. This evidence demonstrates a discriminatory impact on African Americans under Title VI and the Safe Streets Act. *See Chavez v. Illinois State Police*, 251 F.3d 612, 637 (7th Cir. 2001) ("The Supreme Court has long noted the importance of statistical analysis in cases in which the existence of discrimination is a disputed issue.") (internal citation omitted); *Bradley v. United States*, 299 F.3d 197, 206 n.11 (3d Cir. 2002) ("In profiling cases . . . statistical evidence of discrimination may be the only means of proving a discriminatory effect"); *Floyd v. City of New York*, 959 F. Supp. 2d 540, 661–62 (S.D.N.Y. 2013) (statistical evidence of racial and ethnic disparities in police stop and frisk practices, including post-stop outcomes, proved adverse impact under the Equal Protection Clause); *Melendres v. Arpaio*, No. CV-97092513, 2013 WL 2297173 (D. Ariz. May 24, 2013) (statistical evidence proved that certain patrol operations at a sheriff's office disparately impacted Latinos); *Maryland NAACP v. Maryland State Police*,

454 F. Supp. 2d 339, 349 (D. Md. 2006) (disparities in stops and searches of African Americans constituted "powerful circumstantial evidence of racial profiling"). Here, statistical evidence highlights racial disparities at all levels of BPD's street enforcement, from the initial decision to stop pedestrians or vehicles to conducting searches and making arrests. We also found troubling trends in the sample of use of force reports we reviewed, suggesting that force may be used disproportionately against African Americans.

a. Racial Disparities in Stops and Searches

BPD officers subject African Americans to a disproportionate number of pedestrian and vehicle stops on Baltimore streets and search African Americans disproportionately during these stops.

i. Stops

BPD disproportionately stops African Americans standing, walking, or driving on Baltimore streets. The Department's data on all pedestrian stops from January 2010 to June 2015 shows that African Americans account for 84 percent of stops[55] despite comprising only 63 percent of the City's population. Expressed differently, BPD officers made 520 stops for every 1,000 black residents in Baltimore, but only 180 stops for every 1,000 Caucasian residents.

The high rate of stopping African Americans persists across the City, even in districts where African Americans make up a small share of the population. Indeed, the proportion of African-American stops exceeds the share of African-American population in each of BPD's nine police districts, despite significant variation in the districts' racial, socioeconomic, and geographic composition.[56] For example, African Americans accounted for: 83 percent of stops in the Central District (compared to 57 percent of the population), which contains the City's downtown business area; over 93 percent of stops in the Eastern District (compared to 90 percent of the population), which includes predominantly low-income, urban neighborhoods; and 83 percent of stops in the Northern District (compared to 41 percent of the population), which includes many affluent, suburban neighborhoods. Even in the Southeast District—with an African-American population of only 23 percent—two out of three BPD stops involved African-American subjects. Figure 2 illustrates this pattern.

---

55 Stops for which officers did not record the subject's race are excluded from this analysis.

56 The proportion of African American pedestrian stops and population was virtually identical in the Western District, where both figures are approximately 96 percent.

Figure 1 - BPD Pedestrian Stops Per 1,000 Residents, 2010-2015

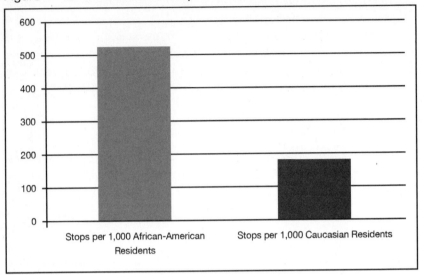

Closer analysis highlights the impact of these racial disparities. Individual African Americans are far more likely to be subjected to multiple stops within relatively short periods of time. African Americans accounted for 95 percent of the 410 individuals stopped at least ten times by BPD officers from 2010–2015. During this period, BPD stopped 34 African Americans at least 20 times and seven other African Americans at least *30 times*.[57] No person of any other race was stopped more than 12 times. One African-American man in his mid-fifties was stopped 30 times in less than four years. The only reasons provided for these stops were officers' suspicion that the man was "loitering" or "trespassing," or as part of a "CDS investigation." On at least 15 occasions, officers detained the man while they checked to see if he had outstanding warrants. Despite these repeated intrusions, none of the 30 stops resulted in a citation or criminal charge. The map on the following page shows the concentration of stops in African-American neighborhoods.

BPD likewise stops African-American drivers at disproportionate rates. From 2010–2015, African Americans made up 82 percent of people stopped by BPD officers for traffic violations, compared to only 60 percent of the City's driving age population. As with pedestrian stops, BPD stopped a higher rate of African American drivers in each of the City's districts, despite large differences in

---

57 As explained in Section II.A.1, there is strong evidence that BPD under-reports its pedestrian stops. Thus, the true number of African Americans who hit these—or higher—stop thresholds may be significantly larger.

Figure 2 - Pedestrian Stops Compared to Population, by BPD District, 2010-2015

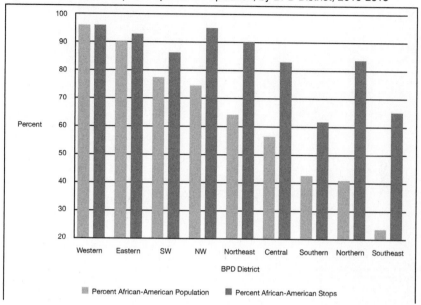

those districts' demographic profiles and traffic patterns. For example, African Americans accounted for 80 percent of vehicle stops in the Northern District despite making up only 41 percent of the district's population, and made up 56 percent of stops in the Southeast District compared to only 23 percent of the population living there.

While there are limitations on using population data to benchmark vehicle stops because the proportion of drivers on roadways does not necessarily match the population living in a particular area, there are strong indications that BPD's high rate of stopping African-American drivers is discriminatory. Indeed, the proportion of African-American drivers on Baltimore roadways is almost certainly less than their 60 percent share of the City's driving age population. Baltimore's traffic patterns are influenced by commuters and visitors from surrounding areas with significantly smaller African-American populations than the City's. BPD's data confirms that 25 percent of the Department's traffic stops involve drivers who live outside the City, overwhelmingly in towns and suburbs within the Baltimore metropolitan area. The presence of these individuals on Baltimore roads lowers the proportion of African-American drivers, as African Americans account for only 27.6 percent of the driving age population in the Baltimore metropolitan area. Moreover, basic population data is likely to overstate the portion of African-American drivers on Baltimore roadways because African Americans are less likely than

BPD Reported Stops, 2010 - 2015, with Percentage Black Population

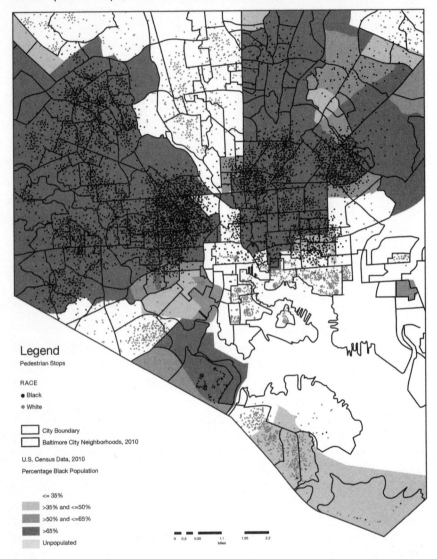

Legend

Pedestrian Stops

RACE

● Black

● White

☐ City Boundary
☐ Baltimore City Neighborhoods, 2010

U.S. Census Data, 2010

Percentage Black Population

<= 35%

>35% and <=50%

>50% and <=65%

>65%

Unpopulated

0   0.3 0.55   1.1   1.65   2.2
                   Miles

other City residents to have access to vehicles.[58] Nationally, 19 percent of African Americans live in households that do not have access to automobiles, compared to 4.6 percent , a disparity that "follows directly from sharp racial differences in household income and poverty." Berube, Deakin, & Raphael,

---

58 According to the U.S. Census Bureau's American Community Survey 2010–2013, 30 percent of Baltimore residents do not have access to automobiles.

SOCIOECONOMIC DIFFERENCES IN HOUSEHOLD AUTOMOBILE OWNER-
SHIP RATES 203 (2008). This trend is pronounced in Baltimore, where over
100,000 African Americans live in poverty, constituting an outsized share of
the City's low-income residents.[59] Consequently, African Americans almost
certainly comprise less than 60 percent of Baltimore drivers, but account for 82
percent of BPD's traffic stops.

ii. Searches

We also found evidence of bias in BPD's searches during pedestrian and vehicle
stops, although our analysis is limited by significant shortcomings in BPD's
data collection. We first examined spreadsheets provided by BPD that purportedly reflect the Department's data on all vehicle and pedestrian stops from
2010–2015, including whether officers conducted a search during each stop. Although these spreadsheets typically record the race of the person stopped and
the district in which the stop occurred, they do not appear to reflect complete
information about searches. BPD's data record that officers conducted searches
in only 1.3 percent of pedestrian stops and 0.5 percent of vehicle stops—rates
that are implausibly low. Interviews with BPD personnel responsible for entering data from officers' stop reports into the spreadsheets confirmed that information on searches is frequently not captured. Other relevant data—such
as the reason for the stop, officers' unit assignments, etc.—also appear to be
recorded inconsistently. In an attempt to address this under-reporting and facilitate more comprehensive analysis of searches, experts retained by the Justice
Department drew a sample of nearly 14,000 hard copy BPD stop reports, manually coded them, and created a new database containing all of the information
recorded on the reports. Within this sample, officers conducted searches in 13
percent of pedestrian stops and 8.2 percent of vehicle stops—far higher rates
than reflected in the data BPD captured in its data entry.

The database we created from hard copy stop reports reveals that BPD officers search African Americans at disproportionate rates. During pedestrian
stops, officers searched 13 percent of African Americans compared to only 9.5
percent of other people—making African Americans 37 percent more likely
to be searched when stopped than other residents. Similarly, officers were 23
percent more likely to search African Americans during vehicle stops. These
differences are significant beyond conventional levels of statistical signifi-

---

59 African Americans account for more than 76 percent of Baltimoreans living below
the poverty line despite making up only 63 percent of the City's population. U.S. Census
Bureau, American Community Survey 2014 One-Year Estimate.

cance.[60] Justice Department experts found that racial disparities in search rates persisted after using regression techniques to control for relevant variables, including the area in which a stop occurred and the assignment and experience level of the officers involved.

These racial disparities suggest that BPD's search practices discriminate against African Americans. Search rate differences do not alone establish disproportionate impact based on race, however, because it is possible that differential search rates are driven by race-neutral explanations. For that reason, the best measure of racial patterns in searches is a comparison of the rates at which officers find contraband during searches, or "hit rates." *See, e.g.,* John Knowles, Nicola Persico & Petra Todd, *Racial Bias in Motor Vehicle Searches: Theory and Evidence,* 109 JOURNAL OF POLITICAL ECONOMY 203 (2001). A lower hit rate for searches of a particular demographic group is evidence that officers apply a lower threshold of suspicion when deciding to search members of that group compared to others.

To the extent that BPD collects hit rate data, it suggests that officers' search decisions are biased against African Americans. Indeed, BPD's data on all stops from 2010–2015 shows that searches of African Americans have significantly lower hit rates than other searches. During vehicle stops, BPD officers reported finding some type of contraband less than half as often when searching African Americans—in only 3.9 percent of searches of African Americans, compared to 8.5 percent of other searches. Search hit rates during pedestrian stops also exhibited large disparities, with officers finding contraband in only 2.6 percent of African American searches compared to 3.9 percent for other searches—a 50 percent difference.[61] These results are statistically significant.

In short, BPD's pedestrian and vehicle stops disproportionately impact African Americans. The large racial disparities in stops persist throughout the City,

---

60 In the fields of statistics and criminology, results are generally considered statistically significant if they would occur by chance no more than 5 times out of 100.

61 This analysis is based on all 3,863 searches that BPD recorded for pedestrian stops and 1,495 searches recorded for vehicle stops from 2010–2015. As discussed above, these data likely fail to capture a significant number of searches that BPD officers actually conducted during this period. The *hit rates* from these searches are nonetheless indicative of bias, however, because there is no reason to believe that there are systematic differences in how BPD records search outcomes based on the race of the person searched. In other words, BPD officers sometimes fail to record their searches at all. But when searches are recorded, there is no indication that officers change how they record the fruits of the search based on the race of the person searched. Nor does it appear that officers disproportionately record searches in certain parts of the City. To the contrary, the proportion of searches recorded in each district roughly tracks the number of stops in those districts. In sum, BPD's data showing that searches of African Americans are less likely to find contraband than other searches is reliable evidence of disproportionate impact.

Figure 3 - Search Hit Rates, 2010-2015

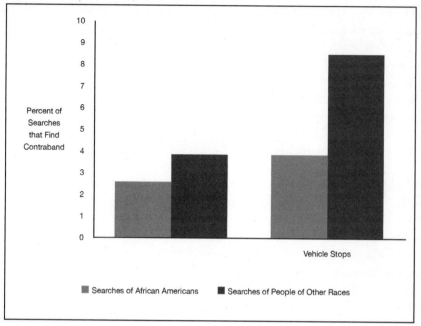

subjecting African Americans to heightened intrusion from the police in their lives. Officers also search African Americans at higher rates during these stops, even though searches of African Americans are less likely to find contraband than searches of people from other racial backgrounds. These differential search rates are not justified by characteristics of the people searched.

Our analysis of racial patterns in BPD's searches was challenging because of the Department's deficient data collection. BPD's failure to record consistent search information not only inhibits our analysis here, it limits the Department's ability to root out discriminatory conduct by its officers. Moving forward, BPD must reform its data collection and analysis systems to ensure that robust search data is tracked and analyzed to prevent and correct discriminatory practices.

b. Racial Disparities in Arrests

The racial disparities in BPD's stops and searches are further reflected in BPD's arrest practices. From November 2010–July 2015, BPD charged African Americans with 280,850 criminal offenses, constituting over 86 percent of all charges filed for which the race of the offender is known.[62] Expressed a different way, African Americans in Baltimore were charged with one offense for every 1.4 residents, while individuals of other races were charged with only one offense per 5.1 residents. This discriminatory pattern is particularly apparent in two categories of BPD's enforcement: (1) warrantless arrests for discretionary misdemeanor offenses such as disorderly conduct and failing to obey an officer's order; and (2) arrests for drug possession. In both cases, officers arrest African Americans at rates far higher than relevant benchmarks.

i. Racial Disparities in Misdemeanor Street Arrests

BPD's warrantless arrests for discretionary misdemeanor offenses exhibit substantial racial disparities. Our analysis of these arrests is based on data the State of Maryland tracks for all criminal charges made by law enforcement officers. For each charged offense, this data captures the agency making the arrest, the race and gender of the person arrested, and the arrest's disposition. As explained in Section II.A, *supra*, the disposition data records whether each arrestee was committed into jail, issued a criminal or civil citation, released without charges, or released because of mistaken identity. For arrests that do not result in immediate release, the data also record whether reviewing officials at the State's Attorney's Office found that the arrest lacked probable cause or otherwise declined to charge the offense. Analysis of this data reveals that African Americans account for the overwhelming majority of BPD's discretionary misdemeanor arrests, and that reviewing officials are more likely to dismiss charges against African Americans—indicating that officers apply a lower standard when making them.

As an initial matter, BPD officers arrest African Americans for several common misdemeanor offenses at high rates. Although they make up only 63 percent of Baltimore's population, African Americans accounted for: 87 percent of the 3,400 charges for resisting arrest; 89 percent of 1,350 charges for making a false statement to an officer; 84 percent of the 4,000 charges for failing to obey an order; 86 percent of the more than 1,000 charges for hindering or obstruction; 83 percent of the roughly 6,500 arrests for disorderly conduct; and 88 percent of the nearly 3,500 arrests for trespassing on posted property. Figure 4 highlights the magnitude of these disparities by expressing the number of arrests for these offenses per 1,000 Baltimore residents.

---

62 After removing duplicates from data provided by the State of Maryland, we found that BPD filed 331,764 criminal charges during this period. Of these charges, 5,641 were excluded from analysis because the arrestee's race was not recorded.

Figure 4 - Misdemeanor Charges Per 1,000 Residents, 2010-2015

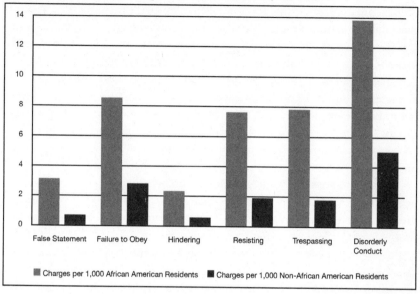

These disparities are even more pronounced where officers arrest individuals solely for a misdemeanor street offense, unconnected to a more serious charge. In such cases, African Americans comprise 91 percent of trespassing charges; 91 percent of failure to obey charges; 88 percent of hindering charges; and 84 percent of disorderly conduct charges. BPD also charged 79 people solely with "resisting arrest," despite not arresting them for any other crime. African Americans accounted for 90 percent of these charges.

In addition to these common misdemeanor offenses, BPD enforces other minor charges almost exclusively against African Americans. For example, BPD charged 657 people with "gaming" or playing "cards or dice," of whom 652—over 99 percent—were African Americans. Although we are not aware of any data tracking the precise rate at which people of different races play cards or dice, it is extremely unlikely that African Americans comprise 99 percent of those doing so. Notably, in some cases, BPD has expended significant resources to enforce these minor offenses against African Americans. For example, BPD has used a helicopter unit known as "Foxtrot," which typically coordinates officers' response to shootings and other serious crimes, to enforce misdemeanor gambling offenses against African Americans. In early 2016, a Foxtrot unit alerted patrol officers that a group of young African-American men were playing dice on a street corner. Officers on the ground responded to this intelligence by confronting the group and arresting one of the men, who was charged solely with "playing dice."

The differential rates at which BPD supervisors release without charges or local prosecutors decline to charge BPD's misdemeanor arrests underscore their discriminatory nature. To arrest for a misdemeanor offense, BPD officers must have probable cause that an offense occurred. As explained above, in some cases reviewing officials at booking or the State's Attorney's Office disagree with officers' probable cause determinations and decline to charge arrestees. If officers apply a consistent, unbiased standard when making arrests, the rate of such declinations should be roughly equivalent across racial groups for arrests on any particular offense. However, our outcome analysis shows large racial disparities: misdemeanor arrests of African Americans are dismissed or declined at significantly higher rates than other arrests.

During their initial review of arrest documents, booking officers and prosecutors dismissed charges against African Americans at significantly higher rates than arrests of other people. This disparity exists for every common misdemeanor offense we examined, as evident in Figure 5 below. Officials dismissed charges against African Americans for trespassing at a rate 52 percent higher than the rate at which they dismissed other trespassing arrests; dismissed African American resisting arrest charges at a 57 percent higher rate; failure to obey charges at a 33 percent higher rate; false statement charges at a 231 percent higher rate; disorderly conduct charges at a 17 percent higher rate; and disturbing the peace charges at a 370 percent higher rate. These disparities are statistically significant. Notably, the racial disparities in outcomes for these highly discretionary, non-violent offenses are not present for less discretionary felony offenses. We found that reviewing officials' initial review resulted in dismissal of charges for first degree assault, burglary, and robbery at nearly identical rates across racial groups. The implication of these findings is that there are no underlying conditions that cause officials to dismiss African-American charges at higher rates. Instead, the large racial differences in the proportion of dismissed charges for misdemeanor street offenses demonstrate that, where officers have wider discretion to make arrests, they exercise it in a discriminatory manner.

In sum, BPD disproportionately arrests African Americans for common misdemeanor street offenses. The proportion of African Americans arrested for these offenses is far higher than their share of Baltimore's population, and reviewing officials determined that arrests of African Americans for these offenses are significantly more likely to lack probable cause or otherwise not merit prosecution. Taken together, these facts demonstrate that BPD arrests African Americans for misdemeanor offenses based on lower evidentiary thresholds than it uses when arresting people from other racial backgrounds.

Figure 5 - Percent of Charges Dismissed Upon Initial Review, 2010-2015

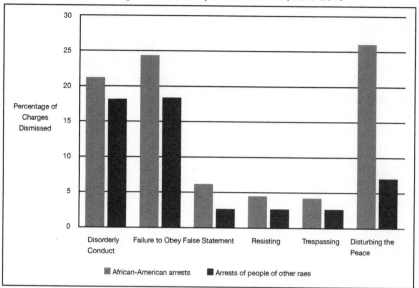

ii. Disproportionate Arrests for Drug Possession

There are large racial disparities in BPD's enforcement of laws criminalizing possession of controlled substances. We analyzed drug possession charges for several reasons: such charges make up more than one third of all BPD arrests; stakeholders and community members we interviewed frequently expressed their belief that BPD focuses on African Americans for heightened drug enforcement; and data on the drug arrests can be compared to relevant benchmarks on drug usage to assess whether BPD enforces drug laws disproportionately. For this analysis, we compared BPD's drug arrests to: (1) survey data on drug usage; and (2) the rates of drug arrests in jurisdictions similar to Baltimore. We find that BPD arrests far more African Americans for drug offenses than would be expected based on drug usage and population data, and that this disparity is not attributable to any legitimate law enforcement objective. Indeed, BPD's rate of African-American drug arrests is significantly higher than the rate of such arrests by law enforcement agencies in cities with similar demographic profiles and socioeconomic challenges. These analyses reveal that BPD's drug enforcement disproportionately impacts African Americans.

BPD arrests African Americans for drug possession offenses at rates far exceeding their drug usage: To assess the racial impact of BPD's drug arrests, we first aggregated all drug possession offenses[63] for which BPD made at least 3,000 charges from November 2010–June 2015. BPD charged approximately 100,000 people for drug possession under these offenses. Eighty-nine percent of those charged were African American.[64] BPD made 254 drug arrests for every 1,000 African-American Baltimore residents while making only 52 drug arrests per 1,000 residents of other races.[65] African Americans were thus five times more likely than others to be arrested for drug offenses.

Figure 6 - Drug Possession Charges Per 1,000 Residents, 2010-2015

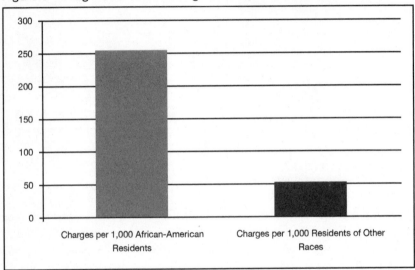

---

63 Some criminologists believe that, when comparing drug arrests to survey data on drug usage, the most accurate comparison includes police arrests for drug possession and drug distribution because law enforcement officers may charge individuals possessing controlled substances with intent to distribute them. Accordingly, we also compared BPD's rate of charging individuals for all drug possession *and distribution* offenses to data on drug usage. This comparison yielded nearly identical results. African Americans account for 90 percent of possession and distribution offenses charged by BPD, compared to 88.5 percent of possession charges alone.

64 We excluded a small number of charges for which the race of the arrestee was not recorded.

65 These figures include only drug offenses for which BPD made at least 3,000 charges from 2010–2015. The total number of all drug arrests is higher, as indicated in the analysis of Bureau of Justice Statistics data discussed below.

The racial disparities in BPD's enforcement are far higher than any demographic differences in the rates at which individuals use drugs. While the observed prevalence of illicit drug use varies somewhat by data source, most comprehensive surveys indicate that African Americans use drugs at rates that, at most, only modestly exceed other population groups. The Center for Disease Control's (CDC) National Survey on Drug Use and Health found that, in 2013, 8.7 percent of African Americans over age 12 had used drugs within the past month, compared to 7.7 percent of Caucasians. The 2012 survey reported similar figures, with 9.1 percent of African Americans and 7.4 percent of Caucasians reporting drug use.[66] In other words, the CDC survey found that African Americans were between 1.1 and 1.2 times more likely to use drugs than Caucasians, yet BPD arrests African Americans for drug possession 5 times as often as others.[67]

BPD's disparate rate of arresting African Americans for drug crimes cannot be explained by differences in drug usage within Baltimore as compared to the nation as a whole. To the contrary, drug use in Baltimore appears broadly similar to national averages. For example, data maintained by the Substance Abuse and Mental Health Services Administration (SAMHSA) shows that the rate of marijuana use from 2010–2012 averaged 8.2 percent in Baltimore, compared to a national average of 7.0 percent. For drugs other than marijuana, SAMHSA surveys show that usage in Baltimore averaged 3.3 percent during this period, compared to a national average of 3.4 percent.

BPD arrests African Americans for drug possession offenses at higher rates than similar cities: A second measure of BPD's disproportionate drug enforcement is the agency's high rate of arresting African Americans for drug possession offenses compared to law enforcement agencies in cities with comparable demographic profiles, crime rates, and economic profiles. Expert criminologists retained for our investigation identified five cities most comparable to Baltimore for purposes of this analysis: Atlanta, Cleveland, Detroit, Memphis, and Milwaukee. These cities reported overall drug usage rates in line with Baltimore's 8.2 percent, including: 9.0 percent in Milwaukee; 13.6 percent in Detroit; and 6.5 percent in Atlanta.[68] The comparison cities likewise reported usage rates similar to Baltimore's 3.3 percent for drugs other than marijuana. Cleveland reported 3.5 percent non-marijuana

---

66 *See* National Survey on Drug Use and Heath, CENTER FOR DISEASE CONTROL (Aug. 4, 2016), http://www.cdc.gov/nchs/data.

67 Ninety-nine percent of BPD's arrestees for drug possession were either African American or Caucasian.

68 *National Survey on Drug Use and Health Table 5*, SUBSTANCE ABUSE AND MENTAL HEALTH SERVICES ADMINISTRATION (August 4, 2016), http://www.samhsa.gov/data/sites/default /files/NSDUHsubstateChangeTabs2012/NSDUHsubstateChangeTabs2012.htm.

usage, Atlanta 3.1 percent, and Detroit 3.7 percent.[69] Despites these similarities in rates of drug *use*, however, we found that BPD makes far more drug *arrests* than agencies in Baltimore's peer cities.

To make this comparison, we collected data from the Bureau of Justice Statistics (BJS) on drug arrests in Baltimore and the five comparison cities. The most recent period for which BJS data is available is 2010–2012. We used the 2010–2012 BJS data for all cities—including Baltimore—to standardize how arrests are categorized and reported.[70] We then controlled for population differences among these cities by measuring arrest rates based on the number of drug arrests per 1,000 residents in each racial category. The results show that BPD's rate of arresting African Americans for drug crimes dramatically exceeds the rate of such arrests by agencies in the comparison cities. Indeed, for each of the three years we examined, Baltimore drug arrests of African Americans were between *200 and 500 percent higher* than the comparison cities.[71]

Figure 6 - Drug Possession Charges Per 1,000 Residents, 2010-2015

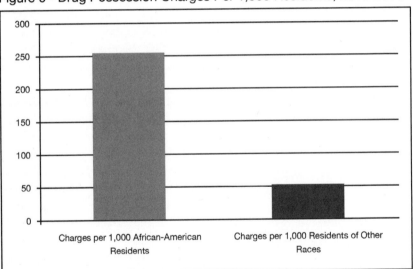

69 *Id.*

70 The BJS data on drug arrests in Baltimore differs slightly from the data BPD provided to us during the investigation, but the small differences do not impact our analysis. Indeed, for all three years we examined, the BPD data show that the agency arrested an even larger number of African Americans than the data reported to BJS. The analysis presented here thus may slightly understate the magnitude of BPD's disparate drug arrests of African Americans when compared to agencies in other cities.

71 BPD also arrests non-African Americans for drug possession offenses at somewhat higher rates than the national average and the comparison cities. As explained above, however, the *proportion* of BPD drug arrests of African Americans is far higher than would be expected

Figure 7 - Drug Possession Arrests Per 1,000 African-American Residents, 2010-2012

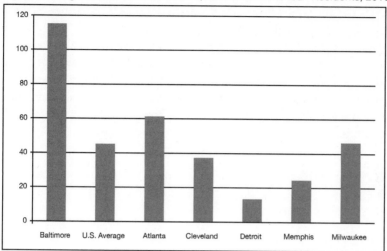

c. Use of Force

The consequence of the large racial disparities in stops, searches, and arrests may also manifest itself in what may be disproportionate use of force against African Americans by BPD. We found that African Americans accounted for roughly 88 percent of the subjects of non-deadly force used by BPD officers in a random sample of over 800 cases we reviewed. This trend is consistent across different types of non-deadly force, including tasers, the most common weapon used by BPD officers. While these patterns merit attention, we draw no firm conclusions about their relative impact on African Americans because we did not compare the rates of force to any "benchmark" of encounters in which force is warranted. Nevertheless, this rate of force is significantly higher than the proportion of African Americans in Baltimore's population, heightening our concerns.

In sum, we find large racial disparities in BPD's pedestrian stops, vehicle stops, searches, and arrests. We further identified troubling indications that BPD officers disproportionately use force during encounters with African Americans on Baltimore streets. As explained further below, BPD's disparate stops,

---

based on drug usage data and population statistics. The comparison to law enforcement agencies in similar cities demonstrates that these disparities are not driven by legitimate responses to socioeconomic conditions. Rather, BPD's discriminatory drug enforcement renders it a significant outlier.

searches, and arrests of African Americans are not part of a calibrated, proportionate strategy for responding to criminal activity. These disparities establish disproportionate impact under the Constitution and the nondiscrimination provisions of Title VI and the Safe Streets Act. Title VI and the Safe Streets Act prohibit law enforcement agencies that receive federal financial assistance from engaging in practices that have an unnecessary disparate impact based on race. Because BPD's disparate stops, searches, and arrest are not done in a manner necessary to achieve BPD's legitimate public safety goals, they violate Title VI and the Safe Streets Act.

2. Racial Disparities in BPD's Enforcement, Along with Evidence Suggesting Intentional Discrimination Against African Americans, Exacerbates Community Distrust

The policing practices that cause the racial disparities in BPD's stops, searches, and arrests, along with evidence suggesting intentional discrimination against African Americans, undermine the community trust that is central to effective policing. Indeed, we heard from many community members who were reluctant to engage with BPD officers because of their belief that the Department treats African Americans unfairly. *See also* Jack Glaser, *Suspect Race: Causes and Consequence of Racial Profiling* 96–126 (2015) (racial profiling has a "high risk" of undermining efforts to control crime and promote public safety). These concerns were acknowledged by BPD leadership and officers, who explained that the lack of trust—particularly in many of Baltimore's African-American communities—inhibited officers' efforts to build relationships that are a key component of effective policing.

Starting in the early 2000s, BPD implemented a "zero tolerance" policing strategy. This strategy encouraged officers to take discretionary enforcement actions, including stops, searches, and arrests for misdemeanor offenses like loitering and disorderly conduct. As described above, this enforcement strategy focused on African Americans and predominantly African American neighborhoods for discretionary enforcement actions, and it led to officers frequently stopping, searching, and arresting individuals without the required constitutional justification. We also found evidence of officers using racial slurs or making other statements exhibiting bias while taking enforcement actions against African Americans.

The Department has had notice of concerns about the impact of its zero tolerance strategy on African Americans and predominantly African-American neighborhoods for many years, but for many years it failed to take adequate steps to ensure that its policing efforts are non-discriminatory. BPD did not institute a "Fair and Impartial Policing" policy until 2015, leaving officers without critical guidance on how to lawfully perform their duties. We likewise found no evidence that BPD has performed any analysis to determine if its enforcement strategies and activities disparately impact African Americans, even though it has collected the basic data to perform such assessments for years. Indeed, every analysis we include in this report is based on BPD's own data, but BPD never developed systems to conduct this analysis. We also found that BPD repeatedly fails to investigate complaints of racial bias. In the approximately six years of complaint data we received from BPD, we found only one complaint that BPD classified as a racial slur. This is implausible. By manually reviewing and performing text searches on BPD's complaint data, we found 60 more complaints that alleged that BPD officers used just one racial slur—"n****r"—but all these complaints were misclassified as a lesser offense.

Recently, City and BPD leaders have acknowledged that the zero tolerance policing strategy has harmed the City's predominantly African-American communities. *See supra* at 17-18. During our investigation, one of BPD's top officials told us that "stop and frisk killed the hopes and dreams of entire communities." The City's and BPD's recognition that its zero tolerance policing strategy has had a significant, unwarranted impact on Baltimore's African-American communities has led to recent changes in the Department, including implementing the "Fair and Impartial Policing" policy in 2015, and efforts to improve its collection of data on its enforcement activities. We commend the City and BPD for these efforts.

Still, many BPD supervisors continue to reinforce zero tolerance enforcement. Officers patrolling predominantly African-American neighborhoods routinely receive orders to "clear corners" by stopping or arresting African-American youth standing on sidewalks. This practice has continued despite concerns raised by officers themselves, who have told BPD leadership that these actions lack legal justification, are time-consuming, and counterproductive. In some cases, supervisors have issued explicitly discriminatory orders, such as directing a shift to arrest "all the black hoodies" in a neighborhood. And when officers have expressed concerns about such directives, the Department has failed to take corrective action. To restore the community's confidence in BPD and ensure that its policing services are being provided equitably, BPD must continue to improve its policies, training, data collection and analysis, and accountability systems.

The assessment of discriminatory intent focuses on "circumstantial and direct evidence of intent as may be available." *See Vill. of Arlington Heights v. Metro. Hous. Dev. Corp.*, 429 U.S. 252, 266 (1977). "The impact of the official action . . . may provide an important starting point" for assessing discriminatory intent. *Id.*; *see also Williams v. Hansen*, 326 F.3d 569, 585 (4th Cir. 2003). In addition to evidence of disparate impact, other factors include: direct statements that exhibit bias; an agency's departures from its own procedures and accepted practices in the field; and the relevant historical context. *Arlington Heights*, 429 U.S. at 266–68; *Sylvia Dev. Corp. v. Calvert County*, 48 F.3d 810, 819 (4th Cir. 1995).

a. BPD's Enforcement Activities Disproportionately Impact African Americans

The magnitude of the racial differences in BPD's stops, searches, and arrests are evidence that BPD's disproportionate enforcement may constitute intentional discrimination. We found consistent racial disparities in BPD's stops, searches, and arrests that are not attributable to population patterns, crime rates, or other race-neutral factors.

- BPD stops African Americans disproportionately in each of its nine police districts, despite significant variation in the districts' demographic characteristics and crime rates. Moreover, BPD has used pedestrian stops as a regular part of its discretionary enforcement—documenting over 300,000 stops in five years—despite their demonstrated ineffectiveness for ferreting out crime. Only 3.7 percent of pedestrian stops uncovered evidence of criminal activity—and the rate of criminal activity found during stops of African Americans was lower than stops of others. Supra at 28.
- Racial disparities in BPD's search rates persisted after controlling for the area in which a search occurred and numerous other factors, including the unit assignment and experience level of the officers involved. And searches of African Americans were less likely to find contraband compared to searches of people from other racial backgrounds, indicating that officers apply a lower threshold of suspicion when deciding to search African Americans. Supra at 53.
- There is also substantial evidence that the large racial disparities in BPD's enforcement of drug possession statutes are not explained by rates of drug usage. While survey data on drug usage shows that African Americans use banned substances at rates similar to or slightly higher than other population groups, BPD arrested African Americans for drug possession offenses at five times the rate at which it arrested others. BPD also arrested African Americans for drug possession offenses several times more often than law enforcement agencies in cities with similar crime rates and demographic and economic characteristics. Supra at Section II.B.1
- The consistent racial disparities in outcomes from BPD's misdemeanor arrests also do not appear to be attributable to non-racial factors. For every misdemeanor offense we examined, supervisors at Central Booking and prosecutors dismissed a significantly larger share of charges brought against African Americans than others. This consistent pattern

suggests that, for these highly discretionary offenses, BPD is disproportionately likely to arrest African Americans based on insufficient evidence. See supra at Section II.B.1.

Together, these findings provide substantial evidence that BPD's disparate stops, searches, and misdemeanor arrests of African Americans
are not part of a calibrated, proportionate strategy for responding to
criminal activity.

In addition, BPD's disproportionate enforcement against African Americans is suggestive of intentional discrimination because the racial disparities
are greatest for enforcement activities that involve higher degrees of officer
discretion. In the five years of arrest data we reviewed, African Americans accounted for a larger share of charges for highly discretionary misdemeanor
offenses than for other offenses, including: 91 percent of those charged solely
with trespassing, 91 percent of charges for failing to obey an officer's orders,
88 percent of those arrested solely for "impeding" and 84 percent of people
charged with disorderly conduct. As noted above, booking supervisors and
prosecutors dismissed a significantly higher portion of charges made against
African Americans for each of these charges. This pattern indicates that, where
BPD officers have more discretion to make arrests, they exercise that discretion
to arrest African Americans disproportionately. Moreover, the racial disparities in dismissal rates exist only for highly discretionary misdemeanor arrests,
not felony arrests. That is, booking officials and prosecutors dismissed charges
at nearly identical rates across racial groups for felony charges like first degree
assault, burglary, and robbery for which there is little officer discretion about
whether to arrest suspects. For every discretionary misdemeanor offense that
we examined, however, officials dismissed charges against African Americans
at significantly higher rates—indicating that officers apply a lower standard
when arresting African Americans for these offenses.

b. BPD's "Zero Tolerance" Strategy Focused on African-American Neighborhoods

In addition to this statistical evidence of disparate impact, we also have evidence that racial disparities occurred, at least in part, because of BPD's reliance
on "zero tolerance" enforcement tactics in predominantly African-American
neighborhoods. BPD employed these tactics without adequate oversight, training, or analysis, despite frequent community concerns about their impact. We
also found evidence of direct orders that encourage discriminatory treatment.

Zero tolerance tactics in African-American neighborhoods prioritized officers making large numbers of stops and arrests for minor offenses, despite

knowing the potential impact of these practices. For example, in the approximately five and half years of data we examined, BPD recorded nearly 55,000 pedestrian stops in its smallest police district—the Western District, with a population of a little more than 37,000 people that is 97 percent African American—while making only 21,000 stops in the predominantly white Northern District, with a population of approximately 91,000.[72] Expressed differently, BPD made 146 stops for every 100 residents in the predominantly African American Western District while making only 22.5 stops per 100 residents in the predominantly white Northern District—a more than 6 to 1 disparity. We found that disparities in BPD's stops of African Americans persist across all of BPD's nine police districts.

We heard concerns from numerous officers that zero tolerance tactics have resulted in unconstitutional stops and arrests, and that they are counterproductive. The Fraternal Order of Police's 2012 *Blueprint for Improved Policing* noted how zero tolerance tactics are counterproductive:

> Comstat numbers drive everything in BPD, which has led to misplaced priorities . . . As a result, officers in the BPD feel pressure to achieve numbers for perception's sake," and "[t]he focus on assigning blame for less-than-satisfactory numbers during Comstat, rather than problem-solving, is completely unproductive and weakens the collective morale of the BPD."

> The *Blueprint* concluded that BPD "must discontinue the practice of rewarding statistically driven arrests."

Nevertheless, many BPD supervisors continue to encourage patrol officers to use zero tolerance tactics. Based on our observations during numerous ride-alongs and conversations with BPD officers, instructions to "clear corners" remain a regular feature of patrolling certain predominantly African-American neighborhoods. These activities frequently lack any legal basis. One officer informed us that she stops and disperses youth standing on sidewalks because "it looks bad." The same officer, while responding to a call about a gang fight, stopped to engage an African American man and his four-year-old son who were sitting on a fence by a playground where the young boy had been playing. The officer told them that they "couldn't just stand around" and "needed to move." A second officer, after explaining to his supervisor that he had no legal basis to clear a corner, was told to "make something up." BPD has

---

72 These stops also fell disproportionately on African Americans. Despite making up only 41 percent of the Northern District's population, African Americans accounted for 83 percent of stops in the district.

continued this practice despite its impact on African-American residents and its lack of effectiveness for fighting crime. Indeed, we found that BPD's pedestrian stops—and searches conducted during these stops—uncover criminal activity at extremely low rates. *See supra* at Section II.A.2. And the rate of finding criminal activity when stopping and searching African Americans is lower still. *Id.*

In some cases, BPD supervisors have instructed their subordinates to specifically target African Americans for enforcement. A sergeant told us that in 2011 her lieutenant—a commander in charge of setting enforcement priorities for an entire police district during the shift—ordered the sergeant to instruct officers under her command to "lock up all the black hoodies" in her district. When the sergeant objected and refused to follow this order, she received an "unsatisfactory" performance evaluation and was transferred to a different unit. The sergeant filed a successful complaint about her performance evaluation with BPD's Equal Opportunity and Diversity Section, but BPD never took action against the lieutenant for giving the order to target "black hoodies" for enforcement. Similarly, as described above, in 2012 a BPD lieutenant provided officers under his command with a template for trespassing arrests that suggested officers would arrest exclusively African-American men for that offense. As in the first example, this directive is especially concerning because it came from a shift commander. *See supra* at 63. These statements targeting African Americans for enforcement reinforce the statistical disparities in enforcement outcomes that we measured. The enforcement activities ordered by the BPD commanders—arresting African Americans for trespassing and finding any possible basis to arrest "black hoodies"—are consistent with the racial disparities we found in BPD's discretionary stops, searches, and misdemeanor arrests.

c. Statements Exhibiting Bias Against African Americans

We also found numerous examples of BPD officers using racial slurs or other statements that exhibit bias. Officers' use of racial language was a recurrent theme during the hundreds of interviews we conducted with members of the Baltimore community. The frequency of this conduct is difficult to quantify, however, because BPD erects many formal obstacles to filing complaints, community members often do not file complaints because they believe doing so would be fruitless, and BPD fails to properly document and classify allegations that are made. *See infra* at 139. Even when individuals successfully make a complaint alleging racial bias, BPD supervisors almost universally misclassify the complaint as minor misconduct—such as discourtesy—that does not reflect its racial elements.

Indeed, BPD's internal affairs records contain only one complaint that officers categorized as a racial slur allegation in the six years of data we examined. Our interviews with hundreds of Baltimore residents, along with other complaints we have received from the Baltimore community, demonstrates that this number is implausibly low. Because of this, we manually reviewed the narrative descriptions of a subset of the complaints that were not classified as alleging racial bias, and we identified more than one hundred examples of officers allegedly using racial epithets, slurs, and making threats when interacting with African Americans in that subset. Indeed, we found 60 separate allegations between 2010 and 2016 that officers used the word "n****r" that were not classified as complaints alleging use of racial slurs or other racial bias.[73] As explained further below, BPD misclassifies and fails to investigate complaints of racial slurs and racial bias, allowing a culture of bias against African Americans to persist. Several examples highlight the types of statements we found that exhibit bias towards African Americans:

- The City paid $95,000 in 2012 to settle a lawsuit brought by an 87-year-old African-American grandmother who alleged that she was shoved against a wall after she refused to allow an officer to enter her basement to conduct a warrantless search. After shoving the woman to the floor, the officer allegedly stood over her and said, "Bitch, you ain't no better than any of the other old black bitches I have locked up."
- In 2014, a middle-aged African-American man alleged that a sergeant in Southeast Baltimore stopped him near Patterson Park and strip-searched him in public. When the man protested and said he would contact a lawyer, the sergeant allegedly told him, "Get your n****r ass out of here." BPD found the complaint "not sustained" without interviewing any of the involved parties.
- One Baltimore firefighter and an emergency medical technician told us that, prior to a march led by a prominent African-American pastor in 2015, a BPD officer told the firefighters "they're going marching and there's going to be a problem. What y'all should do is turn them hoses on them."
- In 2013 a white male BPD officer made a racially-charged threat to an African-American teenager while booking the youth into Baltimore's juvenile facility on a failure to appear charge. The incident stemmed from an argument about George Zimmerman, who had been acquitted

---

73 Use of "racial epithets undoubtedly demonstrate racial animus." *Jones v. Robinson Prop. Group*, 427 F.3d 987, 993 (5th Cir. 2005). Many courts have recognized that particular slurs are extremely probative of racial animus. *See Spriggs v. Diamond Auto Glass*, 242 F.3d 179, 185 (4th Cir. 2001) ("Far more than a 'mere offensive utterance,' the word 'n****r is pure anathema to African-Americans."); *Brown v. E. Miss. Elec. Power Ass'n*, 989 F.2d 858, 861 (5th Cir. 1993) ("the term 'n****r is a universally recognized opprobrium, stigmatizing African-Americans because of their race."); *Boyer-Liberto v. Fontainebleau Corp.*, 786 F.3d 264, 280 (4th Cir. 2015) (use of the slur "porch monkey" is about as odious as the use of the word n****r).

of murdering Trayvon Martin four days earlier. In response to the teen-ager referring to the officers present as "Zimmermans," a white officer threatened the juvenile by referring to the outfit Martin wore at the time he was killed: "Put a hoodie on and come to my neighborhood, you will see." The officer also threatened the youth by stating, "If you come to my neighborhood I'll throw you in the water and feed you to the crabs. I will then let the crabs get fat off you and then sell them to your family." When BPD investigated the incident, the officer admitted to "talking about the crabs and throwing him in the river," but claimed to internal affairs in-vestigators that he "could not recall" whether he made the remark about the hoodie. BPD sustained a complaint against the officer for "miscon-duct" and making an "inappropriate comment," but the investigative file contains no record of discipline. The officer remains employed at BPD.

- In a complaint from August 2011, an African-American man alleged that during a vehicle stop, an officer warned a second officer to "be careful" because the occupants of the car "might do voodoo on you"—an appar-ent reference to their heritage and accents. A second officer made monkey noises throughout the encounter. BPD closed the complaint without making an investigative finding.

- An African-American man told us that, while out walking in April 2015, officers stopped him, accused him of looting, and called him a "low life n****r."

The use of racial slurs and other racially charged statements described above, as well as others we uncovered during our investigation, typically occurred while officers were conducting stops or searches of African Americans. This is consistent with the areas in which we found large statistical disparities in BPD's enforcement.

d. BPD Misclassifies Complaints of Racial Bias and Fails to Investigate Racial Bias Allegations

BPD fails to record complaints of racial bias or affirmatively misclassifies com-plaints to mask their racial components. BPD also fails to investigate allega-tions of biased enforcement.[74] By not using its own procedures to deter and correct biased conduct, BPD exacerbates relationships with Baltimore's African-American communities. Numerous individuals told us that BPD either refused

---

74 Prior to enacting its "Fair and Impartial Policing" policy in 2015, BPD only had a general prohibition against discrimination, which did not provide sufficient guidance to officers on how to conduct their policing activities in a non-discriminatory manner, although it did provide a basis for BPD to discipline officers.

to accept complaints—even for egregious, racially-motivated misconduct—
or did not take their complaints seriously. Many community members thus
feel that BPD is biased against African Americans and does not respond their
concerns.

i. BPD's defective procedures for recording and classifying complaints of racial bias

BPD's internal affairs database reflects only five complaints from 2010–2016
that BPD supervisors classified as alleging use of a racial slur or other racial
bias.[75] The absence of such records stems from at least two procedural deficiencies. As discussed above, BPD erects significant obstacles to filing complaints.
And even when community members succeed in filing a complaint of racial
bias according to BPD's requirements, supervisory officers almost universally
misclassify those complaints to mask their racial elements. As a result, BPD
does not investigate the frequent allegations of race-related misconduct made
against its officers and has no mechanism to track such allegations to correct
discriminatory policing where it occurs.

Most notably, BPD supervisors affirmatively misclassify complaints of
racial bias, precluding the Department from investigating or tracking bias allegations. A commander at BPD's Internal Investigation Division told us BPD requires all complaints claiming officers used a racial epithet to be categorized as
"racial slur" complaints, and BPD's disciplinary matrix makes clear that "conduct relating to a person's race" is a serious offense that may result in termination. Yet in nearly every case in which an officer allegedly used a racial slur,
BPD officials categorized the allegation merely as "discourtesy" or using "inappropriate language." For the complaints in which our manual review found
that BPD recorded allegations that officers used the word n****r, supervisors
failed to classify the complaint as a racial slur or other allegation of racial bias
98 percent of the time.

BPD similarly misclassified nearly all of the complaints we identified that
alleged other types of racial discrimination in BPD's enforcement. Out of the
dozens of complaints that our manual review found to allege "racial profiling"
or "racial discrimination," BPD supervisors classified only four as alleging any
type of racial bias. And even those complaints triggered no meaningful review.
BPD referred two of the complaints to command investigation units tasked
with addressing only minor allegations, and closed a third complaint seven
minutes after opening an internal affairs "investigation." Although we found
that BPD routinely misclassifies other complaints due to systemic deficiencies

---

75 We refer in this section only to complaints alleging bias by BPD officers towards members of the African American community in Baltimore.

in its practices, *see infra* at 138, we did not find anything approaching the level of systematic misclassification of complaints we found relating to alleged racial discrimination, such as the 98 percent misclassification of use of the word n****r. Moreover, the complaints that are misclassified allege racial discrimination on their face, such as the use of a racial epithet. Failing to recognize the potential for racial discrimination in the use of a racial epithet is difficult to attribute to a lack of training, policy guidance, or other systemic deficiency. This systematic misclassification of complaints, particularly when the classification is not difficult, indicates that the misclassification is because of the racial nature of the complaint.

BPD's practice of obscuring racial elements of misconduct impedes any significant disciplinary action, even in cases where an officer admitted to using a racial epithet. Several examples highlight this practice. In a case from 2010, an officer admitted that he said "you know, you're acting like a real n****r right now" during an encounter with a young African-American male he had stopped for "loitering." The officer's partner, who was African American, filed the complaint after witnessing the incident. The complaint was initially categorized as a "racial slur" complaint. Before issuing an investigative finding sustaining the allegation, however, the lead BPD investigator changed the categorization in BPD's internal affairs database from "racial slur" to "inappropriate comments, profanity, or gestures to a departmental member." This change in classification, shortly before the allegation was sustained, indicates an intent to disguise and excuse the racial motivation for the enforcement action. The incident resulted in minimal discipline against the offending officer.[76] Other aspects of the investigation are equally troubling. The detective who downgraded the complaint also expanded his review of the incident to investigate the officer who reported the racial slur for "neglect of duty," ostensibly based on the officer's failure to provide the African-American man with a citizen contact receipt. We are concerned that the expanded investigation may have been done in retaliation for reporting a fellow officer's racial bias. Despite the complaint's clear misclassification in violation of Department policy, BPD supervisors signed off throughout the chain of command.

In another incident from 2010, an African-American man stated that he witnessed officers use excessive force during an arrest and punch a fourteen-year-old boy who attempted to film the arrest on his cell phone. The African-American man recounted that the officers used "the word 'n****r' frequently" and asked him if he "take[s] it up the ass by Allah." When the man went to the district headquarters to report the misconduct, he was met by the same officers who told him, "what brings your black ass back here?" and "you

---

76 The officer was not fired or suspended. Instead, he received a letter of reprimand, was required to attend sensitivity training, and forfeited thirty days of his leave.

can take your black ass down to Kirk Avenue[77] before the bus leaves because you know how you black people like the bus." Despite the seriousness of the allegations and the fact that the complaint identified two witnesses, BPD never investigated the incident's alleged racial motivation. Instead, detectives categorized the allegations as "misconduct," "excessive force," and "unwarranted action," and administratively closed[78] the case without conducting a single interview.

ii. BPD fails to investigate racial bias allegations

BPD further impedes accountability for discriminatory policing by departing from its procedures for investigating biased conduct. BPD supervisors repeatedly fail to seek evidence that could corroborate bias allegations and result in officer discipline. For example, a 2011 complaint described an incident in which two white officers told an African-American man who had double-parked his car and was blocking the street to "move this car, n****r!" The man was double parked in order to assist his aunt into her home in Northeast Baltimore and was not charged with any offense. The man's complaint—the *one* complaint BPD correctly categorized as a "racial slur" in the more than six years of data we examined—was assigned to be investigated at the command level[79] and administratively closed six months later. The file BPD provided has no record of the investigation or any attempt to identify the officers involved.

BPD conducted a similarly inadequate investigation in a 2010 case that also alleged race-motivated misconduct. There, an African-American man alleged that while being held in a cell at the Southwest District, several officers called him a "monkey" and a "n****r" while beating him. The investigative file, which consisted solely of a few summary paragraphs about the incident, revealed that the investigating officer administratively closed the case without even reading a related incident report because "it was locked in the report box at the time of my investigation."

In another example, BPD failed to adequately investigate a complaint that an officer called an African-American woman a "black b***h." BPD never inter-

---

77 Kirk Avenue refers to the location of BPD's Internal Investigation Division, or "IID." Under BPD policy, members of the public should be able to file external complaints of officer misconduct both at district headquarters, and also at the IID.

78 As discussed further in Section III.C.1, *infra*, internal investigations should be issued one of four possible findings: sustained, not sustained, unfounded or exonerated. We found that BPD frequently disposed of cases with minimal or no investigation by labeling them as "administratively closed."

79 As described further in Section III.C, *infra*, under BPD policy, "minor" misconduct can be investigated and handled at the command level by "command investigations units."

viewed the officer accused of using the offensive term. Instead, he was asked only to complete a written questionnaire that omitted the racial component of the woman's allegation. The questionnaire asked whether the officer "at any time call[ed] or refer[red] to [the woman] as a bitch?" BPD found the allegation not sustained based on the officer's written denial. The omission of the racial component of the woman's allegation indicates that BPD investigators intended to conceal the racial nature of the interaction and avoid determining whether the heightened discipline required for using a racial slur should be imposed.

e. Baltimore's History of Residential Segregation

BPD's "zero tolerance" policing strategy has focused on predominantly African-American neighborhoods that have been segregated for generations due to government policies that systematically prevented African Americans from acquiring wealth, and obstructed their ability to move into neighborhoods with better jobs or schools.

Starting in the early 20th Century, the City sponsored residential segregation programs that forced the large number of African Americans who settled in Baltimore during the "Great Migration" to live in economically depressed neighborhoods. Baltimore was the ninth most segregated city in the country when the Great Migration ended in 1970,[80] and the most recent U.S. Census Bureau data shows that the City remains extremely segregated.[81] In its lawsuit against Wells Fargo for discriminatory lending practices, the City of Baltimore itself acknowledged that its minority communities have been "victimized by traditional redlining practices," and that the city itself remains highly segregated:

> [E]ven though Baltimore is 64% African-American and 32% white, many neighborhoods have a much higher concentration of one racial group or the other. For example, the African-American population exceeds 90% in East

---

[80] See Douglas S. Massey and Nancy A. Denton, *Hypersegregation in U.S. Metropolitan Areas: Black and Hispanic Segregation Along Five Dimensions*, 26 Demography 3, 1989. The Great Migration refers to a mass relocation of African Americans between 1910 and 1970 when six million African Americans migrated from rural Southern states to settle across the country. When the Great Migration ended around 1970, nearly half of all black Americans were living outside the South, compared to ten percent when the Migration began. Baltimore is affected by "hyper-segregation," a term sociologists use to refer to the nearly complete division of races following the Great Migration. *See* Isabel Wilkerson, THE WARMTH OF OTHER SUNS 8–10, 398 (2010).

[81] According to the 2010 census, the dissimilarity index for Baltimore is 71.8, which indicates the percentage of African Americans that would need to move to less segregated areas for the population to be distributed equally with whites.

Baltimore, Pimlico/Arlington/Hilltop, Dorchester/Ashburton, Southern Park Heights, Greater Rosemont, Sandtown-Winchester/Harlem Park, and Greater Govans. It exceeds 75% in Waverly and Belair Edison. At the same time, the white population of Greater Roland Park/Poplar, Medfield/Hampden/Woodberry, and South Baltimore exceeds 80%, and the white population of Cross-Country/Cheswolde, Mt. Washington /Coldspring, and North Baltimore/Guilford/Homeland exceeds 70%.

City of Baltimore v. Wells Fargo, No. 1:08-cv-00062-JFM (D. Md. Oct. 21, 2010).

City leadership encouraged and supported this segregation by passing the country's first block-by-block segregation ordinance, which made it a crime for African Americans to move to majority white blocks, and vice versa. At the time of the ordinance's enactment in 1910, the New York Times described it as "the most pronounced 'Jim Crow' measure on record" and noted that "[n]othing like it can be found in any statute book or ordinance record of this country."[82] The Supreme Court later struck down a similar ordinance in Buchanan v. Warley, 245 U.S. 60 (1917), but the effect in Baltimore was minimal. White property owners, with support from City leadership, continued to enforce the rule informally by requiring homeowners in certain white neighborhoods, like the affluent Roland Park area in North Baltimore, to sign covenants barring African Africans from owning or renting their property. The mayor directed City building and housing inspectors to institute a practice of citing for code violations anyone who rented or sold property to African-Americans in those neighborhoods. See Antero Pietila, NOT IN MY NEIGHBORHOOD 35, 53–54 (2010).

The federal government also contributed to Baltimore's segregation by instituting policies that further isolated African Americans. During the Great Depression, the government's Home Owners' Loan Corporation (HOLC) created maps of 239 cities, including Baltimore, to rate residential areas for market value and risk. Baltimore's neighborhoods with large African-American populations were colored red on the map to signify HOLC's conclusion that these neighborhoods were "hazardous," leading to the term "red-lining." See HOLC 1937 map (following page).[83] After the Great Depression, the Federal Housing

---

82 Baltimore Tries Drastic Plan of Race Segregation, N.Y. Times, Dec. 25, 1910, at 34, 43, http://timesmachine.nytimes.com/timesmachine/1910/12/25/105900067.html?pageNumber=34.

83 HOLC devised a system of rating neighborhoods based on their perceived suitability to receive home mortgage loans, ranging from the ostensibly most suitable "A" areas to the least suitable "D" areas. HOLC classified the "A" areas, colored green on the map, as most

Administration (FHA) carried on HOLC's legacy well into the 1960s. The FHA promoted home-ownership in white suburban neighborhoods, and tolerated further red-lining by private banks and insurance companies. *Id.* at 61–74.

The legacy of this government-sanctioned discrimination continues to impact the African-American community in Baltimore today. The City remains highly segregated, and African-American residents live disproportionately in neighborhoods with social and economic challenges. More than 100,000 African-American residents live in poverty, constituting more than three-fourths of Baltimoreans who do so.

BPD leadership is acutely aware of the challenges posed by this backdrop. Former Commissioner Batts explained that when he was appointed to lead BPD in 2012 "it was like going back a little bit in time. It's about black and white racism in [Baltimore]. It's all the things you dealt with in the 1960s."[84] Commissioner Davis has also recognized the challenges officers face in addressing racism and poverty, among other social problems: "when cops hear that they have the burden to address racism and poverty and education and homelessness . . . I think cops misinterpret that message with, 'how do you expect me to do that?'"[85] Recently, BPD has taken several commendable steps towards addressing these concerns, including issuing a "Fair and Impartial Policing" policy and launching an educational program for officers that addresses some of the racial dynamics in the City's history.

Nevertheless, many challenges remain. BPD needs to ensure that it employs law enforcement strategies that do not discriminate against African Americans and predominantly African-American neighborhoods. Working together with the community will promote proactive, constitutional, and effective policing.

In sum, BPD's stops, searches, and arrests disproportionately impact African Americans and predominantly African-American neighborhoods and cannot be explained by population patterns, crime rates, or other race-neutral factors.

"in demand" for home mortgage loans. The "B" areas, colored blue on the map, were rated as "still desirable." The yellow-coded "C" areas were rated as "definitely declining." The red "D" areas were rated as too "hazardous" for general lending practices. Baltimore residents living in the D areas were generally unable to obtain mortgages. *See Not in My Neighborhood*, at 67–70.

84 *Q&A C-SPAN: Anthony Batts* (C-SPAN television broadcast Jan. 20, 2015), https://www .c-span.org/video/?323886-1/qa-anthony-batts.

85 http://www.baltimoresun.com/news/maryland/bs-md-davis-challenges-20150711story .html.

This disparate impact violates Title VI and the Safe Streets Act. We also found evidence suggesting intentional discrimination against African Americans. This racial discrimination undermines community trust in BPD.

C. BPD USES UNREASONABLE FORCE

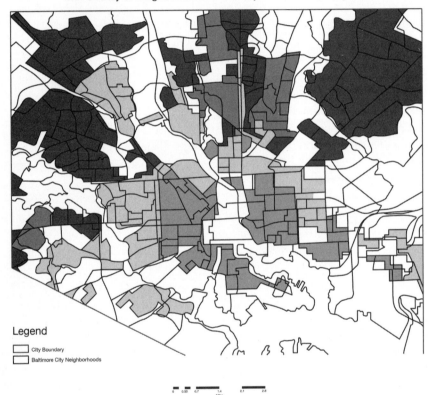

Home Owner's Loan Corporation (HOLC) 1937 Map
with Overlay of Neighborhoods in the City of Baltimore, Maryland

Based on our review of nearly a thousand of BPD's own investigative files of its officers' uses of force, we find reasonable cause to believe that BPD officers use unreasonable force[86] in violation of the Fourth Amendment, and fail to make

---

86 Throughout this letter, we use the terms "unreasonable" and "excessive" interchange-ably; both terms refer to force that exceeds constitutional limits, or in other words, is

reasonable modifications necessary to avoid discrimination in violation of Title II of the Americans with Disabilities Act, contributing to the pattern or practice of conduct that violates the constitution and federal law. BPD's unreasonable force is not limited to officers' use of any specific weapon; we found it throughout the use of force files we reviewed.

The Fourth Amendment guarantees the "right of the people to be secure in their persons, houses, papers, and effects, against unreasonable searches and seizures." U.S. CONST. amend. IV. This protection from "unreasonable" seizures prohibits an officer from using excessive force when making a seizure. "Determining whether the force used to effect a particular seizure is 'reasonable' under the Fourth Amendment requires a careful balancing of the nature and quality of the intrusion on the individual's Fourth Amendment interests against the countervailing governmental interests at stake." *Graham v. Conner*, 490 U.S. 386, 396 (1989) (internal quotation marks omitted). The determination must be made while viewing the incident "from the perspective of a reasonable officer on the scene, rather than with the 20/20 vision of hindsight." *Id.* at 396, 399.

To determine whether force used by a law enforcement officer is reasonable, we look to (1) "the severity of the crime at issue;" (2) "the extent to which the suspect poses an immediate threat to the safety of the officers or others;" and (3) "whether [the suspect] is actively resisting arrest or attempting to evade arrest by flight." *Estate of Armstrong v. Vill. of Pinehurst*, 810 F.3d 892, 899 (4th Cir. 2016) (alteration in original) (internal quotation marks omitted). "To properly consider the reasonableness of the force employed we must view it in full context, with an eye toward the proportionality of the force in light of all the circumstances." *Id.* at 899 (internal quotation marks omitted). "[O]fficers using unnecessary, gratuitous, and disproportionate force to seize a secured, unarmed citizen, do not act in an objectively reasonable manner. . . ." *Meyers v. Baltimore County*, 713 F.3d 723, 734 (4th Cir. 2013) (internal quotation marks omitted).

Our evaluation of BPD's use of force was informed by many sources, including: (1) interviews with hundreds of individuals who have had encounters with officers or witnessed those encounters; (2) interviews of the Department's officers, supervisors, and command staff; (3) an extensive review of nearly one thousand of the Department's reports and investigations of officers' uses of force; (4) the Department's policies and training materials; and (5) analysis by our expert police consultants.

The nearly one thousand force cases we reviewed included a randomly selected, statistically significant sample from all use of force incidents by BPD

---

disproportional in light of the severity of the crime suspected, threat posed to officers or others, and level of resistance. When using the term "unnecessary," we mean that force was used when the incident could have been resolved without resorting to any force at all.

officers occurring between January 1, 2010, and June 19, 2015. The sample of 814 cases was identified by our statistical experts from the universe of all 2,818 incidents of force, including both deadly force and less-lethal force, identified by BPD. The sample size accounted for a number of factors, including the type of weapon used by officers and whether the force was used against people with mental health disabilities or in crisis.

Because of their critical nature, we also attempted to review all uses of deadly force by BPD occurring from January 1, 2010, through the duration of our investigation, and we reviewed what was provided to us through May 1, 2016. However, though we identified for BPD on multiple occasions additional deadly force cases that we had not received, BPD was never able to find and produce case files for all deadly force investigations from this time period. The Department informed us that it is unable to locate the files for twenty firearms discharges from the time period that we requested. Because of this lack of documentation, we were unable to conclusively determine the number of deadly force incidents that occurred during the time period we reviewed. This failure is quite concerning. The Department's inability to maintain the files for officers' firearms discharges reflects a serious deficiency in the oversight of officers' uses of deadly force. For a number of other shooting cases, BPD provided us with supplemental information nearly a year after we initially requested the complete files. In the end, we were able to review over one hundred investigations of BPD's uses of deadly force. We carefully reviewed each of the force files we were provided, both deadly force and less-lethal force, to determine whether each use of force was justified under applicable legal standards. Our review of individual use of force reports and investigations informed our determination of whether a pattern or practice of excessive force exists within BPD.

We note that, in a number of cases—of both deadly and less-lethal force—the reports and reviews of force provided too little information about the circumstances surrounding the use of force to allow our team and experts to determine whether the force was reasonable. This is troubling because, despite the lack of adequate information to determine whether these uses of force were reasonable, BPD supervisors still approved all but a handful of these uses of force. This systematic failure to provide adequate oversight of use of force requires correction. Even given the significant number of cases in which we were unable to make a decision, however, we were nevertheless able to make determinations in a sufficient number of cases to conclude that there is a pattern or practice of excessive force at BPD.

While reviewing BPD's force investigations, we noted a number of trends. First, in a significant number of cases, officers use aggressive tactics that escalate encounters and stifle public cooperation, leading to the use of physical force when it is not necessary to resolve an incident. Officers approach incidents involving mere quality of life violations in a confrontational manner and fail to use basic conflict resolution skills, creating conflict where it did not exist before. BPD trains officers to be aggressive, inculcating an adversarial mindset in its recruits and teaching them to, for example, point a weapon at unarmed and innocent civilians to control a scene. Tactics such as these unnecessarily escalate encounters, increase tensions and lead to unnecessary force.

Second, officers use excessive force against individuals with mental health disabilities or in crisis. When families in Baltimore confront a family member experiencing a mental health issue, they often call 911 to request an officer to safely escort their family member to a hospital for a mental health evaluation and, if necessary, commitment. In too many of these calls, officers arrive at the homes of families, knowing they are being called to assist with a mental health incident, without a plan to account for the mental health issue. Because of their lack of planning and proper tactics, they end up in violent confrontations with individuals with mental health disabilities or in crisis and use force, sometimes deadly, against these vulnerable individuals.

Third, officers use unreasonable force against juveniles. It is apparent that officers have not received guidance nor have been trained on well-established best practices for police interactions with juveniles that account for their developmental stage and prevent the unnecessary criminalization of overwhelmingly minority youth. The lack of policy and training for these interactions results in excessive force being used against youths.

Finally, officers use unreasonable force against people who present little or no threat to them or others. One such group includes individuals who are already restrained and under officers' control. Another group is individuals who are fleeing away from officers. Officers in Baltimore engage in a high number of foot pursuits, a tactic with a number of attendant risks, including endangering officers and community members. Due to the risks inherent in foot pursuits, agencies must exercise careful oversight over foot pursuits and provide proper guidance and training on when it is appropriate to engage in foot pursuits and how to do so safely. BPD fails to do so. In some cases, the people who officers pursue have not committed serious crimes and present no threat to officers or community members, but these pursuits end with BPD officers using significant force. Additionally, in some cases when individuals flee in vehicles, officers use unreasonable force after any potential threat to them has subsided.

The Department's failure to provide officers with the necessary guidance, skills, and oversight to resolve incidents in a way that keeps them and community members safe underlies officers' constitutional violations. The Department fails to provide proper policy guidance on how and when it is appropriate to use force. It also fails to properly train officers on how to operationalize its policies and, in some cases, has improperly trained its officers by teaching incorrect legal standards or improper tactics that lead to officers' unreasonable force. Finally, the Department fails to exercise proper oversight to address potentially unreasonable force and remedy bad tactics when they occur. These failures have led to the systemic use of unreasonable force that we observed in our investigation.

1. BPD's Overly Aggressive Tactics Unnecessarily Escalate Encounters and Result in Excessive Force

BPD officers' aggressive tactics in their encounters with civilians unnecessarily escalate situations and contribute to officers' systemic use of unreasonable force. Officers use aggressive tactics in encounters that begin consensually or in cases where officers stop individuals for low-level and highly discretionary violations such as "loitering," as well as violations that officers charge based on civilians' conduct during the encounter, such as "failure to obey," "resistance" or "disorderly conduct," as discussed *supra* at Section II(A). In these encounters, officers issue commands without explanation rather than communicating respectfully, explaining the purpose for their approach and providing subjects an opportunity to voice their concerns.[87] When subjects do not immediately comply with officers' commands, rather than attempt to problem-solve or use conflict-resolution skills, officers resort too quickly to physical force even if individuals do not present a threat to them or others. Even where force is justified, officers frequently use a high level of force when only a low level of force is objectively reasonable. Officers use these tactics against individuals with mental health disabilities or in crisis, who have committed no crime, and also on juveniles. The force used by officers in these situations is often unnecessary and disproportional to the suspected violation, threat, and resistance posed by civilians under *Graham. See Armstrong*, 810 F.3d at 900 (internal quotation marks omitted) ("The problems posed by, and thus the tactics to be employed against, an unarmed, emotionally distraught individual who is creating a disturbance or resisting arrest are ordinarily different from those involved in law enforcement efforts to subdue an armed and dangerous criminal who has recently committed a serious offense."). *Cf. Waterman v. Batton*, 393 F.3d 471, 477 (4th Cir. 2005) ("[T]he reasonableness of the officer's actions in creating the dangerous situation is not relevant to the Fourth Amendment analysis."). In addition to

---

87 Citizens who do not understand why they are being stopped and feel they are being treated unfairly and disrespectfully are less likely to comply with officers' orders. *See* Tom R. Tyler, *Procedural Justice, Legitimacy, and the Effective Rule of Law*, 30 Crime & Justice 283, 350–51 (2003) ("When people judge that legal authorities and institutions are making their decisions fairly, they view those authorities as more legitimate and more willingly defer to and cooperate with them in personal encounters and in their everyday law-related behaviors.").

contributing to officers' unconstitutional conduct, these tactics greatly undermine BPD's efforts to repair its damaged relationship with some segments of Baltimore's community.

For example, in a 2014 incident, an officer informed a young man, Matthew,[88] that he could not smoke inside a public market and asked him to leave. Matthew left and the officer followed him outside. Once outside, the officer asked him for identification to issue a civil citation. According to the Department's use of force report, the Matthew "became agitated and started to argue" with the officer, attracting a crowd. The young man refused to provide identification and moved backward. The officer grabbed the young man by his jacket, at which point he pulled away and fled. Two officers pursued Matthew for blocks and when they eventually caught up with him, "used arrest and control techniques" to tackle him and "stop him from further fleeing." "While trying to control him on the ground and place him in handcuffs," he "sustained abrasions to the left and right side of his face and a cut to his upper lip," requiring two stitches. The officer arrested Matthew for being "disorderly," but according to the arrest database that BPD provided, the State's Attorney's Office declined to formally charge the young man.

The officer repeatedly escalated this encounter, using unnecessarily aggressive tactics against a young man who had not committed a crime, resulting in the man being subjected to excessive force. The decision to grab the man by his jacket, after he had obeyed the officer's warning by leaving the market, escalated the encounter and led to the man resisting the officer's force by pulling away. The officer's decision to then pursue the young man, for a mere civil citation, also escalated the encounter. Other than calling off the pursuit (which would have been appropriate), as discussed in more detail *infra* at page 91, the most likely way to end the pursuit was by using force. Tackling, and using control and arrest techniques resulting in two stitches and abrasions to his face, was disproportionate in light of the civil violation the young man had committed, and where he posed no threat to officers or anyone else. *See Graham*, 490 U.S. at 396.

In another example, in a 2010 incident, a major who was patrolling in uniform in an unmarked police vehicle "observed several people on the steps of an apartment building." He asked the group "if everyone lived there." One of the group, a young 5'6", 147-pound African-American man, Daniel, asked the major "what the problem was." The major "told the suspect there was no problem and he can go back to his steps." The major reported that Daniel

---

88 We use pseudonyms for individuals who were the subject of force with BPD officers to protect against disclosing personally-identifying information. We also do not identify BPD personnel by name, as the purpose of these illustrations is not to assess individual liability but to support and illustrate the findings of a pattern or practice.

"walked in front of [the major's] vehicle acting in a [sic] agitated state wearing and adjusting some type of athletic gloves and taking his shoes off." An older African-American man "was instructing [the young man] to 'stop acting like this.'" Daniel began "yelling at this older male in a threatening manner and challenging him." The major called for backup, withdrew his taser,[89] and ordered Daniel to "sit on the curb." A lieutenant arrived as backup. The major reportedly told the lieutenant that the young man "was warned to desist but to no avail and is ready to fight . . . he needs to be arrested before he hurts someone." The investigating sergeant reported that the subject moved to one side of the street and sat on the curb. The major informed the lieutenant that Daniel "was the aggressor and he continued to be a threat." There is no indication in the report that Daniel stood up from his seated position on the curb. Nevertheless, the lieutenant "immediately pushed [Daniel] to the ground with [a] left foot kick to the chest." Daniel had committed no crime, was seated on a curb and obeying officer's commands at the time the lieutenant unnecessarily and unreasonably kicked him in the chest. This incident, involving a lieutenant and a major, was investigated by a lower-ranked sergeant, undermining the credibility of the investigation. The major, who was involved in the incident, ultimately approved the sergeant's investigation, though the major lacked the independence to objectively determine whether the force used was appropriate.

Officers also use heavy-handed tactics when civilians simply refuse to obey their commands and escalate encounters by resorting to force too quickly, including against individuals who are not being arrested for any crime, with mental health disabilities or in crisis.[90] We determined that approximately 20

---

89 A "taser," or an "Electronic Control Weapon" (ECW) is a weapon that "'can be used either in 'probe' mode or in 'stun' mode. In probe mode, two probes are fired from a distance, attached to thin electrical wires, to lodge in the skin of the subject. The [t]aser then delivers a fixed five-second cycle of electricity designed to cause electro-muscular disruption, effectively freezing the subject's muscles and thereby temporarily disabling him. In stun mode, the probe cartridge is removed and the [t]aser's electrodes are applied directly to the subject. The [t]aser operator can then deliver a painful electric shock, the duration of which is completely within [the operator's] control. In stun mode, the [t]aser does not cause muscular disruption or incapacitation, but rather functions only as a 'pain compliance' tool.'" *Meyers,* 713 F.3d at 728 n.3 (alterations in original) (quoting *Meyers,* 814 F. Supp. 2d 552, 555 n.3 (D. Md. 2011)).

90 A "crisis" incident is one in which someone experiences or displays intense feelings of personal distress (*e.g.,* anxiety, depression, anger, fear, panic, hopelessness); a thought disorder (*e.g.,* visual or auditory hallucinations, delusions, sensory impairment, or cognitive impairment); obvious changes in functioning (*e.g.,* neglect of personal hygiene); or catastrophic life events (*e.g.,* disruptions in personal relationships, support systems or living arrangements, loss of autonomy or parental rights, victimization, or natural disasters). This could be a result of mental illness (including substance use disorders), an intellectual disability, a personal crisis, or the effects of drugs or alcohol.

percent of use of force files BPD provided involved individuals with mental health disabilities or in crisis. In one of many such incidents we reviewed, in 2013, three officers and one sergeant responded to a call to transport an individual to a hospital for a mental health evaluation. According to their report, the officers arrived at the back of a house and found a woman, "Ashley," the subject of the petition, sitting on the ground with a clenched hand. Ashley reportedly had a "small" build and was yelling "don't shoot me." One officer asked her to empty her hands and she refused, stating, "you have to shoot me first I am not giving it up [sic]." There is no indication that the officers attempted to verbally persuade Ashley in any way to open her hands or calm her down. Rather, the officers physically attempted to force her hands open. Ashley resisted the officers' physical attempts and began to "kick[] and swing[]" at them. According to the report, one officer used a taser in drive-stun mode "to try to calm [her] down." Because drive-stunning an individual causes great pain, it did not calm her. The technique also carries a heightened risk of serious harm or injury when used on individuals with mental health disabilities or in crisis. *See* Police Exec. Research Forum & Cmty. Oriented Policing Servs., *2011 Electronic Control Weapon Guidelines* 14 (2001) (hereinafter "PERF & COPS, *2011 Electronic Control Weapon Guidelines*"). Ashley continued to resist. In response, the officer drive-stunned her two more times, with similar results. The officers were eventually able to physically pry open Ashley's hands, which held two vials, the contents of which emptied onto the ground. Ashley was transported to the hospital for a psychiatric evaluation. Use of the taser in drive-stun mode three times against a woman experiencing crisis, who was unarmed, posed no serious threat to the officers or others, and was not being arrested for any crime, was unnecessary and unreasonable. Problematically, it appears the only investigation of this incident was conducted by the sergeant who was at the scene. A sergeant who participated in the incident lacks the necessary objectivity and independence to fairly assess whether officers on the scene acted appropriately. Having an involved sergeant investigate the force undermines the integrity of the investigation.

Aggressive and violent police interactions, such as those described above, have left some Baltimore residents with the belief that encounters with BPD officers will result in their being subjected to unnecessary force. Community members told us in interviews that even when they believe they have done nothing wrong, they flee from interactions with officers, believing that it is better to run at the sight of an officer rather than take the risk that an interaction with the officer will result in unnecessary and excessive force being used against them.[91] Indeed, officers' unnecessary and unreasonable force during

---

91 While flight in a high crime area may give officers reasonable suspicion to conduct a

arrests for highly discretionary charges such as "loitering," "disorderly conduct," "resisting" or "failure to obey" an officer's commands, confirm these
community members' fears.

The fault for officers' systemic use of these heavy-handed tactics lies with
BPD as an agency. Through training used for many years—some of which is
still ongoing—BPD teaches officers to use aggressive tactics. We reviewed a
number of training materials, such as BPD's Academy-Level training on Use
of Force, Defensive Tactics, and BPD's in-service training on "Characteristics
of an Armed Person." We also observed in person BPD's training on foot patrols and interactions with people with mental illness.[92] Through its Defensive
Tactics training, for example, BPD instructs officers to point their firearm at
individuals when they need to control a scene. In the cases we reviewed, and in
media reports, we saw this troubling tactic in operation. BPD groups this tactic
on par with "command presence," "verbal commands," and using a "firm grip."
Pointing a gun at an individual for general control is an inappropriate use of a
firearm and is a threat of deadly force where the underlying offense, if any, does
not justify deadly force being used. See Holland v. Harrington, 268 F.3d 1179, 1192
(10th Cir. 2001) (explaining that an officer's pointing of a firearm "involves the
immediate threat of deadly force" and thus "should be predicated on at least
a perceived risk of injury or danger to the officers or others, based upon what
the officers know at that time"). Pointing firearms directly at individuals is also
dangerous because it can lead to accidental discharges; limit officers' ability to
use other, more appropriate force when one hand is occupied with holding a
firearm; and lead to unnecessary use of deadly force. During our review, we
saw instances in which officers drew and pointed their firearms at individuals
when the use of deadly force did not appear to be justified, including an incident that resulted in an accidental discharge that fortunately did not strike
anyone. In part through aggressive tactics such as these, BPD's trainings fuel
an "us vs. them" mentality we saw some officers display towards community
members, alienating the civilians they are meant to serve.

Moreover, the Department has failed to equip officers with sufficient de-
escalation skills and tactics. The Department had no comprehensive training
on de-escalation techniques until 2015, when it added de-escalation training to
the Academy's Use of Force curriculum for new recruits. We commend the Department for its efforts and desire to implement de-escalation training. Nevertheless, work remains to ensure that these de-escalation skills are sufficiently
emphasized within the Academy's Use of Force curriculum. Even with the new
Academy training, these skills must be constantly refreshed through in-service

---

Terry stop under Illinois v. Wardlow, 528 U.S. 119, 124–25 (2000), flight alone does not provide
a justification to use the amount of force we observed in many cases.

92 Throughout this Report, the term "mental illness" includes substance use disorders.

training for experienced officers after they leave the Academy. BPD does not sufficiently prioritize these skills in the in-service training courses it offers.

The other trends we identified below through BPD's own force investigations—using force against vulnerable groups and individuals who are not a threat—also reflect officers' aggressive tactics that result in unreasonable force.

2. BPD Uses Unreasonable Force Against Individuals with a Mental Health Disability and Those in Crisis and Fails to Make Reasonable Modifications When Interacting with Individuals with Mental Health Disabilities

BPD officers routinely use unreasonable force against individuals with mental health disabilities or those experiencing a crisis[93] in violation of the Fourth Amendment. Additionally, by routinely using unreasonable force against individuals with mental health disabilities, BPD officers repeatedly fail to make reasonable modifications necessary to avoid discrimination in violation of Title II of the Americans with Disabilities Act of 1990 (ADA), 42 U.S.C. §§ 12131–12134. Since 2004, BPD has provided some specialized training to its new officers on how to interact with individuals with disabilities and those in crisis. But this training has not been provided to all officers. Moreover, the Department does not have a protocol requiring that a person with this training be dispatched to a crisis call. The result is that BPD officers frequently fail to de-escalate encounters with unarmed individuals with mental health disabilities and those in crisis. Indeed, their tactics often escalate these encounters. Instead of requesting an officer trained in handling crisis events or a mobile crisis team made up of trained mental health professionals, officers handcuff and detain people with mental health disabilities and those in crisis and resort too quickly to force without understanding or accounting for the person's disability or crisis.

For example, BPD officers often are called to the scene to escort individuals likely to have disabilities to a hospital for a mental health evaluation (referred to as an "emergency petition" under Maryland law), and possible civil commitment. Frequently, these individuals have committed no crime and present no significant threat to officers or other members of the public. "Where a seizure's sole justification is preventing harm to the subject of the seizure, the government has little interest in using force to effect that seizure. Rather, using force likely to harm the subject is manifestly contrary to the government's interest in initiating that seizure." *Armstrong*, 810 F.3d at 901. In the course of engaging with these individuals, usually to transport them for medical treatment, BPD officers resort to using unreasonable force if individuals fail to comply with their commands.

---

93 For a definition of "crisis," *see* note 90, *supra*.

Under the Fourth Amendment, "officers who encounter an unarmed and minimally threatening individual who is "exhibit[ing] conspicuous signs that he [i]s mentally unstable" must "de-escalate the situation and adjust the application of force downward." *Id.* at 900. Similarly, the ADA, which applies to BPD's services, programs, and activities, including on-the-street encounters, arrests, and transportation to a hospital for mental health evaluation, *see* 42 U.S.C. § 12132; 28 C.F.R. § 35.130(a), requires BPD to "make reasonable modifications in policies, practices, or procedures when the modifications are necessary to avoid discrimination on the basis of disability." *See also* 28 C.F.R. 35.130(b)(7); *Title II Technical Assistance Manual* § II-3.6100, at 14.[94] BPD's obligations apply when officers respond to a scene where they know or reasonably should know that an individual has a mental health disability.[95] For example, BPD has knowledge of an individual's disability when BPD is called for an emergency petition, when a mother calls 911 and says her son has schizophrenia and is not eating, or when a person is exhibiting apparent signs of mental illness.

Training BPD officers on how to interact with individuals with mental health disabilities is a reasonable modification to policies, practices, and procedures to afford people with mental health disabilities the equal opportunity for a police intervention that is free from unreasonable force. *See Estate of Saylor v. Regal Cinemas, Inc.*, 54 F. Supp. 3d 409, 424 (D. Md. 2014) (holding that the failure to provide appropriate training for officers to interact with individuals with developmental disabilities, which resulted in the death of a 26-year-

---

94 The ADA's obligation to make "reasonable modifications in policies, practices, or procedures" is not limitless. A modification is not required if it would "fundamentally alter the nature of the service, program, or activity." 28 C.F.R. § 35.130(b)(7). The requested modifications here would not "fundamentally alter" BPD's programs. As discussed in further detail in Section II(C)(5), *infra*, BPD already offers some policing services specifically tailored toward individuals in crisis, although significant work remains to fully develop this program. Additionally, the requested modifications are consistent with BPD's obligations under the Constitution. BPD would not have to make the requested modifications if the person requiring the modification poses a direct threat to the safety of an officer or others. *See* 28 C.F.R. § 35.139. A direct threat is "a significant risk to the health or safety of others that cannot be eliminated by a modification of policies, practices, or procedures, or by the provision of auxiliary aids or services." 28 C.F.R. § 35.104. In many of the incidents we reviewed involving individuals with mental health disabilities or in crisis, however, the person against whom force is used does not meet the definition of "direct threat" as that term is used in the ADA.

95 Guidance on ADA Regulation on Nondiscrimination on the Basis of Disability in State and Local Government Services, 28 C.F.R. pt. 35, app. B, at 686 (2015) (Law enforcement agencies and officers are "required to make appropriate efforts to determine whether perceived strange or disruptive behavior . . . is the result of a disability"), *available at* https://www.gpo.gov/fdsys/pkg/CFR-2015-title28-vol1/pdf/CFR-2015-title28-vol1-part35-appB.pdf.

old man with Down Syndrome after officers attempted to force him to leave a movie theater, properly stated a claim under Title II of the ADA). Among other things, such training should result in officers employing appropriate de-escalation techniques or involving mental health professionals or specially trained crisis intervention officers.

Rather than employing such de-escalation tactics, we found that BPD officers often resort too quickly to using force against individuals with mental health disabilities or in crisis. We found that on many occasions, the officers' unreasonable use of force involved use of tasers in drive-stun mode. As the Fourth Circuit has recognized, "[d]eploying a taser is a serious use of force. The weapon is designed to cause . . . excruciating pain and application can burn a subject's flesh." *Armstrong*, 810 F.3d at 902 (internal quotation marks and citations omitted). The court noted that "using drive stun mode 'to achieve pain compliance may have limited effectiveness and, when used repeatedly, may even exacerbate the situation.'" *Id.* at 902 (quoting PERF & COPS, *2011 Electronic Control Weapon Guidelines*, at 14); *see also Armstrong*, 810 F.3d at 897 n.3 (internal quotation marks and citations omitted) ("Tasers generally have two modes. In dart mode, a taser shoots probes into a subject and overrides the central nervous system. Drive stun mode, on the other hand, does not cause an override of the victim's central nervous system; that mode is used as a pain compliance tool with limited threat reduction."). Even Taser International, the company that manufactures tasers, has cautioned against using the drive stun mode on "emotionally disturbed persons or others who may not respond to pain due to a mind-body disconnect." *Id.* at 903.

Nonetheless, BPD officers have repeatedly used drive-stuns while responding to people with mental health disabilities and those in crisis, causing unnecessary pain and suffering without any noticeable benefit. In fact, these uses have often, if anything, exacerbated the situation. In a 2011 incident we reviewed, several officers responded to a call about a domestic disturbance, at which point they were flagged down by "Michael," standing outside without shoes in January weather, smelling of alcohol. His wife, present on the scene, informed officers that she had not been assaulted, but that her husband was intoxicated and that she was packing things to leave for the night. Michael yelled profanities and stated that he wanted to die. Instead of using de-escalation techniques, calling for help from an officer trained in crisis intervention techniques or a mental health professional, or working to connect Michael with appropriate treatment services, the officers attempted to physically force Michael into handcuffs, and when he resisted, drive-stunned him with a Taser five to six times. One officer specifically noted in his report that "[t]he Taser seemed to have a minimal affect [sic] upon [Michael] possibly due to his level of alcoholic intoxication and mentally disturbed state." After handcuffing him, the officers took Michael to the hospital for stabilization. He was never charged with a crime. The force used by the officers was unreasonable because he had not committed a crime and did not appear to pose a threat to officers or his wife. It was also ineffective in rendering Michael compliant, and caused unneeded suffering without any appreciable benefit.

In another 2011 incident, nine officers responded to a call for service regarding a man, "Christopher," standing in the street with no clothing on. In this case, there is no documented attempt to have a specially-trained officer at the scene. When the officers encountered Christopher, they reported that he was speaking religious verses and arguing with himself. They believed he had a mental illness and decided to transport him to a hospital to be evaluated. There is no indication in the reports that the officers sought to have Christopher go with them voluntarily, and instead they sought to place him in handcuffs, even though he was not under arrest. In order to handcuff him, one officer held his left arm, a second officer held his right arm, and a third officer attempted to apply the handcuffs. Christopher reportedly "became aggressive and violent," attempting to grab and bite officers. The officers and Christopher fell onto the ground. From the officers' reports, it appears that six additional officers were on the scene and available to assist in bringing Christopher under control, but there is no indication that they attempted any control techniques on Christopher. There is also no indication that de-escalation techniques or other reasonable modifications were used, such as attempts to verbally calm Christopher, create distance or slow down the incident.

Instead, the transport van driver exited his van and promptly drive-stunned Christopher. Using a taser in drive-stun mode is to be avoided unless it is necessary to "creat[e] a safe distance between the officer and subject." PERF & COPS, 2011 Electronic Control Weapon Guidelines, at 14. BPD had no policy or training so limiting the use of drive-stuns, even against individuals with mental illness or in crisis, at this time. Thus, the van driver continued to drive-stun Christopher, an individual in crisis, "a few more times in his chest and back area"[96] until Christopher became compliant. As a result of the encounter, Christopher and two officers received minor injuries, and Christopher was transported to the emergency room for treatment. Before the officers' attempts to handcuff him, he had not committed any violent offense, and presented no immediate physical danger to the officers or the public at large. Christopher was never arrested or charged with a crime. In 2016, BPD issued new guidance limiting officers' uses of tasers, a positive step forward. Additional work remains, however, to ensure that officers abide by the new guidance.

---

96 In an October 2009 Training Bulletin, Taser International recommended that its Tasers, the leading brand of ECWs, not be used on individuals' chests, to avoid controversy about whether such shots affect the human heart. *See* TASER Int'l, *Training Bulletin 15.0 Medical Research Update & Revised Warnings* (Oct. 15, 2009).

In many incidents involving individuals in crisis, the use of force was precipitated by officers' perceived need to bring the individual into immediate custody at all costs, including handcuffing them and placing them into a police vehicle for transport in order to provide necessary mental health treatment. During this detention process, a number of uses of unreasonable force against individuals with mental illness and crisis have occurred when they had committed no crime at all—instead, BPD's interaction with the individual was precipitated by calls for help from a loved one, friend or concerned citizen. That a person has committed no crime "weighs heavily" against a finding that the use of force by law enforcement was reasonable. *Bailey v. Kennedy*, 349 F.3d 731, 744 (4th Cir. 2003) (finding that blows and kicks against a man resisting arrest for an unwarranted emergency medical evaluation were unreasonable). In many incidents, however, officers have failed to distinguish between people in crisis who are being escorted to the hospital for treatment, and people who have committed crimes and are being placed under arrest. From our review of BPD's force reports, it appears that officers make little, if any, effort to de-escalate or engage peaceably with the person in crisis, resorting to the use of force as a first option in order to transport the individual for treatment. If they do not submit to handcuffing or respond immediately to officers' commands, they are often subjected to uses of force in order to physically restrain them, rather than neutralize a threat. The only difference is that the final destination will be an emergency room, rather than jail.

In one such incident, in 2010, several officers responded to a call from the father of a man, "James," in mental health crisis. The father informed the officers that James was the subject of an emergency petition, had a history of mental illness and hospitalization, and was unarmed. The petition itself indicated that James was not taking his medication, wearing a winter coat in hot weather, and yelling at people on the street and his father. When they could not convince James to open the door, officers attempted to pry the door open with a crowbar, then sprayed two bursts of mace in an attempt to force him out of the apartment. Once inside, a lieutenant deployed his taser in probe mode, striking James, when he resisted being handcuffed. Despite the fact that James had committed no crime and there is no indication in the force report that he was a threat himself or the officers other than resisting handcuffing, the officers resorted to a high-level of force to detain the man. *See Armstrong*, 810 F.3d at 900 (internal quotation marks omitted) ("The problems posed by, and thus the tactics to be employed against, an unarmed, emotionally distraught individual who is creating a disturbance or resisting arrest are ordinarily different from those involved in law enforcement efforts to subdue an armed and dangerous criminal who has recently committed a serious offense."). Using effective deescalation techniques and calling for assistance from a mental health provider or crisis intervention trained officer would have likely prevented the use of force against James.

In another incident, two officers encountered a "possible mental patient" inside a vacant dwelling. The man, "David," was "yelling incoherently" and would not come out of the building when ordered. The officers entered, and when David became louder and placed his hands in his pockets, one officer pointed a taser at him as a threat, purportedly to protect himself and to persuade David to comply with the order to exit the building. David told the police officers that tasers did not work on him. In response, the officer deployed one cycle of his taser in probe mode, striking the man "to eliminate the need for a fight." Without waiting to assess whether additional force was necessary, the officer used a second cycle. David was handcuffed and transported to the hospital. The only justification offered by the officer for the second taser cycle was that it was necessary "to gain his full compliance." For many people with mental health disabilities or in crisis, the appearance of officers pointing weapons may convey the impression that they are being threatened or arrested, rather than provided treatment that is intended to help them. The use of a taser against David in this context was unnecessary and unreasonable where it had the sole purpose of bringing him into the physical custody of the officers for treatment, and David presented no immediate threat to himself or others. Using effective de-escalation techniques and calling for assistance from a mental health provider or officer trained in crisis intervention techniques would have likely prevented the use of force against all of these individuals.

Tragically, some encounters with people with mental health disabilities or in crisis have resulted in uses of deadly force that may have been avoided had officers used tactics to account for the mental state of the individuals involved. For example, in a 2012 incident, a single officer was the first to arrive on the scene in response to a call by a man, Zachary, who informed the dispatcher that he had "a weapon" and was "about to do something crazy." After the officer was dispatched, another officer and sergeant stated over the air that they would respond as backup. The officer did not wait for backup to arrive, however, or request the presence of a specially trained crisis intervention officer, despite the fact that he had prior information that Zachary had a weapon and was in crisis. The officer also made no attempt to contact Zachary inside the house before approaching the door, or consider less-lethal options for intervention. Instead, the officer went up to the door, alone, and with his gun already drawn. When Zachary opened the door with a lit cigarette in one hand, and a knife in the other, the officer reportedly ordered the man three times to drop the knife, and when he did not comply, the officer fired, killing him. After radioing dispatch to inform that he had arrived on the scene, less than two minutes passed before he announced that Zachary had been shot two to three times. Although there is insufficient information to make a determination about the shooting itself, this incident shows how different tactics could have changed the outcome.

Officers' use of arrest techniques, including force, handcuffing and prisoner transport vans to detain people with mental health disabilities or in crisis for emergency petitions when they present no immediate threat to officers or the public, may cause people to perceive that they are being attacked or arrested, rather than transported for treatment. This perception may escalate the encounter, resulting in additional force.

In some cases, officers resort to arresting individuals with mental health disabilities or in crisis in situations where treatment—instead of jail—would more effectively serve the goals of public safety and welfare and could prevent the need for unnecessary force. For example, in one case, officers responded to a "mental case" and found a man, "Robert," speaking to his mother, who explained that her son had a mental illness and that she was afraid of him. The officers told Robert to leave and put a shirt on, which he did, and then returned. Officers then told Robert he had to leave, or would be arrested. When he refused, officers handcuffed him and sat him in a chair while waiting for a transport van to arrive. This decision to arrest and handcuff Robert, a person in crisis, led to unreasonable force. While waiting, Robert repeatedly stood up in what the officer believed was an attempt "to flee," and was "kicking his legs" to "create space around himself." After being told several times to stop standing and stop kicking, and that he would be struck in the leg with a baton if he did not comply, Robert refused to comply. He attempted to stand again, in what officers reportedly believed was another attempt to flee. One officer struck him in the right shin with his baton. This force used against Robert, while he was handcuffed, was unreasonable because he had not acted violently, did not present any evident threat to the officers or his mother, and the officers had been informed that he had a mental illness. This force could have been avoided by using de-escalation techniques before handcuffing Robert or by calling a mobile crisis team for assistance. In this incident, as with all of the above incidents involving individuals with mental health disabilities or in crisis, officers did not seem to understand that individuals' mental illness or intoxication might diminish their ability to comply with orders. Moreover, the officers in this incident believed—contrary to the Department's policy—that they could not emergency petition Robert because he had not displayed any signs of mental illness in their presence, despite his mother's call for assistance based on that mental condition and her explanation of his history of hospitalization. Instead, the officers arrested him and charged him with disorderly conduct, trespassing, resisting arrest, and failure to obey. All charges against him were subsequently dismissed.

BPD routinely uses unreasonable force against people with mental illness or in crisis, even when they have not committed any crimes and when the officers know or should know that the individual has a mental health disability. As a result, individuals are exposed to serious harm that exacerbates their disability and the crisis that precipitated the request for BPD assistance. This unreasonable use of force against individuals in crisis violates the Fourth Amendment. And BPD further violates Title II of the Americans with Disabilities Act by failing to make reasonable modifications to its policies, practices and procedures, such as training in de-escalation, effectively using specialized crisis intervention trained officers, and involving mental health professionals as necessary to avoid discrimination against individuals with disabilities.

3. BPD Uses Unreasonable Force Against Juveniles And Ignores Widely Accepted Strategies For Police Interactions With Youth

BPD officers frequently use unreasonable force against juveniles without implementing widely accepted techniques and tactics for engaging with youth. Courts have recognized that an individual's age can be a factor in whether the force used against them was reasonable. *See Graham*, 490 U.S. at 396 ("the test of reasonableness" . . . "requires careful attention to the facts and circumstances of each particular case. . . ."); *Doe ex rel. Doe v. Hawaii Dep't of Educ.*, 334 F.3d 906, 909–10 (9th Cir. 2003) (noting Plaintiff "was eight years old" in analysis under *Graham* of whether force was reasonable); *Ikerd v. Blair*, 101 F.3d 430 (5th Cir. 1996) (finding a reasonable jury could conclude a deputy used excessive force where "the appellants produced evidence that Deputy Varnado, a 300-pound man, violently jerked Laura, a ten-year-old child, out of her living room chair and dragged her into another room"). We found that BPD officers engage in unnecessary and excessive force with youth and fail to adjust their tactics to account for the age and developmental status of the youth they encounter.

For example, in a 2011 incident, an officer noticed a 5'2", 85-pound female youth standing with a male in a "known area for high drug trafficking." The officer in charge who investigated the force reported that the involved officer "was familiar with the female juvenile and her past history for selling CDS." The involved officer's incident report does not mention any history of selling drugs but states that she "suspected [the female was] a missing juvenile." Regardless of the basis for stopping the youth, the officer got out of her patrol vehicle "to identify" the female. When she did so, the youth and the male began to "walk away very quickly." The officer commanded the individuals to "stop" but they did not comply. The officer again commanded the two to stop. When they continued to not comply with her command, the officer discharged her taser in probe mode at the young 85-pound female, "which gave an electric shock." The youth "stopped and supported herself on [a] fence," and the officer "discontinued the electric discharge[]." When the officer discharged her taser, she did not have probable cause for an arrest. There is also no indication in BPD's own reports that the youth was threatening the officer or others; rather, she was simply walking away. Even assuming that there is reasonable suspicion for a stop, refusing to obey an officer's command to "stop," when the officer has no probable cause to arrest and there is no threat to the public or officer, does not justify the use of a taser. The officer's use of a taser was unnecessary and excessive.[97] The chain of command failed to identify any issues with the officer's use of force.

In another incident, in 2010, two officers approached a group of individuals who were standing on a sidewalk in a residential neighborhood and "verbally warned this small crowd to disperse." A juvenile, Brian, and his sister walked onto the steps of their home, remaining outside. When one of the officers approached Brian's sister to "warn her about loitering," she informed the officers, yelling and cursing, that she lived in the house. The officers did not appear to dispute her claim that she lived in the house. Their reports do not show that any effort was made to confirm whether it was her home. Nevertheless, the officers continued to "warn" her to leave and "cease causing a disturbance." They eventually attempted to arrest her for "non-compliance." One of the officers walked up the steps of the siblings' stoop to attempt to make the arrest. Brian attempted to block the officer, and the officer began to "struggle" with the juvenile. According to civilian witness statements that are summarized in the Department's reports, the officer punched Brian in the face. The officer also used oleoresin capsicum, or "OC" spray, against both siblings and arrested them for loitering, resisting arrest and assault on a police officer. All of the officer's uses of force against the siblings, who were standing on or in front of their own property, were unreasonable. These individuals were placed into the criminal justice system for standing on their own steps.

Allegations of BPD's unreasonable use of force against juveniles are not new. BPD has a history of problematic encounters with youth that pre-date the period of our review. For example, in 2007, officers arrested a seven-year-old child for sitting on a dirt bike during an initiative to confiscate dirt bikes. Allegedly, although the dirt bike was turned off, it was not "securely locked or otherwise immobilized" in violation of Baltimore City Code. According to Court documents filed by the family's attorney, officers attempted to confiscate the bike and "maliciously and unreasonably grabbed [the child] by his shirt collar and dragged [him] off the bike." According to the same documents, the

---

97 Behind where the youth and her male companion were stopped, officers found bags of "a green leaf substance suspected to be [m]arijuana." Additional bags of the green leaf substance fell out of the man's pants. The youth was arrested for a controlled substance violation and taken to a juvenile detention center.

child's mother informed officers that she intended to file a complaint, and the officers, in turn, arrested the child. The family alleged he was handcuffed to a bench at the district station for hours, and detained and questioned without his parents' consent. He was eventually released and never formally charged. This incident garnered widespread media attention in Baltimore and invoked a community outcry about BPD's aggressive tactics, particularly against a seven-year-old child. Despite the outcry and widespread attention, BPD failed to create policy guidance or comprehensive training for officers' interactions with youth.

In addition, three officers were criminally charged this year for assaulting a youth who had been in crisis and was restrained in a 2015 incident. According to a complaint filed about the incident, when the child was admitted to the hospital for evaluation of a mental health condition, independent witnesses on the scene indicated that he had no injuries. In his hospital room, he was handcuffed with both hands behind his back but was being unruly—yelling and kicking his legs. One of the officers reportedly ordered hospital staff to leave the room and reportedly slapped or punched the youth in the face repeatedly. The nurses observed the officers being verbally abusive to the child and observed injuries to his face when they returned to the youth's room.

Research has established that adolescent development affects the manner in which juveniles comprehend, communicate, and behave. These unique realities of adolescent development warrant specific policies and tactics for officers' interactions with juveniles. The International Association of Chiefs of Police (IACP) has recognized this need and created guidance for officers' interactions with youth.[98] Specific strategies for officers include "[a]pproach[ing] youth with a calm demeanor, conveying that you are there to help them" because "[a]ggression may cause the youth to shut down and make the situation worse."[99] BPD officers are not provided guidance on the causes and unique qualities of youth behavior and communication or trained on the skills and tactics necessary for interacting with youth. Officers use the same overly aggressive tactics they use with adults, unnecessarily escalating encounters with youth. As the President's Task Force on 21st Century Policing notes, "[u]se of physical control equipment and techniques against vulnerable populations—including children . . . can undermine public trust and should be used as a last resort."[100]

We reviewed numerous other cases that also raised concerns about officers'

---

98 Int'l Assn. of Chiefs of Police, *The Effects of Adolescent Development on Policing* 2 (2015), available at http://www.iacp.org/teenbrain).

99 *Id.* at 4.

100 Final Report of the President's Task Force on 21st Century Policing 15 (May 2015).

interactions with juveniles. These cases demonstrate that BPD fails to adjust its tactics, even when dealing with youth. They also show that BPD needs to provide detailed and comprehensive policy guidance and training for interactions involving juveniles, and to hold officers accountable if they fail to abide by their training and guidelines.

4. BPD Uses Unreasonable Force Against People Who Are Not a Threat to Officers or the Public

a. BPD Uses Unreasonable Force Against People who Are Already Restrained

BPD uses unreasonable force against people who are already restrained and pose little or no threat to the officer or the public. In some instances, these individuals may continue to verbally resist or not submit to officer's demands, but this type of passive resistance or non-compliance does not justify using force. This practice contravenes well-settled law.

In *Meyers*, the Fourth Circuit determined that an officer's use of force was excessive and unreasonable where the officer repeatedly administered electrical shocks from a taser on an individual who was no longer armed, was no longer actively resisting arrest and was physically restrained by several other officers. 713 F.3d at 734. "We also have stated in forthright terms that 'officers using unnecessary, gratuitous, and disproportionate force to seize a secured, unarmed citizen do not act in an objectively reasonable manner.'" *Id.* (quoting *Bailey v. Kennedy*, 349 F.3d 731, 744–45 (4th Cir. 2003)); *see also Champion v. Outlook Nashville, Inc.*, 380 F.3d 893, 902 (6th Cir. 2004) (citing cases) ("We have consistently held that various types of force applied after the subduing of a suspect are unreasonable and a violation of a clearly established right."). The Court in *Meyers* also indicated that "any 'unnecessary, gratuitous, and disproportional force'" against unarmed and secured individuals was objectively unreasonable regardless of the type of weapon used, whether arising from a gun, a baton, a taser, or other weapon. 713 F.3d at 734–35 (quoting *Jones v. Buchanan*, 325 F.3d 520, 532 (4th Cir. 2003) (fists)) (citing *Park v. Shiflett*, 250 F.3d 843, 852–53 (4th Cir. 2001) (pepper spray)).

In Baltimore, BPD officers use excessive force against restrained individuals, often when those individuals are awaiting transport to Central Booking after being arrested for committing low-level street offenses. For example, in a 2011 incident, three BPD officers responded to an anonymous tip about persons using illegal drugs inside a pick-up truck. Arriving on scene, the officers located illegal drugs and drug paraphernalia in the truck's cab. The three occupants—two women and one man—were removed from the vehicle and arrested for controlled substance violations. While waiting for a prisoner transport vehicle, one of the women, "Sarah", began "moving around" in a perceived attempt to wander away or escape. Sarah attempted to get up on six occasions and "each attempt to rise was met with a verbal warning to stop" and an admonition that the next time she tried to "escape" the officer would use force to against her. Sarah again tried to stand up and the officer, already holding his police baton in his hand, struck Sarah in the leg and then "managed to maintain physical control over her." This baton strike appears to be used as punishment for failing to follow the officer's commands rather than necessary and reasonable force to control Sarah, who was not actively aggressive and was being detained for a minor drug offense. Sarah later told the investigating supervisor that she was not attempting to escape; rather she was trying to stand up because her knees were in pain from kneeling on the hard pavement for such a long time. In this situation, other less forceful techniques should have been employed—for instance an escort position, joint manipulation, or utilizing leg restraints if escape was truly a concern. Moreover, BPD specifically trains its officers that impact weapons should not be used when individuals are non-compliant or passively resisting. Rather, striking an individual with an impact weapon should only be used to stop an attacker who is actively attempting to inflict injury. Nevertheless, this strike against a restrained individual was summarily approved by the chain of command.

In a 2014 incident that we reviewed, a CitiWatch operator who was monitoring security cameras placed throughout Baltimore notified BPD patrol officers that he observed an unknown male, later identified as "Brandon," conduct a hand-to-hand exchange of suspected narcotics. An officer and a trainee responded to the scene and entered a local store to interview Brandon. After producing identification, the officers smelled an odor of marijuana emanating from Brandon, whom they then patted down for weapons, but found none. As they were exiting the store, BPD officers noticed a baggie containing a white powdery substance on the floor near the entrance where Brandon had been standing. According to their force reports, having seen no one else enter or leave the store, the officers determined that the baggie belonged to Brandon, handcuffed him and took him outside to wait for a transport wagon.

When a BPD sergeant arrived on scene, Brandon was sitting on the ground in handcuffs. The sergeant began speaking to Brandon and reportedly observed another small baggie containing a white powdery substance and a clear sandwich baggie containing green plant material under Brandon's tongue. According to the sergeant, he asked Brandon to spit out the baggies, but Brandon clenched his mouth "and attempted to destroy the narcotics/evidence by swallowing them." The sergeant placed his hand on Brandon's cheeks and, most troublingly, on his throat and then applied pressure—"not to restrict his breathing, but just to keep him from swallowing the illegal narcotics/evidence which could have also put [Brandon's] life at risk." When Brandon refused to spit out the suspected narcotics, the sergeant ordered the police officer trainee on the scene to tase Brandon, even though he was restrained. The trainee drive-stunned Brandon on his legs. When Brandon did not spit out the baggies, the sergeant ordered the trainee to drive-stun Brandon three additional times. Brandon spat out "several" small baggies and was transported to the district for processing.

The use of force on Brandon's neck—a handcuffed detainee who did not pose a threat to officer safety, and who was being arrested for what the officer's described in their own report as a "street level drug transaction"—was excessive and unreasonable. Although some force to prevent the destruction of evidence or to protect Brandon may be reasonable, the sergeant's application of pressure to Brandon's throat was a use of lethal force that was not justified by the possible destruction of evidence or even the potential threat to Brandon of swallowing the narcotics. If Brandon had actually swallowed the baggies, officers should have transported him to a hospital for treatment by trained medical professionals. The officer's use of his taser on Brandon was also highly questionable, if not excessive.

In a 2010 incident, two BPD officers and a lieutenant arrested a 5'6," 160-pound man for littering after observing him throw a cigar wrapper on the ground and then empty the tobacco contents from the cigar. The officers handcuffed and sat 19-year-old "William" on a curb, and conducted a search incident to arrest. They removed William's shoes and recovered a blue Ziploc bag containing what they suspected was marijuana. According to the force reports, William began to yell profanities and accuse the officers of planting the drugs. One officer placed William against a wall while they waited for a transport vehicle. William continued to yell, then pushed off the wall and began to run. After only a few steps, an officer pushed William to the ground. According to the force report, William continued to flail and try to "strike the officers by head butting, kicking, shouldering and spitting." The officers attempted to gain control of William, but were unable. A crowd formed around the officers and William. Although William was in handcuffs and three officers were present to control the restrained man, the officers resorted to tasing the man in drive-stun mode "approximately six times." The lieutenant and one of the officers also reportedly kicked William several times either in an effort to get him to the ground or to keep him on the ground; the reports are unclear. When the drive-stuns were reportedly ineffective, and William reportedly pushed away the taser and continued to fight, the lieutenant ordered the officers to move away and deployed two bursts of pepper spray in William's face. The officers were then able to hold William on the ground and place him in a transport vehicle. The inability of three officers to control William is concerning and reflects insufficient training on arrest and control techniques. While we take no position on the reasonableness of much of the force used in this incident, the use of the taser on a handcuffed individual "approximately six times" was un-reasonable. The use of taser on a restrained individual is rarely reasonable, and tasing the person in drive-stun mode six times is unreasonable and excessive in almost any case. A drive-stun is to be used only to create distance. William suffered abrasions on his knees, arm, back and a small fracture of left shoulder. He was charged only with littering and disorderly conduct.

BPD officers also use excessive force against restrained detainees who refuse to exit BPD transport vehicles, in some cases when being transported to the hospital for an emergency petition evaluation. In a 2010 case we reviewed, a BPD transport officer responded to a call about a person with possible mental illness in a wheelchair who was allegedly exposing himself to take him to a hospital for an evaluation. Although the incident report is vague, difficult to read, and lacks any follow-up investigation, it appears that the officer ap-proached the man, "Timothy," who was "agitated and disorderly," and asked for identification. Timothy produced his identification and then jumped out of the wheelchair and kicked the patrol car. When the officer attempted to take Timothy into custody, Timothy began kicking, and the officer tased him and took him into custody. Timothy was transported to an area hospital for an emergency petition evaluation. Upon arriving at the hospital, Timothy refused to come out of the transport vehicle and kicked at the BPD transport officer. The transport officer gave Timothy several commands to stop kicking or he would be tased. A second officer stood outside witnessing the events, but there is no indication that he made any effort to intervene. After the transport officer gave Timothy a third command to stop kicking, the transport officer deployed his taser in drive-stun mode.

The reasonableness of the first taser incident cannot be determined because there were conflicting accounts of what occurred, there was no supervisory in-vestigation, and the incident reports contain little detail. However, tasing Tim-othy the second time while he was restrained in the back of a transport vehicle was unreasonable. In *Orem v. Rephann*, 523 F.3d 442 (4th Cir. 2008), *abrogated on other grounds by Wilkins v. Gaddy*, 559 U.S. 34, 39 (2010), the Court of Appeals addressed whether the use of a taser against an arrestee who was being trans-ported to jail in a police officer's car constituted excessive force. Because the sub-ject was already in custody, the court analyzed the excessive force claim under the Fourteenth Amendment's standard of whether the officer "inflicted unnec-essary and wanton pain and suffering." *Orem*, 523 F.3d at 446; *but see Kingsley v. Hendrickson*, 135 S. Ct. 2466 (2015) (holding that excessive force claims brought by pretrial detainees need only meet the *Graham* standard of objective unreasonableness). In doing so, the court held that the use of a taser on a de-tainee who was already in handcuffs and restrained in the back of a police car was clearly unlawful, despite the fact that the detainee was extremely unruly and uncooperative. *Orem*, 523 F.3d at 446–47; *Cf. Wernert v. Green*, 419 F. App'x

337, 342–43 (4th Cir. 2011). Here, Timothy was transported to an area hospital because BPD officers determined that he needed an emergency psychological evaluation. Timothy was in crisis and kicked at the transport officer, but he was restrained and was not currently a danger to himself or a threat to the officers. There was no urgent need to remove Timothy from the transport vehicle. Instead of having patience and attempting to de-escalate the situation—or asking for assistance from the other officer on scene or qualified medical personnel in the hospital—the transport officer resorted to a high level of force to gain compliance from a person in crisis who may not have understood his commands. The use of the taser in this instance, and in other similar BPD force files we reviewed, was punitive rather than necessary and reasonable.

Nevertheless, in determining that the officer's actions conformed to Departmental Guidelines, the supervisor justifying this use of force wrote: "The X26 Taser fills the action void with a force less than either espantoon[101] or deadly force to elicit compliance from individuals who are about to be arrested. It allows members to use a relative mild force and provides a safer option than suffering or inflicting serious injury." The supervisor's determination that drive-stunning a restrained, mentally ill person is "mild" and justified because it prevents suffering or serious injury illustrates a lack of appreciation for the seriousness of the force used and the possibility of harm that could result. *See Bryan v. MacPherson*, 630 F.3d 805, 825 (9th Cir. 2010) ("The physiological effects, the high levels of pain, and foreseeable risk of physical injury lead us to conclude that the X26 and similar [tasers] are a greater intrusion than other non-lethal methods of force we have confronted."). It also demonstrates an ignorance of applicable Fourth Circuit law that prohibits the use of a taser in these circumstances. *Orem*, 523 F.3d at 446–47.

In a strikingly similar 2014 incident, a BPD officer responded to a domestic violence call, took the subject into custody, and transported him to the district station. When officers ordered "Eric" to exit the transport wagon, he refused and stated "I want the police to shoot me. I have nothing to live for." The officers warned Eric several times that he would be tased, but when he refused to comply with their commands, the sergeant on the scene ordered one of the officers to tase Eric. The taser probes struck Eric in the arm and buttocks. Subsequently, the officers transported Eric to the hospital for an emergency petition. This use of force on a passively non-complaint person in crisis was unreasonable. The officers resorted to force simply to gain compliance from Eric, not because they needed to gain control over him. In doing so, BPD officers disregarded an individual's constitutional rights in favor of expediency. The sergeant who ordered the officer to tase Eric—and also investigated the use of force, despite the conflict of interest—justified the taser deployment by citing

---

101 An "espantoon" is one type of baton used by BPD officers.

what appears to be a version of the Department's Training Guidelines titled "Electronic Shock Devices," that had been replaced in 2010, four years before the incident took place.

b. BPD Uses Unreasonable Force Against Persons who Are Fleeing from Them and Present Little or No Threat of Harm

A significant number of incidents we reviewed involved BPD officers using force against individuals who were fleeing from officers and presented little or no threat of harm to them or others. Many of these incidents involved officers who chased civilians on foot, often without suspicion that they had committed any serious crimes. Such foot pursuits increase the likelihood that officers will use force in order to stop an individual that is not reasonable in light of the threat posed or crime committed by the person. Foot pursuits of individuals for low-level offenses are also an unsafe tactic that unnecessarily endangers officers and community members.

Similarly, we found a number of cases in which officers shot at vehicles that were fleeing or moving away from them, after any threat of harm to them or others had subsided. Such shootings are unreasonable.

i. In Foot Pursuits, BPD Uses Excessive Force Against Individuals Who Are Fleeing From Them and Tactics That Endanger Themselves and Community Members

BPD officers used excessive force against individuals during foot pursuits. When officers encounter civilians who flee from them, officers nearly always give chase, without weighing the severity of any suspected crime, whether the person poses a threat, and any alternative, safer means to affect a stop or seizure. Once engaged in a foot pursuit, BPD officers then often used force to end the pursuit regardless of whether they had only reasonable suspicion to conduct a stop, or probable cause to make an arrest. *See Cortez v. McCauley*, 478 F.3d 1108, 1126 (10th Cir. 2007) ("[P]olice have historically been able to use more force in making an arrest than in effecting an investigative detention."); *see also Rabin v. Flynn*, 725 F.3d 628, 632–33 (7th Cir. 2013) ("When an officer's use of force during such a *Terry* stop becomes so disproportionate to the purpose of such a stop in light of the surrounding circumstances—and the purpose may include ensuring the safety of the officers or others—then the encounter becomes a formal arrest (which must then be justified by probable cause.")) (citations omitted). Often, the force officers used to end the pursuit was disproportional to the suspected crime and the threat posed by the civilian. *See Armstrong*, 810 F.3d at 899 (internal quotation marks omitted) ("To properly consider the reasonableness of the force employed we must view it in full context, with an eye toward the proportionality of the force in light of all the circumstances."). Based on the force reports we reviewed, the frequency with which officers engaged in foot pursuits, without considering the seriousness of the suspected crime, any alternative means to stop the individual, and risks to themselves, the suspect, and others is concerning.

Foot pursuits are generally a high-risk tactic and have civil rights implications. *See generally* IACP, *Protecting Civil Rights: A Leadership Guide for State, Local, and Tribal Law Enforcement*, p. 133. In particular, at the end of a foot pursuit, when officers seize an individual, they may experience an adrenaline rush; actions taken under such circumstances may impede an officer's ability to exercise proper judgment and appropriate restraint. For this reason, police departments should, and generally do, give careful consideration to foot pursuits in policy and training.

BPD has not engaged in the careful consideration that foot pursuits require as a policy and training matter. BPD has no policy on foot pursuits to guide, and hold accountable, its officers' conduct. An internal report in 2013 recommended that the Department issue a policy on these pursuits, and its internal documents indicate that it has intended to draft a policy to guide officers' conduct in pursuits for a number of years. However, to date, BPD has not issued any policy on this issue. BPD's training on foot pursuits for both new and experienced officers also is deficient. Only in 2015 did BPD create a specific training on foot pursuits for its recruits in the Academy. Previously, its training on this tactic was spread throughout several different courses, leaving it to officers to tie the lessons together. Additionally, the skills that officers learn in the Academy must be refreshed frequently throughout an officer's career through in-service training. For experienced officers, BPD provided in-service training on foot pursuits for the first time in 2015.

BPD officers resort to excessive force to end foot pursuits, or after a pursuit has occurred. For example, in the 2010 incident discussed *supra* on page 31, an officer reportedly in an area "known for violent crime and narcotics distribution" recognized an African-American man who had previously fled when the officer had attempted to conduct a field interview and again fled at the sight of the officer. The officer reportedly pursued the man because he believed he was "involved in criminal activity" though he did not identify any specific crime he suspected. He also reportedly believed he "may be armed with a concealed weapon" because of his "actions, loose clothing and the surroundings." Such generic and vague descriptions are insufficient to justify using serious force against a person. *Smith v. Ball State Univ.*, 295 F.3d 763, 771 (7th Cir. 2002) (applying *Graham* and finding force used in a Terry stop reasonable because it was "measured, brief, and appropriate to accomplish the purposes of the investigative stop."). Here, the officer pursued the man on foot for eight blocks. During the pursuit, the officer deployed his taser in probe mode two times on the man, and then finally used a drive-stun to stop the individual.[102] The officer then frisked the man and found he was not carrying any firearms. To strike the man with two deployments of a taser in probe mode and one in drive-stun was excessive in these circumstances. A lieutenant who arrived on the scene interviewed the man and asked why he had run from the officer. The man informed the lieutenant that "he was scared." Officers released the man without charging him with any crime.

Separate from the risk of excessive force, BPD officers also use unsafe tactics when they engage in foot pursuits, needlessly endangering themselves and community members. The risks of engaging in a foot pursuit may outweigh the benefits in a number of cases. Particularly when officers are acting alone, pursuits are not advised. Indeed, the International Association of Chiefs of Police (IACP) has also cautioned that "[n]ormally, conducting a foot pursuit alone is far too dangerous an undertaking to be permissible."[103] In our reviews of BPD's files, officers engage in solo foot pursuits frequently, even when, in some cases, they believe the person they are pursuing to be armed. Engaging in a solo pursuit of an armed person is dangerous to the officer, and may make it more likely that shots may be fired, increasing the danger to community members. BPD officers repeatedly fail to consider the risk factors inherent in foot pursuits. They too frequently employ tactics that are unsafe for officers, the individuals they pursue, and the community.

When officers decide to pursue a suspect, even though they must decide quickly whether to pursue, they should assess the seriousness of the suspected violation at issue, the dangerousness of the pursuit under the circumstances, whether the person they intend to pursue poses an immediate and serious threat or could be apprehended later or through other means. The need for the suspect's immediate apprehension must be weighed against the risks to officers and the public caused by engaging in a foot pursuit. If officers know the identity of the suspect, his or her immediate apprehension is likely unnecessary without exigent circumstances. However, if circumstances require that the suspect be immediately apprehended, officers should contain the suspect and establish a perimeter rather than engaging in a foot pursuit, particularly if officers believe the suspect may be armed. Officers may then conduct a sweep in a coordinated manner within the contained area to locate the suspect, with the assistance of surveillance if this is available. This recognizes that the safety of the officers and community members is paramount when alternative tactics are available to resolve the incident. Containing a suspect and establishing a pe-

---

102 Striking a stationary individual with a taser in probe mode, if at a distance, can be difficult; striking a moving person while an officer is also running has a low likelihood of being effective.

103 Int'l Ass'n of Chiefs of Police, *Foot Pursuits Concepts & Issues Paper* 2 (Feb. 2003).

rimeter also slows the incident down, decreasing the need for rushed decisions or judgments made in adrenaline-filled circumstances, and decreases the need to use force to apprehend a suspect.

Officers should be encouraged and incentivized to choose safe and professional courses of conduct. Indeed, the IACP recommends that "[b]ecause of the inherent and demonstrated dangers involved in foot pursuits, it should be a matter of agency policy that officers should not be criticized or sanctioned for making a rational and professionally informed decision not to engage in or to terminate a foot pursuit." BPD, to the contrary, indirectly encourages foot pursuits by placing a heavy emphasis on officers' arrest numbers. As discussed above in Section II(A)(1) some supervisors still assess officers, at least in part, by the number of arrests they make, regardless of the severity of the underlying crime. This incentivizes officers to pursue individuals for even minor infractions to increase the number of arrests they make. Additionally, pressure from past City officials to lower the rate of violent crime also has encouraged officers to pursue and seize individuals who may be armed, in an attempt to seize and remove their guns from the street. This is a high-risk strategy that, if engaged in, must have strict controls and oversight to ensure that officers' actions are constitutional and that officers and the public are not exposed to unnecessary risk. Our investigation finds that such controls and oversight are not present, and that officers do not appear to be engaging in pursuits of individuals who they suspect are armed in a manner that keeps them and others safe.

For example, in a 2014 incident, a uniformed officer patrolling in an area allegedly known for drug trafficking and violence turned on his lights and sirens to respond to a call for service regarding "a silent alarm at a nearby block." As he did so, he noticed Andrew, "an unknown black male observe [his] marked uniform presence and flee on foot." The officer noted that Andrew was "holding his left side" which the officer believed to be "a characteristic of an armed person." The officer abandoned the call for service that he had been responding to and instead pursued Andrew, an unknown individual, alone, on foot. Andrew entered a residential home from the back porch and locked the door behind him. The officer, "[b]elieving that he might be armed, and fearing that the house he entered might not have been his, and also fearing that any evidence or contraband/weapons he may have on him would be destroyed/concealed," "forced entry into the house, damaging the door in the process."[104]

---

104 It is not clear that the officer had cause to enter the home without a warrant. *See Brigham City, Utah v. Stuart*, 547 U.S. 398, 403 (2006) (internal quotation marks omitted) ("It is a basic principle of Fourth Amendment law that searches and seizures inside a home without a warrant are presumptively unreasonable."). While officers in "hot pursuit" of a fleeing suspect are granted an exigency exception to the general principle prohibiting a search of a home without a warrant, it is not clear that this qualifies as a "hot pursuit" where the officer

If Andrew *had* been armed, the officer's choice of tactics—forcing entry without backup—could have resulted in the officer being shot. Andrew ran to the front door where the officer caught up to him and attempted to make an arrest—the officer did not specify the crime for which he was attempting to make the arrest. While the two were "struggl[ing]" at the front door, a pit bull charged at them from inside the house. The officer withdrew his service weapon "fearing" that he would "have to shoot the dog." Eventually, to avoid the dog, the officer let Andrew run out the front door and continued to pursue on foot. The officer then decided to tase Andrew because he believed Andrew "was involved in illegal activity," suspected he "had entered an unknown house," "might be armed," and "had already resisted all attempts to apprehend him." The officer tased Andrew two times, as the first deployment was not effective. After taking him into custody, the officer discovered that Andrew was not armed, had no contraband, and was eventually determined, at a later, unknown time, to have an open warrant. The reason for the officer's force listed in his use of force report was that the "suspect refused to comply."

This officer repeatedly used unsafe tactics that endangered himself, the individual he pursued, and a homeowner, and damaged a homeowner's property. He chose to engage in a foot pursuit in an allegedly violent area, alone, while believing the person he was pursuing to be armed. There is no indication in the report that he called for backup or considered discontinuing the pursuit at any time. He forced entry into an unknown home, where the person he was pursuing was inside and at a tactical advantage to the officer. If Andrew had actually been armed, as the officer suspected he was, the officer could have been shot. The officer damaged a home by breaking the door, potentially increasing the danger to the homeowner he was trying to protect, and pointing his firearm at the homeowner's dog while struggling with a man, creating a risk of harm to the homeowner's property. The officer's use of force against Andrew was highly questionable, if not clearly unreasonable, particularly given the officer's own training on the likelihood that the individual was armed.

Like the officers in the above accounts, officers frequently cite factors learned in BPD's training on "Characteristics of an Armed Person" such as "grabbing one's waistband" or "wearing loose clothing." Officers appear to use these factors to justify the force they use during or following pursuits, asserting that they believe individuals who exhibit any one of these factors to be armed. BPD provides their training on "Characteristics of an Armed Person" to teach officers to identify when a person may be armed, which may provide reasonable suspicion for a stop. BPD training instructors warn students that there may be false positives, and informed us that they instruct students that *eighty percent*

---

had insufficient basis to believe the man had committed a specific crime, or that any other exigency existed here permitting the officer to enter the home. *See id.*

of individuals who show characteristics of an armed person—such as wearing loose or baggy clothing, or grabbing their waistbands while running—will *not* be armed.[105] Despite purportedly being trained on false positives, BPD officers nevertheless frequently engage in foot pursuits and use force on individuals based solely on factors such as "wearing loose clothing." We found that this results, at times, in the use of excessive force.

Some of the incidents we reviewed involved officers shooting at individuals who were fleeing from them and who officers suspected were armed. In a number of cases involving BPD officers' uses of deadly force, it was not clear that the individuals officers shot at had actually threatened the officer or others with serious or deadly harm. Without an immediate threat, simply being in possession of a firearm does not justify using deadly force. *Tennessee v. Garner*, 471 U.S. 1, 11 (1985); *Cooper v. Sheehan*, 735 F.3d 153, 159 (4th Cir. 2013) ("[T]he mere possession of a firearm by a suspect is not enough to permit the use of deadly force. Thus, an officer does not possess the unfettered authority to shoot a member of the public simply because that person is carrying a weapon. Instead, deadly force may only be used by a police officer when, based on a reasonable assessment, the officer or another person is threatened with the weapon.").

However, because the investigations of these incidents were so incomplete, as further explained below in section II(C)(5), it is difficult to determine based on the information provided in BPD's investigative files whether officers faced any immediate threat before firing. For example, in a 2013 case, four officers traveling in two unmarked vehicles pursued a suspect after they heard gunshots. The suspect allegedly raised a firearm while running, then ran through the yard of a residence, though the officers' statements regarding the suspect's actions are inconsistent. The officers parked their vehicles and gave chase on foot. At some point during the foot pursuit, the suspect may have tossed his gun (one witnessing officer stated in his interview that the suspect tossed his gun when he "jumped on" a bush before the officer heard the next gunshot) which struck the suspect. When asked whether the potential gun toss occurred before or after he was shot, he stated he had not seen the actual gun toss. Another officer found a gun near a bush several feet from where the suspect lay after being shot. The interviewers did not thoroughly examine whether the potential gun toss occurred before or after the officer shot at the suspect. The four officers involved in this case were interviewed for only 5, 8, 8, and 14, minutes.

---

105 It is highly unlikely that only eighty percent of individuals who are wearing loose or baggy clothing are unarmed. Nevertheless, this training gave officers clear notice that even a person who is displaying some of the characteristics of an armed person is most likely to be unarmed. BPD officers also appear to be relying too heavily on only a single characteristic of an armed person, rather than a set of characteristics that, when combined, together indicate that a person is armed.

During these cursory interviews, the interviewers made no efforts to probe the basis for the officer's initial statement that the suspect had tossed his gun, and did not question the other officers about whether and when the potential gun toss occurred.

Officers should have policy guidance and training on when and how to safely engage in foot pursuits, given the frequency with which officers conduct them in Baltimore, and the risks involved for both officers and the public. It is critical that BPD provide officers with policy guidance on how to assess whether circumstances warrant engaging in a foot pursuit, and sufficient training on how to conduct these pursuits safely, without needlessly endangering themselves, suspects, and the public.

ii. BPD's Discharges of Firearms at Moving Vehicles Are Highly Dangerous, Ineffective, and May Be Constitutionally Impermissible

BPD officers shot at moving vehicles in eight cases during the time period we reviewed. Shooting at a vehicle that is fleeing away from officers is unreasonable except in rare circumstances. *See Waterman v. Batton*, 393 F.3d at 482 ("[O]nce Waterman's vehicle passed the officers, the threat to their safety was eliminated and thus could not justify the subsequent shots."); *cf. Plumhoff v. Rickard*, 134 S. Ct. 2012, 2021 (2014) (finding officers' use of deadly force against fleeing suspect reasonable where suspect engaged in "outrageously reckless driving," leading officers on a chase that exceeded 100 miles per hour and passing more than two dozen vehicles, several of which were forced to alter course). In some of these cases, although the factual descriptions were incomplete, it appeared officers may have fired shots at individuals in moving vehicles as the vehicle was fleeing away from them. At that point, the vehicle itself no longer posed a serious threat to the officers, and if it posed a threat to others, shooting at it likely increased the threat, rather than eliminating it. *See* Police Exec. Research Forum, *Guiding Principles on Use of Force* 44 (Mar. 2016) ("Shooting at vehicles must be prohibited. . . . unless someone in the vehicle is using or threatening deadly force by means other than the vehicle itself."); IACP Nat'l Law Enforcement Pol. Ctr., *Use of Force Concepts & Issues Paper* 5 (Rev. Feb. 2006). The investigations of these incidents often left critical questions unanswered, however, making it difficult to determine whether the officers faced an immediate threat of serious harm before discharging their weapons. Nevertheless, supervisors and investigators generally approved officers' decisions to fire shots at moving vehicles.

Additionally, shooting at a moving vehicle is a highly dangerous tactic and an ineffective way to stop the vehicle. Using firearms against a moving vehicle often creates greater risks than it eliminates. If a driver is shot while a vehicle is in motion, the vehicle itself may become out of control and a danger, to officers and innocent bystanders in its path, rather than coming to a stop. Further, a moving vehicle is a difficult target to shoot with accuracy; shots fired may miss the intended target and hit bystanders or passengers in the vehicle. Thus, shooting at a moving vehicle should be permissible in only extreme circumstances. Since 2006, the IACP's model policy on Use of Force has accounted for these risks, requiring:

> Firearms shall not be discharged at a moving vehicle unless a person in the vehicle is immediately threatening the officer or another person with deadly force by means other than the vehicle. The moving vehicle itself shall not presumptively constitute a threat that justifies an officer's use of deadly force. An officer threatened by an oncoming vehicle shall move out of its path instead of discharging a firearm at it or any of its occupants.

Two illustrative incidents identify some of our concerns with BPD's use of firearms on fleeing vehicles, although we make no finding on whether the force used in either of these incidents was unreasonable. In one 2013 incident, an investigation into a possible drug transaction ended with an officer firing seven shots at the front, side and rear of a vehicle as it drove away. One of three officers on the scene observed what he suspected was a drug transaction in progress in a car parked near a gas pump and signaled to the other two officers to investigate. One officer approached to the driver's side door of the vehicle and the other to the passenger side. The officer at the driver's side, reportedly fearing the driver was reaching for a weapon, opened the driver's side door and reached inside while the car was still running; he does not appear to have ordered the driver to turn the engine off. Rather than reaching for a weapon, the driver had put the car into drive. With the officer's torso inside the vehicle, the driver hit the gas and the car sped forward. The officer, becoming caught halfway into the car, was dragged by the car. He reached for his weapon and fired one shot toward the driver of the car, missing both the driver and the officer standing on the other side of the vehicle. The officer's gunshot reportedly caused the driver to jerk the car, dislodging the officer from the car. The vehicle turned to exit the parking lot, driving towards the third officer who had observed the incident. According to BPD's documents, the third officer stepped out of the way of the oncoming vehicle and then fired seven rounds, two of which hit the front windshield, and five of which hit the right side passenger windows, and rear passenger door, shattering the rear windshield and hitting the rear roof of the car. The officer admitted—during a brief, 15 minute interview BPD investigators conducted 258 days after the incident—that he shot at the vehicle as it was fleeing away from him. It appeared he shot at the vehicle, which had fled the wrong way down a one-way street, to disable it, though BPD officers conducting his interview did not clarify this point. BPD determined all force in this incident to be reasonable.

In another incident from 2013, two officers were on foot, directing traffic near a crowded nightclub. A civilian car traveling the wrong direction struck the two officers from behind, knocking them to the pavement. The car then started to leave the scene. One of the two officers fired eight shots at the vehicle as it was fleeing away from him. In this case, investigators determined the discharges to be inappropriate. In our review, we observed additional incidents of firearms discharges at moving vehicles which, even if they were not unreasonable, endangered members of the public.

The disparate treatment of the officers in these two incidents may have resulted from the lack of clear policy guidance on when officers might be justified in shooting at moving vehicles. The Department's 2001 "Use of Deadly Force Guidelines" instruct officers that they "may not shoot at vehicles moving away from them unless the vehicle turns around and attempts to injure them or someone else and adequate cover is not available." However, Guidelines function differently from policies—they are not binding on officers. The prohibition on shooting at vehicles moving away from officers was not made clear in policy until May 2016. The Department now prohibits shooting at moving vehicles unless confronted with a deadly threat, other than the vehicle itself. This new policy prohibiting shooting at moving vehicles, regardless of whether they are fleeing, is a positive step forward.

5. BPD's Deficient Policies, Training, Crisis Intervention Program, and Lack of Oversight Underlie The Pattern Or Practice Of Excessive Force and Violations of the Americans With Disabilities Act

BPD's deficient policies, training, crisis intervention program, and failures in oversight over force incidents underlie the pattern or practice of unconstitutional force we observed. It is the Department's responsibility to articulate policies that provide sufficient guidance, both in quality and content, to officers on when and how it is appropriate and lawful to use force against members of the public. BPD's policies fail to provide this guidance. It is also the Department's responsibility to train officers to ensure they understand how the Department's policies are to be operationalized, and to provide officers with skills they need to safely and constitutionally resolve the broad spectrum of incidents they encounter on the street while minimizing the need to resort to force. The Department has failed to provide such training. The Department is likewise charged with investigating incidents of force to ensure they comply with its policies and the law, and where they do not, remedying officers' conduct through retraining and discipline, as appropriate. The Department has failed to exercise proper oversight over incidents of force and address deficiencies when they occurred, allowing officers to continue using unreasonable force and unsafe tactics. In addition, BPD fails to adequately prepare officers for their interactions with individuals with disabilities or in crisis, and to partner effectively with other social service providers in these incidents. Thus, the responsibility for the pattern or practice of unconstitutional force we observed lies with the Department as an agency.

a. BPD's Deficient Policies Have Contributed To and Permitted BPD's Pattern or Practice of Excessive Force

Deficiencies in BPD's policies regarding the use, reporting, and investigation of force have contributed to officers' systemic use of excessive force. Overall, BPD's policies regarding when and how to use force: (1) are missing critical elements; (2) are scattered across multiple documents, making it difficult for officers to synthesize their guidance; (3) included elements that were not enforced; and (4) are sometimes inaccessible to some officers. These policies fail to provide officers with clear and consistent guidance that officers need to safely and constitutionally conduct their law enforcement activities. BPD issued revisions to its policies governing officers' uses of force on July 1, 2016. The policies appear to have improved in some respects and the Department is to be commended for its initiative and efforts. However, the recent updates may require additional amendments to correct the patterns or practices of unconstitutional force our investigation uncovered.

BPD's policies on use of force, and on use of specific weapons were, until very recently, missing critical elements. BPD implemented its first policy governing officers' use of batons in 2016. The Department's first policy governing the use of oleoresin capsicum, or "OC" spray was implemented in 2015. Despite the previous lack of policy guidance on the use of these weapons, the Department had issued these weapons to its officers for decades. It is a fundamental responsibility of the Department to provide controlling guidance to officers regarding when they are permitted to use the weapons the Department has supplied them. Previously, officers' use of these weapons was governed only by "Training Guidelines," but these training guidelines did not establish clear standards for officer conduct.

While the Department implemented a policy on Electronically Conducted Weapons, or tasers, in 2007, this policy failed to provide officers with necessary guidance on when it would be appropriate to use a taser. Training Guidelines regarding tasers, which were issued in 2010, similarly failed to provide any restrictions on officers' use of these weapons. Instead, both the policy and Guidelines simply provided officers with descriptions of the various modes that the weapon may be used in, without providing proper limitations on those uses. Neither the policy nor the training guidelines were updated when the Department of Justice's Office of Community Oriented Policing Services, in conjunction with the Police Executive Research Forum, released ECW Guidelines in

March 2011, which recommended restrictions such as not using a taser more than three times on a particular individual.

Importantly, until its 2016 policy update, BPD did not require a number of types of force by BPD officers to be reported. This included takedowns, punches, control holds and pain compliance techniques, unless a subject complained of pain, or injury resulted. Our review of BPD's reports suggests that, in practice, force involving an officer's hands was generally only reported if the subject sustained injuries requiring medical attention. Our review of BPD's force cases, interviews with community members in Baltimore, as well as interviews with officers, demonstrated that a significant volume of force by BPD officers involves officers using their hands against individuals in close encounters—types of force that BPD did not require officers to report until very recently. Force that is not documented cannot be managed or monitored. In our interviews with community members, many members of the public described experiences in which officers used force such as takedowns and control techniques without sufficient justification. These incidents have led to the deep frustration that some members of the public feel towards BPD.

Until July 2016, BPD policies on force failed to encourage any de-escalation strategies. It is critical that officers be provided guidance not only on when and how force may be used, but also that they be encouraged to use tactics that minimize the need for force. Using force against members of the public is not only an intrusion to the subject of force, it also creates risks for officers entangled in these encounters by heightening tensions and creating situations in which officers may also, in turn, be injured. BPD's new policies have taken some steps to incorporate de-escalation principles, but significant work remains to ensure that de-escalation strategies are understood and utilized throughout the Department. Additionally, although BPD implemented a policy governing contacts with youth in June 2015, the policy fails to provide any guidance on the unique qualities of youth behavior and development or prescribe specific techniques for officers' approach and interactions with youth.

Second, in addition to missing critical elements, BPD's guidance on when and how to use force, as well as to report, investigate, and review uses of force is scattered throughout many policies, training guidelines, and their various updates. For example, the rules governing officers' uses of their service weapons are contained in at least four separate policies and a "Training Guideline" on the use of deadly force, rather than a single, cohesive policy. Additionally, when the Department updates a policy, each update is written in a new and separate document. One policy can have many updates, and thus officers are expected to keep track of many different documents simply to understand a single policy. To understand all of the applicable policies governing force, officers must be aware of and synthesize dozens of documents. There is no cohesive, comprehensive guidance for officers that is digestible and workable. Having this critical guidance scattered throughout dozens of disparate documents makes it difficult to understand and operationalize what guidance the Department does provide its officers about use of force. In interviews, officers expressed concern that policies were simply implemented and distributed without sufficient guidance regarding the meaning of provisions. A number of officers we spoke with expressed confusion about the contents of recently updated policies, including the Department's new use of force policy.

Third, until recently, officers had insufficient access to Departmental policies. Officers received a policy manual in the Academy upon joining the Department, but later updates to policies were not distributed in a manner that ensured officers received and reviewed the updated policy. Officers receive policy updates through their email, which many officers do not frequently check or have access to because Department computers in the precincts are old, outdated, and frequently break down. Officers were not required to sign off on whether they had received policy updates and the Department had no tracking mechanisms in place to ensure that all officers had received, much less understood, policy updates. To its credit, the Department has realized that this is a significant problem, and has purchased a new software application to track the distribution of new and updated policies and proficiency testing of officers on the new or updated policies, but that application had not yet been rolled out by June 2016.

Finally, the Department does not uniformly and consistently enforce its policies. For example, a 1999 policy on reviewing and investigating firearm discharges that was in effect until 2012 included a requirement that each discharge be reviewed by an "ad hoc board" consisting of a number of chiefs and other personnel appointed by the Commissioner. To our knowledge, based on the documents we reviewed, such a review board was never constituted under this policy during the period of our review. Instead, under former Commissioner Batts, a new policy regarding a Use of Force Review Board was implemented in 2014, under which a number of reviews were conducted. As we describe in more detail in Section III(A) below, the Department's failure to consistently enforce its policies has contributed to the pattern or practice of excessive force that we found.

These deficiencies in policy guidance, organization, distribution, and enforcement contribute to the pattern or practice of unconstitutional force we observed.

b. BPD's Training On Force Is Severely Lacking, Leading To Officers' Systemic Constitutional Violations

BPD officers are trained in the Academy when they initially join the Department, and then through mandatory annual in-service training. Training at both levels—at the Academy and through in-service—is lacking. As described in more detail in Section III(A)(1) below, BPD's training generally fails to provide officers with sufficient instruction on how to operationalize policies. It lacks the integrated, scenario-based training that equips officers with the tactical skills necessary to conduct law enforcement activities in a safe and constitutional manner, including strategies that decrease the need for force.

BPD's Defensive Tactics training teaches officers an erroneous legal standard for excessive force. It separates excessive force into (1) "perceived" excessive force; (2) "intentional" excessive force; and (3) "unintentional" excessive force. This separation between "perceived," "intentional" and "unintentional" excessive force has no place under well-established Fourth Amendment standards governing excessive force. An officer's subjective intent is irrelevant for Fourth Amendment purposes. *Graham*, 490 U.S. 386, 397 (1989) ("the reasonableness inquiry in an excessive force case is an objective one: the question is whether the officers' actions are objectively reasonable in light of the facts and circumstances confronting them, without regard to their underlying intent or motivation") (internal quotations and citations omitted). Indeed, the Supreme Court explicitly rejected the notion that excessive force required intent or malice decades ago, declaring that "[a]n officer's evil intentions will not make a Fourth Amendment violation out of an objectively reasonable use of force; nor will an officer's good intentions make an objectively unreasonable use of force constitutional." *Id.* According to BPD's Defensive Tactics training, the "appropriate" consequence for "unintentional" excessive force, a category of force that does not exist in the legal landscape, is "remedial training"—no other consequence is identified. This training is a disservice to officers, because it is inconsistent with how courts will consider their use of force. The category of "perceived" excessive force is also problematic because it appears to discredit the complainant—whether the complainant is another officer or a community member.

BPD's training on "Characteristics of an Armed Person" also appears to be ineffective. While instructors teach students that eighty percent of individuals who show characteristics of an armed person—such as wearing loose or baggy clothing, or grabbing their waistbands while running—will *not* be armed, this issue of false positives does not appear to be taught in an effective manner. No scenarios involving false positives are employed in the training that would allow officers to internalize and retain this lesson. Additionally, it is critical to learn how to safely and constitutionally approach and investigate an individual who may be armed. In a training on the same subject, sponsored by the Department of Justice and the IACP and held at BPD's training center for law enforcement agencies throughout the region, the instructor spent a significant amount of time refreshing students' knowledge of Fourth Amendment law and principles. In that training, the instructor repeatedly reinforced throughout the course that a person who displays one of these characteristics is not necessarily armed; each characteristic should be one factor in an officer's analysis. It does not appear that BPD's own training on "Characteristics of an Armed Person" provides officers with such critical guidance.

Additionally, until recently, BPD had no comprehensive training on de-escalation strategies to guide officers on how to resolve incidents without resorting to force. It created a short course on de-escalation in 2015, a positive step forward. However, given the novelty of de-escalation tactics within BPD's curriculum, it is important that leadership within the Department make clear to officers that this skill-set is critical to keeping officers, as well as community members, safe. The Department must ensure that de-escalation is sufficiently emphasized and integrated into all of its courses involving force such that officers understand it is a critical tool for resolving incidents.

Similarly, officers have been provided with little to no training on tactics and techniques for interacting with youth, including on how to engage with juvenile witnesses or victims. Because their developmental state affects the manner in which adolescents comprehend, communicate, and behave, BPD officers must be trained on these unique realities and equipped with skills and techniques to account for them when interacting with youth.

The Department provided a brief training, running from May through June of 2016 for officers on its new use of force policy and 26 other policies the Department reviewed and updated. We were able to attend one of the first sessions of the training and hear from consultants about a later session. Our observations based on the first session we attended gave us serious initial concerns about the adequacy of the training, but it appears the training substantially improved with time. We applaud the Department's desire to issue new guidance and training to its officers, but we have some concerns about the adequacy of the training being provided, given the ambitious scope of what the Department intends to cover. It is clear to us, however, that the Department is committed to improving the guidance it provides to officers on use of force, and we look forward to working with the Department to make sure it is successful in its efforts.

c. BPD's Lack of Oversight Of Officers' Uses of Force Has Contributed to the Pattern of Excessive Force

As a whole, BPD fails to exercise oversight of its officers' uses of force. Of the 2,818 force incidents that BPD recorded in the nearly six-year period we reviewed, BPD investigated only ten incidents for excessive force based on concerns identified through its internal review. Of these ten incidents, it found only one use of force to be excessive. During the same period, twenty-five officers were sued four or more times in cases alleging violations relating to use of force, stops, searches, arrests, or discriminatory policing. The few incidents that the Department internally noted as problematic are also striking considering the many incidents we determined to be unconstitutional.

Like that of many departments, BPD policy sets out different investigative requirements for different levels of force that officers use. BPD officers' use of force is investigated through one of two routes. First, for most incidents of force other than shootings, officers notify their supervising sergeant after using force. The sergeant travels to the site where force was used, and conducts an investigation at the scene. The chain of command then reviews the sergeant's investigation and either returns it for further investigation or makes a decision on whether the officer's force was reasonable. The process for these investigations is outlined in a policy that has been in place since 2003; it remained in place until July 2016. Until November 2014, all uses of force other than shootings were to be investigated in this manner by an officer's chain of command. For ease of reference, we refer to these as "chain of command investigations."

In these chain of command investigations, if BPD investigators or reviewers believed that a use of force may have been unreasonable or out of policy, in order to investigate that concern, a supervisor in the chain of command would have to file an internal complaint of excessive force with Internal Affairs. Internal Affairs would then also separately investigate the complaint through its processes. We found that, in practice, internal complaints were exceedingly rare—the data we reviewed indicated only ten such complaints had been made during the period of our review. Indeed, one sergeant we spoke with about his force investigations of officers under his command indicated that he would not feel comfortable filing a complaint with Internal Affairs if he suspected an officer under his supervision had used unnecessary or unreasonable force. Instead, he would call his chain of command and inform them of the situation, leaving it to them to make the decision of whether to file a complaint about the officer for Internal Affairs to investigate.

The second route that an administrative investigation of force may take is reserved for officers' use of deadly force. The process for investigating these deadly force cases changed a number of times during the period of force incidents we reviewed. From the beginning of our period of review, in 2010 until early 2014, this second route was reserved for officer-involved shootings, which were investigated by officers in BPD's Homicide Unit. In January 2014, BPD instituted a specialized "Force Investigation Team" (FIT) to investigate shootings and other uses of force that have "the potential to cause serious physical injury or death." The FIT functioned only until July 31, 2015, when it was replaced as an interim measure by the Homicide unit in 2015, and then by a Special Investigation Response Team (SIRT) in September of 2015. The SIRT has the same jurisdiction as the former FIT and currently investigates shootings as well as other serious use of force cases. For ease of reference, we refer to these as "deadly force investigations."

Based on our review of BPD's force investigations and our interviews with BPD officers and sergeants, it appears that the chain of command fails to thoroughly and objectively evaluate officers' uses of force. BPD's investigative files of force incidents are missing critical elements necessary to allow the chain of command to understand and adjudicate the force incidents. This is perhaps unsurprising, because, until this year, BPD provided no training whatsoever for sergeants on how to investigate their officers' uses of force, or for lieutenants, captains or majors, regarding their responsibilities and obligations in reviewing force investigations. Similarly, BPD also fails to thoroughly and objectively investigate officers' uses of deadly force. BPD's deadly force investigations likewise lack critical information necessary to evaluate the force used and reflect bias on the part of investigators. These investigations are also subject to unreasonable delays, to the detriment of both officers and the community.

i. BPD's Investigations of Less-Lethal Force Cases are Missing Critical Elements that are Necessary to Evaluate the Propriety of the Force Used

In BPD's chain of command investigations, critical information that is necessary to investigate force incidents is routinely missing. Investigators routinely fail to interview any civilian witnesses, witnessing officers, the involved officer, and the person against whom force was used. In many cases, there are no witnesses—civilian or officer— interviewed even though witnesses were present on the scene. For example, in one 2014 narcotics arrest at a public housing complex during which a taser was deployed, there were reportedly 20 to 30 civilian witnesses gathered at the site of the arrest, and the officer felt it necessary to call in additional units for backup to deal with the crowd. However, the force report did not include a single civilian witness statement. Although the report states that "[t]here were no civilian witness[es] who wished to provide a statement," there is no indication of the efforts the officers made in attempting to obtain statements from witnesses.

From our interviews, it appears that some people may refuse to speak with officers because of the distrust they have of the police. While BPD's policy on use of force reporting requires that "notations of a neighborhood canvass for witnesses must be included," many other reports we reviewed did not include such a notation. Even in the instances where it appeared an investigator spoke with a civilian who had witnessed the incident, investigators did not record the civilian's statement or provide the civilian's account in their own words. Instead, the investigator summarized the civilian's statement for the investigative file. If the investigator misses relevant information, or misunderstands a civilian's statement in any way, or if the investigator biases the civilian's statement in any way—whether intentionally or not—this cannot be remedied by the chain of command's review.

We also found that, in cases where a civilian's account appeared to be inconsistent with information provided by an officer, investigators appeared to summarily dismiss the civilian's account or credit officers' accounts over civilians' without sufficient investigation. For example, in a 2014 incident, a sergeant responded as back-up to assist two plainclothes officers with an arrest for CDS possession. He observed them "engaged in an ongoing struggle in the street" when he arrived on the scene. Even though the sergeant was on the scene in a supervisory role when the use of force was taking place, he also investigated the officers' force. When attempting to locate witnesses, he reported "several citizens in the block" stated, "They didn't have to beat him like that," "Another case of police brutality," "They picked that man up and dumped him on his head," and "Somebody has it on video. It will be on youtube tomorrow," though he was unable to gain contact information for the person with video. Shortly after the incident, a woman formally complained to the Department about the incident, and the same sergeant responded to address her complaint. Despite these statements from witnesses, the sergeant dismissed the five complaints of the force used and determined "[b]ased on the facts of this incident, witness interviews, and reviews of CCTV footage" that the officers had used appropriate force.[106] In addition to our concerns about how the different witness and officer accounts were reconciled in this investigation, this is one of a number of cases we saw where sergeants who were involved in an incident where force was used investigated that incident. The sergeant's supervision of the use of force undermines the integrity of his investigation of the force as well as the individuals' complaints of the incident—he lacked the independence and objectivity to investigate either the force or the complaints.

Officers' statements, when they were provided, were only in written form, often lacked details of the force used and why it was necessary, and used vague and boilerplate language, preventing reviewers from understanding the nature of the threat that officers faced and the nature of the force that officers used. Often, the only documented basis for using force was that the subjects were "resisting," with no detail about which actions taken by the suspect while he or she "resisted" necessitated force by the officer. Descriptions of the force itself were likewise often vague. In some cases where a taser was used, officers re-

---

106 The sergeant requested video from "Citiwatch," but the video was "on pan mode during the entire incident." He reported that the parts which "capture the incident are grainy, but gave no indication that unnecessary force was used." The video was not produced to us with the investigative file.

ported they used the taser on an individual "a few" or "several" times or until he or she "complied" or "became subdued," rather than specifying the number of times that they deployed their taser. The specific number of times that a taser is deployed is critical to assessing the reasonableness of its use under the circumstances and must be reported. Similarly, in almost all instances in which officers employed a takedown technique, the officers did not specify the type of technique used, such as a straight arm bar, joint manipulation, or pressure points. Without knowing the specific actions that officers took, it is difficult to evaluate whether they acted reasonably under the circumstances. For example, during a 2010 incident, three plainclothes officers approached two men, who they believed were involved in distributing narcotics, to arrest them. Reportedly, as the officers approached, one of the two men punched one of the officers and ran. Two of the officers gave chase. When they caught up with the individual, the involved officers reported that the individual began to "violently resist" and "during the struggle," was reportedly "tackled to the ground several times," during the course of which the suspect "struck his head against a fence." According to the investigating sergeant's report, the suspect suffered head injuries in this altercation requiring 37 staples. It is difficult to assess whether the officers' force here was reasonable without more information about how the suspect resisted the officers and what techniques the officers used on the suspect that caused a head injury requiring 37 staples. The suspect in this case was not interviewed, depriving BPD of critical information to assess the incident. In their review of this incident, the chain of command approved the force without asking for any additional information, despite the vagueness of the officers' accounts. This was the case in many of the incidents we reviewed.

Officers' written statements, when any were provided, were also often nearly identical—facially lacking in independence. The officers' accounts appeared to have been copied after they agreed upon a single account of the incident. Indeed, because of this, officers' accounts sometimes referred to themselves in the third person because the account had been electronically copied into the force report. We also found that the language investigators used in their reports indicated a lack of objectivity, such as a description that officers "were forced to use" a taser, baton, OC spray, or other weapon. This language does more than simply state the facts, and indicates bias in favor of the involved officers.

We also found that inconsistencies between officers' statements were not routinely reconciled or addressed. In one incident, in which a sergeant pointed out inconsistencies between officers' accounts, it appears the chain of command took issue with the sergeant's investigation and report that highlighted the inconsistencies. In a 2011 incident, an investigating sergeant, to his credit, explicitly reported that two officers' "versions of events differ[ed]" regarding whether a juvenile was sprayed with OC spray before or after he was handcuffed—a significant fact that could affect the reasonableness of the force used, and whether it had been in or out of policy. *See Tracy v. Freshwater*, 623 F.3d 90, 98–99 (2d Cir. 2010) (jury could find officer's application of pepper spray to be unreasonable where plaintiff claimed he was handcuffed and not resisting); *Henderson v. Munn*, 439 F.3d 497, 502–03 (8th Cir. 2006) (officer not entitled to qualified immunity at summary judgment where jury could find that he had applied pepper spray to non-resisting plaintiff's face while plaintiff was lying on his stomach and handcuffed with his hands behind his back); *Vinyard v. Wilson*, 311 F.3d 1340, 1347–49 (11th Cir. 2002) (officer not entitled to summary judgment where he had pulled over and applied pepper spray while arrestee was yelling and arrestee had been arrested for minor offenses, was handcuffed and secured in backseat of police car, posed no threat to the officer or herself, and there was a partition separating her from the officer). According to the sergeant's report, when he realized that the officers' reports varied on this point, he called them both into his office to "question them, about what had happened." The witnessing officer stated that "his administrative report was correct" and submitted it. The officer who used OC spray "with-drew his administrative report, stating he was getting worried about how this investigation was progressing and stated that he wanted to talk to the FOP prior to submitting his administrative report." The sergeant reported these facts—that the officers reported inconsistently about whether force was used on a handcuffed person, and that the involved officer withdrew his report—to his chain of command. He submitted his investigation for approval. A lieutenant colonel responded, "NOT APPROVED; RETURNED FOR CORRECTIONS," and stated, "YOU NEED TO SEE ME IMMEDIATELY REGARDING THIS SUMMARY!" There is no documentation of the conversation between the sergeant and the lieutenant colonel. In the final report produced to us, the second page of the witnessing officer's report is missing; the document specifically notes that it is two pages long, yet only the first page is provided. The first page of the witnessing officer's report simply states the facts about the beginning of the incident and provides no information about the force that was used and whether it was used after the juvenile was handcuffed. Ultimately, it appears the sergeant identified an inconsistency in this case, and the chain of command not only refused to address it, but may have attempted to cover up the report that identified potentially problematic officer conduct.

Witnesses' accounts, both officers' and civilians', are important not only for determining whether an officer's use of force was within policy, but also in assessing whether the officer's tactics were appropriate, and whether there are any issues on which the officer would benefit from additional training, mentoring, or guidance. The lack of specifics in these statements prevents supervisors from improving officers' performance and preventing future misconduct. One sergeant informed us during an interview that judging an officer's tactics is simply not part of a use of force investigation; he did not deem it to be his job to "second-guess" an officer's tactics. This is a failure in supervision—it is a sergeant's job to mentor officers in areas where they may benefit from additional guidance. The sergeant's statement here reflects a lack of understanding of the role of a supervisor, and indicates a Departmental failure to train sergeants on how to be effective supervisors.

Our investigation also found that critical evidence was often missing from the chain of command force investigations. We did not see a single chain of command investigation in which photographs of the subject's injuries were provided. These photographs are taken by Crime Lab technicians, but, as a matter of protocol, they are not kept with the investigative file. Among the over eight hundred chain of command investigative files we reviewed, we did not see any indication that a lieutenant or major had requested to see photographs of the subject's injuries in any case. Similarly, taser downloads verifying the number of times that officers deployed their tasers were not included in investigative files, thereby preventing the chain of command from confirming the accuracy of officers' reports. These deficiencies in chain of command investigations prevent supervisors from being able to exercise real oversight over officers' uses of force. Without details of incidents provided by civilian witnesses, involved and witnessing officers, and evidence such as taser downloads or photographs of injuries, officers' use of force cannot be critically examined.

Finally, we found evidence that serious incidents involving use of force by officers went entirely unreported. Indeed, because it was not required to be reported by policy, much of the force used by officers with their hands was not reported, even when it—and not the force reported—was the source of injuries to officers. In the 2011 incident involving a juvenile above at [page 306], for example, the sergeant reported that the officers "fought" with the juvenile. The involved officer was transported to a hospital and treated for abrasions and bruises to his knee. His knee injuries were severe enough that he was unable to work for a number of days. However, the use of force report was created to report on the officers' use of OC spray. An injury report alleges the juvenile kicked the officer in the knee but the use of force report does not provide any specific information about the fight between the officers and the juvenile that caused the officer's injury, other than that the youth was making threatening statements, and "kicking" and being "combative" while officers were attempting to handcuff him. It does not include any details about the officers' use of their hands during the fight. These failures in exercising oversight of officers' use of force are attributable in part to BPD's prior deficient policy on reporting use of force. The policy on reporting use of force, through multiple provisions, allowed investigators and reviewers to ignore allegations of excessive force. It stated that "[w]hen allegations of excessive force arise[]," investigating sergeants were to inform the complainants of the "the reporting requirements for complaints of excessive force" and provide the complainants with the telephone number and address of the Internal Affairs Division. The policy did not require an investigating sergeant to address the complaint him- or herself in any way or to ensure that Internal Affairs was notified of the complaint. These policy failures allowed significant force, and allegations of excessive force, to go entirely uninvestigated.

ii. BPD's Deadly Force Investigations Lack Critical Analysis and Information that is Necessary to Evaluate the Threat Faced and Force Used

Like its chain of command investigations, BPD's investigations of officers' use of deadly force, including officer-involved shootings, lack critical information needed to evaluate the propriety of the force, reflect a bias in favor of involved officers, and include unreasonable delays. This is concerning, as "[t]he intrusiveness of a seizure by means of deadly force is unmatched. The suspect's fundamental interest in his own life need not be elaborated upon. The use of deadly force also frustrates the interest of the individual, and of society, in judicial determination of guilt and punishment." *Garner*, 471 U.S. at 9. Officers' uses of deadly force must be critically examined to ensure that they conform with the Department's policies and law. Even when the use of deadly force is justified, much can be learned by critically examining incidents to improve tactics and lessen the need to use such force.

In our investigation, we requested investigative files for all deadly force incidents, including all officer-involved shootings, between January 1, 2010 and May 1, 2016. Troublingly, BPD informed us that they could not locate the investigative files for twenty officer-involved shootings that occurred in that timeframe, and could provide no explanation for their absence. These included lethal shootings of members of the public, including one lethal shooting, as well as firearms discharges against animals and unintentional discharges. Failing to maintain files of such high risk incidents is a serious omission, inhibiting effective oversight and eroding public confidence that BPD takes seriously its responsibility to oversee its own use of force.

Our review of BPD deadly force investigations revealed many of the same problems that were present in the chain of command investigations. Transcripts of interviews were routinely excluded, and it appears that they were not created in many cases. Inconsistencies between witness accounts, officer statements, and physical evidence were frequently not investigated. Moreover, documents and evidence that one would expect to see in an administrative investigation of an officer-involved shooting, such as crime scene logs, photographs of the subject or the scene, and crime lab reports, were frequently missing from the investigative files we reviewed. As in the chain of command investigations, we saw evidence that involved officers conferred with other involved and witnessing officers about the incident before speaking with investigators. Investigators also failed to question officers about their conduct before the shooting, to ascertain—even if the shooting was lawful—what tactical, training or other issues could be identified.

We also found that significant delays in BPD's deadly force investigations diminished the integrity of the investigations. As a matter of practice, BPD investigators do not interview officers who discharge their weapons until after the State's Attorney's Office issues a letter declining to prosecute the officer for any potential criminal act. Often, the State's Attorney's Office takes many months, and in a number of cases, over a year, to determine whether to prosecute, and, if not, to issue a declination letter. In one extreme case, for a shooting that occurred on August 29, 2010, the State's Attorney's Office did not issue a declination letter until October 16, 2012, over two years later. Many law enforcement agencies conduct parallel administrative investigations of officer-involved shootings, understanding that precautions can be taken to ensure that the officer's statements are segregated and do not taint any potential criminal investigation. BPD does not conduct such parallel investigations.

We also found significant differences between BPD's practices when interviewing witnesses and its practices when interviewing officers that suggest a bias in favor of the officer. For example, when interviews of the officers finally did occur, they were conclusory and superficial, often lasting no longer than ten or fifteen minutes, with some ending after five minutes. Officers were generally not asked any critical questions about the threat they faced or their decision-making process leading up to their deadly force. For example, in a lethal 2013 shooting, the Internal Affairs detective's interview of the shooting officer lasted only five minutes, which included form questions about the nature of the interview which were not particular to the facts of that case. The actual substantive interview of the officer lasted three minutes. BPD's interviews of civilian witnesses, on the other hand, often last hours, and the investigators ask specific, probing questions, demonstrating their ability to be thorough and exacting. We also found that BPD has a practice of conducting "pre-interviews" with officers before turning on the recording device; at times, investigators stated that they had done a "pre-interview" on the record. For example, in another 2013 officer-involved shooting, an investigator from Internal Affairs stated, "Sir, please just as we did before we went on the tape, just tell us what happen [sic]." The officer then provided a canned and prepared presentation about a shooting, summarizing the incident, from beginning to end. The entire interview, on tape, lasts only eight minutes. Pre-interviews impede the integrity of the investigation. Because of this, pre-interviews in investigations of officer-involved shootings have been discouraged since the at least the early 1990s. See, e.g., JAMES G. KOLTS & STAFF, THE LOS ANGELES COUNTY SHERIFF'S

DEPARTMENT 140 (1992), available at http://www.clearinghouse.net/chDocs
/public/PN-CA-0001-0023.pdf.

These investigative deficiencies prevent BPD from being able to evaluate
whether officers who used deadly force faced an immediate threat of serious
harm, and whether their force was justified. Moreover, by failing to critically
evaluate officers' tactics and decision-making prior to their use of deadly force,
including opportunities to de-escalate, the Department fails to help officers improve their skills and potentially decrease the need to resort to deadly force.
To effectively oversee its use of force, BPD must take steps to remedy these
deficiencies.

d. BPD Has Inadequate Policies, Programs, and Training to Guide Officer Interactions with Individuals with Disabilities or in Crisis, and Fails to Coordinate Adequately with Other Social Services Providers

BPD's inadequate policies, training, and programs regarding officer interactions with individuals with a disability or in crisis also contribute to the systemic use of excessive force in violation of the Fourth Amendment and the
failure to provide reasonable modifications necessary to avoid discrimination
in violation of the Americans with Disabilities Act. The vast majority of individuals with mental health disabilities, including substance use disorders,
or intellectual or developmental disabilities (I/DD) in Baltimore are working,
learning, and living in the community and will live their lives without any
involvement with BPD. Some individuals with disabilities, however, who are
not able to access sufficient home- and community-based services to meet their
needs may be unable to avoid crisis, maintain housing and employment or,
for youth, to engage with school, leading some to come into contact with law
enforcement. According to a 2009 Baltimore City Community Health Survey,
23 percent of residents reported having unmet mental health needs.[107] The rate
was notably higher for black residents (33.4 percent) and for all individuals with
less than a bachelor's degree in education (28.6 percent).[108] This disparity was
reflected again in a 2011 Maryland Behavioral Risk Factor Surveillance System
study, which found that 19.5 percent of black residents and 15.1 percent of white
residents reported that their mental health was "not good" for eight or more
out of the past 30 days.[109] Law enforcement officers are often the first respond-

---

107 See BALTIMORE CITY HEALTH DEP'T, HEALTHY BALTIMORE 2015, at 11 (2015), http:
//health.baltimorecity.gov/sites/default/files/HealthyBaltimore2015_Final_Web.pdf.

108 Id.

109 See BALTIMORE CITY HEALTH DEP'T, HEALTHY BALTIMORE 2015: INTERIM
STATUS REPORT 28(2013) available at http://health.baltimorecity.gov/sites/default/files
/HB2015InterimUpdateOct2015Optimized_2.pdf.

ers when people with mental health disabilities are experiencing a crisis, and the same is true in Baltimore.[110] It is therefore incumbent upon BPD to provide clear guidance to its officers on how to interact with individuals in crisis, but that guidance is lacking.

i. BPD's Crisis Intervention Practices Are Inadequate

BPD's crisis intervention policies and procedures are inadequate to safely and lawfully serve individuals in crisis. Based upon our investigation, including our review of use of force files, reports, and training materials, as well as interviews with BPD employees, community members, and service providers, it is clear that BPD officers are not prepared to effectively and safely respond to individuals experiencing crisis. Consequently, BPD officers frequently resort to unreasonable force against individuals in crisis and fail to make reasonable modifications necessary to avoid discriminating against people with disabilities.

BPD itself recognized the challenges that police officers face when responding to individuals in crisis. But the program it launched in 2004, called Behavioral Emergency Services Team (BEST) has proven to be ineffective.[111] First, since 2009, BEST training has been offered only to new recruits in the training academy. Crisis calls are among BPD's most challenging calls for service, and officers early in their careers are typically not well prepared to handle these complex incidents while also adjusting to their many new duties as a police officer. An effective crisis intervention response program would provide at least a basic level of crisis intervention training to all officers, including new officers in the academy, but it would also ensure that at least some of its more experienced officers had received a high level of crisis intervention training. These experienced, highly-trained officers are the ones well positioned to handle the complex situations that interactions with individuals in crisis present. Because BPD only offers crisis intervention training to new recruits, many officers are not trained to identify whether an individual is in crisis or engaging in behavior related to a disability, to interact effectively with people with disabilities, to de-escalate a crisis, and to connect the individual with local resources to provide treatment or support. BPD should regularly provide in-service training to

---

110 *See, e.g.*, Law Enforcement and Mental Health, NAT'L ALL. ON MENTAL ILLNESS, https://www.nami.org/Get-Involved/Law-Enforcement-and-Mental-Health (last visited May 25, 2016) ("With our failing mental health system so inadequate, law enforcement agencies have increasingly become *de facto* first responders to people experiencing mental health crisis.").

111 The BEST program has trained over 800 officers since its inception. During the first five years of the project, it trained an average of 70 officers each year. Since 2009, the training numbers average 136 officers per year.

refresh the lessons recruits learned in the academy once they have experience in patrol. Our investigation revealed that insufficiently trained BPD officers have escalated interactions that did not initially involve criminal behavior, resulting in the arrest of, or use of force against, individuals in crisis, or with mental health disabilities or I/DD, or unnecessary hospitalization of the person with mental health disabilities or I/DD.[112] When BPD officers have discretion about whether to make an arrest, agency policies and procedures should direct them to consider whether it would be appropriate to decline to arrest or issue a citation, and instead connect individuals to community-based services without further criminal justice involvement.

Second, dispatchers do not receive training on BPD's BEST program and BPD has no mechanisms in place to ensure that BEST-trained officers are dispatched to crisis-related calls for service. Nor does the Department collect data on whether and how often BEST-trained officers respond to calls involving individuals in crisis. Moreover, other officers and community members do not know to request a BEST-trained officer when a crisis does occur. During an interview on crisis intervention, for example, one district commander bluntly stated "We don't do that here." Similarly, many Baltimore City mental health service providers indicated they were unaware of the program or had only a limited familiarity with the concept of BEST training, and an even smaller number stated that they request BEST-trained officers to respond to individuals in crisis.

Third, BPD policy does not require that a BEST-trained officer be dispatched to calls involving individuals in crisis. In fact, the only BPD policy we found that specifically addresses individuals in crisis is an order describing the process for executing a petition for an emergency evaluation. And until BPD amended the policy in July 2015, it failed to provide any guidance to officers on how to identify and interact with an individual in crisis or mention utilizing BEST-trained officers. Indeed, this policy is both underdeveloped and unnecessarily restrictive. The policy suggests that de-escalation techniques and BEST-trained officers are only needed in situations where someone is going to be taken to the hospital for an emergency petition evaluation. It is unsurprising, therefore, that

---

112 Under Title II of the ADA's "integration mandate," public entities must administer services, programs, and activities in the most integrated setting appropriate to the needs of qualified individuals with disabilities. 28 C.F.R. § 35.130(d). The Supreme Court in *Olmstead v. L.C.*, 527 U.S. 581 (1999), further held that Title II prohibits the unjustified institutionalization of individuals with disabilities. The Court held that public entities are required to provide community-based services to persons with disabilities when (a) such services are appropriate; (b) the affected individuals do not oppose community-based treatment; and (c) community-based services can be reasonably accommodated, taking into account the resources available to the entity and the needs of others who are receiving disability services from the entity. *Id*. at 607.

many BPD officers see detention for an emergency petition, arrest, or inaction as their only options when responding to a crisis situation.

Officers in the field also stated that it is not a common practice to seek out BEST-trained officers for assistance with crisis calls. Similarly, during our review of force reports, there was no indication that BPD officers rely on BEST-trained officers to help them respond to crisis calls, even when they request back up for a call involving an individual in crisis. We reviewed one force file where BPD officers, responding to a call for an assault where people experiencing homelessness were known to stay, encountered an individual clearly in crisis, naked, hiding in the woods, bleeding and yelling. Instead of requesting the assistance of a BEST-trained officer, BPD officers asked dispatch to request that an officer armed with a taser respond to the scene. When one arrived, the officers yelled at the man to walk out of the woods, and that he would be tased if he did not comply. The officers' report indicated that the man had his arms "tucked up under his arm pits" and "positioned himself into a fighting stance[.]" Allegedly believing that the man might charge, the officer tased him, striking him in the groin and causing him to fall to the ground. When they approached him, he started kicking his legs and grabbing at the trees. The officers responded by cycling the taser five additional times. None of the four officers present on the scene were BEST-trained.

Not every encounter with an individual in crisis will or should result in arrest or an emergency petition evaluation. Employing sound crisis de-escalation techniques could prevent unnecessary and unreasonable force with individuals in crisis and also prevent needless incarceration and hospitalization.

ii. BPD Does Not Partner Effectively with Community Service Providers

Our investigation found that there are existing services in the community that BPD fails to utilize sufficiently, many of which may prevent an individual from experiencing a crisis or may prevent recurring instances of crisis. The City of Baltimore provides a range of services for people with disabilities to which the police should be connecting individuals, including community mental health clinics where individuals can receive mental health and substance use assessments, individual and group therapy, and medication management; Assertive Community Treatment teams, which are mobile teams of psychiatrists, social workers, nurses and mental health professionals who provide mental health treatment and support services; and the array of crisis services, such as community-based psychiatric crisis intervention and addictions treatment services. These include a telephone crisis hotline, mobile crisis teams (mental health professionals including psychiatrists, social workers, and nurses who can be dispatched to any Baltimore City location to provide immediate assessment, intervention, and treatment), medical detoxification for individuals addicted to substances, and in-house and community case management.

Although there appears to be a sufficient array of services to meet the needs of many individuals with disabilities, there does not appear to be sufficient capacity in many of those services to meet the need. Gaps in Baltimore City's community mental health service system increase the community's reliance on the police as mental health first responders. If a person with mental health disabilities is not adequately connected to services or is not getting her mental health needs met by the mental health system, she may end up in crisis, and BPD will likely be called to intervene. BPD, alone, cannot solve the problem of insufficient mental health services or capacity—although BPD's collaboration with the mental health service system could result in greater reliance on the mental health system to serve people in crisis, rather than law enforcement. What BPD can control, however, is how effectively it uses the resources that exist in the community.

BPD's BEST program does not partner effectively with the behavioral health community, consumers of these services, and their families. Until relatively recently, BPD's approach to crisis intervention has been limited to its academy training program. Beginning in 2014, the BEST coordinator formed the Collaborative Planning and Implementation Committee (CPIC) with the purpose of bringing together a body of stakeholders from the behavioral health community to act as an advisory board for further developing BPD's BEST program. CPIC is a substantial undertaking, and we are encouraged that BPD is taking this important step toward greater collaboration between BPD and Baltimore's behavioral health community, and, ultimately, toward providing effective crisis intervention services to the people of Baltimore. Progress has been slow, however, and during our site visits, it was apparent that BPD officers had not been trained on diversion to community-based treatment as an alternative to jail or short-term acute hospitalization, demonstrating that additional work remains for CPIC. BPD should continue to find ways to build and strengthen relationships with local providers that serve individuals with disabilities or in crisis.

Finally, BPD should better track when it connects people to service providers. It is difficult to fully assess BPD's efforts to connect individuals with disabilities to services because BPD does not aggregate data on mental health calls and does not track connection to services.

iii. To Remedy the ADA Violations, BPD Should Strengthen its Crisis Intervention Policies, Training, Community Partnership, and Data Collection Practices

In order to prevent further ADA violations, BPD should strengthen its crisis intervention policies, training, community partnership, and data collection practices. BPD must develop and implement policies and procedures for all officers on responding to individuals with mental health disabilities to ensure that officers make reasonable modifications necessary to avoid discrimination. BPD must develop and implement effective training for all officers and dispatchers that focuses on identifying individuals with mental health disabilities and effectively responding to individuals with mental health disabilities, including making reasonable modifications and diversion to treatment services. To better ensure the success and efficacy of these efforts, BPD should work collaboratively with the mental health community, including mental health agencies, providers, advocates, and consumers and their families, to develop the policies, procedures, and trainings. BPD must ensure appropriate officer accountability for protecting the civil rights of people with disabilities. BPD should collect, aggregate, and analyze information on officer interactions with individuals with mental health disabilities. BPD should use the data and information to make further improvements to policy, procedures, training, and accountability measures as necessary to avoid discrimination.

6. BPD's Transport Practices Create a Significant Risk of Harm

Our investigation revealed significant deficiencies in BPD's transport practices that place detainees who are being transported at significant risk of harm. A lack of video monitoring and data collection surrounding BPD's transport practices prevented us from reaching a conclusive determination regarding a practice of "rough rides" or constitutional violations in transportation. Nonetheless, we found evidence that BPD officers routinely fail to safely secure arrestees in transport vans with seatbelts. In multiple instances in the past, this failure has resulted in serious injuries and, in some circumstances, death. This risk of harm should be remedied.

a. BPD Has a History of Not Securing Arrestees

BPD relies on specially outfitted vans to transport detainees from the location of arrest or crisis to the district station, Central Booking, or the emergency room.[113] BPD's use of these vans has, at times, been the subject of considerable controversy and has led to some reforms, but these have not been consistently carried through in practice. For example, in 1997, BPD arrested Jeffrey Alston for speeding. According to testimony at a later trial, he was placed into a chokehold by BPD officers during the arrest and thrown unsecured into a transport

---

113 Most BPD cruisers do not have partitions, or "cages," and are therefore unsuitable for transporting people who have been arrested.

van. As a result of the treatment and transport, Alston was left quadriplegic. A civil jury found in favor of Mr. Alston, and the City ultimately settled with him for $6 million. Following this incident, BPD issued a General Order requiring officers to ensure every individual placed in a van is secured with seat or restraint belts. The Police Commissioner reaffirmed this requirement in 1999, issuing a memorandum stating that it is the responsibility of the officer to "[e]nsure that prisoners transported in prisoner transportation vehicles are secured with a seat belt."

Despite its longstanding policy that officers must secure detainees, BPD has received repeated indications that officers routinely fail to comply with seatbelt policies, sometimes with tragic results:

- In 2005, Dondi Johnson, Sr. was arrested for urinating on a public street and transported in a van by a BPD officer. During a subsequent trial, officers admitted that neither the driver of the van nor the arresting officers secured Mr. Johnson in the back of the van. While transporting him, the driving officer testified that she heard several bangs from the back of the van, and that she reached the district station in half the time it would have taken if she had driven at the speed limit. When the van was opened, Mr. Johnson was found face-down on the floor and in pain. Hospital records revealed that Mr. Johnson described being hurt while falling after the van took a sharp turn, and an expert witness testified that the nature of the injury was such that the van must have been driven in an aggressive manner. Mr. Johnson died shortly afterward due to complications from paralysis. A jury found in favor of Mr. Johnson's family, awarding $7.4 million in damages.
- In 2013, Christine Abbott sued BPD officers, alleging that she and her boyfriend were subjected to a "rough ride" in addition to other constitutional violations. The suit stated that officers threw her into the back of the police van, failed to secure her, and drove erratically. Ms. Abbott claimed she was violently thrown around the interior of the van during the ride and sustained injuries. In a deposition, the transporting officer acknowledged that Ms. Abbott was not secured during the ride. The City settled the case with Ms. Abbott for $95,000.

b. BPD Continues to Place Detainees At Risk During Transport

Our investigation found that BPD continues to place detainees at significant risk during transport. Following each of the Johnson and Abbott lawsuits, BPD undertook inspections of its transport vans to determine if officers were properly securing arrestees. An audit conducted by BPD from April 12, 2012, through May 14, 2012, inspected 18 vehicles, two from each BPD district. The audit found that *none* of the 34 arrestees in those vehicles were secured with seatbelts.

BPD conducted similar audits of nine vehicles in April 2014 and September 2014, and another shortly after the death of Freddie Gray in April 2015. With each audit, BPD inspected one transport vehicle from each of the districts, one time. The April 2014 audit found that one out of 11 arrestees was not secured by a seatbelt. The September 2014 audit found that all of the 15 arrestees in the inspected vehicles were secured. The April 2015 audit found that 13 out of 14 detainees were secured. While this represents a significant improvement from 2012, the audits were limited in scope and sample size, and as described below, are contradicted by the statements of officers about BPD's actual practices. According to the documents produced to us in our investigation, BPD has not conducted any further inspections of the transportation process, nor has it gathered any data to ensure that detainees are consistently secured in vans.

Given the limitations of the BPD audits, we attempted, through several methods, to obtain information from BPD about injuries that occur during transport. BPD neither collects data about injuries that detainees incur during transport nor tracks data on the source of injuries reported by detainees after they are accepted at Central Booking or the emergency room. Thus, we attempted to obtain injury data directly from Central Booking and to match it to injury data available in BPD's incident and force reports. These data were insufficient for us to reliably match and analyze them.

We also attempted to obtain videos BPD maintained of detainees during transport. BPD transport vans originally contained cameras to show drivers the detainees in the rear of the van. Many of these cameras ceased to function shortly after the vans were put in use, however, and have not been repaired. Because of these failures, we were unable to obtain video of detainees and conduct an evaluation of their treatment during transport. Without functioning video, data collection on injuries, or more frequent inspections, we could not confirm that detainees are still routinely being transported while unsecured.

Given such difficulties in obtaining data about BPD transport practices, we conducted an anonymous poll of recent arrestees during bail review hearings throughout the month of March 2016, with assistance from lawyers at the Maryland Office of the Public Defender. Sixty of the 298 polled arrestees reported that they had been unsecured for at least a portion of the ride to Central Booking—more than 20 percent of the arrestees polled. Several of the respondents indicated that they hit their head, neck, or back during the ride, and/or reported minor injury. While this survey was limited in scope, it was larger than any of the audits conducted by BPD. And, despite its limitations, the results suggest that BPD continues to fail to secure arrestees during transport, placing them at significant risk of harm.

We also obtained significant anecdotal evidence from officers that detainees were often unsecured while being transported by BPD officers, particularly before Freddie Gray's transport last year. One officer who spoke to us described the transportation process before Freddie Gray's death as "load and go," often with little regard for seatbelts. Other officers repeatedly told us that they knew of or had heard about "rough rides" that had taken place in the past, although they declined to give us specifics.

c. BPD Transport Equipment Continues to Place Detainees At Risk

Our evaluation of BPD transport vans heightens our concern regarding transportation practices. Many vans used by BPD remain unsuitable for safe transportation because of a lack of functioning seatbelts and video observation equipment, although BPD has made a number of changes over the last few months to address this problem. Until recently, all vans featured a rear compartment split down the middle by a dividing wall, creating two parallel sections to enclose detainees, with three seats facing inward in each section. While each seat features a seatbelt, this was not always the case: for some time, many vans had no seatbelts. Moreover, though vans are now equipped with seatbelts, we observed on our ride-alongs that some are broken. The space inside each of the transport vans is limited, making it possible for detainees being transported, if not properly secured, to strike their head on the divider or walls relatively easily; and there is virtually no padding to protect the person from injury. The physical layout of the van also creates significant concerns for officer safety. In order to belt in multiple individuals, the officer has to climb into the van, exposing his weapons and equipment to those seated in the first two seats. Once inside the compartment, the officer runs the danger of being harmed by an individual in the van or even locking himself inside. Officers reported to us that such lock-ins occur with some frequency.

BPD is currently retrofitting older vans with a partition, or "cage," that has a different format. The new cage features an open compartment accessed from the rear doors of the van, with seating for four people; two on each side of the van, facing inward. There is a separate, smaller compartment, accessed from the side of the van, with seating for two people sitting side by side, facing the door. Each seat is equipped with a seatbelt and a strap for the detainee to grip for stability while seated with hands cuffed behind his or her back. The newer vans also have video cameras in the rear compartments that can be viewed by the driver and have the capability to record.

However, significant challenges remain, even with the new system. Officers reported that the video recording function has yet to be enabled. There is no clear line of sight from the driver to the rear compartments and sounds are muffled by the barrier. Accordingly, if any person in the rear compartment is hurt or otherwise requires assistance, the driver may remain unaware of the person's condition. This is contrary to a recommendation by the International Association of Chiefs of Police that officers should maintain visual contact with people they transport at all times, through either video or direct observation.[114] Similar to the older vans, the interiors are small and lack padding, so anybody riding in the back, if unsecured, could be injured if the manner of driving caused them to hit the walls, seats or floor. Even when functioning, the seatbelts are positioned in such a way that a person with hands cuffed behind his back can unbuckle himself by turning his body. This raises additional concerns for people in crisis, as well as for officer safety with uncooperative detainees.

BPD has also made other efforts to improve their transportation practices and procedures. After the 2012 audit, officers were briefed on the requirement to seatbelt arrestees. Following Freddie Gray's death and the 2015 audit, BPD sent officers who operate the transport vehicles to academy training, and conducted a brief training during "roll-call" at the beginning of shifts. The training and certification program is short, however, consisting of only four hours of instruction. And while it purports to cover a wide range of topics, from proper handcuffing and search techniques to identification of mental health and medical issues, the training does not cover driving techniques. BPD has also indicated that new patrol cars coming into the departmental fleet will be equipped with protective partitions allowing for the transport of detainees, but it is not clear when BPD will have a sufficient number of equipped cars to eliminate the need for transport vans.

Thus, despite such improvements, BPD still has a great deal of work to do. Most fundamentally, BPD must improve its oversight and monitoring of its transportation practices to ensure that its own policies are followed, and that arrestees are consistently transported in a manner that is safe and secure.

D. BPD UNLAWFULLY RESTRICTS PROTECTED SPEECH

The people of Baltimore have a constitutional right to observe and verbally criticize the police. "Since the day the ink dried on the Bill of Rights, the right of an American citizen to criticize public officials and policies is the central meaning of the First Amendment." *McCurdy v. Montgomery County*, 240 F.3d 512, 520 (6th Cir. 2001) (internal quotation marks and citations omitted). We found that BPD officers routinely infringe upon the First Amendment rights of the

---

114 IACP Law Enforcement Policy Center, "Transportation of Prisoners Concept and Issues Paper," originally published August 1990, revised October 1996, March 2005, and September 2015.

people of Baltimore City, typically in one of three ways. First, we found that BPD unlawfully stops and arrests individuals for speech they perceive to be disrespectful or insolent. Second, we found that officers retaliate against individuals for protected speech through the use of excessive force. Third, we have concerns that BPD improperly interferes with individuals who record police activity.

1. BPD Unlawfully Detains and Arrests Members of the Public for Protected Speech

BPD detains and arrests individuals for speech perceived to be rude, critical, or disrespectful. These arrests—described by the officers in their own words in incident and arrest reports—violate the First Amendment. For example, an officer in downtown Baltimore in 2011 "felt . . . that it was reasonable" to order a young African-American man to leave the area because he "had no respect for law enforcement" and was "making idle threats towards a uniformed officer." As the young man walked away accompanied by a friend, the two made additional comments mocking the officers and the BPD; 15 minutes later, the officer again spotted the two men in the same area and placed both under arrest for failure to obey. "The freedom of individuals verbally to oppose or challenge police action without thereby risking arrest is one of the principle characteristics by which we distinguish a free nation from a police state." *City of Houston v. Hill*, 482 U.S. 451, 462–63 (1987) (striking down municipal ordinance that made it illegal to oppose or interrupt a policeman as constitutionally overbroad under the First Amendment).[115] By ordering the young men to leave, and then arresting them for their comments, the officer violated their First Amendment right to peacefully and verbally criticize or oppose law enforcement officers without actively interfering with the officers' lawful performance of their duties.

In another incident from 2011, BPD officers arrested a man for disorderly conduct after he refused to leave a public area following an order issued without just cause, and yelled "fuck you" repeatedly at the officer. This arrest was also unlawful, as individuals may not be punished for using vulgar or offensive language unless they use "fighting words," that is, words that "by their very utterance inflict injury or tend to incite an immediate breach of the peace." *Chaplinsky v. New Hampshire*, 315 U.S. 568, 572 (1942). Use of profanity alone is not sufficient to rise to the level of inflicting injury or inciting a breach of peace. *See Hess v. Indiana*, 414 U.S. 105, 107–08 (1973) (finding that profane words were

---

115 As discussed in Section *supra* at 36-39, this order and arrest also likely violate the Fourteenth Amendment's Due Process clause.

not fighting words because they were not a personal insult); *Lewis v. City of New Orleans*, 415 U.S. 130, 132–34 (1974) (invalidating New Orleans ordinance that made it unlawful to curse at a police officer on duty); *Buffkins v. City of Omaha*, 922 F.2d 465, 467–68, 472 (8th Cir. 1990) (arrest was unlawful as use of the word "asshole" towards officers did not constitute fighting words). From our review of their reports, some BPD officers appear to believe that use of vulgar or profane language provides probable cause to arrest or grounds for ordering a person to leave a location.

Indeed, in another case, an officer patrolling the inner harbor on the Fourth of July complained that a man, "Nicholas," bumped his shoulder while walking past. As Nicholas continued walking, the officer said, "Hey, you ran right into me," to which Nicholas replied "fuck you" and continued walking. Although no crime had been committed, the officer pursued Nicholas and demanded his identification. Nicholas continued to walk away from the officer, who attempted to grab his arm. Nicholas swore at the officer again and continued to pull away, at which point the officer informed him he was under arrest. According to the officer's report, after attempting to place the man under arrest, the incident ended in a physical altercation between officers, Nicholas, and his brother, with the brother eventually being tased. Though Nicholas made repeated attempts to walk away peacefully, the officer pursued him and escalated the encounter. According to the officer's report, he believed that Nicholas's attitude and actions indicated "he was purposely looking for a confrontation with law enforcement[.]" However, Nicholas made no obvious threats or aggressive movements toward the officer. His use of profanity did not rise to the level of "fighting words" and was protected by the First Amendment. The officer's pursuit, detention, and eventual arrest was an unlawful exercise of government power to exact personal vengeance for a perceived slight.

BPD officers also violate the First Amendment by arresting individuals who question the lawfulness of their actions. In one reported use of force, an officer described the arrest of a man who approached him during a traffic stop to ask why the officer had stopped his friend. The proffered justification for the arrest was that the man refused to leave the area when ordered to do so by the officer. Nothing in the officer's report indicates that the man physically interfered with the officer's duty or was otherwise committing a crime. He was arrested merely because he continued to stand "near" the officer. Arrests for failing to leave a crime scene are also unlawful. The man had a right to "voice his objection to what he obviously felt was a highly questionable detention by a police officer." *Norwell v. City of Cincinnati, Ohio*, 414 U.S. 14, 16 (1973); *see also Wilson v. Kittoe*, 337 F.3d 392, 402 (4th Cir. 2003) (officers lacked probable cause to arrest an attorney who did not obey officers' orders to leave the scene of the arrest of another person, and that the subsequent arrest of the attorney unlawfully infringed upon his First Amendment rights). The man sustained an injury to his head while struggling during the course of being taken into custody following the unlawful arrest. Despite a clear lack of probable cause, supervisory review found that the officer had acted properly and within policy.

In a similar incident from 2014, BPD officers arrested a man for disorderly conduct because he was shouting at the officers. The man believed they had assaulted his nephew and stolen from him while detaining him on suspicion of "gambling." When he approached the officers, demanding to know which of them had punched his nephew, a crowd gathered, and he was placed under arrest. The man was within his rights to question the officers' actions, and the arrest unlawfully suppressed his speech. Officers arrested him for objecting to their actions and for making vocal inquiries into their conduct.[116] In making these arrests, BPD officers violated these individuals' right to question and criticize police actions. See Norwell, 414 U.S. at 16 (speech protesting officers' actions is protected even if "loud and boisterous" or "annoying" to officers).

"[A] clear and present danger of crowd violence" may be a consideration in determining whether a First Amendment violation occurred. Smith v. McCluskey, 126 Fed. Appx. 89, 94 (4th Cir. 2005) (per curiam) (unpublished) (internal quotations omitted). But the presence of other people alone is insufficient to render otherwise protected speech grounds for arrest, unless such speech "is directed to inciting or producing imminent lawless action and is likely to incite or produce such action." Brandenburg v. Ohio, 395 U.S. 444, 447 (1969). See also State of Texas v. Johnson, 491 U.S. 397, 409–10 (1989) (rejecting the argument that "the potential for breach of peace" satisfies the Brandenburg standard); Patterson v. United States, 999 F.Supp.2d 300, 316 (D.D.C. 2013) ("[C]ursing at an officer in the presence of a crowd, without some indication of a likely violent reaction from that crowd, does not give rise to probable cause to believe that the speaker is engaged in disorderly conduct."); Dormu v. District of Columbia, 795 F.Supp. 2d 7, 21 (D.D.C. 2011) ("[D]isorderly conduct does not occur merely because a crowd gathers to watch a citizen-police encounter."). And unlike the plaintiff in Smith v. McCluskey, the individuals in the above described incidents had not been placed under valid arrest at the time their speech was suppressed. Neither the man's demand to know which officer had struck his nephew, nor the woman's shouts or profanity were evidently directed to produce imminent lawless action on the part of the crowd. Accordingly, their suppression by arrest was unlawful.

These and other arrests for protected speech demonstrate that BPD officers

---

116 Although one officer later told a supervisor that the man had adopted a "fighting stance" before the decision to arrest, this was not corroborated by other officers or civilian witnesses on the scene, who reported that the man merely refused to leave and made repeated demands to know who had assaulted his nephew.

may consider speech critical or disrespectful of their activities to be assaultive or disruptive, and therefore sufficient to justify suppression through the unlawful use of police powers to detain and arrest.

2. BPD Retaliates by Using Force Against Individuals Who Engage in Protected Speech

BPD uses unreasonable force to retaliate against individuals who engage in protected speech critical of law enforcement, in violation of both the First and Fourth Amendments.[117] *City of Houston*, 482 U.S. at 461; *Hartman v. Moore*, 547 U.S. 250, 256 (2006) ("the law is settled that as a general matter the First Amendment prohibits government officials from subjecting an individual to retaliatory actions . . . for speaking out."). We reviewed a number of troubling incidents where BPD officers appeared to use force against individuals simply because they did not like what those individuals said. In one case from 2011, officers tackled and used a taser to drive-stun a young black man who was, in their view, "loitering" near a market during business hours in downtown Baltimore. When told to move, the young man refused and swore at the officers, who then tackled him. Nothing indicated the man was armed, violent, or presented a danger to the officers or others. Supervisors who investigated and approved the incident failed to recognize that the force appeared to be retaliatory, even though the man, when interviewed, told them he believed he was tackled because he cursed at the officers.

Furthermore, we have reviewed many incidents in which BPD officers believe they are justified in using force or arresting a person, based solely on profane or insulting words. We reviewed an incident, for example, in which an officer tased a young man who, according to the officer's report, had removed his shirt and was yelling at club patrons and staff. The officer justified using the taser on the basis that the man approached the officer in an aggressive manner while swearing. Although the report is not altogether clear on what the officer meant by "aggressive," the report does make clear that the man's "mouth"—his words—constituted the weapon or means of attack:

> Indeed, this report appears to indicate the officer felt he was justified in tasing an individual—a high level of force—for this reason. Moreover, the report noted that the individual's "trademark" was "[e]xplicit word this place." If this was in fact the officer's justification for tasing this in-

---

117 Retaliatory force also violates the Fourteenth Amendment when used against individuals who have been arrested are being held as pretrial detainees, for example during prisoner transport. *See Orem v. Rephann*, 523 F.3d 442, 446 (4th Cir. 2008), abrogated on other grounds by *Wilkins v. Gaddy*, 559 U.S. 34, 39 (2010).

dividual, it is grossly insufficient, and it would violate both the First and Fourth Amendments. Although we make no finding about this specific incident because of the vagueness of word "aggressive" in the report, it is notable that the officer's direct supervisor signed off on the report, and a review of the use of force found it to be justified without need of clarification.

We reviewed a number of substantially similar incidents where BPD officers only resorted to force after an individual swore at them. These uses of force in retaliation for protected speech violate the First and Fourth Amendments, and they undermine public confidence in the BPD.

3. Concerns that BPD Interferes with the Right to Record Public Police Activity

We also have serious concerns that BPD officers interfere with individuals who

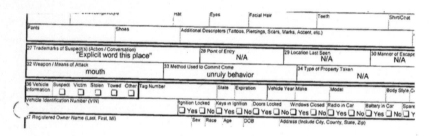

attempt to lawfully record police activity, although we do not make a finding of constitutional violations in this area because we did not find a sufficient number of incidents to warrant such a finding at this time. We nevertheless received and reviewed a number of allegations that BPD officers seize, view, and destroy video and audio recordings that constitute private property without just cause to do so. In 2012, we provided guidance to BPD on the First, Fourth, and Fourteenth Amendment considerations related to the recording of public police activity in a Statement of Interest filed in *Sharp v. Baltimore City Police Dep't.*, No. 1:11-cv-02888-BEL (D. Md. Jan. 12, 2012), 2012 WL 9512053.

That case was brought by the ACLU of Maryland on behalf of a man whose cellular phone was seized by BPD officers during an incident at the Pimlico Race Course in 2011. The City settled the case in 2014 for $250,000. The plaintiff alleged that BPD officers seized, searched, and deleted the contents of his phone after he used it to record officers using force during an arrest of his acquaintance. When BPD returned the phone to him, all of the videos on the device were deleted, including a number of personal videos of his young son. After the man filed suit, BPD moved for partial summary judgment, and the Department of Justice opposed that motion in our Statement of Interest. Shortly thereafter, on May 14, 2012, in advance of the parties' settlement conference, we sent a letter to both parties. In our letter, we described in more detail how these constitutional interests play out in practice, and we gave technical assistance on their implications for policy and training. The parties settled, and, as part of the settlement, BPD agreed to implement a new policy and training program concerning the right to audiotape, videotape, and photograph BPD members during the public exercise of their duties. The new policy was published in 2014. Nonetheless, in the time period since *Sharp*, we have received numerous allegations that BPD officers continue to interfere with the individual right to record police activity, in violation of the First Amendment and their own policy.

One example of the allegations we received stems from an incident in 2015. According to the complainant, a young man was charged with three offenses after filming BPD officers arresting his friend for trespassing outside a nightclub in Baltimore City. The friend was engaged in an argument with security officers at a bar complex about refunding his admission fee. When BPD Officers informed him that he was trespassing and began handcuffing him, his companion, allegedly standing approximately 20 feet away, began to film the incident using his phone. Two other officers on the scene turned and confronted him, grabbing his phone and placing him in handcuffs. While the alleged trespasser was released with only a ticket, the man filming was arrested and charged with three offenses: failure to obey, trespassing, and assault (for what appears to be a later-discovered alleged assault against the nightclub's bouncer). During the arrest process, the man watched as an officer openly went through his phone. When BPD released the man after he spent two nights in jail, he discovered that the video of the incident had been deleted. Ultimately, a state court entered a judgment of acquittal for the assault and failure to obey charges, and the man was acquitted of the trespassing charge at trial. According to the man, the sole justification for his arrest was his attempt to record the officers' interaction with his friend. We also note that, to the extent that the officers thought that the man recording their activities was somehow interfering in their enforcement efforts, the officers do not appear to have made any effort to instruct the man who was recording them to move to a less-intrusive place where he could continue recording.

In addition to these apparent First Amendment violations, BPD officers also appear to have violated the Fourth and Fourteenth Amendments by searching the phone following the arrest, apparently without a warrant, and by deleting the video. When individuals record police officers in the public exercise of their duties, they have a Fourteenth Amendment property right to maintain the possession of their belongings, including recordings and recording devices. *See, e.g., Helton v. Hunt*, 330 F.3d 242, 247–49 (4th Cir. 2003) (striking down statute allowing police to seize and destroy video gaming machines without due process). BPD's policy accordingly prohibits employees from erasing, deleting, or instructing others to erase or delete any recordings from a recording device. By going through the man's phone and deleting the video, BPD destroyed valuable evidence and disregarded the owner's property rights and the Department's own policy.

First Amendment violations acutely affect a community's trust in the legitimacy of law enforcement operations. BPD's sensitivity to criticism and recording of their activity is ultimately both a symptom and a cause of mutual mistrust with the community. There is emerging evidence that video recording can be a valuable tool to reduce use of force incidents and complaints, and protect the rights of both community members and officers.[118] To create an atmosphere of mutual respect and accountability, officers will need to demonstrate the ability to work within the confines of the First Amendment.

In sum, BPD takes law enforcement action in retaliation for individuals' engaging in protected speech or activity in violation of the First Amendment.

---

118 *See, e.g.,* IACP. *The Impact of Video Evidence on Modern Policing: Research and Best Practices from the IACP Study on In-Car Cameras,* available at: http://www.theiacp.org/Portals/0/pdfs/WhatsNew/IACP%20In-Car%20Camera%20Report%202004.pdf (last accessed June 10, 2016).

E. BPD'S HANDLING OF SEXUAL ASSAULT INVESTIGATIONS RAISES SERIOUS CONCERNS OF GENDER-BIASED POLICING

Our investigation also raised serious concerns about how BPD responds to and investigates reports of sexual assault.

1. Evidence of Gender Bias in BPD's Response to Sexual Assault

a. Treatment of Victims of Sexual Assault

By its very nature, sexual assault is a crime about which it can be difficult to ascertain the facts: for example, sexual assault often occurs in a private setting, with no witnesses other than the people involved as the victim[119] and suspect, and victims of sexual assault are often reluctant to report the assault, particularly to law enforcement. For that reason, victim advocates—who act as confidantes and guides for victims as they navigate the criminal justice system, and whose role affords them a unique perspective from which to identify patterns in their clients' experiences—play a critical role in providing information about sexual assaults to BPD.

The information provided to us by victim advocates, and, in some cases, by victims of sexual assault themselves, together with our review of BPD's sexual assault case files and related documents, raise serious concerns about gender bias in BPD's treatment of victims of sexual assault. For instance, officers and detectives in BPD's Sex Offense Unit often question victims in a manner that puts the blame for the sexual assault on the victim's shoulders—for example, with questions suggesting the victims should feel personally responsible for the potential consequences of a criminal report on a suspect or for having engaged in behavior that invited the assault. In their interviews of women reporting sexual assault, for example, BPD detectives ask questions such as "Why are you messing that guy's life up?" BPD officers and detectives also asked questions

---

119 Throughout this findings letter, we have used the terms "victim" and "victim of sexual assault" to refer to people having experienced sexual assault because it is the term generally used in criminal legal definitions of sexual assault and in the criminal justice system. We appreciate, however, that many prefer the terms "survivor" or "victim/survivor," and encourage respect for those preferences.

suggesting that they discredit the reports of victims who delayed in reporting the assault to the police. This type of questioning is inappropriate in a detective interview of a potential victim of sexual assault and suggests gender bias by the detectives.

We were also troubled by statements of BPD detectives suggesting an undue skepticism of reports of sexual assault. One victim advocate told us about a detective in the BPD Sex Offense Unit making comments at a party, in the company of BPD officers and victim advocates, that, "in homicide, there are real victims; all our cases are bullshit." When another person suggested the detective soften the statement, the detective added, "Ok, 90 percent." We also reviewed e-mail correspondence between a BPD officer and a prosecutor in which they openly expressed their contempt for and disbelief of a woman who had reported a sexual assault: the prosecutor wrote that "this case is crazy. . . I am not excited about charging it. This victim seems like a conniving little whore. (pardon my language)."; the BPD officer replied, "Lmao! I feel the same."

In addition, we found indications that BPD disregards reports of sexual assault by people involved in the sex trade—a particularly troubling trend given the vulnerability of those individuals to rape.[120] According to one case report, the suspect had approached the victim with a gun, the victim had called the police right away, and the suspect's interview was almost entirely consistent with the victim's account of the assault—all evidence that could have supported an investigation and prosecution. Nonetheless, the BPD detective made no attempt to corroborate the victim's account of the assault with witness interviews or other evidence and told the suspect that he would not be charged with anything other than possession of a gun.

b. BPD's Treatment of Transgender Individuals

We received allegations of BPD officers' mistreatment of transgender individuals and have concerns that BPD's interactions with transgender individuals reflect underlying unlawful gender bias. We heard allegations that BPD officers make disparaging and inappropriate comments to transgender individuals, and that BPD officers refuse to acknowledge transgender women as women. One transgender woman, for example, described an incident after a traffic stop in December 2015 in which she was asked by the officer whether she identified as male or female, and told the officer that she identified as female. Despite her response, the arresting officer then said to another officer at the scene, "Well, are

---

120 *See, e.g.*, Michele R. Decker et al., *Violence Against Women in Sex Work and HIV Risk Implications Differ Qualitatively by Perpetrator*, 13 BMC PUB. HEALTH 876 (2013), available at http://bmcpublichealth.biomedcentral.com/articles/10.1186/1471-2458-13-876.

you going to transport him?" We also heard from the transgender community
that their interactions with BPD are degrading and dehumanizing and that, as
a result, transgender individuals are afraid to report crime to law enforcement.
The same transgender woman described above, for example, alleged that when
she arrived at intake, the female supervisor who was called to search her said,
"I am not here for this shit. I am not searching that." When she then tried to
ask the supervisor to show her some respect, the supervisor said, "Like I said,
I don't know you. I don't know if you're a boy or a girl. And I really don't care,
I am not searching you." This is not the only example we heard about BPD officers conducting inappropriate searches of transgender individuals. We heard
several reports that indicate that BPD officers lack guidance on the appropriate
process for conducting searches of transgender individuals, including ensuring
that searches are conducted by a person of the appropriate gender.

   BPD's treatment of women victims of sexual assault and of transgender individuals should not reflect gender-based stereotypes and assumptions that may
compromise the effectiveness and impartiality of BPD's response to reports of
sexual assault and discourage women and transgender individuals from engaging with the criminal justice system.

2. BPD Fails to Adequately Investigate Reports of Sexual Assault

BPD seriously and systematically under-investigates reports of sexual assault,
and the sexual assault investigations it does conduct are marked by practices
that significantly compromise the effectiveness and impartiality of its response
to sexual assault. These are not new issues for BPD. BPD's handling of sexual
assault was subject to widespread public scrutiny in 2010, spurred by media reports of BPD's misclassification of rape cases, failure to identify and investigate
reports of sexual assault, and substantial backlog of rape kits. Victim advocates,
for example, criticized the manner in which BPD treated victims of sexual assault—including interrogating rape victims, questioning women in the emergency room, threatening to hook up women reporting sexual assault to lie
detectors, and not informing victims about the status of their cases. Moreover,
victim advocates reported that BPD's Sex Offense Unit was only minimally investigating reports of sexual assault; for example, they were not making efforts
to identify witnesses or submitting rape kits for testing.

   Despite some attempts at reform by BPD and Baltimore City leaders, most
of these problems either remain or have returned. BPD's response to reports
of sexual assault is, overall, grossly inadequate: for example, BPD allows more
than half of its rape cases to linger in an "open" status, often for years at a time,
with little to no follow-up investigation, while fewer than one in four of its rape
investigations are closed due to the arrest of a suspect, a rate roughly half of

the national average; BPD detectives request testing of rape kits in fewer than one in five of BPD's adult sexual assault cases, leaving these rape kits to sit untested in BPD's evidence collection unit; and BPD detectives rarely, if ever, seek to identify or interview suspects and witnesses, even in cases where they are clearly identified by the woman reporting the assault. In addition, BPD investigative policies and practices significantly undermine the quality, effectiveness, and fairness of BPD's response to reports of sexual assault, making it more difficult to uncover the truth when sexual assault allegations are made.

a. Failure to Develop and Resolve Preliminary Investigations

In the majority of BPD's sexual assault cases, BPD fails to pursue investigations beyond the immediate, preliminary response to a report of sexual assault. According to BPD's own data, for example, between 53 and 58 percent of its sex offense cases were in an "open" status each year between 2013 and 2015. In our own review of a sample of BPD's sexual assault cases between 2010 and 2015, we found that more than half of these cases were described by BPD as being in an "open" status and that only a preliminary investigation had been done in a substantial proportion of those "open" cases. One sexual assault case, for example, was identified by BPD as "open," despite the fact that there had been no activity on the case since February 2013. In this case, there had been no request for a lab test kit, no follow-up with the suspect's lawyer to interview the suspect or test DNA, and no indication of communication with the victim over the past three years. Indeed, it appeared from the file that communication with the victim, and BPD's investigation of the case, had slowed and ultimately stopped after the suspect hired a defense attorney.

b. Failure to Identify and Collect Evidence to Corroborate Victims' Complaints

Similarly, BPD makes little, if any, effort to corroborate victims' accounts of their assaults, either by identifying and interviewing witnesses, gathering other types of evidence, or identifying and interrogating suspects. BPD routinely fails to contact witnesses to sexual assaults in the first instance and, where their initial attempts to contact witnesses fail, BPD almost never make a second attempt to contact those witnesses. Even when a victim describes having reported the assault to others in the immediate aftermath of the crime, BPD makes no effort to identify and interview these "outcry" witnesses—in other words, the people who first heard the allegation of sexual assault. In one case, for example, the victim had immediately told her father and other witnesses about the assault; however, BPD made no attempt to contact any of these outcry witnesses to corroborate the victim's story. Similarly, BPD persistently fails to make any efforts to contact eye witnesses to sexual assaults. In one case, for example, the victim and the suspect had been in two different bars together before the assault. The victim believed that the suspect had drugged her, and she had injuries all over her body. After the assault, the victim had run out of a bar and immediately reported the crime. Given these facts, it is reasonable to expect that there would have been numerous people who would have seen the victim and the suspect together at or around the time of the assault and who could have corroborated details of the victim's account. But BPD made no attempt to contact the bartenders of the bars or to identify any other eye witnesses.

In addition to failing to seek out corroborating witness testimony, BPD persistently fails to seek other types of evidence that could corroborate a victim's account of the assault. In the case just described, for example, in addition to neglecting to identify and interview witnesses, BPD made no attempt to review surveillance camera recordings from the two bars visited by the victim and the suspect, no effort to have the victim tested for drugs, and no attempt to gather physical evidence from the scene.

BPD persistently neglects to request lab testing of rape kits and other forensic evidence. Rape kits are only tested if a detective makes a request and all too often, detectives do not request that rape kits be tested. Between 2010 and September 2014, for example, rape kits were tested in only 15 percent of BPD's cases involving sexual assaults of adult victims. Similarly, between January and September 2015, BPD detectives requested testing of rape kits in only 16 percent of BPD's cases involving sexual assaults of adult victims. In the few cases where BPD is requesting rape kit tests, we found that there are long delays in making those requests. In one case, for example, BPD requested a lab test nine months after receiving a report of the sexual assault; it took another five months for BPD to get the results of the lab test.

Similarly, BPD detectives consistently neglect to gather DNA evidence and to request lab tests for DNA evidence from swabs or clothing. In one case, for example, a taxi driver drove an intoxicated woman to his home instead of to the address given to him by a bartender; the woman reported that the taxi driver had then raped her at his home. BPD subsequently interviewed the taxi driver, and he admitted to having taken the woman to his home. A rape kit was submitted and tested positive for semen. However, BPD made no attempt to get a DNA sample from the taxi driver.

BPD also makes minimal to no effort to locate, identify, interrogate, or investigate suspects. We found this to be true even in cases where the suspects had been identified or were easily identifiable on the basis of the victim's testimony. For example, in one case, involving an attempted sexual assault of a woman by the driver of an unauthorized taxi, the detective was able to identify the suspect based on the woman's detailed description of the suspect's car. The detective made no attempt to contact the suspect, however, and the investigation progressed no further. Because sexual assault is a crime that frequently occurs in private settings, it is critical that law enforcement make efforts to gather, preserve, and analyze evidence, especially corroborative evidence, as quickly as possible. BPD's persistent failure to seek out and develop such corroborative evidence, including suspect interrogations, constitutes a significant and damaging omission from their investigations of sexual assault.

BPD fails to identify and follow up on indications of serial suspects in its sexual assault cases. Serial suspects are believed to be responsible for a substantial proportion of sexual assaults—one oft-cited study concluded, for example, that two in three rapists who had never been prosecuted for their crimes were repeat rapists[121]—and thus there may be enormous public safety consequences when law enforcement fails to identify and hold accountable serial rapists. We were troubled to find evidence of such failures in BPD's investigations of sexual assault. For example, we reviewed numerous cases of forcible rapes of women by strangers that presented circumstances suggesting there might be serial rapists involved; however, BPD detectives did not take the steps necessary to make that determination, such as searching for cases presenting similar factual scenarios or identifying other victims in Baltimore or neighboring jurisdictions.

c. Missing or Inadequate Documentation of Investigation

BPD's sexual assault case files, as a general matter, are missing critical information and lack sufficient documentation of the investigation to allow detectives, their supervisors, and prosecutors to effectively evaluate the quality of investigation and to assess and respond to the reported crimes. For instance, we found that BPD's sexual assault case files frequently lack video recordings of victims, witnesses, and suspects, even where the notes in the case file indicate that those interviews had taken place and been recorded. BPD's sexual assault case files generally lack notes from officers and detectives. Where case files do include such notes, the notes provide insufficient information about officers' and detectives' impressions and observations, or about their reasons for making investigative decisions, to present a comprehensive, factual picture of the reported assault. Indeed, across the board, we found that we learned far more about victims' impressions and recollections of their assaults from the forensic medical exam reports than from BPD's own reports.

---

121 David Lisak & Paul M. Miller, *Repeat Rape and Multiple Offending Among Undetected Rapists*, 17 VIOLENCE AND VICTIMS 73–84, 78, 80 (2002).

d. Failure to Collect and Review Data About, and to Appropriately Report and Classify, Reports of Sexual Assault

The information provided to us by BPD in response to our requests for data regarding the department's cases of sexual assault suggests to us that BPD continues to have problems with improperly identifying, reporting, and classifying reports of sexual assault, as well as with collecting, reviewing, and analyzing data about sexual assaults reported to BPD. BPD has previously been subject to public scrutiny for its misclassification of cases of sexual assault and for its failures to appropriately identify or report cases of sexual assault. In June 2010, the *Baltimore Sun* reported that BPD patrol and detectives had classified more than 30 percent of their rape cases as "unfounded"—a classification that is appropriate only for a report of rape that is found, after an investigation, to be either false or baseless; BPD's "unfounded" rate for rape cases at that time was five times the national average.[122] A subsequent review of unfounded cases conducted by the Baltimore City Sexual Assault Response Team (SART) audit unit found that, of the cases reviewed by the SART audit unit, more than half of the sexual assault cases classified as "unfounded" by BPD detectives had been unclassified.[123] According to data from BPD, the proportion of rape cases classified as "unfounded" by BPD has dropped dramatically since 2010; BPD's data reflected a rate of 9.6 percent of rape cases classified as "unfounded" between January 2010 and March 2016. We are concerned, however, that these statistics mask a continuing problem with BPD's understanding and application of the appropriate definitions and uses of the classification categories, as well as with its practices for identifying and reporting sexual assaults. In 2015, for example, BPD described approximately 56 percent of its rape cases as "open." Meanwhile, only 17 percent of BPD's rape cases in 2015 were closed by arrest—a rate less than half the national average for the proportion of rape cases closed by arrest. Also in 2015, according to both data and anecdotal evidence from the Baltimore City SART, only a handful of BPD's cases were closed as "unfounded;" SART data indicated a rate of 6.6 percent of rape cases classified as "unfounded" by BPD between January and September 2015, and BPD presented only a handful of cases classified as unfounded to the SART audit committee for their review. Taken in the aggregate, this data suggests that BPD is keeping the majority of

---

122 *See, e.g.,* Justin Fenton, *City Rape Statistics, Investigations Draw Concern,* BALTIMORE SUN (June 27, 2010), http://articles.baltimoresun.com/2010-06-27/news/bs-md-ci-rapes-20100519_1_rosalyn-branson-police-detective-police-figures.

123 Md. Coal. Against Sexual Assault, *Baltimore City Sexual Assault Response Team Annual Report* 10 (Oct. 5, 2011), http://www.mcasa.org/_mcasaWeb/wp-content/uploads/2011/11/BaltimoreCityAnnualReport_print.pdf.

its rape cases in an "open" status, thus drastically reducing the rate of its rape cases closed as "unfounded"—and creating the illusion of having made meaningful reforms to its procedures for identifying and classifying sexual assaults.

In addition, we were troubled by the fact that BPD was unable to provide us with responses to our requests for basic data about the victim and suspect population, the incidence and nature of cases of sexual assault reported to and handled by the department, and the incidence of cases of sexual assault involving BPD officers. The inability to collect and produce such data suggests to us that BPD, at present, lacks the capacity to effectively assess the effectiveness its own response to sexual assault, to identify trends in the incidence of sexual assault, both in the Baltimore community and within its own department, and to make decisions about how to adjust or improve its response to sexual assault. Particularly in light of the public attention to the serious flaws in BPD's identification, reporting, and classification of cases of sexual assault, BPD's failure to remedy its procedures for collecting and reviewing data about sexual assault represents a significant weakness in the department's handling of sexual assault.

e. Lack of Supervisory Review

Although a supervisory review form is included as a matter of course in BPD's sexual assault case files, these supervisory review forms are almost always left blank. In the rare circumstances where the supervisory review forms are filled out, they include little information and appear to reflect a limited review of what steps have been taken in the investigation, and not an examination of the quality of the investigation or the reasoning for the outcome of the investigation. Similarly, although a "State's Attorney Contact Log" form is included as a matter of course in BPD's sexual assault case files, this form is rarely completed and, when it is filled out, contains very little information. The extremely limited nature of the information provided by the supervisory review form and State's Attorney Contact Log form raises concerns for us about the inadequate supervision and review, both within and external to the police department, of BPD's sexual assault investigations.

III. SYSTEMIC DEFICIENCIES IN BPD'S PRACTICES CONTRIBUTE TO CONSTITUTIONAL VIOLATIONS, ERODE COMMUNITY TRUST, AND INHIBIT EFFECTIVE POLICING

The constitutional violations described in our findings result in part from critical deficiencies in BPD's systems to train, equip, supervise, and hold officers accountable, and to build relationships with the broader Baltimore community. *First*, BPD fails to adequately supervise its officers. This lack of supervision manifests itself in multiple ways, including a failure to guide officer activity through effective policies and training; a failure to collect and analyze reliable data to supervise officer enforcement activities; and the lack of a meaningful early intervention system (EIS) to identify officers who may benefit from additional training or other guidance to ensure that they do not commit constitutional violations. *Second*, BPD lacks meaningful accountability systems to deter misconduct. BPD does not consistently classify, investigate, adjudicate, and document complaints of misconduct according to its own policies and accepted law enforcement standards. Indeed, we found that BPD personnel sometimes discourage complaints from being filed and frequently conduct little or no investigation—even of serious misconduct allegations. As a result, a culture resistant to accountability persists throughout much of BPD, and many officers are reluctant to report misconduct for fear that doing so is fruitless and may provoke retaliation. *Third*, BPD fails to have proper agreements in place to coordinate its activities with other agencies that are operating within its jurisdiction. *Fourth*, BPD fails to adequately support its officers through effective strategies for recruitment, retention, and staffing patterns, and does not provide them with appropriate technology and equipment. *Fifth*, BPD does not engage effectively with the community it polices. BPD's failure to use accepted community policing strategies and transparency mechanisms erodes the community trust that is central to productive law enforcement.

These systemic deficiencies impair officer safety and effectiveness and lead directly to violations of the Constitution and federal law.

A. BPD FAILS TO ADEQUATELY SUPERVISE ITS OFFICERS' ENFORCEMENT ACTIVITIES

1. BPD Does Not Provide Adequate Policy Guidance and Training to its Officers

BPD's inadequate policies and training contribute to the Department's pattern or practice of constitutional violations. Clear, comprehensive, and legally accurate policies and training are essential to the proper functioning of a police department. They provide crucial guidance for officers regarding what practical steps to take to remain in compliance with departmental rules and legal requirements, allow supervisors to properly monitor and instruct officers, and provide consistent guidelines for officer discipline. Here, we find that certain BPD policies and trainings do not fulfill these functions. BPD officers thus lack sufficient guidance to ensure that their enforcement activities are effective, safe, and consistent with the constitutional rights of the people they serve. While BPD has made admirable efforts to update its policies in 2015 and 2016, some outdated and contradictory policies remain in effect, diminishing the impact of the new policies and procedures.

a. Deficient Policies

As we described above in our findings, critical deficiencies in BPD's policies contribute to officers violating the constitutional rights of Baltimore residents. For example, officers' frequent use of tasers to apply constitutionally excessive force is connected to the Department's failure to have any policy governing the use of electronic control weapons until 2015. BPD similarly lacked any policy on baton use—also a frequent source of constitutional violations—until 2016. The Department likewise lacked a fair and impartial policing policy until 2015, despite longstanding notice of concerns about its policing of the City's African-American population. And policy deficiencies also contribute to officers' frequent illegal stops, searches, and arrests by misstating the law on the justification required to stop or frisk individuals suspected of criminal activity. Indeed, several BPD policies do not adequately capture the current state of the law, and others provide insufficient guidance to officers to allow them to align their conduct with constitutional requirements.

Beyond these specific policy deficiencies, however, we found systemic problems with BPD's method of drafting, distributing, and implementing policies that has made it difficult for officers to understand proper procedures and adapt to changing rules. BPD fails to follow widely accepted principles in developing, distributing, and implementing new policies. The International Association of Chiefs of Police, for example, has developed a set of best practices for effective development of operational policy and procedures. Among other recommendations, these principles indicate that staff should be involved in the development of the manual and kept informed of any changes. Chief W. Dwayne Orrick, *Best Practices Guide: Developing a Police Department Policy-Procedure Manual,* International Association of Chiefs of Police, http://www.theiacp.org/portals/0/pdfs /BP-PolicyProcedures.pdf (last visited June 17, 2016). Empirical research has also suggested that officers are more likely to support and comply with policies when they have been provided opportunities to give input, and supervisors clearly explain decisions that they have made. Nicole E. Haas et. al., *Explaining officer compliance: The importance of procedural justice and trust inside a police organization,* 15 Criminology & Crim. Just. 4, 16 (Sept. 2015).

BPD does not follow these accepted methods of policy development. Instead, the Department has historically developed and published policies and amendments in a manner that officers find to be confusing and opaque. As many officers told us, the numbering system alone is a source of confusion. Generally, BPD policies have been organized with titles that included letters and numbers. During one period, however, the letter-and-number system was replaced with a system that included numbers alone. The new system only applied to newly implemented policies, however, and the majority of policies were still classified by letter-and-number. Policies from different eras are written in different formats, and often modified by annexes, memoranda, amendments, and rescissions, instead of replacing the old policy completely, making it difficult for officers to be confident that they had the current, complete policy. While the policy manual has a table of contents, there is no index, and new additions and revisions can quickly make older manuals difficult to navigate. In fact, during our investigation, BPD was unable to locate one of its own amendments to disclose to us. In short, BPD policies do not provide officers with clear guidance that can be rapidly digested and put into practice in the field. Although in early 2016 BPD made efforts to provide clearer and more effective guidance to its officers by distributing a binder of updated, core policies that each officer can use in the field, significant work remains to ensure that all of BPD's policies are clear, internally consistent, and readily available to officers.

BPD likewise fails to provide officers the opportunity to provide input on the policy as it is developed. We spoke with many officers, including supervisors and others in positions of authority, who were frustrated by the lack of input they were able to have on policy development, including the policies developed in 2016. With nearly 3,000 sworn officers and another 1,000 person-nel, BPD will likely receive conflicting input in addition to the helpful ideas generated if it seeks input from officers. Without seeking this input, however, BPD fails to learn critical lessons from the field, and, as importantly, it risks alienating its officers and undermining adherence to the policies it develops. Indeed, during our interviews and ride-alongs, we found that large numbers of officers expressed a lack of confidence in the policy guidance BPD provides.

To ensure that its policies provide officers with sufficient guidance to police within the bounds of the Constitution, BPD must update its policies to make them reflect current legal requirements and develop a system to distribute and maintain policies and procedures in a way that promotes officer confidence and allows officers to use the policies effectively.

b. Deficient Training

Compounding the problems with policy development, BPD relies on deficient training on a broad array of substantive policing functions. This contributes to the pattern or practice of violations of the Constitution and federal law that we observed. Officers have not been properly trained on numerous important topics, from the use of force and de-escalation to stops, searches, and arrests, to how to supervise and investigate misconduct. Absent effective training on how to prop-erly conduct these actions, it is not surprising that BPD officers frequently violate federal law when interacting with the community. Our observations of training programs, review of internal documents, and conversations with BPD personnel revealed that training deficiencies within the Department arise from founda-tional issues in BPD's overall approach to training. The Department has failed to establish a robust training program and lacks the basic organizational capacities, infrastructure, and support required to effectively train police officers to respond to situations that arise in law enforcement encounters.

i. Training Has Not Been a Top Priority Within BPD

Our investigation revealed that one of the fundamental causes of the break-down in training is the Department's indifferent attitude towards its training program. Numerous members of BPD, from line officers to command staff to training personnel, conveyed to us that training is not a priority within the De-partment. Indeed, BPD's former director of the Training Academy released a needs assessment in 2015 that highlighted an "internal culture of placing train-ing second," "expectations for 'rushed' training," and "outside pressure to con-dense training programs" as threats to the current program. *See Baltimore Police Department Training Academy Needs Assessment* (July 2015), at 5. Unfortunately, after the training director sent the needs assessment to BPD leadership, he did not receive a response for months. He also organized three different meetings with patrol commanders to begin making changes based on the needs assessment, but no commanders attended the meetings.

We found that this lack of emphasis on training has a pervasive influence on the Department. A significant number of officers we spoke with had no training beyond Maryland's basic requirements. Officers who had furthered their training did so because of their own personal interest or ambition, often using private funds and overcoming obstacles posed by supervisors or work schedules. Rather than encouraging additional training, supervisors view training as a peripheral activity that is consistently superseded by the need to keep officers on the street. Strikingly, training personnel are also subject to being pulled from their training duties to other tasks: basic training is frequently postponed or shifted due to overtime details for training personnel, leading to the extension of time basic recruits spend at the Academy. *See id.*

Training is crucial for effective and lawful policing in Baltimore. Indeed, keeping officers on the street without proper or up-to-date training is a disservice not only to community members, but to officers because of the impact on officer safety.

ii. BPD Lacks Basic Infrastructure to Train its Officers

The failure to invest in training infrastructure underscores BPD's failure to prioritize this critical component of effective policing. BPD lacks adequate staff to train its officers efficiently; its training facilities are outdated, ill-repaired, and often unable to accommodate modern training methods; and BPD lacks mechanisms to track officer attendance and performance to ensure that officers receive and understand the training they need to engage in safe, effective, constitutional policing.

The training academy is notably under-resourced. The program lost about two-thirds of its staff over the past three years: training staff fell from approximately 60 in 2013 to 20 currently. During the course of our investigation, thirty classes had no primary instructor. Multiple training units, including the ones responsible for supervisor training for new sergeants and lieutenants, were entirely vacant with no personnel staffing them. We also found that student-to-instructor ratios during training classes were often extremely high, undermining effective communication of the material. The Fraternal Order of Police has also highlighted this concern, noting that class sizes for new recruit training have averaged 35–50 officers. *See FOP Blueprint for Improved Policing* (July 11, 2012), at 7. Minimal staffing also poses difficulties for BPD instructors to attend outside courses to develop their training skills.

BPD training facilities are in a similarly troubling state. During the course of our investigation, we were informed that BPD has only 17 computers available to train its nearly 4,000 personnel. The buildings themselves are in disrepair: water cannot be consumed from the faucets, and the buildings often lack workable air conditioning and heating. According to the Academy's recent needs assessment:

> The decrepit state of the academy itself gives the impression of a lackadaisical and uncommitted attitude towards the necessities of training the modern police officer. Recruits, sworn personnel, visiting law-enforcement experts, and civilians get the impression that they are party to a fly-by-night, poverty-stricken department when they find themselves in a crumbling, drafty building.

> See Baltimore Police Department Training Academy Needs Assessment (July 2015), at 12. The needs assessment additionally describes a long list of basic equipment and structures missing from training facilities, from protective headgear to mats for defensive exercises. Our observations confirmed many of these shortcomings.

Equally problematic is BPD's inability to evaluate and track officer training, thus failing to properly enforce training requirements. According to internal documents produced to us during the investigation, practical training exercises do not have a comprehensive evaluation tool that measures the skill and comprehension levels of students; instructors are unable to properly assess recruits' proficiency with defensive tactics or their ability to determine when situations require force; and the current curriculum lacks pre- and post-testing procedures for evaluating how training changed recruits' comprehension of relevant information. Nor is there a mechanism to track the follow-up remedial training required after a disciplinary incident. Numerous personnel conveyed that they do not have a workable tracking system for determining when officers require training or have failed to attend a class. Rather, the current system relies on a single officer updating an Excel spreadsheet with the activities of thousands of officers and formulating a training schedule. Likely due to this deficient tracking system, members of the training staff noted that they often find that officers are "missing" significant amounts of required training.

iii. Despite Efforts to Improve Training, Much Work Remains to Fix the Program

Individuals throughout the Department have highlighted that the Department needs to significantly improve its training program. For example, in 2012, the Fraternal Order of Police's *Blueprint for Improved Policing in Baltimore* includes an entire section focused on training issues and recommendations. *See FOP*

Blueprint for Improved Policing (July 11, 2012), at 6–8. More recently, BPD's July 2015 Training Academy Needs Assessment provides a program analysis, describing major issues in personnel, curriculum, equipment and structures, and budgeting. It also notes that the Academy has been working to address some of these issues. This includes topic-area trainings on, for example, the use of force, de-escalation, and understanding youth. The Academy has also begun to create training videos and providing roll-call trainings on current law, two important steps forward. While this is encouraging, these new initiatives will not be successful without a considerable change in the overall approach to the Department's training. Much work remains, and this work will require dedication from all members of the Department to provide BPD's training programs with the necessary resources and to create an atmosphere that actively encourages training and preparation.

Three particular types of training will need significant work if the Department wants to effectively implement reforms. First, the Department lacks sufficient scenario-based training for its officers. This "real world" training is critical for building officers' skills. The FOP has also noted this deficit: according to the FOP, simulation training on real-life scenarios should be an area of focus for BPD, and officers have frequently noted that simulation training is crucial because it teaches officers how to react in situations that regularly arise. *See FOP Blueprint for Improved Policing* (July 11, 2012) at 7. Such training, especially within a defensive tactics or crisis intervention curriculum, helps students determine the most appropriate actions during law enforcement activities, such as the level of force to be used in an encounter. Fortunately, leaders in the Department have also recognized this need, but much work remains to address it.

Second, BPD's Field Training Officer, or FTO, program needs significant improvement. An effective FTO program is a critical tool for the Department to reinforce the training and values communicated to a new officer during the academy. Likewise, a poor FTO program can undermine the investment the Department has made in a recruit before that training has become ingrained. Generally speaking, BPD does not currently attract and retain the right officers for the FTO positions, and those who do become FTOs receive only one week of training. There is a dearth of qualified FTOs throughout the Department; some districts lack FTOs entirely. The importance and benefit of a strong FTO program have long been recognized. *See, e.g.,* Michael S. McCampbell, *Field Training for Police Officers: The State of the Art* (1987) (discussing research showing that FTO programs can help reduce civil liability complaints and increase a police agency's effectiveness in the community). To achieve the reforms required, BPD needs to invest in this program to ensure that the new officers it adds to the Department have a solid foundation to engage in effective and constitutional policing.

Finally, supervisor and leadership training is a critical need within the Department. Across all levels of BPD, we found that training for these positions was deficient. Our interviews revealed that many Department commanders do not have the opportunity to receive command development training, and the FOP noted a similar lack of training. *See FOP Blueprint for Improved Policing* (July 11, 2012) at 6. The Blueprint describes management training overall as "very insular," because department managers generally "stay in Baltimore." *Id.* In an agency of BPD's size, command-level and supervisory training is critical to ensuring that the values of the agency are reinforced by its leaders on a consistent, day-to-day basis. To create the type of cultural transformation required to address the constitutional violations we found, strong, capable leadership is required. Effective leadership, combined with procedural justice internal to the agency, results in officers who are more likely to behave according to agency standards when interacting with members of the community. *See, e.g. The Final Report of the President's Task Force on 21st Century Policing* (May 2015) at 54.

2. BPD Does Not Adequately Supervise Officers or Collect and Analyze Data on their Activities

Serious deficiencies in BPD's supervision of its enforcement activities, including through data collection and analysis, contribute to the Department's failure to identify and correct unconstitutional policing.

a. BPD Does Not Effectively Use Data to Oversee Officer Activity

BPD fails to collect and record important data on a broad range of police activities, and that, when it does collect data, BPD does not use the data to manage and supervise officer activity. As discussed in Section II.A4, *supra*, BPD's own internal audits and other indications demonstrate that officers fail to record any information on a large portion of the stops and searches conducted on Baltimore streets, contrary to BPD's own policies and procedures. When officers do record the existence of a stop, they do not consistently record important information connected to it. We found that officers likewise often fail to report using force against individuals. And as with stops and searches, even where force is reported, officers do not consistently document important supporting information, such as statements from witnesses and other officers on the scene. These omissions violate BPD's own policy requirements. The policies and procedures are also under-inclusive, however, and do not require information to be gathered that is essential to supervise officer activity effectively.

Even where data is collected, BPD fails to store it in systems that are capable of effective tracking and analysis. Chief among the data analysis challenges is BPD's failure to use integrated systems to maintain information. Information technology officers with the Department informed us that BPD uses 232 separate databases to store information, most of which cannot link to each other. Moreover, most files do not contain unique identifiers that allow supervisors to identify and review information about a single incident that may be stored in separate databases. For example, BPD uses different programs or databases to record stops, arrests, and incident reports. The different information captured on these activities is siloed: BPD's systems do not allow a supervisor reviewing the record of an arrest or use of force that stemmed from a pedestrian stop to access the stop record that is maintained separately. BPD's failure to respond to its pattern of conducting unlawful arrests illustrates the consequences of segregating related data in unconnected systems. As explained above, Maryland maintains data on all arrests by BPD officers for which booking officers find "no probable cause" or otherwise result in prosecutors declining to bring charges. Many of these problematic arrests stem from stops, searches, or other incidents described in various BPD reports. Yet the Department lacks any mechanism to connect problematic arrests to information about the enforcement actions that precipitated them because that information is maintained in separate programs or databases. BPD supervisors thus lack critical information to correct these constitutional violations.

Moreover, BPD conducts minimal pattern analysis of officer activities. The Department does not generate any reports or otherwise track patterns in officers' stops, searches, arrests, uses of force, or community interactions. For example, supervisors do not have access to information about how frequently officers search suspects during stops, the proportion of stops and searches that find weapons or contraband, how often stops or arrests lead to officers using force, or how often arrests lead to charges being dismissed. Because the Department does not track these activities, it lacks information to assess the effectiveness of its policing strategies and resource utilization.

BPD's inadequate data collection and analysis reflects broader deficiencies relating to officer supervision that allow constitutional violations to go uncorrected. As explained throughout our findings on stops, searches, arrests, and uses of force, supervisors conduct minimal substantive review of officers' justifications for these activities. A number of supervisors informed us that they view their role as "documenting" activity rather than assessing whether the activity conformed to policy, or that they believe internal affairs—not direct supervision—is the appropriate vehicle for assessing whether an enforcement action meets policy or constitutional requirements. Indeed, our review did not identify a single stop, search, or arrest that a front line supervisor found to violate constitutional standards—even though numerous incident reports for these activities describe facially unlawful police action. Supervisory review of officers' use of force is similarly limited. As explained further in Section II.C.5, *supra*, the Department sustained only one excessive force complaint that came from internal channels between 2010 and 2015, despite the over 2,800 uses of force that BPD recorded during that time period. These failures are compounded by the data collection and analysis deficiencies highlighted above. Supervisors lack important information about the activities and effectiveness of officers under their command.

BPD's failure to implement systems to collect and analyze data undermines not only BPD's ability to supervise its own activities, but also the ability of City leadership and the community to review the activities of their own police force. The lack of data and data analysis renders BPD opaque to any external entity, making it difficult to ascertain whether BPD is policing in a manner that accords with the priorities of City leadership or the communities BPD serves. BPD must institute more effective data management, so that it can be accountable to its community and leadership.

b. BPD Does Not Use an Adequate Early Intervention System

Related to BPD's failure to supervise its officers and collect data on their activities, the Department lacks an adequate early intervention system, or EIS, to identify officers based on patterns in their enforcement activities, complaints, and other criteria. An effective early intervention system allows sergeants, lieutenants, and commanders to proactively supervise the officers under their command and to continually assess officers' risk of engaging in problematic behavior. EIS is a forward-looking tool that helps supervisors interrupt negative patterns before they manifest as misconduct or unconstitutional activity. Likewise, early intervention systems help supervisors recognize positive patterns that should be encouraged. BPD's EIS does not achieve these goals.

Despite BPD's longstanding notice of concerns about its policing activities and problems with its internal accountability systems, the Department has failed to implement an adequate EIS or other system for tracking or auditing information about officer conduct. Rather, BPD has an early intervention system in name only; indeed, BPD commanders admitted to us that the Department's early intervention system is effectively nonfunctional. The system has several key deficiencies. First, BPD sets thresholds of activity that trigger "alerts" to supervisors about potentially problematic conduct that are too high. Because of these high thresholds, BPD supervisors often are not made aware of troubling behavioral patterns until after officers commit egregious misconduct. Second, even where alerts are triggered, we found that BPD supervisors do not consistently take appropriate action to counsel the officer, consider additional training, or otherwise intervene in a way that will correct the behavior before an adverse event occurs. Third, critical information is omitted or expunged from the EIS that could help address officer training or support needs or help prevent future misconduct. For example, BPD expunges discipline imposed from "command investigations"—more than half of all internal investigations handled by the Department—within one year where an officer voluntarily accepts the command punishment. This expungement is problematic for officer discipline, which is not the function of EIS, but it also inhibits a functional EIS because this critical information is omitted. Together, these deficiencies impede BPD's ability to identify and interrupt patterns of behavior that may compromise safety or lead to future misconduct. Moreover, under the State Law Enforcement Officer Bill of Rights, all complaints that do not result in a sustained finding are eligible to be expunged within three years and thus no longer captured in the Department's EIS system.

It is clear that the Department has been unable to interrupt serious patterns of misconduct. Our investigation found that numerous officers had recurring patterns of misconduct that were not adequately addressed. Similarly, we note that, in the past five years, 25 BPD officers were separately sued four or more times for Fourth Amendment violations. BPD has likewise failed to identify officers in need of support through its EIS. For example, one of the officer-involved shooting files we reviewed revealed that the involved officer—who unloaded his entire magazine at a car driving toward him—had been previously involved in two other officer-involved shootings in the past five years, in addition to a long history of complaints for harassment and excessive force. When interviewed about the most recent shooting, the officer told detectives that he believed he still had post-traumatic stress related to the other shootings. Even under BPD's high EIS thresholds, the officer's conduct had triggered alerts. But based on the records we reviewed, the Department failed to respond to those alerts in a way that could have uncovered the officer's condition or otherwise allowed for an intervention. The officer was criminally charged in the shooting. BPD's lack of an effective EIS exposes officers, the Department, and the public to risk that should be avoided.

B. BPD FAILS TO ADEQUATELY SUPPORT ITS OFFICERS

BPD fails to support its officers through effective strategies for recruitment, retention, and staffing patterns, and does not provide them with appropriate technology and equipment. The Department must address a number of internal challenges—namely, current and projected manpower shortages, and outdated technology, facilities, equipment and insufficient resources— in order to ensure that officers are adequately supported. BPD districts are short-staffed, an issue that is further complicated by challenges the Department is facing in retaining experienced officers, and in recruiting qualified cadets. Additionally, the Department's technology, equipment, and facilities are outdated, creating inefficiencies for officers and the Department, and negatively impacting the Department's relationship with the community. The Department also lacks critical resources to support officers, such as psychological counseling for officers following a traumatic incident.

First, BPD does not have a Department-wide plan to address staffing shortages in patrol; instead, each district deals with its own shortages independently. Districts address their staffing shortages by "drafting," or requiring, officers to work additional hours after their regular ten-hour shift. Officers are "drafted" to work up to an additional ten hours after their regular shift, making for, potentially, a twenty-hour day. Only one district indicated that they attempt to draft officers who are not working the following day after being drafted. Each district has crafted its own process of drafting, and there are variations in each district's procedures. The Department has, however, indicated it is in the process of creating a policy to more consistently address staffing shortages. The Department does not record, track, or assess which officers are drafted, how frequently they are drafted, or for how many hours they are drafted per day or over any period of time. Officers we spoke with consistently informed us of the serious negative impact that drafting has on their morale. Additionally, the potential negative impact that drafting has on officers' decision-making skills after working for up to twenty hours is equally troubling. It would be difficult even for officers who are well-trained and guided by proper policies—which BPD officers are not—after working fourteen to twenty hours, to exercise restraint and good judgment in their interactions with the public. It is difficult to expect ill-trained officers who are provided little to no guidance to do so in such circumstances.

It appears BPD's staffing shortage will not be resolved in the short term. We heard from officers, supervisors, and command staff that many officers join

BPD to gain experience in a high-activity environment, and after three to five years, leave the Department for less-demanding and higher-paid positions with neighboring agencies. *See FOP Blueprint for Improved Policing* (July 11, 2012) at 4, 13. This is a significant drain on the Department's resources, as these experienced officers, if they remained, would be the future leaders of the Department, and critical to the success of the Department's law enforcement efforts. The Department also appears to be confronting challenges in recruiting qualified officers—it has only met a fraction of its goals for the 2016 Academy class. At least one of the Department's background check processes—its psychological testing—has been investigated for allegedly rushing those evaluations, sometimes conducting psychological evaluations for aspiring officers in as little as fifteen minutes.[124] The Department must ensure that in its efforts to recruit a sufficient quantity of officers, it does not sacrifice the quality of officers that the Baltimore community and current employees of the Department deserve.

Second, officers are also challenged by BPD's outdated technology, equipment, and facilities. The Department is hampered by significant technological infrastructure gaps and historically has underestimated the infrastructure required to implement technology. While we applaud the Department's advances, such as its commitment to equipping all officers with body-worn cameras, BPD must also ensure that it updates its technological infrastructure to support such initiatives, as necessary. Likewise, officers suffer from being supplied with outdated, broken, or in some cases, no equipment. As one officer noted to the Fraternal Order of Police in a focus group, "How am I supposed to pull someone over for having a taillight out when my car has two?" *See also FOP Blueprint for Improved Policing* (July 11, 2012) at 10. Officers have no computers in their cars, forcing them to return to the district station to type reports, and even those computers are often not working. Although the Department uses the "PocketCop" application on departmentally issued cell phones, we found that many officers did not have access to it for various reasons, and that it could not be used for many reports. This absence of technology for field-based reporting creates an additional drain on the Department's already limited resources. Taking officers off the street to type reports at the district takes away from time that could be spent on law enforcement or community building activities. It also creates inefficiencies for officers who often must write reports on paper in the field while their memories of incidents are fresh, and then type the same information into computer databases after arriving at the district station at the end of their shift.

These equipment issues not only create inefficiencies for officers and drain

---

124 Kevin Rector, *Provider of mental health evaluations for Baltimore police under investigation*, The Baltimore Sun, Aug. 5, 2015 (9:23 PM), http://www.baltimoresun.com/health/bs-md-police-psych-evals-20150805-story.html.

the Department's resources, they also negatively impact officer morale. The dilapidated state of some of the Department's district stations also lowers officer morale, and affects community relationships. The Department also lacks critical support services for officers, such as adequate psychological counseling or peer support program following a shooting or other traumatic event. Despite its budgetary issues, the City of Baltimore will need to make an investment in its public safety facilities and resources to ensure that officers have the tools necessary to properly serve the residents and businesses of the City.

C. BPD FAILS TO HOLD OFFICERS ACCOUNTABLE FOR MISCONDUCT

BPD relies on deficient accountability systems that fail to curb unconstitutional policing. For years, the Department's process of investigating and adjudicating complaints has been plagued by systemic failures, including: discouraging individuals from filing complaints; poor investigative techniques; unnecessary delays; minimal review and supervision; and a persistent failure to discipline officers for misconduct, even in cases of repeated or egregious violations. BPD likewise fails to provide information about officer misconduct in a transparent manner or receive input on the accountability process from the community it serves. As a result, a cultural resistance to accountability has developed and been reinforced within the Department. This culture further undermines accountability by discouraging officers from reporting misconduct and discouraging supervisors from sustaining allegations of it. BPD's persistent failure to hold officers accountable for misconduct contributes to an erosion of the community trust that is central to effective law enforcement.

Central to BPD's accountability systems is the Internal Investigation Division, or IID. IID investigates and resolves complaints of officer misconduct, both complaints received internally from other officers or BPD employees, and those received from members of the community. Within the IID, "Ethics" detectives investigate complaints that officers engaged in potentially criminal activity, or other allegations that, though not criminal, implicate an officer's integrity or truthfulness. "General internal affairs" detectives investigate all other allegations of serious officer misconduct, including most instances of excessive force. Outside of the IID, each of the nine patrol districts, along with each Specialized Unit within BPD's Operations Bureau, housed a "Command Investigations Unit," or CIU, until January of 2016, when the Department centralized all Command Investigation Units at the IID. Before centralization, each CIU operated independently of the other CIUs and of the IID. The CIUs investigate minor violations of BPD policy, and BPD has authorized district and unit commanders to impose minor discipline in the event an accused officer agrees to the discipline.

When IID sustains the allegations in an investigation,[125] or an officer re-

---

125 When BPD completes an internal investigation, there are four possible outcomes. The Department can sustain an allegation, which means investigators found, by a preponderance of evidence, that a policy violation occurred. Allegations can be found "not

fuses to accept discipline at the command level, the case is sent to the Office of
Administrative Hearings to coordinate the drafting of administrative charges
and, if necessary, to arrange disciplinary proceedings. Under the State's Law
Enforcement Officer's Bill of Rights (LEOBR), officers are then entitled to an
adversarial hearing, or trial board, before the Department can discipline them.
At BPD, trial boards convened to adjudicate certain minor violations of BPD's
command discipline policy typically consist of one person, drawn from a pool
of BPD commanders. Trial boards convened to adjudicate major discipline are
composed of two commanders and one BPD member of the same rank as the
accused officer. If the trial board finds the officer is not guilty of violating BPD
policy, that finding terminates the case and the Department cannot discipline
the officer. But if the trial board finds the officer is guilty, it hears a presentation of mitigating evidence, and then recommends discipline. Ultimately, the
commissioner determines the appropriate discipline, but may only do so if the
trial board first finds the officer guilty. The commissioner may depart from the
Board's recommendation and impose less or more discipline. But if the commissioner imposes greater discipline, the officer is entitled to another opportunity to be heard. The officer may then appeal any discipline imposed by the
Department to the state courts in Maryland.

We found deficiencies throughout these accountability systems that undermine adherence to BPD's policies and procedures and contribute to the violations of federal law that we found.

1. BPD Lacks Adequate Systems to Investigate Complaints and Impose Discipline

BPD's systems for holding officers accountable are plagued by several deficiencies. We found that BPD discourages members of the public from filing
complaints; improperly classifies complaints to mask misconduct; delays investigations of complaints unnecessarily; uses poor investigative techniques to
gather evidence about misconduct; fails to consistently document the results
of its investigations; and does not receive input from the community or share
information about its investigative processes. As a result, the Department is
rarely able to impose discipline for misconduct, and many officers believe that
disciplinary determinations are not made fairly or consistently.

---

sustained," which means that investigators were unable to tell either way. Allegations can
be unfounded, meaning the investigator determined that the violation did *not* occur. Or
allegations may be exonerated, meaning that the action alleged did occur, but that it did not
violate Department policy.

a. BPD Discourages Members of the Public from Filing Complaints

BPD discourages members of the public from filing complaints against officers through the procedural requirements BPD has imposed on filing complaints, and BPD officers and supervisors have actively discouraged community members from filing complaints. These practices pose significant barriers to members of the Baltimore community who try to alert the Department to misconduct by its officers.

As an initial matter, BPD places unnecessary conditions on the filing of complaints. While the Department ostensibly accepts complaints made in person, by telephone, or over email, it requires complaints alleging many common types of misconduct—including excessive force, abusive language, harassment, false arrest and imprisonment—to be signed, notarized, and filed in person at one of just a few locations throughout the City.[126] Additionally, complaints alleging excessive force must be sworn under penalty of perjury. Although IID commanders we interviewed informed us that, despite these requirements, the Department investigates all complaints even if they are not notarized or submitted in person, our review of BPD's files indicated that, in practice, BPD does not investigate unless these requirements are met. For example, in 2013 an individual called BPD's internal affairs to complain about an officer who grabbed him by the neck and called him a "punk ass faggot." Although the individual gave a statement describing the incident over the phone, BPD supervisors closed the case because the complainant did not show up in person at BPD's Internal Investigation Division to "fill out a CRB form and to have his statement notarized." Indeed, the BPD investigator claimed that the man "failed to cooperate" by not submitting a notarized form. These requirements all but ensure that numerous anonymous complaints, or those received over the phone, by email, or in person at any of BPD's nine police districts, will go unexamined.

In addition, we found examples of BPD officers expressly discouraging civilians from filing complaints, sometimes mocking or humiliating them in the process. Some civilians wishing to alert BPD to officer misconduct had to endure verbal abuse and contact BPD multiple times before investigators would move forward with any investigation. As described *supra* at 69–70, for example, BPD officers ridiculed an African-American man attempting to file a complaint that officers used excessive force and racial slurs during an arrest: when the man arrived at the district headquarters to make the complaint, officers told him, "you can take your black ass down to Kirk Avenue before the bus leaves because you know how you black people like the bus." Kirk Avenue

---

126 If the complaint is made by a juvenile, the juvenile must be accompanied by an adult.

is the location of BPD's Internal Investigation Division. In another incident, a woman alleged that a BPD supervisor flatly refused to accept a complaint that officers used excessive force when arresting her son. According to the woman, the supervisor refused to accept the complaint, telling the woman "she could not go against her officers."

To ensure that it learns about potential constitutional violations and other misconduct by its officers, and to rebuild its relationship with many of the communities it serves, BPD must reform its complaint intake procedures and make them accessible to the public.

b. Supervisors Misclassify Complaints and "Administratively Close" Them Without Investigation

After intake of a complaint, BPD investigators frequently misclassify those complaints or administratively close them with little attempt to contact the complainant.

First, BPD investigators often inappropriately categorize complaints as minor allegations that may be resolved at the command level without IID involvement. Appropriately categorizing a complaint is critical because it affects which internal affairs component will investigate, the level of investigation undertaken, and the possible discipline imposed. BPD's policy on command discipline lists categories of cases which "may" be handled by the district, but this fails to provide guidance for officers and detectives about when cases should be referred to IID, or who is responsible for making that decision. Instead, we were told that BPD officers and IID investigators categorize complaints based on "common sense." Moreover, we found that BPD does not use its internal affairs database to consistently review how complaints are categorized, and that is its only mechanism for doing so. This process vests considerable discretion in supervisors, and we found that supervisors frequently use this discretion to classify allegations of misconduct that result in minimal investigation. Indeed, we found that the Department resolved the majority of the approximately 38,000 allegations[127] made against BPD officers from 2010 through 2015 at the command level without referral to IID, resulting in significantly less investigation. Moreover, of these 38,000 allegations, 9,694 allegations were categorized as "supervisor complaints," which, according to BPD commanders, require no investigation at all. Accordingly, allegations handled as supervisor complaints virtually never result in discipline. We found that BPD "administratively closed" 67 percent of supervisor complaints and sustained just 0.27 percent of them, or 1 out of every 370 allegations.

Many complaints that were sent to command investigations or classified

---

127 A single complaint may contain multiple allegations.

as "supervisor complaints" alleged serious misconduct, including allegations that officers committed criminal assault, theft, and domestic violence. In 2014, for example, although a complaint on intake alleged a "sexual assault," the case was assigned to a command investigations unit and categorized as "misconduct/improper search" and "discourtesy." In 2011, a sergeant likewise misclassified a complaint alleging that that BPD officers had been harassing an African-American woman's nephew over the past month by repeatedly stopping him near their home in West Baltimore. Though the woman wished to make a complaint of harassment, the sergeant categorized the complaint as a "supervisor complaint" and closed the case without conducting any interviews of the involved officers or the woman's nephew. This is troubling, particularly given our findings that BPD officers engage in unlawful stops and discriminatory policing.

Second, even where complaints are nominally "accepted," BPD supervisors often "administratively close" them with minimal investigation. Indeed, BPD supervisors administratively closed 33 percent of all allegations received from 2010 through 2015—ensuring that the allegations would result in no further investigation or officer discipline. Administrative closures frequently occur after supervisors make only minimal efforts to contact the complainant. Some of the files we reviewed contained no indication that investigators attempted to contact complainants at all. Many other files showed that investigations languished for months before investigators made any effort to reach out, or that investigators closed cases after complainants failed to respond to a single letter, answer a phone call, or appear for a scheduled interview. By administratively closing complaints, BPD investigators evade BPD policy that requires all complaints to be labeled as sustained, not sustained, exonerated or unfounded. Some BPD officers we interviewed believed it was appropriate to administratively close a complaint when the complainant withdrew his or her complaint, or could otherwise not be reached. Others believed "complaints" that failed to allege a "real" violation of BPD policy should be administratively closed. These administrative closures, combined with BPD's failure to ensure that complaints are appropriately classified, undermine BPD's system of accountability and contributes to the perception shared by officers and community members alike that discipline is inconsistent and arbitrary.

c. BPD Fails to Investigate Complaints in a Timely Manner or with Effective Techniques

When investigations of complaints do proceed, they are hampered from the start by poor investigative techniques and unreasonable delays. These failures limit the Department's ability to discipline its officers by preventing investigators from gathering evidence of misconduct and subjecting evidence to attack during administrative proceedings.

i. Delays Impede Investigations

BPD's misconduct investigations are frequently plagued by delays that compromise the evidence-gathering process and undermine community confidence. As an initial matter, even when BPD nominally "accepts" an external complaint and assigns the case to an investigator, the Department's practice in most cases is to not investigate that complaint until the individual appears in person at BPD's Internal Investigation Division during business hours and participates in a formal, taped interview. By that point, key evidence that could corroborate claims may be lost or destroyed. We found instances in which investigators waited months before canvassing neighborhoods in which alleged misconduct occurs. After such delays, physical evidence is often destroyed, witnesses cannot be located, and witness memories have faded. Other important evidence, such as surveillance video, may also be unavailable.

These delays not only impede effective investigations, they communicate to the community that BPD does not take complaints seriously—even those alleging egregious officer behavior. For example, a man alleged in 2013 that two plainclothes officers punched him in the face, placed him in a chokehold, and spit in his face during an arrest. The man, whose arrest prosecutors declined to pursue, participated in a formal interview at IID during which he provided the investigator with the name of a witness to the incident, and the witness's wife, who could help investigators locate him. The investigator made no effort to follow up with the civilian witness until eight months after the incident occurred. At that time, the investigator went to the car wash where the witness's wife had been working at the time of the incident and was told by the owner that she was no longer employed there. The investigator then recommended to close the complaint as "not sustained" because "[w]ithout testimony from independent witnesses," along with the officers' denial, "there exists insufficient evidence to prove or disprove the allegations." BPD's investigation of a second 2013 complaint alleging serious misconduct suffered even longer delays. The complainant alleged he was hospitalized after two officers slammed him to the ground and unlawfully arrested him for "hindering" and failing to obey due to his refusal to leave the area while officers questioned his brother-in-law. The complaint was not investigated for thirteen months while two command investigation units sent the complaint back and forth. After the case was rediscovered after an audit of IA Pro, it lingered for another four months before a supervisor finally assigned the case to an IID detective. BPD ultimately found the complaint not sustained for "lack of cooperation" when witnesses failed to show up for interviews *seventeen months* after the complaint was filed. According to the investigative file, the Department never interviewed the accused officers.

In another egregious example, an investigator made minimal delayed attempts to look into a woman's complaint that two BPD officers fondled her when conducting a search and called her a "junkie, whore bitch." The investigator assigned to the case made no attempt to contact the woman until four months after she made these serious allegations. And at that point, the investigator merely sent the woman a certified letter seeking information. Two months later, after the letter had come back unclaimed, the investigator went to the residential address the woman had originally provided, only to discover she had been evicted months before. Moreover, the delays precluded investigators from identifying relevant video evidence. The incident occurred in a public location—the Lexington Market—that was likely captured on video surveillance. Yet the detective made no attempt to gather the footage until ten months after the incident. By that time, any video had been deleted. Investigators also waited ten months to reach out to a witness, even though the complainant had provided the witness's contact information at the time she filed the complaint. Ultimately, the investigator learned that the complainant had passed away several months before he first contacted the witness. BPD then found the complaint "not sustained."

In these and many similar cases we reviewed, unnecessary delays precluded BPD investigators from gathering important evidence about allegations of serious misconduct. Going forward, collecting and assessing such evidence in a timely manner will be a critical piece of the accountability system that BPD must build to identify officers' constitutional violations and impose appropriate discipline.

ii. BPD Uses Ineffective Methods to Investigate Misconduct Allegations

In addition to frequent delays that limit the information available about misconduct allegations, poor investigative techniques further compromise BPD's investigations. We identified several key failures that recur throughout the Department's investigative files, including the failure to adequately consider inconsistencies in investigations, as well as inappropriate interviewing methods and notice of allegations.

First, investigators fail to adequately consider evidence and statements from witnesses or other officers that contradict explanations provided by officers accused of misconduct. Indeed, BPD appears to apply a standard that favors officers when evaluating statements made by complainants and involved officers. While BPD's Internal Affairs Manual encourages investigators to be wary of a complainant's inconsistent statements, the Department permits officers to submit addendums that clarify their original statements. And when inconsistencies arise—either from such addenda or other evidence—investigators generally discredit or discount entirely evidence contradicting the accused officer's account. We found investigations in which this took place even where the accused officer's account is contradicted by physical evidence, including photographic or video evidence.

Second, BPD investigators compromise officer interviews by failing to probe beyond reports the accused officer already provided, and performing unrecorded "pre-interviews" with accused officers. As we described in Section II.C.5, *supra* at 107, regarding force investigations, these pre-interviews compromise the integrity of an investigation. Similarly, we also found numerous instances in which officers reviewed their statement or administrative report related to the incident before the interview, and the interview then consisted merely of the accused officer orally reciting his administrative report.[128] IID investigators did not probe beyond this oral recitation. These interview techniques inhibit the function of IID investigators to obtain reliable information from officers accused of misconduct.

Third, BPD risks compromising investigations by providing accused officers with a detailed notice describing the alleged misconduct, often right after a complaint has been filed and before any investigation occurs. While LEOBR provides that officers must receive basic notice of allegations and five days to obtain counsel prior to questioning, BPD frequently notifies officers almost immediately after the Department receives a complaint.[129] This notice often takes place before a detective undertakes any investigation or even attempts to contact the complainant to set up an interview. Moreover, the notice specifically articulates the allegations against the officer—sometimes including the date and time of the incident in question. Providing such detailed notice at the outset of an investigation, which is not required by LEOBR, may compromise certain investiga-

---

128 BPD officers' collective bargaining agreement provides the opportunity to review statements and reports prior to being interviewed.

129 Until early 2016, LEOBR entitled officers to a ten day notice period to obtain counsel prior to being questioned. We note that these waiting periods prescribed by LEOBR may, in many instances, impede effective investigations, and that a similar waiting period is not afforded to members of the public who may have been involved in an incident or were witnesses to the incident. In some instances, we saw evidence that BPD required witnesses to be interviewed immediately, even while the witness's friend or family member was being taken to the hospital as a result of the incident. The best practice is to interview the officer as soon as possible. Additionally, the International Association of Chiefs of Police "opposes any special and/or additional protection for law enforcement officers. Officers' rights should be no greater than those of other private and public sector employees." LEGISLATIVE AGENDA FOR THE 114TH CONGRESS, INTERNATIONAL ASSOCIATION OF CHIEFS OF POLICE 20, http://www.theiacp.org/Portals/0/documents/pdfs/IACP114th LegislativeAgenda.pdf.

tive steps and opens the possibility that a complainant may be retaliated against or intimidated prior to speaking with investigators. Indeed, the Department's own internal affairs audit identified these same potential problems in 2014. The Department nonetheless continues to use its early notification practice.

iii. BPD Fails to Adequately Supervise Investigations

The deficiencies in BPD's investigative techniques persist in part because of ineffective supervision and training. Indeed, we found that most investigators receive no formal investigative training. Lack of training coupled with minimal supervision results in some investigators continuing to rely on poor investigative techniques. For example, one CIU detective who was responsible for all command investigations for an entire district told us that his practice was to allow accused officers to be interviewed by questionnaire—which officers could complete off-site with the assistance of their attorneys—rather than submit to in-person interviews. Although BPD formally discontinued the use of written questionnaires years ago, the practice persists because of inadequate training and oversight. Indeed, this practice has continued even after it was criticized by the Department's own internal affairs audit.

Moreover, BPD supervisors fail to identify deficiencies or questionable findings in investigations. We found that commanders consistently approve investigative findings, even where investigative files are deficient or incomplete. In our review, we found that files frequently omitted basic information, such as the outcome of the investigation or any discipline imposed. We also found key pieces of evidence referred to in the investigator's narrative—including witness statements, photographs, and video footage—were left out of the case file itself. Nevertheless, across all the case files we reviewed, we saw virtually no evidence that supervisors sent cases back for further investigation or clarification. Nor do supervisors meaningfully review investigators' determinations about whether to sustain complaints. Indeed, CIU investigators told us they were not required to have supervisors review and sign off on investigations that resulted in findings of "not sustained," although supervisors must approve an investigation that results in a finding of "sustained."

Additionally, BPD's internal affairs files and database indicate that BPD does not adequately supervise investigators to ensure that they meet investigative deadlines, especially in the command investigations units. Under LEOBR, in order to discipline an officer for misconduct, the Department must complete the internal investigation and bring administrative charges within one year. We reviewed complaints where investigators recommended closing cases because the investigations had extended past the one-year deadline. Indeed, BPD's internal affairs database itself includes possible "findings" that indicate cases were closed due to "expiration."

Finally, BPD has not taken sufficient steps to ensure that investigators do not have a conflict of interest. We found instances in which conflicts of interest could have compromised an internal investigation. For example, one internal affairs detective we interviewed told us that he had been detailed to serve under the supervision of an officer he was investigating at that time, and that the commander knew of the investigation. This is troubling, and it communicates to officers, investigators, and the community that internal investigations are not a priority of the Department.

BPD's failure to ensure that investigations are thoroughly and fairly investigated limits its ability to hold officers accountable for misconduct. Without adequate evidence, the chances of sustaining allegations of officer misconduct are diminished. And even where allegations of misconduct are sustained, the Department's ability to marshal adequate evidence at trial board proceedings is compromised. Consequently, officers frequently do not face internal discipline even where evidence of misconduct exists.

d. BPD Fails to Sustain Complaints and Apply Discipline Consistently

Deficiencies in BPD's complaint intake and investigation contribute to BPD's extremely low rate of sustaining allegations of officer misconduct, which in turn leads to a lack of discipline and accountability in the Department. Discipline for allegations of serious misconduct is rare. Of the 1,382 allegations of excessive force that BPD tracked from 2010 through 2015, only 31 allegations, or 2.2 percent were sustained. These allegations arose out of fourteen separate incidents. In light of the significant evidence of excessive force we found in our investigation, the low rate of sustaining excessive force complaints is troubling. Similarly, BPD completed investigations into 1,359 allegations of discourtesy from 2010 through 2015, and sustained just 2.6 percent of those allegations, arising out of just fifteen incidents. This low number of sustained outcomes is also concerning, considering the number of community members we spoke to who described BPD officers behaving in a rude or abusive manner during encounters with community members.

When complaints of misconduct are sustained, however, the trial board process that follows in order for discipline to be imposed also has several problems that impede accountability. First, the process is beset by delay. The Department reported to us, for example, that some trial boards conducted in 2015 were to resolve cases BPD began investigating in 2011. Delays of this magnitude send a message to officers that misconduct is tolerated, frustrating officers and supervisors who are trying to follow and implement Department policies and procedures. They also signal to the public, and in particular to the complainant, that officers who commit misconduct are unlikely to be held accountable.

Second, officers facing the trial board have substantial powers granted to them by LEOBR and BPD's collective bargaining agreements to shape the membership of the trial board that will hear their case, undermining accountability. Trial boards convened by BPD to adjudicate allegations of misconduct are typically composed of three officers selected from a pool determined by the commissioner. Under LEOBR, each board must include one officer who is "the same rank as the law enforcement officer against whom the complaint is filed."[130] The accused officer has the right to reject assigned Board members a total of three times through the use of peremptory strikes. The officer can exercise these strikes up to and including the day of the hearing itself, potentially dismissing all members of the board. We heard from numerous sources, including many within BPD and City leadership, that this use of peremptory strikes permits officers to assemble a trial board sympathetic to their interests, particularly because the pool of eligible command staff in the Department is limited, and because the command staff members are also part of the same union. The Maryland legislature amended LEOBR in early 2016 to authorize jurisdictions within the state to allow up to two voting or nonvoting civilians to serve on trial boards if authorized by local law or if negotiated through collective bargaining with the police union. To date, BPD does not allow civilians to serve on the trial board.

Although BPD produced a very limited amount of information about trial board proceedings, we saw indications that the construction of the trial boards undermines confidence in the equity of the process. We requested information on all trial boards conducted between 2010 and 2015, and BPD produced only twelve transcripts of trial board proceedings, and no summaries and no written findings for the 139 trial boards the Department reported took place between 2010 and 2015, despite our request that the Department produce "all documentation" concerning trial board cases. In addition, BPD's attorneys told us the Department will only create a transcript of a trial board that results in a guilty finding if the officer challenges the discipline imposed in court. This lack of information is consistent with BPD's own assessment: according to an internal audit, BPD has historically failed to fully track information related to disciplining officers. Such minimal documentation of the trial board process prevents the Department from fully evaluating the proceedings or identifying patterns or deficiencies that may contribute to the Department's failure to discipline an officer.

This lack of consistency and fairness in imposing discipline has a profound effect on officer morale, and it also affects how officers interact with the public. Throughout our interviews and ride-alongs with officers, we heard officers ex-

---

130 Md. Code Ann., Pub. Safety § 3–107.

press that discipline is only imposed if an incident makes it into the press or if you were on the wrong side of a supervisor, not because of the magnitude of the misconduct. Similarly, some officers felt that command staff creates an appearance of addressing problems after a high-profile incident by rushing to issue new policies, without any officer input, and often in conflict with existing policies. By BPD rushing to issue these new policies, officers felt that they were not provided with adequate training to follow the new rules, exposing them to risk even as the Department appeared to address the problem and respond to City politics. This lack of internal procedural justice—officers' sense that they are being treated fairly by their Department—diminishes officer morale and diminishes officers' adherence to Departmental rules. This, in turn, can make officers less likely to treat members of the public fairly and in accordance with BPD policies and procedures, potentially contributing to violations of federal law we found in our investigation. *See, e.g.,* Nicole E. Haas et. al., *Explaining officer compliance: The importance of procedural justice and trust inside a police organization,* Criminology & Criminal Justice, p. 14 (January 2015) (finding that "the perception of procedural justice and trust is associated with higher levels of endorsement of rules and regulations on the use of force").

e. BPD Lacks Effective Civilian or Community Oversight

BPD's accountability system is shielded almost entirely from public view, and the civilian oversight mechanisms that are currently in place are inadequate and ineffective. These flaws damage the Department's legitimacy in the community.

Community members are unable to obtain information about BPD's complaint and discipline systems at almost every step in the process. Complainants face many hurdles in filing complaints, but once they are filed, it is difficult for complainants to obtain information about how the complaints are progressing or whether and when they will be acted upon. Indeed, even when discipline is imposed, notice of this action is only given to a small group within the Department, not to the complainant or to the public except in unusual circumstances where the Department determines that a broader announcement of the discipline is in the public interest. Trial board proceedings have been closed to the public historically. Although they were opened to the public in early 2016, it is too early to determine what effect this has on the community's ability to affect the accountability process. The Maryland Public Information Act, or MPIA, further limits BPD's transparency to the public. The MPIA prohibits disclosure of documents that constitute "personnel records." *See* Md. Code Ann. § 10–616. The statute does not define the scope of this prohibition, but Maryland appellate courts have held that it applies to all materials related to hiring, promotions, and discipline, as well as "any matter involving an employee's status." *See, e.g., Montgomery County v. Shropshire,* 23 A.3d 205, 215 (Md. Ct. App. 2011).

We heard from numerous sources that this provision has repeatedly blocked attempts to access information about the resolution of complaints and other issues of public concern related to BPD's policing activities.

In addition, Baltimore's Civilian Review Board, or CRB, has proven to be ineffective at changing this dynamic, in large part because it has never been provided with adequate authority or resources to perform its intended function. Established in 2000, the Board was meant to be a crucial check on police misconduct by providing an alternative investigative and review process. The Board is made up of civilian representatives from each of the City's nine police districts selected by the Mayor and approved by the City Counsel, along with members without voting power from local advocacy organizations and the local chapter of the Fraternal Order of Police. The Board may accept complaints that allege excessive force, abusive language, harassment, false arrest, and false imprisonment directly from the community. BPD is also required by policy to forward all complaints containing these categories of allegations to the Board. The Board may review BPD's investigations, or it may conduct an independent investigation and make recommendations directly to the commissioner that the complaint be sustained, not sustained, unfounded, or exonerated. It can also request that BPD undertake additional investigation.

The Board has faced several impediments to serving as a meaningful community backstop for accountability. First, the Board relies upon BPD to forward complaints that fall within its authority, except when a complaint is filed directly with the Board, and BPD often fails to forward complaints in a timely manner. Indeed, CRB staff members told us of cases BPD forwarded to the Board only after BPD had already closed its investigation, despite BPD's obligation to share the complaint with the Board within 48 hours of receipt. The Board has no authority to audit BPD to determine if it has received all the complaints that should have been forwarded to it. Second, the Board has insufficient resources and authority to conduct its own investigations. During 2010 to 2015, the Board only had a single investigator to investigate all the complaints that fell within its authority. The Board also cannot compel officers to participate in investigations; indeed, LEOBR provides that sworn law enforcement officers can only be "interrogated" by other sworn law enforcement officers. Finally, when the Board makes recommendations to the commissioner about investigative findings, or recommends that the IID conduct additional investigation, the Board has no way of knowing if BPD acts on its recommendations, much less requiring that BPD do so. The lack of resources and authority that the City currently invests in the Board render it ineffective, heightening community perceptions that BPD is resistant to accountability.

We note that we are encouraged that the Civilian Review Board was recently able to hire several new staff members, and is now coordinating a new mediation initiative for police and community members. Although these are steps in the right direction, the Board will still be unable to fulfill its mission if it is not granted more authority and supported with adequate resources to perform its duties.

2. BPD's Internal Culture is Resistant to Effective Discipline

The longstanding deficiencies in BPD's systems for investigating complaints has contributed to a cultural resistance to accountability that persists in the Department. The cultural opposition to meaningful accountability within the Department is reflected by the lack of discipline for serious misconduct and widespread violations of minor policy provisions; the failure to take action against officers with a known reputation for repeatedly violating Department policy and constitutional requirements; and the reluctance of officers to report observed misconduct for fear that doing so will subject them to retaliation.

a. BPD Has Allowed Violations of Policy To Go Unaddressed Even When They Are Widespread Or Involve Serious Misconduct

In part because of the above failures in investigating complaints against officers, BPD allows policy violations to go unaddressed, even when they occur in large number or involve serious misconduct. For example, the most common allegations of policy violation that fall under command investigations level is that officers fail to appear in court. The Department's internal affairs database indicates that 6,571 allegations were made that officers failed to appear in court between January 1, 2010, and March 28, 2016. For 1,698 of these allegations, the Department did not record any disposition at all, although a "completed date" has been entered for all but a handful of these incidents, indicating that the investigation has concluded. Additionally, the Department "administratively closed" 1,142 of the cases. Thus, nearly half of these policy violations—43 percent—resulted in no action being taken against the officer for failing to appear in court. Without the arresting or witnessing officer's testimony, many of these cases lack adequate evidence to proceed, and are dismissed.

Moreover, we found evidence that some BPD officers engage in criminal behavior that BPD does not sufficiently address. We heard complaints from the community that some officers target members of a vulnerable population—people involved in the sex trade—to coerce sexual favors from them in exchange for avoiding arrest, or for cash or narcotics. This conduct is not only criminal, it is an abuse of power. Unfortunately, we not only found evidence of this conduct in BPD's internal affairs files, it appeared that the Department failed to adequately investigate allegations of such conduct, allowing it to recur.

For example, BPD investigators became aware of one officer's alleged misconduct in March of 2012 when they conducted a "prostitution initiative" "for the purposes of gathering intelligence and obtaining confidential informants relating to police corruption." One of the women interviewed informed BPD investigators that she met with a certain officer and engaged in sexual activities in the officer's patrol car once every other week "in exchange for U.S. Currency or immunity from arrest." The Department administratively closed the case nine months later, without, it appears, referring the matter for criminal prosecution or interviewing the accused officer, or any other potential witnesses.

Ten months after closing the first investigation, the Chief of BPD's Office of Professional Responsibility received an anonymous "Crime Stoppers" tip that the same officer was "having sex in his patrol vehicle" with a different person involved in the sex trade. The Department initiated a new investigation, and assigned the case to a different detective. One day after opening the investigation, an assistant state's attorney directed the detective to subpoena the woman's phone records for a six month-period. The detective waited more than a month to do so, and then did not review those records for another six months, until May of 2014. The records confirmed that the officer and the woman exchanged 237 text messages and five phone calls in the six-month period for which records were subpoenaed. Approximately four months later, the State's Attorney's Office declined to prosecute the officer, though BPD's administrative investigation remained open.

Four months after the State's Attorney's Office declined to prosecute, in February of 2015, BPD received a third, new tip that the same officer was engaging in sexual activities with the same woman involved in the sex trade who was mentioned in the "Crime Stoppers" tip. The new tip came from a neighboring Police Department, which interviewed the woman and subpoenaed her phone records in the course of an investigation. Though BPD's administrative investigation into the "Crime Stoppers" tip remained open, BPD opened a third, separate investigation into the new tip, assigning a new, third detective to investigate the same officer's conduct. The case was assigned "low" priority. The third BPD detective attempted to interview the woman but postponed the interview because she was in ill health. Two days later, the woman passed away. The investigators finally reviewed the officer's phone records, which indicated that the officer had exchanged text messages—some sexually explicit—with several other women whose numbers were linked to online profiles for sex trade services. Finally, months later, Department investigators interviewed the officer two times in connection with the two open investigations. The allegations resulting from the "Crime Stoppers" tip and the third investigation were eventually sustained in the fall of 2015, based largely on the evidence provided by the neighboring Police Department. The officer was allowed to resign from BPD. It is unclear from BPD's files whether any state authorities were notified of the officer's sexual misconduct.

This was not the only case in which allegations were made that officers co-erced sex in exchange for immunity from arrest. We found other complaints of this nature were also not properly investigated. Failing to properly investigate allegations that officers were engaged in sexual misconduct is troubling in light of the concerns of gender bias discussed *supra* at 122–27. Failing to properly investigate and address repeated policy violations and serious misconduct also does a disservice to community members and the vast majority of law-abiding BPD officers who are unfairly tainted by the misconduct of a few. By failing to timely address repeated policy violations and misconduct the Department does harm to its internal credibility and external legitimacy.

b. BPD Has Failed To Take Action Against Offenders Known to Engage in Repeated Misconduct

Our investigation also found substantial evidence that BPD fails to take disci-plinary action against officers BPD knows have engaged in serious or repeated misconduct. One example of this problem is the so-called "Do Not Call" list. BPD has had notice, including from the State's Attorney's Office, that partic-ular officers may be engaging in behavior that is, at a minimum, unethical and impacts their credibility and integrity. Through at least 2011, the State's Attorney's Office maintained a formal "Do Not Call" list of officers prosecu-tors would not call to testify because they believed their testimony would be undermined by issues of credibility or integrity. The size of this list varied over time, and included as many as a dozen officers. BPD was aware of the list— the State's Attorney's office regularly discussed the officers on the list with the Chief of BPD's Office of Professional Responsibility—but failed to take action on the information. Instead, the officers listed remained on the streets, making arrests that could not be credibly prosecuted. At one point, we were told, an entire squad's members were on the list, leading to a number of cases being dismissed. Although the formal "Do Not Call" list has been discontinued, the State's Attorney's Office continues to discuss problem officers with BPD.

BPD's ability to take disciplinary action against officers on the "Do Not Call" list is expressly circumscribed by LEOBR and BPD's contract with the police union. Specifically, BPD cannot take punitive action against the officer "based solely on the fact that [the] officer is included on the list," including demotion, dismissal, suspension without pay, or reduction in pay.[131] Because of this prohibition, BPD has not taken any action against officers that the State's

---

131 Md. Code Ann., Pub. Safety § 3–106.1.

Attorney's Office has notified BPD cannot be called to testify, and these officers remain on duty. Particularly given the evidence of numerous unlawful stops, searches, and arrests that we found, the fact that officers whose arrests are not able to be prosecuted remain on the street is troubling. While LEOBR may prevent the Department from taking disciplinary action against officers solely for appearing on the list, it does not prevent the Department from taking other action, including initiating its own investigation of officers' conduct to independently determine whether discipline, training, reassignment, or other action is appropriate.

We also found evidence that BPD fails to take action against officers with a long history of misconduct that is well known to the Department. Our investigation found, for example, that one officer currently employed by BPD has received approximately 125 complaints from complainants within the Department and from the community since 2010, and many of these complaints allege serious misconduct. Indeed, complaints from different individuals alleged remarkably similar facts—specifically, that the officer subjects civilians to unwarranted strip and cavity searches in public. But the Department has sustained only one complaint against the officer for minor misconduct—for not filing a proper vehicle inventory report, resulting in the loss of a camera valued at $1,200. The officer was "verbally counseled on the proper procedure" for filling out inventory reports. Although we were unable to conclusively determine whether other complaints should have been sustained based on the information BPD provided, such a large number of complaints, including unrelated complaints alleging similar behavior, is troubling. We have serious concerns that BPD is not adequately addressing repeated misconduct by its officers.

c. BPD Officers are Reluctant to Report Misconduct

BPD's systemic accountability failures have also contributed to a culture in which some officers are reluctant to raise concerns to supervisors about problematic policing practices or identify misconduct by their fellow officers. Several officers told Justice Department investigators that they believe their fellow officers have retaliated against them for reporting misconduct or objecting to improper enforcement activities. Other officers expressed fears that they would face such retaliation, and that BPD supervisors would not address any retaliation that occurs. Our review of BPD's internal affairs files underscores these concerns.

Several examples highlight BPD's resistance to internal accountability. In 2014, a BPD lieutenant placed several signs next to the desk of an African-American sergeant with a reputation for speaking out about alleged misconduct in the Department. Among the signs were warnings to "stay in your lane," "worry about yourself," "mind your own business!!" and "don't spread rumors!!!" After the sergeant filed a complaint about the signs, the lieutenant admitted to creating them and placing them next to the sergeant's desk. Yet BPD took no meaningful corrective action. Though the complaint was sustained, the lieutenant received no suspension, fine, or loss of benefits. Instead, he was given only "verbal counseling" instructing him that such behavior is "unprofessional and inappropriate." This minimal response to admitted allegations that a supervisor warned his subordinate to "mind your own business" rather than report misconduct underlines BPD's failure to create a culture of accountability.

In a widely-publicized incident,[132] a former BPD detective in the Violent Crime Impact Division (VCID) faced retaliation after reporting two officers, including his sergeant, for alleged excessive force in the fall of 2011. According to the detective, the VCID unit arrested a man for drug possession after a chase that ended with the man breaking into the home of an officer's girlfriend to hide. According to the officers' reports of the incident, after the man's arrest the sergeant brought him back inside the home to "apologize" to the woman living there. When the man emerged from the home, his shirt was ripped open, he was bleeding, and he had suffered a broken ankle and other injuries. The sergeant claimed that the arrested man injured himself by attempting to headbutt the sergeant and falling to the ground. Concerned that the sergeant and off-duty officer had beaten the man inside the home, the detective asked a different BPD sergeant whether to report the incident to internal affairs. According to the detective, the sergeant discouraged him from reporting the incident, stating "If you're a rat, your career here is done." The detective reported the incident to prosecutors in the State's Attorney's Office, who indicted both officers on criminal charges stemming from the incident. After the detective testified against the officers at trial, a jury convicted the sergeant of misconduct and the off-duty officer of assault and obstruction of justice.

The detective faced significant retaliation for exposing this misconduct. The detective recounted that, after reporting the incident to prosecutors, fellow officers frequently called him a "rat." A sergeant left pictures of cheese on the detective's desk. The detective also told us that a lieutenant denied his transfer request to a violent repeat offender squad because the detective "snitched." The lieutenant allegedly said that the detective was "not the right fit" for the unit

132 See Justin Fenton, *Whistle-blower officer files lawsuit against Batts, BPD,* The Baltimore Sun (Dec. 23, 2014, 6:55 PM), http://www.baltimoresun.com/news/maryland/baltimore-city/bs-md-ci-crystal-whistleblower-ratgate-lawsuit-20141223-story.html; Albert Samaha, *Breaking Baltimore's Blue Wall of Silence,* Buzzfeed (May 14, 2015, 9:09 PM), https://www.buzzfeed.com/albertsamaha/breaking-baltimores-blue-wall-of-silence?; Luke Broadwater, *Baltimore to pay $42K to whistle-blower former officer who found rat on car,* The Baltimore Sun (June 1, 2016, 7:14 PM), http://www.baltimoresun.com/news/maryland/baltimore-city/bs-md-ci-crystal-settlement-20160601-story.html.

because they "have to do things in the gray area." And on two occasions, no one in the detective's unit responded to his calls for backup. The retaliation intensified as the officers' trials approached. In November 2012, the detective found a dead rat on his car with its head severed under his wiper blades. Shortly thereafter, a BPD sergeant allegedly told the detective "you better pray to God you're not the star witness" against the officers. The detective reported the dead rat incident to internal affairs, but stated that investigators did not contact him until May 2014, after the incident received substantial media coverage. The detective ultimately resigned from the Department in September 2014 and now works at a different law enforcement agency. The Department settled a lawsuit brought by the former detective in the spring of 2016.

The alleged retaliation against the detective received significant publicity and has had a chilling effect on other officers in the Department who witness misconduct. In one case, an officer in a specialized drug unit observed one of his fellow officers plant drugs on a suspect after a foot chase. The officer decided not to report the misconduct because he did not want BPD officers to "do me" the way they treated the detective.

Officers also told us that they have faced retaliation for raising concerns about the constitutionality of certain BPD enforcement practices. In 2015, a sergeant banned a patrol officer from working overtime for 30 days after the officer objected to the sergeant's frequent requests to "clear corners," which the officer believed required her to violate constitutional standards by making stops without reasonable suspicion. When the officer raised her concerns with the major in charge of the district, he allegedly defended the punishment by stating that the officer "hadn't made stats for six days." At the time supervisors banned her from working overtime, the officer was a single parent who was known to work overtime frequently to support her family. In a similar incident, detailed in Section II.B.2, *supra*, a sergeant reported that she was transferred and given a poor performance review after objecting to a lieutenant's instruction to target "black hoodies" for enforcement.

In short, resistance to internal accountability persists within BPD. The Department has failed to take adequate steps to ensure that officers feel comfortable reporting misconduct and make clear that it will not tolerate retaliation against officers who do so.

D. BPD DOES NOT COORDINATE WITH OTHER AGENCIES APPROPRIATELY

BPD also fails to appropriately coordinate its efforts with other law enforcement agencies that it has granted authority to exercise concurrent jurisdiction, creating gaps in the reporting of stops, searches, and in the reporting and investigation of the use of force. These gaps impede BPD's ability to ensure that it is appropriately supervising its own enforcement activities and those of agencies exercising concurrent jurisdiction.

The Department has entered into a number of agreements with law enforcement agencies in and around Baltimore City, including the Baltimore School Police Force, and police forces serving the University of Baltimore and Morgan State University. For example, BPD has entered into an agreement with the Baltimore City Public School System, which operates the Baltimore School Police. This agreement considerably expands the school police force's jurisdiction, which otherwise would be limited to school property. Md. Code Ann., Educ. §§4–318 (c) and (d)(1)(2015) (limiting BSP's jurisdiction, in most circumstances, to "property operated or controlled by the school system"). Under the school police force's agreement with the Department, however, the Baltimore School Police are given "concurrent jurisdiction": school police may act with lawful authority—including with the power of arrest—throughout the City of Baltimore. According to the agreement, school police may "exercise full police power anywhere within the jurisdiction of the City of Baltimore" and assist in investigations and follow-up in criminal cases. School police must notify BPD when its officers act outside of school property and within the territorial jurisdiction of BPD. If school police officers make an arrest while exercising concurrent jurisdiction, they must write an official police report, and they must also use BPD field reports or identical forms for incidents occurring in areas of concurrent jurisdictions.

Early in our investigation, we learned that the City has essentially used the Baltimore School Police as an auxiliary force to BPD. During our ride-alongs with BPD officers, we frequently observed school police officers patrolling neighborhoods and responding to calls along with BPD officers. This was particularly true in districts that were understaffed. The files BPD produced to us confirmed that school police are often present with BPD officers during enforcement activities. School police were present, for example, at the scene of several incidents in which BPD officers used force, and school police officers were also mentioned in our review of BPD's internal affairs files.

We have several concerns with the City's use of the school police as an auxiliary force to BPD. First, based on our review of the agreement between BPD and the Baltimore City Public School System, the agreement does not clearly delineate which agency is in charge of an incident when officers from both agencies respond, as we observed numerous times during our ride-alongs. It is unclear whether this responsibility falls to the senior officer on the scene, regardless of that officer's agency, or to BPD officers because BPD is the agency granting concurrent jurisdiction to the school police (regardless of rank), or if the decision is based on other factors. When officers were questioned about it during our ride-alongs, they were also unclear about who would be in control in those circumstances. This creates considerable risks for both the officers and members of the public, because lines of authority are not clear if a crisis of some kind arises.

Second, the agreement is likewise silent on which agency's policies control decisions made during and after an incident, such as an incident involving the use of force. When use of force policies for each agency set different standards for when force may be used, BPD risks having a school police officer, acting under the concurrent jurisdiction granted by BPD, use force in circumstances that BPD would deem out of policy. Similarly, after the use of force occurs, the agreement does not make clear which agency—or both—would investigate the use of force if it involved officers from both agencies, or how that investigation would be conducted. This failure could lead to gaps in accountability for both agencies.

Third, the agreement does not set forth a process for how complaints about alleged officer misconduct will be handled, even if those complaints arise out of incidents where officers from both agencies are present. When we questioned commanders in BPD's Internal Investigation Division about this, they informed us that the Department's practice was to refer complaints received about school police officers to the school police force itself. We found incidents, however, where it appears BPD officers refused to take complaints about school police—and did not refer them to other agencies—without making any effort to ascertain whether the school police were acting with authority granted to them by BPD, or pursuant to the direction of BPD commanders. This failure similarly undermines accountability and community confidence in both BPD and the school police.

Finally, although the agreement requires school police officers to file arrest and field reports, we are concerned that the data from these reports, as well as from other reports on activities such as stops and searches that do not appear to be required by the agreement, are not being properly collected and analyzed. This impacts the ability of BPD and the school police to effectively supervise officer activities. Particularly where BPD is using the school police as an auxiliary force to aid in patrol and other activities when BPD is itself short-staffed, the failure to coordinate efforts to collect and analyze this data can lead to a skewed view of BPD's enforcement activities. As mentioned previously, reliable and accurate data about BPD's enforcement efforts is critical to effective supervision and prevention of unlawful stops, searches, arrests, and use of force.

BPD should take immediate steps to strengthen its agreements with agencies to which it has granted concurrent jurisdiction to remedy these deficiencies.

E. BPD FAILS TO ENGAGE IN EFFECTIVE COMMUNITY POLICING

From participation in grassroots organization meetings to police department interviews, our investigation revealed a significant divide between the police and members of the Baltimore community. Both community members and police officers expressed that the Department has overly focused on narcotics enforcement, gun recovery, and "clearing corners," even when such strategies are ineffective at addressing the community's desire to combat drug crimes and other enforcement priorities. Many officers openly admitted that community relations are BPD's weakest attribute. Some supervisors noted that it is "sad to see" how many of the city's residents, especially those in low-income, predominantly African-American neighborhoods, hate the police. This divide is a significant impediment to constitutional and effective policing in the City of Baltimore.

Central to this divide is the perception that there are "two Baltimores" receiving dissimilar policing services. One is affluent and predominately white, while the other is impoverished and largely black. The notion that residents in more affluent neighborhoods receive better policing services than residents in poor neighborhoods was evident in many of our conversations with community members. The disparities described to us go beyond aggressive behavior and misconduct; some residents spoke about a police non-response to poor, minority areas as well as a lack of thorough investigation into crimes committed in these communities. Many point to the police response following the unrest in April 2015 as an example. We heard from an African-American resident who told us that "during the unrest in Baltimore the rich white people's neighborhoods were protected but stores in the black neighborhoods were left unguarded." In another account, residents in a minority neighborhood at the center of the unrest described their frustration upon hearing that Bolton Hill, an affluent, majority-white area, was granted an increase in officer deployment while their request for foot patrol following a dramatic spike in drug trafficking was denied due to a lack of resources. One resident commented, "The city was pretty much saying Sandtown doesn't matter; the black neighborhood can burn. They were protecting the white people, the richer people." *See, e.g., Over-Policed, Yet Underserved: The People's Findings Regarding Police Misconduct in West Baltimore*, West Baltimore Commission on Police Misconduct and the No Boundaries Coalition (March 8, 2016) at 11.

Our investigation found that, through all levels of the Baltimore Police

Department, from members of command staff down to officers on the street, the Department has not implemented fundamental principles of community policing. Community policing involves building partnerships between law enforcement and the people and organizations within its jurisdiction; engaging in problem-solving together with the community; and managing the police agency to support this community partnership and community problem-solving. *See, e.g., Community Policing Defined* 1–16 (U.S. Dep't of Justice, Office of Community Oriented Policing Services, 2014). Community policing is inherently proactive; it involves identifying leaders within a community that can aid the police in preventing and investigating crime, particularly among those groups that are most alienated from the police, and creating relationships with those leaders that allow the police and the community to work together to make the community safe. This strategy enables law enforcement agencies and the individuals and organizations they serve to develop solutions to problems and increase trust in the police. *See, e.g., Effective Policing and Crime Prevention: A Problem Oriented Guide for Mayors, City Managers, and County Executives* 1–62 (U.S. Dep't of Justice, Office of Community Oriented Policing Services, 2009); *The Collaboration Toolkit for Law Enforcement: Effective Strategies to Partner with the Community* 1–92 (U.S. Dep't of Justice, Office of Community Oriented Policing Services, 2011). To be effective, it must include all ranks, sectors, and units of a police department. *See, e.g., Community Policing Explained: A Guide for Local Government* 1–54 (U.S. Dep't of Justice, Office of Community Oriented Policing Services, 2003). This approach is currently not being implemented by the Baltimore Police Department, although leadership in the Department has made efforts to change this over the last few years. To remedy the constitutional violations we found in our investigation, a comprehensive community policing strategy must be a central component of police reform in Baltimore.

1. The Relationship Between the Police and the Community in Baltimore Is Broken

The relationship between the Baltimore Police Department and many of the communities it serves is broken. During our investigation, we participated in or observed dozens of community meetings, reviewed thousands of documents, including letters and complaints from Baltimore residents, and interviewed hundreds of additional Baltimore residents. Many residents throughout the City of Baltimore, and particularly in impoverished, primarily minority, neighborhoods, described being belittled, disbelieved, and disrespected by officers, spurring some groups to submit detailed accounts, documentation, and even formal reports to us about their experiences with the Department. *See, e.g., Over-Policed, Yet Underserved: The People's Findings Regarding Police Misconduct in West Baltimore*, West Baltimore Commission on Police Misconduct and the

No Boundaries Coalition (March 8, 2016). These accounts included reports of verbal abuse during routine interactions and often involved cursing or threats. In one account, during a traffic stop, a resident politely asked an officer why he had been pulled over. The officer simply told him to get out of the car and, when asked again, began cursing at the resident, even threatening to tow his "fucking car." In another account, a woman asked police officers the reason for conducting a search of her home. She was told to "shut the fuck up bitch and sit the fuck down" because they were "the fucking law." Strikingly, the vast majority of the individuals we spoke with do not want the police to be less involved in their communities; they want police engagement, and they want this engagement to be respectful and collaborative, so they can feel safe in their own communities.

Our interactions with BPD officers and review of the Department's documents confirmed many of the accounts we heard from members of the public. Our review of the Department's own incident reports, for example, revealed numerous instances in which officers spoke in an unnecessarily rude or aggressive manner when interacting with suspects, witnesses, and the general public. And, as described previously *supra*, these aggressive interactions frequently escalated situations and, at times, led to the unnecessary use of force. Interviews with BPD officers throughout the chain of command also revealed that officers openly harbor antagonistic feelings towards community members. We found a prevalent "us-versus-them" mentality that is incompatible with community policing principles. When asked about community-oriented problem solving, for example, one supervisor responded, "I don't pander to the public." Another supervisor conveyed to us that he approaches policing in Baltimore like it is a war zone. A patrol officer, when describing his approach to policing, voiced similar views, commenting, "You've got to be the baddest motherfucker out there," which often requires that one "own the block." Officers seemed to view themselves as controlling the city rather than as *a part* of the city. Many others, including high ranking officers in the Department, view themselves as enforcing the will of the "silent majority."

Many BPD discretionary enforcement actions increase distrust and significantly decrease the likelihood that individuals will cooperate with the police to solve or prevent other crimes, as described in numerous incidents and statistics throughout this letter. In one report, an officer described telling two individuals, a mother and her son, who were standing in the block to leave. They refused, noting that were standing outside of their own home, but eventually moved to the steps of their front stoop. Ultimately, the son, a juvenile with no prior criminal record, was arrested for loitering outside his own home. Supervisors raised no issues with respect to the incident. Similarly, groups of people are often dispersed unless they have a clear reason for gathering in that location. In one internal report, a supervisor describes the actions of an officer, stating, "Officer approached the group to ascertain the reason for the crowd and if there was no legal reason they were going to disperse the crowd." The interaction concluded with an officer using OC spray on the entire group of people. These enforcement activities for behavior that is, at most, a minor offense if even unlawful, alienate community members and decrease their willingness to work with police.

Indeed, our review of documents and our conversations with Baltimore residents confirm that distrust is causing individuals to be reluctant to cooperate with police. It was not uncommon to see marked on incident reports that witnesses were hostile and unwilling to share basic information with police officers. And in many instances, BPD imposed unnecessary negative consequences for optional interactions. For example, a case manager requested that the police reach out to a juvenile who was friends with victims of a homicide case because she was concerned for his safety and wanted to check if he desired to be relocated. Detectives in the Homicide Unit arrived at his house, and the juvenile invited them inside his home to speak about the murder of his friend. During the course of the conversation, the detectives decided that they wanted a formal statement from the juvenile. However, after telephoning his grandmother, who advised him not to speak to investigators, he refused. The detectives insisted that he come downtown, which caused the juvenile to allegedly scream and ball his fists. Ultimately, officers placed him in handcuffs and transported him downtown. We also read numerous incident reports where the person who originally called the police or was in need of assistance refused to cooperate after becoming upset with the manner in which the police responded.

2. BPD Has Failed to Implement Community Policing Principles

Our investigation revealed that one of the fundamental causes of the breakdown in the relationship between the Department and the community it serves is that, throughout much of the Department, community policing principles are not being implemented. During our interviews with command staff, district commanders, and other supervisors, we observed that, in the vast majority of these interviews, the person was unable to accurately describe what community policing is or how BPD implements community policing efforts. Some district commanders had not even considered enlisting the community to help combat crime problems. Most could not identify community organizations willing to do violence prevention work or other partners for community policing on an ongoing basis. And none of the BPD majors we talked with had relationships with community groups who were able to put pressure on violent members of the community to stop the violence. These coalitions can be an effective tool in not only stopping the violence but also building important community relationships. Notably, when a district commander or member of command staff did have a stronger grasp of community policing principles, their description of the specific actions BPD is taking often differed widely from that shared with us by other Department leaders. The Department lacks a common vision for how it is engaging and working with its community.

The Department leadership's lack of vision for community policing has repercussions for the officers they supervise. Most of the officers we encountered during our investigation care deeply about doing a good job, but their approaches are narrowly aimed at enforcement, with an almost exclusive focus on offenders, and lack community-oriented problem-solving. Many officers described little interaction with the communities they patrol, noting that those on patrol simply handle calls for service. Supervisors confirmed this notion. One noted, "Officers basically just handle calls for service." Another described patrol officers by stating that they "go from call to call, so they have no time for community interaction . . . they're controlled mostly by the radio." Many police personnel openly admitted that officers do not regularly attend community meetings—that street cops focus on enforcement with little outreach to or investment in community needs.

Community policing efforts are ad hoc and officer- or major-specific. Those officers we saw interacting with the community in a positive manner did so due to their own interest, noting that such actions were not mandated by command staff. At the command level, one district commander described prioritizing sector officers and sergeants having as many "designed intentional moments" as possible with the community and tracking officers' foot patrol time to encourage such interactions. The same district has been involved in numerous outreach efforts, including listening campaigns, "Cocoa with a Cop," a shoe giveaway, and community walks. However, this district commander's efforts again appear to be an exception to BPD's overall policing strategy. The commander confirmed this, telling us, "I know it needs to happen—so I don't wait for someone to tell me to do it." Furthermore, although this district commander and some others focus on community policing, many patrol officers are receiving conflicting messages. For example, one officer told us, "Commanders say they want community policing, but then they come back around and ask 'How many arrests you made?'" As this question suggests, from command staff to officers, the Department struggles to embrace true community policing and fails to understand how community policing strategies can make it better and more effective at reducing crime and social disorder.

3. BPD Recognizes that It Must Improve Its Relationship with the Communities It Serves, But Much Work Remains

Over the past few years, leaders within the City and within Baltimore Police Department have recognized that the Department needs to do significant work to improve its relationship with the communities it serves throughout Baltimore, particularly those in impoverished and minority neighborhoods. During our investigation and before it, the Department began to make changes to the way it polices to better embrace community policing principles and more effective serve its community. Unfortunately, community policing is still not a philosophy that permeates all aspects of BPD's activities; rather, it currently is a single program that is not integrated with BPD's other law enforcement functions. Indeed, most officers think of community policing as distinct from their regular policing duties.

Currently, the Department's community policing efforts are undertaken exclusively by the Community Collaboration Division (CCD), except for the ad hoc efforts of certain officers and commanders described above. CCD is led by a Lieutenant Colonel, and its philosophy is based on four pillars: community-oriented policing, faith-based involvement, youth engagement, and re-entry programs. Structurally, CCD aims to have one sergeant and four officers per district—with each officer responsible for a "pillar" and the sergeants responsible for supervision. These officers are not under district command; instead, they work out of their own unit downtown.

While it is too early to conclusively evaluate these efforts, we are concerned that these new initiatives will not be successful without substantial changes in the Department's approach. First, the Department's community policing plan is currently too limited in scope, and does not embrace all aspects of the work of the Department. As currently understood by many members of the Department, community policing is the responsibility of the CCD, not the Department as a whole. To be effective, however, community collaboration and engagement has to be practiced by every member of the organization, especially by the uniformed patrol officers who are assigned to neighborhoods. At present, patrol officers largely view the policing strategy as someone else's job. This limited version of community policing will not be effective, particularly given the relatively small number of individuals dedicated to undertake these efforts.

Second, and relatedly, the Department's community policing efforts are not well-integrated with the work of the districts. We express no view on whether community policing efforts need to be led out of the districts or centralized, as they currently are in Baltimore in the CCD. Regardless of where these efforts are led, however, they must be closely coordinated and integrated with patrol and specialized units, and that integration is not yet occurring. This problem is exacerbated by the distinct nature of each district in Baltimore. According to some people throughout the Department, districts work as if they are a separate "kingdom," with distinctly different practices and approaches. This is consistent with our observations. Evidence of the difficulties this poses is already apparent. In some districts, the district commanders were appreciative of the help and support they received from the CCD; other commanders, however, were concerned that they were not aware when the unit was actually working in their area. A few also voiced frustration that they lack control of community engagement in their district, given their experience in the area. One commander noted that it can be difficult to engage and build relationships with some community groups, most notably the faith-based contacts, since this responsibility falls under the CCD. "It's harder for district commanders to have access to these folks," noted one. The major described how the district developed its own initiatives to facilitate community policing and engagement because of the difficulties in coordinating with the CCD.

Third, the Department is not building effective partnerships with existing community groups dedicated to serving their communities, and instead is trying to establish new programs that are led by the Department. During the course of our investigation, we observed a surprising lack of BPD representation at community meetings of grass-roots organizations throughout the City. At the majority of community meetings we attended, we found that members of the BPD—even the CCD—were not present. Often, the community and religious leaders hosting the meeting told us that they had personally reached out to the police department to invite officers to the meeting, but received no response. According to some participants, police officials used to attend their meetings but have not done so since the unrest following the death of Freddie Gray. By not participating in these meetings, the Department is missing valuable opportunities. Attending these meetings would allow officers to build partnerships, gain information, and solve problems that would facilitate effective policing. Notably, during our interviews with them, CCD leadership did not speak to the importance of partnering with grass-root organizations that are not traditional supporters of the police. Instead, the approach to police-community relations is primarily focused on establishing programs to support CCD's four pillars, which are police-led rather than partnering with others who have already established themselves in the community. It is perhaps unsurprising that community activists have described the Department's efforts to improve police-community relations as troubling—that the police are seeking "a 'community rubber stamp' to normalize 'problematic policing practices'" rather than working with the community to find an approach to policing that can gain buy-in.[133]

Fourth, the Department is not consistently enforcing its own requirements for officer community engagement. For example, the Department recently implemented a 30-minute foot patrol requirement, but this obligation is not

---

133 Maggie Ybarra, *A conversation with Police Commissioner Kevin Davis*, City Paper, April 27, 2016, http://www.citypaper.com/news/features/bcp-042716-feature-commissioner-davis-interview-20160427-story.html.

uniformly enforced by command staff. Although we engaged in numerous ride-alongs with patrol officers, only a handful of the officers completed their foot patrol. Additional interviews confirmed that this requirement is not readily enforced across BPD. It is, therefore, unsurprising that some officers fail to integrate community policing efforts into their time on patrol. There are few incentives and little encouragement to do so.

Finally, BPD's policies and training do not consistently embrace community policing principles. BPD's community policing strategy involves few training modules on community policing and communication. We attended one of these in-service trainings, which focused on community policing and foot patrol. The segment on officers' role as "warriors versus guardians" focused primarily on the benefits of being a warrior. Indeed, it seemed that principles of community policing and the role of a police officer as a "guardian" is not yet well understood by the instructors, who emphasized the drawbacks of this approach, making it unlikely that officers will understand how to embrace such principles in their interactions. Better training is needed if the Department wants to teach officers effective community policing practices, and this training needs to be provided and tailored to personnel throughout all levels of the Department.

Community policing and engagement provide a promising route for ensuring officers act in accord with the Constitution and for repairing BPD's relationship with the community. A proactive community policing strategy has the potential to overcome divisive dynamics that disconnect residents and police forces, dynamics ranging from a dearth of positive interactions to racial stereotyping and racial violence. *See, e.g.*, Jack Glaser, *Suspect Race: Causes and Consequence of Racial Profiling 207–11* (2015) (discussing research showing that community policing and similar approaches can help reduce racial bias and stereotypes and improve community relations); L. Song Richardson & Phillip Atiba Goff, *Interrogating Racial Violence*, 12 Ohio St. J. of Crim. L. 115, 143–47 (2014) (describing how fully implemented and inclusive community policing can help avoid racial stereotyping and violence); *Strengthening the Relationship Between Law Enforcement and Communities of Color: Developing an Agenda for Action 1–20* (U.S. Dep't of Justice, Office of Community Oriented Policing Services, 2014). Thus, as the Department strives to correct the problems our investigation identified and to engender trust within Baltimore's diverse communities, a community policing strategy should be a central component of its approach moving forward.

CONCLUSION

For the foregoing reasons, the Department of Justice concludes that there is reasonable cause to believe that BPD engages in a pattern or practice of conduct that violates the Constitution or federal law. The pattern or practice includes: (1) making unconstitutional stops, searches, and arrests; (2) using enforcement strategies that produce severe and unjustified disparities in the rates of stops, searches and arrests of African Americans; (3) using excessive force; and (4) retaliating against people engaging in constitutionally-protected expression. We also identified concerns regarding BPD's transport of individuals and investigation of sexual assaults. BPD's failings result from deficient policies, training, oversight, and accountability, and policing strategies that do not engage effectively with the community the Department serves. We are heartened to find both widespread recognition of these challenges and strong interest in reform. We look forward to working with the Department, City leadership, and Baltimore's diverse communities to create lasting reforms that rebuild trust in BPD and ensure that it provides effective, constitutional police services to the people of Baltimore.

Investigation of the Chicago Police Department

United States Department of Justice

Civil Rights Division and United States Attorney's Office
Northern District of Illinois

JANUARY 13, 2017

EXECUTIVE SUMMARY

On December 7, 2015, the United States Department of Justice (DOJ), Civil Rights Division, Special Litigation Section, and the United States Attorney's Office for the Northern District of Illinois, jointly initiated an investigation of the City of Chicago's Police Department (CPD) and the Independent Police Review Authority (IPRA). This investigation was undertaken to determine whether the Chicago Police Department is engaging in a pattern or practice of unlawful conduct and, if so, what systemic deficiencies or practices within CPD, IPRA, and the City might be facilitating or causing this pattern or practice.

Our investigation assessed CPD's use of force, including deadly force, and addressed CPD policies, training, reporting, investigation, and review related to officer use of force. The investigation further addressed CPD's and IPRA's systems of accountability both as they relate to officer use of force and officer misconduct, including the intake, investigation, and review of allegations of officer misconduct, and the imposition of discipline or other corrective action. We also investigated racial, ethnic, or other disparities in CPD's force and accountability practices, and assessed how those disparities inform the breakdown in community trust.

We opened this investigation pursuant to the Violent Crime Control and Law Enforcement Act of 1994, 42 U.S.C. § 14141 (Section 14141), Title VI of the Civil Rights Act of 1964, 42 U.S.C. § 2000d (Title VI), and the Omnibus Crime Control and Safe Streets Act of 1968, 42 U.S.C. 3789d (Safe Streets Act). Section 14141 prohibits law enforcement agencies from engaging in a pattern or practice of conduct that violates the Constitution or laws of the United States. Title VI and its implementing regulations and the Safe Streets Act prohibit law enforcement practices that have a disparate impact based on protected status, such as race or ethnicity, unless these practices are necessary to achieve legitimate, non-discriminatory objectives.

This investigation was initiated as Chicago grappled with the aftermath of the release of a video showing a white police officer fatally shooting black teenager Laquan McDonald. This aftermath included protests, murder charges for the involved officer, and the resignation of Chicago's police superintendent. The McDonald incident was widely viewed as a tipping point—igniting longstanding concerns about CPD officers' use of force, and the City's systems for detecting and correcting the unlawful use of force.

Over the year-plus since release of that video, and while we have been conducting this investigation, Chicago experienced a surge in shootings and homicides. The reasons for this spike are broadly debated and inarguably complex. But on two points there is little debate. First, for decades, certain neighborhoods on Chicago's South and West Sides have been disproportionately ravaged by gun violence. Those same neighborhoods have borne the brunt of the recent surge of violence. And second, for Chicago to find solutions—short- and long-term—for making those neighborhoods safe, it is imperative that the City rebuild trust between CPD and the people it serves, particularly in these communities. The City and CPD acknowledge that this trust has been broken, despite the diligent efforts and brave actions of countless CPD officers. It has been broken by systems that have allowed CPD officers who violate the law to escape accountability. This breach in trust has in turn eroded CPD's ability to effectively prevent crime; in other words, trust and effectiveness in combating violent crime are inextricably intertwined.

The aim of this investigation was to conduct a thorough, independent, and fair assessment of CPD's and IPRA's practices. To accomplish this goal, we relied on several sources of information.

First, we reviewed thousands of pages of documents provided to us by CPD, IPRA, and the City, including policies, procedures, training plans, Department orders and memos, internal and external reports, and more. We also obtained access to the City's entire misconduct complaint database and data from all reports filled out following officers' use of force. From there, we reviewed a randomized, representative sample of force reports and investigative files for incidents that occurred between January 2011 and April 2016, as well as additional incident reports and investigations. Overall, we reviewed over 170 officer-involved shooting investigations, and documents related to over 425 incidents of less-lethal force.

We also spent extensive time in Chicago—over 300 person-days—meeting with community members and City officials, and interviewing current and former CPD officers and IPRA investigators. In addition to speaking with the Superintendent and other CPD leadership, we met with the command staff of several specialized units, divisions, and departments. We toured CPD's training facilities and observed training programs. We also visited each of Chicago's 22 police districts, where we addressed roll call, spoke with command staff and officers, and conducted over 60 ride-alongs with officers. We met several times with Chicago's officer union, Lodge No. 7 of the Fraternal Order of Police, as well as the sergeants', lieutenants', and captains' unions. All told, we heard from over 340 individual CPD members, and 23 members of IPRA's staff.

Our findings were also significantly informed by our conversations with members of the Chicago community. We met with over ninety community organizations, including non-profits, advocacy and legal organizations, and faith-based groups focused on a wide range of issues. We participated in several community forums in different neighborhoods throughout Chicago where we heard directly from the family members of individuals who were killed by CPD officers and others who shared their insights and experiences. We also met with several local researchers, academics, and lawyers who have studied CPD extensively for decades. Most importantly, however, we heard directly from individuals who live and work throughout the City about their interactions with CPD officers. Overall, we talked to approximately a thousand community members. We received nearly 600 phone calls, emails, and letters from individuals who were eager to provide their experiences and insights.

In addition to attorneys, paralegals, outreach specialists, and data analysts from the Civil Rights Division of the United States Department of Justice and the United States Attorney's Office for the Northern District of Illinois, 11 independent subject-matter experts assisted with this investigation. Most of these experts are current or former law enforcement officials from police departments across the country. Accordingly, these experts have decades of expertise in areas such as the use of force, accountability, training, supervision, community policing, officer-involved domestic violence and sexual misconduct, officer wellness, and more. These experts accompanied us on-site, reviewed documents and investigative files, and provided invaluable insights that informed both the course of this investigation and its conclusions.

During the year it took us to complete this investigation, the City of Chicago took action of its own. Following the release of dashboard-camera video capturing the death of Laquan McDonald, Mayor Rahm Emanuel established the Police Accountability Task Force (PATF). The Mayor charged the PATF with assessing the Police Department and making recommendations for change in five areas: community relations; oversight and accountability; de-escalation; early intervention and personnel concerns; and video release protocols. In April 2016, the PATF issued a report with over a hundred recommendations for improving transparency and accountability. In December of 2016, the City issued a progress report outlining the steps it has taken since April to meet the recommendations made by the PATF.

Perhaps most significantly, the City passed an ordinance creating the Civilian Office of Police Accountability (COPA), which is scheduled to replace IPRA in 2017. The ordinance also establishes a Deputy Inspector General for Public Safety, who is charged with auditing the entire police accountability system and identifying patterns that violate residents' constitutional rights. In June of 2016, the City issued a new "transparency policy" mandating the release of videos and other materials related to certain officer misconduct investigations. CPD also pledged to establish an anonymous hotline for CPD members to report misconduct; began an ambitious process to develop an early intervention system; and developed a draft disciplinary matrix to guide CPD in assigning appropriate discipline for various misconduct violations.

The City embarked on other initiatives during our investigation that are intended to improve policing in Chicago. In early 2016, the City began a pilot program for body-worn cameras, and reported recently that the expansion of the program will be accelerated so that all officers will be wearing these cameras by the end of 2017. In the last few months, CPD began an important force mitigation/de-escalation training course for officers, and revised several policies related to use of force. The City also committed to providing additional training on how officers and emergency dispatchers respond to individuals in mental health crisis, and to improving CPD's training more broadly. As part of its efforts to engage community members and improve police-community relations, the City established a Community Policing Advisory Panel that will help develop a new strategic plan for community policing. The City is also undertaking recruitment efforts aimed at increasing CPD's diversity, and recently retained a consultant to complete a staffing analysis to inform deployment decisions Department-wide.

Many of these planned or implemented reforms are discussed in detail in this Report, alongside our assessment of their impact on the problems our investigation found, and whether CPD and the City need to go further.

As noted, while our investigation was underway and the City moved forward with some reforms, Chicago experienced an unprecedented surge in shootings and homicides. In 2016, there were 762 homicides, nearly 300 more than the previous year and, according to the draft of a new study from the University of Chicago Crime Lab, the largest single-year homicide increase of the last 25 years among the five most populous United States cities. Overall, there were 3,550 shootings, with 4,331 shooting victims, in Chicago in 2016, approximately 1,100 more than in 2015. While shootings and homicides occurred in all parts of the City, they were largely concentrated in Chicago's South Side and West Side neighborhoods. Homicide clearance rates, the rate at which police identify the suspected killer, continued their years-long slide, with CPD clearing only 29 percent of all homicides, less than half the national clearance rate.

During our investigation, DOJ has enhanced its assistance with CPD's reform and violence-reduction efforts. DOJ has allocated additional funding to CPD to support its efforts, provided technical assistance, and continued and expanded its cooperation through DOJ's Violence Reduction Network (VRN), an innovative approach to support and enhance local violence reduction efforts. Since December 2014, CPD and DOJ, through the United States Attorney's Office in Chicago, have hosted nine Community Trust Roundtables across Chicago's most violence-plagued neighborhoods. These recent efforts build on the foundation of DOJ's longstanding collaborative initiatives with CPD.

It has never been more important to rebuild trust for the police within Chicago's neighborhoods most challenged by violence, poverty, and unemployment. As discussed below and throughout our Report, Chicago must undergo broad, fundamental reform to restore this trust. This will be difficult, but will benefit both the public and CPD's own officers. The increased trust these reforms will build is necessary to solve and prevent violent crime. And the conduct and practices that restore trust will also carry out an equally important public service: demonstrating to communities racked with violence that their police force cares about them and has not abandoned them, regardless of where they live or the color of their skin. That confidence is broken in many neighborhoods in Chicago.

At the same time, many CPD officers feel abandoned by the public and often by their own Department. We found profoundly low morale nearly every place we went within CPD. Officers generally feel that they are insufficiently trained and supported to do their work effectively. Our investigation indicates that both CPD's lawfulness and effectiveness can be vastly improved if the City and CPD make the changes necessary to consistently incentivize and reward effective, ethical, and active policing. While it will take time and concerted focus to implement all of the necessary changes, a strong sign of a genuine and unalterable commitment to such change could increase officer morale more quickly, especially among the countless good officers within CPD who police diligently every day, and who disapprove of some officer conduct they see—and many of whom quietly told us how eager they are for the kind of change that can come only from an investigation like the one we have just completed. It is within this current climate, and with these challenges in mind, that we conducted our investigation and make the following findings.

FORCE

We reviewed CPD's force practices mindful that officers routinely place themselves in harm's way in order to uphold their commitment to serve and protect the people of the City of Chicago, and that officers regularly encounter individuals who may be armed and determined to avoid arrest. We likewise recognize that officers have not only a right, but an obligation, to protect themselves and others from threats of harm, including deadly harm, which may arise in an instant.

But even within this context, we, in consultation with several active law enforcement experts, found that CPD officers engage in a pattern or practice of using force, including deadly force, that is unreasonable. We found further that CPD officers' force practices unnecessarily endanger themselves and others and result in unnecessary and avoidable shootings and other uses of force.

As discussed throughout this Report, this pattern is largely attributable to systemic deficiencies within CPD and the City. CPD has not provided officers with adequate guidance to understand how and when they may use force, or how to safely and effectively control and resolve encounters to reduce the need to use force. CPD also has failed to hold officers accountable when they use force contrary to CPD policy or otherwise commit misconduct. This failure to hold officers accountable results in some officers remaining with the Department when they should have been relieved of duty. These officers often continue their misconduct including, at times, again using unreasonable deadly force. More broadly, these failures result in officers not having the skills or tools necessary to use force wisely and lawfully, and they send a dangerous message to officers and the public that unreasonable force by CPD officers will be tolerated. We found further that CPD's failure to meaningfully and routinely review or investigate officer use of force is a significant factor in perpetuating the practices that result in the pattern of unlawful conduct we found. Each of these causal factors is discussed further in this Summary and the accompanying Report.

Our finding that CPD engages in a pattern or practice of force in violation of the Constitution is based on a comprehensive investigation of CPD's force practices and a close analysis of hundreds of individual force incidents. We reviewed CPD's policies related to the use, reporting, and investigation of force, including older versions of polices that were effective during our review period, and CPD's proposed revised policies. We spoke with officers at all ranks, including the Superintendent and the Chief and Deputy Chief of the Bureau of Patrol, to understand how officers are trained to use force, their view of when force is appropriate, and how the policies are interpreted in practice throughout CPD. We also did an in-depth review of officer reports of force, civilian complaints of force, and CPD's and IPRA's review of force, and investigations of allegations of excessive force. We reviewed all documents we were provided related to over 425 incidents of less-lethal force, including representative samples of officers' own reports of force, and of investigations of civilian complaints about officer force between January 2011 and April 2016. We also reviewed over 170 files related to officer-involved shootings.

The pattern of unlawful force we found resulted from a collection of poor police practices that our investigation indicated are used routinely within CPD. We found that officers engage in tactically unsound and unnecessary foot pursuits, and that these foot pursuits too often end with officers unreasonably shooting someone—including unarmed individuals. We found that officers shoot at vehicles without justification and in contradiction to CPD policy. We found further that officers exhibit poor discipline when discharging their weapons and engage in tactics that endanger themselves and public safety, including failing to await backup when they safely could and should; using unsound tactics in approaching vehicles; and using their own vehicles in a manner that is dangerous. These are issues that can and must be better addressed through training, accountability and ultimately cultural change.

Among the most egregious uses of deadly force we reviewed were incidents in which CPD officers shot at suspects who presented no immediate threat. CPD's use of less-lethal force also contributes to the pattern of unlawful conduct we found. We reviewed instances of CPD using less-lethal force, often Tasers, including in drive-stun mode, against people who posed no threat, and using unreasonable retaliatory force and unreasonable force against children. We found also that CPD officers use force against people in mental health crisis where force might have been avoided. These issues are further discussed, along with specific examples, in the Force Section of this Report.

CPD does not investigate or review these force incidents to determine whether its responses to these events were appropriate or lawful, or whether force could have been avoided. The City is currently taking steps to improve its response to persons in mental health or behavioral crisis, in part in response to the tragic shootings deaths of Quintonio LeGrier and Bettie Jones. While we applaud the steps the City has taken, as discussed in our Report, there are important additional steps the City needs to take. The City must do more to ensure that effective, well-trained "crisis intervention" officers respond to these events, and that mental-health or similar crises are analyzed to determine whether changes to the program or CPD's crisis response are warranted.

We found many circumstances in which officers' accounts of force incidents were later discredited, in whole or part, by video evidence. Given the numerous use-of-force incidents without video evidence, discussed further in Section II.C. of this Report, the pattern of unreasonable force is likely even more widespread than we were able to discern through our investigation.

In light of these incidents and many more like them, we support the City's decision to accelerate its plan to ensure that all CPD officers have body cameras so that all officers have them by the end of this year. While we urge the City to go forward with this plan, we hope the City will also heed the concerns set out later in our Report that it work with police unions and community groups on policies and protocols for body-camera usage, and that it develop the supervisory and accountability supports necessary to ensure that body cameras are effective, both at preventing misconduct and exonerating officers where they are wrongfully accused.

Our review further determined that CPD and IPRA do not adequately respond to incidents in which officers used unreasonable or unnecessary force—including force that resulted in a person's death and the officer's stated justification was at odds with the physical evidence. Although IPRA's deficiencies—discussed in the Accountability Section of our Report—have played a central role in allowing patterns of unconstitutional force to persist, IPRA cannot eliminate the pattern of misconduct we found unless CPD's force reporting and investigations change fundamentally as well. As an initial matter, formal and functional gaps in IPRA's jurisdiction mean that many incidents are inadequately investigated or not investigated at all. Where IPRA does act on its jurisdiction, we found that IPRA's ability to fairly investigate force pursuant to its mandate is compromised by deficiencies in how CPD reports force and gathers related evidence immediately after a force incident.

CPD policy requires officers to report force but, in practice, officers are not required to provide detail about the force they used that is sufficient for an adequate review, and most officer force is not reviewed or investigated. Although shootings where a person is struck are investigated, as discussed in the Accountability Section, those investigations are inadequate. As a result of so few force incidents being even nominally investigated, and the low quality of the force investigations that do occur, there is no meaningful, systemic accountability for officers who use force in violation of the law or CPD policy. Nor is there any opportunity for meaningful assessment of whether policies, training, or equipment should be modified to improve force outcomes in the future for officers or civilians. The failure to review and investigate officer use of force has helped create a culture in which officers expect to use force and not be questioned about the need for or propriety of that use. In this way, CPD's failure to adequately review officer use of force on a regular basis has combined with CPD's failure to properly train and supervise officers to perpetuate a pattern of unlawful use of force within CPD.

The City has acknowledged and begun to correct a number of deficiencies related to how officers use and are held accountable for force. In March 2016, CPD began a review of its force policies in an effort to provide clearer direction to officers on the appropriate use of force. CPD released the draft force policies in October 2016 for public comment. The proposed revisions address core force principles such as the sanctity of life; ethical behavior; objective and proportional use of force; use of deadly force; de-escalation; and force mitigation. CPD is reviewing the public feedback and, at the time of this drafting, "will in the very near future incorporate suggestions and improvements to prepare final versions of the policies." CPD also has begun providing all officers with force-mitigation training designed to better equip officers to de-escalate conflicts safely; recognize the signs of mental illness, trauma and crisis situations; and respond quickly and appropriately when force is necessary.

These steps are meaningful and important. But to fulfill their promise, this new approach to CPD use of force must be supported by leadership and enforced by supervisors. Moreover, they must be accompanied by changes to how force is reported and reviewed, not only so that officers can be held accountable when they misuse force, but so that CPD can learn from force incidents and make the policy, training, and equipment changes necessary to make officers and the public safer and more secure.

ACCOUNTABILITY

Police accountability systems are vital to lawful policing. In combination with effective supervision, a robust accountability system helps identify, correct and ultimately prevent unreasonable and unnecessary uses of force. We also investigated the City's police accountability systems and their effectiveness in identifying police misconduct and holding officers responsible.

The City received over 30,000 complaints of police misconduct during the five years preceding our investigation, but fewer than 2% were sustained, resulting in no discipline in 98% of these complaints. This is a low sustained rate. In evaluating the City's accountability structures, we looked beneath these and other disconcerting statistics and attempted to diagnose the cause of the low sustained rates by examining the systems in place, the resources, and leadership involved with the City's accountability bodies, including CPD's Bureau of Internal Affairs (BIA), IPRA, and the Chicago Police Board. We reviewed their policies and practices, interviewed many current and former supervisors, investigators, and other members involved, and we reviewed hundreds of force and misconduct investigative files from an accountability standpoint. We discovered numerous entrenched, systemic policies and practices that undermine police accountability, as described below. We also took into account that the City has taken many steps during our investigation to address many of these accountability deficiencies, including creating COPA, which will replace IPRA as the independent agency responsible for investigating serious police misconduct. Although we commend the City for these and other recent reforms, they do not sufficiently address many of problems we discovered in the City's deeply flawed investigative system.

The City does not investigate the majority of cases it is required by law to investigate. Most of those cases are uninvestigated because they lack a supporting affidavit from the complaining party, but the City also fails to investigate anonymous and older misconduct complaints as well as those alleging lower level force and non-racial verbal abuse. Finally, and also contrary to legal mandates, IPRA does not investigate most Taser discharges and officer-involved shootings where no one is hit. Some of these investigations are ignored based on procedural hurdles in City agreements with its unions, but some are unilateral decisions by the accountability agencies to reduce caseloads and manage resources. And many misconduct complaints that avoid these investigative barriers are still not fully investigated because they are resolved through a defective mediation process, which is actually a plea bargain system used to dispose of serious misconduct claims in exchange for modest discipline. Regardless of the reasons, this failure to fully investigate almost half of all police misconduct cases seriously undermines accountability. These are all lost opportunities to identify misconduct, training deficiencies, and problematic trends, and to hold officers and CPD accountable when misconduct occurs. In order to address these ignored cases, the City must modify its own policies, and work with the unions to address certain CBA provisions, and in the meantime, it must aggressively investigate all complaints to the extent authorized under these contracts.

Those cases that are investigated suffer from serious investigative flaws that obstruct objective fact finding. Civilian and officer witnesses, and even the accused officers, are frequently not interviewed during an investigation. The potential for inappropriate coordination of testimony, risk of collusion, and witness coaching during interviews is built into the system, occurs routinely, and is not considered by investigators in evaluating the case. The questioning of officers is often cursory and aimed at eliciting favorable statements justifying the officer's actions rather than seeking truth. Questioning is often marked by a failure to challenge inconsistencies and illogical officer explanations, as well as leading questions favorable to the officer. Investigators routinely fail to review and incorporate probative evidence from parallel civil and criminal proceedings based on the same police incident. And consistent with these biased investigative techniques, the investigator's summary reports are often drafted in a manner favorable to the officer by omitting conflicts in testimony or with physical evidence that undermine the officer's justification or by exaggerating evidence favorable to the officer, all of which frustrates a reviewer's ability to evaluate for investigative quality and thoroughness.

Investigative fact-finding into police misconduct and attempts to hold officers accountable are also frustrated by police officers' code of silence. The City, police officers, and leadership within CPD and its police officer union acknowledge that a code of silence among Chicago police officers exists, extending to lying and affirmative efforts to conceal evidence. Officers who may be inclined to cover up misconduct will be deterred from doing so if they understand that honesty is the most crucial component of their job and that the Department will aggressively seek to identify dishonest officers and appropriately discipline them. However, our investigation found that IPRA and BIA treat such efforts to hide evidence as ancillary and unexceptional misconduct, and often do not investigate it, causing officers to believe there is not much to lose if they lie to cover up misconduct. Investigators employ a higher standard to sustain claims against officers for making false statements under what is known as a Rule 14 charge and they rarely expand their investigations to charge accused and witness officers with lying to cover up misconduct. Nor, until recently, has the City focused much attention on officers' efforts to conceal by mishandling video and audio equipment or by retaliating against civilians who witness misconduct. The City's failure to prioritize Rule 14 investigations must change. When it is aware of information that an officer lied or otherwise covered up misconduct, the City must actively and aggressively investigate and consistently seek to discipline officers who do so.

We found that inadequate staffing contributes both to these investigative flaws and to the City's decisions to forego or short-circuit so many of the investigations it should be handling. The City has recently committed to providing more funding to IPRA when it becomes COPA, and the agency has already begun to hire additional staff. But COPA's range of responsibilities will also be much broader than IPRA's, and there has not been sufficient analysis to determine whether COPA will have the capacity to do any better than IPRA. We also found that poor training accounted for some of these investigative deficiencies. Investigators and leadership at IPRA acknowledged investigative training was inadequate, and IPRA/COPA is developing plans to revamp and increase training for all staff, especially investigators. While we commend IPRA for this reform, improved training is likewise necessary for BIA investigators as well. Such enhanced training is an important step towards improving the quality of misconduct investigations handled and changing the culture to one that is more determined to resolve investigations and reliably determine whether an officer committed misconduct. However, the depth and breadth of that training is unclear. It should not only cover general investigative techniques, but should include training to eliminate biased investigative techniques as well as training in specific areas, including unlawful entry and seizure, domestic violence and sexual assault, and false statement charges under Rule 14.

In the rare instances when complaints of misconduct are sustained, we found that discipline is haphazard and unpredictable, and is meted out in a way that does little to deter misconduct. Officers are often disciplined for conduct far less serious than the conduct that prompted the investigation, and in many cases, a complaint may be sustained, but the officer is not disciplined at all. The police discipline system, including the City's draft disciplinary matrix, fails to provide clear guidance on appropriate, fair, and consistent penalty ranges, thus undermining the legitimacy and deterrent effect of discipline within CPD.

Finally, we also found deficiencies with the Chicago Police Board's systems, which impair its ability to be an effective component of CPD's accountability structure. The Board should focus on improving its civil service commission function of providing due process to officers accused of misconduct and relinquish its role of providing community input into CPD's accountability system to the Community Oversight Board that the City has committed to creating. The fairness of Police Board hearings can be improved by modifying current rules that bar the officer's "negative" disciplinary history but allow the officer's "complimentary" history as well as favorable character evidence offered by the accused's supervisors. The City can further level the playing field by providing more experienced advocates to represent CPD before the Board and by offering better training for Board members. Allowing Board members to hear evidence directly, instead of a second-hand summary from the hearing officer, and increasing the Board's transparency will further instill community confidence in the Police Board.

TRAINING AND SUPERVISION

CPD's pattern of unlawful conduct is due in part to deficiencies in CPD's training and supervision. CPD does not provide officers or supervisors with adequate training and does not encourage or facilitate adequate supervision of officers in the field. These shortcomings in training and supervision result in officers who are unprepared to police lawfully and effectively; supervisors who do not mentor or support constitutional policing by officers; and a systemic inability to proactively identify areas for improvement, including Department-wide training needs and interventions for officers engaging in misconduct.

Both at the outset and through the duration of their careers, CPD officers do not receive the quality or quantity of training necessary for their jobs. Pre-service Academy training relies on outmoded teaching methods and materials, and does not equip recruits with the skills, knowledge, and confidence necessary to serve Chicago communities. For example, we observed an Academy training on deadly force—an important topic, given our findings regarding CPD's use of force—that consisted of a video made decades ago, which was inconsistent with both current law and CPD's own policies. The impact of this poor training was apparent when we interviewed recruits who recently graduated from the Academy: only one in six recruits we spoke with came close to properly articulating the legal standard for use of force. Post-Academy field training is equally flawed. The Field Training Officer (FTO) Program, as currently structured, does not attract a sufficient number of qualified, effective leaders to train new probationary police officers (PPOs), has an insufficient number of FTOs to meet demand, and fails to provide PPOs with appropriate training, mentorship, and oversight. Finally, in-service training is not provided pursuant to any long-term training plan or strategy. Instead, CPD provides only sporadic in-service training, and does not think proactively about training needs Department-wide. Without a long-term training plan, CPD is often called upon to deliver ad-hoc trainings on tight timelines in response to crises. Consequently, in-service trainings are often incomplete and ineffective at teaching officers important skills and information. The recently-mandated Department-wide Taser training exemplifies CPD's problematic approach to in-service training. Large numbers of officers were cycled through this important training quickly in order to meet a deadline set by the City, without proper curriculum, staff, or equipment. This left many officers who completed the training uncomfortable with how to use Tasers effectively as a less-lethal force option—the very skill the training was supposed to teach.

The City recognizes the need for comprehensive reform of its training program. Its plans for reform are discussed in this Report. While laudable, these plans are still preliminary and amount to verbal commitments with uncertain dates for completion. Academy curriculum revisions, restructuring of the field training program, and development of a proactive, well-planned in-service training program are all needed. CPD must also evaluate whether it has the staff, equipment, and physical space to meet the training demands of the Department, and if not, proactively plan for how to meet training needs going forward. CPD must identify the resources necessary to make these changes, and obtain commitment from the City to provide what is needed.

We found that deficiencies in officer training are exacerbated by the lack of adequate supervision CPD provides to officers in the field, which further contributes to CPD's pattern or practice of unconstitutional policing. CPD does not sufficiently encourage or facilitate supervisors to provide meaningful supervision to officers. Overall, CPD does not hold supervisors accountable for performing certain basic supervisory tasks, including guiding officer behavior or reporting misconduct. Additionally, structural deficiencies in how CPD organizes supervision prevent effective oversight of officer activities. CPD requires supervisors to engage in non-supervisory tasks and manage too many officers at a time. CPD also structures its shift system in such a way that supervisors do not consistently work with the same groups of officers, which inhibits supervisors from learning the needs of officers under their watch. And, much like the deficiencies in CPD's officer training, CPD does not adequately train supervisors on how to provide appropriate supervision. Compounding its supervision problems, CPD does not have a meaningful early intervention system (EIS) to effectively assist supervisors in identifying and correcting problematic behavior. CPD's current behavior intervention systems are underused and inadequate, putting both officers and the public at risk.

Providing robust, meaningful supervision would not only better prevent officer misconduct, it would help CPD better prevent crime in the community. The City and CPD leadership must make the necessary reforms to supervision to protect public and officer safety.

OFFICER WELLNESS AND SAFETY

Policing is a high-stress profession. Law enforcement officers often are called upon to deal with violence or crises as problem solvers, and they often are witnesses to human tragedy. In Chicago, this stress is particularly acute, for several reasons. Increasing levels of gun violence and neighborhood conditions take their toll on officers as well as residents. At the same time, the relationship between CPD officers and the communities they serve is strained; officers on the street are expected to prevent crime, yet they must also be the face of the Department in communities that have lost trust in the police. This makes it particularly difficult to police effectively. And these stresses animate the interactions officers have with the communities that they serve—both positively and negatively. As one CPD counselor explained, it is the "stress of the job that's the precursor to the crisis."

Our investigation found that these stressors can, and do, play out in harmful ways for CPD officers. CPD deals with officer alcoholism, domestic violence, and suicide. And as explained elsewhere in this Report, CPD officers engage in a pattern or practice of using force that is unjustified, disproportionate, and otherwise excessive. Although the pressure CPD officers are under is by no means an excuse for violating the constitutional rights of the citizens they serve, high levels of unaddressed stress can compromise officer well-being and impact an officer's demeanor and judgment, which in turn impacts how that officer interacts with the public. Some officers are able to manage the stress by shifting their focus to working even harder to do their jobs well. For others, it is more difficult. As these officers struggle with the stress of the job, they can close off and push away those they serve and those who want to help. As noted by the President's Task Force on 21st Century Policing, "an officer whose capabilities, judgment, and behavior are adversely affected by poor physical or psychological health not only may be of little use to the community he or she serves but also may be a danger to the community and to other officers." For precisely these reasons, law enforcement agencies can and should do everything they can to support officers' physical and psychological well-being.

Because of how officer wellness can impact officer behavior, and the uniquely tense circumstances facing CPD officers each day, CPD officers need greater support from the City and CPD leadership. CPD and the City should think meaningfully about how to better address the stressors CPD officers face, and how to create an overarching operational plan that includes robust counseling programs, comprehensive training, functioning equipment, and other tools to ensure officers are successful and healthy. CPD should move away from traditional strategies that fail to fully address the issue of officer wellness and react to the changing nature of policing in Chicago and the demographic changes in CPD's police force. CPD needs to transform its officer support system so that officer wellness is an integral part of the Department's operations and reinforces the values of wellness and a culture that encourages officers to seek assistance when needed. CPD also should work to overcome officers' concern that using officer wellness services will negatively impact their career, and to educate officers on the value of these services. In this way, CPD can better support its officers' success, personally and professionally.

DATA COLLECTION AND TRANSPARENCY

A lack of transparency regarding CPD's and IPRA's activities has contributed to CPD's failure to identify and correct unlawful practices and to distrust between CPD and the public. Since the start of our investigation, the City and CPD have instituted steps aimed at increasing transparency regarding CPD's and IPRA's work. For example, the current IPRA Chief Administrator significantly improved IPRA's public reporting by expanding the amount of information regarding misconduct investigations that is regularly posted on IPRA's website. And, following the PATF's recommendation, the City adopted a "transparency policy," which created a portal on IPRA's website where video and other evidence of certain types of police misconduct investigations are posted. These steps go beyond the measures many other agencies put in place.

Our investigation found that additional steps are necessary to ensure the City is as transparent as possible and uses its data to adequately address the patterns and practices identified in this investigation. The City and CPD must improve the ways in which they collect, organize, analyze, track, and report on available data and data trends. Currently, CPD's data collection systems are siloed and do not allow for meaningful cross-system data collection, evaluation, and tracking. As a result, CPD is unable to easily use the data at its disposal to identify trends, including trends in misconduct complaints, training deficiencies, and more. Improving these systems will allow CPD to better understand its operations, and more easily report CPD activities to the public.

The data that is collected and publicly reported by the City is also incomplete, and at times, inaccurate. IPRA reports only on how investigations are resolved by that agency; but, as discussed in this Report, the findings of IPRA investigators can be set aside, and its discipline recommendations greatly reduced. IPRA's reporting, therefore, does not give a full picture of how misconduct investigations are ultimately resolved. Independent evaluation of IPRA's publicly reported data regarding use of force found that the data was, at least historically, inaccurate. And, even though IPRA's public reporting is far more comprehensive now than it was before, CPD does not aggregate or publish the same information for investigations handled by BIA and the districts. Currently, very little information is published about those investigations, even though those entities handle roughly 70% of all misconduct complaints. Finally, the City should also release more information regarding settlements of officer misconduct lawsuits; publicly available data is, at present, limited to the general nature of the allegation (e.g., "excessive force" or "false arrest") and the settlement amount.

Finally, the City should actively engage the public in crafting solutions in this area. Recent public engagement efforts, such as soliciting public feedback on the video release policy, COPA ordinance, and new use-of-force policies, were important steps toward increasing solicitation of public input into contemplated reforms. Improving and expanding upon these recent initiatives will ensure that the public understands and supports, to the greatest extent possible, the additional reforms currently being considered by the City.

PROMOTIONS

Dedicated, highly qualified supervisors are vital to ensuring CPD officers are able to police safely while valuing and respecting the rights of all community members. Under CPD's current promotions system, officers can be promoted to detective, sergeant, or lieutenant based on test scores or evaluation of other merit-based criteria. The merit-based promotion track was created following several lawsuits challenging CPD's promotional exams as discriminatory. The merit promotions system was then later challenged, as part of larger litigation regarding City hiring practices, as unfairly promoting individuals based on political connections rather than true merit. All of these legal battles resulted in several important reforms, including the creation of a City Hiring Plan and corresponding policies intended to organize and structure the merit promotion process.

Despite these important reforms, however, officers we spoke with continue to express skepticism about CPD's promotions system. Much of this is because CPD does not effectively communicate the details of its promotions process to the rank-and-file, and does not provide sufficient transparency following promotional decisions to allay officer concerns. For example, officers are unaware of the metrics used to evaluate individuals who are nominated for merit promotions, or why the officers receiving those promotions were selected. By not sharing this information publicly, and not ensuring Department-wide understanding of the promotions system, CPD has perpetuated an atmosphere of doubt around the promotions process as a whole.

CPD can and should do several things to restore officer and public confidence in its promotions system, and to ensure that the best-qualified candidates are promoted in a fair, lawful, and transparent manner. Promotional exams must be reviewed regularly to ensure they are fair and lawful, and offered often enough to ensure well-qualified candidates have the opportunity to be promoted. Monitoring and oversight of compliance with CPD's merit promotion policies are also necessary to ensure those systems are working as intended, and that merit promotion decisions are as transparent as possible. Without regular review and increased transparency, CPD's promotion processes will continue to be viewed as unfair and ineffective.

COMMUNITY-FOCUSED POLICING

A contributing factor to CPD's unreasonable use of force is CPD's approach to policing. CPD as a whole needs to support and provide incentives to policing practices that are lawful and restore trust among the City's marginalized communities. Within the past several months, CPD and the City have announced ambitious plans to revive community policing in Chicago. Superintendent Johnson has formed a Community Policing Advisory Panel to develop strategies for enhancing community policing within CPD. The Superintendent has pledged to remake the Department's Chicago Alternative Policing Strategy (CAPS), and the Department recently issued a directive expanding community involvement programs in several districts. CPD has several additional community policing–related initiatives underway. We commend CPD for these efforts. This policing approach, when implemented with fidelity to all its tenets, has been shown to be effective at making communities safer while incentivizing a policing culture that builds confidence in law enforcement.

Notwithstanding this recognition, community policing as a true CPD value and driving force fell away in Chicago many years ago, and past attempts to restore it have not been successful. To be successful this time, CPD must build up systems to support and bolster this community-focused approach to policing.

CPD has the officers it needs to make community policing work. During our investigation we observed many instances of diligent, thoughtful, and self-less policing, and we heard stories of officers who police this way every day. We know that there are many dedicated CPD officers who care deeply about the community, are affected by the violence they see, and work hard to build trust between the community and the Department. We heard about officers and command staff who are well-respected and beloved in the neighborhoods they patrol.

But for community policing to really take hold and succeed in Chicago, CPD must ensure that its supervision, training, promotions and accountability systems incentivize and support officers who police in a manner that conveys to community members that CPD officers can be a trusted partner in protecting them, their families, and their neighborhoods. Community policing must be a core philosophy that is infused throughout the Department's policing strategies and tactics.

In recent years, community policing in Chicago has been relegated, through CAPS, to a small group of police officers and civilians in each district. We were told by CAPS staff that CAPS offices were understaffed, and that CAPS officers receive little training on how to accomplish their mandate. Community policing efforts are also poorly funded and institutionally neglected.

In addition to infusing the tenets of community policing throughout the Department, and creating support for community policing beyond the CAPS program, CPD must also change its policing practices so that it can restore trust and ensure lawful policing. The Department has to do more to ensure that officers police fairly in neighborhoods with high rates of violent crime, and in vulnerable communities. A striking feature of our conversations with members from Chicago's challenged communities was the consistency with which they expressed concern about the lack of respect in their interactions with police, whether those interactions come when they are targets of police activity or when they or their family members are the victims of crime. Advocates and members of the Latino, Muslim, and transgender communities each separately raised concerns with us about the Department's response to potential or apparent hate crimes against members of their communities. There was also a sense that CPD relies too heavily on specialized units, such as Tactical (TACT).

This may not be how CPD intends policing to be conducted or perceived in these neighborhoods, but these experiences impact individual dignity and residents' willingness to work with law enforcement, and should not be ignored. CPD must ensure that it is creating incentives and rewarding policing where building community trust is central to all crime-prevention efforts, whether this policing is done by specialized units, beat officers, or CAPS staff.

Additionally, the City must address serious concerns about systemic deficiencies that disproportionately impact black and Latino communities. CPD's pattern or practice of unreasonable force and systemic deficiencies fall heaviest on the predominantly black and Latino neighborhoods on the South and West Sides of Chicago, which are also experiencing higher crime. Raw statistics show that CPD uses force almost ten times more often against blacks than against whites. As a result, residents in black neighborhoods suffer more of the harms caused by breakdowns in uses of force, training, supervision, accountability, and community policing.

Our investigation found also that CPD has tolerated racially discriminatory conduct that not only undermines police legitimacy, but also contributes to the pattern of unreasonable force. The pattern or practice of unreasonable force, coupled with the recurrence of unaddressed racially discriminatory conduct by officers further erodes community trust and police effectiveness. Our review of complaints of racially discriminatory language found repeated instances where credible complaints were not adequately addressed. Moreover, we found that some Chicago police officers expressed discriminatory views and intolerance with regard to race, religion, gender, and national origin in public social media forums, and that CPD takes insufficient steps to prevent or appropriately respond to this animus. As CPD works to restore trust and ensure that policing is lawful and effective, it must recognize the extent to which this type of misconduct contributes to a culture that facilitates unreasonable force and corrodes community trust. We have serious concerns about the prevalence of racially discriminatory conduct by some CPD officers and the degree to which that conduct is tolerated and in some respects caused by deficiencies in CPD's systems of training, supervision and accountability. In light of these concerns, combined with the fact that the impact of CPD's pattern or practice of unreasonable force fall heaviest on predominantly black and Latino neighborhoods, restoring police-community trust will require remedies addressing both discriminatory conduct and the disproportionality of illegal and unconstitutional patterns of force on minority communities.

Finally, during our investigation, we heard allegations that CPD officers attempt to gain information about crime using methods that undermine CPD legitimacy and may also be unlawful. In some instances, we were told, CPD will attempt to glean information about gang activity or other crime by arresting or detaining individuals, and refusing to release the individual until he provides that information. In other instances, CPD will take a young person to a rival gang neighborhood, and either leave the person there, or display the youth to rival members, immediately putting the life of that young person in jeopardy by suggesting he has provided information to the police. Our investigation indicates that these practices in fact exist and significantly jeopardize CPD's relationship with the community.

CPD must root out these practices that harm CPD's interaction with the community. Doing so will better support lawful policing, and allow CPD to gain legitimacy in the eyes of the public and more effectively address crime. With a community-focused approach that incentivizes and rewards officers for policing actively and in a manner that builds strong, positive community relationships, CPD will be better able to carry out its mission lawfully and effectively.

Finally, we find that, notwithstanding the City's recent efforts to address the broad problems within the Chicago Police Department, it is not likely to be successful in doing so without a consent decree with independent monitoring. Fixing the problems our investigation found will be neither easy nor quick. The root causes of these patterns of conduct and systemic deficiencies are complicated and entrenched, which is why they have persisted for so long despite repeated, concerted reform efforts by the City and community members from all walks. As Chicago's Mayor said in stating his intention to cooperate with our investigation, "We need a third party in this City because in the past instances . . . we've never, ever as a City measured up with the changes on a sustained basis to finally deal in whole cloth with that situation."

We applaud the City for this recognition and for agreeing to negotiate a set of comprehensive reforms that will be entered as a federal court order and assessed by a team of independent experts in policing and related fields. Through this commitment, the City has signaled its willingness to go further than any previous City administration to ensure that necessary reforms to the Chicago Police Department are made and take root.

We agree that such an approach is necessary. Our investigation found that the reforms the City already plans to implement, as well as the additional reforms our investigation found necessary, will likely not happen or be sustained without the reform tools of an independent monitoring team and a court order. An independent team of policing and other experts will be charged with assessing and publicly reporting on CPD's and the City's progress implementing reforms. A court-ordered, over-arching plan for reform that is overseen by a federal judge will help ensure that unnecessary obstacles are removed, and that City and police officials stay focused on carrying out promised reforms. Together, an independent monitor and court decree will make it much more certain that Chicago is finally able to eliminate patterns of unconstitutional conduct, and can bolster community confidence to make policing in Chicago more effective and less dangerous.

I. BACKGROUND

A. Chicago, Illinois

Chicago is the largest city in Illinois and the third largest metropolitan area in the United States with approximately 9.5 million residents, 2.7 million of whom live within the city limits. The City is racially diverse: 33% of current residents are black, 32% are white, 29% are Latino, and 8% identify as Asian or multiracial. The median household income in Chicago is $48,522, which is below the national average of $53,889. 22% of the City's residents live below the federal poverty threshold. The unemployment rate for individuals living in Chicago is 5.5%. Black and Latino Chicago residents are disproportionately poor when compared to white Chicago residents. Approximately 35% of black residents and 25% of Latinos live below the poverty line, compared to less than 11% of white residents. The mean household income for black residents is $30,400, as opposed to $61,500 for whites.

Chicago is governed by a Mayor, who is the chief executive, and the City Council, which is the legislative body. The City Council is made up of 50 Alderman elected from each of the 50 wards of Chicago. The City Council is led by a President Pro Tempore, currently Margaret Laurino. The current Mayor, Rahm Emanuel, was elected in 2011 and re-elected to a second term in 2015.

In 2015, Chicago reported 24,663 violent crime incidents. 9,649 of those crimes were robberies, and aggravated assaults constituted over 13,000 reported incidents. The City recorded 478 homicides that year. In 2016, there were 762 homicides in Chicago. According to the draft of a new study from the University of Chicago Crime Lab, this is the largest single-year homicide increase of the last 25 years among the five most populous United States cities.

B. Chicago Police Department

CPD is the primary law enforcement agency in the City and the second largest municipal police department in the United States. The Department is led by a Superintendent and a First Deputy Superintendent who reports directly to the Superintendent. The Mayor appoints the Superintendent of CPD with the advice and consent of the City Council. Mayor Emanuel appointed the current Superintendent, Eddie Johnson, in March 2016. As of June 2016, CPD employed approximately 12,000 sworn officers.

CPD is divided into four major bureaus: Patrol, Detectives, Organized Crimes, and Support Services. There are 22 different police districts in Chicago, and three geographic patrol "areas"—Area North, Area Central, and Area South. Each Area is led by a deputy chief who reports to the Chief of the Bureau of Patrol. Each district is led by a district commander who reports to the Area deputy chief. Each district also has specialty units, including gang, saturation, and tactical teams. All officers employed by CPD are required to live within City limits.

There are several unions in Chicago that represent the interests of CPD officers and supervisors. The Fraternal Order of Police, Chicago Lodge 7, is the CPD officers' union. Sergeants, lieutenants, and captains are all separately unionized under the Policeman's Benevolent & Protective Association of Illinois, Unit 156. Each union has a separate collective bargaining agreement (CBA) with the City. These CBAs include detailed provisions establishing certain terms and conditions of employment. Several CBA provisions relate to areas addressed by our investigation and are specifically discussed within this Report. The supervisors' unions are currently renegotiating their CBAs with the City. The officers' union will begin renegotiating its CBA this year.

C. Chicago's Accountability Systems

CPD's systems for reviewing misconduct allegations are unique and are explained in more detail later in this Report. The Independent Police Review Authority (IPRA), which is external to CPD, serves as the intake agency for all complaints of police misconduct. In 2015, IPRA intake totaled more than 5,000 cases, which were predominantly complaints filed by community members or other officers within CPD.

IPRA is led by a chief administrator, who is appointed by the Mayor and confirmed by the City Council. The Mayor appointed the current Chief Administrator, Sharon Fairley, in December 2015. IPRA's budget is set by the City Council. IPRA employs a staff of roughly 80 civilian investigators, supervisory investigators, attorneys, and support staff.

IPRA only has jurisdiction to investigate certain types of misconduct, including allegations of excessive force, domestic violence, biased-based verbal abuse, coercion, weapons discharges, and deaths in custody. Accordingly, IPRA handles roughly 30% of all complaints of misconduct filed against CPD officers.

On October 5, 2016, the Chicago City Council passed an ordinance establishing the Civilian Office of Police Accountability (COPA), which will replace IPRA in 2017. Because COPA is not yet in existence, this Report focuses on the work of IPRA, but will note changes that are anticipated as a result of the COPA ordinance.

The majority of misconduct complaints do not fall within IPRA's jurisdiction and are referred to CPD's Bureau of Internal Affairs (BIA). BIA is led by Chief Eddie Welch III. There are over 90 sworn personnel assigned to BIA, including officers, sergeants, lieutenants, and one commander. BIA handles investigations related to officer-involved criminal conduct and various rule violations, including abuse of CPD medical leave and CPD's policy requiring that CPD officers live within City limits. BIA also assigns some misconduct complaints to district commanders for investigation.

Chicago has a Police Board made up of nine private citizens appointed by the Mayor with the City Council's consent. The Police Board is not an investigatory body. Rather, it participates in finalizing CPD disciplinary decisions both by presiding over evidentiary hearings in discharge cases and by resolving discipline disputes between IPRA and the Superintendent, as described further below.

There is also an Inspector General for the City of Chicago who serves as the "watchdog for the taxpayers of the City, and has jurisdiction to conduct investigations and audits into most aspects of City government," including some parts of CPD operations. And the police accountability ordinance established a new Deputy Inspector General for Public Safety charged with auditing the police accountability system and identifying patterns and practices that violate residents' constitutional rights.

D. Historical Background of Reform in Chicago

The Chicago Police Department has cycled in and out of the national consciousness almost since its inception, and the last several decades have been no exception. In 1968, images of CPD officers beating protestors at the Democratic National Convention were captured and broadcast on national television. A commission convened in the aftermath of the event found that the violence amounted to a "police riot." No officers were prosecuted. In the 1980s and 1990s, a CPD detective, Jon Burge, and several officers under his command used severe interrogation tactics, such as physical force, suffocations, and electric shocks, to coerce confessions from predominantly black men living on Chicago's South and West Sides. Burge was ultimately fired, and in 2008, decades after the abuse began, he was arrested on charges of perjury and obstruction of justice. He was convicted on all counts, but was allowed to keep his pension from CPD and served only four-and-a-half years in prison. In the 1990s, CPD ran a special enforcement unit within the Patrol Division called the Special Operations Section (SOS). This unit improperly stopped and searched black and Latino community members and seized their cash and other property. Many of the officers working in that unit amassed numerous misconduct complaints. When the activities of the unit became publicly known, it was disbanded, and several officers involved were arrested and sent to prison for robbery and kidnapping. More recently, the circumstances of several officer-involved fatal shootings have generated coverage by national media, including the deaths of Rekia Boyd, Laquan McDonald, Quintonio LeGrier, and Bettie Jones.

In response to these and other incidents, the City has undertaken many reform efforts over the past several decades. In 1972, then-Mayor Richard J. Daley convened a blue ribbon panel that heard four days of public testimony regarding concerns about police abuse. Black and Latino residents testified about illegal stops and searches, excessive uses of force, and unjustified killings of Chicago residents by police officers. The panel issued a report containing several recommendations "for steps that should be taken to eliminate abusive police conduct and improve police performance in Chicago." In 1997, then-Mayor Richard M. Daley appointed the Commission on Police Integrity "in response to the indictment of seven members of [CPD] on charges of conspiracy, racketeering, and extortion." The Commission's charge "was to examine the root causes of police corruption . . . and to propose possible changes to department policies and procedures." The Commission's final report recommended changes to CPD's hiring standards, training program, early warning system, and other "management process improvements." More recently, the City asked a Chicago-based global consulting firm and a local law firm to jointly conduct an independent assessment "of what [CPD] is doing to prevent and address police misconduct and, specifically, to suggest ways the Department can improve." The conclusions of that review were released in 2014, and contained roughly 30 pages of recommendations for changes to CPD's accountability systems. In response to each of these panels and reports, the City and CPD chose to implement some recommendations, and rejected others. Some implemented recommendations lasted; others did not.

Most recently, in the wake of the shooting death of Laquan McDonald by a CPD Officer and the release of dashboard-camera video capturing the incident, Mayor Emanuel quickly responded to widespread community concern by establishing the Police Accountability Task Force (PATF). The Mayor charged the PATF with assessing the Police Department and making recommendations for change in five areas: community relations; oversight and accountability; de-escalation; early intervention and personnel concerns; and video release protocols. In April 2016, the PATF issued a report with over a hundred recommendations for improving transparency and accountability. In December 2016, the City issued a progress report outlining the steps it has taken since April to meet the recommendations made by the PATF. Too little time has passed to know whether the recommendations the City decided to implement will be sustained.

E. Federal Involvement in Chicago

During the thirteen months of our investigation, and particularly in light of the tumultuous year Chicago saw in 2016, the United States Department of Justice (DOJ) has proactively enhanced its assistance with CPD's reform and violence-reduction efforts. Beginning in September 2014, Chicago became part of DOJ's Violence Reduction Network (VRN), an innovative approach to support and enhance local violence reduction efforts. This data-driven, evidence-based initiative complemented DOJ's Smart on Crime initiative through delivery of strategic, intensive training, and technical assistance. Through VRN, Chicago received federal support and resources including training, federal law enforcement support, technical assistance from subject-matter experts, and participation in peer exchanges. This support led to implementation of new strategies, policy enhancements, improved technology, and increased analytic capacity.

In October 2016, at the conclusion of the initial VRN program phase, DOJ extended its commitment to the City of Chicago by offering continued support, technical assistance, and resources through at least March 2017. This additional commitment builds on existing strategies that have shown promise in Chicago, such as focusing on high-risk individuals and high-crime neighborhoods; emphasizing timely inter-agency intelligence gathering and sharing; concentrating on homicides, gun violence, and gang activity; ensuring fidelity to agreed-upon strategies throughout each agency; and incorporating trust-building principles into CPD's violence-reduction efforts. DOJ also is facilitating technical assistance to CPD by federal law enforcement agencies and current and former high-ranking police executives with expertise in reducing violence while increasing community trust. The areas of focus for crime-fighting strategies include development and dissemination of a comprehensive crime fighting plan; assessment and managed evolution of the Compstat command accountability program; and enhancing partnerships with state, local, and federal law enforcement agencies.

Further, in October 2016, DOJ allocated additional funding through its Office of Justice Programs (OJP), which now has professionals working directly with the City and CPD to assess community needs and available services in high crime neighborhoods to identify areas that would benefit from multi-sector public and private investments. The new OJP resources are complementary to, and coordinated with, preexisting collaborative initiatives launched by DOJ and CPD to improve community trust. Since December 2014, CPD and DOJ, through the United States Attorney's Office in Chicago, have hosted nine Community Trust Roundtables across Chicago's most violence-plagued neighborhoods.

These recent efforts build on the foundation of DOJ's longstanding collaborative initiatives with CPD. The United States Attorney's Office and other federal law enforcement partners in Chicago, including the Federal Bureau of Investigation (FBI), Drug Enforcement Agency (DEA), Bureau of Alcohol, Tobacco, Firearms and Explosives (ATF), and the United States Marshals Service (USMS) work closely with CPD on a variety of ongoing enforcement initiatives. Last year, each of these federal agencies increased resources dedicated to working with CPD in an effort to tamp down on the current spike in gun violence.

Indeed, the United States Attorney's Office charged more illegal firearms cases in total, and more as a percentage of its overall cases, last year than it has in any year since 2004. Further, longstanding collaborations include, among other programs: Project Safe Neighborhoods, which seeks to reduce gun violence through strategic enforcement, deterrence, and reentry; Chicago's Violence Reduction Strategy (VRS), which is a targeted deterrence partnership aimed at gangs and violent criminals; and Youth Outreach Forums, a DOJ-funded program aimed at helping at-risk youth, 13 to 17 years old.

F. Investigation of the Chicago Police Department

On December 7, 2015, the United States Department of Justice, Civil Rights Division, Special Litigation Section, and the United States Attorney's Office for the Northern District of Illinois, jointly initiated an investigation of CPD and IPRA. This investigation was undertaken to determine whether the Chicago Police Department is engaging in a pattern or practice of unlawful conduct and, if so, what systemic deficiencies or practices within CPD, IPRA, and the City might be facilitating or causing this pattern or practice.

We opened this investigation pursuant to the Violent Crime Control and Law Enforcement Act of 1994, 42 U.S.C. § 14141 (Section 14141), Title VI of the Civil Rights Act of 1964, 42 U.S.C. § 2000d (Title VI), and the Omnibus Crime Control and Safe Streets Act of 1968, 42 U.S.C. § 3789d (Safe Streets Act). Section 14141 prohibits law enforcement agencies from engaging in a pattern or practice of conduct that violates the Constitution or laws of the United States. Title VI and the Safe Streets Act prohibit law enforcement practices that have a disparate impact based on protected status, such as race or ethnicity, unless these practices are necessary to achieve legitimate, non-discriminatory objectives.

Our investigation assessed CPD's use of force, including deadly force, and addressed CPD policies, training, reporting, investigation, and review related to officer use of force. The investigation further addressed CPD's and IPRA's systems of accountability both as they relate to officer use of force and officer misconduct, including the intake, investigation, and review of allegations of officer misconduct, and the imposition of discipline or other corrective action. We also investigated racial, ethnic, or other disparities in CPD's force and accountability practices, and assessed how those disparities inform the breakdown in community trust.

We relied on several sources of information. First, we reviewed thousands of pages of documents provided to us by CPD, IPRA, and the City, including policies, procedures, training plans, Department orders and memos, internal and external reports, and more. We also obtained access to the City's entire misconduct complaint database and data from all reports filled out following officers' use of force. From there, we reviewed a randomized, representative sample of force reports and the investigative files for incidents that occurred between January 2011 and April 2016, as well as additional incident reports and investigations. Overall, we reviewed over 170 officer-involved shooting investigations, and documents related to over 425 incidents of less-lethal force, including representative samples of officers' own reports of force, and of investigations of civilian complaints about officer force between January 2011 and April 2016. We also reviewed documents provided to us by other City agencies, such as the Office of Inspector General and the City's Law Department.

We also spent extensive time in Chicago—over 300 person-days—meeting with community members and City officials, and interviewing current and former CPD officers and IPRA investigators. In addition to speaking with the Superintendent and other CPD leadership, we met with the command staff of several specialized units, divisions, and departments. We toured CPD's training facilities and observed training programs. We also visited each of Chicago's 22 police districts, where we addressed roll call, spoke with command staff and officers, and conducted over 60 ride-alongs with officers. We met several times with Chicago's officer union, Lodge No. 7 of the Fraternal Order of Police, as well as the sergeants', lieutenants', and captains' unions. All told, we heard from over 340 individual CPD members, and 23 members of IPRA's staff.

In addition to document review and conversations with CPD and IPRA, our findings were significantly informed by our conversations with members of the Chicago community. During the course of our investigation we met with over 90 community organizations, including nonprofits, advocacy and legal organizations, and faith-based groups focused on a wide range of issues. Several of these groups set up meetings for us so that we could hear directly from their clients or membership. We participated in forums where we heard directly from the family members of individuals who were killed by CPD officers. We also met with several local researchers, academics, and lawyers who have studied CPD extensively for decades. Most importantly, however, we heard directly from individuals who live and work throughout the City about their interactions with CPD officers. Overall, we talked to approximately a thousand community members. We received nearly 600 phone calls, emails, and letters during the course of our investigation from individuals who were eager to provide their experiences and insights. We also held several community forums in different neighborhoods throughout Chicago, where community members were able to share their stories in person.

In addition to attorneys, paralegals, outreach specialists, and data analysts from the Civil Rights Division of DOJ and the United States Attorney's Office for the Northern District of Illinois, eleven independent subject matter experts assisted with this investigation. Most of these experts are current or former law enforcement officials from police departments across the country. Accordingly, these experts have decades of expertise in areas such as the use of force, accountability, training, supervision, community policing, officer-involved domestic violence and sexual misconduct, officer wellness, and more. These experts accompanied us on-site, reviewed documents and investigative files, and provided invaluable insights that informed both the course of this investigation and its conclusions.

We thank the City, CPD officials, union officials, and the rank-and-file officers who have cooperated with this investigation and provided us with insights into the operation of the Department. We are also grateful to the many members of the Chicago community who have met with us during this investigation to share their experiences.

II. CPD ENGAGES IN A PATTERN OR PRACTICE OF UNCONSTITUTIONAL USE OF FORCE

We reviewed CPD's force practices mindful that officers routinely place themselves in harm's way in order to uphold their commitment to serve and protect the people of the City of Chicago, that officers regularly encounter individuals who may be armed and determined to avoid arrest, and that our inquiry should be guided by the perspective of the reasonable officer on the scene rather than perfect hindsight. We likewise recognize that officers have not only a right, but an obligation to protect themselves and others from threats of harm, including deadly harm, which may arise in an instant. We also recognize that the City has taken some steps that—if properly implemented—could represent meaningful improvements to the way that officers use force.

Nonetheless, we found reasonable cause to believe that CPD has engaged in a pattern or practice of unreasonable force in violation of the Fourth Amendment and that the deficiencies in CPD's training, supervision, accountability, and other systems have contributed to that pattern or practice. CPD has not provided officers with adequate guidance to understand how and when they may use force, or how to safely and effectively control and resolve encounters to reduce the need to use force. CPD often does not appropriately supervise officers to identify dangerous tactics or behaviors that may indicate officers need additional training or other intervention. CPD also does not review its force practices as a whole to identify problematic trends or patterns that endanger officers and others. When officers use force, CPD often does not adequately review those force incidents to determine whether the force used complied with the law or CPD policy, or whether the tactics the officer used were safe and effective. Consequently, officers are asked to perform a dangerous job with insufficient guidance as to whether their force practices are safe, effective, or legal. These failures have resulted in CPD engaging in a pattern or practice of using force in a manner that is unconstitutional, contrary to CPD policy, and unsafe. Inappropriate use of force by the police (even when no lasting physical injury is involved) results in fear and distrust from many of the people whom the police are committed to protect and whom the police need as partners in that effort.

The use of excessive force by a law enforcement officer violates the Fourth Amendment. *Graham v. Connor*, 490 U.S. 386, 394 (1989). "In determining whether police used excessive force under the Fourth Amendment, the relevant inquiry is 'whether the officers' actions [were] objectively reasonable in light of the totality of the circumstances.'" *Flournoy v. City of Chicago*, 829 F.3d 869, 874 (7th Cir. 2016) (citations omitted); *Fitzgerald v. Santoro*, 707 F.3d 725, 733 (7th Cir. 2013) (citing Graham, 490 U.S. at 396–97). In determining whether force used by a law enforcement officer is reasonable, courts look to "the severity of the crime at issue, whether the suspect poses an immediate threat to the safety of the officers or others, and whether he is actively resisting arrest or attempting to evade arrest by flight." Id. at 396. Whether a particular use of force is reasonable is "judged from the perspective of a reasonable officer on the scene, rather than with the 20/20 vision of hindsight." Id. Courts are mindful that "police officers are often forced to make split-second judgments—in circumstances that are tense, uncertain, and rapidly evolving—about the amount of force that is necessary in a particular situation." Id. at 396–97. An officer's use of force is unreasonable if, judging from the totality of the circumstances at the time of the arrest, the officer uses greater force than was reasonably necessary to effectuate the arrest. *Phillips v. Cmty. Ins. Corp.*, 678 F.3d 513, 519 (7th Cir. 2012) (citing *Gonzalez v. City of Elgin*, 578 F.3d 526, 539 (7th Cir. 2009)).

A pattern or practice of unreasonable force may be found where incidents of violations are repeated and are not isolated instances. *Int'l Bd. of Teamsters v. United States*, 431 U.S. 324, 336 n.16 (1977) (noting that the phrase "pattern or practice" "was not intended as a term of art," but should be interpreted according to its usual meaning "consistent with the understanding of the identical words" used in other federal civil rights statutes). Courts interpreting the term "pattern or practice" in similar statutes have established that statistical evidence is not required. *Coates v. Johnson & Johnson*, 756 F.2d 524, 533 (7th Cir. 1985) ("Neither statistical nor anecdotal evidence is automatically entitled to reverence to the exclusion of the other."). A court does not need a specific number of incidents to find a pattern or practice. See *United States v. W. Peachtree Tenth Corp.*, 437 F.2d 221, 227 (5th Cir. 1971) ("The number of [violations] . . . is not determinative. . . . In any event, no mathematical formula is workable, nor was any intended. Each case must turn on its own facts.").

Although a specific number of incidents and statistical evidence is not required, our investigation found that CPD officers use unnecessary and unreasonable force[134] in violation of the Constitution with frequency, and that unconstitutional force has been historically tolerated by CPD. This finding is based on a comprehensive investigation of CPD's force practices. We reviewed CPD's policies related to the use, reporting, and investigation of force, including older versions of polices that were effective during our review period, and CPD's proposed revised policies. We spoke with officers at all ranks, including the Superintendent and

---

134 Throughout this Report, we use the terms "unreasonable" and "excessive" interchangeably; both terms refer to force that exceeds constitutional limits, or in other words, is disproportional in light of the threat posed to officers or others, the level of resistance, and the severity of the crime suspected. When using the term "unnecessary," we instead mean that force was used when the incident could have been resolved without resorting to the amount of force used.

the Chief and Deputy Chief of the Bureau of Patrol, to understand how officers were trained to use force, their view of when force is appropriate, and how the policies are interpreted in practice throughout CPD and at each level. We also did an in-depth review of officer reports of force, civilian complaints of force, and CPD's and IPRA's reviews of force and investigations of allegations of excessive force. We reviewed over 425 incidents of less-lethal force, including representative samples of officers' own reports of force and of investigations of civilian complaints about officer force between January 2011 and April 2016.

We also reviewed over 170 IPRA files related to officer-involved shootings, which amounts to a significant portion of all officer-involved shootings. The City was not able to accurately identify how many people were shot by CPD officers. We were provided with a list of all incidents involving a weapons discharge between January 2011 and January 2016, but it was inaccurate and incomplete. By comparing this list to other data provided by the City, we were able to identify nine shooting incidents during that time period in which a person was struck that either were not on the list provided by the City or that were not categorized as hits of people. In all, we were able to identify 203 officer-involved shooting incidents in which at least one civilian was shot between January 1, 2011 and March 21, 2016. In those 203 incidents, 223 civilians were shot. We reviewed 151 of these, including all 134 for which the investigation was complete and the disposition was final as of June 2016. In addition to these 151 officer-involved shooting incidents, we also reviewed 22 shooting files that pertained to officer-involved shootings that CPD refers to as "no-hits," meaning that CPD is not aware of anyone being struck during the incident. As described below, the City does not investigate shootings in which it is not aware that a person was struck. Consequently, those files contain very little information about the circumstances of those shootings and did not provide sufficient information to determine whether the force was lawful.

The uses of excessive force we identified were not aberrational. Our holistic review of this information, combined with our investigation of CPD's training, supervision, accountability, and other systems, give us reasonable cause to believe that the unreasonable force we identified amounts to a pattern or practice of unlawful conduct. Below we describe some recurring categories of unreasonable force we identified. We also provide illustrative incidents. In all incidents, the description of events comes from CPD's and IPRA's own records.

A. CPD Uses Deadly Force in Violation of the Fourth Amendment and Department Policy

CPD's pattern or practice of unreasonable force includes the use of deadly force. Our review of CPD's deadly force practices identified several trends in CPD's deadly force incidents, including that CPD engages in dangerous and unnecessary foot pursuits and other unsound tactics that result in CPD shooting people, including those who are unarmed. We also saw a trend in dangerous and unnecessary shootings at vehicles and other unsafe tactics that placed officers and others in danger of being shot.

1. CPD's pattern or practice of unreasonable force includes shooting at fleeing suspects who present no immediate threat

We found numerous incidents where CPD officers chased and shot fleeing persons who posed no immediate threat to officers or the public. Such actions are constitutionally impermissible. See *Tennessee v. Garner*, 471 U.S. 1, 13 (1985) ("Where the suspect poses no immediate threat to the officer and no threat to others, the harm resulting from failing to apprehend him does not justify the use of deadly force to do so."). Moreover, "an officer does not possess the unfettered authority to shoot a member of the public simply because that person is carrying a weapon. Instead, deadly force may only be used by a police officer when, based on a reasonable assessment, the officer or another person is threatened with the weapon." *Cooper v. Sheehan*, 735 F.3d 153, 159 (4thCir. 2013); *Curnow v. Ridgecrest Police Agency*, 952 F.2d 321, 324–25 (9th Cir. 1991) (deadly force unreasonable when suspect holding gun was not pointing it or facing officers). Cf. *Williams v. Ind. State Police Dep't*, 797 F.3d 468, 484–85 (7th Cir. 2015) (deadly force justified not merely by possession of weapon, but by suspect's actions).

In some cases, CPD officers initiated foot pursuits without a basis for believing the person had committed a serious crime. In these cases, the act of fleeing alone was sufficient to trigger a pursuit ending in gunfire, sometimes fatal. During subsequent review, almost without exception, officers' reports of these events were accepted at face value, even where there was contrary evidence.

In one case, a man had been walking down a residential street with a friend when officers drove up, shined a light on him, and ordered him to freeze, because he had been fidgeting with his waistband. The man ran. Three officers gave chase and began shooting as they ran. In total, the officers fired 45 rounds, including 28 rifle rounds, toward the man. Several rounds struck the man, killing him. The officers claimed the man fired at them during the pursuit. Officers found no gun on the man. However, officers reported recovering a handgun nearly one block away. The gun recovered in the vicinity, however, was later determined to be fully-loaded and inoperable, and forensic testing determined there was no gunshot residue on the man's hands. IPRA found the officers' actions were justified without addressing the efficacy of the pursuit or the number of shots fired.

In another case, a CPD officer chased and shot a man. The officer later claimed that during pursuit she ordered the man to stop, at which point the man turned and raised his right arm towards her. According to the officer, the man had pointed a gun at her earlier in the incident and, fearing he was doing so now, she fired. The only gunshot wounds were to the man's buttocks. No weapon was found on the man, but a gun was found on a nearby roof gutter. IPRA found the shooting justified without accounting for the wounds to the man's backside. In another case, a CPD officer chased a man who ran when an officer told him to stop, and then shot the man in the back of the leg. The officer claimed the man had turned to point a gun. After a thorough search of the scene, no gun was recovered. The man, who denied ever turning to face the officer, was found only with a cell phone.

In another case, a CPD officer fatally shot a fleeing, unarmed suspect in the back. The officer told investigators the suspect had turned around to point a black object. This account did not square with the location of the shooting victim's gunshot wounds and appeared contrary to video footage that showed the suspect running away from the officer. Again, IPRA accepted the officer's account, despite the conflicting evidence. IPRA's final report of the incident did not mention the existence of the video.

In another case, video evidence showed the tragic end of a foot pursuit of a man who was not a threat when an officer shot him in the back. The officer, who fired 16 shots, killing the man, claimed on his force report that the man was armed and the man "charged [him] with apparent firearm." The officer shot the man during the foot pursuit, and dashboard-camera footage showed that as the unarmed man lay on the ground, the officer fired three shots into his back. CPD stripped the officer of his police powers after this shooting—his third that year—and the City paid the man's family $4.1 million in settlement.

To be sure, foot pursuits are a necessary and sometimes important part of good policing. There are circumstances in which officers are legally authorized to engage in a foot pursuit, and should. That said, foot pursuits are also inherently dangerous and present substantial risks to officers and the public. Officers may experience fatigue or an adrenaline rush that compromises their ability to control a suspect they capture, to fire their weapons accurately, and even to make sound judgments. Consequently, officers caught up in the heat of a pursuit "often exhibit a tendency to rush into what can be described as 'the killing zone,' that is, within a 10-foot radius of the offender."[135] The adrenaline rush also may make it more difficult for the officer to decrease the amount of force used as the threat diminishes. CPD has long had detailed policies regarding

---

135 ANTHONY J. PINNIZZOTTO ET AL., Escape from the Killing Zone, FBI LAW ENFORCE-MENT BULL., March 2002, at 1.

vehicle pursuits. It does not have a foot pursuit policy. It should. In addition to not having a policy, CPD has not taken corrective action to address problematic foot pursuits. This puts officers and the public in danger and results in unreasonable uses of force.

2. CPD's pattern or practice of unreasonable force includes firing at vehicles without justification

We also reviewed incidents involving officers who either unlawfully fired at fleeing vehicles, or, in violation of CPD policy, who fired after recklessly positioning themselves in the path of a moving vehicle or refusing to move from the path of a moving vehicle. Shooting at a moving vehicle is inherently dangerous and almost always counterproductive. First, bullets fired at the vehicle itself are unlikely to stop or disable it. Second, the bullets may strike a passenger who is not a threat and may be a victim. Third, bullets fired into a vehicle may not result in surrender, but may instead provoke a fight-or-flight response in which the driver is even more determined to escape or stop the source of gunfire. Fourth, disabling the driver may result in a runaway vehicle that endangers the lives of officers or bystanders. Faced with a threat posed by a moving vehicle, the appropriate response ordinarily is to avoid the vehicle's path, take cover, and summon additional resources to maximize safety and obtain a tactical advantage. This approach likewise minimizes the risk of deadly force.[136]

CPD policy has long formally recognized the appropriate tactical response to officers facing threats from moving vehicles. Its deadly force policy for the period September 2002 to February 2015 provided, "When confronted with an oncoming vehicle and that vehicle is the only force used against them, sworn members will move out of the vehicle's path." Since February 2015, CPD policy expressly prohibits "[f]iring at or into a moving vehicle when the vehicle is the only force used against the sworn member or another person."

CPD did not enforce its 2002-2015 policy, however. For example, in one case, an off-duty officer witnessed a reckless driver cause a vehicle collision during a high-speed chase. The officer exited his vehicle and ran to the scene. The motorist, seeking to escape, backed up his car, managing to pin it between the officer's vehicle and a tree. The officer moved in front of the trapped car and fired two shots into the windshield, claiming he did so because he heard the car's

---

136 U.S. CUSTOMS AND BORDER PROTECTION, USE OF FORCE REVIEW: CASES AND POLICIES 6, 8 (Police Executive Research Forum, 2013), available at https://www.cbp.gov/sites/default/files/documents/PERFReport.pdf; USE OF FORCE: CONCEPTS AND ISSUES PAPER 7 (IACP National Law Enforcement Policy Center, Rev. 2006), available at https://www.documentcloud.org/documents/370261-iacp-use-of-force-concepts-and-issues-paper-2006.html.

engine revving. During the IPRA investigation, the officer was never asked to explain why he positioned himself in front of the car or why he could not have stepped out of the way if he believed the car was about to move forward. IPRA found the shooting justified, despite the apparent policy violation and insufficient factual record regarding the officer's claimed need to fire in self-defense.

Our review also included cases involving shots fired at moving vehicles that occurred after CPD's February 2015 change to its deadly force policy. Some of these matters remain under investigation. Absent accountability for violations, the 2015 revisions do not adequately address or resolve the unconstitutional pattern or practice.

3. CPD officers exhibit poor discipline in discharging weapons

We found repeated incidents where officers exhibited poor discipline in discharging their weapons, reflecting disregard for innocent bystanders and constitutional standards.[137] As noted above, for example, in one incident three CPD officers fired a total of 45 rounds, including 28 rifle rounds, at a man during a foot pursuit in a residential area. This man was shot several times, but dozens of the bullets were fired into this residential neighborhood.

In some incidents, officers appeared to fire their weapons merely because others had done so. For example, in one case, two officers chased a man they saw carrying a gun. During the foot pursuit, one officer told his partner he intended to shoot, and then fired 11 shots at the suspect. The partner then fired five shots of his own. Later recounting the incident to IPRA, the partner did not articulate any threatening actions by the man that prompted him to shoot. He stated that the suspect did not turn his body or raise his weapon. Instead, he explained that the first officer began shooting and so he did as well. IPRA did not pursue the matter further and found the use of deadly force justified.[138] On the evidence available to us, the shooting did not meet the constitutional standard because the officer was not responding to a specific, articulable threat.

---

137 During our review of officer-involved shootings, we saw shootings at dogs that appeared to be unnecessary, retaliatory, or reckless. We also observed that there were many complaints from community members that officers unnecessarily or recklessly killed their dogs and that, like other civilian complaints, these complaints were not adequately investigated. These deficiencies in investigation of civilian complaints are discussed elsewhere in this Report.

138 The shooting was of concern for other reasons as well. The first officer claimed the suspect had turned his body to point his weapon at the second officer, prompting him to warn his partner and then pull the trigger. The second officer contradicted this account, claiming the suspect never turned his body and never pointed the weapon. IPRA never pursued the inconsistency and did not mention it in its final report.

4. CPD officers make tactical decisions that unnecessarily increase the risk of deadly encounters

We observed a trend in shootings resulting from CPD officers unnecessarily escalating confrontations or using reckless, untrained tactics, putting themselves in a position of jeopardy and limiting their force options to just deadly force. While these tactical decisions may not always result in uses of force that are unconstitutional, they do result in avoidable uses of force and resulting harm, including deaths. Moreover, these poor tactics are part of the systemic deficiencies that have led to the pattern or practice of excessive force.

a. Failure to await backup and use of unsound tactics in approaching vehicles

Deadly force incidents have occurred when CPD officers failed to await backup and unnecessarily injected themselves into high-risk situations where there was no exigent need to do so. Although not necessarily unconstitutional uses of force, these are avoidable uses of force that present an unnecessary risk to officer and public safety. In one case, an off-duty civilian-dressed CPD officer did not call for backup after witnessing two men exit a car, fire gunshots at an unknown target, and then drive off. Instead, after locating the car stopped in traffic, the officer approached it on foot and engaged the suspects. The officer fired his off-duty firearm at their car upon seeing an occupant of the car point a pistol at him. The officer fired 10 times, wounding but not disabling either suspect. The officer had fired all his ammunition, leaving him defenseless in the middle of the street. In addition, the CPD officer did this in a high-traffic area, thereby exposing bystanders to the risk of errant rounds from a shootout. And, a nearby uniformed state trooper conducting an unrelated traffic stop drew his gun on the CPD officer, because the trooper was unsure whether he had just witnessed an attempted murder.

In another case, two officers were flagged down by a woman reporting that someone in a car had pointed a shotgun at her. The officers spotted the car and radioed for assistance. They did not wait for backup and instead approached on foot alone. As one officer stood adjacent to the passenger side of the suspect's car, he reportedly saw the driver point a shotgun at him. Standing exposed at close range, the officer fired twice, wounding but not disabling the suspect. The suspect drove off without returning fire. Though the officer was justified in firing in self-defense, the violence may have been avoided altogether if the officers had observed sound tactics.

In another case, an off-duty CPD officer spotted the silhouette of a man in a vacant building and suspected the man was burglarizing it. The officer called 911, but did not wait for other officers to arrive. Instead, the off-duty officer summoned the man out of the building. According to a civilian witness, the burglary suspect angrily exited the building, yelling, "You're not a fucking cop." The suspect then advanced on the officer, who struck and kicked the suspect. According to the officer, the suspect then reached into his waistband and withdrew a shiny object, prompting the officer to fire twice, killing the man. No weapon was recovered. Instead, officers reported finding a silver watch near the man's body. IPRA found the shooting justified without addressing the officer's failure to await backup. According to press reports, in November 2016, this same officer shot a man in the back and killed him, claiming the man had pointed a gun at him during a foot pursuit. No gun was recovered.

We further found instances where CPD officers unnecessarily exposed innocent bystanders to deadly risks. In one case, three CPD officers were driving two civilian witnesses assisting in an assault investigation. Along the way, the officers heard gunshots from a nearby restaurant and saw a group of individuals running. The officers decided to confront the suspected gunmen themselves, with their unwilling civilian passengers in tow. The driver officer stopped the unmarked patrol car within a few yards of the suspects and issued police commands. According to the officers, one of the suspects drew a firearm and pointed it toward the officers and the side of the patrol car, where the two civilian witnesses sat exposed in the back seat. Both the driver officer and front passenger officer opened fire. During the IPRA investigation, both officers acknowledged that the confrontation had placed the civilian witnesses' lives at risk and sought to justify their use of deadly force in part because of that risk. While the suspect was indeed armed, one of the civilians in the backseat denied seeing the man point or raise the weapon at officers. IPRA found the shooting reasonable and justified with no stated concerns about the officers' tactics and without mentioning the civilian's contrary account in its final report.

b. Use of dangerous vehicle maneuvers

Other shooting incidents arose out of officers' use of high-risk, untrained vehicle maneuvers designed to box in suspects' cars. In one such incident, officers in two patrol vehicles tried to stop a car reportedly matching a description of suspected narcotics dealers with a gun hidden in the car. The first patrol car initiated the traffic stop by pulling in sideways in front of the suspects' car, thereby exposing the passenger officer to the risk of gunfire or serious injury if the driver had opted to ram the police car. The passenger officer exited the patrol car and fired upon the suspects as they attempted to drive away. Although it is unclear whether the officer's use of force was constitutional, it is clear that the poor stop tactics unnecessarily placed the officer at risk, thereby increasing the likelihood of a deadly force encounter.

On another occasion, officers used a variation of this box-in technique to trap a car in a high-traffic area. Again, an officer in the lead patrol car ended up firing into the suspect's vehicle, although in this case the car had not fled the scene. The officer acknowledged in his interview that they used the vehicle technique in the field despite never having been trained on the technique.

In another case, CPD officers used unmarked police cars to box in a car driven by an armed robbery suspect. After forcing the suspect to stop, the officer in the front patrol car exited and placed himself between his car and the driver's side of the suspect's vehicle. The suspect backed up, striking the rear police car. As this occurred, the front car officer moved in front of the suspect's car. The suspect then placed the car in drive, turned his wheels, and attempted to drive away. The officer from the front car fired a single shot into the driver's window, claiming he feared the suspect would run him over. The officer's bullet struck the suspect through the driver's window, causing the driver to crash his car into an occupied parked car. IPRA found the shooting justified without addressing the officers' tactics.

c. Reckless foot pursuits

As discussed above, we found repeated incidents of unreasonable uses of force stemming from foot pursuits that were initiated with an insufficient basis to conduct the pursuit. We also identified other cases in which foot pursuits were conducted in a tactically unsound, often reckless manner, some of which culminated in an officer-involved shooting. We found multiple instances in which officers began pursuit without first broadcasting over radio dispatch critical information like location and direction of travel. In addition, officers frequently engage in a dangerous tactic known as "partner-splitting," in which officers split off from one another to pursue one or more suspects. In some cases, one officer drives away from the foot chase, seeking to cut the suspect off from the other side of the block. Partner-splitting covers more territory, but it also can compromise the safety of officers who lose their ability to assist or effectively communicate with each other. It also increases the risk that the officers or innocent civilians will be caught in cross-fire. Because it is dangerous to officers and the public, this tactic should be used only when absolutely necessary to protect the public or officers from imminent harm.

Partner-splitting is not a trained CPD technique, but a practice developed in the field. As one CPD officer put it, "My partner and I have an agreement or we call it protocol, if you will, that if I'm driving, I stay in the vehicle and he is going to be the one that's going to pursue on foot." The officer offered this observation during an IPRA investigation of a partner-splitting foot pursuit that left him alone in a backyard with a man he claimed pointed a gun at him, resulting in a fatal shooting. The shooting was deemed justified, with no scrutiny of the tactics that precipitated the event.

This lack of policy, guidance, and oversight of foot pursuits presents not only constitutional and safety concerns, but also exposes the City to sub-stantial damages claims in civil rights litigation. See, e.g., *Quintana v. City of Philadelphia*, Civ. No. 10-6088, 2011 WL 2937426 at *3 (E.D. Pa. July 21, 2011) ("[A]rming police officers without providing any training on the constitutional limitations of the use of deadly force may amount to deliberate indifference, as could failing to maintain any sort of foot pursuit or partner splitting policy for police officers involved in a foot pursuit.") (citations omitted); *Pelzer v. City of Philadelphia.*, 656 F. Supp. 2d 517, 535 (E.D. Pa. 2009) ("[F]oot pursuits tend to be strong in emotion, weak in tactics. . . . A reasonable jury could find the failure to establish [foot] pursuit policies creates a sufficiently obvious risk to the rights of pursuit subjects. . . . A jury may also be able to conclude that the issue of pur-suit and patrol policies are the result of a policymaker's decision, and that the City's omission was the moving factor behind the plaintiff's injury.").

A contributing factor to many foot pursuits that end in unnecessary force is CPD's use of a particular stop technique, often called a "jump out." The practice involves groups of officers, frequently in plain clothes and riding in unmarked vehicles driving rapidly toward a street corner or group of individu-als and then jumping out and rapidly advancing, often with guns drawn. These actions often cause one of more members of the targeted group to walk away briskly or run from the scene. The officers then zero-in on the fleeing person, often with one officer tasked with chasing him on foot. Some of the most prob-lematic shootings occurred when that sole officer closed in on the subject, thus greatly increasing the risk of a serious or deadly force incident.

Such techniques can be particularly problematic when deployed by CPD tactical or other specialized units using unmarked vehicles and plainclothes officers. It can be difficult, especially at night, to discern that individuals spring-ing out of an unmarked car are police officers. In high-crime areas, residents may be particularly unwilling to stick around to find out. For example, in one case, a tactical officer in plain clothes jumped out of an unmarked car, chased a man who ran from him, and ultimately shot the man from behind. Officers claimed the man pointed a gun, but no weapon was recovered. The shooting victim explained to investigators that he ran because a sedan he did not recog-nize had raced through a stop sign and headed toward him. Similarly, in an-other case, two plainclothes officers dressed in black and in unmarked vehicles approached a man and his female passenger as they were getting into their car. According to the woman, the couple did not know they were officers and fled, and an officer shot at the side and rear of the vehicle, killing the man.

CPD should provide officers with guidance and support in conducting field operations in a tactically sound manner that reduces risk to officers and civilians alike. This does not mean a retreat from law enforcement, but rather a move toward practices that are more effective. Policy and guidance are the first step; scenario-based training is the next. As noted by trainers from the FBI Academy, "realistic and practical exercises can instill in officers the skills and mental preparedness that they can call on automatically when confronting offenders. Law enforcement agencies should ensure that officers receive training in such critical issues as formulating action plans, following established policies, knowing their physical and mental conditions, remaining aware of their surroundings, considering offender reactions, and exploring tactical options."

B. CPD Uses Less-Lethal Force in Violation of the Fourth Amendment and Department Policy

Although CPD documents generally include insufficient detail of when and how officers use force, particularly less-lethal force, our review of CPD records made clear that CPD's pattern of unreasonable force includes unreasonable less-lethal force. As discussed in detail below, CPD does not require officers to provide detailed information about the amount and type of force they use. The form on which officers are to report force requires officers to indicate via check box, for example, that they used a Taser[139] or a "control instrument" without requiring them to explain the manner or circumstances in which the force was used. Officers also are not required to provide any details about the amount of resistance they encountered from suspects. Instead, officers use boilerplate, vague terminology like "actively resisted" or "attempted to defeat arrest." In reviewing officers' use of less-lethal force, supervisors generally do not conduct any follow-up investigation or request any additional information from officers to help them understand what happened. As a consequence, CPD's documentation for many uses of less-lethal force do not paint a complete or accurate picture of the amount of force used or why it was used. IPRA investigations of misconduct complaints regarding force are similarly deficient, as discussed in the Accountability Section of this Report.

In many cases we reviewed, due to insufficient information, we were not able to determine whether the force was reasonable. For example, if an officer reported that he used a "kick" because a subject "balled his fists" and actively resisted, we were unable to determine whether the force used was reasonable because we did not know how many times the officer kicked the subject, where on the body the subject was kicked, or whether it might have been necessary. In many cases, however, the information that was reported was sufficient to demonstrate that the force used was unreasonable. If, for example, an officer reported that he or she used a Taser against someone suspected of a minor prop-

---

139 "Taser" is the brand name of electronic control weapons manufactured by Taser International, Inc. CPD uses Taser brand electronic control weapons and refers to these weapons in their policies and forms as "Tasers."

erty crime as the suspect fled, we determined that force to be unreasonable because, as described below, that level of force is unconstitutional on its face. Even using this conservative methodology—taking officers' reports of force at face value and not making inferences—we saw a clear pattern of unreasonable force.

1. CPD's pattern or practice of unreasonable force includes the use of excessive less-lethal force against people who present no threat

CPD's pattern or practice of unreasonable force includes using excessive force against people who do not present a threat and who are suspected only of low-level crimes or, in some cases, no crime at all. For example, officers used a Taser in "drive-stun mode" against a woman in mental health crisis and whose only documented actions were that she failed to follow verbal commands and that she stiffened.[140] Officers provided no narrative of the encounter other than to write that the woman was "a high risk mental" who needed to be transported to a hospital for a "mental evaluation." They noted on the form that the woman was engaged in passive, not active, resistance. This use of force against a woman who was not suspected of any crime was unreasonable and violated CPD policy, which prohibits the use of Tasers against people who only are passively resisting.

The use of unreasonable force to quickly resolve non-violent encounters is a recurrent issue at CPD. This is at least in part because CPD's policy permits the use of Tasers in situations where it is unreasonable, and allows the use of Tasers in drive-stun mode in any circumstance in which "probe mode" is allowed. CPD's policy permits use of a Taser (in any mode) to defeat active resistance, defined by CPD policy as "movement to avoid physical control," without regard to the severity of the crime or whether the person poses any danger to an of-

---

140 Tasers can be used in drive-stun or probe mode. Taser probes shot from a short distance incapacitate a person by causing them to lose control of their muscles. Drive-stun mode requires direct contact between the Taser and the person and simply causes pain. Many agencies restrict the use of Tasers in drive-stun mode because it is less effective in minimizing threats and has a high potential for abuse. See, e.g., DIRECTIVE 10.3: USE OF LESS LETHAL FORCE: THE ELECTRONIC CONTROL WEAPON (ECW) 9 (Phila. Police Dep't, Sept. 18, 2015) ("Personnel must be aware that using an ECW in Drive Stun is OFTEN INEFFECTIVE in INCAPACITATING a subject."), available at https://www.phillypolice.com/assets/directives /PPD-Directive-10.3.pdf; ATT'Y GEN., SUPPLEMENTAL POLICY ON CONDUCTED ENERGY DEVICES § V.4., at 7 (N.J. Attorney General, Rev. March 3, 2016) ("An officer shall not use a [Taser]in drive stun mode unless the officer reasonably believes based on the suspect's conduct that discharging the device in drive stun mode is immediately necessary to protect the officer, the suspect, or another person from imminent danger of death or serious bodily injury."), available at http://www.nj.gov/oag/dcj/agguide/directives/2016-3-3_Supplemental-Policy-on-Conducted-Energy-Devices.pdf

ficer, factors that must be considered in judging the reasonableness of a use of force. Graham, 490 U.S. at 396. CPD recently has proposed changes to its Taser policy. The proposed revised policy makes clearer that officers may not use a Taser unless it is objectively reasonable, necessary under the circumstances, and proportional to the threat or resistance of the subject. This is an important change, but the policy still does not place restrictions on the use of drive-stun mode. And, like any policy, it must be enforced in order to be effective.

Some CPD officers resort to Tasers as a tool of convenience, with insufficient concern or cognizance that it is a weapon with inherent risks that inflicts significant pain. Use of a Taser "is more than a *de minimis* application of force" and is a "very significant intrusion on [a person's] Fourth Amendment interests." *Abbott v. Sangamon County, Ill.*, 705 F.3d 706, 726, 730 (7th Cir. 2013). In an incident we reviewed, a man died after hitting his head when he fell while fleeing because a CPD officer shot him with a Taser. The man had been suspected only of petty theft from a retail store. IPRA deemed this use of a Taser justified. We saw other unnecessary uses of Tasers against people fleeing after committing minor violations, including a man who was suspected of urinating in public, and a 110-pound juvenile who fled after officers caught him painting graffiti on a garage. In all of these instances, as in many others we reviewed, the officers articulated no basis to support a conclusion that the convenient but painful and at times dangerous use of Tasers, rather than a less severe use of force, was necessary.

As with lethal force, some officers escalate encounters unnecessarily. This includes incidents in which CPD officers use retaliatory force against people who object and claim that they were unlawfully stopped by CPD. In one incident, officers had searched and released a man they had detained to determine if he was armed (he was not). The man then yelled at the officers and put his left foot in front of the squad car tire, taunting them to run over his foot so he could sue them. Instead of backing up, going around the man, or trying verbal techniques to calm the man down, the officers got out of the car and ordered him to stop blocking their car. The man then yelled that he was going to beat and kill them. They arrested him for aggravated assault. Officers reported that, during the arrest, he balled his fists and tried to pull away, so they punched and hit him and took him to the ground. In another incident, officers used pain compliance techniques and forcibly brought to the ground a man because he stiffened and locked his arms while they were arresting him for walking his dog without a leash and refusing to present identification. In both of these instances, officers provided no justification for the level of force they used, or why they did not attempt to resolve these situations with common de-escalation techniques.

2. CPD's pattern or practice of unreasonable force includes the use of excessive less-lethal force against children

CPD's pattern or practice of excessive force also includes subjecting children to force for non-criminal conduct and minor violations. In one incident, officers hit a 16-year-old girl with a baton and then Tasered her after she was asked to leave the school for having a cell phone in violation of school rules. Officers were called in to arrest her for trespassing. Officers claimed the force was justified because she flailed her arms when they tried to arrest her, with no adequate explanation for how such flailing met the criteria for use of a Taser. This was not an isolated incident. We also reviewed incidents in which officers unnecessarily drive-stunned students to break up fights, including one use of a Taser in drive-stun mode against a 14-year-old girl. There was no indication in these files that these students' conduct warranted use of the Taser instead of a less serious application of force.

CPD's Taser policy does not address the use of Tasers on children. It should. Prior to using a Taser on a child, officers should be required to factor into their decision the child's apparent age, size, and the threat presented. The use of a Taser in schools and on students should be discouraged and deployed only as a last resort. Tasers are painful and, because of a child's smaller size, children are especially vulnerable to greater injury from them. That is one reason the Police Executive Research Forum warns that Tasers should not be used against young children and that officers should consider a person's age in deciding whether use of a Taser is reasonable.[141] CPD policy contains no such admonition, and this is true even under CPD's proposed revised policies. Moreover, in several of the instances we reviewed, officers used the Taser in drive-stun mode, which as noted above is prone to abuse.

We also found instances in which force was used against children in a retaliatory manner. In one incident, an officer's neighbor called to report that some boys were playing basketball on the officer's property. The officer, on duty, left his district to respond and found the teenage boys down the street on their bikes. The officer pointed his gun at them, used profanity, and threatened to put their heads through a wall and to blow up their homes. The boys claim that the officer forced them to kneel and lie face-down, handcuffed together, leaving visible injuries on their knees and wrists. Once released, one boy called his mother crying to tell her an officer had pointed a gun at his face; another boy went home and showed his mother his scraped leg and, visibly upset, said "the police did this to me." The mothers reported the incident to IPRA. The officer,

---

141 2011 ELECTRONIC CONTROL WEAPON GUIDELINES 21 n.27 (Police Executive Rese. F. & Community Oriented Policing Serv.'s, March 2011), available at http://www.nccpsafety .org/assets/files/library/2011_Electronic_Control_Weapon_Guidelines.pdf.

who had not reported the use of force, accepted a finding of "sustained" and received a five-day suspension. The officer was never interviewed and his reasons for not contesting the allegations are not documented in the file.

In another case, a girl and a boy, both 15 years old, were crossing a street at the light, and one car had already stopped so they could proceed. A uniformed officer in an unmarked car braked hard and changed lanes to avoid the stopped car. The girl claimed the officer got out of the car and yelled profanity (calling her a "fucking idiot" among other things), drawing the attention of a female witness. The girl claimed that when she told the officer that they had the right of way, he pushed her in the back with both hands so hard she fell into a newspaper stand, after which he handcuffed her arms behind her back while she still wore her backpack, hurting her wrists, and did not loosen the cuffs when she complained. The officer called for backup, two officers responded, and the teens were released without charges. The girl reported this incident to IPRA. During the investigation, the officer, who had not reported using any force, claimed the teens were standing in the street obstructing traffic, causing him to slam on his brakes, prompting the teens to laugh at him. He said the teens cursed at him, and he handcuffed the girl for his and her safety because she "was becoming agitated and refused any and all direction." Despite the existence of four witnesses (the two officers, the boy, and the female witness at the very least), the IPRA investigator obtained a statement only from the accused officer. The investigator did not try to call the female witness until 26 months after the incident (yet wrote that she "did not cooperate with this investigation"). By the time the investigator concluded the investigation in April 2014 and deemed her allegations not sustained, the girl had turned 18.

In another case, an officer forcibly handcuffed a 12-year-old Latino boy who was outside riding a bike under his father's supervision. A plainclothes officer, responding to a report of "two male Hispanics running from" the area, detained the boy. According to the boy and his father, the officer approached the boy, ordered him to stop his bike, forcibly handcuffed him, pulled him off his bike, and placed him up against a fence. The boy reported he did not understand the man was a police officer or why he was being detained and told the officer he was only 12. According to the boy, the officer responded that the boy was "old enough to bang," meaning old enough to engage in gang violence. The boy's father approached the officer, explained that his son was only 12 years old, and asked what was going on. Records of 911 calls reflect a caller reporting that a plainclothes officer had a 12-year-old in handcuffs and was refusing to say why. The officer placed the boy in the back of a police vehicle before eventually releasing him. The officer's only apparent basis for this detention was the boy's race, which is constitutionally unreasonable. *United States v. Moore*, 983 F. Supp. 2d 1030, 1033 (E.D. Wis. 2013) ("[P]olice could not, consistent with the Fourth Amendment, stop every black male within their perimeter wearing a dark winter coat on a cold January day"); *United States v. Brown*, 448 F.3d 239, 248 (3d Cir. 2006) (reversing conviction where "about the only thing [defendant] had in common with the suspects was that they were black").

C. Video Evidence Suggests a Broader Pattern or Practice of Unconstitutional Use of Force

Evidence suggests that the pattern of unreasonable use of force identified by our investigation may be even broader than that revealed through CPD documents alone. During our investigation, we reviewed numerous use-of-force incidents captured on video. In many of these incidents, the use of force was facially unreasonable and the videos undercut the officers' descriptions of the incidents. Given the large volume of reported incidents not captured on video, this suggests that the extent of unreasonable force by CPD officers may be larger than is possible to discern from CPD's scant force reports and force investigations alone. Indeed, the inaccurate descriptions of events that were undercut by video we reviewed bore striking similarities to descriptions provided by officers in numerous cases with no video.

In one incident captured on cell-phone video, an officer breaking up a party approached a man, grabbed him by the shirt, and hit him in the head with a baton. In his reports, the officer, using language very similar to that used in many other reports we reviewed, falsely claimed that the victim had tried to punch him. Before the video surfaced, the officer's supervisor had approved the use of force and the victim had pled guilty to resisting arrest. The officer has since been relieved of his police powers and is facing criminal charges for his conduct. In another video, a woman exited her car and placed her hands on her vehicle when officers threw her to the ground, hit her, and deployed a Taser against her. The video indicates that the officer's claim that she had refused to show her hands, thus justifying the force used, was false. Despite the existence of the video, IPRA deemed the force reasonable.

We also reviewed a video of an officer choking, hitting, and slapping a man who had refused an order to leave the area in front of a store where the man was shopping with his family. The officer had not reported having used any force at all, and an officer witness to the event did not report the choking. The man complained to IPRA. Investigators there obtained a copy of the store surveillance video, which confirmed the man's account. The officer was then suspended for 45 days.

In many of these cases, IPRA generally accepted the officer's version of events, which were later undercut by video evidence. The Laquan McDonald shooting is one such incident; our review found many others. In one incident, for example, officers justified unreasonable force by falsely claiming in their reports that a woman had attacked them. In the video, officers can be seen aggressively grabbing the woman, who was being arrested for a prostitution offense, throwing her to the ground, and surrounding her. After she is handcuffed, one officer tells another to "tase her ten fucking times." Officers call her an animal, threaten to kill her and her family, and scream, "I'll put you in a UPS box and send you back to wherever the fuck you came from" while hitting the woman—who was handcuffed and on her knees. Officers can then be seen discovering a recording device and discussing whether they can take it. Supervisors approved this use of force and the officers were not disciplined until after the woman complained to IPRA and produced surveillance video of the event. The City paid the woman $150,000 in settlement of her lawsuit.

Another video shows an officer punching a handcuffed man several times, apparently in retaliation for the man having earlier punched the officer. The officer claimed falsely in his report, again using language very similar to many other reports we read, that the man had been struggling and kicking and that the force had been necessary to control him. Unknown to the officer, the incident was captured on surveillance video of the hospital where officers had taken him for a psychiatric evaluation. The officer's partner also did not report this unlawful force, and supervisors deemed the use of force justified. It was only after the hospital staff who reviewed the video contacted IPRA that anyone was disciplined.

Video evidence is available in only a sliver of force incidents. This underscores the potential value of body-worn cameras—and functioning in-car cameras—to ensuring that the true circumstances of officer uses of force are known, and that officers can be held accountable when they use unreasonable force. As discussed in the Accountability Section of this Report, the Mayor recently has announced that the provision of body-worn cameras to all officers will be accelerated. This is commendable, but must be made part of a broader system of accountability in which protocols are put in place to ensure such equipment is used appropriately and that videos are routinely and randomly reviewed by supervisors to determine whether an incident reveals deficiencies in officer use of force.

D. CPD Does Not Effectively Use Crisis Intervention Techniques to Reduce the Need for Force

When individuals experience a mental or behavioral health crisis, law enforcement officers often are the first responders. Officers who are well trained in interacting with people in crisis can reduce the need to use force, save lives, and keep officers and others safer. Chicago has adopted a Crisis Intervention Team (CIT) approach as a means to safely and effectively respond to incidents involving persons in crisis. However, our review of CPD's force reports revealed that CPD uses force against people in crisis where force might have been avoided had a well-trained CIT officer responded to the scene and employed de-escalation techniques. While not all of these avoidable uses of force are unconstitutional, a meaningful number were, and deficiencies in CPD's CIT response contributes to the pattern or practice of unconstitutional use of force.

CPD's documentation of these incidents is often insufficient to determine whether the force was necessary, appropriate, or lawful. Consequently, all we know are the broad contours of terribly sad events—that officers used force against people in crisis who needed help. In one case, officers used a Taser against an unarmed, naked, 65-year-old-woman who had bipolar disorder and schizophrenia. Officers used a Taser "to subdue a mental who ignored verbal commands" because he was believed to be a danger to himself and others. Officers twice drive-stunned a man who they then transported for a mental health evaluation. Officers used a Taser in probe and drive-stun mode against an unarmed suicidal man who pulled away from the responding officers. Officers, who were responding to a call that a woman was "off meds" and "not violent," Tasered an unarmed woman because she pulled away and "repeatedly moved [her] arm." CPD did not conduct any investigation or review of these incidents to determine whether its response to these events was appropriate or lawful, or whether force could have been avoided.

The shooting deaths of Quintonio LeGrier and Bettie Jones by CPD officers who responded to a call for help with a domestic disturbance laid bare failures in CPD's crisis response systems—the dispatcher did not recognize the call as one involving someone in crisis and did not ask questions that might have resulted in clues that it did; a crisis-trained officer was not dispatched to the scene; the officers did not use crisis intervention techniques; and the officers made tactical errors that resulted in the shooting death of a bystander who had simply opened her door. In part as a response to this tragic event, Mayor Emanuel in December 2015 called for a review of the City's crisis intervention program. The crisis response review led to the announcement of plans for reforms which, if effectively implemented and sustained, could result in important improvements to the City's CIT program. There are additional steps the City should take. The City should do more to ensure that effective, well-trained crisis intervention officers respond to these events, and that crisis incidents are analyzed to determine whether changes to the program or CPD's crisis response are warranted.

1. CPD's crisis intervention team model needs more support to be sustainable

Like many major city police departments, CPD has developed a CIT designed to respond to incidents involving someone in crisis, whether related to addiction, trauma, or mental health.[142] While no process is a guarantee against all poor outcomes, an effective crisis intervention approach can reduce the need for force, including deadly force, and prevent unnecessary entanglement of persons in crisis with the criminal justice system where mental health services will better serve the individual and public safety.

CPD purports to adhere to the "Memphis Model" of crisis intervention response consistent with the recommendations of CIT International.[143] While specialized training is the cornerstone of the Memphis Model, CIT is more than just training.[144] It requires a dedicated cadre of trained officer volunteers large enough to cover all shifts and all districts.[145] It also requires coordination between dispatch and police, policies that facilitate referrals to mental health providers, coordination with such mental health service providers, and continuous evaluation of CIT outcomes.[146] CPD began developing its CIT program in 2002 and made initial laudatory steps. It created a dedicated CIT unit to coordinate the CIT program and training. CPD trained its first cadre of CIT police officers in October 2004. By 2005, CPD rolled out CIT to its first two pilot districts and, as of April 2016, had trained 2,200 officers—18% of CPD's approximately 12,000- member authorized strength. In a 2010 study, CPD personnel reported that CIT training was effective and valuable, and that CIT-certified officers were able to more effectively resolve encounters, noting lives saved and diversion to service providers.[147]

Over the years, however, CPD has reduced the number of personnel assigned to run the CIT unit, from a high of nine people in 2008-2009, to three people as of late 2016. Those three people now bear the burden of training more officers and administering a CIT program that is being asked to do more than

---

142 CIT is a distinct program, different than other mental health awareness training. CPD's recruit training includes a 14-hour mental health module, and officers are now being provided eight hours of CIT training as part of CPD's newly designed force-mitigation training. However, this basic training does not equip officers with the specialized skills needed for crisis intervention. Similarly, CIT overlaps in some respects with de-escalation training, but CIT training is distinct from and more expansive than CPD's current eight-hour de-escalation training.

143 See, e.g., CIT International, CIT is More than Just Training . . . It's a Community Program, available at http://www.citinternational.org/Learn-About-CIT.

144 Id.

145 RANDY DUPONT ET AL., CRISIS INTERVENTION TEAM CORE ELEMENTS (U. of Memphis Sch. of Urb. Aff. and Pub. Pol'y, Sept. 2007), available at http://cit.memphis.edu /pdf/CoreElements.pdf.

146 Id.

147 KELLI E. CANADA ET AL., CRISIS INTERVENTION TEAMS IN CHICAGO: SUCCESSES ON THE GROUND, (J. Police Crisis Negot. 2010, Jan. 1, 2011), available at https://www.ncbi .nlm.nih.gov/pmc/articles/PMC2990632/#R4.

ever. Despite the work of these dedicated individuals and the positive response CIT officers have expressed when employing their skills on scene, CPD has not dedicated adequate resources to the CIT unit, thereby limiting its effectiveness and failing to achieve the promises of effective crisis intervention. In 2016, CPD increased its number of CIT trained officers by approximately one-third and plans to have 35% of the officers in the Department's Bureau of Patrol certified in CIT by the end of 2017. The already overburdened three-member CIT unit has been tasked with training these officers, which has reduced the ability of these hardworking individuals to develop thoughtful, effective, and well-delivered training. And because the staff that comprises the three-member CIT unit is now consumed with increased training demands, it is even more difficult for them to perform other critical functions, including conducting evaluations and follow-up on CIT incidents.

2. CPD should improve its CIT selection process in conjunction with plans to increase the number of CIT officers

As noted, the City has recognized the need for an effective crisis intervention response and has recently announced an ambitious plan to quickly increase its cadre of officers who have received the 40-hour crisis intervention training. The City's commendable desire for a rapid development of the CIT program, however, should not come at the expense of the quality of its crisis intervention response.

Effective crisis response requires a police department to designate and train certain officers to be members of the CIT, and dispatch those officers to all crisis intervention calls. It is important that all CIT officers have volunteered for the assignment. Officers who volunteer are more likely to have a deeper interest in and commitment to working with people in crisis. And they are more likely to develop proficiency and expertise as they become more experienced responding to crisis calls. Volunteers should be screened to determine that they are qualified. Of course, all officers should receive some training in responding to persons in crisis, and it may be useful to provide the full 40-hour CIT training to officers who have not volunteered for or not been accepted to the CIT program. But these officers should not be considered designated CIT officers and should not be dispatched to a crisis call in lieu of a CIT officer.

CPD, understandably eager to improve its crisis response, has deviated from the use of volunteer officers who are dedicated to working with people in crisis. CPD has required certain categories of officers, including all field training officers and sergeants, to take crisis intervention training and has designated those officers as CIT officers. In addition, CPD has dropped most screening for volunteer officers and is simply accepting most volunteers. By making CIT participation mandatory rather than voluntary and failing to screen those who volunteer, CPD has not developed a CIT team consisting of officers optimally suited for this work. While it is true that CPD likely needs more CIT officers to meet the demand of CIT calls, training large numbers of officers who have not volunteered for the task is, in the long run, unlikely to achieve the City's goal of improved crisis intervention response.

The City does not yet know how many additional CIT officers are necessary or where they should be deployed. The City has provided dispatchers with training to recognize when a person is in crisis, and recently developed a straightforward way for dispatchers to identify CIT officers available for dispatch. Already, these laudable steps have resulted in a five-fold increase in the number of calls identified as being crisis related from 2015-2016. This is a positive development because it suggests that dispatchers are becoming adept at identifying these calls and more CIT officers are being directed to handle crisis situations. But it has greatly increased the demand on the small CIT unit and the current CIT officers. And the City does not currently collect data on CIT calls in a way that would allow it to make informed staffing and deployment decisions to ensure an adequate number of CIT officers to cover all shifts in all districts. It has announced plans to do so. Each of these announced improvements should be implemented, supported, and sustained.

3. CPD should analyze crisis incidents to determine whether CIT is functioning effectively

CPD does not have an effective system in place to evaluate its response to CIT calls. CPD has developed a Crisis Intervention Report that is designed to capture important information about its response to crisis calls, including whether the call was recognized and identified as a CIT call before the officer's arrival and whether crisis techniques were employed. Even under CPD's newly revised policies, however, officers do not complete this form if the incident requires any other reporting. Thus, if an officer uses force during the crisis call, the officer will be required to fill out a Tactical Response Report (TRR) and therefore is not required to fill out a Crisis Intervention Report. As discussed above, the TRRs provide very little information about a use of force and include almost none of the information necessary to evaluate whether the crisis response was appropriate. Consequently, CPD has no ability to analyze the most concerning crisis incidents to evaluate its response.

During our review of force incidents, we saw many examples of force, including deadly force, being used against individuals in crisis. We did not see any evidence that CPD had engaged in after-action analysis to determine whether: the force used was reasonable and necessary; the incident had been recognized as a crisis incident and if not, why not; a CIT officer was dispatched to the scene and, if not, whether there were any barriers to dispatching a CIT officer; the officer used crisis intervention techniques; or the incident demonstrated that improvements in policy or training are needed. CPD should develop an after-action review process that answers these questions so that it understands how its CIT team is functioning and can correct deficiencies and build on successes.

CPD also has no mechanism to evaluate the quality of its CIT officers. Once an officer receives the 40-hour training and is certified as a CIT officer, CPD does not evaluate that officer's performance to determine whether the officer is applying the CIT training and is effective in resolving crises, or whether the officer may need some refresher training or additional support, or is not working out as a CIT officer. Although the City is aware of this need, this improvement was not part of the City's recently announced plans for reform. Without analyzing these incidents and the skills and training of its officers, CPD has no way of knowing whether its CIT program is effective, whether refinements in policies and training are needed, and whether the performance of any individual officers should be addressed.

The City's plans to improve its CIT program—including by increasing and improving data collection, providing training to Office of Emergency Management and Communications dispatchers, and increasing the number of trained CIT officers—are important and long needed. But these steps by themselves are not sufficient. Until they are accomplished, the City cannot know how many CIT officers it truly needs. Similarly, until CPD requires officers to accurately document these events and engages in analysis and evaluation of this data, it cannot know whether its training is effective or in need of improvement. We applaud the City's desire to respond quickly to legitimate concerns about its CIT program, but it is important that the response be based on an understanding of the effectiveness of and challenges to its current program. Failure to develop that understanding may, in the long term, impede its ability to improve its crisis intervention response.

E. CPD's Failure to Accurately Document and Meaningfully Review Officers' Use of Force Perpetuates a Pattern of Unreasonable Force

CPD policy requires officers to report most uses of force, but in practice, officers are not required to provide sufficient detail about the force they used, and most officer force is not reviewed or investigated, notwithstanding CPD policy requirements.

In the most serious instances of force—where an officer discharges his firearm in a manner that could potentially hit someone—CPD responds to the scene to conduct a preliminary investigation, but IPRA has the authority to investigate whether the shooting was justified. Because of IPRA's central role in these cases, all aspects regarding the reporting and review of these uses of force—including CPD's initial response to the scene—is discussed in the Accountability Section of this Report.

Below, however, we discuss the reporting and review of other uses of force. CPD policy requires supervisors to investigate all reported uses of force, other than shootings, to determine whether they were in compliance with policy. In actuality, however, most force is not reviewed. As a result of so few force incidents being reported and even nominally investigated, and the low quality of the force investigations that do occur, there is no consistent, meaningful accountability for officers who use force in violation of the law or CPD policy. Nor is there any opportunity for meaningful assessment of whether policies, training, or equipment should be modified to improve force outcomes in the future. The failure to ensure the accurate reporting, review, and investigation of officers' use of force has helped create a culture in which officers expect to use force and never be carefully scrutinized about the propriety of that use.

1. CPD does not require officers to accurately report uses of less-lethal force

CPD's documentation of officer use of less-lethal force is consistently insufficient. Moreover, CPD and IPRA have accepted insufficient documentation even when officers' use of force is suspect, or when people complain about the force officers used against them.

CPD policy requires officers to complete a TRR anytime they use force, except for control holds to handcuff someone and techniques attendant to handcuffing or searching a person that do not result in injury or an allegation of injury.[148] As detailed earlier, TRRs do not require officers to provide a narrative but instead present a series of boxes officers check to indicate in standard terms the force used, such as "elbow strike" or "take down/emergency handcuffing," and the resistance encountered, such as "stiffened," "imminent threat of battery," or "attack with weapon." There is a small textbox on the form for the officer to include additional information, but it is too small to provide an actual narrative of the encounter and officers rarely use it at all. The design of the form also discourages officers from providing important details

---

148 Officers are not required to report the use of escort holds, pressure-compliance techniques, and firm grips that do not result in an injury or allegation of injury; control holds, wristlocks, and armbars utilized in conjunction with handcuffing and searching techniques that do not result in injury or allegation of injury; that force necessary to overcome passive resistance due to physical disability or intoxication that does not result in injury or allegation of injury, or the use of force in an approved training exercise. See GENERAL ORDER 03-04-05: INCIDENTS REQUIRING THE COMPLETION OF A TACTICAL RESPONSE REPORT (Chi. Police Dep't October 30, 2014).

about the force they used. For example, an officer might check that the officer used "kicks," but the TRR contains no requirement that the officer state how many kicks were used, where these blows landed, any injuries they specifically caused, or the order in which events occurred. The form also does not require officers to indicate what alternatives to force they considered or tried, and why these efforts were or would be unsuccessful. If a subject is injured, they must check the box for "injured" but they need not and generally do not document what those injuries were. Officers do often include some description of the encounter either in the arrest report or the case report that is related to the TRR. In reviewing CPD's use of force, we reviewed all of the documents the City provided related to a particular TRR. Even with this additional information, however, the true details of a force encounter were often obscured by a lack of sufficient detail and the use of boilerplate language.

In one typical example, officers documented that they used force on a man who they alleged was trying to interfere with their arrest of his brother for domestic battery. According to the arrest report, the man kept approaching officers as they tried to make the arrest, despite repeated commands not to do so. The officers arrested him for resisting arrest and reported that he tightened his arms and tried to pull away while they were placing him in custody. On the TRRs, the officers checked off "arm bar," "pressure sensitive areas," "control instrument," and "takedown/emergency handcuffing" in describing the force they used. It is impossible for anyone, including these officers' supervisors charged with determining whether the force was reasonable and within policy, to know even approximately how much force these officers used. But what is described could very well be unreasonable—officers provided no details that would justify a takedown, and he appears to have merely been upset that his brother was being arrested. Indeed, in the box in which the supervisor is to document the subject's response to the use of force, the lieutenant wrote that the man said, "I don't know why they arrested me." CPD conducted no follow-up investigation of this use of force.

In many other instances, there are indications in the reports that the force used was more significant than reflected in the opaque description of events. In one incident, officers arrested a man because he "tried to physically interfere" with the arrest of another man. While they were arresting him, he began to pull away and grabbed and pushed the officers. According to the arrest reports, one officer "executed a knee strike." But four officers filled out TRRs, indicating that they each used force against him. In describing their actions, one officer checked the boxes for "takedown/emergency handcuffing" and "closed hand strike/punch;" the second checked "open hand strike," "takedown/emergency handcuffing," "closed hand strike/punch," and "kick;" a third officer checked "wristlock," "arm bar," "takedown/emergency handcuffing," "closed hand strike/punch," and "knee strike;" and the fourth officer checked "knee strike."

None of the officers reported how many strikes they delivered, where they landed, or why each was necessary. All four officers checked the box indicating that the man was injured, but those injuries were not described anywhere. In the man's booking photo, he has abrasions on his face.

For some files we reviewed, the injuries the victims suffered, rather than the explanations by CPD officers, reveal the level of force that CPD officers actually employed. For example, an officer pushed an 18-year-old female student onto his police car, chipping her tooth, because, as he was walking her to his squad car after breaking up a fight between her and another girl outside of their school, she screamed profanities and flailed her arms. The officer reported that the injury occurred when he performed "an emergency take-down maneuver to regain control." The girl was 5'4" tall and weighed 120 pounds, while the officer was 6'1" and weighed 186 pounds. Without requesting any additional information, supervisors approved this use of force. In the girl's complaint to IPRA, she alleged that when she informed the officer he had chipped her tooth, the officer responded that he did not "give a fuck." IPRA exonerated the officer without interviewing him.

It also appears that officers have been instructed on the language they should use to justify force. We saw many instances where officers justified force based on a boilerplate description of resistance that provides insufficient specificity to understand the force used or resistance encountered. For example, officers frequently reported using force because the person "flailed" his or her arms. Officers used a Taser against a man who appeared to be in crisis when he "stiffened his body, pulled away, and flailed his arms;" drive-stunned a man because, when they went to arrest him, he "began to flail his arms wildly;" deployed a Taser against a man who resisted arrest for theft by "flailing his arms;" and drive-stunned a man because, when they tried to arrest him, he "pulled away and flailed his arms."

The examples above are illustrative of problems we found in the hundreds of files we reviewed. In many of these files, it was nearly impossible for us to understand how much force officers used or whether the level of resistance justified the force used. Further, the design of the form, including that there is so little space for officers to provide a narrative account of the force they used, makes it impossible for officers to provide a complete or useful account of the force incident.

2. CPD rarely reviews or investigates officers' use of less-lethal force

CPD supervisors consistently violate CPD's force review policy. CPD policy requires supervisors to conduct investigations of every reportable officer use of non-shooting force. When an officer is involved in a use of force requiring completion of a TRR, the officer is to "immediately notify their immediate supervisor that he or she has been involved in a use of force incident." The officer must "submit his or her completed TRR to their immediate supervisor for review." The supervisor is to "respond to the scene when the injury to a subject or member is of the severity to require immediate medical attention," "ensure that all witnesses are identified, interviewed, and that information is recorded in the appropriate report," and request an evidence technician to take photos of subjects who were injured. When an officer uses a Taser, the officer must request that a supervisor respond to the scene, and a supervisor at least one rank higher than the officer must respond. Supervisors must also obtain a copy of the Taser deployment data sheet and are prohibited from approving the TRR until it has been received and reviewed.

In practice, little of this happens. In the hundreds of TRR files we reviewed, we rarely saw evidence that supervisors responded to the scene unless officers shot someone. Canvasses for witnesses rarely occur and even witnesses who are present are rarely interviewed. Even where TRRs make clear that a subject was injured, no photographs are taken of the injuries. In most instances, a "mugshot" is taken of arrestees, and in the files we reviewed we sometimes saw unexplained injuries to the person's face. TRRs are routinely approved without any evidence in the file that a Taser deployment data sheet was obtained or reviewed. Indeed, when we referenced these requirements in interviews with officers in an effort to gain an understanding of the system, officers and supervisors of all ranks seemed surprised to hear that these requirements existed. None asserted that these requirements were adhered to on any regular basis and most struggled to explain what these policies require.

In practice, a supervisor may interview the subject of the use of force if the subject is immediately available to the supervisor. Otherwise, for example if the person has been transported to the hospital, he or she will not be interviewed, which means that supervisors generally do not interview the subjects of the most concerning uses of force. If the person is available and agrees to speak with the supervisor, the supervisor typically documents one or two sentences that summarize the person's statement. Many of the interview summaries we saw suggest the interview centered more on what the subject did to justify the officer taking action at all, rather than the circumstances of the use of force itself. These interviews are not recorded and in none of the files we reviewed did the supervisor document the questions asked of the person.

After the supervisor's force review is complete, the supervisor is supposed to review the TRR "for legibility and completeness and indicate approval of such by signing the appropriate box." In 2014, this requirement was modified to require that the supervisor "review the member's TRR and, if appropriate, approve the report." In practice, sergeants view this role as ministerial. They play no role in reviewing the force itself for appropriateness. Sergeants we spoke to told us their only role is to ensure the form is filled out correctly, and none had ever refused to sign a report based on an evaluation of the force itself. From at least 2002 until 2014, the task of evaluating the force used was assigned to the watch commander, who was to record the subject's statement regarding the use of force and conduct an evaluation to determine whether the force was within CPD policy. In 2014, these tasks were given to lieutenants.

Despite the lack of detail describing most uses of force and the near total lack of additional information collected, supervisors routinely use boilerplate language to approve the TRRs, often only minutes after the officer submits it, even where there is information in the file indicating the officer violated CPD policy or the law. In the files we reviewed, we saw only a handful in which a supervisor referred the incident to IPRA for investigation or requested additional information from the officer.[149] Our interviews with CPD officers were consistent with these findings. One commander told us he could not recall ever calling for further investigation of a use of force. Another said that he has never seen an unreasonable use of force on a TRR. That same commander also said he had never seen any TRR wherein he identified a better tactical decision, even if the force was reasonable.

Illustrative of the inadequacy of supervisory review of force incidents is the troubling incident discussed above in which officers deployed a Taser against an unarmed 65-year-old woman who was in mental health crisis. The TRR file contains only a cursory description of the incident, and without reviewing the Taser data download or requesting any investigation, the sergeant approved this TRR three minutes after the officer submitted it, and the lieutenant approved it less than 25 minutes after that. There is no indication that the lieutenant asked the officers any questions about whether this force was necessary or whether there might have been something they could have done to avoid using force against this woman, such as seeking assistance from a crisis intervention trained officer.

Our investigation also found instances in which CPD officers used canines against children and conducted no investigation to determine whether these uses of force were reasonable or necessary. In one case, officers allowed a canine to bite two unarmed 17-year-old boys who had broken into an elementary school and stolen some items. In another case, officers deployed a canine to

---

149 Pursuant to City ordinance, supervisors are required to report all Taser uses to IPRA. See CHAPTER 2-57, INDEPENDENT POLICE REVIEW AUTHORITY (IPRA) 2-57-040(c) (IPRA chief administrator has power and duty to "conduct investigations into all cases in which a department member discharges his or her . . . stun gun, or Taser in a manner which potentially could strike an individual, even if no allegation of misconduct is made"). Notwithstanding this ordinance, unless the supervisor specifically requests additional investigation, IPRA does not investigate Taser discharges. We saw several instances where the supervisor did not notify IPRA that a Taser discharge had occurred, despite being required to do so.

locate two boys, ages 12 and 14, who had broken into a school and stolen some candy and basketballs. Fortunately, the canine did not bite them and the boys were uninjured. CPD should have investigated these uses of force to determine whether they were reasonable, yet in both cases supervisors approved the force without an investigation.

F. CPD's New De-escalation Training and Proposed Policy Revisions Should be Expanded and Sustained

In March 2016, CPD began a review of its use-of-force policies in an effort to provide clearer direction for officers on the appropriate use of force. CPD released the draft force policies in October 2016 for public comment. The proposed revisions address core force principles such as the sanctity of life, ethical behavior, objective and proportional use of force, use of deadly force, de-escalation, and force mitigation. CPD is currently reviewing the public feedback and has stated that it will incorporate suggestions and improvements to prepare final versions of the policies. CPD also has begun providing all officers with force-mitigation training designed to better equip officers to de-escalate conflicts safely; recognize the signs of mental illness, trauma, and crisis situations; and respond quickly and appropriately when force is necessary.

We appreciate that CPD has recognized the need to address some of the problems described in this Report. The steps the City has taken are meaningful and important. To be effective, the new approaches to the use of force must be embodied in these polices, and training must be supported by leadership and enforced by supervisors to ensure officers follow them consistently. CPD's past policy rollouts have faced considerable challenges, with policies sometimes issued before officers have been trained on them, leading to confusion and frustration about what is required and why. CPD's Fraternal Order of Police (FOP) union leadership already has expressed concern that the 2016 draft force policies do not adequately address the concerns of officers. CPD must demonstrate more thoughtful planning and commit more resources and time for the training and rollout of force policy revisions so that officers will understand, accept, and be able to safely and effectively implement the new requirements.

Additionally, these revised policies do not improve upon CPD's deficient procedures, discussed above, for reporting and investigating force. In part because of these deficiencies, officers are not held accountable to the current force policies. Until these deficiencies are addressed, revisions to policies and training are unlikely to achieve the necessary changes in how officers use force.

III. CHICAGO'S DEFICIENT ACCOUNTABILITY SYSTEMS CONTRIBUTE TO CPD'S PATTERN OR PRACTICE OF UNCONSTITUTIONAL CONDUCT

A well-functioning accountability system is the keystone to lawful policing. In combination with effective supervision, a robust accountability system is required in order to identify and correct inappropriate uses of force and other kinds of misconduct—with discipline, training, and counseling as appropriate—which in turn helps prevent misconduct. But Chicago seldom holds officers accountable for misconduct. In the five-year period prior to our investigation, Chicago had investigated 409 police shootings and found that just two were unjustified. It is similarly illustrative that the City paid over half a billion dollars to settle or pay judgments in police misconduct cases since 2004 without even conducting disciplinary investigations in over half of those cases, and it recommended discipline in fewer than 4% of those cases it did examine. Our comprehensive investigation of Chicago's accountability structures and systems found clear indications, set forth in detail in this Section, that those structures and systems are broken.

Together with our law enforcement experts, we scrutinized hundreds of misconduct and IPRA force investigations, and closely reviewed related policies and protocols. We looked at the available resources and organizational structure of CPD's accountability components. We talked to scores of current and former IPRA and BIA investigators and supervisors. We also spoke with many line officers, members of CPD leadership, and police union officials about their experiences with and views of CPD's accountability systems. We spoke with members of the public about these same issues.

Our investigation confirmed that CPD's accountability systems are broadly ineffective at deterring or detecting misconduct, and at holding officers accountable when they violate the law or CPD policy. As with most complicated problems that have built up over time and repeatedly been glossed over, we found that many factors contribute to the systemic deficiencies of CPD's accountability system. These are summarized below.

Our investigation revealed that the City fails to conduct any investigation of nearly half of police misconduct complaints and that a number of institutional barriers contribute to this fact. There are provisions in the City's agreements with the unions that impede the investigative process, such as the general requirement that a complainant sign a sworn affidavit and limitations on investigating anonymous complaints and older incidents of misconduct. That said, the union agreements contain override provisions for some of these provisions that the City rarely utilizes. Other barriers have been created solely by the City, such as internal policies allowing investigative agencies to truncate investigations of serious misconduct through mediation, administratively close complaints deemed less serious, and ignore mandatory investigations into uses of force that could identify misconduct or faulty training issues. The City must work to remove these barriers so it can thoroughly investigate all claims of misconduct and uses of force and thus regain community trust.

Our review of files for complaints that *were* investigated revealed consistent patterns of egregious investigative deficiencies that impede the search for the truth. Witnesses and accused officers are frequently not interviewed at all, or not interviewed until long after the incident when memories have faded. When interviews do occur, questioning is often biased in favor of officers, and witness coaching by union attorneys is prevalent and unimpeded—a dynamic neither we nor our law enforcement experts had seen to nearly such an extent in other agencies. Investigators routinely fail to collect probative evidence. The procedures surrounding investigations allow for ample opportunity for collusion among officers and are devoid of any rules prohibiting such coordination. We found that a lack of resources and investigative training contribute to these investigative problems. We also found that investigations foundered because of the pervasive cover-up culture among CPD officers, which the accountability entities accept as an immutable fact rather than something to root out.

In the rare instances when complaints of misconduct are sustained, discipline is inconsistent and unpredictable, and meted out in a way that does little to deter misconduct. Officers are often disciplined for conduct far less serious than the conduct that prompted the investigation, and in many cases, a complaint may be sustained but the officer is not disciplined at all. The police discipline system, including the City's draft disciplinary matrix, fails to provide clear guidance on appropriate, fair, and consistent penalty ranges, thus undermining the legitimacy and deterrent effect of discipline within CPD. And the City's process for finalizing IPRA's and BIA's discipline recommendations further delays and inappropriately influences discipline, and compromises the ability for such discipline to withstand appeal.

We also found deficiencies within Chicago's Police Board that impair its ability to be a fully effective component of CPD's accountability structure. The Board should focus on its function of providing due process to officers and ensuring they are held accountable as appropriate. The Board's current role as conduit for providing community input into CPD's accountability system may be more appropriately handled by the Community Oversight Board that the City has committed to working with the Chicago public to create. We found also that the completeness of Police Board consideration of discipline can be improved by modifying current practices, such as the current rules that bar the officer's "negative" disciplinary history but allow the officer's "complimentary" history, and allowing favorable character evidence by the accused's supervisors to be offered at the liability phase of proceedings.

Throughout the time our investigation has been underway, the City has undertaken positive steps to improve its accountability structure and repair its relationship with the community, and it should be commended for this. But the problems we found are complex and entrenched, and have persisted in part because the City has been unable, and at times has not committed the long-term sustained focus and resources, to eliminate the problem and keep it from coming back.

A. Chicago's Systems for Investigating Police Conduct

Chicago's police accountability system is currently divided among three investigative entities: (1) the Independent Police Review Authority (IPRA); (2) CPD's Bureau of Internal Affairs (BIA); and (3) CPD district offices. IPRA was created in 2007 to replace the Office of Professional Standards and is intended to operate as a civilian disciplinary body that is independent from CPD. IPRA serves two main functions: it receives and registers all complaints against CPD officers and assigns them to either BIA or itself, depending on the claim; and it investigates specific categories of complaints as well as other non-complaint police incidents and recommends discipline where appropriate.

IPRA investigates four types of complaints: (1) excessive force; (2) domestic violence; (3) coercion; and (4) bias-based verbal abuse. It also conducts mandatory investigations, regardless of alleged misconduct for: (1) officer weapon discharges (including gun, Taser, or pepper spray); and (2) death or serious injury in police custody. Over the last five years, IPRA has received almost 7,000 citizen complaints per year and retained investigative authority over approximately 30% of them as falling within IPRA's jurisdiction. In addition, it receives notification of approximately 800 mandatory investigations a year. IPRA is headed by the Chief IPRA Administrator (currently, Sharon Fairley), who is appointed by Chicago's Mayor and operates with an 80-person civilian staff.

BIA investigates complaints that are outside of IPRA's jurisdiction, which consists of approximately 70% of all police complaints. BIA is an entity within the Police Superintendent's Office, and the BIA Chief reports directly to the Superintendent. BIA is responsible for investigating four types of officer misconduct: (1) criminal misconduct; (2) bribery and other forms of corruption; (3) drug or other substance abuse; and (4) driving under the influence, as well as all operational and other violations of CPD rules. BIA receives approximately 4,500 complaints per year from IPRA and refers approximately 40% of the less serious investigations to the 22 individual police districts for investigation.

Given that many of the same problematic practices are common to both IPRA and BIA investigations, below we discuss those different entities' investigations hand in hand. Where the evidence we found demonstrates that a specific problem is particularly acute in one entity, we have made that clear.

After IPRA and BIA complete their investigations, the investigator issues a finding of "sustained," "not sustained," "unfounded," or "exonerated."[150] If one or more of the allegations of misconduct is sustained, the investigator's supervisor makes a discipline recommendation. While CPD is in the process of changing this, historically, the recommended discipline is not pursuant to any applicable guidelines, but rather is based only upon experience and historical precedence. The investigation concludes with a summary report by the investigator.

Investigators' findings recommendations and discipline recommendations for all sustained cases at either IPRA or BIA are subject to several layers of CPD review before they become final decisions. First, except in cases where discharge is recommended, the recommendations are subject to a Command Channel Review (CCR), in which supervisors in the accused officer's chain of command review and comment on the recommended discipline. Next, recommendations, along with CCR comments, are forwarded to the Superintendent for review. Discharge recommendations skip the CCR review and go directly to the Superintendent. If the Superintendent approves the recommendations, the decision is final, but if not, it is subject to another process before the Chicago Police Board, which is made up of nine private citizens appointed by Chicago's Mayor with the City Council's consent. If the Superintendent disagrees with IPRA's recommendations, the Superintendent has the burden of convincing a three-person panel from the Chicago Police Board that the Superintendent is justified in departing from those recommendations.

The Police Board also acts as a reviewing body by adjudicating CPD decisions recommending discharge, or appeals of suspensions over 30 days for sergeants, lieutenants, and captains. Such reviews consist of a full evidentiary hearing before a Police Board hearing officer who makes a report and recommendation, which is reviewed by the full Police Board before a final decision is made. The Police Board's role in accountability, particularly its role in reviewing disciplinary decisions, is discussed in Section III.H., below.

Other than in discharge cases, which are heard only by the Police Board, officers also can challenge final CPD discipline decisions through arbitration, which can either be a summary disposition on the record or a full evidentiary hearing, depending on the officer's rank and the level of discipline recommended. Decisions of the Police Board and arbitrators are subject to adminis-

---

150 "Sustained" means the complaint was supported by sufficient evidence to justify disciplinary action. "Not sustained" means the evidence was insufficient to either prove or disprove the complaint. "Unfounded" means the facts revealed by the investigation did not support the complaint (e.g., the complained-of conduct did not occur). "Exonerated" means the complained-of conduct occurred, but the accused officer's actions were proper under the circumstances. See IPRA RULES § 4.1.

trative review in the Circuit Court of Cook County and can then be appealed to the Illinois Appellate Court and the Illinois Supreme Court.

In October 2016, the City took steps towards creating the Civilian Office of Police Accountability (COPA). COPA, which under current plans will assume IPRA's responsibilities sometime in 2017, appears to have the potential to be a meaningful improvement over IPRA, but gaps also appear to remain within this entity and through all other components of Chicago's accountability systems. COPA, and its limitations, are discussed at the end of this Section.

B. The City Has Put in Place Policies and Practices that Impede the Investigation of Officer Misconduct

City policies and practices prevent investigation of a substantial portion of CPD misconduct complaints and uses of force, including many it is required by law to conduct. Deficient systems and police culture inhibit many other complaints of police misconduct from ever being filed. These deficiencies keep unconstitutional conduct and practices hidden. We discuss below several of the unnecessary barriers to investigation, including: a formal policy against investigating many complaints about force; referral of verbal abuse complaints to a process in which no discipline can be imposed even if misconduct occurred; a failure to investigate anonymous complaints or complaints without a sworn affidavit; and handling many complaints via a so-called "mediation" process that is in fact antithetical to the tenets and goals of complaint mediation. Collectively, through this patchwork of policies and practices, the City fails to conduct any meaningful investigation of nearly half of the complaints made against officers. This is separate and apart from CPD's failure to investigate most of the Taser and "no-hit" shootings required under local law or to conduct any review of the vast majority of officer uses of force that are discussed in the Force Section of this Report.

While IPRA and the City appeared to have acquiesced to, or developed, many of these restrictions to alleviate a crushing docket, the City's new Police Accountability ordinance has set aside significantly more resources for COPA than IPRA currently has. The City should revisit these restrictions in light of COPA's expanded capacity and ensure that they are removed. COPA's capacity, in turn, should be increased further if necessary to allow it to investigate the cases that it has previously been unable to because of the restrictions set out below.

1. The City has unduly narrowed the scope of misconduct allegations that are fully investigated

One way in which the City has acquiesced to narrowing the scope of misconduct complaints it investigates is through the police union contracts' provision requiring a sworn affidavit from the complainant before a claim is investigated.

While officers should certainly not be subject to false claims, this affidavit requirement creates a tremendous disincentive to come forward with legitimate claims and keeps hidden serious police misconduct that should be investigated. Until this affidavit requirement can be changed, however, IPRA and BIA should be acting more aggressively to ensure that this requirement does not stand in the way of investigating meritorious, and sometimes egregious, allegations of misconduct.

Most police misconduct complaints begin with a letter, email, or phone call, through which the complainant provides information about a misconduct incident. But in nearly every case, neither IPRA nor BIA will conduct any meaningful investigation of the complaint unless the complainant meets an investigator in person and provides a complete recorded statement of the incident, and submits a sworn statement that all claims are true and correct under penalties provided by law. The City closes about 40% of all complaints (an average of 2,400 complaints a year) because the complainant did not sign an affidavit. A 2015 report showed that between 2011 and 2014, IPRA closed 58% of its total complaints for lack of an affidavit.

There are many understandable reasons why victims of police misconduct may choose not to submit a supporting affidavit. Chicago residents who have lost faith in police accountability altogether have no interest in participating in that very system. Others fear retaliation—that if they proceed with an investigation, they will be targeted by CPD officers. Many more cannot meet the logistical hurdles necessary to file the affidavit, including taking time off of work during a weekday to sit for a lengthy interview. Additionally, civil rights plaintiffs and criminal defendants—both of whom may have potentially valid misconduct complaints—typically follow their attorney's reasonable advice and refrain from providing verified statements pending their criminal and civil litigation. In fact, for most of the lawsuits in which police misconduct victims received significant settlements or verdicts, IPRA's parallel misconduct investigation was closed for lack of an affidavit. In other words, the City routinely pays large *sums* to police misconduct victims who have filed non-verified complaints in civil litigation describing the misconduct in question but fails to *investigate* these same officers for disciplinary purposes because their administrative complaints are not verified. And even criminal defendants who wish to file affidavits so their complaint can be investigated cannot always do so because certain investigators rarely, if ever, go into Cook County Jail or to state correctional institutions to obtain affidavits that would be willingly given.

CPD's unions correctly note that investigators can "override" the requirement for a sworn affidavit, and we agree that IPRA and BIA should make more use of the override option. IPRA investigators we interviewed relayed that overrides are not encouraged, and no training was provided on how to obtain one. Not surprisingly, this override provision was used only 17 times in the last five years. But, there is also no question that the override option is problematic in a number of respects. To obtain an override, BIA or IPRA must obtain an affidavit from the other agency's director, verifying that she has reviewed "objective verifiable evidence" and affirms "that it is necessary and appropriate for the investigation to continue." Not only does this process undermine the independence of IPRA, and create an additional procedural barrier to investigating misconduct, but requiring that objective verifiable evidence exists before an investigation can be undertaken puts the cart before the horse.

Even though the affidavit requirement and the override exception restrict the City's ability to ultimately sustain a complaint, they should not be used as an excuse to avoid a full and fair investigation that begins immediately upon a complaint being made. Currently, investigators conduct no witness interviews until after securing a sworn affidavit. Yet because investigators already have a statement from the complainant describing the basis of the complaint—albeit not "verified"—most times they have sufficient information to conduct their investigation immediately, before witnesses' memories fade and evidence disappears. Additionally, by interviewing witnesses and canvassing for additional evidence, IPRA and BIA would be in a better position to consider an override request. Undertaking such investigative efforts immediately, even without an affidavit, will improve accountability and help demonstrate to the community that IPRA and BIA are not indifferent to complaints of police misconduct.

CPD's and IPRA's failure to investigate anonymous complaints, pursuant to the City's collective bargaining agreement with officers, further impedes the ability to investigate and identify legitimate instances of misconduct. As noted above, given the code of silence within CPD and a potential fear of retaliation, there are valid reasons a complainant may seek to report police misconduct anonymously, particularly if the complainant is a fellow officer. Indeed, it was an anonymous tip that led to the video release of the Laquan McDonald shooting. IPRA and BIA should have greater discretion in investigating tips and complaints from anonymous sources.

Likewise, the CBA contains other provisions that have the effect of impairing investigations of police misconduct. For example, the CBAs mandate disclosure of a complainant's name prior to questioning the accused officer. Like the anonymous complaint prohibition, this provision is problematic because of the significant fear of police retaliation by many complainants. Experts in law enforcement investigations noted that disclosure of the complainant's identity during the investigation has the potential to chill misconduct reporting without providing discernible benefit to the officer. IPRA and BIA already must provide the accused officer with detailed notice of the misconduct charges as well as copies of all relevant police records; this should allow the accused officer to sufficiently prepare before being questioned. Eliminating this identity disclosure requirement, and clearly communicating it to complainants, should encourage more complainants to come forward without fear of retaliation.

Finally, the City has agreed with CPD's police unions to prohibit investigations into older incidents of police misconduct, even where those incidents may include serious misconduct or be probative of a pattern of misconduct. One CBA provision prohibits IPRA or BIA from initiating any disciplinary investigations into incidents over five years old, absent authorization by the Superintendent, and another requires destruction of most disciplinary records older than five years. Yet, CPD's culture and "code of silence" as described elsewhere in these findings may prevent disclosure of serious misconduct in a timely fashion. Moreover, the document destruction provision not only may impair the investigation of older misconduct, but also deprives CPD of important discipline and personnel documentation that will assist in monitoring historical patterns of misconduct.

IPRA and BIA also fail to investigate certain claims of conduct that they cursorily determine are not "serious" enough to warrant a full investigation. Under its "Excessive Force Protocol," IPRA administratively closes, without any investigation, most complaints alleging excessive force in connection with handcuffing, take-downs incidental to arrest, and displays of an officer's gun, because IPRA determines that the force used was "de-minimis." As our expert noted, however, it is relatively easy for officers to gratuitously cause excruciating pain during the handcuffing process merely by overexerting the amount of force used in a trained finger or wrist lock. Such gratuitous punishment is hardly de-minimis, even if it leaves no marks or lasting injury. Similarly, as explained in more detail in above, BIA does not investigate complaints of verbal abuse by an officer, but instead refers them to district supervisors for "non-disciplinary intervention."

It is reasonable for IPRA and BIA to exercise discretion about the resources to assign to certain types of cases. But there is no system in place to ensure that a properly trained investigator is objectively evaluating these force and verbal abuse complaints and performing a sufficiently thorough preliminary investigation to accurately decide whether a full investigation is warranted. Moreover, such information is not properly tracked and maintained to enable IPRA and BIA to determine trends, or ensure that CPD is properly identifying officers who are appropriate candidates for referral to one of CPD's behavioral intervention programs. *See* Report, Section IV.B.

2. The City does not meaningfully investigate certain types of force unless a misconduct complaint is filed

IPRA fails to investigate several types of force despite being formally required to do so. IPRA has long been required by ordinance to undertake investigations of Taser discharges and officer-involved shootings where no one is hit,[151] yet, in practice, it investigates neither. This problematic practice results in a large number of potentially serious policy or constitutional violations going undetected and undeterred. The pattern of unreasonable force our investigation found both reflects this longstanding failure to adequately review officers' use of force and underscores the necessity of doing so to eliminate this pattern of unlawful conduct.

IPRA's failure to meaningfully investigate Taser discharges has had significant implications. In 2009, IPRA reported just under 200 Taser uses, and as required under local ordinance, was investigating each use. A year later, CPD expanded its Taser program, and uses jumped dramatically to almost 900 and have since leveled off at almost 600 a year over the last five years. In 2010, as Taser uses were expanding, IPRA stopped investigating all but a few of the Taser uses—in particular, those accompanied by a citizen complaint or an override. The former IPRA Chief Administrator explained this investigative change was simply due to the fact that IPRA does not have resources to more thoroughly audit every Taser use.

While the number of Taser discharges may have outpaced IPRA's ability to investigate each discharge, this does not excuse the City's failure to ensure that somebody reviewed officers' Taser use. By placing responsibility for investigating Taser discharges in IPRA, and then failing to ensure that IPRA did so, the City created a system in which no one assesses whether Tasers are being used appropriately or effectively. This, in turn, prevents the City and CPD from uncovering the potential need for retraining or additional policy refinement, and of course from deterring future misuse of Tasers by holding officers accountable for abuse. While the City's new Police Accountability Ordinance removes jurisdiction from IPRA for investigating most Taser discharges, it does not create a structure to ensure that Taser discharges or other less-lethal uses of force will be investigated in the future. Such a structure is needed to ensure CPD's pattern or practice of unreasonable force does not continue.

IPRA's longstanding decision not to respond to or investigate officer-involved shootings in which officers miss their intended targets is also problematic. Although "no-hit" shootings raise the same legal, policy, tactical, and ethical issues as "hit" shootings, IPRA essentially ignores the cases unless they generate a misconduct complaint. In most no-hit cases, IPRA merely collects written reports from the involved and witness officers. IPRA does not investigate the shooting scene, does not interview anyone, and does not

---

151 The City's new Police Accountability Ordinance narrows IPRA's jurisdiction over Taser discharges, as discussed elsewhere in this Report.

conduct any analysis of physical evidence. Nor, in cases where officers fire at people who escape, is there any indication that IPRA or anyone else checks with area hospitals in an attempt to confirm that in fact no one was struck. Once it collects the often-sparse documentation of a no-hit shooting, IPRA closes its file with the finding, "administrative closure" without any comment on compliance with the law or CPD policy.

IPRA receives approximately 35 notifications per year for no-hit shootings. Many no-hit shootings we reviewed raised serious questions that warranted investigation, but were ignored simply because the officer missed his intended target. For example, in one case, an off-duty CPD officer fired multiple times at a car, missing the driver, but injuring him with shattered glass. The written reports in the file (there were no recorded interviews) did not address critical questions, such as where the officer stood in relation to the car, where his bullets struck, or the car's direction of travel. Notwithstanding these glaring omissions and CPD's policy generally prohibiting officers from shooting at vehicles, IPRA closed the file.

The difference between a hit and a no-hit shooting case may only be a matter of bad aim; investigation of no-hit cases is thus vital to uncovering deficiencies in policies, procedures, tactics, equipment, and training that could prevent unnecessary or inappropriate shootings in the future.

In nearly all Taser and no-hit shooting cases, no complainant comes forward. This reluctance, even in questionable shootings, is understandable both because of retaliation fears described above and because of the possibility that such individuals may have been involved in criminal conduct. Nevertheless, the officer may have intentionally or unintentionally engaged in unreasonable force in the incident, or otherwise violated policy. It is thus essential that investigations in these cases occur even in the absence of an underlying complaint.

3. Attempts to expedite investigations through so-called "mediation" allow officers to circumvent punishment for serious misconduct

Many serious misconduct complaints that avoid the investigative barriers described above are not fully investigated but instead are resolved through what IPRA calls "mediation." However, this program is not true police-complaint mediation where parties meet to arrive at a mutually agreeable resolution of their dispute and, often, gain a better understanding of each other's perspective along the way. Such programs, like the one that has been implemented in conjunction with our consent decree regarding the New Orleans Police Department, provide an opportunity for dialogue and understanding between victims of police misconduct and the officers who are the subject of their complaints in the presence of a neutral third party. "Mediation" at CPD, however, is a euphemism for a plea bargain, and is used in a way that often inappropriately, albeit quickly, disposes of serious misconduct claims in exchange for modest discipline, while misleading the public into thinking that accountability has been achieved.

"Mediation" is used by IPRA to resolve an allegation of misconduct, usually by having the officer agree to a sustained finding in exchange for reduced punishment. Mediation is always used before investigations are complete, including before the accused officer is ever interviewed. This premature use of mediation deprives investigators of important information they could use to better determine the severity and breadth of the misconduct.

The complainant is generally excluded from the process altogether, further separating the "mediation" process used by Chicago from the typical mediation used in other departments. Persons who complain of police misconduct are afforded no opportunity to meet with the officers who are the subject of their grievances or provide input into the resolution of their complaints if disciplinary action is taken. At the end of this process, complainants receive a letter that even IPRA leadership admits can be misleading, because it advises that the complaint was sustained but never discloses the precise charge that was sustained or the discipline imposed.

These flaws are particularly concerning given how often IPRA uses mediation. From 2013 through 2015, mediations accounted for approximately 65% of all sustained cases. The investigators we spoke to stated that by December 2012, a year after the pilot program began, they were told to attempt mediation in *every* case. So instead of using mediation only in a limited number of appropriate circumstances, such as allegations where the facts are undisputed and there is no victim, IPRA mediates a wide range of complaints despite the seriousness of the allegations. This includes cases that are facially inappropriate for mediation, such as allegations of excessive force and domestic violence by officers.[152] Approximately 50% of the mediations from 2013-2015 were for domestic violence or a full range of excessive force claims.

Moreover, because IPRA is intentionally lenient in exchange for an officer agreeing to mediation, the discipline imposed for misconduct violations resolved through mediation is often far lighter than the allegation facts merit. We reviewed one complaint where an officer fractured his girlfriend's nose during a domestic dispute. In this case, investigators recognized the serious-

---

152 IPRA's use of "mediation" to resolve domestic violence disputes is problematic because it minimizes the serious, repetitive nature of this abuse and allows abusers to avoid meaningful punishment, which may empower them to continue the cycle of abuse. Using even true mediation (as opposed to IPRA's current plea-bargain mediation) to resolve domestic violence allegations against police officers would be inappropriate, given the dynamics of domestic violence.

ness of the allegations and requested an affidavit override after they could not secure the victim's agreement to participate in the investigation because the victim feared retaliation from the officer and his friends within CPD. It is laudable that the investigators recognized the seriousness of the offense and pursued the investigation without the victim's agreement to participate in the investigation. Yet, in the end, the investigators still sent the case to mediation, and the officer received only a five-day suspension. Another officer received a one-day suspension for admitting that he had shoved his baton into a victim's side. And in over half of these excessive force and domestic violence cases, there was no real discipline at all, but simply a "violation noted" in the officer's record, such as the case in which a CPD officer who participated in mediation received only a "violation noted" after being accused of verbally and physically abusing his wife in public, where there were witnesses to the event.

In addition to mediation often leading to lesser disciplinary penalties, agreeing to mediate a misconduct complaint also allows officers to accept a sustained finding on a less serious charge in exchange for the IPRA investigator dropping more serious charges from the complaint file. For example, one investigative summary publicly available on IPRA's website describes an officer who was accused of verbally abusing her mother and brother, striking her brother in the head, scratching his face and neck, stealing her mother's Social Security check, and charging unauthorized items on her mother's credit card. The accused officer was ultimately arrested for domestic battery. Yet, IPRA allowed the complaint to proceed to mediation, and after admitting to the lesser violation of scratching her brother's face and neck, this officer was given only a two-day suspension.

During the course of our investigation, the City and current IPRA leadership recognized that mediation is currently misused. IPRA officials also admitted that mediation is used to reduce caseloads and preserve resources. While this practice may have saved resources, IPRA staff admitted, and we confirmed, that mediation, as it is currently used, is both inappropriate and a significant impediment to true accountability.

Some, but not enough, of the problems described above were addressed in the new ordinance creating COPA. The ordinance prohibits COPA from using mediation for "complaints alleging the use of excessive force that result in death or serious bodily injury and cases of domestic violence involving physical abuse or threats of physical abuse." The ordinance, however, does not provide sufficient guidance on other circumstances where mediation should not be used as a means to negotiate a plea bargain.

C. Investigations That CPD Does Conduct Are Neither Complete Nor Fair

Our review of hundreds of investigative files revealed that IPRA and BIA investigations, with rare exception, suffer from entrenched investigative deficiencies and biased techniques. These investigative flaws cover not only all complaint-driven investigations conducted by both BIA and IPRA, but also the mandatory investigations into officer-involved shootings handled by IPRA.

Our review of investigative procedures, interviews of current and former investigative personnel, and careful analysis of 400 IPRA and BIA investigations revealed a consistent unwillingness to probe or challenge officers' accounts of the incident, even when these accounts were inconsistent with physical evidence, credible eyewitness statements, or common sense. Investigators have permitted union representatives and attorneys to coach officers in the middle of recorded interviews—with official protocols actually prohibiting investigators from preventing this, or even referring to it on tape. Investigators frequently failed to collect basic evidence needed for the investigations by failing to interview important witnesses—including the accused officer—and failing to collect information from other court proceedings involving the same incident. These deficient practices, set forth in detail below, undermine accountability.

1. CPD's initial response to officer-involved shootings

While IPRA is vested with the authority to investigate officer-involved shootings, the initial evidence gathering and reporting on the scene of an officer-involved shooting is largely in the hands of CPD. Understanding the circumstances surrounding the early stages of an officer-involved shooting investigation is important to appreciating how IPRA officer-involved shooting investigations are compromised—and far from independent of CPD—from the outset.

Under CPD rules, all firearms discharges must immediately be reported to CPD supervisors, and if the shot hits a civilian, it triggers two separate but overlapping investigations: (1) a criminal investigation conducted by CPD's Detective Division to evaluate possible criminal conduct by civilians involved in the shooting; and (2) a mandatory administrative investigation conducted by IPRA to determine whether the shooting officer was unjustified. IPRA does not investigate an officer-involved shooting where no one is hit, as explained previously.

Upon notification of a shooting, IPRA sends investigators to the officer-involved shooting scene, where they must wait outside the taped area until a CPD commander in charge of the scene completes the preliminary assessment, which consists of a walk-through of the area and evidence, as well as individual interviews with the officers and civilians present. At the same time the commander is conducting this preliminary review, many other non-IPRA personnel are allowed within the taped area to also interview witnesses and view evidence, including supervising sergeants, detectives, and union representatives. All of these interviews are conducted outside the presence of IPRA investigators and none are recorded. During these communications and particularly before CPD supervisors arrive on-site, there is no prohibition against officers talking with each other about the shooting, and there is no requirement that they remain separate from each other.

After the commander completes his preliminary investigation, he or she allows IPRA inside the taped area and leads the investigators in a walk-through of the scene and provides a narrative of the incident. Generally, IPRA does not speak directly to witnesses until they convene later at the area headquarters, where, again, CPD controls the flow of information and people. While officers complete police reports and review video, CPD supervisors, detectives, union representatives (often accompanied by union counsel), and sometimes prosecutors from the State's Attorney's Office (SAO) conduct additional, unrecorded private interviews with officers and civilians in one area of the station while IPRA investigators are quarantined in a separate room. Union representatives and attorneys not only interview the involved officers but also may assist in completing police reports concerning the incident.

IPRA is the last in line to interview civilian witnesses and officers. After CPD and SAO interviews are finished and after providing the officer with the two-hour notice required under the collective bargaining agreement (CBA), IPRA is then able to conduct recorded interviews of the non-shooting officers at the station. IPRA is sometimes unable to interview civilians at the station, as it depends on the witnesses' willingness to remain at the station after CPD and SAO interviews, as well as cooperation from CPD detectives who are controlling the station scene. Under applicable CBA provisions, the earliest time IPRA can interview the shooting officer is 24 hours after the incident. However, if IPRA makes a preliminary determination that the shooting is unjustified, it will typically refer the matter to the SAO to consider for criminal charges, and defer the interview until it receives a declination letter from the SAO.

These procedures are highly troubling. Allowing involved officers to engage in private, unrecorded conversations with the commander, supervising sergeants, detectives, and union staff before ever speaking with IPRA allows for the inadvertent or intentional conflating of recollections, or the appearance thereof, and greatly impairs IPRA's investigative abilities. If false or mistaken narratives justifying shootings are created during these private conversations and advanced in reports and officer statements, it is exceedingly difficult for even well-trained and diligent investigators to accurately evaluate whether the shooting was justified. We appreciate that officers have a right to counsel, but there are numerous precautions that can be taken to protect the integrity of the investigation without impinging on this right.

The possibility of officer collusion in this setting is more than theoretical. The release of police cruiser video from the 2014 Laquan McDonald shooting led CPD to fire seven officers for falsifying their reports about the shooting. The officers' written reports generally read the same, stating that the teenager was advancing on officers and threatening officers with a knife. The video of the shooting appears to undercut those seven officers' accounts. Additionally, the release of body-worn camera videos from the July 2016 Paul O'Neal shooting shows officers involved in the shooting speaking to each other about the incident moments after the shooting occurred. Officers can be heard discussing the facts of the incident, including confirming they all had the same perception of events. As concerning, CPD officials condone this behavior, and encourage them to have the conversations without making a record of what was said. One video depicts a CPD command official telling officers who are speaking about the shooting to "talk about that stuff afterwards." The same video captures the official informing one involved officer not to say anything until the administrative process has started, and advising other officers that if they have on a body-worn camera, they should not go near the involved officer until the administrative process has completed.

Notwithstanding these most recent scandals and the many others that preceded it, CPD has not amended its policies to address the risk of officer collusion or inadvertent witness contamination. No CPD policy requires involved or witness officers to separate themselves and avoid speaking to each other about a deadly force incident. This is out of step with accepted practice in many agencies, which follow a protocol similar to this one used by the Los Angeles Police Department:

> After all public safety concerns have been addressed, the [on-scene] commander shall ensure that involved officers and witness officers are transported from the scene, physically separated unless logistical problems (e.g., the number of involved officers and/or supervisors) preclude individual separation, and monitored to eliminate the possibility of contaminating their statements prior to their interview by [Force Investigation Division] personnel.

The on-scene commander must be permitted to communicate with officers and witnesses in addressing public safety concerns (e.g., tasks and communications necessary to preserve evidence, secure the scene, address medical needs, determine whether suspects are at large), of course. Once this is done, however, CPD rules should at a minimum prohibit officers from discussing the incident (other than with counsel) outside of IPRA's presence, and this rule should be stringently enforced with significant penalties imposed for violations.

To the extent these restrictions conflict with CBA notice provisions, such as the provision requiring that IPRA provide witness officers with two-hour notice and accused officers with 24- hour notice before interviews, then these provisions should be renegotiated or, alternatively, all witness discussions with CPD must likewise be delayed until IPRA can participate.

We realize that IPRA is now entitled to more control over an officer-involved shooting scene in the wake of the recent passage of the Illinois Police and Community Relations Improvement Act, 50 ILCS 727, but remain concerned that absent proper oversight and guidance, this law will not, by itself, correct the current organizational and control deficiencies that impact accountability for officer-involved shooting scenes.

Additionally, IPRA should interview the shooting officer as soon as possible after the incident, and should not delay it due to a possible criminal investigation. Neither constitutional rights under *Garrity* nor any other valid investigative principle requires delaying such an interview, and CPD's history indicates that an immediate administrative interview is warranted. If a compelled statement must be taken and a criminal investigation subsequently ensues, IPRA should either assign a "clean" and a "screen" investigative team for the parallel investigations, or it should refrain altogether from performing criminal investigative tasks on behalf of the SAO. Indeed, severing the current relationship where IPRA acts as the criminal investigative arm for the SAO in excessive force cases not only will provide more independence from the SAO but will better ensure that IPRA resources are spent aggressively pursuing administrative investigations rather than serving and acquiescing to the needs and motives of SAO. Finally, the CBA-imposed 24-hour rule should be eliminated for these same reasons, but until this is done, CPD and IPRA should arrive at creative and enforceable ways to ensure that both the shooting officers' well-being and Chicago's broader accountability goals are satisfied.

2. Interviews of officers and civilian witnesses

We identified many cases where investigators failed to take reasonable steps to contact and interview identified civilian eyewitnesses to the incident. For example, in one incident an off-duty officer shot and wounded a burglary suspect who apparently attempted to wrest the officer's weapon from him. During the struggle, the suspect was shot in the chest and abdomen. However, the suspect also sustained a third gunshot wound to his back—an injury not explained by the officer. A witness canvass report identified two residents who reported two loud bangs, a pause, and a final bang. The report plainly raised the question of whether the officer fired the final shot—perhaps the unexplained shot to the back—after the threat was neutralized. Yet IPRA did not interview these two witnesses and instead accepted the officer's account and deemed all three shots justified. Similarly, in one investigation of a complaint of misconduct, an IPRA investigator interviewed an 8-year-old girl who complained that a CPD officer working secondary employment in a school grabbed the girl by her hair, swung her around, and choked her while breaking up a fight in a school hallway.[153] IPRA did not interview the identified student witnesses and entered a non-sustained finding based primarily on the accused officer's written statement.

Moreover, in numerous files we reviewed, *officer* witnesses and even the *accused officers* in misconduct cases were never interviewed. In one misconduct case involving an allegation that officers broke into a home and beat two men, IPRA interviewed a mother and her two children who witnessed the incident and testified in support of the claim. IPRA identified but never interviewed any of the officers involved, discounted the mother's testimony and ignored the children's testimony because of their ages, and made a "not sustained" finding. In another case, a man alleged two officers stopped him on the street and slammed him against a car, requiring hospitalization. Although the hospital records supported the injury described and IPRA identified the officers involved, IPRA never interviewed the officers and instead deemed the allegation "unfounded" because the medical records indicated that the complainant was intoxicated.

Where investigators do seek to interview officers, they frequently do so by sending what is known as a "to/from" memo requesting that the officer provide written answers to general questions about the complaint. One high-ranking IPRA staff member admitted during our interview with him that he believed inadequate staffing caused investigators to rely too heavily on "to/from" statements from officers instead of conducting live interviews. This practice is not as effective as a live interview; it allows for collusion and for answers to be drafted or influenced by others, whereas hearing the officer directly during an interview allows for more spontaneous responses, more probative follow-up questions, and more well-informed credibility determinations.

Finally, in BIA investigations, interviews are not electronically recorded and transcribed. Instead, the BIA investigator types up the questions and answers provided during the interview, and then tenders the final printed version for witness signature. In the context of the other systemic deficiencies noted herein, this practice further undermines the quality of the interview because it prevents an auditor from meaningfully reviewing or evaluating an interview.

---

153 We note that a significant amount of alleged officer misconduct involves officers working secondary employment. While we did not fully investigate CPD's oversight of officers' secondary work, the review that we did undertake indicated that there is a need for a thorough review of the policies and accountability measures related to officers' secondary employment.

3. Officer collusion and witness contamination

Our review of officer-involved shooting and misconduct investigations revealed that IPRA investigators exhibit little interest in whether CPD officers
have colluded with each other or have otherwise been subject to contamination. For example, in one case involving an officer who had shot an unarmed
man in the back, IPRA reviewed and obtained a copy of video footage from the
officer's patrol car that appeared inconsistent with the account the officer had
related to CPD detectives immediately after the shooting. IPRA postponed its
officer interviews for nearly a year while the State's Attorney's Office reviewed
the matter for possible prosecution.[154] Although the incident had become well-
known throughout the Department and the community, IPRA did not ask the
officers if they had seen the video or ask them to relate what they had read,
seen, or heard about the incident.

We found this problem in virtually all officer-involved shootings we reviewed, where IPRA investigators very rarely made any effort to explore the
possibility that involved officers and witness officers were lining up their stories
or had been influenced by outside information such as video footage or press
reports. Instead, officers were given free rein to provide apparently rehearsed
accounts, with no follow-up questions aimed at ferreting out collusion or contamination. This was true even when the officers used very similar language
or otherwise exhibited signs of coordinating their stories. For example, in one
case, two officers involved in an officer-involved shooting separately related the
incident in nearly identical terms, and even included the same digressions at
the same point in the narrative. The IPRA investigator never inquired whether
the officers had spoken to each other prior to their investigative interview or
asked them to identify all persons with whom they had discussed the incident.

Investigators in misconduct complaint investigations demonstrated this
same indifference to witness contamination. They frequently use "to/from"
memos or unnecessarily delay interviews of accused and witness officers for
extended periods, with some case files containing explicit assertions from investigators that an interview delay of months or years is based on the investigator's heavy caseload. And similar to shooting cases, when interviews do occur,
investigators in misconduct complaint cases rarely explore whether the officer
consulted with other officers prior to the interview.

Investigators' routine failure to explore the possibility of officer collusion
or other forms of witness contamination contributes to a culture in which officers have felt free to compare their accounts before meeting with investigators.
Although investigators generally cannot ask officers to disclose confidential

---

154 We discuss the problems associated with IPRA's decision to delay officer interviews
pending a prosecutor's determination in greater detail below.

communications with their attorneys or union representatives, they can and should routinely ask officers to identify all other persons with whom they had discussed the incident. This is routine practice in many other agencies.

4. Hidden witness coaching during officer interviews

IPRA itself undermines the integrity of its investigations by actively enabling officers to receive coaching during the course of an investigative interview. IPRA's investigation procedures manual expressly *requires* investigators to permit legal representatives to consult with officers about questions and their answers *during* a recorded interview.[155] In addition, these procedures *require* investigators to hide the extent of this consulting by turning off the tape recorder whenever officers or their representatives request—even if (and often because) a critical question is pending. The procedures likewise require investigators not to state on the record who is requesting a pause in the recording, why the request was made, how long the parties were offtape, and not to mention anything that occurred while off-tape. In striking contrast, IPRA's procedures for civilian interviews *require* that time on and off tape be recorded.

Although these procedures are limited by their own terms to misconduct investigations— i.e., cases where the officer is accused of specific offenses that may lead to discipline—IPRA applies them in practice to officer-involved shooting investigations as well, despite the fact that in virtually all cases, the officer has not been accused of any particular offense.

The important protections provided by the right to counsel do not explain or justify these practices. We have not identified any other agency that permits witness coaching to occur in the very presence of investigators, much less requires those investigators to cooperate with others in the room to conceal such efforts from the tape recorder and omit any mention of them in the investigative file. At CPD, however, the practice is institutionalized, with IPRA investigators often starting their interviews by inviting officers to use a hand signal if they want the investigator to turn off the tape recorder.

We found these coordinated, coach-and-conceal efforts reflected in many of the investigations we reviewed. Moreover, we found that it was not uncommon for officers to change the course of the narrative or walk back statements they had made after their legal representatives whispered a few words. Consider, for example, this exchange in an interview of a witness officer:

---

155 See IPRA STANDARD OPERATING PROCEDURES MANUAL SECTION E, Accused Members, § C.6. (Rev. Jan 1, 2015).

INVESTIGATOR: Okay. Do you remember hearing anything that your partner might've said during this whole incident? After you exited the uh squad car and you positioned yourselves, do you remember hearing your partner saying anything either commands to the offender or comments to you or anything like that?

OFFICER: I remember hearing my partner say police as he announced his office. Investigator: Okay. Was that before or after he fired shots?

OFFICER: Before.

INVESTIGATOR: Okay. All right. (pause)

UNION ATTNY: (whispers to client)

OFFICER: Partner also uh stated he has a gun.

INVESTIGATOR: Okay. Do you remember when he said that, when your partner said that? Officer: Inside the dumpster pen.

INVESTIGATOR: Okay.

UNION ATTNY: (whispers to client)

OFFICER: Uh as I ordered the offender to put his hands up is when I heard my partner say that, he, he's gotta gun.

These practices are particularly troubling given that witness and subject officers almost invariably share the same attorney and union representative. Under such circumstances, where the representative is coaching witnesses, the legal representatives are in a position to (1) take careful note of what a witness officer states in one IPRA interview and (2) share that information with the next witness or involved officer to be interviewed. Because communications between officers and their legal representatives are generally privileged, IPRA lacks the means to determine the extent to which such information-sharing occurs.

5. Use of leading and otherwise inappropriate questions

IPRA investigators not only routinely facilitated witness coaching by officers' legal representatives, but at times directly sought to influence officers' statements—in the officer's favor—by asking unnecessary leading questions during investigative interviews. For example:

INVESTIGATOR: Was [the victim] given a sufficient number of verbal commands to drop his weapon before an exchange of fire ensued?

Another example similarly illustrates this practice:

INVESTIGATOR: Okay. Was there time available or a split-second decision to fireyour weapon?

OFFICER: It was a split-second decision.

We found essentially the same exchange in other cases, such as this one:

INVESTIGATOR: Okay. Was there time available or a split-second decision
    to fire your weapon?
OFFICER: Yes.
INVESTIGATOR: Which one?
OFFICER: It, oh it was a split second.

In other instances, the investigator asked leading questions evidently aimed
at eliciting from officers a statement that they feared for their lives when they
used deadly force. This line of questioning of an officer who shot an unarmed
teenager is illustrative:

OFFICER: Then he stumbled to the ground, and then he came up. That's
    what I'm saying—he—how he jumped the fence, he stumbled to the
    ground, came up with his hands still in his waistband. That's when
    I left one round.
INVESTIGATOR: And when he came up, he was facing you?
OFFICER: Yes.
INVESTIGATOR: Okay, so he—as he's standing back up again, he still had
    his hands in his waistband?
OFFICER: Correct.
INVESTIGATOR: And you felt like he had something in his—in his hands?
OFFICER: Correct.
INVESTIGATOR: And you—you were in danger?
OFFICER: Yes, I was—I was in fear—I was in fear of my life.
INVESTIGATOR: You were in fear for your life so you fired how many
    times?
OFFICER: Once.

IPRA reviewers also routinely asked officers leading questions about
whether they experience "tunnel vision" or "auditory exclusion" that might
impair their ability to provide a completely accurate account. We were told
that such questions are asked because stress can impair sense perception.
However, strikingly IPRA does not pose the same leading questions to civilians—not even civilians such as crime victims wounded by gunfire. Similarly, it bears noting that neither Illinois law nor CPD policy provides for any
"cooling off period" before investigators may interview civilians. Instead,
stated concerns about the impact of stress on perception and memory appear
strictly confined to police officers.

IPRA investigators also pose leading questions that assume the truth of matters in significant dispute. For example, in one case involving a man shot in the buttocks as he fled officers, the IPRA investigator asked a CPD officer, "And uh could you tell which hand let's see, yeah, which hand the [fleeing man] held the weapon in?" Prior to that question, the officer had not said anything to the investigator about seeing a weapon. In another case, also involving a fleeing suspect shot in the back, an officer had told the IPRA investigator that the suspect had not offered any physical resistance other than running away. The IPRA investigator then stated, "Right. Okay. And he was reachin', he had the hand on his weapon." The officer then replied, "Correct." Another case, involving shots fired at a vehicle, included this exchange:

> INVESTIGATOR: As [the vehicle] turns I guess that's what you're seein' is the window rolled down?
> OFFICER: Yes. Investigator: And you think they're about to start shootin'?
> OFFICER: I think the driver is about to start, yes.

6. Failure to probe officer accounts, even when inconsistent with other evidence

Investigators rarely asked officers probing questions about their accounts of officer-involved shootings or the alleged misconduct. This reluctance to ask probing questions was particularly evident in cases where the physical evidence—often gunshots to the rear of a subject, or a lack of a weapon recovered at the scene—appeared inconsistent with the officer's story.

For example, in one case, an officer claimed that as he struggled to extract a suspect from a car, the suspect pointed a gun at him, leading him to shoot the suspect in the abdomen. However, the seated suspect somehow had sustained one of his gunshot wounds to the buttocks. IPRA did not pursue the apparent conflict. In another case, an officer fatally shot a man in the back during a foot pursuit. The officer claimed that he fired because the man faced him while pointing a gun. However, IPRA learned the night of the shooting that the man had been shot in the back. IPRA did not pursue the apparent inconsistency or press the officer for details about his position or that of the shooting victim. In a third case, an officer reported shooting a fleeing suspect in the back after he had allegedly turned to point an object the officer thought was a gun. However, video footage of the incident showed the suspect running away when the officer fired. IPRA never pursued the discrepancy or asked the officers present about what was depicted on the video. This failure to probe officer accounts of incidents even in the face of apparently inconsistent other evidence undermines accountability.

7. Failure to adequately address physical evidence

Our review of IPRA's investigative files identified other deficiencies and irregularities that related to the collection, analysis, and reporting of physical evidence. Although the IPRA procedure manual states that "physical evidence is crucial to any case," and "investigators should pay close attention to physical evidence," we found IPRA files lacking in key respects. CPD routinely swabs recovered weapons and suspects' hands for DNA and gunshot residue (GSR) so it may determine whether an individual held or fired a weapon. Most officer-involved shooting files we reviewed noted the collection of DNA or GSR evidence. Rarely did the files contain the lab results of DNA tests or an explanation for why they were missing. More frequently, we saw lab results for GSR tests, but in most cases, IPRA only mentioned the results in the rationale for their finding when the results corroborated the officers' accounts.

This outcome is troubling, especially in cases where there were sharp disputes between officer and civilian witnesses. For example, in one case, an officer shot a man in the elbow following a foot chase. According to the officer, he saw the man turn and point a gun at him. The officer reportedly told the man, "Drop the gun," and then fired when the man continued pointing the weapon. The officer then claimed the wounded man threw the gun over a fence as he was falling to the ground. Two other officers, located further away, provided a similar account. However, a nearby resident told IPRA she had seen the conclusion of the foot pursuit but had not seen any gun, and instead saw the man begin to raise both hands after an officer shouted, "Show me your hands." A second witness reported hearing the same command followed almost immediately by gunfire. Under the circumstances, analysis of the recovered weapon bore special importance, especially because the gun lacked any recoverable fingerprints. Still, IPRA's final report, which accepted the officers' version, did not mention the outcome of DNA or GSR tests or state whether they were still pending.

We found IPRA files lacking in other critical respects relating to the collection and analysis of physical evidence. First, virtually none of the files included a copy of crime-scene logs or any other documentation identifying who entered or exited the crime scene or when they did so. Second, many files lacked a report regarding crime-scene measurements or even a scaled diagram of the crime scene that identified the location of key evidence such as expended shell casings, bullet fragments, and the like. Third, few files reflected even a rudimentary effort to analyze bullet trajectories. Fourth, nearly every file lacked any photographs depicting the point of view of any civilian eyewitnesses IPRA interviewed, making it difficult to evaluate the reliability of their accounts.

8. Lack of appropriate use of evidence from civil and criminal proceedings

Some police misconduct allegations are the subject of a criminal prosecution or private civil litigation. IPRA and BIA investigators do not properly review these cases, or, where appropriate, incorporate evidence from these proceedings, in order to inform or strengthen administrative investigations. Additionally, in other cases—particularly within BIA, where the same investigators handle both the criminal and administrative investigations—investigators improperly rely on the outcome of a parallel criminal investigation when deciding whether to substantiate administrative charges based on the same conduct, even though the standards for civil and criminal violations are very different. Both practices result in investigators not using the information at their disposal to properly conduct and resolve administrative complaints.

a. Ignoring evidence from civil and criminal proceedings

The failure of IPRA and BIA to collect information from parallel criminal prosecutions or civil litigation involving the same alleged police misconduct represents a missed opportunity. Some misconduct cases are also the subject of a parallel criminal investigation. Motions to suppress in these criminal cases, as well as the underlying criminal trial, may yield important information that allows BIA or IPRA investigators to discover additional evidence or witnesses, or that assists in credibility determinations of officer witnesses. Yet there is no system that requires investigators to review parallel criminal proceedings, and no such periodic review of such criminal proceedings is done.

Similarly, in excessive force cases, it is not uncommon for the same conduct that IPRA or BIA has jurisdiction to investigate to be litigated in a Section 1983 civil rights lawsuit. Where there is an open IPRA or BIA investigation that is also the subject of a parallel civil case, investigators do not appropriately review and incorporate information from that parallel case into their administrative investigation. Moreover, there is no dependable procedure in which new civil lawsuits alleging police misconduct trigger investigations by IPRA or BIA. Indeed, many such complaints never make it to BIA or IPRA for consideration, and even when they do, no disciplinary investigation is automatically opened since a lawsuit is not deemed to satisfy the complainant affidavit requirement described above. Though IPRA has the authority to override the affidavit requirement, it rarely exercises it in these circumstances.

However, once a police misconduct lawsuit is settled or judgment is entered in favor of a plaintiff, a City ordinance requires IPRA to review the case in question for a possible disciplinary investigation. But IPRA has no timely systematic review process to comply with the ordinance, and often such settled lawsuits will sit on IPRA shelves for months or years before being reviewed at all. And when reviewed, many of these lawsuits—even though settled—still fail to clear the complainant affidavit requirement, and thus no investigation is ever conducted. And for those settlements that are substantively reviewed and investigated by IPRA—i.e., because they include a supporting affidavit—the complaints almost never result in a sustained finding, despite the fact that the City judged the case worthy of paying large amounts of money to the complainant. During our investigation we discovered that of the hundreds of misconduct settlements IPRA reviewed over the seven-year period from 2009–2015, it recommended discipline in less than 4% of them.

The City should review settlements and judgments on a broader scale to spot for trends, identify officers most frequently sued, and determine ways to reduce both the cost of the cases and the underlying officer misconduct. The City's Office of Inspector General (OIG) recently issued an advisory report criticizing the City's risk management systems as a whole. In particular, the OIG found that because the City does not analyze trends, including trends in police misconduct, or take action on the basis of such analysis, the City "spends tens of millions of dollars annually to pay claims." In response to OIG requests for information, the City's Department of Finance (DOF) admitted that the City "has no comprehensive program in place to examine claims against the City (including small claims, settlements, and judgments)," and that the limited analysis DOF does specifically excludes police misconduct claims. The City responded that a "risk management working group" is being convened, but that police misconduct claims will not be a part of that review, citing the pending conclusion of this investigation. This response should be corrected now that this Report has been issued.

b. Erroneously closing administrative investigations when investigators are unable to prove criminal charges

We also reviewed BIA *administrative* investigations that appear to have been closed simply because there was not enough evidence to hold the officer *criminally* liable. Unlike criminal investigations, in which findings are based on a "beyond a reasonable doubt" standard, findings in administrative investigations are based on the significantly lower "preponderance of the evidence" standard. This standard is appropriate because, if it is more likely than not that an officer has committed misconduct, the Department must take action to ensure it does not continue. In addition, even where officers' conduct may not have violated any criminal code, it may have violated numerous CPD policies. However, in cases we reviewed that were investigated by BIA, it appeared that BIA did not pursue or sustain administrative charges because criminal prosecution was declined, notwithstanding the possibility of policy violations.

In one case, the BIA investigator documented that he was not sustaining any violations in the administrative investigation because the elements of two crimes the officer had initially been charged with, criminal sexual abuse and unlawful restraint, were not met. That case involved an allegation that a CPD officer attempted to rape a woman at a party. Numerous witness accounts of what took place before and after the attempted rape were consistent, including that the victim reported the assault to the witnesses. The file also contains evidence of numerous text messages sent by the accused officer following the incident, including one in which the officer joked with his friend, "I thought she was an easy lay." The officer was later arrested, and the victim identified him in a lineup. Prosecutors originally classified the criminal allegations against the officer as potential felonies, but eventually dropped the case. The administrative investigation in the file mirrors the criminal investigation, indicating that BIA did no additional work in the administrative case other than talking to the victim again. In the investigator's summary of the administrative investigation, the investigator finds the victim's allegations unfounded, stating "the criminal charge of criminal sexual abuse was Nolle Prosequi by the Cook County State's Attorney office because the elements of this offense were not met. In addition, the elements of criminal sexual abuse were not met in the administrative investigation."

9. Superficial investigation documentation and investigative bias in favor of officers

We also identified numerous shortcomings in IPRA and BIA's final reports concerning officer-involved shootings and other misconduct complaint investigations. For example, the reports typically do not discuss or even cross-reference inconsistencies between officer statements and physical evidence or civilian eyewitness accounts. Similarly, very few point out inconsistencies between officers' written reports and their interview statements. They often gloss over or simply fail to mention conflicts between officer accounts of the incident. For example, in one case, two officers were running next to each other as they pursued a man carrying a gun. One officer told IPRA the man had turned toward his partner, so he fired repeatedly. However, the partner contradicted this claim. He told IPRA the man had not turned toward him and had not raised his arm. IPRA chose not to mention these conflicting statements or otherwise indicate that the two officers' stories appeared to be at odds with each other.

In another case, an officer shot a teenager in the back, claiming the boy had turned toward him and pointed a weapon. A firearm was located nearby, but on the other side of a tall hedge. During his IPRA interview, the officer was unusually vague when asked how the gun ended up where it did. First, the officer stated that as the boy fell to the ground, "the gun went over the hedge." Next, he said the gun "just went over" the hedge, and finally said the boy *apparently* threw it over" the tall hedge (emphasis added). IPRA did not pursue the matter further with that officer. A second officer, who stood nearby, denied seeing the teenager with a gun. Each interview lasted less than 15 minutes, and the IPRA report failed to include the second officer's denials or otherwise indicate that the second officer's account appeared to be in substantial tension with the first officer's.

IPRA reports sometimes omitted mention of crucial physical evidence that appeared to undermine officer accounts. One of the most troubling cases in this respect involved an officer who shot an unarmed suspect in the back at close range. The officer had reported to arriving CPD detectives that the man had pointed an object she mistook for a gun and opened fire. Those detectives briefed IPRA on this statement when it arrived at the scene. However, less than 24 hours later, IPRA had obtained police video footage that showed the confrontation. Far from supporting the officer's story, the police video, recorded at close range, showed the suspect running away from the officer. Nonetheless, IPRA issued a report that accepted the officer's story at face value. The report did not even acknowledge the police video.

We found other IPRA reports that either exaggerated or misstated evidence in a manner favorable to the officer. In one case, for example, officers shot a man in the leg after he reportedly pointed a gun at them. IPRA accepted the officers' accounts, though they were disputed by a civilian witness at the scene. In finding the shooting justified, the IPRA report stated that the shooting victim had admitted to treating physicians that he had pointed his gun at the police. However, the medical records referenced by IPRA in support of this conclusion actually reflect that the claim about pointing the gun was made by a CPD officer, not the shooting victim.

Finally, in sexual assault and domestic violence cases, we also found that investigators were quick to credit officers' versions of events despite the availability or potential availability of additional evidence. For example, in one case, a CPD officer's wife called the police to report that her husband had pointed his gun at her during an argument. The investigation revealed that the officer had a 19-year history of physically abusing her. The victim's son told investigators that he had pulled out a barbeque fork during the incident to protect himself and his mother. The officer admitted to pulling out his gun during the argument but said he did so because his son had come at him with the fork, and had punched him. The IPRA investigator's summary report noted that there were "conflicting descriptions" of the physical altercation, and that the officer "denied committing the alleged act." The investigator also noted that "although it is undisputed that [the officer] pointed his weapon at [the victim's son], the described sequence of events is in conflict, and the appropriate finding is not sustained." Throughout the case summary report, the investigator credited the officer's version of events and said, despite two contrary witnesses and the officer's history of domestic abuse, that because the officer claimed the alleged events did not occur, there was not enough evidence to sustain any of the allegations of misconduct.

10. Racial and ethnic disparities in the City's handling of misconduct complaints

IPRA and BIA sustained only 1.4% of all closed complaints from January 2011 through March 2016. It is not surprising, given the deficiencies discussed above, that so few filed complaints were sustained. What these deficiencies do not explain are the racial and ethnic disparities in sustaining complaints of CPD misconduct, particularly complaints of excessive force.

Our analyses show that, overall, complaints filed by white individuals were two-and-a-half times more likely to be sustained than complaints filed by black individuals, and nearly two times as likely to be sustained than complaints filed by Latinos: 1% of misconduct complaints filed by black residents, and 1.4% of complaints filed by Latino residents, resulted in at least one allegation being sustained, compared with 2.7% of the complaints filed by whites.[156] A closer analysis revealed that the disparity in sustained rates based on the race or ethnicity of the complainant was even greater at the individual allegation level. Black complainants had 2.4% of their individual allegations sustained; Latinos had 3.2% of their individual allegations sustained; and whites had 8.9% of their individual allegations sustained. In other words, for each allegation contained in a complaint, a white complainant is three-and-a-half-times more likely to have the allegation sustained—and the officer held accountable for his or her misconduct—than a black complainant, and twice as likely to have the allegation sustained than a Latino complainant.

Disparities in how IPRA resolves allegations of excessive force are even starker. 2% of all allegations of excessive force involving black complainants and only 1% of such allegations against Latino complainants were sustained, as compared to 6% of allegations of excessive force involving white complainants. In other words, whites were three times more likely than black complainants to have CPD uphold their allegations of excessive force, and six times more likely than Latino complainants to have their excessive force allegations sustained.

---

156 We analyzed CPD's complaint data by comparing the race of the complainant and the findings outcome. A single complaint can include multiple allegations, and each allegation will have a separate finding. We deemed a complaint sustained whenever at least one allegation was sustained. Thus, for example, if a complaint included five allegations, one of which was sustained and the others unfounded, then the complaint was noted to have had at least one allegation sustained.

This does not necessarily indicate that the complaint process is biased, as these numbers do not say anything about the quality of the complaint. While our investigation did not determine why these disparities exist, these disparities are significant and should thus prompt IPRA and BIA to take a close look at their practices to ensure that they are not discounting complaints based on the race or ethnicity of the complainant. Such a practice would itself be a disservice to Chicago's black and Latino residents, and would send the message to CPD officers that CPD and the City have a higher tolerance for misconduct against black and Latino complainants, which could in turn lead to disproportionate abuse of individuals within these groups and undermine community trust in CPD. It is thus imperative that the City work to better understand the reasons behind these disparities and eliminate them to the extent they have no race-neutral, legitimate basis.

11. Inadequate training of investigators

The investigative problems we found are in part attributable to the lack of training investigators receive both at the start of their work as investigators and throughout their career. Like the deficiencies in CPD's training more broadly, *see* Report, Section IV.A., the City does not provide investigators with sufficient training to do their jobs competently and effectively. Investigators we spoke with stated that they do not receive adequate formal training, and they learned how to do their jobs from observing supervisors and co-workers.

As with the lack of general training for investigators, we found that the lack of specific training in how to investigate domestic violence and sexual assault allegations appeared to further undermine BIA's and IPRA's ability to conduct these investigations effectively. Victims of sexual assault and domestic violence may be more likely than other complainants to be reluctant to participate in the investigation beyond reporting due to feelings of shame, however unwarranted. For sexual misconduct in particular, victims may be reluctant to participate in the investigation because the nature of the misconduct and of investigations means that victims may have to retell intimate and embarrassing details numerous times to complete strangers. Domestic violence victims may be particularly unwilling to continue participation in an investigation when the perpetrator is a police officer, given the potential impact of a sustained domestic violence finding on an officer's career.

Investigations we reviewed indicate that investigators handling these cases may not understand these dynamics, including how to interact with victims in a manner that encourages their participation in the investigation. One investigator told us that it was "up to [the survivors of domestic violence] if they wanted to talk," and admitted that he had not received any training on how to get domestic violence victims to trust him and provide information about their assault. An IPRA investigator we spoke to admitted that many of the investigators handling domestic violence cases believe that an incident does not qualify as domestic violence unless it is "a punch in the face," and that, as a result, many allegations of abuse that do not meet this threshold are not investigated. These misconceptions impact the intensity with which IPRA investigates these claims. For example, in one complaint, the girlfriend of a CPD officer alleged that he pushed her to the ground and hit her on the head with an object, injuring her, and that the officer had assaulted her on four different occasions in the past. Two days after the initiation of the complaint, the victim told the investigator that she did not want to pursue the case further because the officer agreed to seek anger management counseling, and because the two had decided to "work on their relationship." In light of the considerations in domestic violence cases described above, the investigator in this case should have attempted to gain her trust and cooperation to enable the investigation to move forward. Instead, IPRA closed this case.

The City recognizes that investigators need more training, and IPRA is beginning to substantially revamp and increase training for all staff, especially investigators. As part of the newly formed COPA, the City plans to create new trainings for all staff, including a one-week "on-boarding program" for all COPA employees and a new investigator/legal staff academy. IPRA's current Chief Administrator informed us that the academy will last five to six weeks, and will cover topics such as investigative policies and procedures, case management practices, crime scene management, external investigative resources, and investigative skill building. The creation of these new training programs is an important step towards improving the quality of misconduct investigations and changing the culture to one that is more determined to resolve investigations and reliably determine whether an officer committed misconduct. CPD has not informed us of similar plans for BIA investigators, although such training is necessary for those investigators as well.

In addition to the new general training plans described above, the City should also improve allegation-specific training to ensure investigators are equipped to properly handle the nuances and complexities of more complicated allegations. Although IPRA's Chief Administrator informed us that the new training program will cover investigative subject areas, including training in each of the areas under IPRA's/COPA's jurisdiction, the depth and breadth of that training is unclear.

D. Insufficient Staffing Contributes to IPRA's Investigative Deficiencies

Although lack of resources cannot account for all of the investigative deficiencies we found during our investigation, it is clear that the City has given IPRA a tremendous responsibility without providing sufficient resources to accomplish the mission effectively. Many of the troubling shortcuts we found in individual investigations, as well as the policy decisions that prevent cases from being meaningfully investigated, have the hallmarks of an overwhelmed agency working in a constant state of triage. The City has recently committed to providing more funding to IPRA when it becomes COPA, and the agency has already begun to hire additional staff. But COPA's range of responsibilities will also be much broader than IPRA's, and there has not been sufficient analysis to determine whether COPA will have the capacity to do any better than IPRA. The City should be mindful of the concerns discussed below and ensure that it provides resources to COPA adequate for it to succeed.

IPRA's historically high caseload was in part due to the sheer size of CPD and in part due to the large volume of cases it inherited from OPS. When IPRA replaced OPS in 2007, it took on a tremendous backlog of cases, which continued to grow for several years, causing some investigators to carry as many as 60 investigative files. Operating with fewer than 90 total staff, IPRA struggled to work through this backlog while keeping up with new complaints filed against CPD's 12,000-plus sworn members. Although no comprehensive staffing study has been done to determine how many investigators are needed at CPD, IPRA's current staff is too small by any estimate. As described by a former high level IPRA official, "IPRA was never given the resources for the volume it was expected to handle."

In addition to causing the investigative delays described below, IPRA's burdensome workload has negatively impacted its investigatory methods and even its findings. IPRA investigators and supervisors agreed that the resource issue incentivizes investigators to reach not-sustained findings. They explained that it is easy and less work to develop a case enough to justify a not-sustained finding, but that it takes a lot more work to push the case to either a sustained or unfounded finding. Investigators are also inclined towards not-sustained findings because they know the case will not need approval beyond their immediate supervisor. Our review of investigative files indicates that this admission might plausibly explain many instances in which IPRA's findings appeared at odds with the facts.

Insufficient resources also incentivize IPRA investigators to close cases prematurely. Investigators told us that high caseloads led supervisors and IPRA leadership to implement new procedures designed to close cases more quickly, even though they represent poor investigative practice. IPRA staff reported the following examples of such problematic procedures, each of which is discussed elsewhere in this Section, that in their view are directly attributable to inadequate staffing:

- The development of the Excessive Force Protocol that allows for administrative closure, without investigation, of force complaints deemed to be minor, even though proper investigation of such complaints might reveal more serious misconduct.
- Declining to investigate officer firearm discharges where the officer did not hit a subject (either intentionally or unintentionally, e.g., because the officer had bad aim), even though IPRA supervisors agreed that such investigations would reveal deficiencies in training or policy in need of correction.
- Referral of many cases to "mediation," because it eliminates the need to interview the officer or write a summary report (and the investigator does not need to attend the mediation), even though mediation may be inappropriate given the conduct alleged.
- Administratively closing investigations of Taser use, even though such investigations are mandatory.
- Relying too heavily on "to/from" statements from officers instead of demanding live interviews, even though live interviews would, among other things, allow investigators to probe behind officers' statements and make vital credibility determinations.
- Reducing the number of people who review investigative summary reports, regardless of the finding.

All of these procedures sacrifice accountability because they preclude IPRA's ability to conduct meaningful misconduct investigations in all circumstances.

Lack of resources also means that investigators are not engaging in other important oversight and accountability tasks that would benefit CPD, the City, and the community as a whole. For example, as noted elsewhere in this Report, IPRA is supposed to review settlements entered into by the City in civil rights lawsuits filed against police officers. IPRA staff admitted that these mandatory investigations of settled cases sometimes sat piled up on a shelf for years because such reviews were too time consuming to tackle given their current caseloads. Moreover, although IPRA staff acknowledged that ideally they would be tracking and collecting valuable investigative information from parallel police misconduct lawsuits that are ongoing, they reported being unable to do so due to large workloads. IPRA recognizes that beyond investigating individual allegations of misconduct, with proper resources, the agency could also proactively engage CPD in efforts aimed at preventing future misconduct, such as providing policy and training recommendations to CPD; performing broad-based trend analysis based on its investigations; and monitoring individual officers who are subject to a high number of complaints. Unfortunately, insufficient staffing has prevented IPRA from undertaking these important tasks.

IPRA leadership is enthusiastic about again taking on these tasks and more under the new accountability ordinance once COPA is in place. But it is far from clear whether COPA's increased funding will sufficiently cover its new expanded responsibilities. Without a meaningful evaluation of needs, and a steadfast commitment to meeting those needs, there is little doubt that high caseloads, with the profound impact this has on the quality and timeliness of IPRA's investigations, will remain.

E. Investigations Lack Timely Resolutions, Undermining the Quality of Investigations and Credibility of the Process

IPRA expects, and its enabling ordinance requires, that it will complete investigations within six months. However, this is rarely accomplished. In cases where IPRA sustains the allegations in a complaint, it takes an average of two-and-a-half *years* to complete the investigation. Members of the Department and the public alike are frustrated with how long it takes CPD and IPRA to complete these investigations.

1. Structural deficiencies cause investigative delays

Structural deficiencies within Chicago's investigative entities allow complaints of officer misconduct to go unresolved for unreasonable amounts of time. Investigations are often delayed at the outset because of the affidavit requirement, as discussed above. IPRA and BIA often take weeks and months before securing an affidavit. Not only does this delay the preservation of evidence through witness interviews, but the more time investigators spend chasing complainants for affidavits, the less time they spend trying to complete other investigations, thus causing additional delays.

And after an affidavit is secured, the investigative agencies do not appear to follow strict deadlines for the completion of various steps or the investigation as a whole. While IPRA gives its investigators some guidance on how long it should take to complete some investigative steps, these do not appear to be firm deadlines, nor do there appear to be repercussions for when investigators fail to meet them. Nor are there deadlines for supervisory review, resulting in reviews taking anywhere from one week to six months. While internal deadlines are sometimes easier set than kept, providing clear guidance about important investigative deadlines and prioritizing tasks helps promote timely investigations. Some investigations are inherently more complex than others, and adherence to tight deadlines will be difficult, if not impossible. However, without any firm deadlines for investigative activities, these investigations have strung out for years, often transferring between several investigators before even basic steps are complete.

Another policy causing delay is the unwillingness of IPRA and BIA to pursue administrative charges against an officer while criminal charges are contemplated or pending in court. The Chief of BIA stated that BIA will never conduct parallel investigations, and will always wait for a declination of charges from the State's Attorney's Office before continuing an administrative investigation. IPRA investigators acknowledged following the same practice. This means that administrative investigations remain open for months, if not years, awaiting the resolution of a criminal case that, in nearly every instance, is not prosecuted.

Most investigators interviewed believed incorrectly that such practice is required under *Garrity v. New Jersey*, 385 U.S. 493, 500 (1967) (holding that an officer cannot be compelled to make a statement against his will for the purposes of an administrative investigation that will then later be used against him in a criminal investigation). However, parallel administrative and criminal investigations can and do occur as long as precautions are taken to not taint the criminal investigation with any evidence from compelled interviews in the administrative investigation. Given that both IPRA and BIA investigators generally provide investigative assistance to prosecutors in criminal investigations, pursuing parallel investigations may require additional resources, and in some cases, a valid reason may exist for deferring administrative investigations pending the outcome of a criminal investigation. However, when at all possible, IPRA and BIA should pursue the administrative misconduct investigation notwithstanding parallel criminal investigation, even if this requires staffing a "clean" and a "screen" investigative team for purposes of *Garrity*.

Finally, although we are not able to quantify it, our investigation found that another factor contributing to delayed investigations is the lack of resources described above. In many investigations not involving parallel criminal proceedings, important witness interviews did not take place for months or years after the incident, and the investigators admitted in the file that such delays were due to burdensome demands in other investigations."

2. Investigative delays undermine investigative outcomes and reduce public and officer confidence

The consequences of delayed resolutions of investigations are severe. Most importantly, lengthy delays can make it impossible for investigators to uncover the truth: memories fade, evidence is lost, and investigators may not be able to locate those crucial witnesses needed to determine whether misconduct has occurred. Our review of investigative files shows that many witnesses, and particularly the accused, are not interviewed for months or years after the incident. A Chicago Tribune report reflected consistent results, showing an average four-month delay in officer-involved shooting cases before the shooter was interviewed, and in 15 cases the interview occurred over a year after the shooting.

Delayed investigations also compromise CPD's ability to make discipline recommendations withstand appeal. Not only do protracted investigations enable the accused officer to argue the case should be dismissed on due process or statute of limitations grounds, but it greatly compromises the City's ability to present a strong case during the layers of appeal afforded to officers. CPD's discipline case typically relies on civilian witnesses who may not be available years after the incident or may not be cooperative or invested in the case since they have little to gain and much to lose by testifying openly about police misconduct in front of the accused officer.

Apart from the negative impact on outcomes, investigative delays also undermine the message that the City takes these complaints seriously. It disheartens complainants to learn that an officer they know to be abusive remains on the force for years after being the subject of a credible complaint of serious misconduct. These delays are unwelcome to officers as well: CPD and IPRA delays in completing misconduct and force investigations were one of the first and most frequent complaints we heard from officers from the outset of this investigation. Accused officers who have not engaged in misconduct are burdened with the scrutiny of being under investigation, and may be stuck doing "desk duty" for years while investigations languish. During our investigation, we heard from many officers who described understandable frustration with having their careers put on hold, sometimes for years, while the investigation creeps forward.

F. CPD and the City Do Not Take Sufficient Steps to Prevent Officers from Deliberately Concealing Misconduct

When officers—at any rank—conceal misconduct, it thwarts, often insurmountably, efforts to investigate and hold officers accountable. IPRA and BIA treat such efforts to hide evidence as ancillary and unexceptional misconduct, and often do not even investigate it.

1. Code of silence

One way to cover up police misconduct is when officers affirmatively lie about it or intentionally omit material facts. The Mayor has acknowledged that a "code of silence" exists within CPD, and his opinion is shared by current officers and former high-level CPD officials interviewed during our investigation. Indeed, in an interview made public in December 2016, the President of the police officer's union admitted to such a code of silence within CPD, saying "there's a code of silence everywhere, everybody has it . . . so why would the [Chicago Police] be any different." One CPD sergeant told us that, "if someone comes forward as a whistleblower in the Department, they are dead on the street."

When officers falsify reports and affirmatively lie in interviews and testimony, this goes well beyond any passive code of silence; it constitutes a deliberate, fundamental, and corrosive violation of CPD policy that must be dealt with independently and without reservation if the City and CPD are genuine in their efforts to have a functioning system of accountability that vindicates the rights of individuals who are abused by CPD officers.

We cannot determine the exact contours of this culture of covering up misconduct, nor do we know its precise impact on specific cases. What is clear from our investigation, however, is that a code of silence exists, and officers and community members know it. This code is apparently strong enough to incite officers to lie even when they have little to lose by telling the truth. In one such instance, an officer opted to lie and risk his career when he accidentally discharged his pepper spray while dining in a restaurant—a violation that otherwise merits minor discipline. Even more telling are the many examples where officers who simply witness misconduct and face no discipline by telling the truth choose instead to risk their careers to lie for another officer. We similarly found instances of supervisors lying to prevent IPRA from even investigating misconduct, such as the case discussed elsewhere in this Report in which a lieutenant provided a video to IPRA but recommended that the case be handled with nondisciplinary intervention rather than investigated, describing the video as only depicting the use of "foul language" and affirmatively denying that it contained any inflammatory language or that the victim made any complaints—both patently false statements as demonstrated by the video. High ranking police officials and rank-and-file members told us that these seemingly irrational decisions occur in part because officers do not believe there is much to lose by lying.

Rather than aggressively enforcing and seeking discharge for violations of CPD's Rule 14, which prohibits making false statements, enforcement in this area is rarely taken seriously and is largely ignored. The IPRA enabling ordinance makes it discretionary for IPRA to initiate Rule 14 investigations incidental to one of its delegated mandatory investigations. Investigators rarely exercise this discretion, and it is so little used that there is much confusion even over whether BIA or IPRA would have jurisdiction over such a Rule 14 investigation. Provisions in the CBA add to the obstacles facing Rule 14 enforcement. Under the FOP contract, investigators cannot base Rule 14 charges on a video unless the officer is first allowed to view the video and correct prior false statements, regardless of their materiality.

Not only are Rule 14 investigations not encouraged, but past IPRA leadership prohibited investigators from initiating such Rule 14 investigations without obtaining approval from the IPRA Chief Administrator, sending a strong message to investigators not to expand their investigations into collateral Rule 14 charges. Such Rule 14 requests required a de facto higher standard of proof and were rarely approved. One IPRA supervisor told us that while investigating an incident involving an off-duty officer in a bar, she discovered the officer lied in a police report but was denied permission to bring Rule 14 charges. In another case, an investigator sustained a Rule 14 charge for making false statements in his interview, but IPRA leadership rejected this recommendation and directed the report be changed to exonerated.

The former IPRA Chief Administrator explained his reluctance to authorize Rule 14 charges: "we don't make Rule 14 allegations in a cavalier way, because we realize how significant it is and how devastating it can be to a police officer's career . . . it impacts their credibility as a witness, and in so many instances can be a career killer." Of course, no legitimate investigative body should make any misconduct allegations in a cavalier way. But the reason for not doing so should be based upon a firm commitment to act only based on the evidence, not undue concern about an officer's career. After all, officers who lie cannot be effective officers, should not be testifying in court proceedings, cannot instill confidence in the community, and discredit and demoralize the many honest officers on the force.

In practice, IPRA rarely asserts Rule 14 charges when officers make false exculpatory statements or denials in interviews about alleged misconduct, even when the investigation results in a sustained finding as to the underlying misconduct. This is true even in some cases we reviewed in which video shows the accused officer lied about the underlying misconduct or tried to cover up evidence. One case we reviewed included witnesses statements and a video showing the accused officer lied in a police report about the basis for arresting the complainant, but no Rule 14 charges were made and the officer received a two-day suspension following mediation. In another case, the video shows an officer punch a handcuffed woman in a massage parlor and then shows the officer looking for the video recorder he realized had captured the abuse. IPRA failed to discipline the officer for the obvious cover-up attempt and settled the physical abuse claim in mediation for an 8-day suspension.

Nor do investigators hold witness officers responsible for covering up misconduct of others. Investigators do not diligently review the investigative records to determine whether witness officers have lied in police reports or whether supervisors have blindly approved reports without attempting to determine whether the reports are fabricated. In one case we reviewed, the complainant alleged an officer punched him while handcuffed in a hospital, which was denied by both the accused officer and his partner. A video later surfaced showing that both officers lied, but Rule 14 charges were never brought against the *witness* officer. Indeed, our investigation revealed that there were only 98 Rule 14 charges sustained over the last five years. Only one of these sustained cases was initiated by IPRA against an officer *witness* who IPRA discovered lied to cover up misconduct of another. Moreover, in many of the cases where Rule 14 charges were brought and sustained against accused officers for lying, the discipline imposed was less than discharge. Almost one-third of all the sustained Rule 14 cases had a recommended punishment of 25-day suspension or less, and some of the discharge recommendations were reduced or overturned on appeal.

Furthermore, even in the rare case where a Rule 14 charge is made and results in a sustained finding, officers face little risk that such finding will impact their ability to testify in criminal cases in support of the prosecution. We learned in our investigation that there is no system in place to ensure that all officer disciplinary findings bearing on credibility, including Rule 14 findings, are supplied to the State's Attorney's Office and criminal defendants, even though this is required under *Giglio v. United States*, 405 U.S. 150 (1972).

The Laquan McDonald case demonstrates that Rule 14 violations are ignored by IPRA. Neither the IPRA investigators nor the IPRA Chief Administrator considered pursuing Rule 14 charges against any of the officers who witnessed the shooting and completed reports that seem inconsistent with the video footage, nor against the supervisors who approved such reports. Not until Chicago's Office of Inspector General took over the case were Rule 14 investigations opened and sustained findings made. The point here is not to prejudge whether such Rule 14 charges arising out of the McDonald shooting should have been sustained or will survive challenge, but rather to highlight by example the reluctance of IPRA investigators to even initiate a Rule 14 investigation. IPRA's unwillingness to open Rule 14 investigations or bring Rule 14 charges, even when there is evidence that officers attempted to conceal misconduct, only perpetuates the code of silence. It is critically important that IPRA change its historical practice and pursue Rule 14 charges against officers, including witness officers, whenever there is evidence of deceit, concealment or cover up.

Finally, IPRA and BIA investigators must not just sit back and wait for a testimony-impeaching video to appear. Instead, they should be collecting all available information and assessing whether officer's stories match the evidence. A valuable source of such information includes judicial proceedings where judges occasionally make affirmative findings that an officer's testimony is not credible. This information should be critical not only to police officials who supervise those testifying officers, but also to IPRA and BIA to better evaluate credibility in pending and future investigations involving those officers. More importantly, they should be evaluating whether the circumstances surrounding a judicial credibility finding would support a sustained Rule 14 investigation. For example, in investigating the many administrative charges against one CPD officer, including a fatal officer-involved shooting, it would have been helpful for IPRA investigators to know that a judge had found this officer to have lied in court testimony in 2011. Yet prior to our investigation, there was no system in place for CPD or IPRA to collect such judicial information. Not surprisingly, none of the Rule 14 charges brought against officers in the last five years was based on false testimony in court. This indifference to judicial proceedings involving officer credibility is particularly troubling in the criminal context where IPRA and BIA should have already had a system in place to evaluate whether suppression hearings should trigger administrative investigations into 4th Amendment violations.[157]

2. Tampering with video and audio

Real-time audio and video footage of alleged misconduct is one of the most effective tools in overcoming the code of silence and making credibility determinations. Such evidence provides direct insight into what actually took place, has been shown to deter unfounded misconduct complaints, and minimizes the risk that witnesses will later give false statements about the incident, increasing accountability and the public's confidence in the accountability system. Yet, CPD has done very little until recently to ensure that police conduct is captured on audio and video.[158]

Not until the public release of the McDonald shooting video—captured on only two of the five car cameras and excluding all related audio—has CPD made much effort to ensure that cameras and microphones entrusted to of-

---

157 After our investigation began, the State's Attorney's Office announced it had begun reviewing cases in which officers' testimony had been questioned by judges and had begun issuing "disclosure notices" notifying criminal defense lawyers that a judge has discredited an officer's testimony. This is a positive step for the CPD accountability system and the Cook County criminal justice system but will require oversight to ensure that this program is effective and that it continues when public focus turns elsewhere.

158 CPD and IPRA also do not sufficiently gather or make use of the audio and video showing misconduct that is available. This problem is discussed separately in this Section.

ficers are working properly and are not tampered with. A January 2016 CPD report following the McDonald video release found that the audio capability of 80% of the Department's dash-cams was either not working or had been tampered with. The report stated that officers had routinely removed microphone batteries, destroyed antennae, and stashed mics in the glove compartment boxes of their squad cars.

CPD's law enforcement partners have similarly expressed frustration with the Department's failure to capture officer conduct, despite having video and audio recorders. Former Cook County State's Attorney Anita Alvarez, for example, called the lack of audio in police dash- and body-cam videos was "frustrating" and "something . . . the Police Department has to address." Similarly, our investigation revealed that officers consistently failed to check or sync their dash-cam mics with the in-car system, rendering them useless. Yet IPRA and BIA have rarely investigated whether these instances were deliberate attempts to tamper with video or audio recordings, and, if so, taken any disciplinary action.

Shortly after our investigation began, the CPD Superintendent warned beat officers that they would be disciplined for failure to follow proper dash-cam protocol. The reminder that officers should follow this policy was probably needed: prior to the McDonald case, it is hard to find any inquiry into the suspicious failure of most of CPD vehicles' dash-cams.

In the aftermath of the release of the McDonald video, the Department pledged to expand its body-worn-camera initiative, announcing in September 2016 that all CPD patrol officers will have body-cams by the end of 2018. However, in a December 2016 press release, CPD announced that the initiative was being fast-tracked and that all officers in the 22 police districts will have body-cams by the end of 2017, a year ahead of schedule. This is a positive accountability reform. But body-cams will not be any more successful than dash-cams unless CPD works with police unions and community groups on policies and protocols for body camera usage and develops better accountability measures. Currently, the CPD policy on the use of such cameras is insufficient, and in many instances directives are vague or confusing. There is no policy directing supervisors as to when or whether they regularly review recordings to ensure proper use of the cameras and identify officer training opportunities or conduct concerns. Further, current policy does not explicitly provide that an officer who deliberately fails to use his or her assigned body-cam properly will face discipline. It should therefore come as no surprise that a recent high-profile use-of-force incident in a July 2016 shooting of an unarmed teenager by an officer wearing a body camera was inexplicably not captured on audio or video. It appears that officers have become used to ignoring CPD rules requiring them to use dash- or body-cams because such behavior was not being investigated or punished. It will take committed effort for CPD and IPRA to undo this attitude.

Transparency tools like dash- and body-cameras have perhaps unmatched potential to simultaneously confront the Department's recognized code of silence and make the City safer for both officers and civilians. They can do neither, however, if they are not used. We are encouraged by the City's respect for and focus on the powerful accountability tools of audio and video. Strong foundational policies and long-term oversight is necessary to ensure their potential is realized.

3. Complainant and witness intimidation

We identified a significant number of incidents where the evidence supports concluding that CPD officers intimidated potential complainants or witnesses from filing or testifying regarding misconduct complaints.

We heard from numerous advocates and individual victims of police abuse that officers who engaged in force against a civilian routinely file baseless police assault and battery charges against the victim and other witnesses to the misconduct. In 2006, a patron in a restaurant claimed that after being beaten up by several off-duty officers, he and witnesses to that incident were falsely arrested for battery to cover up the incident. In another case in 2009, the City settled for $100,000 a lawsuit alleging a CPD lieutenant falsely arrested him for battery to cover up the officer's abuse of the plaintiff. In 2014, the City settled another lawsuit for $30,000 where a driver alleged an off-duty officer aimed his gun at him and then filed false battery charges to cover it up when other officers arrived on the scene.

Filing false assault charges not only constitutes an independent civil rights violation, but is powerful discouragement to potential complainants and witnesses regarding police misconduct. Criminal assault charges against witnesses also undermine their credibility when testifying about the misconduct, as we know from the 2006 restaurant incident mentioned above.

Failure to investigate and discipline for witness and complainant intimidation not only prevents CPD from resolving allegations of misconduct, but undermines the integrity of the system as a whole. Moreover, using complainant non-cooperation as a rationale for closing cases where the complainant explicitly alleges intimidation sends the message to CPD officers that witness intimidation can be an effective tactic. In one illustrative case in which a woman alleged that an officer had raped her, she refused to provide BIA the officer's name, and refused to sign an affidavit, telling the investigator that the officer had told her that he had "bigger power" over her and would "fuck her up" if she went to the hospital or the police. The woman alleged that the officer had also threatened her girlfriend, a possible witness to the rape. Despite providing a detailed account of the alleged rape—on two separate occasions—to the investigator, the investigator did not follow up on the results of the rape kit, did not attempt to interview a known witness, and did not canvass for witnesses at the location where the victim and the officer reportedly met. Nor does the investigator appear to have sought an affidavit override. The BIA investigator instead closed the investigation, "based on the victim's refusal to cooperate any further."

G. The City's Discipline System Lacks Integrity and Does Not Effectively Deter Misconduct

On the rare occasions when an allegation of misconduct is sustained, and the even rarer occasions when the sustained finding results in true discipline, CPD initiates a convoluted, lengthy process of determining, and revisiting, the appropriate discipline through several layers. The lack of guidance for determining the initial disciplinary penalty; the many opportunities for second-guessing and undermining the penalty; and the amount of time this process takes, has made CPD's disciplinary policy illegitimate in the eyes of officers and the public alike, and rendered it ineffective at deterring misconduct and contributing to a culture of integrity.

1. Discipline system

Once an IPRA or BIA investigator determines that an allegation against an officer should be sustained, the investigator and/or the investigator's supervisor recommends discipline. The discipline that an investigator can recommend ranges widely. Despite the sustained finding, sometimes no discipline is actually imposed, or the only discipline that is imposed is that a violation is noted on the officer's record. A "violation noted" penalty is only slightly less meaningless than a "no discipline imposed" resolution, as it will only remain on an officer's disciplinary history for one year. During the January 2011 through March 2016 time period we reviewed, 28.4% of sustained findings resulted in "no discipline imposed" or only a "violation noted." Investigators can also recommend that the officer receive a "verbal reprimand," which amounts to a supervisor addressing the officer's wrongful conduct verbally, but nothing more. Sustained findings were resolved with "verbal reprimand" in 24.8% of the closed cases we reviewed. Investigators can also recommend suspension from one to 365 days, and in certain circumstances, discharge from CPD. CPD officers received suspensions in 45.6% of sustained cases we reviewed, with an average recommended suspension of 7.8 days. However, the average is inflated by a small number of cases that resulted in lengthy suspensions. The most frequent suspension length was one day; the median suspension length was three days. Discharge occurred in nine cases, or 1.1% of the cases during the time period we reviewed. The investigator's recommendation to sustain an allegation and impose discipline is subject to review within IPRA, including review by IPRA's general counsel and the chief administrator, prior to the recommendation leaving IPRA. While CPD is currently developing a matrix of disciplinary penalties to guide this decision-making process, CPD's unions have not signed off on it, and it has significant deficiencies, as discussed below.

After the recommended discipline is finalized at either IPRA or BIA, there are many layers—up to seven—of review before it is final and can be imposed. First, except in cases where discharge is recommended, the recommendation is subject to a Command Channel Review (CCR), in which supervisors in the accused officer's chain of command review and comment on the recommended discipline. Next, the recommendation, along with CCR comments, is forwarded to the Superintendent for review. Discharge recommendations skip the CCR review and go directly to the Superintendent. The Chief of BIA makes a final disciplinary decision that is forwarded to the Superintendent for review after the BIA investigator's recommendation has gone through the CCR process.

The Superintendent has 90 days to respond to discipline recommendations by IPRA, or the discipline is deemed accepted. There is no time limit for Superintendent review of BIA disciplinary recommendations. At any point along this path, the command channel can essentially start the process over again by sending the case back to the investigative unit and asking for more investigation.

Once a disciplinary recommendation reaches the Superintendent he can approve it or, if he disagrees with it, he must meet with IPRA's Chief Administrator to attempt to resolve the dispute. If they cannot agree, a three-person panel of the Chicago Police Board will resolve the disagreement. See Section IV.H. The Superintendent can also ask for more investigation to be done, possibly restarting the review process, or even overturning the sustained finding. Once the Superintendent has approved a disciplinary recommendation, it is "final" unless it must be submitted to the Police Board for a full hearing. See Section IV.G. In these instances, discipline is not final until approved by the Board, a process which generally takes additional years.

CPD officers can and frequently do challenge the "final" disciplinary decision. If the recommended discipline is suspension of 10 days or less, the officer can go through a binding "summary opinion" process. If the recommended discipline is suspension for a period between 11 and 30 days, the officer may also challenge the discipline by filing a grievance, which will be decided through arbitration. Finally, if the recommended discipline is suspension between 31 and 365 days, the officer may appeal the decision to the Police Board or an arbitrator, at the officer's election. Under the grievance procedures, if the parties are unable to settle during the initial negotiations with the officer's commanding officer or in mediation, the officer is entitled to a full evidentiary hearing before a neutral arbitrator. Decisions of an arbitrator through the grievance proceedings as well as appeal decisions by the Police Board are subject to administrative review in the Circuit Court of Cook County and can then be appealed to the Illinois Appellate Court and the Illinois Supreme Court. Pursuing the grievance procedure adds an average of three extra years to the disciplinary process.

Only after these steps are completed can discipline actually be imposed on an officer. And, when a suspension finally is imposed, an officer can serve the suspension by using paid vacation or furlough days, resulting in no loss of income to the officer.

2. CPD's disciplinary system is ineffective

The outcomes of officer-conduct investigations are critical to holding officers accountable for misconduct and deterring future misconduct. *See McLin by and through Harvey v. City of Chicago*, 742 F. Supp. 994, 1001 (N. D. Ill. 1990 ("A failure to discipline officers, resulting in increased abusive behavior by police officers, has been recognized to be a policy for which municipal liability may attach."); *Sassak v. City of Park Ridge*, 431 F. Supp. 2d 810, 816 (N.D. Ill. 2006) (noting that failure to discipline allegations often support a finding of municipal liability because "a policy of condoning abuse may embolden a municipal employee and facilitate further abusive acts."). CPD's system for imposing discipline on officers who it has determined have committed misconduct suffers from systemic deficiencies that undermine its fairness, consistency, and effectiveness.

a. CPD's disciplinary process takes too long and needlessly introduces opportunities to undermine accountability

Having individuals at all levels weigh in on disciplinary recommendations, and even send cases back for more investigation, creates needless opportunity to undermine accountability. Additionally, these multiple layers of review make discipline unduly slow to be imposed. The City's current process thus leaves both victims and officers unclear how, when, or if an officer will be held accountable for misconduct the officer committed, sometimes for years after a finding has been sustained. On top of the delays that occur while an investigation is still with BIA or IPRA, once an investigative finding is made, the additional layers of review by the CCR, Superintendent, or Police Board can result in years of additional delay from the time when an allegation is sustained until discipline is actually imposed and served.

The City should take measures to reduce delays in this process, but should ensure that in doing so it does not introduce new problems. One example of this complicated dynamic involves the City's use of "summary opinions." An officer's right under his collective bargaining agreement to challenge imposed discipline can result in even further delays. The most recent FOP collective bargaining agreement created the "summary opinion" process, which was intended to resolve discipline grievances more quickly. This option has allowed for more speedy resolution of these matters. The Police Accountability Task Force found that, when summary opinion was used, the average time from the misconduct to the issuance of the arbitrator's opinion was 447 days, as compared to 1,049 days under the older system that did not allow for summary opinion.

In addition to these delays, CCR undermines accountability more directly. While the accused officer's supervisory chain should certainly receive notice of the disciplinary decision, which would allow them to better supervise their officers, little value is gained and much is lost in the current process. As the Mayor's Police Accountability Task Force recently stated, "Command Channel Review (CCR) provides a platform for members who are potentially sympathetic to the accused officer to advocate to reduce or eliminate discipline." The Task Force also found that arbitration decisions overturning discipline quote reviewers who not only disagreed with the discipline but opined that the allegation should not have been sustained at all. The Task Force's conclusions are consistent with our findings on this point. Indeed, we recommended to the City during the course of this investigation that it modify the CCR process, and instead have discipline decided at a disciplinary conference headed by a single individual whose decision is reviewed directly by the Superintendent. We further recommended that investigators should never recommend discipline following a sustained finding. The disciplinary conference process we recommended is used in law enforcement agencies across the country to improve accountability systems. With the latest version of the draft disciplinary matrix, discussed below, the City appears to have rejected our suggestions and decided to leave this broken process in place with only superficial changes.

By eliminating unnecessary layers of review, and holding necessary reviewers to strict deadlines, the City would be able to decrease how long it takes for a complaint to reach final resolution, and better ensure that discipline is not overturned. This, in turn, would enhance certainty and speed, increasing officer and public confidence that the complaint adjudication system is fair and efficient, and giving it far greater deterrent value.

b. Lack of appropriate guidance for determining discipline results in too much discretion and inconsistencies in how discipline is decided

A lack of clear guidance on appropriate penalty ranges undermines the legitimacy and deterrent effect of discipline within CPD.

Prior to the start of our investigation, investigators' disciplinary recommendations were not guided by any formal standards. Instead, the discipline recommended following a finding of misconduct was entirely up to the discretion of the investigator and his or her supervisor. This resulted in disparities in discipline recommended both across incidents involving the same offense, and even within a single incident as it proceeds through various layers of review. For example, we reviewed one incident where investigators recommended a 150-day suspension for various misconduct violations; command channel reviewers disagreed, and recommended between six and eight days for those same violations; and the IPRA administrator finally recommended a 60-day suspension. This case is currently pending before the Police Board, and the ultimate discipline that will be imposed (for an incident that occurred in January of 2011— six years ago) is still unknown.

In recent months the City has been developing a "disciplinary matrix" that outlines presumptive penalties for misconduct violations by offense type. There are three categories of penalties for each offense type: mitigated, presumptive, and aggravated. In other words, for each offense type, there is a presumptive penalty range, but also a "mitigated" range that can be imposed if certain mitigating circumstances are presented, or a heightened "aggravated" range if there are aggravating circumstances present. The City also created a "guidelines" document to explain what each offense category encompasses, and how to use the disciplinary matrix, including the factors to consider when imposing discipline and mitigating down or aggravating up from the presumptive penalty.

During this investigation, we reviewed and provided feedback on the first draft matrix and guidelines. The City incorporated some of the changes we suggested, but did not incorporate some of the more difficult but critical modifications that we believe are necessary to ensure the disciplinary system will be fair, impartial, and transparent. For example, the current versions still remain unnecessarily vague. There are several "miscellaneous" categories that do not provide sufficient direction for what offenses are included in those categories. Another category, "failure to ensure civil rights," is described as a violation where the "member fails to ensure that a person's civil rights are not violated." Because these categories are so sweeping, it is unlikely that they will be applied consistently and fairly.

The current draft matrix also still prescribes unusually low punishments for conduct that is inconsistent with constitutional, respectful policing, and allows for mitigation in circumstances where doing so would be inappropriate. For example, the latest version of the matrix allows a mitigating range for the offense of "verbal abuse-racial/ethnic," meaning the use of language that is racially or ethnically derogatory.

Moreover, although the guidelines reference how second and third offenses should be considered, the matrix itself does not account for progressive punishment for subsequent offenses. The language in the guidance suggests only that third offenses result in a penalty "at or near the top end of the Aggravated Pen-

alty Range . . . except in extraordinary circumstances." Those circumstances
are not defined, leaving decision makers unclear when a subsequent offense
merits harsher discipline. Without clear, well-defined guidelines for how subsequent offenses will be punished, the matrix system does not ensure sufficient
accountability for repeat offenders.

Other disciplinary ranges in the matrix are so large that they provide no
useful guidance. For example, for "Crime Misconduct" categories such as "Conspiracy to Commit a Crime," "Other Misdemeanor Arrest," and "Sex Offense,
Other" the discipline range is 31 to 365 days. If the offense is "aggravated,"
separation is permitted. Yet, it is difficult to imagine conduct that is serious
enough to warrant discipline on the upper end of the presumptive range, yet
not serious enough to warrant separation. Moreover, it is unclear why the City
believes that an officer found to have engaged in some of these offenses should
remain on the police force at all. In any event, the ranges provided for these
types of offenses allow for too much variation and discretion, which may result
in unfair disparities.

Finally, adherence to the draft disciplinary matrix is not mandatory. As currently drafted, the guidelines state that "the CR Matrix is to be used as a *set of
guiding principles* in the administration of discipline. It does not prohibit the [de-
cision-maker] from assessing a different penalty where unique and exceptional
circumstances may warrant." (emphasis added). "Unique and exceptional circumstances" is not defined, and CPD does not provide even a single example of
such circumstances, or illustrate how they fairly factor into discipline. At best,
this lack of specificity leaves well-meaning individuals to guess whether a given
set of circumstances is unique or exceptional. At worst, this language leaves the
door open for less well-disposed individuals to favor or disfavor officers according to whim. In both instances, it would be difficult to hold anyone accountable
for poor decisions.

The creation of the disciplinary matrix and guidelines is an important step
towards providing greater consistency and clarity in discipline for officer misconduct, but the deficiencies described above still allow for too much discretion and the imposition of discipline that is incongruent with the offense.

H. Chicago's Police Board

The Police Board has a long history of overturning the Superintendent's misconduct findings and proposed discipline, but this trend has changed over the
past year. While this change is welcome and appropriate, our investigation indicated that there are structural challenges to the Board's process that, unless
addressed, may prevent this change from taking hold long term. We found also
that the Police Board's effectiveness is undermined by the same investigative
deficiencies that render CPD's accountability ineffective more generally. Below

we discuss these challenges to assist Chicago's efforts to ensure that the Board continues to become, and remains, a stronger component of CPD's accountability structure.

1. Background of Chicago's Police Board

Created in the wake of a crisis (the Summerdale Scandal of 1959), Chicago's ninemember Police Board was expected by many Chicagoans to function primarily as an independent accountability check on CPD. But the Police Board arguably has undermined accountability by routinely overturning or reducing the Superintendent's disciplinary decisions, often overturning sustained findings altogether, even in instances where Board members may believe the officer in fact committed misconduct. This misconduct includes the unreasonable use of deadly force and other violations for which the Superintendent and IPRA recommended termination.

To understand why the Police Board is perceived as an ineffective accountability mechanism, despite the best efforts of many of its members, it is important to recognize the Board's built-in structural conflict. Through a combination of policy and practice, the Board has evolved into an amalgam of at least three, typically separate, types of police/civilian entities.

It appears clear that, at least when it was formed, the Board was meant to serve some of the functions that *police commissions* serve in some other large cities (such as Los Angeles). That is, by its authorizing municipal ordinance, the Board is tasked with adopting "rules and regulations for the governance of the police department of the city," and with influencing the selection of Police Superintendent by nominating the names of three candidates to the Mayor, from which the Mayor is to select. As confirmed by several Board officials during our conversations with them, the Board has "never" really fulfilled its duty of adopting CPD rules and regulations.

The Police Board has instead evolved into a combination of civil service protection panel and independent-oversight backstop, but without sufficient guidance as to how to effectively navigate this difficult dual role. The Police Board in some respects acts as a *civil service commission*, part of a system meant to "protect efficient public employees from partisan political control." *See Glenn v. City of Chicago*, 628 N.E. 2d 844, 850 (Ill. App. 3d 1993). In this role, the Board has viewed itself as focused on ensuring procedural due process for any officer subject to discipline. The Board officials we spoke with emphasized, for example, the Board's role in giving the officer a robust opportunity to "confront the evidence" against him or her, and to ensure that the officer receives "due process."

The Board also appears to see itself, however, as serving the role of an *independent oversight agency*, having a responsibility to the broader Chicago community to ensure that the values and views of the public are reflected in the Department's misconduct findings and imposition of discipline. Board officials thus emphasized their role ensuring that the hearing process is "transparent," and that "ordinary citizens" have input into discipline, and that they are "not all lawyers" and that they represent people who live both in Chicago's "wealthy" and "poor" areas. Similarly, the Board's website lists "holding monthly public meetings that provide an opportunity for all members of the public to present questions and comments to the Board, the Superintendent of Police and the Chief Administrator of [IPRA]" as one of its "primary" powers and responsibilities.

There is no inherent conflict between ensuring that officers' procedural rights are protected and that the Chicago public has insight into how the police officers who serve them are held accountable for misconduct. However, as Chicago's Police Board demonstrates, it is difficult for one entity to serve as both an arbiter of appropriate discipline and a conduit for public-police discourse, and impossible without a clear mandate and a set of balanced protocols. The Police Board lacks such a mandate or protocols, so rather than balancing these two roles effectively, has seemed to vacillate between them. The public, police officers, and Board members alike are frustrated with public meetings during which the Board does not engage with the public and has no authority to address the concerns raised by the public, and at which the Superintendent and IPRA leadership may or may not show up to address public concerns and report on what they have done to address previously raised concerns. It appears clear that the Board's civilian outreach functions would be better placed in another entity, like the Community Oversight Board that the City reports it has committed to implementing within the next six to nine months.

Moving these civilian outreach functions to another entity would allow the Police Board to focus its efforts on where its greatest focus already lies and where it has its greatest potential impact: deciding CPD disciplinary matters in which the Superintendent is recommending discharge or lengthy suspensions.[159]

2. The Police Board's role in deciding disciplinary cases

The Police Board is required to decide disciplinary cases in which the Super-

---

159 As part of its role deciding certain disciplinary matters, the Board is assigned the responsibility of resolving disagreements between the Superintendent and IPRA over the recommended discipline for officers found to have committed misconduct. Where there is a disagreement, the Superintendent bears the burden of overcoming the IPRA Administrator's recommendation. See CHICAGO POLICE BOARD RULES OF PROCEDURE, SECTION VI (April 16, 2015). The frequency of such disagreements has varied over time, and the Board reportedly has overwhelmingly refused to overturn IPRA's recommendations. There have been no such disagreements since 2014, and in 2014 there was only one.

intendent has recommended termination of an officer, or suspension over one year, or suspension of a supervisor (rank of sergeant or above) for over 30 days. At the officer's election, the Board also reviews officer suspensions that are between 31 days and one year.[160] The Board's decision is *not* subject to Superintendent approval or veto, and may not be challenged via arbitration.[161]

a. Past trends in Police Board discipline decisions

The Police Board has long been known for reversing many of the Superintendent's findings of misconduct, including most of the cases in which the Superintendent proposes discharging an officer. According to the Police Board's 2014 Annual Report (the most recent available), of the 16 discharge cases the Board decided, it upheld the Superintendent's discharge in only six, or 37%. It found "not guilty" in another six cases, thus going beyond refusing to discharge to wiping the slate entirely clean in another 37% of the cases in which the Superintendent had sought to discharge an officer. In another four cases, the Board reduced the Superintendent's recommendation of discharge to a suspension or reprimand.[162] Similarly, of the 27 cases the Board decided in 2013, the Board upheld the Superintendent's recommendation of termination in only 11, about 40%, and overturned the sustained finding in an additional two. This trend was longstanding: a 2009 study by the Chicago Justice Organization found that the Board upheld the recommended discipline for a sworn officer in only 37% of the cases it heard.[163]

---

160 Officers and supervisors may request Board review of a suspension of 30 days or less where the union decides not to arbitrate an officer's grievance.

161 The Police Board's decision can be appealed only to Cook County Circuit Court via petition for administrative review. Either party may appeal the Circuit Court's decision to the Appellate Court of Illinois. The Court will overturn the Board's findings of facts only where they are against the manifest weight of the evidence. The Court presumes the Board's findings of fact to be prima facie true and will find them contrary to the manifest weight of the evidence only where the opposite conclusion is "clearly apparent." The Court will overturn the Board's imposition of discipline only where the decision was arbitrary or unreasonable, taking into account the Board's "wide latitude" to determine what punishment was appropriate to "punish the conduct of the officer . . . and deter future conduct by other officers." *McDermott v. City of Chicago Police Bd.*, 2016 IL App (1st) 151979, ¶ 35.

162 In another five cases the officer resigned, and one case was otherwise dismissed prior to decision. The Board was more likely to uphold the Superintendent's suspension cases in 2014, upholding two of the three cases it heard, and, in an unprecedented decision, discussed below, recommending an increase in the penalty in a third case.

163 It is unclear how dependent this change is on the individuals currently on the Board. As discussed below, there are several structural changes that can be made to the Police Board to improve its functioning at an institutional level, and increase officer and public confidence that its decisions are fair and impartial.

This historically high rate of overturning the Superintendent's misconduct and disciplinary determination would not have been concerning if it reflected the Board's accurate determination that the Superintendent had erred in finding misconduct or in levying heavy discipline. And certainly there appear to have been many instances where this was the case and the Board served its important function of ensuring that police officers are not unfairly or unduly harshly punished. But our investigation, including our conversations with past and current Board officials, makes clear that it too often has been the case that Board officials have overturned the Superintendent's findings of misconduct and/or the level of proposed discipline—including in cases where they firmly believe that the officer committed the alleged misconduct.

The statistics set out above, alongside a review of the type of misconduct and discipline the Board has overturned over the years, makes clear that this dynamic has had a negative impact on officer accountability and police legitimacy in Chicago. The Board has, for example, reduced a case that resulted in an in-custody death (and a $1.3 million dollar settlement) from discharge to reprimand, and reinstated an officer, despite a criminal conviction, for falsifying a field sobriety test that led to the arrest of a citizen. The City has paid out nearly $400,000 in five lawsuits related to this officer's DUI stops.

b. Recent changes in Police Board discipline decisions

The Board's trend of overturning the Superintendent's recommendation to discharge an officer is changing. Over the past year, the Board tended to uphold the Superintendent's discharge recommendations far more frequently. In 2016, the Board sided with the Superintendent in the eight cases in which he recommended discharge. Additionally, in two discharge cases where the Board had previously found the officer not guilty, the City appealed the Board's decision and, upon remand, the Board imposed a 31-day suspension in one case and discharge in another. In another case on remand, given instructions to impose a penalty less than discharge in a case in which it had previously agreed with the Superintendent's proposed discharge, the Board imposed a suspension of five years. The Board reduced the Superintendent's recommended discharge, to an 18-month suspension, in only one case. In the one suspension case the Board decided, it affirmed the Superintendent's 60-day suspension. In seven other cases, the officer resigned after the Superintendent filed charges with the Board.

In 2014, the Board took the unique step of increasing and officer's discipline. It ordered an officer's discharge in a case in which the Superintendent had recommended a 60-day suspension. The Appellate Court found this to be a legitimate exercise of the Board's authority. *See Lesner v. Police Bd.*, 2016 Ill.

App. (1st) 150545. This is potentially an important step forward in allowing the Board to serve a valuable, unique role in ensuring appropriate officer accountability in Chicago.

c. Challenges to effective Police Board review

As discussed below, there are numerous changes the City can and should make to ensure that the Board, as an institution, garners and retains greater confidence among CPD officers and the broader public.

It is worth noting at the outset that even if the Board corrected these structural challenges, many members of the public in Chicago might still find the Board a disappointment and even question its utility. This is because the Police Board only reviews cases where IPRA and the Superintendent have already determined that the officer committed misconduct. The Police Board does not provide independent civilian input into whether officers who were not found to have committed misconduct should have been.[164] Nor does the Board have any authority or ability to ensure that IPRA completes investigations more quickly or more competently, or that an officer be recommended for discharge if neither IPRA nor the Superintendent have done so. The Police Board thus does not, and was not meant to, address the broad concern in Chicago—a concern that our investigation finds to be well-founded—that the Superintendent and IPRA sustain far too few allegations of misconduct, and propose discipline that is too low in the cases they do sustain.

Nonetheless, even as the Police Board cannot make up for problems in other components of the City's accountability processes, in the past it has done great harm by exacerbating the City's accountability failings through unnecessarily overturning so many of the very few cases that the City has managed to sustain. While this trend appears to have reversed itself in the past year, the discussion below is meant to help the City ensure this remains the case.

i. Description of Board hearing process

The Board conducts hearings pursuant to Rules of Procedure, most recently amended in April 2015. These Rules provide the framework for a quasi-trial process, with pre-hearing motions practice and hearings, which can last several days, in which the rules of evidence do not apply, although hearsay evidence is not admissible. At these hearings, the City has the burden of demonstrating,

---

164 Several Police Board officials with whom we spoke expressed concern in particular about IPRA's handling of allegations against officers of domestic violence, including IPRA's failure to sustain such allegations and to "mediate" a resolution. Both of these topics are covered elsewhere in the Accountability Section of this Report.

through the presentation of documentary evidence and live testimony, that the Superintendent's sustained finding is supported by a preponderance of the evidence. The officer has the right to cross-examine all witnesses and otherwise challenge the testimony, and offer evidence in defense and mitigation. Should the City prevail at the "liability" phase, the trial proceeds to a "penalty" phase. Contract attorneys called hearing officers, of which there are three, have sole authority over the hearing itself. These hearing officers are attorneys from private practice and the only requirement is that they have five years' experience as an attorney. Their main functions, according to the Board officials with whom we spoke, is to create a good record for the Board's consideration; to present the case impartially to the Board; and to write up the Board's decision. Board members are provided with transcripts and video recordings of the hearing and meet privately to confer. The Board's final vote on each case is made at a public meeting. In 2012, these Rules were amended to require all Board decisions to be supported by written findings. These written decisions are posted on the Police Board's website.

Our investigation indicated that there are several elements of the Board's hearing process, and the City's accountability processes more generally, that contribute to officers avoiding accountability when they appear before the Police Board.

ii. Information available to Board unfairly skewed in officers' favor

The hearing officer and Board do not have full access to the officer's complaint and disciplinary file: due to restrictions in the collective bargaining agreement, even sustained findings of misconduct are available to the Board only if they occurred within the past five years. Nor does the Board know the officer's disciplinary or lawsuit history at the "liability" phase, even where that history could provide powerful probative evidence of whether the officer has a history of dishonesty, or whether the officer's current alleged misconduct is consistent with misconduct the officer has repeatedly been accused of, or even found to have committed, in the past. Even as the Board is denied access to this potentially critical information, it is given the officer's complete "complimentary" history—spanning the entirety of an officer's career.

In addition, the officer is permitted to have other officers, including commanders, testify as character witnesses for the officer, *at the liability phase* of proceedings, even where the charges do not place the officer's character at issue, notwithstanding the fact that the Superintendent is recommending discipline, often termination, for the officer. While this is styled as "character witness" testimony in support of "evidence in mitigation," its inclusion at the liability phase belies this label, as do the statements of some Police Board officials that the testimony of CPD supporting officers and commanders "means a lot" and that they "give their testimony more weight" (although other Police Board officials told us they give this testimony "no weight"). The Superintendent recently filed a motion to keep this information under seal or move it to a separate post-liability hearing. Board officials told us the Board denied this motion because it would extend the proceedings one month.

The format of the Board's hearing process may also undermine the effectiveness of the Board because it deprives the Board of the ability to directly assess the evidence. Because the Board reviews transcripts and video recordings of the hearing after it is completed, it is unable to ask clarifying questions or otherwise direct the proceedings to ensure the Board, as fact-finder, gets the information it needs to make a decision. Instead, it must rely entirely on the hearing officer. The precise extent to which the Board relies upon these hearing officers is unclear. One Board official told us that the hearing officer is "not allowed" to make credibility determinations; another Board official told us that the Board will in fact ask the hearing officer for credibility determinations. Regardless, it is clear that the quality of the hearing officer impacts the Board's ability to make a decision. In one case, the Board reported it had to send the case back because the hearing officer had done such a poor job creating a record, "we couldn't make sense of it."

iii. City has in the past not effectively advocated for accountability

The relative inexperience of the attorneys representing the City and Superintendent, compared to the attorneys representing the officers, has undermined accountability, although this is reportedly improving. The Board told us that they feel compelled to let off officers they are sure committed the misconduct, because "the City messed up on the evidence." Board members and others report that attorneys for the officers, all former state's attorneys, have extensive trial experience and, in the words of one Police Board member, "make the Superintendent have to work." At the same time, according to Police Board members, the City's attorneys have little trial experience, and, in the past, have had to handle the trial on their own. In the words of one Board official, there is a "big disparity in experience and effectiveness" between City and officer attorneys. Still other advocates point to the potential for conflict: the City is advocating to discharge the officer even as it may be defending the City in civil litigation stemming from the same incident. One long term observer of the Police Board and Corp Counsel's office asserts that this problem is exacerbated because the "firewall in the Corp Counsel's office has not been honest or effective." The City reportedly has recently begun to outsource representation of the City at some Board hearings, and sending better prepared attorneys (and more than one attorney) to others. Board members report that the quality of the City's representation has increased in recent months "dramatically" as a result. The City should continue to build on these efforts.

iv. Board members and hearing officers lack training

The Board's own lack of training regarding adjudicating police misconduct further undermines its effectiveness. Board members are generally not lawyers and have no background in policing or accountability. One Board member told us of voting against a Superintendent's sustained finding of an unlawful search, even though the Board member agreed the search was unlawful, because of the amount of drugs the officers found during this "clearly" illegal search. Hearing officers can be similarly inexperienced, with a "wide variance in quality," and problems creating a clear record for the Board's consideration.

For at least the past 20 years, there has been no set or required training for either group. The training as described by one Board member consists of little more than a binder of materials; a tutorial on the burden of proof; the opportunity to watch an academy class on use of force; and an offer to go on a ride-along. The Board's Executive Director conceded that "this is one area that needs improvement." One former Board member pointed out that Board members should have a respect for policing, but that the Board would also do well to "put [Board members] in the homes of people on the West or South Side for a day and see what they go through."

That the lack of training impacts Board decisions appears evident from some of the decisions themselves, described above, as well as in the disagreements we heard directly from Board members about proper application of the rules, such as when an officer should be discharged for lying, or whether officers should ever be found guilty for using profanity. Poor decisions may have been avoided with better training for both hearing officers and Board members.

v. Lack of investigative timeliness and quality undermines accountability

Board consideration of the Superintendent's recommendations is unquestionably compromised by the poor quality and lack of timeliness of IPRA and BIA investigations discussed elsewhere in this Report. According to Board officials, among cases decided since 2010, the median time from the date of the incident to charges being filed is four years for IPRA cases and over two years for BIA cases, and our conversation with Board members and a review of Board decisions makes clear charges are sometimes filed much longer than this after the date of the incident. In one case we reviewed, charges were filed in 2014 for incidents that took place sometime between 1999 and 2003. In other cases, the Board is unable to affirm the Superintendent's charges of excessive force because the charges were brought more than five years after the incident, in violation of Illinois' statute of limitations on excessive force charges brought against officers.[165] In one such case, the Appellate Court upholding the Board's decision not to affirm the Superintendent's findings based on this lack of timeliness, stated:

> [W]e find it necessary to express our dismay with the unreasonable length of time the Superintendent took bringing charges in this case . . . . The Superintendent brought charges more than six years after the incident, without any explanation other than a "mix-up" occurred. A delay of this magnitude does nothing to foster the public's interest in effective oversight and supervision of police officers nor does it foster the protection of a police officer's right to due process in defending serious disciplinary charges. The passage of an unreasonable amount of time adversely affects witness availability and recollection and the officer's ability to present a meaningful and effective defense to unjustified charges.[166]

Board members and accountability advocates expressed similar concerns about the impact of delays on Board hearings. As one former Board member stated, the cases before it were "so old and so stale" that it was "unfair to the police officers; unfair to the witnesses; unfair to the victims." This lack of quality and timeliness has ramifications much broader than undermining the Police Board's ability to hold officers accountable, but this impact is particularly harmful given the severe nature of the misconduct that the Board often considers.[167]

vi. The Police Board's lack of transparency

The Police Board's process provides a greater window into officer discipline than is available in many police disciplinary processes; in this respect the Police Board represents an advance over accountability systems that rely solely upon opaque internal processes and arbitration. But the Board also provides less transparency than is available through most police civilian oversight entities, and

---

165 65 ILL. COMP. STAT. 5/10-1-18.1 (1992).

166 *Castro v. City of Chicago Police Board*, 2016 IL App (1st) 142050, ¶ 42.

167 The Board process itself adds significant delay to the accountability process. As per the Board's 2014 Annual Report (the most recent available), in 2013 and 2014 the median number of days from the Superintendent filing charges to Board decision was 198, or over six-and-a-half months. According to the Police Accountability Task Force Report, in 2015 this median was 209 days. In our review of 2016 cases (excluding cases in which the officer resigned) the median was 266 days, and it took the Board an average of 301 days after the Superintendent filed charges to render a decision. The Board should develop and implement a plan to reduce the length of time it takes it to resolve the cases that come before it.

less than it professes it should. The City and Board have both asserted that the Board is intended to provide transparency as an "essential value" to "increase the public's and police officers' confidence in the process for handling allegations of police misconduct." It is thus incumbent upon the City and Board to make reasonable efforts to be as transparent as possible.

There are several steps that the Police Board can and should take to be more transparent and increase confidence in its process. First, the Board could post all materials related to its hearings on its website, including transcripts and videos. Currently, members of the public must request hearing transcripts through public records requests, and the City does not release videos of the hearings.[168]

The Board could also increase transparency by tracking and publishing more detailed case-specific and aggregate data about its decisions, and making this information available in a timely manner. Currently, the Board provides only vague anonymized data in untimely annual reports (the most recent one was in 2014). Even the Board's monthly reports to the Superintendent containing complaint statistics must be requested through public records requests. Some groups have requested materials and attempted to analyze and publicly report on Board statistics. But CPD officers and the public should not have to rely upon the voluntary efforts of a third party to have access to data about the Board's work, and this system leaves the public guessing about whether publicly available data is accurate or complete.

I. The City's Police Accountability Ordinance and Similar Efforts to Correct the Problems Our Investigation Identified

As discussed above, the City's Police Accountability Ordinance created COPA, which will replace IPRA as the independent agency responsible for investigating serious police misconduct. Besides the name change, COPA's main differences with its predecessor include (1) expanded investigative authority, (2) a guaranteed budget floor, (3) authority to hire independent counsel, (4) a five-year ban on former police officers serving as investigators, and (5) a modified mediation program. These changes and other recent IPRA-initiated reforms are positive steps to enhance police accountability.

But the reforms do not directly address the many problems we identified with IPRA's deeply flawed investigative system. For example, as discussed above, it is

---

168 The City's ostensible reason for not releasing videos is that witnesses might not be willing to testify if they knew video of their testimony would be released. This argument is unpersuasive, as it ignores the availability of image-blurring technology and the ability to redact witness names, and the fact that the City currently makes no attempt to redact the names of witnesses from the transcripts it releases. It also ignores that the Board's hearings are already open to the public.

not clear that COPA's increased budget will be enough to satisfy both its existing investigative duties conveyed from IPRA as well as COPA's expanded investigative obligations. And while the new law attempts to correct IPRA's inappropriate use of mediation, it can still be used for many serious cases not appropriate for mediation and defers until later the precise policies under which the new mediation program will operate. Allowing for independent counsel and limiting new employees with police backgrounds will enhance independence, but may not be sufficient. Finally, if none of these changes fixes the defective investigative practices identified in the Accountability Section under IPRA, then COPA's expanded investigative authority simply exacerbates these investigative problems.

The City believes that IPRA's newly published operational rules will increase investigative oversight, facilitate coordination with the Law Department, and improve processes for affidavit overrides and officer-involved shootings. The test will be in how well these new rules are implemented. The City likewise highlights its plans for new investigator training, as discussed above, and new information technology. These plans are a positive first step. COPA is just beginning to engage consultants, who will help diagnose the training and IT problems and only then will set out to develop a plan.

COPA's success in the public eye will depend on how well it addresses the credibility crisis that IPRA faced for most of its existence. The City understands this, which in large part drove its decision to change IPRA's name to COPA. Indeed, all of new changes contained in the COPA ordinance as well as the recent programmatic reforms could have been accomplished without creating COPA. However, the City believed that IPRA's reputation in the community was so badly damaged that it needed a new name. But the City must do more than a name change to repair the broken trust that surrounds this investigative agency, particularly since most residents remember the last time the City employed this same rebranding strategy eight years ago when it replaced OPS with IPRA.

Finally, COPA's companion ordinance creates a new deputy inspector general for public safety who will be charged with initiating reviews and audits of CPD, COPA, and the Police Board. These are welcome changes from an accountability standpoint, and certainly the Inspector General's Office has a level of community support and respect that surpasses the other agencies in Chicago's police accountability network. The description of how these new duties will be interpreted and implemented has yet to be decided, and will impact this position's effectiveness. Moreover, while this new deputy inspector general has authority to make recommendations to COPA and CPD that may impact misconduct investigations, it has no enforcement power. The City has made important strides in improving accountability, but the systemic and entrenched nature of the deficiencies we identified cannot be remedied by these reforms alone.

IV. CPD DOES NOT PROVIDE OFFICERS WITH SUFFICIENT DIRECTION, SUPERVISION, OR SUPPORT TO ENSURE LAWFUL AND EFFECTIVE POLICING

A. Training

Our investigation revealed engrained deficiencies in the systems CPD uses to provide officers with supervision and training. CPD's inattention to training needs, including a longstanding failure to invest in the resources, facilities, staffing, and planning required to train a department of approximately 12,000 members, leaves officers underprepared to police effectively and lawfully. Officer errors and misconceptions that result from lack of training are not corrected in the field, because CPD has neither structured supervision in a way that will adequately support officers, nor invested in programs and systems that will detect when officers are in need of help or exhibiting behavior that must be corrected. Officers' ability to stay safe, protect public safety, and police within constitutional standards suffers as a result.

To set and maintain a culture of policing safely, effectively and constitutionally, a law enforcement agency must provide its officers strong training both at the outset and throughout their careers. Proper training gives officers the confidence and knowledge to police safely and effectively. Training at all levels—pre-service, in-service, and in the field—should foster communication, problem-solving, and analytical skills; facilitate acceptance of community policing principles and tactics; and encourage creative thinking. Training also shows officers how effective policing is not only consistent with, but bolstered by, police tactics that abide by the law and build stakeholder trust. Effective training is delivered through meaningful content, not just hours sitting in a classroom. A solid foundation of recruit training, field training for new officers, and ongoing in-service training ensures a culture of respectful and lawful policing that is active and effective. Through the course of their careers, police officers confront stressors, discouragements, and shifting legal and policy ground. Effective training helps them navigate those challenges, and is crucial not only for the safety of the public, but also for the safety of the officers themselves.

CPD and the City of Chicago have not provided such training to CPD officers for many years, to the disservice not only of those officers but to the public they serve. CPD's Academy training and post-Academy field training program do not sufficiently prepare new CPD officers for their jobs, and the absence of meaningful, regular in-service training prevents officers from reinforcing previously-learned material and gaining knowledge of current policy, legal issues, tactical developments, and police operations.

Officers at all ranks—from new recruits to the Superintendent—agree that CPD's training is inadequate. The City has announced steps that, if properly resourced and effectively staffed, could represent critical improvements to the way that officers are trained throughout their police careers. These announcements are welcomed, but cannot be allowed to languish or to be handled in a quick, reactive manner, which is how officers characterized prior trainings that were only provided in response to a crisis of the moment. As the City's training consultant stated, "implementation will be complicated and will be a long term process." It also will be costly and involve difficult decisions. Our investigation makes clear both that this effort is well worth it, and that the City must sustain focus on its ambitious set of reforms.[169]

1. CPD Academy training does not instill in new recruits a culture of service towards all Chicago communities or the tenets of constitutional policing

Academy training is foundational to building the knowledge and skills needed to protect public safety and earn community trust. Effective Academy training not only teaches recruits of their obligations under law, policy, and widely accepted law enforcement standards; it is also the first opportunity to acculturate new officers with the Department's values and priorities. Academy training should therefore instill recruits with the ethos that protecting all facets of the Chicago community, especially those that are most beleaguered by crime, is their core function and primary responsibility. This ethos is sometimes framed as a "guardian" mindset, as opposed to an inordinately fear-based "warrior" mentality.[170]

Unfortunately, CPD's Academy does not meet these objectives. Instead, it has, for many years, suffered from severe deficiencies that impede recruits' preparedness to police constitutionally and safely. CPD's Academy provides recruits with approximately 1,000 hours of training on a variety of topics, includ-

---

169 During the course of our investigation, the City acknowledged problems with CPD's training systems and sought immediate input from our investigative team on potential reforms. In response, we assisted CPD with securing immediate substantial technical assistance from another large city agency. The City also hired an independent consultant to conduct a full review of CPD's training program to identify deficiencies and potential solutions. At the City's request, our team spoke with this consultant to share our observations in order to assist his review. At the conclusion of the consultant's review, the City agreed to let us meet with the consultant to discuss his recommended reforms but did not provide a copy of the consultant's report or relate the conclusions he reached that justified the reforms he recommended.

170 SUE RAHR, ET AL., FROM WARRIORS TO GUARDIANS: RECOMMITTING AMERICAN POLICE CULTURE TO DEMOCRATIC IDEALS (New Perspectives in Policing Bull., April 2015), available at https://www.ncjrs.gov/pdffiles1/nij/248654.pdf; Seth Stoughton, *Law Enforcement's "Warrior" Problem*, 128 HARV. L. REV. F. 225 (2015), available at http://harvard-lawreview.org/2015/04/law-enforcements-warrior-problem/.

ing firearms, use of force/control tactics, gangs, vehicle stops, law enforcement driving, and report writing. However, there has been insufficient attention to whether training content matches recruit training needs; the validity of training materials; and to whether this content is effectively delivered. The Academy program relies on outdated materials that fail to account for updates in legal standards, widely accepted law enforcement standards, and departmental policies.

As just one example, a class we observed on deadly force involved officers viewing a video made roughly 35 years ago, prior to key Supreme Court decisions that altered the standards used to evaluate the reasonableness of use of force. The tactics depicted in the video were clearly out of date with commonly accepted police standards of today. Following the video, the instructor spoke for approximately thirty minutes, but did not give detailed information on justified versus unjustified use of deadly force or the standard of objective reasonableness—all essential topics for deadly force training. The training itself was inconsistent with CPD's force policies, further undermining its utility in teaching recruits their obligations under Department policy and constitutional law. Several recruits were not paying attention, one appeared to be sleeping, and there was minimal attempt made to engage the students in the lesson. In fact, the instructor arrived to the class ten minutes late and dismissed students twenty minutes early from this critical class on how CPD officers should use deadly force. The impact of this poor training was apparent. At the academy and during ride-alongs, our retained training law enforcement expert asked several PPOs to articulate when use of force would be justified in the field; only one PPO out of six came close to properly articulating the legal standard for use of force.

We observed over 60 hours of training at the CPD Academy, and found that poor delivery of Academy training was pervasive. Rather than pursue widely accepted teaching methods centered on adult learning principles, in particular scenario-based training and encouraging hands-on skills, CPD continues to employ ineffective strategies to train its new recruits. CPD's Academy curriculum is over-reliant on the PowerPoint/lecture model of classroom instruction, broadly acknowledged as one of the least effective ways to train new recruits. One CPD training supervisor referred to this type of training as "check-the-box" training, meaning that the emphasis is on making a record of having provided the training as opposed to actually providing effective instruction. As discussed further below, these problems with training content and delivery are compounded by significant inadequacies in staffing and facilities.

In observing one of the scenario-based trainings that was offered, we found that Academy staff seemed unfamiliar with how to properly run or evaluate role-play exercises. As part of this training, recruits were "dispatched" to a call for service inside of the training building, and all staff instructors were inside the building role-playing in the scenario. No staff instructors were on the outside of the building to watch and evaluate the approach of the recruits, nor were any instructors assigned as evaluators. If they had been outside the building, the instructors would have noticed the recruits parking in front of the location of the call—a practice that exposes them to unknown dangers and places them at a tactical disadvantage. After observing this, our expert concluded that "trainings such as this instill bad tactics and often, bad tactics lead officers into a situation that requires a use of force that could otherwise have been avoided." Our discussion in the <u>Force</u> Section of this Report confirms that this training may well have instilled bad tactics that have led to avoidable force.

To be sure, we did observe some scenario-based training that seemed well-done, particularly during the newly developed Force Mitigation/Mental Health training, as well as in other contexts at the Academy. We observed one instructor during a scenario give proper instruction on handcuffing and cautioning that a subject may react if he is in pain, noting the importance of not jumping to an unwarranted conclusion that the subject is resisting. The instructor conducted a solid de-brief following the exercise and ensured the students understood the material. However, we did not observe this quality of instruction in many other trainings we observed.

Many of the Department members we spoke with during ride-alongs, district tours, interviews, and small-group meetings confirmed the inadequacies described above. One officer said that Academy instructors are unable to go "off script" and deviate from the PowerPoint lectures, and that at least one Academy instructor was teaching an outdated procedure that had not been used in years. Speaking about instruction at the Academy more generally, another officer told us that "[CPD's] training was fast, sloppy, and it's getting people in trouble." A training official lamented that "CPD is using litigation to measure training effectiveness," i.e., the lack of quality training is resulting in civil lawsuits. Another officer put it more starkly, stating simply, "our co-workers are going to die because of no training."

Because training and the evaluation of its impact on new recruits is so deficient, CPD cannot properly identify which recruits need further training or even dismissal, resulting in new recruits policing Chicago communities who, despite their best intentions, from the outset are illequipped and perhaps incapable of policing effectively and constitutionally. Indeed, while precise figures regarding Academy attrition rates are difficult to obtain, CPD officials expressed that the attrition rate is "very close to zero" and thus well below normal levels present in police academies across the country. CPD recognizes that changes are needed. In the last few months, CPD began to plan for potential changes to the Academy training program, including, among other things, forming a "Recruit Curriculum Working Group" to review the current curriculum and suggest changes; searching for new instructors; and creating "feedback loops" to identify trends and deficiencies where training must be improved. As stated earlier, CPD and the City's recognition of these issues is laudable, but must be accompanied by concrete plans to implement these changes, including through additional resources and staffing.

2. CPD's Field Training Program undermines effective and lawful policing

Similar to the Academy, CPD's post-Academy Field Training Program is poorly structured and operates in a manner that actively undermines, rather than reinforces, constitutional policing. In a functioning field training program, once recruits graduate from the Academy, they are paired, one-on-one, with an experienced Field Training Officer (FTO) for hands-on mentorship, training and evaluation. A strong field training program is essential for reinforcing the policies and practices recruits learn at the Academy. When done correctly, FTOs serve a vital role in engraining within probationary police officers (PPOs) an ethic of effective and constitutional policing that will guide them throughout their carriers. Conversely, a weak FTO program can blunt even the most effective Academy training program.

CPD's FTO program suffers from longstanding systemic deficiencies that have disabled the program's ability to serve this function. One high-ranking official in CPD's Education and Training Division repeatedly referred to the Field Training Program as a "hot mess;" another official described the program simply as "terrible." A third supervisor told us that FTOs are simply "warm butts in a seat" and that is all that matters to CPD. CPD officials also told our retained law enforcement training expert that it was common knowledge that anyone entering the field training program would make it through, meaning that, much like the Academy, the FTO program is not set up to distinguish capable recruits from ill-suited ones. Significant changes to the Field Training Program are necessary to ensure PPOs are adequately prepared to police constitutionally and safely.

CPD does not currently deploy a sufficient number of qualified FTOs to meet the field training demands of the Department. During our tours and ride-alongs in various CPD districts, we consistently observed FTOs responsible for two PPOs at a time, and were told by CPD officers that FTOs can even supervise three PPOs at a time. Three PPOs per FTO is bad practice, and even two per FTO may undermine the effectiveness of the program. When FTOs are assigned more than one PPO, they are not able to develop the rapport conducive to the sometimes difficult redirection new recruits need. Nor is the FTO able to adequately observe and provide instruction.

One reason CPD's Field Training Program remains unsuccessful is that the selection process knowingly discourages many of the most-qualified officers from serving as FTOs and allows problematic police officers to continue acting as FTOs. CPD officers wishing to serve as FTOs must meet certain minimum qualifications to be considered. Interested officers apply in response to a vacancy announcement and sit for an exam. Officers' leadership, mentorship, or instructional skills are not necessarily considered in selecting new FTOs. An officer's disciplinary record bears on his or her eligibility to serve as an FTO only where the officer has sustained misconduct investigations that resulted in suspensions of more than seven days in the last twelve months, or three or more sustained investigations resulting in suspensions of any length in the last five years. Another reason for the failures of the program is that officers working as FTOs must be willing to relinquish control of their district and shift assignments. This dis-incentivizes officers with significant experience, who because of their years of service qualify via CPD's assignment system for coveted posts and shifts, from applying for FTO positions. Additionally, being an FTO is not viewed by CPD officers as a prestigious position because unlike other departments in which serving as an FTO is a stepping stone to promotion, CPD FTOs receive no such benefit. Working as an FTO comes with a pay increase, but the amount is viewed by officers we spoke with as negligible—only a little more than $3,000 per year. As one supervising training official described it, serving as an FTO is a "road to nowhere."

The Department has done little to make this crucial training position more attractive, despite the fact that these problems with CPD's FTO program are not new. In 1997, the mayoral Commission on Police Integrity noted that "the FTO program is currently understaffed and in need of a complete overhaul." More specifically, the Commission recommended that the "number of FTOs should be expanded from its current level of 67 officers to at least 200 officers." The Commission also recommended increasing the FTO salary to attract a larger number of officers to the position and "to ensure that good patrol officers want the job." By 2014, CPD had added some, but not many, new FTOs, and committed to building the program to at least 150 FTOs. Yet, years later, CPD has not met even this limited goal, or heeded decades of recommendations that the FTO program be substantially expanded. FTO pay was never significantly increased, and the program was never adequately expanded. Currently, there are only around 107 FTOs for the entire Department. The Deputy Chief in charge of Training estimates that the number of FTOs actually available, due to furloughs and medical absences, is closer to 60 to 75.

Further, because the City does not consider the limited number of FTOs when hiring new recruit classes, recently-graduated PPOs are often forced to wait for Field Training Program spots to become available before being assigned to an FTO. In the past, PPOs awaiting placement in the Field Training Program were assigned to "hot zones" around the city—areas of high crime—to increase police visibility. This practice, referred to by some officers as "Operation Impact Zone," placed PPOs on foot patrol in locations where they do not have the experience or training necessary to deal with situations that may arise. Although the PPOs are just there to provide presence, and are not supposed to take any action in response to criminal activity, this type of assignment can still negatively impact PPOs' views of their job; they are justifiably unprepared and overwhelmed by these assignments, which impacts their acceptance of community policing principles, decreases their confidence, and clouds their perception of those communities. Placement of inexperienced officers as a show of force also negatively impacts those communities' views of CPD. Such placements could last up to three months while the PPO awaits placement with an FTO. Although we were told that "Operation Impact Zone" has ceased, we understand that PPOs may still be assigned to foot patrols downtown or on parade routes, without adequate supervision, while awaiting openings in the Field Training Program. No matter where they are assigned, placement of PPOs on patrols without an FTO prior to completion of the Field Training Program is dangerous, and demonstrates CPD's disregard of the training necessary for new officers to do their jobs safely, effectively, and lawfully.

When recruits are able to enter the FTO program, they do not receive sufficient supervision and guidance. In addition to supervising too many PPOs at one time, we observed that FTOs do not operate according to any uniform protocols. One more experienced FTO we spoke with reported receiving no training prior to becoming an FTO. Although there is now a five-week FTO training program in place, more senior FTOs may have not received any training at all. Even with a five-week training, we observed that there is no consistency in how FTOs teach and mentor their PPOs, meaning that the quality and content of instruction varies significantly Department-wide. Our retained law enforcement training expert observed FTOs and PPOs interacting and found that the FTOs did not provide proper redirection. For example, our expert observed a PPO driving erratically and making rude and disrespectful comments about the community in the presence of the FTO, but the FTO did not correct this behavior. And further demonstrating how problematic CPD's poor FTO instruction and overall training program can be, CPD's FTOs frequently tell PPOs to "throw out" what they learned in the Academy because the FTOs will show them how to "be the police." The quality of the supervision and training a PPO receives from his or her FTO directly impacts whether the PPO's policing will reflect the Department's values. FTOs' unwillingness to reinforce Academy training, whether because they accurately judge it to be inadequate or because they do not respect CPD's core values, sends a perilous message to recruits and undermines any improved polices or procedures intended to inculcate a culture of respectful and constitutional policing.

Finally, CPD does not evaluate the effectiveness of the FTOs or the FTO program as a whole. Although, pursuant to the hiring criteria for FTOs, an FTO may be relieved of FTO responsibilities if he or she demonstrates a lack of knowledge, skills, or abilities for the assignment, training academy personnel confirmed that FTOs are never actually evaluated in this regard. FTOs are under the command of the Bureau of Patrol, and therefore despite serving a critical role in the training of new officers, they are not evaluated or held accountable by the Education and Training Division. Neither the Bureau of Patrol nor the Education and Training Division engages in regular auditing of the Program or solicits feedback to determine areas for improvement, and the City's proposed reforms make no mention of how any of its proposed changes will address this need.

As with other aspects of CPD's training program, CPD recognizes that the FTO program is in need of a significant overhaul. CPD has acknowledged that several changes are needed, including hiring more FTOs, identifying ways to incentivize more qualified officers to apply for FTO positions, "upgrading the supervisory structure" for the FTO program so that there are supervisors in the districts who oversee the program, and putting systems in place to ensure that the FTO program is more closely coordinated with the Academy. The City also is planning on "upgrading the system for evaluating FTOs" and PPOs. These reforms, however, like the proposed reforms to CPD's Academy, are in the very initial stages, and CPD has no concrete plan for how, or by when, these goals will be accomplished.

3. CPD provides only sporadic in-service training

Once a CPD officer leaves the Academy, he or she is not required to participate in any live, regular annual training for the remainder of his or her career. Instead, CPD's mandatory inservice training consists of last-minute reactive trainings, as described below; videos played at roll call; and "e-learning" courses provided online. One officer summarized CPD's entire post-Academy training program as "Watch a Video."

The impact of the lack of in-service training cannot be overstated. Without regular, mandatory training, CPD officers do not receive ongoing instruction on critically important topics, such as proper use of force, responding to persons in mental health crisis, handling domestic violence calls, or updates in the law regarding stops and searches. This prevents officers from accepting and emulating a culture of constitutional and fair policing. It also inhibits officer confidence that they know how to do their jobs safely and effectively.

CPD also does not provide regular refresher trainings on important basic skills that can help reduce the need for the use of force, including deadly force. These include proper handcuffing techniques and pursuit tactics. At a minimum, generally accepted police practices dictate at least 40 hours of continuing education per year, which usually includes roughly 24 hours of force-refresher skills. Several CPD officers reported to us that, once they left the Academy, they were not required to retrain on any basic skills. CPD officers must qualify on their firearms annually, but qualification is not training. As discussed in the Force Section of this Report, our review of CPD force, including hundreds of force incidents and several video-recorded incidents of CPD uses of force, revealed CPD officers engaging in dangerous tactics that indicate they do not remember or were never taught basic police skills. This results in officers approaching suspect vehicles in a manner that puts officers and civilians in jeopardy; firing at fleeing vehicles in inappropriate circumstances; using force unreasonably; and failing to render aid to suspects who have been shot. Consistent with our review, interviewees were unanimous in their belief that the lack of continuing training has a direct connection to the improper use of force in patrol and other field assignments.

In-service training also is necessary to teach officers about changes in law, technology, community expectations, and developments in national police practices and for presenting changes to Department policy. CPD does not use regular in-service training to meet either of these important objectives. Instead, officers reported that they do not receive sufficient training when policies change, and they worry that they will be criticized for not adhering to a policy that was never explained to them. By not providing regular in-service trainings, CPD makes it unnecessarily difficult for officers to remain aware of changes to law and policy and how to operationalize those changes.

In lieu of actual in-service training, CPD disseminates new information to Department members through roll call, using techniques that are not effective for adult learning and often not appropriate for the complexity of the material being presented. In-service training comes primarily through videos or announcements by supervisors at roll call, or videos available through e-learning modules. Supervisors acknowledge that officers do not pay attention to these trainings. CPD also more generally recognizes that this is an ineffective way to provide new material or refresh previously learned lessons, as roll-call trainings and e-learning videos do not teach skills, and it is difficult to measure learning.

CPD recognizes that providing real in-service training is necessary to build a more effective and qualified police force, and is just beginning to develop plans to institute a comprehensive in-service program. CPD informed us that, going forward, it would like to provide 40 hours of mandatory in-service training for all Department members through a combination of Academy-based and district-based training. CPD still needs to do an assessment of what courses are needed most; create a process for developing, vetting, and reviewing those courses; and identify how and when that training could be delivered. CPD has also not considered whether additional in-service training may be necessary up front, given that there has not been any regular in-service training for years. Once again, CPD's plans for in-service training, while ambitious and potentially beneficial to the Department, are very preliminary, and it remains to be seen whether CPD's stated commitment to more in-service training will actually translate into the sustainable, effective provision of such training in the months and years to come.

4. CPD does not provide training that is proactive, organized, and tailored to Department needs

Until a few weeks ago, CPD did not have a committee tasked with identifying the Department's training needs and establishing priorities, or making sure that training is delivered efficiently, timely, and effectively. The training committee is in the first stages of developing a training plan.[171] The previous absence of a committee and plan has prevented CPD from providing training that is proactive and comprehensive. Currently, although most training is coordinated through the Training and Education Division, there are no protocols for the development, coordination, or delivery of training. Proper planning in this area would help CPD allocate its resources to meet the greatest departmental needs and deliver a cohesive message to Department members about the vision, mission, and culture of the agency. Developing a comprehensive training plan will help in developing trainings that give officers the ability to connect policy to practice, which, in turn, will increase officer confidence that their training as a whole has taught them how to police safely, lawfully, and effectively.

In particular, CPD has not attempted to ascertain the training needs of experienced officers or where additional training might benefit particular units or the Department as a whole. CPD does not actively solicit suggestions from Department members for future trainings, or follow through on requests from officers for training on particular topics. And, as noted elsewhere in this Report, CPD does not use data to evaluate trends of problems within the Department, including patterns of excessive force or other misconduct. CPD has recognized this failure and reports that it plans to develop "feedback loops" from various

---

171 Like many of the other recent training reforms noted above, the City apparently recognized the significant problems attendant to providing training without any strategic plan or guiding committee. The City recently informed us that it established a new "Training Oversight Committee" chaired by the First Deputy Superintendent. This committee is reportedly responsible for establishing, implementing, and overseeing all CPD training, creating strategic plans, and conducting periodic needs assessments. The formation of this committee is an important step. However, as discussed more fully below, additional steps are necessary to ensure the work of the committee is widely accepted and that its goals and objectives can, and will, be met.

stakeholders to inform training. This prospective reform is critical; the historic failure to proactively evaluate trends has blinded CPD to understanding where additional trainings could both improve performance and community relations, and decrease harmful incidents and CPD's exposure to liability.

CPD's overall lack of planning results in training that is ad hoc, disorganized, and reactive to the most recent crisis, rather than thoughtful, proactive, and demonstrably responsive to officers' training needs. Because there is no regular, mandatory in-service training, post-Academy training is offered primarily in response to crises, such as high-profile officer-involved shootings or other uses of force. City leadership is, and should be, responsive to the legitimate concerns of its constituents; but at the same time, CPD should be given time, space and resources to develop thoughtful and effective training that is sustainable.

Instead, training staff are told to "get it done" and "make it work" quickly. Such trainings are often scheduled with only a few days of notice. As a result, the Education and Training Division is not given sufficient time to identify or develop an appropriate curriculum or secure trainers with subject matter expertise. Similarly, although the Academy has a set curriculum, recruit classes often begin on short notice, leaving Division staff little time to secure qualified subject matter experts to train on the various topics. As a result, trainers are often ill-equipped to present the material they are scheduled to teach, decreasing the potential impact of the training.

This haphazard approach to training also hinders officer buy-in that the training being provided is important and valuable for their jobs. Officers feel that CPD trains only in response to crises, rather than pursuant to measured, thoughtful consideration of officers' training needs and desires.

CPD's recent experience introducing Investigatory Stop Reports (ISRs) underscores the consequences of CPD's approach. ISRs require officers to document their stops and searches more systematically than they had done previously. Although instituted in CPD to resolve an ACLU lawsuit,[172] documenting stops and searches in the manner captured by ISRs is a practice that has been in place for many years in other large-city police departments. In Chicago, the new ISR forms were quickly rolled out without a thoughtful, comprehensive training plan that took into account officers' predictable concerns and the broader context. Instead of taking the opportunity to instruct officers about how to conduct lawful and safe stops and searches, the ISR training focused only on how to fill out the new form. The training failed to anticipate or address officers' fears that filling out these forms would subject them to individ-

---

172 American Civil Liberties Union of Illinois, Landmark Agreement Reached on Investigatory Stops in Chicago (Aug. 7, 2015), available at http://www.aclu-il.org/landmark-agreement-reached-on-investigatory-stops-in-chicago/.

ual liability. Supervisors did not receive training before their subordinates did, and were therefore unprepared to provide guidance; officers found the forms onerous and confusing, and did not understand why the changes were instituted. When officers belatedly received training, they found it inconsistent and contradictory. CPD's failure to plan or deliver this training properly increased officers' frustration and fear that this change was being driven by the need for political cover instead of as an integral part of policing the community safely and effectively. As a consequence, many officers do not support the reforms or understand how to implement them effectively. This reaction likely could have been minimized if CPD had appropriately planned this training, and delivered it in the context of a robust in-service training program that addresses connected issues, such as constitutional policing and CPD policies on stops, searches, and arrests.

Similarly, in response to the release of the Laquan MacDonald video in November 2015, the City mandated that all CPD officers be trained on Taser use by June 1, 2016. Effective training on this skill requires small class sizes so that officers have the opportunity to practice using the device in various scenarios, and engage with the instructor to ensure they understand the concepts, including when and how it is appropriate to use a Taser. It also requires a thoughtful curriculum that provides officers with direction on how to avoid the need to use force, while giving them confidence in using the weapon where necessary. CPD, however, quickly cycled large numbers of officers through poorly designed training. As a result, officers were not effectively taught how or when to use the Taser as a less-lethal force option. Many CPD officers told us the training they received did not adequately prepare them to use Tasers in the field. One officer told us that officers had been requesting Taser training for years, but those requests went unfulfilled until the City suddenly changed course. As he put it, "the City's lack of preparation is now our emergency."

This crisis-driven approach to in-service training does a disservice to both CPD officers and the public. Advanced planning and organization is necessary to ensure that trainings are effective in positively impacting officer safety and teaching officers the skills they need to do their jobs.

5. CPD's Education and Training Division lacks the resources it needs to provide training that is coordinated, forward-thinking, and effective

a. CPD has insufficient and inexperienced training staff

CPD's Education and Training Division, which runs the Academy, specialized trainings, and the FTO program, is perennially understaffed and staffed with individuals who are not sufficiently trained or prepared to teach the subject matters they are assigned. We found that many instructors are not properly prepared to teach the materials they are assigned, and are not chosen for their qualifications or abilities, but rather only on how they score on a written test. We also found that Academy curriculum is not vetted in any manner by experts in curriculum design and/or instruction, resulting in gaping omissions and gross misapplications of materials developed. We found that the person tasked with developing and teaching the instructor's training course (where teachers are trained on how to teach) was well qualified and had expertise, but the course itself does not use sufficient evaluation instruments for CPD to determine whether, following the training, the trainees are sufficiently prepared to teach.

CPD now recognizes the need for additional training staff, but leadership must be committed—for the long term—to providing the resources necessary to ensure a sufficient number of competent, well-qualified trainers. CPD must invest in recruiting and hiring trainers and curriculum development staff who will develop and deliver progressive, effective training programs, and retrain or replace existing staff to ensure these roles are carried out successfully.

b. CPD has inadequate training space

CPD's training facilities are in disrepair. CPD has made few physical upgrades to its main training facility since it was built in 1976. Training equipment is old and frequently breaks down. This makes conducting trainings difficult, and potentially dangerous. Poor upkeep of C   PD's training facilities also signals to those who work there, those who train there, and to the public, that training is not valued by CPD.

The current facilities used by CPD are also insufficient to meet the training needs of a department as large as CPD. The spaces CPD currently uses for outdoor drills and exercises are not secure. Features typically used to support recruit training are non-existent. CPD lacks, among other facilities, an outdoor shooting range, a driver training area, marching/drill grounds, and mock buildings for scenario-based training. Storage for firearms at the training facilities is not secure. Our expert found CPD's shooting range at the Academy to be "exceptionally substandard." Indeed, firearm training is provided indoors in a building with ventilation so inadequate that it is unhealthy for participants.

One of CPD's scenario training buildings, which houses the Training and Tactics Unit, is dangerous, both because of the dilapidated, inadequate facility, and the lack of adequate safety protocols. When we visited, this facility did not have locked main doors. The armory room—a former school office—was unlocked with loaded guns left in open, unlocked cubbies in a room left unattended. Training guns and ammunition were stored close to guns loaded with live rounds. The close proximity of these materials, without adequate controls or labels, created a serious risk that the real guns would be mistaken for training ones, or that the guns and ammunition could go missing or be stolen.[173]

CPD leadership recognizes that the training facilities are inadequate. However, CPD has not dedicated adequate resources to remedying these conditions, significantly impacting the quality and breadth of trainings CPD is able to provide. The need to allocate additional resources to the Education and Training Division is especially urgent in light of the City's stated plans to hire nearly 1,000 new officers. This hiring would require the Education and Training Division to run huge classes through the Academy each month—while completing recently mandated specialized training, such as the force mitigation/de-escalation training, for the approximately 12,500 current officers. The Division does not have sufficient personnel, equipment, or space to meet these demands.

6. CPD's current plans for reform

CPD recognizes that whole-scale changes are needed to its training program, and that these changes should be guided by a comprehensive training committee and plan. CPD told us of an ambitious dashboard of changes to its Academy, in-service, pre-service, and FTO training. Currently these plans amount to verbal commitments with uncertain dates for completion. These plans should be committed to writing. Some of the changes CPD would like to make—such as limiting Academy instructor tenure, or adding new incentives to encourage quality officers to serve as FTOs—may impact the City's collective bargaining agreements. Moreover, CPD must identify the resources necessary to make these changes or obtain commitments from the City to provide what is needed. CPD should be empowered with the resources and support it needs to make changes in the best interest of the officers and the public they serve.

We commend CPD for conducting a review of its training program using an expert consultant, and for recognizing and accepting the longstanding deficiencies with the training program that this expert identified. CPD's willingness to identify these problems and work towards solutions is an important first step in bringing CPD's training program in line with national standards. However, as CPD's own expert put it, "the devil is in the details." With many of the recommendations CPD reportedly embraced, CPD has not yet worked out whether these reforms are possible given CPD's current infrastructure, resources, and personnel, and if the reforms *are* possible, precisely how they

---

173 A second facility used for scenario training is on a public street, in close proximity to an elementary school. Conducting scenario trainings in such a setting puts the public at risk.

will be accomplished, and by when. As noted by CPD's consultant, significant external pressures are necessary for any organization to follow through with plans as ambitious as these.

B. Supervision

Instead of encouraging the chain of command to instill proper policing tactics and respect for constitutional policing in CPD officers, CPD provides little incentive, or even opportunity, for supervisors to meaningfully guide and direct CPD officers. CPD provides even less incentive for supervisors to hold officers accountable when they deviate from CPD policy and the law. The City has long known that CPD's direct supervision of officers is inadequate, including through the fact that multiple reports in the last two decades have highlighted deficiencies in CPD's supervisory practices. Yet, City and CPD leadership have not made the necessary reforms to CPD's supervision structure and processes, and community and officer safety suffer as a result. Providing robust, meaningful supervision would better prevent officer misconduct and would significantly help CPD police safely and effectively.

Our conversations with rank-and-file Department members, and our observations throughout each of CPD's 22 districts, illuminated the breadth and depth of CPD's failure to provide proper supervision. Our overarching impression of supervisors from officers is that, with notable exceptions, supervisors do not lead. We were told on several occasions that sergeants are "not there to ruffle any feathers." Rather than ensuring that officers under their watch are policing constitutionally, many sergeants instead focus on keeping their subordinates out of trouble when there may be reason for discipline. Supervisors do not review the personnel records of the officers they are supervising, either because they do not know how, they do not have access to the information, or they do not see the value in doing so. See Report, Section IV.D. Consistent with this broad sense among officers, supervisors told us they are wary of intervening to correct rule or tactical errors, because "no one wants to be the bad guy." As one commander framed the problem, "supervisors lack courage to hold officers accountable." We also heard from several Department members that supervisors, particularly sergeants and lieutenants, are more concerned with being "friends" with their subordinates than providing adequate supervision. As one deputy chief told us, "we have a culture where we [the supervisors] are people's friends rather than supervisors." Another deputy chief stated that supervisors stay "too close" to their former peers after being promoted, which is why "many of them do not step up to the task" of adequately supervising and holding accountable those under their command.

It has long been recognized that first-level supervisors, through their action or inaction, profoundly affect the performance of the officers under their command.[174] In the patrol setting, sergeants are most directly involved in setting the tone of policing on the street. Sergeants who take a lax approach to supervision foster an environment in which mediocrity and misconduct flourish. As one former police manager observed,

> Police officers are extremely sensitive and attuned to what fellow officers do and do not do. Officers know who files false injury claims, who the second car is on a "man with a gun" call, who steps over the line with excessive force, and who is likely to get lost for a full tour of duty. When officers in the middle of the bell curve see that these people are not dealt with, they sometimes begin to imitate their behavior. Similarly, when those in the middle of the bell curve see fellow officers take extra calls, quickly respond as backup, and testify clearly and honestly, they begin to imitate them as well.[175]

It is readily apparent that there is a critical failure of leadership at the first line of supervision within CPD. Officers provide little documentation of their activities—particularly with respect to use of force—and sergeants consistently take a hands-off approach to the means by which officers take enforcement actions. As discussed in the Force Section of this Report, supervisors provide very little supervision of officers' use of force. With the exception of officer-involved shootings, officers are not required to provide details of the incidents in which force was used, and little is done to investigate whether the force used was reasonable, and/or whether policies, training, or equipment should be modified to improve force outcomes in the future. Sergeants informed us that, in reviewing a use of force, their role simply is to ensure the form is filled out correctly. Our review of files confirmed this—in most of the Tactical Response Report (TRR) files we reviewed, we saw no evidence that sergeants took steps to determine what force officers had used and whether it was appropriate, lawful, or safe. Supervisors do not hold officers accountable for the force they use, and supervisors are themselves not held accountable for failing to investigate whether

---

174 *See*, e.g., ROBIN SHEPARD ENGEL, HOW POLICE SUPERVISORY STYLES INFLUENCE PATROL OFFICER BEHAVIOR (Nat'l Inst. of Justice, June 2003), available at https://www .ncjrs.gov/pdffiles1/nij/194078.pdf (a study of leadership styles in urban police departments that found that an active leadership style "was more likely than the others to influence officer behavior" and that this "influence can be either positive or negative; for example, it can inspire subordinates to engage in more problem-solving activities, or it can result in more frequent use of force").

175 STEPHEN J. GAFFIGAN, POLICE INTEGRITY: PUBLIC SERVICE WITH HONOR 36 (Nat'l Inst. of Justice & Cmty. Oriented Policing Serv.'s 1997), available at https://www.ncjrs.gov /pdffiles/163811.pdf (comments of former Metropolitan Police Department Captain Swope).

force used by officers under their command was proper. This failure to provide first line supervision of officers' use of force contributed to the pattern or practice of unconstitutional force we found. CPD has not taken the necessary steps to transform supervision within CPD. As discussed further below, CPD does not provide sufficient training for supervisors. CPD also fails to hold supervisors accountable when they do not hold officers accountable or do not provide the oversight and direction that might prevent officers from committing misconduct or policing poorly. As discussed below, supervisors who do not report the misconduct of their subordinates—or worse, supervisors who cover up that misconduct—are rarely held accountable, with exceptions in a few high-profile cases. At the same time, CPD does not properly incentivize or reward the courageous and diligent supervisors who swim against this tide to provide close and effective supervision to officers, including through holding officers accountable for violations.

These practices, in combination, send a clear message to all ranks within CPD that close, meaningful supervision is neither valued nor rewarded, which in turn has predictably led to a lack of effective supervision throughout the Department.

1. CPD's supervisory structures and responsibilities do not provide for meaningful supervision of all officers

CPD does not demand that supervisors perform fundamental supervisory tasks, such as direct observation and meaningful evaluation of officer performance, including the quality of arrests or uses of force, or mentoring officers. Many supervisors we spoke with are committed to effective, safe, and constitutional policing within their districts; yet, systemic flaws in what CPD expects of them and the priorities that CPD sets prevent line supervisors from meeting those goals.

a. CPD requires that first-line supervisors spend too much time doing nonsupervisory tasks, at the expense of providing officers supervision

CPD first-line supervisors do not engage in the supervisory tasks typically expected of their positions. Most CPD supervisors with whom we spoke appeared uncertain or reluctant about the role they can and should play in identifying and addressing positive or negative police behavior. Although there are many well-meaning supervisors within CPD's ranks, a large number do not make sufficient efforts to communicate with, observe, instruct, or mentor their subordinates. This results in missed opportunities for subordinates' learning and job improvement, and allows both lackadaisical policing and inappropriately aggressive policing to go unaddressed.

CPD sergeants generally spend their shifts on administrative tasks rather than interacting with and guiding their officers. One officer told us that in general, he would not see a sergeant after roll call. When sergeants do go into the field, too often their supervision is tentative and formalistic. One sergeant told us when he goes into the field, he spends his time "logging" his officers, that is, driving around and laying eyes on each car twice per shift. This means that the sergeant checks boxes and does administrative work instead of providing meaningful oversight or analysis of officer activity.

The lack of true supervision is in part due to the failure of supervisors to see these tasks as part of their role. It is also attributable to the myriad duties placed on supervisors that could, and should, be done by other entities. Sergeants, for example, are bogged down with tasks that would be more appropriately assigned to civilian administrative assistants. CPD employs fewer civilian employees than other large police departments, leaving supervisors to take on administrative tasks that do not involve police work. CPD leadership recognizes that the low number of civilian employees working for CPD results in officers and supervisors spending too much time doing administrative and other tasks, and that additional efforts to change this are needed to bring CPD "up to industry standards." In the last year, the City began a push towards "civilianizing" certain jobs, that is, hiring civilian staff to do work now being done by officers and supervisors. However, during the course of our investigation, we found that the administrative demands on sergeants serve to shift much of the supervision responsibility to lieutenants, even though they too are overburdened with administrative work.

b. A too-broad span of control and lack of unity of command prevents supervisors from performing critical supervisory functions

Even if sergeants and lieutenants understood their role as supervisors and were able to dedicate their entire shift to supervision-related tasks, CPD deploys far too few patrol supervisors to ensure adequate supervision of all officers. The number of officers under a supervisor's watch, often referred to as the "span of control," must be narrow enough for supervisors to be able to interact with the officers, observe their performance, and assist when needed. Prior consultants to the City recommended no more than 10 officers assigned to each sergeant on every watch at each district. Experience in Chicago and elsewhere, however, makes clear that the ratio may need to be even smaller than this in some circumstances. A span of control of seven officers to one sergeant is a generally accepted industry standard, although the appropriate ratio will depend in part on the dynamics of the particular district and assignment. CPD frequently operates under a span of control far greater than this recommended limit, even in the busiest districts. One captain told us that sergeants *should* only supervise

8 officers at a time, and at least one sergeant told us he supervises 12 cars at a time—meaning, potentially, 24 officers, assuming two officers per car. Another officer told us that he has seen 2 supervisors in charge of 70 officers at a time. Yet another officer relayed to us an example where a single sergeant was responsible for an entire district during the day shift. The district included 25 officers on patrol, plus 14 officers stationed in 7 different high schools throughout the district. This left one sergeant in charge of nearly 40 officers spread out over a wide geographic area. In each of these examples, CPD's span of control far exceeds industry standards, which prevents sergeants from providing adequate supervision and jeopardizes the safety of the community and the officers themselves.

CPD's rotational system of scheduling also prevents supervisors from maintaining "unity of command," meaning that officers are not consistently scheduled to be supervised by the same sergeants or lieutenants, or assigned to the same beat. Currently, CPD patrol officers work pursuant to a rotational schedule, where they rotate the days off that they have each week. Officers are not assigned the same days off as their supervisors, meaning that they do not consistently interact with the same supervisor on every shift. This prevents supervisors from establishing mentoring relationships with officers and providing guidance targeted to the particular needs of each individual officer. The lack of consistency also inhibits supervisors from identifying changes in an officer's behavior that may indicate the officer is in need of assistance or disciplinary intervention. Officers complained that this prevents them from getting to know their beat well and doing their job effectively.

These issues are not new. The 2014 study of CPD's supervision and accountability structures conducted for the Safer Report, which the City commissioned, recommended changes to staffing and operational patterns to increase monitoring of officer behavior. In particular, the Safer Report strongly recommended switching from the current rotational system to a "patrol squad system," wherein each patrol sergeant is responsible for developing and monitoring a designated group of officers. It noted that the current system "limit[s] the sergeants' ability to develop officers under their command and creat[es] inconsistencies in management styles and expectations." The Safer Report also warned CPD that its current ratio of sergeants to police officers and lieutenants to sergeants is low, and that "maintaining a healthy ratio of supervisors to subordinates is critical to ensuring proper supervision of each officer." CPD did not adopt the Safer Report's recommendation and made no changes to either span of control or unity of command.

CPD leadership recently publicly recognized that reduction in span of control is needed to allow for "more hands-on guidance and direction in difficult situations." As part of the City's recent efforts, in late September 2016, the Superintendent announced plans to hire 112 sergeants and 50 lieutenants over the next two years to "provide valuable guidance to officers on the street." We agree that more supervisors are needed. However, promoting additional officers alone will not resolve the span of control problems that have plagued CPD for years, especially if the City does not deploy officers and supervisors pursuant to a comprehensive staffing analysis. Notably, CPD recently pledged to develop a "fair, transparent, and objective methodology" to determine where to assign new officers and supervisors. CPD noted that the new study will be more "in-depth" than a previous 2010 study by the same group that analyzed the number of patrol officers needed each shift in each district, because it will consider more variables than just calls for service.

The City must not only plan for the effective deployment of new supervisors, but also address the more deeply entrenched problems in supervision that have previously evaded reform. CPD must actively engage in reforming its culture, the structure and scope of supervisory responsibilities, and its adherence to a rotational schedule that does not consistently place supervisors with the same subordinates. Adding additional supervisors alone will not solve the lack of meaningful supervision within CPD.

2. Supervisors are not trained to provide meaningful supervision

CPD does not adequately train its sergeants and lieutenants to provide meaningful supervision. This failure to train both reflects and contributes to CPD's culture of lax supervision.

Out of the 165 hours of pre-service sergeant training, only 7 hours are dedicated to instruction on leadership, when most new sergeants do not have any previous experience as supervisors. For the May 2015 lieutenant training, out of 134 hours of training, there were no courses dedicated to leadership and supervision skills. Nor do the course schedules for either the sergeant or lieutenant trainings reflect courses in professional development, interpersonal relationships, or other important managerial topics.

The insufficiency of CPD's leadership training is not a recent revelation. The Safer Report recommended adding an informal mentorship program for newly minted sergeants to provide "on-the-job" training designed to teach them how to supervise and monitor other officers for the first time. This suggestion was not adopted. The Safer Report also suggested that supervisors be given more courses in leadership, including courses in "Progressive Coaching," and that CPD should offer these courses on a regular basis rather than only at the Academy. However, in-service training remains as irregular for supervisors as it does for other CPD officers. CPD recently informed us that it will be "upgrading" its supervisory training to provide more training on issues relevant to supervisors, but, like other recently proposed reforms, there is no actual plan in place yet, nor information on the tangible changes CPD envisions or how those changes will be achieved.

3. Supervisors are not held accountable for failing to report misconduct

The supervision failures described above are perhaps most acute when it comes to CPD supervisors' unwillingness to step in to correct their officers' problematic behavior. Under CPD policy, supervisors are obligated to report information regarding misconduct by subordinate officers. Yet, CPD culture discourages supervisors from reporting the misconduct of subordinates.

As one captain told us, sergeants in particular are disinclined to report misconduct because they have to work with their officers every day, and they want to avoid conflict. A lieutenant told us that supervisors are concerned about branding a subordinate officer with a negative employment record by formally reporting their misconduct. A deputy chief told us that CPD operates under a culture "where we are people's friends rather than supervisors," and that "no one wants to be the bad guy." And another deputy chief stated that the widespread supervisory failure to hold officers accountable has caused accountability to become CPD's biggest problem.

This failure to report is particularly strong where the officer committing misconduct is regarded as having impunity because of that officer's connections within the Department. CPD officers we spoke to referred to this as someone who "has a phone call," meaning the officer has the protection of a powerful person in the Department who can influence assignments, promotion, and discipline. Supervisors decline to discipline these officers because any such efforts would not only be futile, but could be counterproductive to their own careers. In turn, these CPD members reportedly are able to engage in misconduct with impunity.

Moreover, IPRA and BIA fail to hold supervisors accountable consistently for their failure to report officer misconduct. Rather, one investigator indicated to us that he uses potential "failure to report" charges against a supervisor as a bargaining chip to get accused officers to mediate their misconduct complaints. In other words, if an investigator wants to encourage an officer to mediate a misconduct complaint, the investigator may tell the officer that if he or she rejects mediation, the investigator will launch a separate investigation against the officer's supervisor for failing to report the alleged misconduct. Investigators told us that this practice was effective in resolving misconduct complaints quickly through mediation.

This failure of supervisors to report misconduct also includes the failure to accept and report complaints of officer misconduct that community members make at the districts. CPD policy requires supervisors to accept, record, and forward such complaints to IPRA, yet supervisors often do not do so. An IPRA investigator told us that individuals who call 911 or a district police station to ask for a CPD supervisor to report officer misconduct are told that their complaint will not be documented by CPD, and that they should call IPRA instead. In another example, two teenage boys and their mothers complained to a supervising sergeant at a CPD district that an officer slammed one of the boys to the ground, cuffed him, shoved a gun in his face, and threatened to blow up the boy's house. The sergeant refused to report the complaint to IPRA as required. The mothers filed a complaint directly with IPRA, and the officer involved in the misconduct was eventually disciplined; IPRA did not, however, sustain allegations against the sergeant for failing to report the officer's misconduct. In another IPRA investigation, a complainant said that she asked a desk sergeant how she could file a complaint of officer abuse and was told to "get the fuck out of the station." This allegation in her complaint was never investigated by IPRA. In yet another file we reviewed, the complainant stated that CPD officers pulled him over, abused him, and stole his car keys, leaving him stranded. The complainant told IPRA that he went to a district to file his complaint, but the sergeant he spoke with refused to take it down.

This evidence and the statements from officers at all ranks within CPD are consistent with the findings of the 2014 Safer Report, which noted that "discovering and addressing misconduct is too often viewed as the responsibility of IPRA and BIA, and not of the offending officer's immediate supervisor and chain of command . . . this attitude is misguided and must be changed." The Mayor's Police Accountability Task Force (PATF) report two years later found the same, explaining that "CPD has fostered a culture in which supervisors turn a blind eye to misconduct and do not provide sufficient oversight to ensure that officers perform their duties with integrity." The City's recently proposed changes to CPD's accountability system do not adequately address this important facet of CPD's culture and supervision structure. More changes are necessary to ensure that supervisors hold their subordinates accountable for misconduct, and if they fail to do so, that they will be held accountable themselves.

4. CPD's "early intervention system" exists in name only and does not assist supervisors in identifying or correcting problematic behavior

Compounding CPD's supervision problems, the Department does not use long-available supervisory tools, such as a comprehensive early intervention system (EIS), to identify patterns of concerning officer behavior and prevent patterns of misconduct and poor policing from developing or persisting. A well-designed EIS would allow CPD to track officer conduct, proactively assess risk for future problematic behavior, and intervene when necessary to improve behavior through non-disciplinary corrective action, such as additional training, counseling, or other supportive programs. Currently, despite having spent significant time and resources building an EIS, CPD does not have a functioning system. Instead, there are several semiconnected data-collection, intervention, and counseling programs, each of which suffers from inefficiencies that render them essentially useless. In a positive development, the City recently began an initiative to revamp and revise its EIS once again. However, for this initiative to have the best chance of success, the City and police unions must negotiate collective bargaining agreements that enable an EIS that is accurate, complete, and that allows for meaningful support of officers by redirecting problematic behavior.

a. Performance Recognition System

One CPD system, an electronic "dashboard" referred to as the Performance Recognition System (PRS), is a computer data-tracking program designed to "assist[] Department Supervisors in recognizing exceptional or adverse behavior related to job performance of members under their command." Data is entered into the system by Human Resources, and supervisors are obligated by policy to "monitor and track, on a continual basis," the information contained in the PRS dashboard.

During conversations with district command staff, we learned that CPD supervisors do not understand how the PRS works or how to use the information it presents. In particular, supervisors do not understand what they are supposed to do when the dashboard shows that "early performance indicators" are present for an officer assigned to their district. For each officer, the various indicators are marked in the dashboard as green, yellow, or red. These indicators include data points such as the number of Summary Punishment Action Reports (SPARs) and complaints filed against the officer; the officer's arrest and TRR numbers; the officer's use of medical leave; and more. The dashboard also provides two ratios: the ratio of complaints to arrests, and the ratio of TRRs to arrests. The thresholds used to determine if an indicator is green versus yellow or red is apparently set by CPD's Human Resources Office. For the TRR ratio, for example, officers with more than a certain percentage of arrests involving force are marked in red. However, at least one commander responsible for using the dashboard did not know the threshold that would turn a TRR ratio from green to yellow or red, including whether the threshold is static or relational (i.e., whether it varies, depending upon, for example, officer assignment). He opined that a straight comparison of number of arrests to number of arrests involving force would be problematic, in that it would mark in red an officer who was involved in only one arrest, but that arrest happened to involve force. Indeed, the commander showed us one officer's record in the PRS dashboard that marked the officer in red; the officer had been involved in two arrests, one of which involved force, meaning that the officer had used force in 50 percent of his arrests. The commander agreed that the ratio was artificially high because the officer had been involved in so few arrests, and intervention in that case was probably inappropriate. Yet, he noted that there is no meaningful guidance given to supervisors about when "red" indicators should trigger a response. Nor does policy dictate what that response should be. Instead, the PRS policy gives examples of potential supervisory responses to "early performance indicators" in vague terms, such as "coaching," "counseling," "reviewing Department training tools," and "field monitoring," and provides little to no guidance regarding the circumstances in which each different form of response should be adopted.

The dashboard is also underused. The command staff we spoke with reported that they rarely use the PRS. Supervisors also question whether data that they enter into the PRS is actually saved. Although supervisors are supposed to review the system regularly, most do not, and CPD does not audit supervisor adherence to this or any other aspect of the PRS policy. The problems with the PRS become cyclical: supervisors do not use it because it is inaccurate, and it is inaccurate because CPD does not use it properly or consistently. As we were told by one supervisor, "the info in the PRS is not accurate[;] . . . you got garbage going in so you got garbage going out."

b. Non-disciplinary intervention, Behavioral Intervention System, and Personnel Concerns Program

CPD also offers three separate intervention programs to which officers can be referred on the basis of certain behavioral criteria, but each of these programs suffers from shortcomings that prevent appropriate enrollment and undermine effectiveness.

First, officers may be subject to "non-disciplinary interventions" when they engage in less-serious transgressions, such as using foul language or being disrespectful. This program triggers intervention by a supervisor after multiple incidents, and the interventions available are limited. They include, among other things, speaking with the officer, reminding the officer of available counseling programs, and instructing the officer to review training videos on courtesy and demeanor. Subsequent incidents trigger increasing interventions, including additional conversations and involvement of rank further up the chain of command.

If there are four or more incidents that would otherwise qualify for non-disciplinary intervention, or if the officer is involved in more serious allegations of misconduct, CPD can refer the officer to the Behavioral Intervention System (BIS) or Personnel Concerns Program (PCP). By policy, Human Resources recommends enrollment in BIS based on the existence of several "performance data," including sustained misconduct charges, low performance grade, or a pre-set number of instances of other misbehaviors such as tardiness, being absent without permission, or medical roll misuse. The ultimate decision of whether to enroll a member in BIS generally rests with the member's commander, although Human Resources may override a commander's decision not to enroll his or her subordinate. Employees enrolled in BIS undergo a physical examination, including drug testing, but are not required to undergo a psychological evaluation. Once placed in BIS, CPD may give employees counseling services or an individual performance plan.

The final option available is the PCP. CPD places Department members into PCP when they are involved in more serious transgressions, such as sustained excessive force charges, domestic violence, or five or more sustained misconduct investigations in the last five years. CPD members who fail to comply with an individualized performance plan under BIS can also be placed in PCP. PCP is essentially the "last stop" for officers exhibiting problematic behavior to correct that behavior and remain on the force.

The BIS and PCP programs are ineffective methods for identifying and remedying patterns of negative behavior. First, policy and officers' collective bargaining agreements prevent these systems from considering the full range of behaviors that could be indicative of a problem. Policy prohibits maintaining misconduct allegations older than five years in PRS, or in some circumstances, considering them at all. With one exception, investigations of misconduct complaints that result in a "not sustained" finding are not considered, no matter how recent, even though a finding of "not sustained" indicates that the incident could neither be proven nor disproven.[176] Given the historical failures of CPD and IPRA to properly investigate and sustain allegations of misconduct, the universe of complaint and disciplinary data entered into PRS is egregiously incomplete.

In addition to the fact that policy restrictively limits eligibility for intervention, CPD also does not consistently refer for intervention the individuals who are identified as eligible. Pursuant to CPD policy, an officer's chain of command, BIA, or IPRA may refer the officer for BIS. However, there are no quality checks to ensure that the appropriate officers are actually being referred. A high-level official in Human Resources told us that, "if a recommendation [for intervention] is not made up the chain to HR, it falls through the cracks" and an otherwise eligible officer will never be enrolled. Another official told us that the BIS program is not getting the appropriate amount of referrals. Leadership at CPD does not enforce the BIS and PCP policies; consequently, BIA, IPRA, and the chain of command do not take seriously their obligation to identify and refer problematic officers.

---

176 The one exception is that officers with three "not sustained" excessive force complaints in one 12-month period may be referred to BIS.

Our review of CPD's data confirms that the Department enrolls very few officers in its interventional programs, especially for a department of its size. Between January 2010 and July 2016, CPD enrolled only 38 officers in BIS. An additional 60 members were referred for enrollment, but never enrolled. Notably, 56 of those members were referred to BIS because of their alleged involvement in a domestic incident. An additional nine officers were flagged as eligible for BIS, but their command staff declined to recommend them. 28 officers were referred for enrollment, but removed from the program; the data that CPD provided us did not explain why. Finally, between March and June 2016, after the start of our investigation, CPD identified an additional 50 officers as eligible for the program, but as of mid-July, their status in the program was still listed as "pending." In 2015, only seven officers were enrolled in BIS all year, most for having too many SPARs in a single year.

Review of CPD's complaint data compared to the BIS enrollment program also confirms that there are a significant number of Department members with lengthy complaint histories who were never referred to or enrolled in BIS. Between January 1, 2010 and March 2016, 1,627 CPD members were the subject of five or more misconduct complaints; 350 of those had 10 or more complaints. While there may be innocuous explanations for such complaint numbers for some of these officers, these numbers are high enough to indicate that substantially more than 38 officers should have been enrolled in BIS during this time period.

CPD leadership is aware that these programs are grossly underused. As noted recently by the PATF, CPD "does not use any metrics to measure or assess the effectiveness of the programs." CPD must commit to fixing this broken system with a solution that is well thought out, capable of easy and robust implementation, and supported by all stakeholders.

c. The lack of a functioning early intervention system, coupled with inadequate supervision, has placed officers and members of the public at risk

These longstanding, systemic deficiencies in CPD's early intervention systems have prevented CPD from taking two steps that are crucial to ensuring officer safety and wellness, as well as ensuring policing that is effective and lawful. First, CPD does not adequately and accurately identify officers who are in need of corrective action; and second, CPD does not consistently or sufficiently address officer behavior even where CPD identifies negative patterns. Because of these failures, CPD officers are able to engage in problematic behaviors with impunity, which can—and do—escalate into serious misconduct. This has dramatic consequences for the public. It also impacts the health and safety of officers, who either do not get the support and services they need, or are forced to work alongside individuals who are not receiving such support.

In particular, we found that the current EIS does not adequately identify patterns or trends of misconduct related to force and domestic violence. One officer, for example, was the subject of several complaints of domestic violence over the course of just a few years that CPD did not detect or act upon for a significant period of time. After the officer's ex-wife brought four separate allegations of domestic violence and harassment between 2007 and 2008, many of which were closed for no affidavit or deemed not sustained, IPRA finally disciplined the officer for domestic violence, and gave the officer a 15-day suspension. The officer then went on to engage in domestic violence on two more occasions, which resulted in serious injuries to the officer's victims.[177] Likewise, Officer Giraldo Sierra, who killed Flint Farmer in June of 2011, was involved in three shootings within one year, and three domestic violence allegations in the years prior—yet he was not listed by CPD as an individual who was even considered for enrollment in BIS at any point in 2010-2011. Our review of use-of-force files also found two egregious examples of excessive force where, in each incident, the officers involved had extensive histories of complaints of excessive force but were not on the BIS roster. See Report, Section II.B.2. (discussing incident involving officers who used a baton and Taser on a girl at school, and incident involving the forcible removable of 12-year-old boy from his bike). One of the officers involved in the first incident had five separate complaints involving excessive force in the year prior to the incident described; the officer involved in the second incident had ten.

We also reviewed media reports describing a sergeant who was recently involved in his second fatal shooting in three years. This sergeant allegedly was the subject of a BIA investigation in 2004, prior to his promotion, for violating a rule prohibiting CPD employees from owning businesses that sell alcohol. Per CPD policy, this is a rule infraction that could potentially result in termination. See Employee Resource E01-11, Secondary Employment, at IV.G (noting that

---

177 Following the fifth and sixth separate incidents of this nature, which involved physical abuse of the officer's wife and children, CPD and IPRA sustained the complainant's allegations of domestic violence. To CPD's credit, given the severity of the misconduct, the Superintendent recommended termination from the Department. However, the Police Board reversed this recommendation and instead suspended the officer for a period of days, during which the officer was required to attend counseling and evaluation through the Employee Assistance Program. See In re Edward Feliciano, No. 12 PB 2824, available at https://policeboardproduction.s3.amazonaws.com/uploads/case/files/12PB2824_Decision.pdf. As noted elsewhere in this Report, the counselors who work in that program have no specialized training in domestic violence, and are ill-equipped to address these issues. See Report, Section IV.C. The Police Board's ability to overturn the recommendation of the Superintendent in this case is also illustrative of how Chicago's Police Board can undermine accountability more generally. See Report, Section III.H.

Department members are prohibited from engaging "directly or indirectly in the ownership . . . or operation of a tavern or retail liquor establishment," and that "violation of this policy will result in discipline, up to and including separation."). According to media reports, the individual went on disability leave shortly after that investigation was initiated, and the investigation went dormant as a result. The officer came off disability seven years later in 2011, but the investigation remained stagnant. CPD officials learned of the open investigation after the officer was involved in a fatal shooting of an unarmed man in 2013, but still, the original complaint remained open.[178] The officer was then promoted to sergeant through the merit promotion process, despite the open investigation, and later was involved in his second fatal shooting of an unarmed man. Had there been a functioning, effective EIS system in place, the open investigation could have been caught much earlier—before the officer received a merit promotion, and perhaps before he was involved in his second lethal shooting of an unarmed man.

Finally, we reviewed one investigative file that is emblematic of both supervisors' unwillingness to directly supervise their officers *and* CPD's failure to have a comprehensive EIS. In this incident, a young man was stopped by a CPD officer when he was walking through an alley. After questioning the individual, the CPD officer handcuffed the individual and placed him against the officer's vehicle. In cell-phone video capturing the incident, the officer is seen pushing the individual against the vehicle, as the individual complains repeatedly, in a calm voice, that the handcuffs are too tight and causing pain. The officer repeatedly calls the individual "motherfucker," curses at him, and threatens him, saying "make a move like that at me again, I will fucking show you exactly what I can do." The officer appears to be deliberately provoking the man to "make a move" to give the officer an excuse to use more force. When the individual says that he was not moving, that he had been previously injured in the arm, and the handcuffs were digging into his bones, the officer appears to deliberately push down on the handcuffs, causing additional pain, and continues to repeatedly use profanity while speaking to the man. The individual sought medical attention for injuries he sustained as a result of the incident. An unknown individual eventually filed a complaint with IPRA, and the cell-phone footage of this interaction was posted on Face-

---

178 According to CPD's chief spokesman, in response to this revelation the Superintendent ordered an audit of why the 2004 complaint was never investigated to completion. However, the spokesman noted that the audit would be conducted by Internal Affairs—the same agency that lost track of the complaint. See Jeremy Gorner, Discipline of cop involved in 2 fatal shootings fell through the cracks, CHI.TRIB., Dec. 12, 2016, available at http://www .chicagotribune.com/news/local/breaking/ct-chicago-police-shootings-john-poulos-met-20161212-story.html.

book. When the officer involved in the incident saw the Facebook footage, he alerted his lieutenant of the incident and the existence of the video. The lieutenant reviewed the video and, despite the aggressive nature of the interaction and overtly hostile attitude of the officer, sent a letter to his commander saying that he thought the appropriate response would be non-disciplinary intervention. The lieutenant justified this recommendation by saying that the incident did not involve "racially offensive or otherwise inflammatory language" and that the "subject makes no known complaints which are visible in the video"—two statements that are patently false.

This is a clear example of a CPD supervisor neglecting to hold an officer accountable for obvious misconduct. Moreover, if CPD had a functioning EIS at the time of this incident, the supervisor would have seen that the officer had three prior excessive force complaints, some involving similar allegations of the use of profanity and threats, in the prior year-and-a-half. The officer was a clear candidate for BIS, yet no referral was ever made. The IPRA investigation remains ongoing.

d. The City's past reform efforts have been unsuccessful and more is needed to ensure the success of present efforts

The City needs to take a new approach to reforming its EIS system. The City is currently making another attempt to establish a functional EIS system; this effort is described below. But without a focused, determined plan that builds on lessons learned from past unsuccessful reform attempts, it will be difficult for this new effort to succeed.

Previous efforts to create a data-informed, well-structured EIS within CPD have been unsuccessful. For example, in 1994, the City purchased a promising EIS software program called BrainMaker, designed to analyze data points and pick out patterns indicative of problematic behavior and identify officers at risk of being fired from the Department. Use of this program would have put CPD on the cutting edge of EIS technology nationwide. Union leadership felt this system unfairly targeted officers and subjected them to unfair, adversarial questioning from Internal Affairs. The City stopped using BrainMaker after only two years and all the data and reports it produced "went missing."

The City chose instead to rely on the system that CPD still uses today, despite repeated warnings of its shortcomings. The current system came about following the 1997 Report of the Mayor's Commission on Police Integrity. In that report, the Commission urged CPD to implement a meaningful EIS, noting that "small problems become big ones if left unattended." The Commission also recommended that CPD look at unit-wide trends, rather than analyzing only individual officers, and analyzing civil liability judgments in addition to misconduct complaints. At the time, the Commission was hopeful that expanding the behavioral intervention programs would result in more officers being involved in the programs and improved outcomes. According to the PATF's final report, following a grievance filed by the Fraternal Order of Police challenging the inclusion of certain officers in the BIS program, the City agreed to remove them from BIS, and the program was never expanded as suggested.

More recent studies of CPD's systems reaffirmed the need for reform. A 2007 study noted that nearly 90% of individuals with multiple complaints were never flagged by the EIS, including officers who amassed more than 50 abuse complaints within five years. This study also discussed how, of the 33 officers with 30 or more complaints between 2001-2006, fewer than half had been flagged for intervention. Seven years later, the City was again informed, via the Safer Report, that CPD needed to revise its BIS and PCP programs, including updating the data collection systems to make them more user friendly. In particular, the Safer Report recommended integrating the command staff PRS with systems used by investigative agencies into a single, streamlined case management system. Doing so, according to the study's authors, would eliminate a significant shortcoming of the current system: "the inability to track an officer's conduct throughout her career." Despite these repeated criticisms, the City has not successfully made the changes necessary to improve supervision and accountability in the Department. The PATF Report also highlighted these deficiencies, recommending that CPD develop a structured, tiered EIS system that utilizes appropriate data, supports supervisor training on its use, and provides for evaluation of the program's efficacy.

The City is currently engaging in a promising effort to study and reform the system, but, despite the best intentions of all involved, there are indications that this attempt may not be any more fruitful than past attempts, unless the City lays the necessary groundwork and stays focused until the EIS is fully integrated into CPD culture. The new project is managed by researchers from the University of Chicago, who successfully developed a new EIS system for the Charlotte-Mecklenburg Police Department in North Carolina,[179] and the University of Chicago Crime Lab. The City launched this partnership in the spring of 2016 to study CPD's data systems and develop a comprehensive EIS tool based on predictive data unique to Chicago. The effort represents an ambitious and potentially transformative approach for the Department. However, CPD has not fully addressed concerns that prevented the success of prior reform efforts. For example, there are plans to involve union representation in the development of the system, but the project managers are taking guidance from the City on how and when to do so—and union involvement has not yet occurred. There is no evidence that the

---

179 University of Chicago, Center for Data Science and Public Policy, *Building Data-Driven Early Intervention Systems for Police Officers*, available at http://dsapp.uchicago.edu/public-safety/police-eis.

City or CPD engaged with the unions early on, before beginning this new effort, to determine whether CPD's unions will support the new effort.

The City should commit itself to improving its supervision efforts on all fronts: in the systems and management that supports direct, front-line supervisors, and in the data collection and intervention programs that give CPD a high-level view of potential negative behavior patterns. Until both of these areas are meaningfully and permanently addressed, officer morale and efficacy will continue to suffer, and a culture of constitutional policing will never take root.

C. Officer Wellness and Safety

Policing is a high-stress profession. Law enforcement officers often are called upon to deal with violence or crises as problem solvers, and they often are witnesses to human tragedy. In Chicago, this stress is particularly acute for several reasons. CPD officers are confronted with increasing levels of gun violence in some of the neighborhoods they police. Gun violence and neighborhood conditions take their toll on both residents and officers alike. At the same time, the relationship between CPD officers and the communities they serve is strained; officers on the street are expected to prevent crime, yet they must also be the face of the Department in communities that have lost trust in the police. This makes it particularly difficult to police effectively. These stresses animate the interactions officers have with the communities that they serve—both positively and negatively. As one CPD counselor explained, it is the "stress of the job that's the precursor to the crisis." The President's Task Force on 21st Century Policing put it well, noting that "the 'bulletproof cop' does not exist. The officers who protect us must also be protected—against incapacitating physical, mental, and emotional health problems as well as against the hazards of their job. Their wellness and safety are crucial for them, their colleagues, and their agencies, as well as the well-being of the communities they serve."[180]

All of these stressors can, and do, play out in harmful ways for CPD officers. CPD officers grapple with alcoholism and suicide, and some engage in domestic violence. And as explained elsewhere in this Report, CPD officers are part of a Department that engages in a pattern or practice of using force that is unjustified, disproportionate, and otherwise excessive. Although the pressure CPD officers are under is not an excuse for violating the constitutional rights of the citizens they serve, high levels of unaddressed stress can compromise

---

180 FINAL REPORT OF THE PRESIDENT'S TASK FORCE ON 21ST CENTURY POLICING 62 (Office of Community Oriented Policing Services, May 2015).

officer well-being and impact an officer's demeanor and judgment, which in turn impacts how that officer interacts with the public. Some officers are able to manage the stress by shifting their focus to working even harder to do their jobs well. For others, it is more difficult. As these officers struggle with the stress of the job, they can close off and push away those they serve and those who want to help. For precisely these reasons, law enforcement agencies can and should do everything they can to support officers' physical and psychological well-being.

Officer wellness in CPD is not an integral part of the Department's operations. Given how officer wellness impacts officer behavior and the especially tense circumstances facing CPD officers each day, CPD officers need greater support. CPD does not have an overarching officer-wellness plan that includes robust counseling programs, comprehensive training, functioning equipment, and other tools to ensure officers are successful and healthy. The resources CPD provides are insufficient to meet Department needs, both because the programs are not robust and because the programs do not account for the needs of the increasing diversity of the officers that make up the Department. Furthermore, Chicago currently lacks an integrated platform of inter-related services—such as integrated training, counseling, and intervention programs—designed to enhance both the Department's organizational health as well as the wellness of personnel.

The Department should reinforce the value of wellness and support a culture that encourages officers to seek assistance when needed. CPD can then better prepare its officers for success, which in turn, will help prevent officers from posing harm to themselves and the communities they serve.

1. CPD must commit to providing officers necessary wellness support

a. CPD must dedicate more resources to support officers

CPD's support for officers' physical and mental wellness is provided almost entirely through its Professional Counseling Service/Employee Assistance Program (EAP). EAP provides vital services to the Department, but is understaffed and under-resourced. In contrast to similar-sized departments using the in-service model, which provides professional counseling services through on-staff counselors rather than contracting with independent professional counselors, CPD has devoted fewer resources to support EAP's growth. The ratio of trained counselors available to CPD personnel is considerably less when compared to other departments of comparable size and with similar service delivery models. CPD's EAP is staffed by three clinicians to serve the Department's roughly

13,500 sworn and unsworn personnel.[181] In comparison, the Dallas Police Department also staffs three full-time counselors to provide services for a force that is a quarter of CPD's size (3,400 sworn officers). The Miami-Dade Police Department, while also considerably smaller than CPD with approximately 2,900 sworn officers and 1,700 civilians, has six counselors and one graduate student intern to provide counseling services to its employees. The Los Angeles Police Department, the third largest department in the country, has thirteen counselors available to provide counseling to their roughly 10,000 officers and 3,000 civilian personnel. While CPD does have four certified substance abuse counselors, as well as officers trained to provide peer support services,[182] this staff is insufficient to meaningfully address the needs of a department the size of CPD.

Although the number of professionals necessary for a successful EAP will vary according to the type of program and scope of services provided, the officer wellness consultant we retained to assist with our review of CPD's program found the number of staff dedicated to Chicago's EAP too low to support the programs CPD currently offers. This is especially true given that the EAP in Chicago is intended to provide counseling services to both Department members *and* their families. Indeed, we found that EAP counselors are overextended. EAP reports its accomplishments and activities to the Bureau of Support Services on a monthly basis. At the end of 2015, EAP's three clinicians had provided 7,498 mental health consultations/appointments to Department and family members, including 4,074 clinical interviews, 1,560 informal interviews, and 1,847 telephone interviews. This is laudable, but EAP officials recognize that they could do more, and better, with more resources. One counselor

---

181 This is approximately a 1:4,000 counselor-to-officer ratio, and does not account for family members or retired officers who are also entitled to EAP's counseling services. *See* E06-01, III (D): CHICAGO POLICE DEP'T, EMPLOYEE RESOURCE (Chi. Police Dep't, Feb. 21, 2016), *available at* http://directives.chicagopolice.org/directives/data/a7a57be2-12aaf135-2a912-aaf1-37fbc7d8d466f49f.html ("All of the services offered by the Professional Counseling Service/EAP are available to Department members, a member's immediate or extended family, and retired sworn members."). While we found no published guidelines for the appropriate ratio in the police context, the Employee Assistance Professionals Association's (EAPA) standards and guidelines state: "EAP staffing patterns, and the number of professionals, vary according to the type of program and the scope of services provided. Whether the EAP is internal or delivered by external contractors, the number and qualifications of EAP professionals should match program needs." EAPA Standards and Professional Guidelines for Employee Assistance Programs at 14 (2010). EAPA recommends considering the size and distribution of the workforce, the diversity of the employees, and the scope and design of the EAP, among other factors when determining the necessary staffing levels for an EAP. *See id.*

182 CPD's Peer Support Program has 300 volunteer members who do not offer counseling, but will offer support to officers in times of need and will also refer officers to clinicians or drug and alcohol counselors.

explained that "the problem really is there are so few of us and so much to be done." Every day, counselors check the phones and "triage," many times having to rearrange scheduled appointments, shorten meetings to fit in more people, or cancel others, to address more serious crises. The unmet need is perpetual: EAP offers a one-day stress management program that teaches officers how to manage stress, depression, anxiety, PTSD, and other issues, but according to counselors, there is always a waitlist. The significant strain on the scant resources CPD allocates to officer wellness prevents officers from accessing these services in a timely, meaningful fashion.

b. CPD should better encourage and facilitate the use of available employee support programs

CPD should embrace the concept of officer wellness and support as integral to officer *and* Department well-being. By failing to fully integrate and normalize participation in EAP, CPD risks reinforcing the stigma surrounding seeking help and discouraging officers from using the limited resources currently available.

Even though EAP's small staff is consistently inundated with work, the number of officers who should or could use EAP's services is greater than the number who actually do, primarily because of cultural resistance to accessing these services. Internal CPD culture casts seeking assistance for personal issues as a sign of weakness. As described by one official, "there's still a stigma" associated with going to EAP. Indeed, officers told us that some Department members believe that seeking counseling is a sign of weakness. For the vast majority of officers in need of support, the onus is on them to seek it out, but many will not do so, even in times of need, for fear of being ostracized. Coworkers who see that an officer is in need are equally hesitant to contact EAP on the officer's behalf. One sergeant told us that the burden is on partners to report an officer in crisis, but they will not because they do not want to be seen as "rats." We collected anecdotal evidence from officers who were involved in traumatic incidents such as shootings, and from supervisors, that there is not adequate support from CPD after these incidents.

A former CPD officer who fatally shot an individual, and was shot himself in the incident, told us that his gun was taken away from him after the shooting but was given back to him after his mandatory furlough without any discussion of whether he was ready to carry it again. The officer said that he had also sought assistance from CPD headquarters because he wanted to talk with a psychologist about his experience, but CPD told him that they had no one to recommend. This former officer did not believe that CPD provided him adequate support even though he openly sought help. Beyond shootings, officers have difficult jobs in which they routinely place themselves in danger to help others, and may become witnesses to incidents that cause them to need additional support, such as the death or catastrophic injury of a child. Officers should be provided support services when they experience trauma, whatever the cause.

CPD should better emphasize the importance of officer wellness programs and the value to officers of such programs before, or entirely independent of, being involved in an incident that would result in a mandatory referral. Our investigation found that CPD could better emphasize the importance of officer wellness in several ways. First, CPD does not proactively communicate to officers the services that are available and how using those services can benefit both the officer and the Department. CPD does not provide officers with sufficient information regarding the support services available to them and their families, the practical benefit these services may have, or how to access them. Similarly, CPD misses opportunities to integrate officer wellness principles into existing trainings and promote use of CPD's existing programs. For example, probationary police officers attend stress management training and professional counseling services training. However, the stress management training we observed did not offer any information about EAP or its services.

Relatedly, CPD also does not reinforce the importance of officer wellness through readily available avenues *outside* of the EAP. For example, themes of police legitimacy, procedural justice, and officer wellness could, and should, be woven into all CPD trainings. Trainings on use of force, tactics, and other aspects of CPD operations should capitalize on the opportunity to instruct officers in how to deal with the stressors they will encounter on the job, such as hostile reactions from community members, observing violence or its aftermath, interacting with victims of crime, and policing in communities made up of people with backgrounds that are different than the officers' backgrounds. Likewise, CIT and de-escalation trainings teach officers to identify dangerous behaviors and how to interact with individuals in crisis, which they too can use in their personal life and in identifying coworkers who may be in crisis. CPD does not currently have a template for how these topics should be addressed through trainings.

This lack of cohesive messaging about the services that are available also results in officers misunderstanding how seeking help for stress, including participating in the employee support programs CPD offers, will impact their careers. For example, officers are concerned that if they seek counseling through EAP, they will automatically have their Firearm Owner Identification (FOID) Card taken away, which will prohibit them from having a gun, and therefore working anything other than a desk position in CPD. This is not the case; under Illinois state law an individual's FOID card will be taken away if the person is committed for *in-patient* psychiatric services. An officer's FOID will not be taken away merely for using EAP's services, but CPD's failure to correct this misconception may result in officers not seeking help when needed. Officers also expressed concerns that they would be punished for using EAP or that they would be reported to the Department by the counselors. Union representatives told us that CPD officers need a "safe place to talk out issues" without repercussions, but that is precisely the purpose of EAP. CPD is not publicizing EAP or encouraging its use in a way that would minimize misconceptions and maximize officer participation.

CPD could also develop and implement programs other than EAP that would assist with behavioral intervention. As discussed above, CPD should be monitoring officer conduct to flag officers who might be experiencing personal issues and could be candidates for one of the Department's intervention programs. With a properly functioning EIS that identifies officers who would benefit from the support systems, CPD might be able to provide the assistance necessary to avoid crises, especially in cases where the officers would not seek the help on their own. This, in turn, would increase officer wellness and overall Department health.

In each of these areas, CPD leadership could seize upon critical opportunities to advocate for officer health and wellness, and encourage and guide officers to appropriate and necessary supports. Without prioritizing and planning for officer wellness, officers receive the message from leadership that officer wellness is not valued, which discourages officers who want to succeed but feel overburdened and unsupported in that goal.

c. CPD should adapt its current officer wellness programs to CPD's female workforce

CPD's current EAP, in addition to being under-resourced, has also not adjusted to the changing nature of policing, or of CPD's police force. The system is set up to provide counseling for CPD members, but the expertise of the current counselors is limited. As currently structured, with only three clinicians with limited expertise, not all officers will be able to access services that are appropriate, tailored, and attuned to their specific needs. Although EAP clinicians make referrals to outside providers, without a more robust, comprehensive counseling program, CPD can and should do more to ensure that all officers in the Department are supported and capable of using CPD's officer wellness programs.

Women officers we spoke with during our investigation noted that they feel particularly unsupported in the Department, both because of its culture and because the available support systems do not take into account the particular needs of female officers. To adequately provide support to all members and their diverse needs, CPD should expand and improve its program to ensure that services provided are culturally appropriate, sensitive to differing circumstances, and attentive to the issues facing all officers.

d. CPD should improve other areas of its operations to improve officer wellness, safety, and morale

While officer support programs are critically important, the protection of officer wellness, safety, and morale depends upon a wide range of practices within the Department, many of which are currently not adequately supportive of officers. We heard from union representatives that restrictions on when and how officers may use vacation and elective leave time hurts morale. Also, CPD sends a negative message to its officers via the Department's deteriorating equipment. Several officers we spoke with described how outdated, malfunctioning equipment not only prevents them from doing their jobs safely and effectively, but makes them feel that the Department is not sufficiently concerned about their safety, efficiency, or professionalism. In particular, officers mentioned that their in-car cameras and computers frequently broke down, making it difficult to complete reports and enter data from the field, or look up information necessary to police their beat. One officer told us that in his district, 11 of the 14 in-car police cameras were broken, and that CPD does not have the sufficient staff to fix the cameras as they break. This impairs the value that cameras provide as a policing tool, and makes officers' jobs more difficult. Others noted problems with CPD's squad cars, saying that there were often not enough cars for a shift, which forces officers to ride three to a car at times. And many of the cars CPD does have are old and run down. A supervisor described CPD's cars as "dangerous and an embarrassment" to the force. These problems with CPD's equipment contribute to officers feeling unsupported in their work, and negatively impact officer safety, effectiveness, and morale, and in turn, community safety.

2. The unaddressed stress that CPD officers face harms officers, their families, and the public

During our investigation we heard that officer suicide and suicide threats are a significant problem in CPD. In fact, when we met with officials from EAP in May 2016, they had just handled an officer suicide threat the night before. One CPD official told us that CPD's rate is 22.7 suicides per 100,000 Department members. The FOP shared figures showing that CPD's suicide rate between 2013 and 2015 was 29.4 per 100,000 based on available information. This would mean that CPD's officer suicide rate is more than 60 percent higher than the national average of 18.1 law enforcement suicides per 100,000. As a CPD official noted, "in police work, we consider the bad guys the enemies and we have got to change that because it's destructive" and ignores that more officers die of suicide than in the line of duty. Recognizing the prevalence of officer suicide in CPD could help move the Department toward providing better interventions for officers in crisis. Indeed, the FBI credited "an increase in peer support programs, a decrease in resistance to personal assistance, and improvement in proactive mental health checkups" for the decrease in officer suicides nationally in 2012.[183]

Many CPD members also struggle with alcohol and substance abuse. Indeed, EAP served more Department and family members (8,565 consultations) for alcohol and substance abuse than it did for other mental health issues (7,498 consultations). While EAP is serving those officers who seek the help, the Department could do better to alleviate the stresses that may lead to these destructive behaviors, and that implicate public safety, by making wellness central to CPD's culture, from the moment a recruit enters the training academy through an officer's entire time on the force.

Finally, as discussed elsewhere in this Report, IPRA handles many complaints of domestic violence filed against CPD officers. Despite this, CPD does not address officer-involved domestic violence in CPD policies or academy trainings, or proactively inform officer family members how to get help and support if they need it. CPD employs one civilian who serves as a "domestic violence advocate," who can serve as a support person within the Department for victims of officer-involved domestic violence. Moreover, EAP seems particularly ill-suited to deal with domestic violence problems, as EAP officials do not have adequate specialized training or expertise in domestic violence, notwithstanding the fact that this is a known problem at CPD. Nor does CPD offer other robust intervention programs to detect, prevent, and appropriately respond to domestic violence by officers. CPD must institute reforms and dedicate adequate attention and resources to issues of officer wellness so that these and other officer personal and inter-personal issues are addressed appropriately.

D. Data Collection and Transparency

Deficiencies in how the City and CPD collect, analyze, and publish data regarding police activities contribute to the Department's failure to identify and correct unconstitutional policing. These deficiencies also inhibit transparency regarding CPD's practices. For decades, Chicago has failed to develop a comprehensive, integrated system to track and make public basic information about its police force. Instead, information is siloed, inaccurate, and incomplete. In addition, by failing to analyze and use important data, and by not reporting on that data publicly, the City is missing an opportunity to improve public transparency, and in turn, the relationship between CPD and the public.

---

183 Brian R. Nanavaty, *Addressing Officer Crisis and Suicide: Improving Officer Wellness*, FBI LAW ENFORCEMENT BULL. (Sept. 8, 2015), available at https://leb.fbi.gov/2015/september /addressing-officer-crisis-and-suicide-improving-officer-wellness.

1. CPD's data collection systems are siloed and disconnected

CPD uses an enormous and cumbersome data collection system to try to document policing activity. The system contains numerous "modules," which are comprised of thousands upon thousands of data-entry fields. When thousands of people (IPRA, BIA, officers, command staff, Human Resources, and more) are inconsistently filling out a few data fields, let alone thousands, the quality of data to support policing services is compromised. And, when police contacts are not properly documented, supervisors are not able to properly review activity, command staff are not able to properly discern patterns and deficiencies, and oversight bodies are not able to properly monitor activity and complaints.

CPD's data collection tools are filled with inefficiencies. CPD primarily relies on a system called CLEAR for its data collection, but there are several discrete, disconnected modules within that system, and information is generally not accessible across these modules. For example, several years ago, CPD used a program called CRMS to collect information about personnel investigations. CPD then migrated to use a program called AutoCR to track complaints against officers; but the rollout of AutoCR was never completed, and now both AutoCR and CRMS contain largely duplicative data, with one system used by IPRA and another by BIA. Both modules remain in CLEAR. Additionally, the TRR and AutoCR modules in the system do not communicate with each other. As discussed elsewhere in this Report, TRRs are supposed to be filled out every time an officer is involved in a reportable use of force. A portion of these force incidents result in a complaint being filed with IPRA; yet, because the TRR and AutoCR modules are siloed, CPD does not automatically match up TRRs with subsequent complaints. In fact, even though the TRR database includes a field for "CR number obtained," indicating that the TRR is the subject of an IPRA complaint, that field often does not accurately reflect the existence of an IPRA investigation.

Moreover, personnel within CPD often lack access to the data that would help them perform their duties. Commanders reported being able to view only the complaint/disciplinary histories of officers if they are entering a Summary Punishment Action Report (SPAR); otherwise, they believe they do not have the ability to know the histories of their officers and take those histories into consideration when making assignments. Similarly, when an officer is assigned to a new district, the officer's new commander is unable to access the officer's personnel record, complaint record, or other relevant information that would assist the commander with providing appropriate assignments and supervision.

This approach to data collection and maintenance undermines the utility of the data that CPD stores. Command staff are not currently using this data to support or inform officer supervision or officer activity. CPD needs to create a single case management system that will easily allow it to track and share the data it collects. Under the accountability rubric, this data would include CRs, SPARs, TRRs, NDIs, furloughs, medical absences, and related information. Without a streamlined, easy to use data platform, the data CPD collects will remain largely unused, which will continue to impede effective policing and CPD's ability to provide close, well-informed supervision or promote account-ability within the Department.

2. The City provides the public with data that is incomplete, inaccurate, untimely, and insufficient to allow the public to determine if CPD is policing constitutionally and effectively

In addition to insufficiently tracking and analyzing data for CPD and the City's own benefit, the information provided to the public regarding the activities of CPD is also woefully inadequate. The City does not consistently provide its constituents with data regarding crime trends, arrests made, case clearances, or other common police metrics. Nor does the City publish sufficient meaning-ful information regarding officer misconduct. Data that is published is often outdated or incomplete. These deficiencies are impediments to the public's un-derstanding of, and trust in, CPD's ability to detect misconduct, including the use of unreasonable force, and hold officers accountable for misconduct.

CPD has not published an annual report since 2010. In fact, public reporting on crime trends city-wide has not occurred for years; the most recent report covered murder crime trends from 1998-2007. Some statistical reports were historically provided more frequently, but reports have not been issued for the last few years. For example, the most recent "Domestic Violence Quarterly Sta-tistical Report" was released in June of 2014; prior to that, the reports were indeed quarterly. CPD publishes daily crime statistics through a "data portal," but this data is limited to criminal activity. There is no other data published on the website that relates to police-community interactions. Pursuant to a set-tlement agreement with the American Civil Liberties Union, CPD is required to track and report data regarding investigatory "stop and frisk" practices to a court-appointed monitor, who will issue a public report twice each year. Once this agreement terminates, however, CPD will be under no obligation to report this data, and CPD policy does not mandate data collection and public report-ing more broadly. CPD recently stated that it would resume issuing annual reports in 2017, and that the first report would include data for the previous six years when reports were not published. In addition, the Mayor recently issued an end of year "progress report" highlighting the status of Chicago's police reform efforts. These are helpful steps towards greater transparency, but they are not entrenched in policy or otherwise permanent reforms.

The City also should improve public transparency regarding officer misconduct investigations. To be sure, transparency regarding misconduct investigations has greatly improved in recent months, to the credit of the current Chief Administrator at IPRA. Prior to the start of our investigation, until a complaint was fully investigated, the City did not make available the actual allegations filed against officers; police reports that are associated with allegations of criminal misconduct; investigative testimony; or audio or video of incidents where misconduct was alleged. Moreover, until recently, IPRA published only abstract summaries of sustained cases. These abstracts, which were essentially summaries of summaries, did little to illuminate the course of an investigation or the evidence considered. The summaries also covered only sustained cases, leaving the public to wonder how conclusions were reached in the vast majority of cases. Prior administrations also posted redacted summary reports, but only of officer-involved shootings. Under the current administration, IPRA now publishes redacted summary reports, within 30 days of closing the case at IPRA, of all cases, not just shootings, regardless of the investigation's outcome—a positive step towards better transparency. The City also publishes aggregate complaint and investigation data mainly through quarterly reports from IPRA. The reports provide various counts of investigations initiated and completed, such as the number of complaints filed by incident type and the number of complaints that were closed, but this does not provide the public with an accurate picture of police misconduct in Chicago. For example, the reports address only the total number of complaints; they do not account for the total number of *allegations* made against CPD officers. Each complaint could contain several distinct allegations.

IPRA's recent changes to its reporting are improvements, but the City can and should do more to ensure the public has access to as much complete and accurate information as practicable.[184] Indeed, the City's investigative agencies could better report on the types of cases they handle, including the volume, issues involved, and outcomes of those cases. The IPRA quarterly reports also do not provide relevant demographic information of complainants or accused officers. IPRA breaks down the number of incidents filed against each district and specialized unit, but does little else to identify patterns or trends among its data. More specifically, IPRA does not analyze complaint data to identify racial, ethnic, gender, or other disparities that may be present. This prevents the public from seeing how policing is affecting certain communities, and impedes the City's ability to address patterns and root causes of misconduct.

There are also questions about the accuracy, and therefore the usefulness,

---

184 In the past, IPRA also produced Annual Reports. However, IPRA has not released an Annual Report since 2012. *See* IPRA, *Publications: Annual Reports*, available at http://www.iprachicago.org/category/annual-reports/ (last accessed Jan. 12, 2017).

of the limited data that is reported by IPRA. For example, the Office of Inspector General (OIG) recently concluded that public reporting by IPRA on CPD's use of force prior to 2015 "was inaccurate and incomplete." In particular, the OIG found serious deficiencies and discrepancies in IPRA's reporting of weapons discharges, noting that IPRA's data reported in its quarterly reports "did not match the number of actual incidents in any category during the time periods reviewed." As noted in the Accountability Section of this Report, we found issues with IPRA's investigations that would prevent accurate reporting of misconduct occurring within CPD. Specifically, IPRA consistently miscategorizes complaints and fails to separately investigate all allegations of misconduct that are raised by a complainant. These and other errors in IPRA's data collection and reporting therefore render the quarterly reports useless.

Even where accurate, the limited information given in IPRA's quarterly reports gives an incomplete picture of how misconduct investigations are resolved. IPRA findings can be, and frequently are, challenged by the chain of command and/or set aside by the Superintendent. The information provided by IPRA represents only the first step in resolving a misconduct allegation— the findings of IPRA. However, there is no additional public reporting on how often investigators' recommendations are overturned, or what discipline is ultimately imposed. Additional layers of review, including arbitration and involvement of the Police Board, may change the ultimate findings and the discipline that is imposed. As discussed elsewhere in this Report, annual reports from the Police Board provide some of this information in aggregate form, but no information is given regarding individual cases. Further, the last report was published in 2014. The information made public by IPRA is therefore misleading, as it does not tell the public how a misconduct complaint was ultimately resolved and what discipline was imposed.

The lack of transparency regarding officer misconduct complaints is not confined to IPRA. BIA and supervisors at the district level barely report publicly *any* information regarding misconduct investigations under their purview, even though, combined, they investigate roughly 70% of all misconduct allegations filed against officers. BIA only publishes a short annual report, consisting of a list of complaint log numbers. It does not publish summary reports or abstracts of any cases it investigates. District command staff publishes nothing on the investigations conducted at the district level—in fact, all of their investigations are conducted and tracked on paper, rather than electronically, thereby making it difficult for command staff to collect, analyze, and publicly report on those investigations. Community members seeking information about the outcome of a particular investigation at BIA or the district are forced to obtain that information through other channels, such as public records requests. The lack of transparency regarding BIA and district investigations leaves broad gaps in the information that is publicly available regarding misconduct investigations.

Complainants themselves are often kept in the dark about the status of their cases. Individuals complaining of officer misconduct do not receive periodic updates from investigators. Several complainants told us that they were left unaware of what was happening with their complaint for months, or even years—and some never heard back at all. At the conclusion of an investigation, complainants typically receive only a form letter stating the finding, i.e., whether the allegation of misconduct was sustained, not sustained, unfounded, or exonerated. No additional explanation is given. Complainants are not told what steps were taken to investigate their claims, leaving them to wonder whether the investigation was sufficient. Chicago also does not tell complainants the discipline imposed as a result of the complaint. And, as discussed elsewhere in this Report, if "mediation" is used to resolve a complaint, the complainant is not involved or consulted before or during that process; they are merely informed at the end that their complaint was resolved. Chicago's failure to meaningfully communicate with complainants at all stages of the investigative process undermines complainants' confidence that their allegations are taken seriously and that appropriate steps are being taken to resolve their concerns.

Finally, as discussed elsewhere in this Report, the City frequently settles civil rights lawsuits brought under 42 U.S.C. § 1983, and loses such cases at trial. In addition to not internally analyzing these lawsuits to identify trends, CPD also keeps the details of these settlements from the public, thereby avoiding public scrutiny of CPD's deficiencies. For most cases, the only transparency provided is a spreadsheet of all judgments and settlements handled by the City's Law Department; this spreadsheet lists complaints against the police, but contains only the plaintiff's name, the amount of the settlement, and a vague description of the claim settled (e.g., "excessive force," or "false arrest"). Until the Chicago Reporter created its database, based on court records and material requested through public records laws, little information about these settlements was publicly available. The City's limited release of information regarding settlements further contributes to public distrust and the perception that the City wishes to keep officer misconduct concealed from public scrutiny.

3. Recent reforms to improve transparency are positive steps, but more is required and changes must be sustained

The City and CPD have taken steps during the course of our investigation to increase transparency, but these changes—both actual and promised—must go further to ensure transparency is permanently supported and encouraged within CPD and IPRA.

The City recently instituted or committed to institute certain measures intended to increase transparency. These welcome reforms are in the initial stages. For example, CPD announced it would resume publication of annual reports, and the IPRA website now contains significantly more information regarding the results of misconduct investigations. CPD and IPRA should continue to publish this type of information regularly. As another example, in early 2016, the City announced a new "transparency policy" at the request of the Police Accountability Task Force. This policy, which was published in draft form, mandates the release of video and audio footage associated with certain incidents of police misconduct within 60 days of their occurrence, "unless a request is made to delay the release." The policy applies to incidents where an officer "discharges his or her firearm, stun gun, or Taser in a manner that strikes, or potentially could strike, an individual, even if no allegation of misconduct is made" and "those where the death of, or great bodily harm to, a person occurs while that person is in police custody."

This policy represents a significant step towards improving the transparency of investigations into CPD misconduct. Pursuant to this new policy, IPRA recently posted materials from 150 open investigations, including videos, case incident reports, tactical response reports, and officer battery reports. While the policy covers incidents that clearly are of heightened public interest, it is nonetheless limited in scope, and the City should apply it to other categories of force and civil rights violations as well. IPRA's website notes that the Mayor has adopted the policy, but a final version of the policy is not posted anywhere on CPD or the City's website, and is not part of CPD's directives system; the IPRA website only links to the policy as recommended by the Task Force. This policy should be finalized and permanently adopted.[185]

Perhaps as importantly, providing true transparency means not just increasing public access to information about problems, but encouraging public involvement in crafting solutions to those problems. The City should continue to meaningfully involve the community in developing proposed reforms. This is particularly important given the potentially monumental changes on the horizon for the City's transparency and accountability systems. We applaud the City's recent efforts to seek public input on proposed reforms, such as the COPA ordinance and CPD's new use-of-force policies. The City should engage in similar efforts for other anticipated reforms, and ensure that the public comments solicited are genuinely considered and addressed. Involving the community in this way will increase public confidence in and cooperation with CPD, which will improve CPD's ability to police safely, constitutionally, and effectively.

---

185 It is also worth noting that on June 6, 2016, CPD's officer union filed an "unfair labor practice charge" with the Illinois Labor Relations Board, challenging IPRA's release of video as a violation of the union's collective bargaining agreement. The dispute is set for a hearing in early 2017.

There is no dispute that more work is needed to restore the public's faith in CPD. Some of that work may be accomplished through improvements to CPD's data collection, analysis, and publication practices. Above all, to instill meaningful change in this area, any reforms instituted by CPD and the City must be formalized and permanent, so that they survive changes in leadership in CPD and City government.

E. Promotions

Dedicated, competent leaders are essential to ensuring that CPD promotes safe, effective policing tactics while valuing and respecting the rights of all community members. In Chicago, a lack of transparency around promotional systems and decisions, and years of litigation regarding CPD's promotion process, have created a narrative among the rank-and-file that CPD does not value good leadership, and that current leaders are unqualified to lead. Despite attempts at reform, officers we interviewed continue to view the promotions system with skepticism, which has decreased officer morale and undermined effective supervision. CPD's promotions system should be regularly reviewed, and revised if necessary, with the aim of increasing transparency and ensuring the promotion of candidates who will make CPD better able to police effectively and respectfully, while continuing to abide by court orders put in place to ensure that candidates are not unlawfully excluded from promotions on the basis of race or sex.

1. CPD's current promotions system

Under CPD's current promotions system, candidates interested in a promotion to detective, sergeant, or lieutenant take a two-part test. The first test consists of multiple choice questions testing job knowledge regarding policies and procedures, and is graded on a pass/fail basis. Candidates who pass this qualifying exam then move on to a second part of the exam, which is designed to evaluate the skills and application of knowledge consistent with the promotion position. The second part of the exam is scored and candidates are ranked based on their score on the second part of the exam and placed on a list of individuals eligible for promotion.

Candidates who appear on the list of individuals eligible for promotion to detective, sergeant, or lieutenant, may be promoted in one of two ways. First, candidates are ranked by their score on the second part of the exam, and candidates may be promoted based purely on that rank. At least 70% of promotions for sergeant and lieutenant are made from the individuals who complete both tests and are ranked highly on the lists; at least 80% of the promotions to detective are made this way.

Second, candidates who pass the qualifying exam may be nominated for a "merit" promotion regardless of their score or rank on the second part of the exam. CPD has used a merit system for lieutenants starting as early as the mid-1990s, and for sergeants as early as the late 1990s. The system was created to identify CPD members with supervisory potential who do not necessarily score well on promotional exams, given that previous promotional exams had an adverse impact on minority eligibility for promotions.

Notably, CPD adopted a hiring plan (Hiring Plan) regarding merit promotions in 2011—and readopted a revised Hiring Plan in 2014—pursuant to the Settlement Agreement in *Shakman v. Democratic Organization of Cook County, et al.*, a lawsuit alleging politicized hiring and promotions in several City agencies, including CPD.[186] The *Shakman* orders also gave the City's Office of the Inspector General the authority to audit and monitor compliance with the Hiring Plan. Concurrently, CPD revised its Merit Board to match the requirements laid out in the Hiring Plan, and to provide more structure for the merit selection process.

Under the hiring plan and related CPD policies, for the rank of lieutenant and below, merit nominations can come from chiefs, deputy chiefs, commanders, and directors. A Merit Board consisting of five deputy chiefs and the Director of Human Resources interviews and evaluates the merit nominees. In considering which nominees to recommend to the Superintendent for merit promotions, the Merit Board can review the nominee's complimentary history and performance evaluations, but they can only consider the nominee's disciplinary history as permitted by the nominee's collective bargaining agreement. The Superintendent retains discretion to ultimately select the nominees receiving merit promotions, and is not bound by the recommendations of the Merit Board in making the final decision.

In contrast to this dual-track promotions system for detectives, sergeants, and lieutenants, captains are promoted exclusively by a board and do not sit for an exam. Individuals interested in being selected for promotion to the rank of captain submit application materials in response to a job announcement, are screened by Human Resources to determine eligibility, and then, if eligible, evaluated by the "Captain Screening Board." Individuals who pass the screening board are then evaluated by the Merit Board, similar to the Merit Board's evaluation of candidates for the rank of lieutenant and below.

---

186 *See* City of Chicago's Unopposed Motion for Entry of an Order Approving a City of Chicago Police Department Hiring Plan for Sworn Titles, *Shakman v. Democratic Org. of Cook Cnty.*, Case No. 69-C-2145 (N.D. Ill. Oct. 14, 2011).

2. CPD's promotions system, as a whole, is regarded as unfair

a. CPD's tests have been challenged as discriminatory and unfair

The promotional examinations for CPD have been subject to legal challenges under Title VII of the Civil Rights Act of 1964, as amended, 42 U.S.C. § 2000e, *et seq.* (Title VII) for decades.[187] Title VII prohibits an employer from using a neutral employment practice that results in disparate impact on the basis of race, color, religion, sex, or national origin, unless such practice is "job related for the position in question and consistent with business necessity," and there exists no alternative employment practice that would result in less disparate impact and equally serve the employer's legitimate interests. 42 U.S.C. § 2000e-2(k).

The legal challenges of discriminatory impact and allegations of improper exam procedures[188] underscore the continuing need for careful review of the examination's content and procedures. We find the Seventh Circuit instructive in its emphasis of "the City's responsibility to re-examine the promotional process for currency." *Allen*, 351 F.3d at 315. We urge CPD to review its promotional exams and procedures for continued compliance with Title VII in order to ensure the lawful promotion of the best possible candidates in a transparent and fair environment. Ensuring fairness and non-discrimination in promotional testing will help CPD promote the best candidates, which in turn, will ensure that CPD has a cadre of supervisors who are willing and able to provide officers with adequate supervision, guide them on how to police effectively and consti-

---

187 Several of these lawsuits claimed that CPD's promotional exams discriminated against African-American officers, Latino officers, and female officers, and were not consistent with Title VII requirements. *See, e.g., Banos v. City of Chicago*, 398 F.3d 889, 890 (7th Cir. 2005) (minority sergeants challenged 1998 promotions to lieutenant); *Allen v. City of Chicago*, 351 F.3d 306, 307 (7th Cir. 2003) (minority officers challenged 1998 promotions to sergeant); *Bryant v. City of Chicago*, 200 F.3d 1092, 1094 (7th Cir. 2000) (minority sergeants challenged 1994 promotions to lieutenant); *United States v. City of Chicago*, 549 F.2d 415, 420 (7th Cir. 1977) (plaintiffs alleged discrimination against African-American, Latino, and female officers in hiring and promotions). White officers have also sued, claiming the tests discriminate against them. *See, e.g., Majeske v. City of Chicago*, 218 F.3d 816, 818 (7th Cir. 2000) (non-minority officers challenged 1989 detective promotions); *Barnhill v. City of Chicago*, 142 F. Supp. 2d 948, 950 (N.D. Ill. 2001) (white male officers challenged 1998 promotions to sergeant).

188 Separate from, and in addition to, litigation concerning the tests' discriminatory impact, promotional examinations also have been tainted with allegations of cheating or cronyism in the exam's preparation or administration. A 1998 promotional exam was heavily criticized when groups of officers allegedly conferred with one another during bathroom breaks and subsequently changed their exam answers, and some test takers were given exams that were copied poorly, leaving portions of the questions unreadable. The City Inspector General is also currently investigating allegations that three recently promoted lieutenants were coached by a high-ranking official who helped develop the August 2015 lieutenant exam. Although the investigation is ongoing, allegations of improper exam procedures make CPD officers doubt the fairness of the exam process.

tutionally, and hold them accountable when necessary, all of which are critical to preventing, detecting, and appropriately responding to unreasonable uses of force.

b. CPD's merit promotions are viewed as political and lack transparency

One of the major complaints from officers we interviewed is that CPD's promotions system lacks transparency regarding the nomination and qualification process for merit promotions. This has led many officers to believe that merit promotions are a reward for cronyism, rather than a recognition of excellence that was overlooked by the testing process. Many of the officers we spoke with—minority and non-minority alike—told us that they feel merit promotions are not truly based on "merit," but rather the "clout" you hold in the Department or "who you know." In other words, officers believe that CPD leadership gives merit promotions to individuals who are unqualified to serve as leaders, merely because those individuals have connections up the chain of command or have advocates in positions of power outside of CPD who call in favors or lobby on their behalf. Female officers in particular feel that they are frequently overlooked for merit promotions. This belief undermines officers' faith in CPD supervisors and their acceptance of CPD's systems of accountability and supervision.

In reality, there are documented instructions and guidance for merit promotion nominators and decision makers, but this information is not widely known. Nominators are required to attend "nominator training" in order to be eligible to make nominations, and are instructed by policy to follow the "Merit Selection Assessment Dimensions" contained in the "Nominator Manual" for the rank being filled. However, CPD has not proactively informed the rank-and-file of those dimensions or the content of the nominator training. The nominator and merit selection manuals are apparently posted on CLEAR, but typically officers we spoke with did not know this information was accessible, and remain unaware of the assessment dimensions used to evaluate potential merit nominees. This leaves officers to speculate about what criteria nominators consider when nominating individuals for merit promotions, which, in turn, increases officer skepticism that truly meritorious criteria are used at all. Finally, although the Superintendent must fill out a written justification memorandum explaining the basis for his or her merit selections, nothing about the reasoning is made public, the justification is often cursory, and candidates who were eligible but did not receive merit promotions are never provided an explanation for why they were not selected.

CPD has moved in a positive direction by establishing the Hiring Plan, allowing oversight by the Office of the Inspector General, and introducing new policies and manuals that, in part, describe the information that may be considered by the Merit Board. However, some of these new policies are written in vague terms that would allow problematic promotions to go undetected, and indeed, we know of at least one example where an individual received a merit promotion based on "clout" rather than merit, even after the new procedures outlined in the Hiring Plan were in effect: a recent inquiry from the City's Inspector General found that, as part of the 2013 sergeant merit promotion process, an officer assigned to the then-Superintendent's security detail was inappropriately promoted to sergeant.[189]

The OIG's current role providing oversight of this process is important to ensuring that the process operates as intended. CPD should also itself continuously review the current nominator manuals, policies, and other materials to ensure the systems are working properly. CPD should also review ways in which it can increase transparency surrounding the process. Given the skepticism expressed to us during our investigation, despite several notable areas of progress, CPD has not sufficiently communicated the details of the merit promotion policies to the rank-and-file.

c. Promotional exams are not offered with sufficient frequency

Numerous officers noted that they lack the chance to be promoted because CPD does not schedule promotional exams with sufficient frequency. For example, the last sergeant's exam was completed in January 2014. Before that, the sergeant's exam was last administered in March of 2006—nearly eight years prior. The last lieutenant exam was given in 2015; prior to that, the last exam was in 2006. Officers reported to us that they had been on the force for nearly a decade without being given an opportunity to make detective; indeed, no detective exam was offered between September 2003 and May 2016. The lack of regular

---

189 The officer was, in fact, ineligible for a merit promotion, because the officer had failed the sergeant's exam. The officer was nominated by a commander who had worked for CPD for only two weeks, after the Superintendent's Chief of Staff requested that the commander make the nomination, even though the commander had no knowledge of the officer's qualifications. Human Resources staff did not verify that the officer was eligible for promotion, and despite his failing score, included him on the list of eligible candidates that was forwarded to the Merit Board. The Merit Board nevertheless voted not to recommend promotion, but the Superintendent overrode that recommendation. The Superintendent never submitted a justification memo for this decision, as required by the new policy, but CPD's Human Resources still processed the promotion. The error was not discovered until the newly-promoted sergeant completed supervisor training and the City's own Human Resources department reviewed the hiring materials and discovered that the sergeant was ineligible for that position. The sergeant was then demoted, but the City is now facing a lawsuit over the controversy. The OIG found that, at several steps in the promotional process, the merit promotion policies were either ignored, or there were not enough safeguards in place to catch errors. The OIG recommended several changes based on its review of this incident.

promotional tests increases the frustration and lack of confidence in the promotional system as highly qualified and enthusiastic candidates are forced to wait to take promotional exams for years after they reach eligibility.

The City has recognized this problem and pursuant to the City's new Hiring Plan, eligibility lists must be retired after six years, "unless there is a lack of available funds for testing," in which case the list will be retired "as soon as practicable." City consultants highlighted this problem in 2014, and recommended that the Department administer promotional tests at least every four years. Although the six-year limit contained in the Hiring Plan is an improvement over past practices, CPD should continue to evaluate whether scores on previously administered tests accurately reflect current knowledge and skills, and whether more frequent testing, through validated testing instruments, would result in promotion of the most qualified candidates.

3. CPD must review and revise its promotional exams and merit system as necessary to ensure that the best-qualified candidates are promoted in a fair, lawful, and transparent manner

Despite the long history of litigation and the myriad litigation-initiated reforms, including the addition of the merit promotions system, there remains a broad officer sense that CPD does not promote people fairly. Prior reform efforts have not convinced officers that CPD's promotions system is fair and that the City values strong, quality leadership. Concerns remain about whether the promotion structure as a whole ensures that CPD is promoting the most competent, effective, and dedicated officers to supervisory positions. CPD should engage in regular and careful review of its procedures to ensure that they are fair and sufficiently frequent to result in the promotion of effective, ethical, and otherwise highly qualified officers.

Further, as noted above, CPD should take concrete steps to enhance the transparency of the promotions system. Some recent efforts, including the expansion of the OIG's role, are laudable, and should be expanded and sustained. We note that previous attempts to create transparency in the merit promotion process were scaled back or rescinded following changes in leadership. For example, one former Superintendent published a list of command staff who nominated officers for merit promotions alongside the names of the individuals they nominated. This measure was intended to increase accountability; officers would be aware of whether or not they were nominated, and command staff who nominated individuals for political rather than meritorious reasons could not hide those nominations from public scrutiny. However, the policy of publishing this information was rescinded immediately when the next administration took over. It is imperative that steps taken towards transparency through the 2014 changes be maintained and built on, rather than reversed.

V. CPD MUST BETTER SUPPORT AND INCENTIVIZE POLICING THAT IS LAWFUL AND RESTORES TRUST AMONG CHICAGO'S MARGINALIZED COMMUNITIES

True community policing is an overarching ethos that creates both direction and space for officers and communities to treat each other with respect and with trust. This relationship serves as the foundation for working together to establish crime prevention priorities and develop solutions to public safety problems. Implemented correctly, community policing helps people feel neither over- nor under-policed, and incentivizes and empowers many people to work with the police—and others to at least not work against them. To be successful in this way, community policing must be supported not just by an entire police department, but by an entire city.

Within the past several months CPD and the City have announced ambitious plans to revive community policing in Chicago. Superintendent Johnson has formed a Community Policing Advisory Panel, comprised of national experts, police command staff, and local community leaders, to develop strategies for enhancing community policing within CPD. The Superintendent has pledged to remake the Department's Chicago Alternative Policing Strategy (CAPS), the formerly robust CPD community policing initiative. The Department also recently issued a directive establishing the "Bridging the Divide Program," focused on improving youth-police relationships, in eight districts, with further expansion planned. As part of this approach, Superintendent Johnson has said that "the job of every officer is to reduce crime and help restore trust." CPD has several additional community policing related initiatives underway.

We commend CPD for its renewed emphasis on community policing. This policing approach, when implemented with fidelity to all its tenets, has been shown to be effective at making communities safer while incentivizing a policing culture that builds confidence in law enforcement. As such, it is a promising path that can lead to eliminating the patterns of unlawful conduct our investigation found, increasing community trust in CPD, and reducing crime in Chicago.

The importance of community trust in reducing crime can be seen in homicide clearance rates. In 2016, CPD was able to identify a suspect in only 29 percent of all homicides, which is less than half the national rate for 2015. Identifying suspects in homicides is recognized as an important factor in preventing future homicides. And there is broad consensus, including throughout Chicago, that increasing community trust and confidence in CPD is necessary for CPD to be able to clear more homicides. As Superintendent Johnson recently stated, "The first thing we have to do is improve our trust with the community—especially the minority community and CPD—that will help raise the clearance rate, because those individuals will be more comfortable in coming to us and giving us the information we need to hold these individuals accountable." We heard this same message during many of our conversations with residents of Chicago's high-violence neighborhoods. As one woman told us, "You can get a lot of things done if I have a relationship with you and I can trust you, then I can tell you some stuff. But if I can't trust you, I can't tell you anything . . . [CPD] need[s] to build relationships with the people in the community."[190]

Chicago was formerly a leader in advancing community policing and continues to recognize the promise of this approach. As the Mayor has stated, "Chicago is where the whole idea of community policing began. . . . It remains the best and most comprehensive approach we have in changing the everyday conditions that breed crime and violence and then breed mistrust." CPD's Superintendent Johnson has repeatedly called community policing his "core philosophy."

Notwithstanding this recognition, community policing as a true CPD ethos and driving force fell away many years ago, and past attempts to restore it have not been successful. To be successful this time, CPD must build up systems throughout the Department, to support and bolster this community-focused approach to policing. Community policing will struggle to be successful in Chicago if it remains a series of disconnected initiatives, no matter how well-meaning and well-executed. As stated in the report from the Task Force on 21st Century Policing, community policing must be "infused throughout the culture and organizational structure" of a police department.

A. CPD'S MOVE TO RESTORE TRUE COMMUNITY POLICING WILL BE DIFFICULT BUT IS PROMISING

Infusing community policing throughout City and police systems—from training and supervision to transparency and accountability—while dismantling practices that undercut this effort, will be a lengthy endeavor requiring sustained commitment and focus. Once achieved, however, this trust-building approach to policing will better promote both public safety and respect for constitutional rights.

---

190 Our discussion of the importance of trust in clearing homicides is not meant to diminish the importance of other factors. Many other factors, including the number of detectives assigned to the unit investigating homicides, and to each homicide case, as well as the timeliness of detective response to the scene of a homicide, are important factors in increasing clearance rates. Further, as discussed below, how CPD handles homicides is itself an important factor in building community trust and confidence in law enforcement.

1. CPD has many officers who are already policing in a community-focused manner

CPD has the officers to make community policing work. During our investigation we observed many instances of diligent, thoughtful, and selfless policing, and we heard stories of officers who police this way every day. While on a ride along, we observed officers patiently talk to a troubled young man until they convinced him to remove a belt from around his neck. During an interview with a patrol officer, we learned that he had paid for and installed a koi pond at the school where he works because he "wanted to do something for the kids here." This same officer volunteered to coach the girls' cross-country team at a local school when no one else would take the role.

Chicago residents provided us with story after story of officers who care deeply about the community, are affected by the violence they see individuals commit against each other, and work hard to build trust between the community and the Department. We heard about officers who are well-respected and beloved in the neighborhoods they patrol. We were told about a district commander who knew and interacted with all of the community groups in his district and handed out his personal cell-phone number to residents. We know there are many more like him. Many of the officers with whom we went on ride-alongs took the time to stop and talk with kids or shopkeepers who obviously knew them and were happy to see them. We saw a field training officer and his probationary police officer walk around the neighborhood frequently during our ride-along with them, taking the time to visit with children at a community center and shop. We spoke to officers who organized and secured officer attendance for a CPD-sponsored daddy-daughter dance, to step in for those fathers who, for whatever reason, were absent from their children's lives. We spoke with "Purpose over Pain," an advocacy and support group committed to ending gun violence. The group—run by one of its founders who began the group with her then-husband, a CPD officer—related to us that CPD officers attend its events and are deeply involved in its mission. We were impressed by the attitude and efforts of the CPD officer who led the "Building the Divide" program, a program that promises significant strides in humanizing officers and residents to each other. The Department is currently planning to restart this program in eight districts.

Another of the many examples of such policing that we observed personally occurred while on a ride-along with an officer in the Fifth District. The officers we were with responded to a call in one of Chicago's public housing projects. We observed an officer deal with a potentially volatile incident with skill and patience. By treating both parties with dignity, compassion, and respect, the officer was able to resolve the incident successfully rather than having it escalate, which might have occurred had the officer approached the situation differently, as we have seen from other CPD officers. This officer told us that the resolution was not atypical for him, and that he believed most situations like that could easily be defused with patient and respectful interactions by police officers. Throughout our time with this officer, it was clear he had a warm rapport with the people in the neighborhood he patrolled. He had grown up in the area and knew many people in the neighborhood. It was clear that this officer knew the importance of connecting, on a real and personal level, with residents. He told us that he considered establishing those relationships as one of the keys to success for an officer working his or her beat. As a result of Chicago's requirement that officers live within the City, many officers talked to us, with pride and concern, about policing in the same neighborhoods they grew up in.[191]

From these observations and others, it is clear that many Chicago police officers help community members every day in meaningful and tangible ways. Most of these efforts never make the news because they are part of an officer's daily routine: watching carefully to detect wrongdoers before they can do wrong, diligently patrolling, notwithstanding the disrespect and cold stares that are too often part of the job, and risking their lives to protect complete strangers.

2. For community policing to be successful it must be infused throughout CPD's policing strategies and tactics

Of course, the realities of police work can create challenges to policing with care for even the most well-meaning and dedicated officer. For community policing to be successful within CPD, the Department and City will need to take a holistic approach that will translate the discrete programs and initiatives currently underway into a department-wide ethos that resets the CPD culture. This will require both a sustained shift of resources to systems and initiatives consistent with a community-based policing focus, and a transformation of many of the CPD systems discussed elsewhere in this Report, including Training, Supervision, and Accountability.

Inculcating community policing throughout CPD will also require a remaking of CPD's existing community policing structure. Examining the

---

191 Media reports of course include many additional accounts of officer dedication to the community, as well as officer heroism. For example, CPD officers operate a youth baseball league in one of the most challenged neighborhoods in Chicago, with several officers volunteering their time to coach 9–12-year-olds in the league. CPD's "Shop With a Cop," an established annual event that occurs every holiday season, gives children the opportunity to spend a day shopping, eating, and bowling with police officers. News stories also recount stories of officers assisting people changing flat tires in the middle of the night; buying groceries for elderly neighbors; pulling people and dogs from building fires; pulling a teenage boy from the bottom of a pool and saving him from drowning; and many instances of officers assisting individuals with gunshot wounds—sometimes being credited with saving their lives.

shortcomings of these current community policing efforts may be helpful in bringing about greater success moving forward.

From 2000 to 2010, Chicago's commitment to community policing waned. Even as CPD's overall budget went up, its budget for CAPS was cut. Community policing within CPD began to be implemented half-heartedly and superficially to the point where, today, community policing is largely seen as illegitimate by many officers and community members.

In recent years, community policing in Chicago has been relegated to a small group of police officers and civilians in each district. CAPS typically has a sergeant, two police officers, and a civilian in each district responsible for setting forth a community policing agenda and coordinating community policing activities in the entire district. The officers receive little training on how to accomplish their mandate, and there is little to no involvement by patrol officers or commanders in planning and implementing community policing strategies. Community policing efforts are also poorly funded. Districts receive approximately $9,500 a year to carry out all of CAPS' work if the district is in a high crime area, and $8,000 if not. Approximately half of the money is budgeted for community meetings and events while the other half is budgeted for youth programs and events. This money is far less than what is needed to cover the expenses staff incur in organizing events, so CAPS staff either rely on donations from businesses or pay out of their own pockets. We were told by community policing staff that funding was an "enormous challenge" in developing community policing strategies and events.

Given the lack of resources and emphasis put on community policing, CAPS for the most part focuses on hosting community meetings. But these meetings are not effectively advancing community policing within CPD. Effective community policing is responsive to residents' input regarding community needs, and seeks residents' insights into the best way police can help address those needs. At its core, community policing "takes seriously the public's definition of its own problems." Chicago has attempted to meet this tenet of community policing by sponsoring regularly scheduled meetings in each of CPD's districts. But as currently run, these meetings generally are not an effective way for CPD to learn about neighborhood problems or the concerns of the spectrum of residents who make up each neighborhood. According to some residents, the meetings "are not a place to go if you have an agenda other than what the police want to discuss." This was consistent with our observations. From our interviews with community policing staff and observations of several meetings, it became clear that the purpose of the meetings was to discuss neighborhood criminal activity to the exclusion of broader issues involving the police that are also of importance to the community. One community policing staff person said that community meetings are not meant to address citizen concerns about officer use of force or explain Department policy, telling us that residents should "raise it with someone else." For example, complaints received by community policing officers at the meetings were frequently referred to the saturation, tactical, and gang teams for enforcement—teams by whom some in these communities felt victimized and dehumanized. In one CAPS meeting we saw, an officer was actively antagonistic to community members, responding with hostility after misinterpreting an attendee's statement, and getting increasingly louder and more aggressive as the attendee tried to defuse the situation.

Not surprisingly, CAPS meetings are not generally well-attended and do not reflect a broad spectrum of residents. Although several CAPS sergeants stated that the community meetings were well attended, at the meetings we observed, there were usually only a handful of residents attending. Given other priorities such as jobs, school, and child care, as well as transportation challenges and concerns about possible retaliation, these meetings may not attract large numbers of residents every week. There is a need for CPD to be more creative in finding ways to more meaningfully connect with those who will likely rely on its services the most. The Department has a long way to go in this respect: one young man told us that one CPD officer's reaction upon recognizing him while he was working at the young man's church internship this summer was to say, "You're one of those motherfuckers who sits in CAPS meetings and complains." Statements like this, particularly alongside the conduct of officers described elsewhere in this Report, reinforce the broadly held view among some in Chicago that CPD's approach to community policing is not genuine, and mostly operates as a "surveillance" tool to assist the Department in executing its enforcement strategy.

To be successful moving forward, CPD also must better recognize, reward, and encourage positive community policing efforts. Most community policing officers we spoke to told us that their work is given low priority within the Department. We were mostly met with amused smiles when we asked if their work was recognized by CPD. One community policing officer told us, "We acknowledge the work that we do." CPD officers outside CAPS with whom we spoke were generally dismissive of CAPS and community policing, calling it "not effective." One patrol officer told us he makes an effort to go to CAPS meetings "when he can;" another officer told us that, due to constant enforcement initiatives, officers didn't have time to attend community events. In addition to being disheartening—officers should make the time to connect with residents in the neighborhoods they patrol—the many comments like this that we heard reflect officers' understanding of the Department's priorities. Similarly, the Department's "Bridging the Divide" program was very popular with community members when it was launched, but suffered from poor participation by officers. The Department recently issued a directive requiring participation in this program in eight districts. This effort is laudable, but will not likely be successful if CPD cannot tap into and incentivize the many good officers who are eager to build genuine positive connections with Chicago's youth and families.

B. CPD Must Change Practices to Restore Trust and Ensure Lawful Policing

To turn around policing in Chicago, CPD and the City must focus their efforts on improving relationships within neighborhoods that have Chicago's highest rates of crime, poverty, and unemployment, and with communities that are otherwise marginalized. These efforts include recognizing that Chicago's policing practices have had an unnecessarily negative impact on these communities, and working to change practices to increase police legitimacy and community trust.

Chicago recognizes that it must focus on changing the way it polices, particularly in these communities, and that it must rebuild trust in light of past experiences of both community members and police officers. As Superintendent Johnson has stated publicly, "We recognize that we did treat certain parts of this City inappropriately. And that was our fault. So we have to correct that."

We commend Chicago for recognizing the critical importance of this effort, and urge them to continue and redouble their efforts.

1. CPD must do more to ensure that officers police fairly in neighborhoods with high rates of violent crime, and in vulnerable communities

Any effort to restore trust and ensure lawful policing in Chicago must focus on Chicago's predominantly black and Latino neighborhoods, especially those with high rates of violent crime. Many individuals in these communities experience policing in a fundamentally different way than do white individuals and white communities. Restoring trust and bringing about effective policing will be difficult unless CPD eliminates unnecessary, harmful differences in how people in these communities are treated, and takes affirmative measures to demonstrate its dedication to treating the residents of these neighborhoods fairly.

a. CPD must ensure it is responsive to victims of crime in Chicago's high-crime neighborhoods and other vulnerable communities

Strikingly, residents of Chicago's most challenged communities consistently expressed concern to us about their treatment when they or their family members are the victims of crime. An oft-repeated concern was that officers do not put sufficient emphasis on solving more significant crimes, or at least do not convey their concern to victims of such crimes.

Black and Latino residents in particular told us of feeling disregarded by CPD when they tried to get help after being victimized by crimes. One middle-aged man told us that after being assaulted and having his nose broken outside a store, he reported the crime and told the police there was video footage, but the police told him to go to the store himself to retrieve the video. An Englewood resident told us that a CPD sergeant told him flatly she would not help him get rid of a drug house on his street. One student we met with told us how he once tried to flag down an officer for help, but the officer just drove by. Many residents in predominantly black or Latino areas complained about response times when they call the police for assistance.

The many family members of homicide victims with whom we met similarly expressed a lack of confidence in CPD because of how they had been treated. Their experience with CPD, after a family member had been murdered, had made them feel that CPD does not genuinely care about the murders of young black men and women, and do too little to investigate and resolve those homicides. A young man told us how, after his brother was killed, he would go to the station to talk to someone about the investigation and officers would roll their eyes and say dismissively, "we're working on it." Families told us of detectives not interviewing key homicide witnesses or suspects, declining to obtain relevant video footage, and failing to update parents on the status of investigations, or even return their calls. One woman said that the Department switched the detective who was handling her son's homicide investigation without telling her. Another woman stated that she has to resort to getting information "on the street" about her son's case instead of from the detective, who told her that she "calls too much." This same woman told us that it took a week after her son was killed before anyone at CPD reached out to her. One mother told us that she felt CPD did not think her child was worthy of having his homicide solved. Yet another mother complained that police did not investigate the murder of her son, but sent her a bill for the cleanup of his body. Undoubtedly, many CPD detectives, like many other CPD officers, including those who helped start and participate in the aforementioned support group for those affected by gun violence, care deeply about victims of homicides. Our conversations with scores of family members of homicide victims made clear that CPD needs to do more to convey their commitment and care to these communities.

We also heard many concerns regarding CPD's investigation of potential hate crimes or hate incidents. CPD's Civil Rights Unit is charged with investigating all hate crimes and hate incidents in Chicago, yet has only two investigators.[192] Under CPD's current policy, officers are to notify the Civil Rights Unit when there appears to have been a hate crime or other criminal or quasi-criminal incident motivated by hate. An official familiar with the investigative process explained that the Civil Rights Unit must be notified before the Unit can run a parallel hate crime investigation. This official told us that front line officers need better training to recognize potential hate crimes, or these crimes will go uninvestigated. Indeed, the Civil Rights Unit did not learn about a rash of anti-Semitic and anti-Muslim graffiti in the Rogers Park neighborhood over the summer until there was a televised news report. We were also told that the Unit sometimes has to push to investigate crimes that appear to be hate-motivated because detectives minimize the seriousness of such crimes, saying things like, "a crime is a crime," or "so they got called a name."

Advocates and members of the Latino, Muslim, and transgender communities each separately raised concerns with us about Chicago's response to potential or apparent hate crimes against members of their communities. For example, a Latino church in the Pilsen neighborhood was vandalized numerous times over the past year with anti-immigrant messages stating "Rape and Kill Mexico" and drawings of swastikas. While CPD eventually investigated the incidents as a hate crime, church members were distressed that the church was vandalized six times before CPD acted. The church had installed a security camera after the fifth incident, and it was not until there was a video of the perpetrator that CPD seemed to take the incidents seriously. The church told us that it had been a "struggle . . . to get anyone in authority to hear us and to do work to protect us. We fear we won't be heard until a tragedy occurs." Advocates from the Muslim community voiced similar concerns and frustrations, telling us that in their view CPD is "reticent about looking at potential hate crimes." A Muslim advocacy organization told us that they receive around 200 discrimination complaints per year, and estimates that up to 30 percent could be hate-related. Yet, CPD reported only three hate crimes against Muslims between 2013 and 2015. Leaders in the transgender community are likewise concerned by the investigations of the murders of several transgender women in recent years. The Civil Rights Unit was not asked to open a hate crime investigation into any of these murders. Not only are members of this community upset that these crimes were never investigated as hate crimes, but they are also concerned that CPD's failure to solve any of the murders reflects a lack of commitment to these cases.

Indeed, CPD needs to work harder and more effectively to address concerns of all Chicago communities, including Chicago's transgender residents who voiced concerns about their treatment by CPD officers. CPD updated its Gen-

---

192 The New York City Police Department's Hate Crimes Task Force has 26 officers (including 20 detectives plus additional supervisory staff) and two civilians assigned to it.

eral Order governing interactions with transgender individuals in December 2015, which is commendable. However, the community has expressed concerns about the policy, including that it fails to ensure that transgender individuals are classified by their gender identity and does not require officers to ask an individual their preference regarding the gender of the officer to conduct a search. CPD might have more effectively addressed these concerns had CPD's outreach to the transgender community been more extensive. For example, the Department only has one LGBT liaison, which is insufficient to ensure collaboration and ongoing partnership with this community.

Several CPD officers told us that some people in these neighborhoods and communities seem accustomed to crime. These officers seemed not to recognize the role that police can play in normalizing crime if they fail to respond vigorously to violent crime no matter how often it occurs. The high incidence of violent crime in these neighborhoods and the effects that it has on entire communities make it more important, not less important, that CPD respond seriously to these events. Failing to do so creates the perception for some that crimes committed against those living in these areas are not important to CPD. Indeed, we heard from other officers that CPD leadership responds with greater interest to crimes in some parts of the City, with one commander telling us that he will "catch holy hell" if a "white woman has her iPhone stolen" in the wealthy part of Chicago he commands. CPD must ensure it consistently makes clear to officers that crime does not matter more if it is committed in more advantaged communities.

b. Many residents of Chicago's high-crime neighborhoods experience policing as overly harsh and unfair

Proactive policing is an important part of public safety, when implemented consistently with constitutional and community-oriented policing principles and as part of a thoughtful public-safety plan. However, where proactive tactics are used in a manner that seems dismissive of community concerns, such tactics erode community trust, endanger citizens and officers, and encumber crime solving, particularly over time, as distrust creates an intractable unwillingness to aide investigations.

Even as many residents feel that CPD is not sufficiently concerned when they are victims of crime, they often feel that CPD polices too harshly in their neighborhoods, and too often assumes that they are the perpetrators of crime. This sense may be due in part to CPD's reliance on specialized units to conduct "hot spot" type policing in these neighborhoods, rather than beat officers. These specialized teams, such as the tactical (TACT), gang, saturation, and narcotics units, do not answer service calls, but aggressively seek out problematic activity by conducting traffic stops, making contacts, and effecting arrests.

Many of these officers drive unmarked vehicles and do not wear the traditional police uniform. They instead wear either plainclothes or a uniform consisting of a black shirt, khaki pants, and black boots. This attire sends the message that these officers are not meant to be neighborhood police officers, but instead operate outside CPD's normal police channels. As CPD officers put it, the saturation teams "are jump out squads." Officers also told us of a policing "tactic" of randomly stopping their police vehicle and opening one door: if anyone runs, an officer will get out and give chase; if no one runs, they will close the car door and drive on. In addition to the unnecessary, dangerous situations this approach can get officers into, discussed in the Force Section of this Report, policing like this does little to promote community confidence or efficiently address crime. As one of our police experts put it, in some respects, Chicago's policing strategy in these neighborhoods seems to involve little more thought than having officers go out and "stir stuff up."

CPD incentivizes this tactical-oriented policing approach by elevating members of specialized units to special status. According to officers, being a member of a specialized unit or team carries prestige, and is considered as a "step up" for those uninterested or unable to obtain promotions to sergeant or other command positions. A TACT sergeant told us that officers are selected for TACT teams based on their "aggression, hustle, and effort," and "a patrol officer who rides around and just answers calls is not aggressive. Aggressive officers seek out crime between their radio assignments." This officer told us that his TACT officers "like to hunt" for offenders. One TACT officer we spoke to proudly touted the 1,300 arrests he had made in 11 years. The quality, impact, or even legitimacy of those arrests appeared generally unimportant to most of those that we spoke with throughout CPD. At one COMPSTAT meeting we observed, officers were told to go out and make a lot of car stops because vehicles are involved in shootings. There was no discussion about, or apparent consideration of, whether such a tactic was an effective use of police resources to identify possible shooters, or of the negative impact it could have on police-community relations.[193]

While people in Chicago's downtown areas only rarely see this type of policing, this is how residents in certain segments of the City experience policing on a daily basis. As a result, many residents in those neighborhoods feel, as we were told often in conversations with community members, as if CPD is an occupying force. One youth told us that the nature of the police presence in his neighborhood makes him feel like he is in "an open-air prison." One resident

---

193 CPD is currently working on a relaunch of COMPSTAT that is intended to improve its utility and reputation within CPD. We encourage CPD to ensure that COMPSTAT incorporates integrity and constitutional policing components, as well as community insights, into its use.

told us, "they patrol our streets like they are the dog catchers and we are the dogs." One officer told us that the law is unquestionably enforced differently in some neighborhoods: when "kids" on the North Side of Chicago get caught with marijuana, they get a citation; kids on the South Side get arrested. This officer's commander confirmed this approach when he told us that his policing philosophy in areas with violence is to make arrests because that was how he "was brought up."

In addition to feeling unduly harsh to residents of these neighborhoods, this type of policing has resulted in many residents, especially young people, feeling unfairly targeted and stereotyped by police. Young people we spoke with individually and during community meetings told us many stories of officers who, while unwilling or unable to help them when they needed help, followed and "harassed" them as they went about their daily lives. Young people told us of being stopped and searched by police, handcuffed, and having background checks conducted before being let go, while doing everyday things like walking to the store. A young woman told us of being stopped and frisked on her way to her father's funeral. People also told us that even programs nominally put in place to protect them, such as CPD's Roadside Safety Checks and DUI Saturation Checks, are conducted in ways that make the programs feel like excuses to search residents and their cars.

Young black residents told us they are commonly stopped and suspected of engaging in criminal activity, or of being gang members, based solely on their appearance. As one resident told us, "they see you with [certain types of clothing] and they think you are a criminal. Wear dreads and you get stopped." A young girl stated that "[they are] always think[ing] [we're] gangbangers." Residents with whom we spoke were very concerned about the presumption of gang affiliation, not only because of the assumptions it made about people, but because it also provides a false narrative that can follow these individuals in future interactions with the police and the criminal justice system.

Latino residents of these communities voiced similar concerns. As one Latino resident stated, "there is guilt by association." Latinos stated that there is a tendency for officers to "lump everyone together." One Latino outreach worker told us that he was pulled over multiple times, mostly by TACT teams or non-uniformed officers. During these stops, officers would search the vehicle, and after finding nothing, would let the outreach worker and any passengers in the car go. These stops became so prevalent that the outreach worker's employer eventually had several conversations with CPD to try to stop these needless intrusions.

Of particular concern to us were officers who did not appear to recognize when profiling was unlawful. One *sergeant* told us that "if you're Muslim, and 18 to 24, and wearing white, yeah, I'm going to stop you. It's not called profiling, it's called being pro-active." CPD's own officers, especially, but not only, its black officers, acknowledge profiling and harassment by CPD. A lieutenant told us, "I'm a black man in Chicago, of course I've had problems with the police." Black CPD officers shared stories of being profiled by their own Department. One black officer said that he has been stopped many times by police in the Englewood neighborhood for no reason other than he is a black man in a nice car. Another black officer told us that when she lived in Englewood, she was profiled and stopped many times by officers. Another officer acknowledged that sometimes officers harass youth, but stated that sometimes what looks likes harassment may on occasion be officers interjecting themselves out of concern, such as officers who try to "clear a corner" out of concern for kids when they have information that the corner may be targeted for a shooting. Officers recognize the impact this type of policing has on residents and their perceptions of CPD. We were informed that when officers encounter black men on the street, men sometimes lift their shirts without being asked.

During our meeting with members of Chicago's Arab American Police Association, officers raised similar concerns about cultural sensitivity and the treatment of Muslims in particular. They explained that many times non-Muslim CPD officers will offend cultural norms unintentionally because of "ignorance and lack of training."

This may not be how CPD intends policing to be conducted or perceived in these neighborhoods, but these experiences offend and humiliate people and diminish residents' willingness to work with law enforcement. Nor can these consequences be excused by the rates of violence in some of these communities. As it endeavors to better partner with the residents of these communities, CPD must do a better job—*especially* in these communities—demonstrating that it presumes community residents to be allies rather than suspects, absent individualized evidence to the contrary. Practices that facilitate and support officers gaining close familiarity with the people and dynamics of the neighborhoods they police is an important aspect of encouraging this mindset. More broadly, CPD must ensure that it is incentivizing and rewarding conduct by all personnel—whether specialized units, beat officers, or CAPS staff—that builds community trust.

2. The City must address serious concerns about systemic deficiencies that disproportionately impact black and Latino communities

CPD's pattern or practice of unreasonable force and systemic deficiencies falls heaviest on the predominantly black and Latino neighborhoods on the South and West Sides of Chicago, which are also experiencing higher crime. The impact of these widespread constitutional violations, combined with un-addressed abusive and racially discriminatory conduct, have undermined the legitimacy of CPD and police-community trust in these communities. Many low-income black neighborhoods suffer the greatest harm of violent crime in Chicago, and therefore have more police contacts. As a result, residents in these neighborhoods suffer more of the harms caused by breakdowns in uses of force, training, supervision, accountability, and community policing. Our investigation also found that CPD has tolerated racially discriminatory conduct that not only undermines police legitimacy, but also contributes to the pattern or practice of unreasonable force. As CPD works to restore trust and ensure that policing is lawful and effective, it must recognize the extent to which this type of misconduct contributes to a culture that facilitates unreasonable force and corrodes community trust. We have serious concerns about the prevalence of racially discriminatory conduct by some CPD officers and the degree to which that conduct is tolerated and in some respects caused by deficiencies in CPD's systems of training, supervision and accountability. In light of these concerns, combined with the fact that the impact of CPD's pattern or practice of unreasonable force fall heaviest on predominantly black and Latino neighborhoods, restoring police-community trust will require remedies addressing both discriminatory conduct and the disproportionality of illegal and unconstitutional patterns of force on minority communities.

a. The pattern or practice of unreasonable force disproportionately burdens minority communities

As described throughout this Report, our investigation found that Chicago's black residents collectively have a very different experience with CPD than do Chicago's white residents. Many low-income black and Latino neighborhoods suffer the greatest harm of violent crime in Chicago. Residents in these neighborhoods, not surprisingly, have more frequent police interactions. With these interactions come the harms of unreasonable force that arise from CPD's systemic deficiencies outlined here and throughout this Report. The result is that Chicago's black and Latino communities experience more incidents of unreasonable force. These are the very communities who most need and call on the police to fight violent crime, and where police and community trust and cooperation is most important.

Blacks, Latinos, and whites make up approximately equal thirds of the population in Chicago, but the raw statistics show that CPD uses force almost ten times more often against blacks than against whites. For example, of all use-of-force incidents for which race was recorded between January 2011 and April 18, 2016, black individuals were subject to approximately 76% (19,374) of the uses of force, as compared to whites, who represented only 8% (2,007) of the force incidents. In some categories of force, blacks were even more overrepresented: black individuals were the subject of 80% of all CPD firearm uses and 81% of all

Taser contact-stun uses during that time period. CPD's data on force incidents involving youth also showed stark disparities: 83% (3,335) of the incidents involved black children and 14% (552) involved Latino children.

These data strongly support what we repeatedly and consistently heard from both law enforcement and community sources: Chicago's black and Latino communities live not only with higher crime, but also with more instances of police abuse. Starting from a young age, black and Latino people, especially those living in Chicago's most challenged neighborhoods, have a vastly different experience with police than do white people. These negative, often tragic, interactions form the basis of minority communities' distrust of police.[194]

b. Recurrence of unaddressed racially discriminatory conduct by officers further erodes community trust and police effectiveness

Our investigation found that this pattern or practice of misconduct and systemic deficiencies has indeed resulted in routinely abusive behavior within CPD, especially toward black and Latino residents of Chicago's most challenged neighborhoods. Black youth told us that they are routinely called "nigger," "animal," or "pieces of shit" by CPD officers. A 19-year-old black male reported that CPD officers called him a "monkey." Such statements were confirmed by CPD officers. One officer we interviewed told us that he personally has heard coworkers and supervisors refer to black individuals as monkeys, animals, savages, and "pieces of shit."

Residents reported treatment so demeaning they felt dehumanized. One black resident told us that when it comes to CPD, there is "no treating you as a human being." Consistent with these reports, our investigation found that there was a recurring portrayal by some CPD officers of the residents of challenged neighborhoods—who are mostly black—as animals or subhuman. One CPD member told us that the officers in his district come to work every day "like it's a safari." This theme has a long history in Chicago. A photo from the early 2000s that surfaced years later shows white CPD officers Jerome Finnegan and Timothy McDermott squatting over a black man posed as a dead deer with antlers as the officers hold their rifles. Finnegan was later sentenced to 12 years in prison for being part of a corrupt group in the Department's Special Operations Section that carried out robberies and home invasions in predominantly black neighborhoods, while McDermott was fired when the photo surfaced.

---

194 Devon W. Carbado, *From Stopping Black People to Killing Black People: The Fourth Amendment Pathways to Police Violence*, 1 CAL. L. REV. 102 (forthcoming 2017) (discussing how police interactions expose people "not only to the violence of ongoing police surveillance, contact, and social control but also to the violence of serious bodily injury and death").

This mindset has desensitized many officers from the humanity of the people of color they serve, setting the stage for the use of excessive force.[195]

We reviewed data related to complaints of racially discriminatory language and found repeated instances where credible complaints were not adequately addressed. Our review of CPD's complaint database showed 980 police misconduct complaints coded as discriminatory verbal abuse on the basis of race or ethnicity from 2011 to March 2016. Thirteen of these complaints—1.3%—were sustained. We found 354 complaints for the use of the word "nigger" or one of its variations. Four, or 1.1%, of these complaints were sustained.

Generally, these complaints were sustained only where there was audio, video, or other irrefutable evidence. One of the four sustained complaints was sustained because the officer admitted using the racial slur; another was sustained because there was an audio recording of the officers using the slur. The third sustained complaint was sustained because the victim's husband was a police officer in a neighboring municipality who took extraordinary measures to document the incident. In that case, the officer was suspended for 15 days for the incident, which involved an altercation with the victim at a dog park that involved the officer telling her: "Fuck you, you fucking nigger, you should keep your big mouth shut." When the woman's husband told the officer that the officer should not speak that way to the woman, the officer responded: "Why? Because she's pregnant? I don't care if she's pregnant. I'll beat her fuckin' ass too." As a police officer himself, the woman's husband knew to call the police, request contact cards, get witnesses' information, and go directly to the district station to file the complaint.

The fourth sustained complaint had been generated internally by a lieutenant when she learned of a recording of a police officer yelling, "Don't move nigger!" at a man he was chasing during a foot pursuit. The slur had been broadcast over the police radio. The allegation against the officer was sustained, as were allegations of failing to report misconduct against a lieutenant and another officer. These results are the exception, rather than the rule; most racially charged language used by CPD officers is neither recorded nor directed towards another member of law enforcement who knows how to respond in a way that will ensure the officer is held accountable.

Chicago has settled several lawsuits that alleged racially discriminatory treatment by CPD officers. In one suit, the victim asked the officers why he was under arrest to which they responded, "We got something for big mouthy niggers like you" before beating him. In 2013, a CPD officer arrested a Chinese-American citizen working at a massage parlor and used excessive force. A video of the incident captured an officer screaming, "I'll put you in a UPS box and

---

195 *See* Phillip Atiba Goff et al., *The Essence of Innocence: Consequences of Dehumanizing Black Children*, 106 J. PERSONALITY & SOC. PSYCH. 526 (2014).

send you back to wherever the fuck you came from," and another officer hitting her in the head while she was on her knees.

Finally, we found that some Chicago police officers expressed discriminatory views and intolerance with regard to race, religion, gender, and national origin in public social media forums, and that CPD takes insufficient steps to prevent or appropriately respond to this animus. While CPD policy prohibits Department members from using social media to convey "any communications that discredit or reflect poorly on the Department, its missions or goals," this policy is apparently not well-enforced, even against supervisors. For example, one officer posted a status stating, "Hopefully one of these pictures will make the black lives matter activist organization feel a whole lot better!" with two photos attached, including one of two slain black men, in the front seats of a car, bloodied, covered in glass. Several CPD officers posted social media posts contain disparaging remarks about Arabs and Muslims, with posts referring to them as "7th century Islamic goat humpers," "Ragtop," and making other anti-Islamic statements. One CPD officer posted a photo of a dead Muslim soldier laying in a pool of his own blood with the caption: "The only good Muslim is a fucking dead one." Supervisors posted many of the discriminatory posts we found, including one sergeant who posted at least 25 anti-Muslim statements and at least 43 other discriminatory posts, and a lieutenant who posted at least five anti-immigrant and anti-Latino statements. Given these statements, our observations and conversations with officers during the course of our investigation, and other publicly available commentary, such as the comments posted anonymously on popular CPD officer blogs, it appears that more CPD officers have made similarly derogatory statements, often without repercussion.

Even when CPD learns of overtly discriminatory statements, its response reflects a lack of sufficient concern about such conduct. For example, in June 2015, Chicago learned about an officer who had posted racist comments and had called for a race war on social media forums after a reporter from ABC 7 News contacted IPRA and sent the agency the posts. The investigative file indicates that the case was still pending as of December 2016. Indeed, underscoring both the inadequacy and impact of CPD's response to overtly racist behavior, we found nearly 100 troubling public posts made by the same officer as recently as June 2016, many exhibiting racial animus.

In response to our question about what changes he would like to see among Chicago police officers, one black teen responded, "act as if you care." This simple request from a young Chicago resident encapsulates the kind of policing we heard people asking for in the hundreds of conversations we had, and in the scores of community meetings we attended during our investigation. People living in Chicago's marginalized neighborhoods want policing that demonstrates that CPD has genuine concern about the safety and well-being of all Chicago residents, no matter where they live or what they look like.

The conduct of those officers who have engaged in the racist and abusive behaviors described here, unchecked due to the systemic and cultural failings described in this Report, hurts the many well-intentioned officers. CPD will not be able to convince residents in these neighborhoods that it cares, no matter how earnestly it launches community policing initiatives, if it does not take a stronger, more effective stance against unnecessarily demeaning and divisive officer conduct.

3. CPD must stop using dangerous practices, such as "guns for freedom," to coerce people into providing information

During our investigation, we heard allegations that CPD officers arrest individuals and attempt to gain information about crime using methods that undermine CPD's legitimacy and may also be unlawful. In some instances, we were told that CPD will attempt to glean information about gang activity, the locations of weapons, or drug activity, and refuse to release the individual until he provides that information. In other instances, CPD will take a young person to a rival gang neighborhood and either leave the person there or display the youth to rival members, immediately putting the life of that young person in jeopardy by suggesting he has provided information to the police. Our investigation indicates that these practices in fact exist.

We commend the CPD officers who are working *with* community members to protect the public from gun violence, including by removing illegal guns from the streets. However, when officers use unlawful arrests and detentions or improper intimidation tactics to coerce information, they erode community trust and undermine the work of CPD and the community to rid the City of violent crime.

We were told by many community members that one method by which CPD will try to get individuals to provide information about crime or guns is by picking them up and driving them around while asking for information about gangs or guns. When individuals do not talk, officers will drop them off in dangerous areas or gang territories. We reviewed a publicly available video that appears to capture one instance of an officer displaying a youth in police custody to a group of individuals gathered in a rival gang territory. The video shows CPD officers standing around a marked CPD vehicle with the back doors wide open and a young male detained in the rear. Officers permit a crowd of male youths to surround the car and shout at the adolescent. The crowd can be seen flashing hand gestures that look like gang signs and threatening the cowering teenager in the backseat. One of the males in the crowd appears to have freely recorded the interactions all while CPD officers stood beside the open vehicle doors. The video does not show any legitimate law enforcement purpose in allowing the youth to be threatened.

Residents told us that this has happened for years, with several individuals recounting their personal experiences. A young black man told us that when he was 12 or 13 years old, he and his friends were picked up by CPD officers, dropped off in rival territory, and told to walk home. Another black teen told us that his brother was picked up in one location, dropped off in another location known for rival gangs, and told: "Better get to running."

We also talked with several individuals who gave credible accounts of being detained by CPD officers for low-level offenses (for example, failure to use a turn signal) or on false pretenses, and then were told that they would not be released until they brought the officers guns. We heard community members refer to this practice as "guns for freedom." One man told us of an incident that happened within the past few months, in which he was arrested for driving on a suspended license and told by officers that "everything would go away" if he brought the officers two guns. Officers released him on bond and told him he had one week to bring the officers the guns. They warned him that if he did not bring the guns they would put him away "forever." This person told us of a friend who had a similar experience several years ago. Other individuals with whom we met during community meetings told us similar stories of CPD officers offering to release them from custody if they provided officers with a weapon. A pastor at a Latino church told us that his congregants reported being picked up by CPD officers seeking information regarding guns or drugs, but when they either could not or would not provide such information, the officers removed the congregants' shoelaces and dropped them off in rival neighborhoods. Another man told us that he saw officers surround his seven-year-old niece seeking information about who sold drugs and which gangs were running in their neighborhood.

A recording from November 2015 appears to capture part of a "guns for freedom" incident on video. The video is part of a case in which an individual alleges that police coerced him into producing weapons to gain his own release and the release of a friend. According to the individual who produced the gun, police first required him to tell them where guns were located, and then demanded that he bring them a gun. The man claims he had to buy the gun he brought to the police. The video recording appears to show the man placing the gun in a trash bin and police officers retrieving the gun later that day. The officers' incident report does not mention any arrest and instead claims that the man directed them to "the location of multiple firearms being hidden in the 5th and 22nd district."

In addition to the likely illegality of this conduct, its impact on community trust cannot be overstated. The fear and anger created by these practices was obvious when we talked with individuals who reported these experiences. As the attorney for the man in the November 2015 incident noted during a media interview, "if there was any trust that's built up by officers on the street, that trust is clearly and quickly destroyed." His words underscore what we found more broadly throughout our investigation: when practices like this are allowed to persist, CPD allows abusive officers to set the culture, undermining the hard work of CPD's many good officers.

Our review of CPD's misconduct investigations revealed more than 100 complaints of similar conduct; these complaints were only very rarely sustained, even when internally generated complaints arising from the same incident were sustained. In other cases, investigators failed to follow through on the investigation despite possible corroborating evidence.

Through the publicly available videos noted above, the conversations we had with community members, and the hundreds of complaints that have been made about this conduct over the past few years alone, it is clear that this is a concern CPD should address. Indeed, CPD TACT officers complained to us that while supervisors' direction now is to stay out of trouble, previously the guidance from supervisors was: "If you get me a gun, we'll take care of you."

There may be circumstances in which giving an arrestee who is lawfully arrested based on probable cause leniency or even immunity in exchange for recovering illegal firearms is appropriate. Such practices should be pursued, however, under policy and supervision to ensure they are safe, effective, and within constitutional limits. CPD must ensure that officers consistently police in a manner that builds and preserves police legitimacy.

C. A Trust-Building, Community-Focused Approach to Policing Will Better Promote Lawful Policing and Public Safety

When community policing was more fully supported and broadly implemented in Chicago in the 1990s, studies found it had a substantial impact on public safety and community confidence in CPD. Researchers found, for example, that blacks experienced a 22% decrease in fear of crime in their neighborhoods, and a 60% decrease in perceived social disorder. At the same time, blacks, Latinos, and whites all reported better relationships with police officers.

In the last decade, community-focused policing has worked to bring down crime and rebuild trust in other cities—including big cities and cities with high rates of violent crime. New York has reduced its crime rate while at the same time lowering the number of stops and arrests it makes. Community policing can also be instrumental in bringing about the relationships that are helpful in bringing up homicide clearance rates, one of the most critical problems currently facing Chicago.

No police department is perfect, but other police departments, and Chicago's own history, have shown that it can better support lawful policing, gain legitimacy in the eyes of the public, and more effectively address crime, if it roots out unlawful and divisive practices and infuses its systems with a community-focused approach.

VI. RECOMMENDATIONS

Throughout this Report, we make several recommendations to the City and CPD related to our findings. These recommendations are gathered and offered in more detail below. Through the changes we have identified, CPD will be better poised to police constitutionally and effectively, and improve trust between officers and the communities they serve. We look forward to working cooperatively with the City and CPD on how to best craft and implement these recommendations.

A. Use of Force

CPD should re-orient officers' approach to the use of force to avoid using force except when necessary, and should provide officers with the policy guidance and training to develop and maintain proficiency in de-escalation. CPD should also implement a system of force reporting and investigation to better detect and respond to instances of unreasonable or unnecessary force. Additionally, providing officers with the tools and training to better respond to persons in physical or mental health crisis and those with intellectual disabilities will help avoid injuries, increase community trust, and make officers safer. CPD should:

1. Adopt use of force practices that minimize the use of force.

a. CPD has begun the process of revising its force policies to better reflect the sanctity of human life, the need to avoid the use of force, and de-escalation and force mitigation consistent with officer safety. CPD should continue this process to ensure these concepts are incorporated throughout CPD's force policies, including its canine and Taser policies, and that policies provide sufficient guidance to officers;

b. CPD has begun training officers in safely using de-escalation methods so that force may be avoided. CPD should continue this process and should incorporate these concepts throughout CPD training;

c. Develop, train and implement a foot pursuit policy that makes clear that foot pursuits are dangerous and that sets forth guidelines for foot pursuits that balance the objective of apprehending the suspect with the risk of potential injury to the officer, the public, and the suspect. The policy also should address unsafe foot pursuit tactics to ensure the risks of foot pursuits are not increased;

d. Ensure that officers are trained in sound tactics to avoid unnecessarily exposing officers to situations in which deadly force may become necessary;

e. Revise and reinforce policies against shooting at or from a moving vehicle, and provide additional training on avoiding dangerous vehicle maneuvers;

f. Revise Taser policies consistent with best practices, including implementing restrictions on the use of Tasers in drive-stun mode; limitations on Taser use in situations that pose inordinate risk to the suspect; limitations on Taser use on vulnerable people (e.g., the elderly, pregnant women, people in mental health crisis); restrictions on Taser use to situations in which it is necessary and proportional to the threat or resistance of the subject; and discouragement of the use of Tasers in schools and on students, and requiring officers to factor into their decision to use a Taser a child's apparent age, size, and the threat presented for proportionality and appropriateness. CPD should emphasize in training that Tasers are weapons with inherent risks that inflict significant pain and should not be viewed as tools of convenience;

g. Prohibit the use of retaliatory force, force used as punishment, force used in response to the exercise of protected First Amendment activities (e.g., filming), and force used in response to speech only rather than in response to an immediate threat;

h. Equip officers with appropriate first-aid supplies, train them in their use, and require officers to render aid to injured persons consistent with the officer's training;

i. Equip all patrol officers and supervisors, and officers who regularly interact with the public, including tactical officers, with body cameras, and develop a body camera policy delineating officers' responsibilities regarding the consistent and appropriate use of body cameras and the retention and review of body camera footage.

2. **Change the reporting and review of force to accurately capture the totality of the circumstances in force incidents.**

a. Develop and implement use-of-force reporting requiring officers to complete a narrative force report that describes with particularity the force used and the circumstances necessitating that level of force, including the reason for the initial stop or other enforcement action. Witness officers should also complete reports for serious uses of force (e.g., firearms discharges and other forms of deadly force). Injuries to officers and persons against whom force was used should be photographed;

b. Develop and implement supervisory review of force that requires the supervisor to conduct a complete review of each use of force, including gathering and considering evidence necessary to understand the circumstances of the force incident and determine its consistency with law and policy, including statements from individuals against whom force is used and civilian witnesses;

c. Develop and implement a system for higher-level, interdisciplinary review of incidents involving all types of firearms discharges, successful canine deployments, Taser uses, use of chemical weapons, and force resulting in injury to the person against whom force was used;

d. Discipline or otherwise hold accountable officers who fail to accurately report their own uses of force, officers who fail to accurately report another officer's use of force when policy requires it, and supervisors who fail to conduct adequate force investigations;

e. Collect and analyze data on uses of force to identify racial and other disparities in officer uses of force.

3. Revise the initial response to officer-involved shootings to prevent collusion and the contamination of witnesses.

a. Adopt a policy requiring that IPRA investigators participate in the preliminary assessment during the immediate aftermath of an officer-involved shooting to the same extent as the CPD commander in charge and CPD investigators conducting administrative or criminal investigations;

b. Adopt policies and practices that preclude involved and witness officers from speaking with one another, or with civilian witnesses, about the shooting incident until after they have been interviewed by IPRA investigators, except to the extent necessary to ensure public safety. To that end, require that, where possible, involved officers, witness officers, and civilian witnesses be transported to the station separately and their conversations be monitored to avoid contamination prior to interviews;

c. Except to the extent necessary to ensure public safety, prohibit involved officers and witness officers from using cell phones before they speak with the on-scene commander;

d. Consider prohibiting involved officers, witness officers, and civilians from viewing footage from dashboard cameras, body cameras, surveillance cameras, or cell phones before their interview with IPRA. In all cases, inquire of witnesses and officers whether they have viewed any recordings prior to the interview;

e. Require that interviews with involved officers and witness officers be recorded and IPRA investigators be present (except that an officer may speak with his or her attorney in private) and that interviews with civilian witnesses be recorded unless it would interfere with investigation. In cases where interviews are not recorded, the reason for failing to record the interview should be documented;

f. Revise CBA provisions or other restrictions on how soon officers may be interviewed following an officer-involved shooting; and

g. CPD and IPRA should develop appropriate protocols to conduct concurrent, bifurcated investigations with specific measures to ensure that the integrity of criminal investigations is not compromised.

4. Implement policies and develop training to improve interactions with people who are in crisis.

a. Devote appropriate resources to improve CPD's existing CIT program. Develop and implement policy and training to better identify and respond to individuals with known or suspected mental health conditions, including persons in mental health crisis and those with intellectual or developmental disabilities ("I/DD") or other disabilities;

b. Screen and designate volunteer officers who have expressed an interest in becoming CIT specialists and are well-suited to this work.

CPD should continue to offer CIT training for officers who wish to develop crisis intervention skills, but reserve participation in the CIT program to the selected officers;

c. Provide crisis intervention training to CIT-designated officers, who will respond to critical incidents involving persons in crisis. This training should include how to identify and respond to common medical emergencies that may at first appear to reflect a failure to comply with lawful orders (e.g., seizures, diabetic emergencies);

d. Ensure that there are enough CIT officers on duty throughout the City and throughout the day to help ensure a CIT officer is available to respond to calls involving an individual in crisis;

e. Require that, wherever possible, at least one CIT officer will respond to any situation concerning individuals in mental health crisis or with I/DD where force might be used;

f. Improve the quality of the current CIT 40-hour training program, which will in turn require obtaining sufficient CIT training staff and resources so that training can focus on requiring CIT candidates to demonstrate competency in the necessary skills;

g. Collect data on CIT calls to allow CPD to make informed decisions about staffing and deployment so that a CIT officer is available for all shifts in all districts to respond to every CIT call;

h. Develop a CIT reporting system (apart from the use-of-force reporting system) so that each deployment of a CIT officer is well documented. CIT officers should submit narrative reports of their interactions with persons in crisis so the appropriateness of the response can be evaluated in an after-action analysis; and

i. Implement an assessment program to evaluate the efficacy of the CIT program as a whole and the performance of individual CIT officers. A portion of a CIT officer's performance review should address skill and effectiveness in CIT situations.

B. Accountability

A well-functioning accountability system (in combination with effective supervision) is the keystone to lawful policing. The City and CPD must create impartial, transparent, and effective internal and external oversight systems that will hold officers accountable in a timely manner for violations of law, CPD policy, or CPD training. To that end, the City and CPD must:

1. Improve the City and CPD's accountability mechanisms for increased and more effective police oversight.

a. Work with police unions to modify practices and procedures for accepting complaints to make it easier for individuals to register formal complaints about police conduct;

b. Adopt practices to ensure the full and impartial investigation of all complaints, and assessment of patterns and trends related to those complaints;

c. Revise IPRA/COPA mediation policies and procedures to: 1) require complainant notification of and participation in mediation; 2) incorporate principles of restorative justice; 3) create clear, objective standards for referring cases to mediation; and 4) prohibit mediation for resolving certain categories of complaints, including use of force and domestic violence complaints;

d. Revise BIA policies and procedures to require that investigators record interviews and include transcripts of all interviews with victims, witnesses, or suspect officers in every file. CPD policy should dictate that summaries of interviews will be accepted only where obtaining a recorded or transcribed interview is not feasible;

e. Enforce CPD policies prohibiting officers from falsifying reports and providing false information or testimony during interviews by providing strict disciplinary penalties, up to and including termination, for those officers who violate them; and

f. Put systems in place that ensure administrative charges are fully and timely investigated, even where CPD and the State's Attorney's Office are investigating potential criminal charges, or have decided not to pursue criminal charges, for the same conduct.

2. Ensure investigative agencies have the appropriate resources, training, and structure necessary to conduct investigations thoroughly, efficiently, and fairly.

a. Conduct a staffing analysis, and create a staffing plan based on that analysis, to ensure that both BIA and IPRA/COPA have the staffing and resources to perform their responsibilities effectively;

b. Improve the timeliness and quality of BIA/IPRA/COPA investigations through the creation of case management protocols, including streamlined procedures and target deadlines for the completion of investigations; and

c. Develop and implement mandatory and comprehensive training for BIA/IPRA/COPA investigators, Police Board members, and hearing officers on police practices, civil rights law, evidence collection and assessment techniques, interview techniques, and other pertinent issues. The training for IPRA/COPA investigators should also include training on implicit bias and proper witness interviewing techniques. Investigators tasked with investigating domestic violence and sexual misconduct complaints should receive specialized training on the dynamics of those incidents and interview techniques for domestic violence and sexual misconduct victims.

3. Implement changes to the City's discipline and discipline review systems, including the Chicago Police Board, to ensure disciplinary decisions are fair, timely, and transparent.

a. Revise how disciplinary decisions are made, including streamlining the number of disciplinary decision makers and the layers of review of disciplinary recommendations, to facilitate quicker final resolution of complaints;

b. Revise CPD's disciplinary matrix to ensure that it provides meaningful guidance to those making disciplinary recommendations and findings;

c. Consider moving the Police Board's police commission and civilian oversight duties to another entity (such as a Community Oversight Board), to allow the Police Board to focus on its critical function of reviewing Superintendent/IPRA misconduct and disciplinary findings;

d. Create a cadre of trained and experienced attorneys within IPRA/COPA to advocate before the Board;

e. Modify CPD and IPRA policy, and address related provisions in the CBAs, to ensure that the Board has access to the information necessary to make a fair and informed decisions;

f. Ensure selection criteria for Police Board members and hearing officers include requisite competence, impartiality, and expertise;

g. Post all Police Board materials, including video recordings of hearings, on the Board's website in a timely manner; and

h. Track and publish more detailed case-specific and aggregate data about Police Board decisions, and make this information available in a timely manner.

C. Training

Training is the foundation for ensuring that officers are engaging in effective and constitutional policing. To that end, CPD should:

1. Provide training that is comprehensive, organized, based on adult-learning principles, and developed with national best police practices and community policing principles in mind.

a. Revise Academy curricula and lesson content to ensure consistency with CPD policy and current law, particularly with respect to the use of force, and revise lesson-delivery methods to include lessons that are consistent with adult learning principles and include more scenario-based trainings;

b. Revise end-of-course Academy evaluations to ensure recruits graduate the Academy with sufficient knowledge and skill to police safely and lawfully;

c. Revitalize CPD's Field Training Program by increasing incentives provided to FTOs in order to ensure a sufficient number of high-quality FTOs; improving the training provided to FTOs and, in turn, the quality of supervision and guidance that FTOs provide; creating a standardized curriculum for each FTO to use when training PPOs; increasing the rigor of FTO evaluation of PPOs; creating better supervision of FTOs and regularly evaluating the Field Training Program to identify areas in need of improvement; and

d. Implement a mandatory in-service training program, based on a comprehensive evaluation of Department needs, that includes high quality training through live, scenario-based trainings; provides updates on law and Department policy; and presents officers and supervisors with opportunities to refresh important skills and tactics.

2. **Take steps to ensure the creation of a well-planned, comprehensive training program that is carefully tailored to Department needs and is properly resourced.**

a. Formalize CPD's creation of a training committee in CPD policies, including outlining the committee's goals, membership, responsibilities, and deliverables;

b. Recruit, hire, and train additional instructors, and develop and implement rigorous testing, evaluation, and training of all instructors to ensure subject-matter competency and skill in instruction; and

c. Improve CPD's physical training facilities and equipment.

D. Supervision

Patrol officers must receive proper supervision and guidance in order to ensure that they are engaging in constitutional and effective policing and that they are held accountable if they engage in misconduct. This requires that patrol supervisors receive the tools, training, and support they need to perform their supervisory duties effectively. To that end, CPD should:

1. **Reform CPD's supervisory structures and incentives to provide all officers with meaningful direction and oversight.**

a. Develop and implement policies that establish clear requirements and provide specific guidance to ensure the appropriate supervision of all officers;

b. Ensure that supervisors closely monitor officers under their command, review officer uses of force, and direct and guide officers to use force only where necessary, in a manner that is safe, and that comports with the principles and values set forth in CPD's revised force policies;

c. Hold supervisors accountable if they fail to report misconduct that they observe, fail to accept and refer to IPRA a misconduct complaint, or otherwise fail to take appropriate steps to ensure officer accountability;

d. Implement appropriate span-of-control ratios in all districts and reform shift scheduling to allow for unity of command;

e. Re-examine the responsibilities of supervisory staff at districts to allow supervisors to maximize time spent providing mentorship, oversight, and accountability of officer activities;

f. Provide new supervisors with adequate training on supervisory skills, including leadership and management, and provide all supervisors with regular training on issues relevant to their supervisory responsibilities; and

g. Incentivize and reward supervisors who provide close and effective supervision.

2. Ensure CPD supervisors have the appropriate tools and information necessary to provide meaningful supervision.

a. Commit to putting in place a new and fully integrated EIS system that will allow for early identification of problematic behavior trends and appropriate interventions, and involve all relevant stakeholders in the process early on to ensure its ultimate success; and;

b. Ensure that data collection and tracking systems are adequate Department-wide to support this effort, and audit their use to ensure that these systems are used consistently and appropriately.

E. Officer Wellness and Safety

Officers must receive the support they need from the Department to perform their policing responsibilities well and safely, and to address the stressors related to their work. To better support its officers, CPD should:

1. Evaluate and respond to the needs of CPD officers.

a. Conduct a needs assessment to determine what additional resources officers desire or need to reduce the stressors of their jobs;

b. Expand the Employee Assistance Program by hiring additional counselors, substance abuse specialists, and other staff with specialized training and skills in certain topics, including post-traumatic stress disorder, domestic violence, women's issues, and depression;

c. Coordinate a communication strategy to inform all CPD members of the services available through the Employee Assistance Program and ensure that references to the range of available counseling and support services are included in Academy trainings, including the stress management and wellness trainings;

d. Explore alternative methods for providing officer support, including anonymous support hotlines and group meetings; and

e. Revise and implement new protocols for evaluation and treatment of officers involved in, or who witness, traumatic events, not limited to officer-involved shootings.

2. Incorporate officer wellness principles into all facets of CPD operations.

a. Explore and evaluate other methods to increase officer access to employee supports and services, including how using those services can benefit CPD officers, and encourage officers to use these programs; and

b. Conduct a Department-wide technology and equipment audit to determine what equipment is outdated, broken, or otherwise in need of replacement, and develop a plan with timelines for repair or replacement of equipment as needed.

F. Data Collection and Transparency

To increase transparency and community trust, it is critical that the City improve its data collection systems and publicly report and release information relevant to its policing and accountability efforts. Accordingly, the City, through CPD and IPRA/COPA, should:

1. Improve City data collection systems.

a. Examine and evaluate current data collection mechanisms and technology to determine where there are gaps and inefficiencies;

b. Create a plan to improve and synthesize City and CPD data collection systems by dates certain; and

c. Develop systems to ensure that data is appropriately and timely analyzed to identify trends or patterns in policing activities, including officer use of force and police misconduct complaints. The City and CPD should use data collection systems to track and identify patterns or practices of constitutional violations, so that corrective action can be taken where necessary.

2. Increase transparency regarding CPD and IPRA/COPA activities.

a. Seek input from community members regarding the type of data and information they believe is important for CPD and IPRA to disseminate;

b. Develop and implement policies mandating regular public reporting of crime trends and CPD policing activities;

c. Develop and implement policies mandating regular public reporting of misconduct investigations, including investigations handled not just by IPRA or COPA, but also BIA and the districts. These policies should cover regular reporting on complaint patterns and trends, investigation outcomes, and discipline (both recommended and imposed);

d. Finalize and formally adopt, as part of CPD and IPRA policy, the video release policy, with consideration of expanding the universe of complaints the policy covers; and

e. Develop and implement policies that would increase transparency related to City settlements of police misconduct complaints.

G. Promotions

To ensure constitutional and effective policing, CPD must promote competent, capable leaders, and ensure confidence amongst officers that deserving, well-qualified candidates will be selected for promotions. CPD must review its promotions systems to ensure all qualified candidates have a chance to be promoted, and improve transparency around the promotions process to better inform officers of how promotional decisions are made. To that end, CPD should:

1. Ensure promotions are fair.

 a. Continue to review promotional exams to ensure they are valid and fairly administered;

 b. Schedule promotional exams with sufficient frequency to allow qualified candidates frequent opportunity for promotion throughout their careers; and

 c. Review and revise, as necessary, the merit promotion process, to ensure that policies and procedures are followed, and that the system is working as intended.

2. Increase transparency around the promotions process.

 a. Devise and implement mechanisms for teaching officers about the policies and procedures guiding the merit promotion process;

 b. Develop mechanisms for improving transparency regarding those who receive merit promotions, and the reasons those candidates were selected; and

 c. Continue, and potentially increase, oversight of the merit promotions process through the Chicago Office of the Inspector General, and ensure that the OIG's role in overseeing this process is communicated to both officers and the public.

H. Community Policing

CPD should adopt, and incorporate in its policing approaches, an ingrained and permanent community policing philosophy that humanizes officers and residents to each other and builds trust between the community and the police; incentivizes police-community partnerships; and effectively uses these partnerships to solve crime and address community concerns. To that end, CPD should:

1. **Develop community policing as a core component of CPD's policing strategies, tactics, and training.**

   a. Develop and implement, with the help of community members from Chicago's diverse groups, comprehensive recruit and in-service training to officers on how to establish formal partnerships and actively engage with diverse communities, to include understanding and building trust with minority communities, Muslim communities, immigrant and limited English-proficiency communities, persons with disabilities, and lesbian, gay, bisexual, and transgender communities;

   b. Incorporate community policing and problem-solving principles into Academy training, and require regular in-service training on topics such as procedural justice, de-escalation, bias-free policing, diversity and cultural sensitivity;

   c. Create liaison officers in each district that will be responsive to, and specifically address, the concerns of minority communities, including LGBTQ individuals, Muslims and other religious or ethnic minorities, individuals with limited English-proficiency, and individuals with disabilities. District liaison officers should have monthly meetings to coordinate Department-wide outreach efforts and strategies;

   d. Develop systems that encourage and facilitate opportunities for officers to actively engage with communities while on patrol and gain more familiarity with residents through one-on-one interactions;

   e. Increase opportunities for officers to have frequent, positive interactions with people outside of an enforcement context, especially groups and communities that have expressed a high level of distrust of police; and

   f. Measure, evaluate, and reward individual, supervisory, and agency performance on community engagement, problem-oriented-policing projects, and crime prevention.

2. **Ensure that officers police fairly and compassionately in all neighborhoods, including in those with high rates of violent crime and in minority communities.**

a. Develop and implement a policy that specifically and comprehensively addresses and prohibits discriminatory policing and biased-based policing;

b. Provide initial and recurring training to all officers that sends a clear and consistent message that bias-based profiling and other forms of discriminatory policing are prohibited, and ensures that officers are capable of interacting with and providing services to all communities;

c. Provide training to supervisors and commanders on detecting and addressing bias-based profiling and other forms of discriminatory policing;

d. Provide safeguards for officers who report bias-based profiling and other forms of discriminatory policing;

e. Provide training to supervisors, detectives, and officers on how to detect and report potential hate crimes or hate incidents;

f. Work with community members from Chicago's diverse racial, religious, ethnic, gender, and disability groups to create and deliver cultural awareness training in partnership with CPD, and to inform and suggest the development of additional measures that may improve police-community relations;

g. Enforce Department rules regarding appropriate language, respect, and social media use;

h. Collect and analyze enforcement data (including use of force data) to identify patterns of unequal enforcement on the basis of race or ethnicity, and devise and implement operational changes based on this analysis. Publish stop, search, arrest, and force data bi-annually with the analysis of trends, and the steps taken to correct problems and build on successes; and

i. Capture and track complaints alleging racial and other bias-based profiling or discrimination, along with characteristics of the complainants. Analyze this data to identify and correct any patterns of discrimination.